THE AMERICAN ALPINE JOURNAL
2007

Ivar Tollefsen on Ulvetanna in Queen Maud Land, Antarctica (p. 267). *Robert Caspersen*
Cover: Chomolhari (7,326m), on the border between Tibet and Bhutan. Slovenian teams climbed
new routes on the shadowed north face and the sunlit northwest pillar (p. 14). *Marko Prezelj*

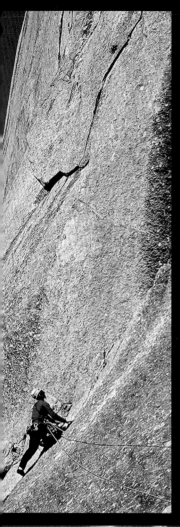
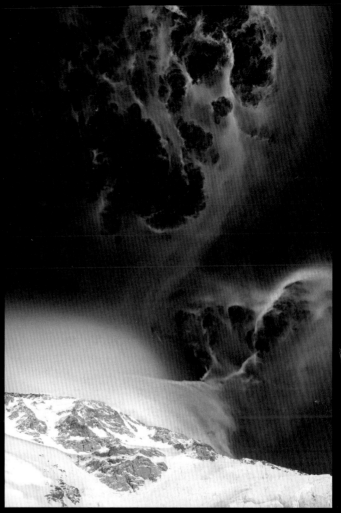

Clockwise from upper left:

On the first ascent of Let's Go Home on the south-southwest face of the First Tower on the southwest (Severence) ridge of Trango II (p. 344). Behind and on the far side of the Trango Glacier is Uli Biaho Tower (6,109m). *Jakub Radziejowski*

Fresh weather coming soon to Denali (p.164). *Marko Prezelj*

Waiting for dinner on the Trango Glacier, Pakistan (p. 343). *Jakub Radziejowski*

Josh Wharton switching to sneakers for a pitch of ice at the end of day two on Shingu Charpa (p. 353). *Kelly Cordes*

Ruben van Walen on the first ascent of Percolator Addicts, Cordon Granito, Chile (p. 240).
Menno Boermans, www.mennoboermans.eu

Corporate Friends

of the

AMERICAN ALPINE JOURNAL

We thank the following for their generous financial support of the 2007 AMERICAN ALPINE JOURNAL

BENEFACTORS:

PATRONS:

Black Diamond

ASOLO

Friends

OF THE

AMERICAN ALPINE JOURNAL

We thank the following for their generous financial support:

BENEFACTORS:
Yvon Chouinard
H. Adams Carter American Alpine Journal Fund

PATRONS:
Ann Carter
Gregory Miller
Louis F. Reichardt, M.D.
Mark A. Richey
Edith Overly
Peter D. McGann, M.D.

SUPPORTERS:
John Harlin III
Richard E. Hoffman, M.D.
William R. Kilpatrick, M.D.

SPECIAL THANKS TO:
Z. Wayne Griffith Jr.
Allen Scott Moore
Dag Wilkinson
Steven Schwartz
Glenn Porzak
Neal E. Creamer
Robert J. Campbell

THE AMERICAN ALPINE JOURNAL
710 Tenth St. Suite 140, Golden, Colorado 80401
Telephone: (303) 384-0110 Fax: (303) 384-0111
E-mail: aaj@americanalpineclub.org

ISBN 978-1-933056-05-0

Robert Caspersen on pitch 14 (A3) of the north face of Ulvetanna in Queen Maud Land, Antarctica (p. 267).
Stein-Ivar Gravdal

THE AMERICAN ALPINE JOURNAL
2007

VOLUME 49 ISSUE 81

CONTENTS

The Matterhorn puts on a fresh coat of summer snow for the Alpine Club's 150th anniversary celebration.
John Harlin III

CLIMBS AND EXPEDITIONS

Including: The Boys of Everest: Chris Bonington and the Tragedy of Climbing's Greatest Generation, *by Clint Willis;* The Wall: A Thriller, *by Jeff Long;* Strange and Dangerous Dreams: The Fine Line Between Adventure and Madness, *by Geoff Powter;* The Climbing Essays, *by Jim Perrin;* K2: The Price of Conquest, *by Lino Lacedelli & Giovanni Cenacchi;* To the Ends of the Earth: Adventures of an Expedition Photographer, *by Gordon Wiltsie;* No Shortcuts to the Top: Climbing the World's Highest 14 Peaks, *by Ed Viesturs and David Roberts;* World Climbing: Images from the Edge, *by Simon Carter;* Three Cups of Tea: One Man's Mission to Fight Terrorism and Build Nations–One School at a Time, *by Greg Mortenson and David Oliver Relin;* An Eye at the Top of the World: The Terrifying Legacy of the Cold War's Most Daring CIA Operation, *by Pete Takeda;* Thin Ice: Unlocking the Secrets of Climate in the World's Highest Mountains, *by Mark Bowen;* Summit: 150 Years of the Alpine Club, *by George Band;* Himalaya: Personal Stories of Grandeur, Challenge & Hope, *edited by Richard C. Blum, Erica Stone, and Broughton Coburn;* Ice Soldiers, *by Paul Watkins;* Illustrated Atlas of the Himalaya, *by David Zurick and Julsun Pacheco;* Burbage, Millstone and Beyond, *edited by David Simmonite.*

Remembering Doug Coombs, Charles Duncan Fowler, Johann Wolfgang "Hans" Gmoser, Samuel Harlow Goodhue, Richard K Irvin, Sue Nott, John Cameron Oberlin, Todd Richard Skinner, Henry Bradford Washburn, Jr.

Submission Guidelines www.AmericanAlpineClub.org/AAJ

The American Alpine Journal

John Harlin III, *Editor*

Advisory Board
James Frush, *Managing Editor*
Rolando Garibotti
Mark Jenkins, Mark Richey

Senior Editor
Kelly Cordes

Associate Editors
Lindsay Griffin
Dougald MacDonald

Art Director
Lili Henzler

Photo Guru
Dan Gambino

Contributing Editors
Steve Roper, *Features*
Joe Kelsey, *Climbs & Expeditions*
David Stevenson, *Book Reviews*
Cameron M. Burns, *In Memoriam*
Frederick O. Johnson, *Club Activities*
Chris Barlow, *Intern*

Cartographer
Martin Gamache, Alpine Mapping Guild

Translators
Molly Loomis   Martin Gutmann
Tamotsu Nakamura   Caroline Ware
Henry Pickford   Thad Eggen
Rolando Garibotti   Daniel Seeliger
          Silvina Verdún

Indexers
Ralph Ferrara, Eve Tallman

Regional Contacts
Malcolm Bass, *Scotland*;
Drew Brayshaw & Don Serl, *Coast Mountains, BC*;
Chris Simmons & Alasdair Turner, *Washington Cascades*;
Raphael Slawinski, *Canadian Rockies*; Antonio Gómez
Bohórquez & Sergio Ramírez Carrascal *Peru;* Rolando
Garibotti, *Patagonia*; Damien Gildea, *Antarctica*;
Harish Kapadia, *India*; Elizabeth Hawley, *Nepal*;
Tamotsu Nakamura, *Japanese expeditions*;
Lindsay Griffin, *Earth;* Mark Watson, *New Zealand*

With additional thanks to
Abdul Ghafoor, Colin Haley, Mike Layton,
José Luis Mendieta and *Desnivel* magazine,
Northwest Mountaineering Journal, Anna Piunova,
Joe Puryear, Marcelo Scanu, John Scurlock,
Servei General d'Informació de Muntanya,
Mark Westman, Josh Wharton

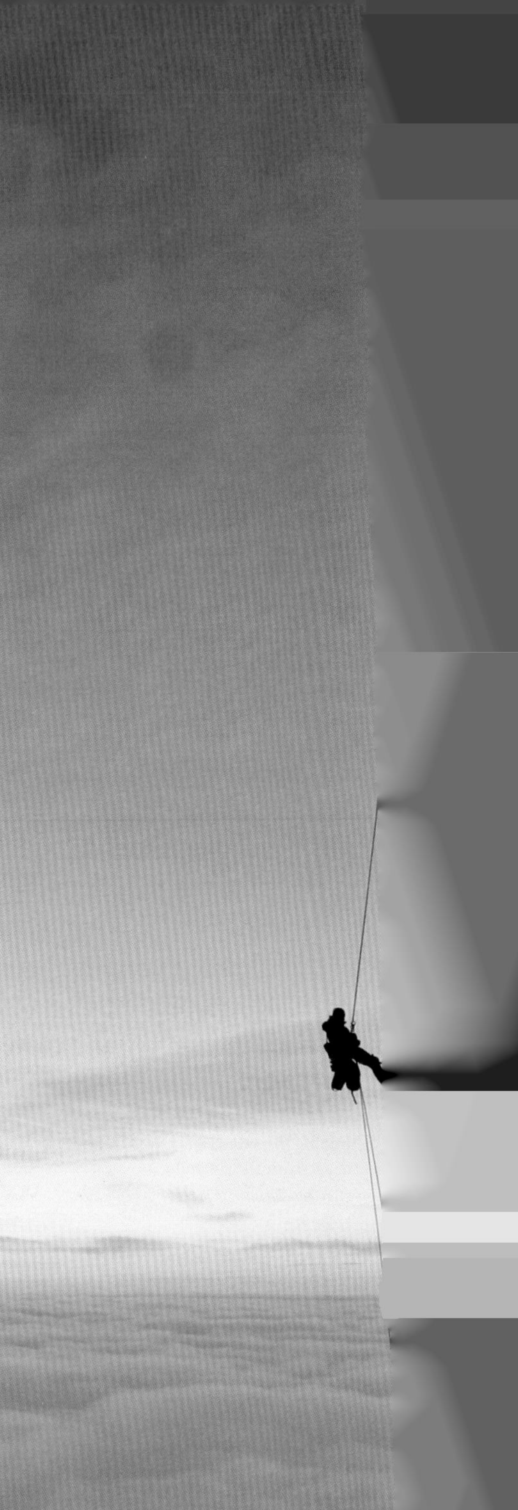

Robert Caspersen returning to camp 3
(650m up) after summiting Ulvetanna
in Queen Maud Land, Antarctica
(p. 267). *Ulvetanna 2006*

THE AMERICAN ALPINE CLUB

OFFICIALS FOR THE YEAR 2007
*Directors ex-officio

HONORARY PRESIDENT
Robert H. Bates

President
Jim Donini*

Secretary
Charles B. Franks*

Honorary Treasurer
Theodore (Sam) Streibert

Vice President
Steve Swenson*

Treasurer
Charlie Sassara*

DIRECTORS

Terms ending February 2008	*Terms ending February 2009*	*Terms ending February 2010*
Steven M. Furman	Ellen Lapham	Cody J. Smith
Steven Schwartz	Greg Miller	A. Travis Spitzer
Charlotte Fox	Conrad Anker	Danika Gilbert
Nancy Norris	Jack Tackle	Mark Kroese
Ralph Tingey	John R. Kascenska	Paul Gagner

SECTION CHAIRS

Alaska
Harry Hunt

New England
William C. Atkinson

Central Rockies
Greg Sievers

Southeast
David Thoenen

Northern Rockies
Brian Cabe
Tom Kalakay

Blue Ridge
Simon Carr

New York
Philip Erard

Sierra Nevada
Dave Riggs

Cascade
Al Schumer

Oregon
Bob McGown

Southwest
David Rosenstein

Midwest
Benjamin A. Kweton

EDITORS

The American Alpine Journal
John Harlin III
Kelly Cordes

Accidents in North American Mountaineering
John E. (Jed) Williamson

The American Alpine News
Dougald MacDonald

STAFF

Executive Director
Phil Powers

Director of Operations
Charley Mace

Controller
Jerome Mack

Marketing Director
David Maren

Membership Director and Grants Manager
Jason Manke

Membership Coordinator
Dana Richardson

Executive Assistant
Janet Miller

Events Coordinator
Brittany Griffith

Library Director
Gary Landeck

Catalog Librarian and Processing Archivist
Maria Borysiewicz

Ranch Manager
Drew Birnbaum

Ranch Assistant
Matt Bressler

PREFACE

One hundred and fifty years ago, when Europe was in the final grip of the "Little Ice Age," glaciers tumbled into low valleys and a dozen Britishers founded the Alpine Club, the first of its kind. The Alpine Club would be a place where members "might dine together once a year, say in London, and give each other what information they could," William Mathew suggested to a friend in 1857. He continued, "Each member, at the close of any Alpine tour in Switzerland or elsewhere, should be required to furnish, to the president, a short account of all the undescribed excursions he had made, with a view to the publication of an annual or bi-annual volume. We should thus get a good deal of useful information in a form available to the members."

In June of 2007 I was fortunate enough to share in the Alpine Club's sesquicentennial celebration in Zermatt, at the foot of the Matterhorn. On the first day we took the impressive cable car up the Kleine Matterhorn, where we disembarked to climb the neighboring Breithorn, 4,164m. I tied into a rope with Doug Scott, a past president of the Alpine Club and, along with Dougal Haston, the first person to climb the imposing south face of Everest—and then survive an open-air bivouac above 8,000 meters. Also on our rope was Stephen Venables, current Alpine Club president and the first British climber to summit Everest without bottled oxygen, via a new route on the Kangshung Face, no less. Fourth on the rope was Steve Goodwin, the current editor of the *Alpine Journal*—the British equivalent of the *American Alpine Journal*, only roughly a half-century older. Along the way we chatted with another roped team, this one including George Band, 78, who had climbed the Breithorn 50 years ago as part of the Alpine Club's centennial celebrations; four years earlier he had been on the team that first climbed Everest; two years after that he made the first ascent of the world's third highest peak, Kangchenjunga. I felt like I'd stepped into a history book.

But the stories on everyone's lips weren't nostalgic memories of high conquest and broken legs (Scott: the Ogre; Venables: Panch Chuli V). Instead, we were all swapping tales of shrinking glaciers, changing climbing seasons, and vanishing icefields. The lift up to the Kleine Matterhorn swooped over glaciers that seemed to be running backward, leaving vast piles of morainal debris to mark their former glory. Venables pointed to glacial tongues he used to ski down that now are piles of rubble. To reach some glaciers in Chamonix, steel ladders recently were installed to span polished rock that was covered in ice when I played there as a kid in the 1960s. In Switzerland the average temperature has risen almost two degrees Celsius since 1970, with another three to five degrees predicted in the next few decades. Just since the 1980s, Alpine glacier mass has shrunk by over 20 percent (50 percent since 1850), and scientists predict the glaciers will vanish almost entirely—except for the high-altitude accumulation zones—by the end of our century, maybe even by midcentury.

It wouldn't be fair to hold 21st century Alpine glaciers to their 19th century past. The Little Ice Age was drawing to a close just as the Industrial Revolution ramped into high gear. This happened to coincide with what's been called the Golden Age of alpinism—the mid 1800s, when the Alpine Club was founded. Most Alpine peaks were climbed for the first time during these decades, and most of the significant summits were pioneered by British climbers employing Swiss guides. Switzerland during that time was arguably the poorest country in Europe, with villagers trapped by the isolation of their rugged valleys. It was Brits on holiday that finally put money into Swiss pockets. As it turns out, many of those Brits could afford their holidays because of rising fortunes back home, where modern machines produced goods at formerly unimaginable rates. The machines were powered by coal, and giant smokestacks belched its byproduct—CO_2—into the atmosphere as never before, unwittingly launching our age of "Greenhouse Catastrophe," with consequences that are only beginning to be understood 150 years later.

I was on the south flank of Mont Blanc during the record hot summer of 2003, when up to 10 percent of glacial mass in the Alps was lost in one big heat wave. Mark Jenkins and I were searching for new-route potential in the region where my Dad had put up two routes in the 1960s, but when we reached a viewpoint overlooking the monstrous Frêney and Brouillard faces we stared dumbfounded as continuous streams of rock poured off the bone-dry walls; the glaciers below were solid black from debris. Boxcar-sized pillars periodically pealed off the nearby walls, echoing

Celebrating the 150th anniversary of the Alpine Club, left to right: George Band, Walter Bonatti (honorary member), Doug Scott, and Stephen Venables. *John Harlin III*

between peaks. French guides wouldn't climb Mont Blanc that month for fear of unstable seracs, and for a while the Swiss "closed" the Matterhorn when melting permafrost caused massive landsliding on the Hornli Ridge. From our vantage, it looked like climbing was over.

But little is cut and dry when it comes to climate change. The next day, September 1, the heat wave collapsed into storm, and three days later Mark and I waded through a meter of fresh snow that had cemented in all the unstable rock. Two years later, this time in late September, I was on the north face of the Eiger. Almost no one climbs that face in the summer anymore because it's too dry and prone to rockfall. But recent storms had plastered the face with ice, gluing in all the loose stones, and the single falling rock we saw was broken off by a party above.

It was stories like these that flowed between participants at the Alpine Club's birthday bash. We compared notes on what was in shape where and when, from Mt. Kenya's Diamond Couloir to snowfall patterns in Pakistan. Old rules didn't apply, and everyone wanted to learn the new rules in order to better plan their next excursion. No one thought that climbing would end, but we stared wistfully at the sight of gorgeous glaciers snaking down from Monte Rosa, wondering what would be left for participants at the Alpine Club's bicentennial ascent of the Breithorn. And if these glaciers have indeed all melted by then, what would this mean for the state of the rest of the world?

For thoughts on what you can do to help monitor glacier changes (and maybe even help do something to slow the process), please read Joe Stock's "The Front Lines of Climate Change," beginning on page 117 of this *Journal*. And keep in touch with the American Alpine Club, because we'll soon be initiating an online clearinghouse for updated mountain info and photos, so we can keep track of changing approaches and route conditions worldwide. You can already find the *American Alpine Journal* online in free searchable and downloadable PDF format (www.AmericanAlpineClub.org/AAJ). But those editions featured yesterday's conditions. What will tomorrow's be?

JOHN HARLIN III, *Editor*

THE WINDS OF CHOMOLHARI

A test of will on a cold Tibetan wall.

MARKO PREZELJ

"**S**omeday you will be perfect," said the charming shopkeeper in Lhasa, through a teasing smile. She gently touched my badly sunburned nose with her finger and consoled me. Someday I will be perfect...maybe. I giggled the whole day.

Ten years earlier. I had broken my ankle badly and was waiting for a flight in Kathmandu, spending my spare time in Pilgrims Book House. Browsing through some Chinese books, I noticed a small black and white photo of an attractive pyramidal mountain with a distinctive ridge. Among the Chinese characters I could read the name "Chomolhari" in English and a height of a bit more than 7,000 meters. Two years later, I returned to Kathmandu and looked for that strange book, but I couldn't find it.

Later still, I noticed a photo of this mysterious mountain while browsing on the Internet. The photo was taken in Bhutan. The mountain had the same name but looked completely different from what I remembered, so I concluded it must lie on the border between Tibet and Bhutan. I learned that a Japanese expedition had stood on its top in 1996.

I wrote to Tamotsu Nakamura, a Japanese expert on Tibet. He promptly responded to my query, saying he would try to find some color photos, and ended with a kindly, "Please wait."

This was the right thing to say. Patience is undoubtedly a virtue that is neglected in the modern age. The best information eventually came from Roger Payne, who had tried to climb the peak's prominent northwest buttress in 2004; due to strong winds and bad weather, he and Julie Ann Clyma had only managed to reach the summit by approximating the 1996 Japanese route. It was clear to me that such a tempting objective would not stay hidden for long. We made our plans and finally received a permit to climb Chomolhari a week before our scheduled departure; our Chinese visas came through the day before our flight. I don't need to explain how we felt about that.

⌂

In Beijing a short van ride led us to the Chinese Mountaineering Association, where an employee charged us $350 for two rides across town and dinner, a few hours in all. Any notion that China was cheap quickly turned into paranoia that we would spend our money too soon. We boarded the new Beijing-Lhasa train with our luggage in the evening, and after a 48-hour journey that was both picturesque and boring we arrived in Lhasa. The journey had just begun.

"Do you have something to ask for me?" This was the mantra of our guide, Lobsang. The 24-year-old Tibetan was a prime example of a successful Chinese education. The self-confidence with which he tried to mask his complete inexperience turned to confusion every time things didn't go according to plan, along with, "Sorry, I don't understand," or, "Sorry, this is not possible." Every time he prepared us for bad news, he started kindly: "I'm very sorry for you..."

Chomolhari (7,326 meters) looms over base camp. Boris Lorencic and Marko Prezelj gained the northwest pillar on the right from the glacier below the north face. Four teammates climbed the north face via the couloir directly above the tent; they then followed the east ridge to the summit. *Marko Prezelj*

He led us through the Potala and expertly described certain sights. He only spoke about the Dalai Lama in the past tense. To a question about the contemporary Dalai Lama, he abruptly answered that he had fled. So, a deserter?

The first time I was in Lhasa was in 1988. Then the town had an entirely Tibetan character, although the omnipresence of police and army troops gave a strong feeling of the government's power. Now Lhasa is an entirely Chinese town. Tibetan pilgrims are merely a welcome attraction for tourists. I could hardly wait to leave.

△

Lobsang pointed to a snowy pyramid ahead of us. Although I had seen it for a while, I leaned forward to show my interest. To the right of the snowy mass I saw something that could be Chomolhari.

"Look!" shouted Damijan and Samo, almost at the same time.

Now we nervously shifted in our seats and raved like children in front of a toyshop. A white cloud covered the top of the mountain. There had been a lot of fresh snow. The driver understood our excitement and stopped by a lake.

It had been ten years since I had first seen Chomolhari in a photograph. Now, the physical confrontation was so sudden that I sensed the primal fear of the group. While our Chinese companions cheerfully ate lunch by our vehicles, the guys ate silently inside, out of the wind. The excitement over our new toy was obscured by countless doubts. We had hoped for much less snow on the mountain. Our conversation had stopped. Just as well: It had been obscuring the silence inside—the collective doubts—that we had to face eventually. My lunch of cold

Chomolhari's steep northwest pillar, seen from the bivy site during the ascent of Chomolhari II's northwest face. *Marko Prezelj*

chicken leg wasn't too appetizing as I thought of avalanches and snow plodding. The portion of insecurity on the menu would be heftier than we'd expected—it wouldn't just spice up this climb; rather, it threatened to overpower all the other flavors, spoiling the taste entirely.

That night we camped in a stone yak pen. The tempo of civilization began to fade. We smiled to each other while secretly tormenting ourselves inside—life doesn't get any better.

In the morning Samo and Rok went to check out the Japanese route, which we intended to use for our descent. The rest of us hiked to a glacial lake where we planned to set up base camp. For Tibetans this lake is sacred, and it filled us with excitement. The turquoise lake, the glacier descending into it, and the pyramidal peak looming above all created a magnificent backdrop. Each of us tried to express his emotions, but we ended up laughing at each other when it became clear we were just talking. We ignored the insecurity fluttering around like a bat. Back at the trailhead, we prepared loads and waited for the two inspectors, who came back with the message that the Japanese route was completely unsafe. One mystery was solved; there would be more to come.

After moving our supplies to the lake and establishing a base camp, Lori and I climbed an arête to a pointy peak along the ridge to the west. The mists cleared to reveal a neighboring peak, from which Rok and Samo waved to us. It was nice to feel the proximity of fellow men.

Back in base camp, impatience soon overtook the relaxed atmosphere. When could we go higher? The usual eagerness of the youngest members of our team caused us to nearly sprint toward the eastern neighbor of Chomolhari after a single rest day. I had incorrectly estimated

Rok Blagus acclimatizes on 6,972-meter Chomolhari II (aka Tserimkang or Jangmo Gopsha), with Chomolhari shrouded in clouds. *Marko Prezelj*

Approaching the bivouac below the north face, where both teams began their climbs. Lorencic and Prezelj started climbing just left of the ice pillar above the two climbers. *Rok Blagus*

this summit to be approximately 6,700 meters high; it was actually 200 meters higher. We paid the price for our initial fast pace and then, more slowly, made our way toward the shelter of a big serac in the middle of the face. I started digging a ledge into the snow in midafternoon. Lori and I set up our tent on a snow ledge, and then we all rested and cooked while watching the sunset. We had Chomolhari at the tips of our fingers. Our teasing expressed both friendship and our worries about the coming days.

In the cold morning, after a good night's sleep, we crept out of our tents and climbed toward the summit. At the ridge the wind gained strength. Before I stepped onto the summit cornice, I asked Matej to belay me. We all took turns approaching the top, then started descending immediately. When I got close to the tents, I saw that the wind had buried one of them with snow; the other was hanging only by a buried shovel and swaying in the wind with all of its contents inside. The third was fluttering loudly. I quickly pulled down two of the tents and started to dig out the covered one. Matej and Tine decided to descend to the base rather than fight with the wind. The rest of us dug deeper into the ice, hoping for better shelter and another night at altitude to strengthen our acclimatization.

That night we realized our mistake. The wind continuously filled up the gap between our tents and the ice wall with snow, threatening to suffocate us. We dug them out repeatedly until dawn freed us and we dashed down to base camp.

While we had been struggling above, the wind had been taking its toll below, tearing down the kitchen tent, the dining tent, and two smaller tents. The sense of failure was complete. We sat and consoled each other by the broken dining tent. Ongchu, our cook, walked around in a daze and from time to time moved a piece of the ruins. When he finally excavated his stove, we jumped to his assistance, hoping for some tea, and with our combined energies we set up the tents again. Team spirit won out. Now we strengthened the camp as if we expected

Prezelj leads toward the first bivy on the pillar in a blinding windstorm. *Boris Lorencic*

a windstorm. What this wind meant for the climbing conditions on Chomolhari we didn't discuss. We all needed a bit of rest first.

After three days, thoughts of climbing crept back into our minds. Rok confidently declared that he and Samo would first climb the left couloir on Chomolhari and then maybe a more serious line. This was an ambitious, if not presumptuous, plan. The rest of us packed our gear to find a route through the glacier to the base of the face.

After just a few steps on the glacier, it became clear that this would not be an easy walk. For a while the four of us made some progress, and then we sat on our "weights" and waited for the other two, who were hurrying toward us. Soon we were laughing as Samo explained that "Junior" had changed his mind and they would be joining us. We slowly made our way to a steep serac beneath the north face, where we cached some gear.

After two days of rest and easy climbing around base camp, we were all sufficiently sharp for an attempt. We all moved to a bivouac below the face. After weeks of not having much appetite I found dinner that night very appealing—this is always a good sign. In the morning I had no troubles getting up. After some tea, we packed up, put on our packs, and started climbing.

Four lights quickly crossed the glacier and climbed onto the north face to our left. Lori and I started up the couloir right above our bivy. Now we were separated, each with our own sins, desires, and enigmas. After 50 meters in the couloir it became warm, and I pulled off my hood.

"Head lamp!" I screamed as my light slid off my helmet and bounced down toward Lori. I expected him to stop it, but my screaming startled him and he dodged the dark falling object. It stopped about a hundred meters lower on the glacier, so I asked him if he could get it. He put down his pack and descended, and I slowly continued up through the crusty snow. Strangely, this work was not as unpleasant as usual. I merrily pointed my boots into the snow and judged the characteristics of the slope ahead of me, aiming to find the crust that was strong enough to support my weight. I waited for Lori and we roped up. After three long pitches, we reached the sunny slope on the top of the couloir.

I sat in the snow, taking in the rope and watching the summit of the mountain, from which the wind was spinning snow off to the north. From the east, the sun cast sharp shadows and created an iridescent halo over the mountain, making a frightening backdrop. If this mountain was really the home of a goddess, as Tibetans believed, we would need her blessing. Lori arrived, and a smile and a few words easily redirected the flow of my thoughts.

Roped up, we simulclimbed the snowy arête over breakable crust. The gusty wind carried sharp snow crystals. At first I thought about backing off, but then I decided to continue so we could see as much new ground as possible. Slowly, I started to become accustomed to the blowing snow.

We reached a rocky barrier in the afternoon. At its foot a small cornice hid a rocky eave. I thought we could set up a tent there, but I wanted to have a look higher first. Each additional meter would serve us well. But it turned out there would be no point in moving on. The face was steep and contained difficult passages, and we weren't as full of energy as we had been in the morning.

Under the rocky barrier behind the cornice, we carefully dug out a ledge for our tent. It was a great shelter. We only heard the wind when a bit of snow fell down the tent wall, like sugar sprinkling over a doughnut. I cooked late into the night and thought about the next morning. The comfortable shelter provided room for my growing ambition. "If we start light tomorrow, we may even reach the top. We'll get down somehow."

Lori nodded as he napped.

So we started climbing early in the morning. We only took one light pack. The first pitch offered difficult climbing, and interesting passages followed one after another. The snow was often soft

Shelter from the wind: the first bivy site. *Marko Prezelj*

and blown into small cornices that forced us onto steeper terrain than we had hoped. It quickly became clear that it was still a long way to the top. The wind pelted us with piercing snow crystals. Lori grimaced with the cold. I wanted to laugh, but somehow I didn't feel like joking. I even stopped taking pictures. The climbing was great: The sculptor wind had demonstrated fantastic creativity.

We called Damijan at base camp on the radio. "When will you reach the top?" he asked. That was really an indecent question. Although we could see base camp, it was obvious he couldn't see us—we were only tiny dots on the mountain.

In half a day we reached a small triangular snow slope beneath the second rocky step. A demanding pitch over steep rock followed. Above us was a chimney blocked by a big cornice and a rock overhang with a long ice pillar next to it. It would take a long time and a lot of energy to climb the chimney, so I led toward the left, hoping to find a passage over narrow bands of ice and snow. It went quickly at first, but these bands became smaller as the terrain got steeper, and the snow-ice often didn't stick to the rock. The climbing demanded total concentration.

From the end of this pitch I traversed right to a rock horn, from which we descended diagonally to reach the exit of the chimney. Another pitch brought us to the edge of the upper snowfield. Here, strong wind covered us with snow continuously. A snowy funnel led up to a steep rocky wall. We stared up at the barrier.

"There, on the right, is some shelter." Lori pointed to a potential bivouac site.

"Yes, I can see that. But our route goes above, on the arête."

"We can go around to the right side."

"We chose the arête, let's climb there."

I didn't wish to discuss this any further. I climbed to the end of the snow funnel and found a snowy slope that led left to a small ramp, from which I hoped we could gain the arête.

We were out of time. After locating a bivy site with a bit of protection from the wind, we decided to return the next day with all of our gear. We started to descend toward our tent, some 500 meters lower. The rappels continued until the evening when, tired but satisfied, we

Prezelj and Lorencic bivouacked three times at their lower campsite—twice on the way up the northwest pillar and again during the descent—and once at the higher camp. *Marko Prezelj*

Serious fun: Prezelj finds interesting mixed climbing in the middle rock band. *Boris Lorencic*

crawled into our shelter.

That night was calm in our den. In the morning, we packed up everything and reclimbed the known terrain with our heavy loads. The hardened snow in our day-old steps sped our progress.

From the edge of the triangular snowfield, beneath the second rock band, I watched four tiny dots descend from the summit of Chomolhari. I was happy and proud that they—we—had succeeded. I even caught myself thinking that we could turn around now.

◇△

Around midday we reached the chimney we had skirted the day before. During our descent, we had rappelled through this chimney and then fixed a thin tag line, which we now used to quickly climb 20 meters to the top of the chimney with heavy packs. Above, I once again led the same delicate pitch I had climbed the day before. We continued up the snowfield through constant spindrift to reach our bivy site.

After quickly digging through wind-blown snow, we undertook the longer mining process into the hard ice below. We entered the tent before sundown. I cooked and tried to gauge the level of our motivation.

"What do you think?"

"In this wind..."

I tried to hide any doubts. I know far too well the moments when doubts and guessing reach epidemic proportions. Mixed with fear, they propel a person toward comfort, leisure, and certainty. The second-guessing strikes suddenly and becomes totally incapacitating. Like diarrhea.

In the morning, the cold, fatigue, and anxiety about the steep ground above us worked

Summit views across high, dry Tibet. *Marko Prezelj*

like a sedative, and we started slower than I would have liked for a summit day. I climbed toward the steep ramp leading to the arête and then faced my mistake. It was a dead end. Restarting, I climbed a long pitch over the wall on the right and made a hanging belay in the ice. Lori climbed to me and said, "I'm totally fucked up."

It would be better if he hadn't said that. I had sensed it anyway.

"I'm a bit cold," I said. I changed the subject. "We can't go straight up. Do you see that overhang?"

"Yes...."

"Well, I'll check it out to the left around the corner."

Piled up doubts and the cold were dragging both of us down. I was chewing on that familiar feeling when curiosity and doubt unite into a tasteless mixture. What if there was no passage behind the corner? How long could we stand this cold? I felt as if one of us only had to say the word "descend" and we would turn downward. Lori's eyes spoke of his desire to go down, but with his words he still approved of my stubborn search for a passage.

I stepped to the base of a chimney and began using my tools in a way that reminded me of the climbing stunts at mixed crags. I could afford these risks because the chimney offered some deceptive shelter and because the rare protection that I set up was quite good.

"If I peel we'll have a good reason to turn back," I thought boldly, just as a pick of my tool slipped down the crack.

At the top of the chimney, I realized with relief that only a snowy ridge separated us from the summit. I felt a strange victorious melancholy, almost like it would be OK if we started descending now. I had proved to myself that my assumptions were correct; the mystery was solved. Each time Lori moved, I gave him tension to speed up. When he reached me, he gasped, "I can barely feel my fingers. My toes are numb."

"OK, we've climbed all the difficulties, now we can go down," I said, verbalizing the thought I'd seen in his eyes for the last few hours. He stared at me and said, "What? Are you crazy? We are going to climb this last part!"

Yes! All I needed was a bit of encouragement to change my mood. The decision was now absolute: "To the summit." A few doubts still gnawed at me as I started up a steep, rocky step covered with sugary snow, but it only hardened my conviction not to give up. Above this step I saw the ridge leveling toward the horizon. I sat in the snow and pulled the rope toward me. The sun shined on us and added noticeable warmth.

We unroped and I removed my harness, which had been bothering me since the morning. I slowly plodded toward the top, calm and relaxed. On the summit I looked around and took a picture of Lori. The view was so extraordinary it bordered on mystical. Looking toward mysterious Bhutan brought to mind the legend of the goddess who had allowed us onto the summit. We were satisfied that the wind, obviously a guardian of the goddess, had been relentless and yet merciful to us. We had withstood the test of will. The test of endurance continued.

△

At first, the descent flew by. As we rappelled, I proudly noticed the features I had used earlier for drytooling. When we reached the tent, I estimated we had enough time to continue, so I took it down. Thus I selfishly avoided a discussion about another bivouac at our high camp. Lori arrived at the tent site with the news that the rope was stuck. Without words and with no will, I climbed back to the anchor. My fatigue was overwhelming. To feel safe I had to rest every few meters.

With the rope freed, we slowly descended from the bivy. Gusts of wind hit us with hard snow crystals. The spindrift poured over us as we rappelled down the rocky step. The humming of the rope provided a nice musical backdrop.

At the lower bivouac, I waited for Lori and told him I wanted to keep descending.

"Are you kidding? Are you nuts?"

He was right, there was no point. A bit of rest would do us good. We set up the tent in the old spot, and I lay down on my sleeping bag. "I'll rest a bit and then I'll start cooking," was the thought that accompanied me to sleep. When I started to feel cold, I moved inside the sleeping bag. "Cooking? Later." I turned to the other side and slept until morning.

When we started again, I went first and then waited at the top of the couloir. I watched Lori descend at the edge of a wind-blown flag of snow stretching far toward the east. A mixture of worry, relief, and resignation kept me company. When Lori reached me, we didn't speak much. His look said more than can be put into words. I thought about belaying, but the snow in the couloir was soft. I started descending the couloir, looking back up at Lori. A visible connection meant the same as being roped up.

I decisively stepped over the bergschrund as if to deliberately cross the line between the world of insecurity and the world of comfort. My foot broke through a hard crust covering a crevasse. "Ugh, it's not over yet," I thought as I pushed myself up and jumped toward comfort. At our bivy site below the face, I sat down on my pack and watched dots moving among the rocks at the end of the glacier. The guys were coming to greet us.

A feeling of friendship and thoughts of home finally tore me away from the mountain. My concentration, which had been at the verge of perfection over the last five days, was slowly evaporating. I returned to the foot of the couloir a couple of times and looked for Lori. He was downclimbing slowly and carefully. An hour of waiting passed quickly because I had already been to someplace warm in my mind.

Lori reached me, limping. I knew he wanted to rest, but now wasn't the time. I encouraged him without offering any false sympathy, and then moved along.

My reunion with the other expedition members was hearty and genuine. The adventure we had consumed had bordered on overdose. Now that we were together again the whole experience had the strongest and purest taste. We sat on stones and indulged in idleness. Damijan walked ahead to meet Lori. When they returned, we felt a touch of solemnity because now we were really all together.

"Do you know what he said when we first met?" asked Damijan mischiefly. "He said, 'I'm finished.'"

We burst into laughter. According to civilized etiquette, we should have shown sympathy to the tired newcomer. But our spontaneous reaction had a much better effect. Lori had a relaxed smile that wouldn't wear off for days. Teasing in this respect was actually praise. We mercilessly repeated his quote at every opportunity and thus strengthened our friendship in a tribal way.

It's true. Someday I will be perfect...maybe...

SUMMARY:

AREA: Himalaya, Tibet-Bhutan

Ascent: First ascent of the northwest pillar (1,950m, ED2 M6+ 80°) of 7,326-meter Chomolhari, Boris Lorencic and Marko Prezelj, October 12-17, 2006. The expedition, which also included Rok Blagus, Tine Cuder, Matej Kladnik, and Samo Krmelj, along with doctor Damijan Mesko, also climbed the north face of Chomolhari and several new routes on neighboring peaks. See Climbs and Expeditions for details.

A NOTE ABOUT THE AUTHOR:

Marko Prezelj, born in October 1965, lives in Kamnik, Slovenia, and is a husband and father, mountain guide, and photographer. He has been practicing alpinism for the last quarter of a century. He says, "An experienced mountain guide recently told me, 'There are two kinds of people: people who climb (and have sex), and others who only talk about it.'"

Marko Prezelj (left) and Boris Lorencic on top. *Marko Prezelj*

Translated from the Slovenian by Ivana Odic, with assistance from Steve House.

SUEÑOS DEL TORRE

A 4,500-foot ice climb linking the south face and west ridge of Cerro Torre.

COLIN HALEY

"Goddamn it, guys! We gotta go climb some mountains!" Our friend Freddie Wilkinson threw the finished bottle of whiskey onto the ground and fell backward over a log. Getting drunk on nine-peso whiskey had become the most athletic activity among the climbers at Campo Bridwell, and everyone seemed ready to explode if the weather ever got good. Three weeks of waiting had delivered only a 12-hour weather window—just long enough for us all to make brief attempts and get totally knackered. Despite the bad weather, I remained optimistic, perhaps as a result of the company of climbers whom I admire and mountains I have dreamed of.

My dad began to take me alpine climbing in the Cascades when I was 10 years old. I was immediately obsessed, and it wasn't long before I stumbled upon a picture of Cerro Torre. I had never seen, before or since, a mountain more spectacular and beautiful, and Cerro Torre became my dream. When I was 15 I found an article by Rolando Garibotti about Cerro Torre's Compressor Route, and I was extremely excited to find that Rolo made it sound easy. Only 5.9? I lead 5.9! A2? A couple of days later I began to teach myself how to aid climb, and I decided I'd be ready to climb Cerro Torre when I was 17.

Two years later, fortunately, I had gained enough sense to realize I wasn't ready for Cerro Torre, but my dreams of Patagonia lived on, and at 19 I finally had the opportunity to visit this ultimate alpine-climbing playground. I met my friend Bart Paull in El Chalten over my winter break from school in 2003, and we climbed Poincenot, Guillamet, and Aguja de la S. Although I had only climbed some of the easiest routes in the Fitz Roy region, the climbing was fantastic and I was hooked. I returned two years later, and after another route on Guillamet with Argentine friends, Mark Westman and I climbed Mermoz, Fitz Roy, St. Exupéry, and Rafael. It was the most successful climbing trip I'd ever had, but still Cerro Torre beckoned from across the Torre Glacier, and I finally felt I was ready.

In October 2006 I managed to convince Kelly Cordes to join me in attempting Cerro Torre. Five years earlier, I'd felt privileged merely to exchange e-mails with Kelly, and our previous climbing experience together consisted of only two days of cragging in Yosemite, but I knew him to be a nice guy and his past accomplishments spoke enough of his abilities. I wanted to try the west face of Cerro Torre, and Kelly agreed but suggested we might consider a direct start via the Marsigny-Parkin Route.

Cerro Torre's west face, or Ferrari Route, begins in earnest at the Col of Hope, between Cerro Torre and Cerro Adela, and climbs 600 meters to the summit. Traditionally, the Col of Hope has been reached from the northwest by a couloir rising out of the Cirque of the Altars. The Cirque of the Altars must be reached either by a long ski across the icecap or by a traverse through the col between Cerro Stanhardt and Aguja Bifida. However, in 1994 Andy

Colin Haley leads the vertical headwall on the upper west face of Cerro Torre. He finished the pitch as darkness fell, ending the first day of his and Kelly Cordes' ascent. *Kelly Cordes*

The Cordes-Haley linkup combined 800 meters of the 1994 Marsigny-Parkin Route on Cerro Torre's south face with 600 meters of the 1974 Ragni di Lecco Route (west face and upper west ridge). The two descended by the southeast ridge (Compressor Route), generally following the right skyline in this photo. *Rolando Garibotti*

Parkin and François Marsigny established a new route to the col, À la Recherche du Temps Perdu. Their route climbed 800 meters of ice gullies on the left margin of the south face to reach the Col of Hope directly from the Torre Valley. From the Col of Hope, Marsigny and Parkin climbed partway up the west face but were beaten back by the infamous Patagonian weather; they retreated to the Cirque of the Altars. Their new line to the Col of Hope, and their ensuing epic retreat via the icecap, earned them the Piolet d'Or. In the years since, the Marsigny-Parkin route had been repeated to the Col of Hope by Bruno Sourzac and Laurance Monnoyeur and by Dani Ascaso and Pepe Chaverri, but no one had yet continued to Cerro Torre's summit. Kelly's idea seemed ambitious but inspiring, and I concurred that we should make it our primary objective.

High pressure finally arrived at the last hour of our trip, and on January 4 we strolled out of Campo Bridwell under sunny skies, crossed the Rio Fitz Roy tyrolean, and made our way up the Torre Glacier. The past weeks of storm had tried our patience and seeded doubts about the feasibility of our goal, so we stopped on a boulder to discuss our options. Should we proceed with our planned linkup or bet with higher odds of success and traverse through the Stanhardt-Bifida col? Our monocular revealed only a small level of detail on the Marsigny-Parkin, and Kelly thought it might just be snow over rock. I was more optimistic and felt that perhaps neither of us would ever see a more opportune time for an attempt. The weather forecast was excellent, and I reasoned that the recent fluctuations between storm and warm weather would have created good ice conditions. I convinced Kelly that we should stick with our primary goal, but I also knew that we would both be very disappointed should we arrive at the base and find my optimism misguided.

After a couple of fitful hours of sleep, we departed the Niponino Bivouac at 2:30 a.m. on January 5, our packs adequately light to make us feel totally unprepared and heavy enough to feel like a burden. We left behind any real bivouac equipment, but brought a stove and a dinner for each of us. We hiked peacefully up the glacier below the south face, and at 5:30 Kelly headed over the bergschrund as the sky began to lighten. Seventy meters of rope disappeared quickly. I shouted to Kelly that I was climbing and soon was delighted to find the gully filled with perfect grade 4 alpine ice. We had brought two small Ropeman ascenders to make simul-climbing steep terrain safer, and it was a good thing, for I was bathed in sunlight only five minutes into the pitch and moving quickly was mandatory. With the sun's arrival bits of ice began to rain down, and I became particularly conscious of the serac looming over us. The serac that threatens the first half of the Marsigny-Parkin had shown no sign of activity during our entire trip, but once it is above your head it is hard to ignore.

Kelly set the first belay after about 150 meters, thankfully beneath an overhang, and by the time I had caught my breath and rehydrated he was off again. From there a tricky mixed traverse (M5) led into the next gully to the left, followed by short vertical ice steps for a 100-meter lead. On the third lead the rope stopped moving for a long time as Kelly grappled with a routefinding error and some mixed climbing to get back on track. I shifted anxiously from

Kelly Cordes starts another long lead on the Marsigny-Parkin Route. Cordes led all the way to the Col of Hope; Haley led from there to the summit. *Colin Haley*

crampon to crampon, and when the rope began to move again I eagerly climbed up to Kelly's belay, 200 meters higher and out of the serac's trajectory.

I hadn't expected such long lead blocks, but Kelly was obviously on a roll and I handed him the rack once again. The fourth lead gained another 200 meters, and in addition to more steep ice it contained a hospitable section of 60-degree snow that allowed a pleasant rest for my calves.

"I think this one will take us to the col," Kelly said, looking above the belay. "Mind if I keep leading? You can take all the west face, and then it'll be even."

I certainly didn't mind Kelly leading more, for he was still moving fast, but did he really expect me to lead the entire west face? As I followed the fifth lead up to the Col of Hope, I wondered if I were up to such a task.

△

We were both in need of rest, but the Col of Hope actually turned out to be a rather steep stance, so I trailed the rope up to a snow mushroom above and stomped out a picnic area on top. The view across the icecap and up the west face was breathtaking; the rime towers, mushrooms, and gargoyles were like no alpine terrain I had ever seen. The Marsigny-Parkin had passed quickly, but eight hours of almost constant climbing had us both worked, and it was only after about two hours of eating, drinking, and melting snow that I finally headed into the rime.

I soon reached the first major difficulty, the Helmet, and was curtly introduced to the style of climbing on the west face. The key was to look for grooves and depressions, where the ice was slightly more consolidated and a little bit of chimney technique reduced the outward pull on my tools. Nonetheless, the bulge at the top of the Helmet was unavoidable, and I zenned my way through with some luck and the use of a picket as an ice tool.

The mixed pitches above the Helmet were moderate, and in the evening sun I soon had a belay set at the base of the long headwall pitch, which had been rumored to be overhanging. Heading up at 9:30 p.m., I left one of our nine screws in the belay and promised not to fall before placing good protection. After about 20 meters I clipped my pack to an old V-thread, perhaps left by the successful Franco-Argentine ascent of the west face the previous summer. I had unpacked the skinny rope for hauling the backpacks, but because it was only 60 meters and our lead rope was 70 meters, I could not leave my pack at the belay stance.

About 30 meters out I placed my first screw, which left six screws for the remaining 40 meters of dead-vertical ice, and one for the belay. Fortunately, the ice on this pitch was mostly of good quality, the climbing no harder than solid AI5, and the angle not truly over-hanging. But at the end of a long, tiring day I found it quite challenging. I chose the wrong exit groove at the top and had to make a quick pendulum off my last screw to gain the correct finish. I finished the pitch just as headlamps became necessary, relieved to find a fixed piton to equalize with my remaining ice screw.

△

We had hoped to climb through the night, but by the time the packs and Kelly arrived at the belay it had become clear that navigating the convoluted mushrooms of the sum-mit ridge would not be feasible in the dark. But the dropping temperature and the arrival of a light wind made it clear that sitting out in the open would be a very cold proposition. We spied a slight depression half a rope length away, and although it wasn't much Kelly went to

Haley starts the first of two rime-ice tunnel pitches near the top of the climb. These tunnels were lined with good ice and provided chimney rests. *Kelly Cordes*

Haley armed his tools with prototype "wings" designed to provide additional security in the soft rime ice. *Kelly Cordes*

work immediately and we soon had a small cubby in which to escape the wind. A few warm drinks helped to pass the time, and our freeze-dried dinners provided a small amount of comfort, except when the package ruptured inside my jacket, soaking my base layers with chicken soup.

The night was long enough to be extremely uncomfortable, but not dangerously cold, and after six hours we crawled stiffly back into the rime world. Above us lay only three mushroom pitches before the summit plateau, but all with sections of steep unconsolidated rime, so I attached a prototype pair of "wings" to the top of my tools that I hoped would give more purchase. Black Diamond had manufactured these aluminum wings to extend horizontally on both sides of the pick but still leave the front of the pick to penetrate real ice. Fortunately, on the first two pitches we discovered natural ice tunnels that ran straight through the bellies of the mushrooms. Formed by the wind, these fantastic, fully enclosed tunnels were lined with good ice and provided quick and easy passage underneath what would have been difficult rime climbing. They were the perfect size, wide enough to allow me to swing my tools but tight enough to let me lean back for a chimney rest.

On top of the second mushroom, only one difficult pitch remained, but here climbing directly up the rime was necessary. A vertical groove ran up the pitch for about 25 meters and then faded into blank rime for about 10 meters before an exit tunnel could be reached. I took all four pickets with me, leaving only Kelly's plunged ice tools in the belay, and started up the groove. The climbing in the groove was reasonable, although the protection was not. As the groove grew progressively shallower, I began digging a vertical trough just deep enough to allow for some chimney technique. However, as the terrain continued to steepen my trough grew deeper, and eventually I tunneled inside the mountain for a few meters. I punched my way back outside near the top of a section of genuinely overhanging snow, forming a gigantic snow V-thread and the only decent protection on the pitch. Two terrifying aid moves off pickets gained the easier terrain above and eventually a natural tunnel to finish the pitch. Kelly followed the pitch with both packs, using ascenders on the section that I had aided, and then we joined the Compressor Route (above the bolted headwall) to quickly climb the easy summit mushroom.

It was surreal to finally stand on top of a mountain that I'd been dreaming of for so long, and I could tell that it meant something to Kelly as well. The view from the summit is a spectacular contrast: the polar landscape of the icecap less than one kilometer to the west, and the lush beech forests and pampas only a few kilometers to the east. We must have spent at least an hour relaxing on the summit before burying one of our pickets as a deadman and beginning the long descent of the Compressor Route. The descent was straightforward but long, allowing us plenty of time to marvel at all the bolts, admire all the fine terrain, and notice the reek of ammonia emanating from our worn-out bodies. We started the rappels with both ropes, but soon realized it was unnecessary and made almost all of our rappels with only the lead rope.

To future parties on the Compressor Route, I would highly recommend a single 70-meter rope, which is sufficient for all the rappels and much preferable for most of them.

Headlamps were necessary again right after pulling the last rappel, and we began our stumble down-glacier back to Niponino, making sure to get off route several times and descend chossy gullies. Kelly swears he heard disco music, that nutter. I went with trusty visual hallucinations, transfixed by bobbing lights above the horizon. We arrived at Niponino at 2:30 a.m., exactly two days after departing, and were warmly greeted with delicious polenta by friends who were just waking to attempt other climbs. We spent the next two days hauling unhealthily heavy packs down to El Chalten, and departed Patagonia on the morning of January 9.

⚐

We did not climb any new terrain, but nonetheless I feel that our linkup was significant because it shows another natural route to the summit to be feasible. Under good conditions, I think this linkup is an excellent way to start the west face, albeit with some objective hazard. It doubles the amount of technical climbing required but vastly shortens the approach. I believe that our linkup is one of only three completed routes to Cerro Torre's summit without using at least some of Maestri's bolt ladders (the other two being the standard West Face and Arca de los Vientos). Our descent, however, was of course greatly eased by this historical trail of compressed air and compressed difficulty that sadly renders Cerro Torre a compressed mountain.

As with any intense experience, it takes a few days or weeks to digest a difficult climb, and I found myself at first confused. "What the hell just happened? Did we really just climb Cerro Torre? Whoa, far out!" It still feels improbable that I climbed my perfect mountain, that I was finally able to achieve my ideal. With the dream completed and thereby destroyed, I will need to search for new inspiration.

SUMMARY:

AREA: Cerro Torre, Patagonia

ASCENT: Alpine-style linkup of À la Recherche du Temps Perdu (800m, Marsigny-Parkin, 1994) on the south face of Cerro Torre with the upper 600 meters of the Ragni di Lecco Route (Chiappa, Conti, Ferrari, Negri, 1974) on the west face and west ridge; descent by the southeast ridge (Compressor Route). The combination was 1,400m, AI6 M5, with two aid moves off pickets and a pendulum; Kelly Cordes and Colin Haley, January 5-7, 2007.

A NOTE ABOUT THE AUTHOR:

Colin Haley, 22, has lived all his life in Seattle, Washington, where he is a student of geology at the University of Washington. Years of climbing in the North Cascades have given him a fondness for bad weather and a forté in downclimbing steep, unconsolidated snow. He writes, "I would like to thank the American Alpine Club for the Mountain Fellowship Fund grant that helped make this climb possible, and for its continuing support of young alpine climbers."

Cordes (left) and Haley, after 48 hours on the mountain. *Kelly Cordes*

THE ENTROPY WALL

A direct route up Mt. Moffit's north face.

JED BROWN

The little-known north face of Mt. Moffit, a 2,300-meter wall. The Brown-Haley route takes on the steep rock wall. The 1989 Miller-Teale route climbed the ice to the right of the rock face. *Jed Brown*

The Hayes Range has long been a sort of local range for Fairbanks climbers. It doesn't have the glamour appeal of Denali or the Ruth Gorge, and access is a problem. (The Talkeetna pilots don't like flying there—distance and uncertain weather make the trip a significant financial risk—and the interior has a shortage of pilots equipped for glacier landings.) As a rule, there is never more than one climbing party at a time in the entire range.

In addition to this remote feel, the range is immature in that it hasn't been picked over for decades by good climbers. Few have heard of Mt. Shand, Peak 10,910', or Mt. Balchen, but these mountains offer plenty of opportunities for those looking for adventure.

In the eastern Hayes Range, the north face of Mt. Moffit rises 2,300 meters above its own private spur of the Trident Glacier. The glacier is bordered on the east by the still unclimbed northeast ridge and on the west by the northwest ridge, which, with four ascents to date, qualifies as the "normal route." This configuration means that the only time sunlight touches the face is for a couple of hours at dawn and dusk near the summer solstice, when the sun barely sets. Active seracs on both sides of the cirque make it a dangerous place to hang out. However, not far away is an idyllic meadow at the base of the northwest ridge, which, if not for the overzealous ground squirrels, would make the perfect base camp.

Jed Brown leading the 13th pitch on the first day.
Colin Haley

Brian Teale, who has been putting up hard ice and mixed routes in Valdez ever since it became Alaska's premier ice climbing destination, completed the first route on Moffit's north face with Harvey Miller in 1989. They climbed a 2,300-meter ice line to the right of the huge rock wall in the center of the face. The lower third of the route was a frozen waterfall to the left of the fall line of seracs high on the right side of the face. The upper part presented a choice between sustained but objectively safe ice and mixed climbing to the left or somewhat lower-angled ice, threatened by seracs, to the right. After the lower part of the route, they were eager to find more moderate terrain. With reluctance, they went right. They reached the summit after spending more than a day under the seracs. Brian's only comment was, "It was like playing Russian roulette with only one chamber empty." Although their route was certainly one of the biggest in Alaska that year, they stuck with the local ethic of the day and did not report it.

⟁

In March of 2002, after my first season of ice climbing, I got my first real taste of alpine success with the second ascent of the Cutthroat Couloir on McGinnis Peak, just east of Moffit. By June, I had convinced myself that I was ready for Moffit. Jeff Benowitz, Fairbanks climber and alpine mentor, and I flew into the mudflats next to the Trident Moraine with plans for the left variation to the Miller-Teale route. There had been two weeks of splitter weather before we flew in, so of course we had two weeks of crap. After we completed the approach in the rain, the clouds parted to reveal four independent, simultaneous avalanches. We never set foot on the face, and the more I looked at it the more I felt that I just wasn't ready for such an objective.

In May 2006, I took the opportunity to return to Moffit with Alaskan legend Carl Tobin (formerly of Fairbanks, now from Anchorage) and Aaron Thrasher (also from Anchorage). Combining my age with Aaron's still fell well short of Carl's, but we were tasked by Carl's wife, Nora, with checking his knot. Our objective was an ephemeral ice line that occasionally was visible on the 1,400-meter rock wall to the left of the Miller-Teale. Based on reports coming from the rest of the Alaska Range, it was a dry year, so I figured the left variation of the Miller-Teale would make a good contingency plan. We flew from Talkeetna to the Trident Glacier and proceeded to get three days of snow. The rock wall was completely ice-free and the snow above the Miller-Teale was not stable, so it was time to find another objective.

Since we had a big rock rack but modest ice gear, we went to the northeast ridge. We had 24 hours of good weather, but after a few pitches of time-consuming climbing over nasty gen-

Brown belays at the sweet snow-mushroom bivy ledge where the pair spent their second night on the wall. *Colin Haley*

darmes, and realizing that we had done less than 10 percent of the hard climbing, we took our last opportunity to bail without having to reverse the ridge. After a dozen harrowing 70-meter rappels down a gully on the east side of the ridge, we realized we should have reversed the ridge. More bad weather arrived, and, low on rack and motivation, we soon commenced the two-day hike to the road.

△

I spent the fall of 2005 in Yosemite, and there I met Colin Haley, who had two weeks, a ton of motivation, and $30 (which included his share of the gas to get back to Seattle). Our climbing styles were compatible, and after a few long routes we parted with vague plans to do something in Alaska the next season. Somewhere along the way, I commented that Moffit's north face looked like a granite and diorite north face of North Twin with 900 meters of snow and ice above it. He replied, "Send me a fucking picture!" On July 4, moments after the flight ban resulting from the North Korean missile test in 2006 was lifted, we flew into the Trident Glacier mudflats, set on a direct route on the north face.

During the first few days of unsettled weather, we made the 25-kilometer round trip to get the rest of our food from the airstrip. On July 9, my handy FM radio caught the Fairbanks

Colin Haley leads the roof over the snow-mushroom bivy (pitch 26). *Jed Brown*

forecast for "mostly sunny followed by two days of partly cloudy," so we sorted the rack and awoke at 1 a.m. We set foot on the face with two nights of food and three of fuel, just as the 3 a.m. sun touched the upper reaches. As expected, the granite bands offered high-quality climbing while the diorite was easier but looser. We led in blocks, with the leader in rock shoes, carrying or hauling the small pack, depending on the terrain. The follower wore boots and followed with the bigger pack, jugging when it was faster. After 19 pitches, we bivied on top of a pillar of granite. So far, the route had gone almost all free at 5.9. The most exciting part for me was dodging a microwave-size block that Colin's rope had knocked loose on an icefield near the end of the day.

While eating dinner and considering the weather, Colin commented that even if a storm came in we were committed to going over the top. The last thing I wanted to do was rap, but with 700 meters of unknown hard climbing and another 900 meters of easier ground before we could descend, it seemed a bit premature to rule out bailing. We still had enough rack to reach the ground, but Colin is driven. I chose not to think about it.

I got the first block in the morning. At the top of the first pitch I considered the consequences while staring up at a series of dripping diorite roofs as it began to snow. Colin sensed my hesitation and weighed in: "Get up there. It doesn't look that bad." After some nailing through loose blocks and back-cleaning twice, I finished the pitch and it was Not Too Bad.

Above a small band of ice, the main headwall began. There were three systems that looked like they might go, but I was only confident in one of them. It had the added bonus of bringing us to a huge snow mushroom under a roof that had been clearly visible from our base camp in the meadow. I had glassed it with binoculars in May and jokingly suggested that it would offer an expansive bivy, protected by the large roof. Indeed, after doing three pitches of mixed free and aid, I discovered that the bivy was better than I could have hoped. Situated under a three-meter horizontal roof, it had a perfectly level swath of snow two meters wide and 15 meters long, complete with railing. Even though we had only done six pitches, we hadn't gotten much sleep the night before and couldn't pass up such a sweet bivy. I was relieved that Colin agreed. After dinner, I lay giggling while rocks from the overhangs far above motored by like chopped Harleys.

In the morning, Colin aided the spectacular thin hand crack through the roof. When he neared the end of the rope, I felt a tug. Obediently, I paid out an armload of slack and was greeted with another tug. "Stop lowering me!" He had pulled a small cam from behind a loose block and taken his first ever aid fall. A few minutes later he was above the block and had the rope fixed. He had back-cleaned the roof, so I took the swing out over the void. It's less scary when all you can see is cloud below. One more rock pitch and we hit the upper icefield.

We knew there was a mixed headwall at the top of the face, but now it looked more intimidating than we had figured. Colin got the first two pitches, and then it was my turn. A short tension traverse and some hooking brought me to a slush-filled slot. When the slush ran out, it was time for a few moves of granite squeeze chimney streaming with water, followed by a leaning ribbon under some froth, and finally straight-up WI4+. Back in the meadow, Colin had talked me into taking only two stubbies and one normal ice screw. Since he was belaying on screws, that left me one stubby and a bit of conviction that I could reach the one crack far

Brown starts pitch 31, searching for the best exit route to the upper snow slopes. *Colin Haley*

above for some rock gear to belay on. I made it with a couple meters to spare, but was soaking wet and getting cold in a hurry.

In thermodynamics, entropy is a measure of disorder in a system.
The Second Law of Thermodynamics states that the total entropy
of an isolated system never decreases.

We had reached the end of the intrusive rock and, hoping to make the ice slopes above, I grabbed some rack and started moving in an attempt to keep hypothermia at bay. I should have brought more slings because the rope drag was horrendous for the final bit of loose hooking to an uninspiring six-piece belay. One more pitch of steep climbing put us on the upper slopes. We packed our main rope, now frozen and nearly filling a backpack on its own, and set off simul-climbing on the skinny rope. Two long pitches later, we unroped as the sun began to rise.

Soon, the angle eased enough to stop for a brew, so we kicked out a flat spot and started melting snow. I had the warmer sleeping bag (−5° C), and Colin had the belay jacket. After a couple of hours, the wind was moving enough snow that we both were cold. It was time to go. More clouds had come in, and it looked like the weather was for real this time. We summited in a whiteout a couple of hours later. We couldn't dig a cave since, in the interest of saving weight, Colin had talked me out of bringing the shovel blade. Lacking a compass, we considered the time of day and the direction of a brief glimpse of sun, and headed in the direction we hoped would get us to the northwest ridge. After a bit of stumbling around blindly, we were indeed

As the clouds lift, Brown realizes he is off-route and descending Moffit's southwest ridge. The two reversed course and headed down the northwest ridge. *Colin Haley*

The Brown-Haley route on the north face of Mt. Moffit. The rock wall is approximately 1,400 meters high. Another 900 meters of snow and ice lie above the rock. *Jed Brown*

on a ridge, but in a brief clearing it became apparent that we were on the southwest ridge. That would take us very quickly to the saddle between Moffit and Shand, but getting back to our camp would be epic, to say the least. The icefall leading down the east fork of the Trident had not been traveled in 60 years and looked like a mighty unhealthy proposition. The alternative would be to descend a route that Jeff Benowitz and company had done on Shand, but it had a bit of technical terrain and there was an icefall that way, too. We went back up to the junction and turned down the proper ridge. A few more hours of descending brought us back to the tent, 38 hours after waking up at the mushroom bivy.

The damned snafflehounds had eaten my dry socks and my toothpaste, chewed my T-shirt into Swiss cheese, and filled the tent with fecal matter. I had learned my lesson in May and left the tent open, so at least they didn't chew holes in that. Our food was safely clam-shelled in a pair of sleds, and we happily began devouring it while several inches of rain were deposited at camp and the face became plastered with snow. We both agreed we had just done the biggest and most committing climb of our lives. I tried acting tough by suggesting "what next?" But for the first time Colin seemed to have had enough. We briefly entertained notions of climbing McGinnis on the way out, but we were fooling ourselves and just walked by. After some amusing antics with two people in a four-pound pack raft made for one and a shovel blade on an ice tool for a paddle, we made it across the Delta River and stepped onto the Richardson Highway.

SUMMARY:

AREA: Eastern Hayes Range, Alaska

ASCENT: First ascent of the Entropy Wall (2,300m, VI 5.9 A2 WI4+) on the north face of Mt. Moffit (3,969m), by Jed Brown and Colin Haley, July 10-13, 2006.

A NOTE ABOUT THE AUTHOR:

Jed Brown, 23, was born in Alaska and calls Fairbanks home. He is a Ph.D. student at ETH Zürich, doing numerical analysis of ice flow.

"I read about this in *Freedom of the Hills!*" Brown prepares a makeshift paddle for crossing the Delta River. *Colin Haley*

THE McNEILL-NOTT MEMORIAL ROUTE

A new line on the south face of Mt. Foraker.

WILL MAYO

Maxime Turgeon finds steep water ice on the south face of Mt. Foraker. *Will Mayo*

W as the sky falling? The serac had avalanched with a vicious cacophony. The moment was surreal: the mind trying to recognize the cause of the roar, the delay between sight and sound too difficult for the brain to assimilate immediately. We had descended merely hours before, and now we watched a serac pummel our route, filling the entire cirque at the base of Mt. Foraker's south face with a cloud of powder blown up by debris. Thirty minutes earlier, Max and I had stood chatting with Karen McNeill and Sue Nott at the very spot where the debris had landed. After the cloud subsided, we could once again see Karen and Sue, unharmed, two dots at the bergschrund at the base of the Infinite Spur. After much swearing and exclamation, and then silence, we continued up to the shoulder, headed back to base camp. It was 8 a.m. on May 14, 2006.

Maxime and I rested on the shoulder for over an hour. I sat in the blazing sun, nauseated by the irony of our mad descent in fear of a storm that hadn't yet materialized, only to barely miss being pulverized by a serac avalanche. I was relieved to be safely off the south face; I felt like we had made the wrong decision; Maxime was disappointed, saying it was like the "Magnificent Failure." I apologized—we had descended due to my ambivalence about the weather. Maxime generously offered that it could have gone either way, the storm could have moved in and swallowed the mountain with its gales. We were up against an essential alpine paradox: Alpine climbing is not about summits; without a summit an alpine climb is incomplete.

Sue Nott (left) and Karen McNeill share a laugh at Kahiltna Base Camp, before starting their attempt on the Infinite Spur. *Will Mayo*

△

In March 2006, Maxime Turgeon and I were given an American Alpine Club Lyman Spitzer Cutting Edge Award for an attempt on the south face of Mt. Foraker. We pushed a new line up to the French Ridge by way of a snow-covered ice gully followed by stacks of brilliant thin-ice and mixed climbing, including two of the hardest and most dangerous mixed pitches I have ever done in the alpine.

At 6 a.m. on May 12, as we surmounted the bergschrund at the base of the face at 8,000 feet, the "above-the-schrund" enthusiasm swept over me. We dispensed with the initial gully rapidly and swept upward on sublimated thin ice that trickled down the steep granite gullies and corners. It was really happening. We were light and fit and moving fast on virgin terrain on a proud alpine face, actualizing all of the dreams and hard work that a devotion of one's life to climbing embodies. The thunk of a well-placed tool in ice, the scrape of a crampon skating off an edge of rock, the steady, regular heaves of deep breathing; the distillation of my existence happens here, the coming together of the past, the present, and the future. The scorched smell of steel striking granite doused with adrenaline-laced sweat washes memories of mountain euphoria over me.

> *The past and present wilt—I have fill'd them, emptied them.*
> *And proceed to fill my next fold of the future.*
>
> ...
>
> *Do I contradict myself?*
> *Very well then I contradict myself,*
> *(I am large, I contain multitudes.)*
> —Walt Whitman

The culmination of the crux pitch involved solid M6 climbing while wearing my pack, a pendulum into a shallow, melted-out chimney filled with loose spikes of granite suspended in lacy, meringuelike snow-ice, and then no gear till the belay. Upon reaching the stance, Maxime congratulated me heartily for the lead. The euphoria now gone, I turned to him and said, "I'm done. Let's go down. This is too dangerous. I have kids." Maxime's lip curled into a smile of disbelief. I imagined his unspoken thought: "And this fact is just occurring to you now?" Maxime argued that the initial snow gully would be too slushy at this time of day to descend safely. He encouraged me, saying he thought we were past the crux. We continued upward; Maxime led the last two stellar mixed pitches brilliantly. Directly above, a gargantuan serac emerged into view. I realized with feelings of fear and guilt that we had spent most of the day climbing directly under its menacing hulk.

After the initial 2,500 feet, the route consisted mostly of hard alpine ice and reasonably well-consolidated snow, with occasional moderate mixed terrain. As we slogged up the concrete ice of the hanging glacier that fed the serac (now safely below us), I noticed that a tune from the musical *West Side Story* was stuck in my head. *I feel pretty.* My toes throbbed. *I feel pretty.* My feet cramped. *I feel pretty and witty and gay.* My crampons were worn, stubby shells of their former selves, so dull it was hard to believe they had been brand-new that morning. *And I pity any girl who isn't me today.* We'd been listening to *West Side Story* incessantly before I left for Alaska—my girlfriend, my two daughters, and me. I smiled thinking of the photos I had taken of Karen and Sue at base camp, nestling a scarlet Beanie Baby lobster on their shoulders. The doll was

Will Mayo starts a steep mixed lead on the McNeill-Nott Memorial Route, on the south face of Mt. Foraker. *Maxime Turgeon*

the mascot of my eldest daughter's third-grade class. They had sent Lobby the Lobster with us to Alaska as our base camp mascot. I was looking forward to showing the girls the pictures of Lobby with these two amazing, inspirational women. Somehow, I imagined that just having those pictures justified the trip, regardless of how our climb went.

After 40 hours on the face (including two rest stops along the way—one nocturnal, one diurnal), we reached 13,500 feet, the point where the French Ridge abuts the massive, towering summit structure of Mt. Foraker. The wind whipped up and the ominous darkness of a high-energy low-pressure system seemed to become visible to the southwest, over the Gulf of Alaska. Having endured two southwesterly Alaska Range windstorms at two different high camps, both of which lasted four days and nearly terrified the life out of me, I was unwilling to proceed. I carried only a summer-weight sleeping bag, no tent, and no shovel. I can't imagine surviving a windstorm up there so equipped. Maxime was surprised by my assessment of the weather—it seemed good enough for him. So we continued. Shortly thereafter, around 10 p.m., my concern about the weather and the increasing winds influenced Max to concede and retreat.

We rappelled and downclimbed the entire face in nine hours, leaving much of our rack behind. We moved as fast as we could while rappelling the lower 2,500 feet, ridiculously exposed to the serac once again. On countless occasions we rappelled from single nuts, single pins, and single V-threads in four-inch-thick ice. We made our final rappel over the bergschrund shortly after 7 a.m. on May 14, pulled the ropes, stuffed them uncoiled into our packs, and ran out from under the face, still wearing our parkas and sweating profusely.

As we were downclimbing the gully, two figures approached in the cirque below. It was Karen and Sue, on their way to attempt the Infinite Spur. We reached them at the center of the cirque and explained why we had bailed. Karen remarked on our small packs with envy; we remarked on the size of their packs with sympathy. We chatted about the weather for a bit. Karen put on her hat and spun her ice axe, ready to go. Sue said

Do you want Flax 'n Oats or Apple 'n Cinnamon? Mayo kicks back at a rest stop. *Maxime Turgeon*

with a grin as she turned toward the Infinite, "Well, hopefully we'll see you in 10 days!" Her tone made it clear she was being optimistic. We wished them well and turned toward the shoulder that begins the retreat route from the cirque. We stopped partway and Max dressed his raw and swollen shins—too few socks. We began hiking again, and soon the serac calved and roared its menacing roar.

△

The perfect weather held. We watched Karen and Sue, two dots in the distance. We knew they must have been shocked by the magnitude of the serac avalanche—they probably were dusted by the powder cloud. I felt afraid and excited for them. The south face of Mt. Foraker is the most magnificent and yet the most terrifying place I have ever been. I secretly wished they would walk down the slope and come toward us and the comfort of the sun. But they did not; they just sat there. As we finally turned to go we gave one last look. Karen and Sue hadn't moved.

After our climb Maxime and Louis-Phillipe Ménard climbed a significant new line on the south face of McKinley. [Editor's note: See story on page 47.] I climbed the Mini-Moonflower on Mt. Hunter alone and spent a lot of time brooding in base camp. We all started to worry about Karen and Sue after two weeks had passed. My girlfriend, Katy Klutznick, joined me at base camp at the commencement of the rescue effort. The U.S. Army Pave Hawks flew search sorties, and the National Park Service Lama chopper, dangling "the claw," retrieved

The McNeill-Nott Memorial ascends about 5,200 vertical feet before intersecting the French Ridge at 13,200 feet. *Maxime Turgeon*

clues. All this seemed to exacerbate Katy's existing trepidation about the intimidating Alaska Range. We climbed most of the approach couloir to the northeast ridge of Mt. Hunter. We skied around the glacier a bit. Mostly, we hung around base camp, hypothesizing about Karen and Sue's disappearance.

I don't think about Alaska 2006 without thinking about them; their loss cast a pall over the entire experience. Climbing is large; it contains multitudes. The south face of Mt. Foraker was beautiful and terrifying, a glowing success and a magnificent failure. While climbing I am most alive and also most aware of what I have to lose. Do I contradict myself? Max and I easily could have been the ones who disappeared on Mt. Foraker last year. And still, I am counting the days with nervous excitement until my return to the Alaska Range this spring.

SUMMARY:

AREA: Alaska Range

ASCENT: First ascent of the McNeill-Nott Memorial Route (5,200', WI5+ M6R A0) on the south face of 17,400-foot Mt. Foraker, reaching the 1976 French Ridge route at ca 13,200 feet, Will Mayo and Maxime Turgeon, May 12-14, 2006.

A NOTE ABOUT THE AUTHOR:

Will Mayo, 34, is an insurance agent who lives in Northfield, Vermont. He loves his daughters more than anything else in the world.

THE CANADIAN DIRECT

Walking a fine line on the south face of Mt. McKinley.

MAXIME TURGEON

Mt. McKinley's south face, as seen from the East Fork of the Kahiltna Glacier. The Canadian Direct ascends the steep, rocky buttress to the right of the climber for about 4,000 vertical feet, and then continues up the American Direct (1967) to reach the summit ridge. See Climbs and Expeditions for a photo showing the route line. *Maxime Turgeon*

"Hey, are you the guys who were on the south side of Foraker? Joe Reichert wants to talk with you on the radio."

As soon as I heard his voice, I knew that Joe, a climbing ranger, was worried about Karen and Sue. How many days was it since I'd seen them at the base of Foraker? Seventeen!

"Yes, they told us, 'Hopefully, we'll see you guys in 10 days,' but they had brought 14 days of food and fuel."

"OK, thanks, Max. They had a radio, so if they didn't call they must be getting down the Sultana Ridge. And what about you guys? How did it go down in the Northeast Fork?"

"Actually, we changed our minds and went into the East Fork."

"And what did you do over there?"

"The Canadian Direct! You know that buttress, the one that many parties had looked at, between the Japanese Direct and the American Direct...."

Six days had passed since we'd last seen Joe. We were almost back down to Kahiltna Base Camp, but every step felt like the last one we'd ever be able to take. Less than 24 hours earlier, we had been totally lost at 19,200 feet on Denali. We had no radio, and no one had known about our plans. Now our feet were so trashed by three days of nonstop effort that our socks felt like sandpaper. The snow on the glacier had transformed into a sugary mixture that wouldn't support our weight. Our packs' painful shoulder straps, shearing our trapezius muscles, made us feel a bit less guilty about the rope that we had left behind when we reached the summit ridge on Denali.

Foraker's Sultana Ridge filled the horizon in front of us. We wished we could see two small dots coming down through that complex structure of seracs and crevasses, but for a while now we hadn't even been sure of what was real and what was not. We probably hadn't exchanged a word for over seven hours, and we didn't feel any need to. The rope between us was enough to tell us exactly what was going on in each other's minds, and now it was clearly transmitting the desire for a good meal and dry clothes.

In the morning, lying on thick mattresses in the warmth of base-camp manager Lisa Roderick's shelter, we awoke to the good smell of pancakes, eggs, and hash-brown potatoes. There was still no news of Sue and Karen, and Lisa was really worried. At first the women hadn't wanted to bring a radio, but Lisa made them understand that she was the one who would be upset if they were overdue. Did they run out of batteries, or were they out of range?

The next afternoon, as we pulled our sleds for the last time up Heartbreak Hill, we saw the Lama fly out of base camp carrying the "jaws." Soon we caught sight of it coming back over the east ridge of Foraker with a backpack dangling at the end of the cable. We knew then that something bad had happened.

△

On May 19, Louis-Philippe Ménard (LP) joined me at base camp. Denali was to be my second climb of the season; I had already climbed a new line on Mt. Foraker with Will Mayo, though we did not reach the summit. [The story of Mayo and Turgeon's climb on Foraker begins on page 42 of this *Journal*.] My new partner and I planned to go as high as possible on Denali to see how we would do at altitude before attempting a more serious route. A day later we were already at the 14,300-foot camp on the west buttress. We spent a day going back down to 12,000 feet to have a look at the Fathers and Sons Wall and found that the conditions were not good. After a rest day we continued to 17,000 feet, where LP started to feel a little altitude illness and descended. The next night we traded places, but at 3 a.m. a party of climbers woke LP at 17,000 feet to help them bring down one of their friends, who was showing signs of cerebral edema. Reunited at the 14,300-foot camp, we gave up our plans to go to the summit for acclimatization.

Our plan until this point had been to climb something on the southwest face, reaching it by going down the West Rib Route, but the forecast for the next three days called for 60 mph to 80 mph winds from the northeast. Looking over the Washburn photos of the mountain, an obvious feature on the south face grabbed our attention. Just a few words were needed before we forgot all the effort we had made to bring all our gear up to 14,300 feet. A few hours later, we were heading back to base camp to have a look at the south face from the East Fork of the Kahiltna.

After a full rest day we went to Lisa's place to ask for the weather report. In the background the south face of Denali was barely breaking through a thick layer of clouds. It looked so far away. We could easily have borrowed a radio from her, but with weather reports being what they are in the Alaska Range, we weren't sure we wanted to hear them once we were on the route. We headed back to the comfort of our multiple mattresses and sleeping bags and dozed off.

On May 27 we started skiing into the East Fork to set up our camp at the base of the icefall below the south face. Around 7 p.m. the low clouds began clearing from the valley, so we grabbed our skis and went to scope our prospective line. It didn't take much to convince us of its quality. Back at camp we geared up for an attempt the following morning: two 40-liter packs; a double bivy sack and one sleeping bag between us; 44 ounces of fuel, gels, bars, and oatmeal; two 60-meter ropes

Louis-Philippe Ménard starts the seventh pitch on the lower buttress. *Maxime Turgeon*

and a light alpine rack. Our packs weighed less than 20 pounds each. We planned for four days to climb the route and make it back down to the 14,300-foot camp on the West Butt.

⟁

At 7 a.m. we were trying to follow our wands from the previous night through the complex icefall below the Ramp Route, guarding the south face. "It's so fractured! How can this be a route?" The crust under our skis barely supported our weight. My aching hip complained every time I sank into the snow and had to pull my skis back onto the crusty surface. On the way back from Foraker I pushed a little too hard, and now I was paying the toll. Would I be able to tolerate it for all the hours of constant effort and sleeplessness to come?

We had not even reached the base of the Czech Direct when the sun hit the lip of Big Bertha, 5,000 feet overhead. We had to spend as little time as possible under this huge serac, and we couldn't even think of stopping for a breath of rest. We'd agreed to play Russian roulette, but not with five bullets. At 9 a.m. we stepped across the schrund and were clear of Big Bertha, but the sun was now warming up the whole face, and the sound of bouncing rocks was like a metronome, forcing us to quicken our steps. At every safe spot we found, we stopped to catch our breath. It was so warm that even in the ice sections we could climb bare-handed. We ran through many 5.5 to 5.8 pitches on great granite, and by 3 p.m. we were at 14,000 feet and ready for a brew stop. Two hours later, a big rock bounced right beside us. Our hearts raced, and very soon we began stretching the rope again.

As soon as the sun turned around the Cassin Ridge, everything got much quieter. The temp dropped dramatically, and the climbing got much harder, forcing us to spend a lot of time belaying. Minutes now felt like hours and the tension was building. We grew more and more frustrated at each other for being slow. We needed a ledge to stop and take out the sleeping bag, but it was too steep. Finally, after climbing all night, we manteled over the top of the lower buttress at 16,000 feet at 10 a.m. and crumpled onto a snow ledge.

For the first time we realized how high we were. Kahiltna Peak looked so small below our feet. Across a col at the far end of the south buttress, we could see the site of Kahiltna Base Camp—we were right at the lowest point on the wall I could see from base camp when I landed there three weeks earlier, and now I realized how far away the summit still was. Back at base camp we'd been so sure we wanted to be completely independent on this face, but now we felt that a little Talk-About would have been nice to have. A good weather report, even a suspicious one, would have been really comforting. On the horizon the French Ridge of Foraker hid the big, wild valley on the south side, where I had been just a couple of weeks ago. I spotted our high point below the 16,800-foot plateau under the summit. On the other side, the Sultana seemed to go on forever. I realized even more how committed we had been back there, and our current position wasn't any more reassuring.

Turgeon follows a pitch bare-handed on the sunny south face. *Louis-Philippe Ménard*

At 2 p.m. we started climbing again, making our way toward the upper buttress, where we would join the American Direct for its last 3,000 feet. We headed for an obvious groove right in the center of the buttress. At its base we found a bolt, probably placed by the American or the Japanese climbers that had passed this point a couple of decades ago. I clipped it and kept simul-climbing, but soon I found myself scratching on the rounded edge of the groove. When I finally managed to make a belay I was shaky and my heart was hammering in my head. LP took over, and the climbing remained insecure. Two pitches later we finally exited onto lower-angled terrain and found ourselves in hip-deep snow. In the last couple of hours the weather had changed drastically, and now it was snowing heavily and the wind was picking up. We were really slow, and even with some extra Clif Shots we felt out of energy. At 17,500 feet, LP stopped; when I finally joined him, he told me he couldn't take one more step. He sat down and I automatically started chopping a ledge.

It was 10 p.m. and without even lighting the stove we squeezed into our double bivy sack together. It grew warm really fast in our Gore-Tex cocoon, but spindrift constantly came in through the air hole we left open. The fabric flapped in our faces, and our leg cramps made our situation intolerable. Minutes seemed to last forever. At 6 a.m., after eight hours of torture, we couldn't endure it any more.

"Do you think we can rap down from here?"

"Fuck, no!"

"Then let's move!"

We manteled onto the southeast spur at 7 p.m. in a whiteout. We both were extremely stressed. We could barely see 15 feet ahead of us, and we knew almost nothing about the terrain

Turgeon leads the Gravel Pitch, "the only loose pitch of the route, but a really loose one." *Louis-Philippe Ménard*

Ménard climbs past the gendarme on the upper buttress (American Direct), just after leaving the Canadians' brief bivouac at about 17,500 feet. *Maxime Turgeon*

around us. We didn't even need to talk. Our only option for getting out of there alive was to follow the cornice toward the summit and then head down the West Butt. After many hours of slogging we were at 20,200 feet, where we could see what seemed to be the slope giving access to the summit. In our minds, we had stopped climbing a while ago, when we started to try to save our butts. The idea of expending even one more calorie just to put our feet on the highest point didn't even register.

We started angling toward the Football Field, but we couldn't judge the angle of the slope and fell every 10 steps. At about 11 p.m., when the GPS indicated 19,200 feet, the slope seemed to steepen in front of us, so I turned around and started to downclimb. I couldn't see any farther than my boots. Suddenly, both of my feet cut loose and I was flying through the air. I hit the snow and the rope tightened and then went slack again. Then I saw LP fly over me and land in the snow. When the tumbling finally stopped, it took us a while to realize what had happened. We had fallen over a 15-foot serac wall. Fortunately, we weren't hurt, but our synthetic pants and jackets were all ripped and the filling was coming out from everywhere. Where were we? There could have been a 1,000-foot wall right under us and we wouldn't know it. It would have been suicidal to continue in those conditions.

We started to empty our packs and establish a bivy. When I tried to light the stove, I couldn't get any pressure in the bottle. I threw it down and told LP it wasn't working. "Man, that's not an option! It needs to work!" he shouted at me. After warming up the pump and replacing some parts, we managed to light it. We were all wet and so was our only sleeping bag. After no more than two hours, hypothermia started to take over and we hadn't melted more than a quart and a half of water. The weather hadn't improved at all. We were trapped much higher than either of us had been before, and nobody on the mountain had any idea where we were. Should we leave everything and try to find our way to Denali Pass? If we didn't find it, we'd be dead. We shouldered our packs, crossed our fingers, and headed straight down until the GPS showed 18,200 feet. If we kept that altitude and headed west, we should end at Denali Pass.

Neither of us had ever seen the pass and hallucinations were starting to create an imaginary col. Something that looked like a rock wall appeared on our right, but then it went all white and flat again. Then it reappeared, getting bigger and bigger. When we got close enough to be sure it was the pass, we both fell onto our knees. We might not believe in any god, but something must have guided us through that whiteout. In less than an hour we were down to the 17,000-foot camp, where friends hooked us up with hot drinks and oatmeal.

It's hard to define all the reasons that compel someone to walk the thin line between life and death. There is probably a good deal of insouciance in this balance, but such experiences also cause something powerful, something indelible, to happen deep inside us. The bond between two people that emerges from such experiences is linked to feelings of extreme distress and profound joy, and these can't be shared with anyone else. LP and I now understand more than ever the spirit in which Sue and Karen wanted to live their lives. We will always remember them as partners linked by total engagement, by the desire to experience their climbs in complete detachment.

Climbers are probably the most selfish people I know, making all their life choices in order to pursue such self-rewarding experiences. To everyone around us, please forgive us for this.

SUMMARY:

AREA: Mt. McKinley, Denali National Park, Alaska

ROUTE: Alpine-style ascent of the Canadian Direct (8,000'/4,000' new, Alaska Grade 6, 5.9 M6 AI4), on the south face of Mt. McKinley (20,320'), between the American Direct (1967) and Japanese Direct (1977), finishing on the American Direct; Louis-Philippe Ménard and Maxime Turgeon, May 28-30, 2006. The two climbed from the bergschrund at around 12,000 feet to 19,100 feet on the summit ridge (southeast spur) in 58 hours, reaching a high point of about 20,200 feet before descending via the west buttress.

A NOTE ABOUT THE AUTHOR:

Maxime Turgeon, 26, lives in the suburbs of Montreal, Québec. He has an engineering degree and has worked briefly in the aircraft industry, but now makes a living as a mechanic, welder, and carpenter between climbs. He says, "I'm not really someone that doesn't like to work, but I have so many climbing projects coming up that I don't see how I can have a full-time job right now." His and Ménard's new route on the north face of Mt. Bradley in Alaska was featured in the 2006 American Alpine Journal.

Turgeon (left) and Ménard, just after reaching the summit ridge. The top was near, but the end of the ordeal was not. *Maxime Turgeon*

FREEING ZION'S THUNDERBIRD WALL

A big payoff for a long apprenticeship in sandstone climbing.

MICHAEL ANDERSON

Mike Anderson figuring out Zion sandstone on the first free ascent of the Lowe Route (15 pitches, 5.13a R) on Angels Landing, December 2004. *Andrew Burr*

What could cause overworked grown men to piss away their valuable time bickering like old married couples? Why, the Internet, of course! Throw in some winter weather and a handful of climbers who are, shall we say, "past their prime" and you have a recipe for an honest-to goodness e-mageddon. In January 2005 the conditions were in good nick for just such a furor when a well-meaning bystander posed an innocent question about the climbing history of Zion National Park. Just like that, the gates of e-halla opened, unleashing the wrath of decades-old drama, the likes of which no high school reunion could match. As more and more Zion legends caught wind of the pissing contest, the melee intensified, leaving no survivors. Good times!

Though the public airing of these personal soap operas was quite entertaining in its own right, I was looking for information about actual climbs. Amid one such engagement, prolific Zion climbing pioneer Dave Jones offered up a simple folk ditty about his one-time mentor. "The Ballad of Timber Top Mesa" recounts the saga of Ron Olevsky's struggle to climb one of the region's biggest walls:

> *Dangle once had a rack on Timber Top,*
> *New as it could be.*
> *Knifeblades, baby angles to part the sandstone rock*
> *The route t'would not be free!*

> *Timber Top will always be,*
> *Home sweet home to me.*
> *Good ol' Timber Top,*
> *And Dangle's rack fallin' free…*
> *And Dangle's rack fallin' free….*

Details were sketchy in the ensuing carnage, and since I have little reason to believe any of the various contradictory reports, I will refrain from elaborating. Suffice to say, I was intrigued and started to do more research on Timber Top Mesa's Thunderbird Wall.

⟁

About a year later, I'm revisiting these thoughts while asking myself the age-old climber's question: "Why didn't I just stay home and watch reruns of the 'A-Team'?" Three thousand feet above the creek bottom, I can easily see over all the nearby towers and mesas. I'm clinging to some sort of amorphous blob of biomass that is drooling down the wall. Evidently vines and roots connect us to the rock, but I can't identify them.

"Dirt!" I yell to Eric Draper, as I dig out a tiny ledge for a foothold. If I can get a few feet higher, I'll be able to place a cam and re-place my underpants. After several days on this wall I have sand in every crevice; my hair is a rat's nest of dirt and moss. Grabbing a fistful of venous dirt, I weight the new foothold, press down, and stretch out for an undercling…got it! Moments later, I lasso a stout pine and yell, "Off belay!" I'm now one pitch from the third ascent of the Thunderbird Wall. Though we had started the climb eight days earlier, this was only our fourth day on the route. Mixed in there somewhere was a 1,300-mile round trip between Zion and my Colorado Springs home, five days of work, family, and some training—welcome to my life.

I had hopes that this route would become the new high point in my efforts to solidify hard free climbing in Zion. After liberating a handful of routes—some popular classics, some obscure adventure routes—I wanted to build on those experiences.

At nearly 2,000 feet, the north face of Timber Top Mesa is among the highest sand-

56   THE AMERICAN ALPINE JOURNAL, 2007

stone walls in the world. Its sole route, the
Thunderbird Wall, was finally climbed by
Ron Olevsky and Earl Redfern in 1986 after
five attempts and the aforementioned lost
rack. Astonishingly, the undisputed founder
of modern Zion climbing, Jeff Lowe, had
attempted the wall as far back as 1971. At
the time, such classic routes as Spaceshot,
Touchstone, and Desert Shield were still
unclimbed. Lowe is a different cat, though.
He wanted big adventure, and he knew Zion
was the place to find it.

Even today, climbing on Timber Top
Mesa is a solitary affair; in 1971 it must have
felt like the dark side of the moon. Nevertheless, Lowe and Cactus Bryan had made a
bold alpine-style attempt on the wall. "We
had a full range of nuts, and that's what we
brought," Lowe told me recently. "I was way
into clean climbing, and I was almost to the
point of completely swearing off aid climbing." Despite their meager gear, they made
it an impressive 1,500 feet up the wall. At
that point they encountered dense vegetation
on lower-angled rock and called it quits. It
never occurred to Lowe and Bryan that later
climbers would decide the summit is super-
fluous. When I brought this to his attention,

Mike Anderson finds complex face climbing on a bolted
variation to the classic Spaceshot (9 pitches, 5.13a),
June 2005. *Andrew Burr*

he just laughed. "Yeah, I could've claimed something I guess, but who cares? It was just a good
adventure with Cactus, who was a great partner."

Thirty-five years later, my friends and I have come to the same wall, looking for the same
things: adventure and friendship.

△

I had mostly just sport climbed with Chris Alstrin when he told me about his plan for an
adventure climbing film and invited me to participate on a route in Zion. When you set out to
free a route, whether it's a boulder problem or a big wall, you usually hedge your bets by select-
ing a route that is, as far as you know, close to going free. The Thunderbird Wall was a mystery.
I did have a topo, but we might have been better off without it. It said one pitch was 5.10 and
the rest were hard aid. I would never attempt a route like that in the absence of peer pressure,
but, if the "naked quarter mile" incident during one of my college track meets was any indication, I don't handle peer pressure very well.

My trusty partner Rob Pizem was psyched to share the climbing duties with me, and I
invited Zion local Eric Draper to help carry gear...er, shoot photos. Our team was in place. From
scoping the wall, we reasoned that a conspicuous roof on the fifth pitch (marked A3+ on our

Rob Pizem changes corners on the second-pitch variation to Thunderbird Wall. *Eric Draper*

topo) would make or break the climb. When we finally got onto the wall in May, we freed what we could and aided the rest, gunning for that roof just to try to figure out whether this whole production would be in vain.

The team eventually overcame my utter incompetence at aid climbing, and on day two we were over the roof, ready to try some free climbing on a toprope. We envisioned a two-pitch variation at the start, and Rob gave it a try. The key to the variation would be switching between two cracks. The rock was a strange gray color, formed by white rock spackled with black lichen. Rob reached to his right to the second crack, a chimney that made jamming out of the question. Instead, he side-pulled the edge of the chimney in an iron-cross position, and, with no footholds available, cut his feet and kicked them over to the opposing wall in unison as my jaw dropped.

"Your eyes got about this big!" Rob hollered, motioning the size of a softball.

"That was crazy!" I replied. "It looks cool, but, man, I never would have thought of that!" Higher, I tried some moves on the roof, and, after watching me climb, Rob was convinced the route would go. I don't recall anyone asking my opinion, but someone made the decision that we would forge ahead. On May 29, our fifth day of working on the wall, Chris and I unceremoniously topped out for the third ascent while Rob and Eric were hard at work below, preparing our route for free climbing with a few bolts and some cleaning. All that remained now was to climb it in style.

◬

In 2004 I threw my hat into the Zion free-climbing ring. I was looking for something big, and Angels Landing was the obvious objective. The steep, dramatic north face lacked a single free line. The Lowe Route served up all I could handle, with persistent physical climbing and some very intimidating pitches, including a crux 5.13a R pitch with serious consequences. I gained a lot from that experience, learning to appreciate challenging routes like this and why they should be preserved. Honestly, I was tempted to cut corners. I considered preplacing gear, or even bolting the crack, but I'm glad I didn't. Leading that pitch required everything I had, physically and mentally, and I'll always have that experience to draw from, in climbing or otherwise.

I do have regrets about that climb, though, as I freed the route over three days, using fixed ropes. I wanted to climb it in a day, but life's circumstances forced me to finish the project

A foreshortened view of the Thunderbird Wall route on Timber Top Mesa. *Mike Anderson*

in December or abandon it. With the short days, a one-day ascent was impossible. That regret has since committed me to attempting one-day ascents.

A few months later my brother Mark and I made the first free ascent of the ultra-classic Spaceshot. Climbing ground-up in a pseudo yo-yo style, we didn't practice a pitch until those preceding it had been freed. I don't know if this is better style, but it certainly made the process more exciting. Every attempt brought new pitches to try, rather than rehearsing moves ad nauseam. This was risky because we might be stymied high on the wall but wouldn't realize it until we were already heavily invested. But the approach was great fun, and I applied it to several of the other free climbs I opened.

The Dunn Route on Angels Landing and Freeloader on Isaac tempered my nerves by exposing the darker side of Zion climbing with their wide cracks and loose rock. They also provided the perfect venue for Rob and I to work through the awkward challenges of a budding friendship. We earned each other's trust while forging a strong partnership.

Through these experiences I learned what it takes to pioneer hard free climbs in this big sandbox, and I also developed my framework for how they should be done. I experimented with the tricks of the trade and evaluated their legitimacy.

△

Two days after our aid ascent of Thunderbird, Chris and I were back at it, barreling across the Utah desert in Chris' Saab toward Zion. Chris' A/C didn't work, but unfortunately his cockpit thermometer did, so we were constantly reminded of how hot we were. The leather seats were a nice touch—they created a nice little microclimate between my legs, something along the lines of deli meat that has been in the fridge a few months too long. We tried our best to "think cold" as we put the miles behind us.

The next morning we awoke as early as we could after the 10-hour drive and hit the all-too-familiar Lee Pass Trail into Zion's backcountry. I was an emotional wreck. We were on our way to try our first ground-up free attempt on Thunderbird, and to make matters worse we had a deadline. Chris, our aspiring filmmaker, was leaving for Peru in two days. We had to send the wall in 24 hours to earn immortality in the form of civilization's most highly revered memorial, the climbing video. I forced my mind to think of anything besides the Thunderbird Wall: circus midgets, having breakfast with leprechauns, and they're eating scrambled eggs, which come from birds, thunderbirds—damn it! I reviewed all the reasons we might fail: I hadn't tried all the pitches; I wasn't sure I could do all the crux moves; the route needed more cleaning; it was too hot; there were too many mosquitoes. Fortunately, this wasn't my first bout with preclimb anxiety; it happens every time. Things usually work out fine, so I went through the motions as I always do.

Rob started the wall at about 10 that morning with a brilliant lead of the intimidating first pitch. Pitch two would be the first crux, and besides rappelling by it I hadn't learned much about the moves. Rob took a short fall at the start, but then quickly fired it on lead. He put me on belay and began his patented spray-down: "There's a foothold on the face for your right foot, left hand match in the pod, now bump your right hand up the crack, stem to the left, you got it, dude!" he shouted. At the top of the left crack I milked a hand jam while contemplating the footloose traverse to the right. This is where Rob had done his double-foot dyno into the next crack. I hate dynos, so I did my best to make the move statically. I reached right and found the best sidepull on the edge of the crack. With my arms in an iron cross pose, I cut my feet from the left crack and let

Mike Anderson reaches for the iron-cross move on the crux fifth pitch of Thunderbird Wall, a short variation to the aid climb. *Eric Draper*

them drag across the wall. I hooked my right heel around the edge of the crack, and stabbed at a dish on the face with my left foot. This allowed me to kick my right foot to a hold and rock over it to reach Rob's belay.

I believe Zion sandstone is the ultimate free climbing medium, and my previous climbs had opened my mind to its possibilities. Any climber who has visited Indian Creek has experienced the stunning cracks common to the Utah desert. Throw in some finely sculpted finger buckets, and you start to get the idea. Because they are so steep and monolithic, I'm always surprised when the walls in Zion yield a free climb. The key passages are often subtle and convoluted, but much of the joy of the process is piecing these puzzles together.

Pitch five, Thunderbird's crux, would be a case in point. "I'll probably just go up to work out the moves, then we can pull the rope and I'll try for the send," I told Rob. It had been nearly two weeks since I tried these moves on toprope, and I wasn't optimistic. The aid route climbed a knifeblade-size crack in the back of a left-facing dihedral. About 30 feet up, a large roof jutted out, capping the dihedral. The aid route would be impossible to free climb, but I had learned on Angels Landing and on Touchstone Wall that the patina on Zion's lower-angled faces often forms tiny face holds. Sure enough, I had pieced together an unlikely sequence on the less-than-vertical arête forming the right side of the dihedral.

"OK, I got you good," Rob said. I stood high off the belay flake and reached out the right side of the dihedral to grab a two-inch-thick flake plastered to the wall. Its jagged shape made for easy free climbing, but its hollow ring was unnerving. I climbed lightly. About 10 feet up, I moved left, back into the dihedral. With my heart beating in my throat, I dug deep to bust out two brutally powerful lieback moves off two-finger piton scars. This bought me enough altitude to reach a good foothold that would allow me to oh-so-tenuously reach right to a good pinch on the arête. I exhaled slowly, pressed off the left wall, and slid my open palm across the pink sandy face. An eternity passed and then my fingers curled around the corner. I latched the pinch and breathed. A few more balancey moves got me around the corner and onto a slab. Switching modes from power to technique, I forced slow, steady breaths to compose myself for the steep slab finish. Beyond my wildest expectations, I held it together for 15 feet to pay dirt. "Woo-hoo!" I yelled.

We had eight hours of daylight and nearly a dozen pitches remaining, so we sprinted toward the top. On the 5.12 eighth pitch, Rob led bravely above a couple of spooky knifeblades I had fixed earlier. As I followed the pitch I realized it was a critical passage for the free ascent. A knifeblade crack splitting a blank wall slowly widened to good hands. A flake provided a few key handholds, which disappeared just as the crack widened to fingers. With no other features within a hundred feet of this crack, the free route would have been impossible if the seam didn't open up soon enough or the flake vanished.

Pizem stretches to clip a preplaced piton on the 5.12 eighth pitch. *Eric Draper*

The next pitch had its own spice. About 50 feet to the right across a slab was a wide crack system, a fast lane to the summit if we could get to it. We could see a reasonable traverse across a steeply sloping ledge that would take us there, but the ledge was about eight feet below the last handhold we could reach. For once, gravity was in our favor: All Rob had to do was let go. He stuck the downward slab-dyno and persisted past thin, funky gear as the 5.12 "fast lane" took its time widening to protectable dimensions.

Every pitch had its own style and character. I got my own 5.12R spice on the 12th pitch, with tricky gear in a flared crack high on an exposed slab, as the waning sun splashed golden light over the upper reaches of Timber Top Mesa. After finishing the 14th pitch, we rappelled to a good ledge for the night, then started again early the next morning. For the final pitch I belayed off a stout ponderosa pine 50 feet below the rim. This last stretch featured numerous grumpy bushes woven into the heavily fractured Carmel Formation sandstone. Equalized gear and slow, steady breathing encouraged me up the 5.11 moves onto the summit, which we reached at 8:30 a.m. for the sub-24-hour ascent.

A few years earlier, lightning had sparked a forest fire that engulfed the summit, and the scattered remains of a once-great forest greeted me. Out of this wreckage, lush fields of scrub oak and wildflowers had taken over. The harmony of this contrast impressed me. I have frequently noted that the desert oasis of Zion is itself a contrast—a constant reminder of my own life. My professional life versus recreation, my family versus my friends, and my two-year quest for free climbing in a land of aid routes. Like this fragile desert ecosystem, I'm hopeful that all these elements will continue to prosper in balance.

SUMMARY:

Area: Kolob Canyons, Zion National Park, Utah

Ascent: First free ascent of the Thunderbird Wall with variations (16 pitches, VI 5.13- R) on the north face of Timber Top Mesa, Michael Anderson and Rob Pizem, May 31-June 1, 2006. Both climbers led or followed every pitch free. Previously, in late May, Anderson, Pizem, Chris Alstrin, and Eric Draper climbed the route to prepare it for free climbing, making the third ascent of the Thunderbird Wall in the process. They added six protection bolts to variations of the original route and fixed three pitons on the original aid line.

A NOTE ABOUT THE AUTHOR:

Michael Anderson is a captain in the U.S. Air Force, currently stationed in Colorado Springs. He is 30 years old and has been climbing half his life. Though his experience spans the spectrum from sport climbing to big mountains, he is currently smitten with free climbing on big walls. Since December 2004, he has made the first free ascents of 10 big routes—mostly Grade V and VI— in Zion National Park.

ENCOUNTERS WITH JANAK

A seven-year itch for a 7,000-meter Himalayan beauty.

ANDREJ STREMFELJ

The southwest pillar of Janak Chuli (7,041m), climbed by Andrej Stremfelj and Rok Zalokar in 2006, forms the left skyline. Stremfelj and Miha Habjan climbed the prominent, diagonaling ice line on the right side of the face in 2005 but could not continue to the summit. *Andrej Stremfelj*

I first saw Janak in 2000, when I led an expedition of 10 young alpinists to the Himalaya. One of our goals was Janak Chuli, but, having arrived in Nepal, we discovered the mountain was still not on the list of allowed peaks. After Andrej Markovic was killed on Jongsang, we unanimously decided to halt the expedition. However, while everyone else was eager to get home and heal their wounds, I was in no hurry. My wife, Marija, and daughter Katarina were already on their way to base camp, and besides I would never miss an opportunity to discover another hidden part of the Himalaya.

Janak rose at the end of the Broken Glacier. The south face glowed in the afternoon sun, and a route up its southwest pillar, leading straight to the top, was plain to see. I was immediately captivated by the mountain, in part because its 7,000-meter-plus summit was still unclimbed. In the following years, Andrej's father, Marjan, asked me to accompany him to his son's grave, and I agreed. Unfortunately our expedition in the autumn of 2005 was cancelled shortly before leaving. But I had intended to take advantage of this journey for a quick side trip to Janak and had made arrangements with a young climber, Miha Habjan, who had proved himself on Dhaulagiri. Since we both had our minds completely set on Janak, we decided to go anyway.

After succeding on an unclimbed peak, 6,842-meter-high Lashar I, we were well-acclimatized and we headed for Janak. I was eager to climb the pillar, but Miha was battling a throat infection and favored an easier line leading up the gully

Rok Zalokar leads the crux pitch during the second day of climbing on Janak, aiming for the crucial ice traverse. *Andrej Stremfelj*

on the right side of the face. We would need our full strength for a route like the pillar on Janak, so we decided for the gully.

We climbed the face in a day, belaying only the last five pitches. On top of the wall the wind was blowing so hard and the cloud cover was so thick that we had to abandon our plan to continue to the summit during the night. Since we had neither a tent nor sleeping bags, we had to protect ourselves from the wind as quickly as possible. We spent half of the night digging and the other half snoozing and shivering in a shallow hole. The early-morning sun filled my heart with hope. However, clouds arriving from the south put my feet back on the ground.

Suddenly, the only important thing was getting down as fast as possible. It started snowing after the first rappel, and soon avalanches began to sweep down the wall. Fifteen anchors, 15 rappels—we just hoped it would eventually end. Hell lasted until we reached the bottom of the face.

△

The decision to return in the spring was easy. I had promised to help a group of alpinists and mountaineers from Novo Mesto with an ascent of 7,140-meter Pathibhara Chuli (a.k.a. Pyramid Peak). Of course, I also wanted to attempt Janak again, this time via the southwest pillar. Miha and I had learned enough about the mountain to know the pillar was climbable. Unfortunately, Miha had already made other plans. In fact, all the alpinists with whom I would want to share a tent on Janak already had named their objectives for the year.

A splendid bivy site: Unfortunately, the two climbers had no sleeping bags or insulated pads inside their tent. *Rok Zalokar*

All of a sudden I thought of Rok Zalokar. As the head of the commission for alpinism within the Alpine Association of Slovenia, I had shaken his hand earlier that year and presented him with an award for the previous year's most promising young alpinist. After the ceremony I approached him and asked about his plans. He said he had nothing special in mind; in fact it was time for him to start studying. Now, just as I had almost despaired of finding a partner for Janak, I dialed Rok's number. He was a bit surprised and started talking—to himself more than to me—about his studies and the shortage of time to raise money. I said he could continue his studies after we returned, but opportunities for a good ascent like this were rare. The finances would be my concern. He promised to let me know in an hour or two. It did not take long for him to call, and Janak once again moved to the front of my mind.

The members of our expedition were mainly older alpinists who hadn't climbed anything remarkable for a long time, if ever. They all focused on climbing the easier European 4,000-meter peaks, Kilimanjaro, and Aconcagua. At the airport, when they met Rok, a colorful and powerful 23-year-old, they kept their thoughts to themselves. After we had become friends, Rok and I exchanged our impressions of this meeting and had a good laugh. As the leader of the expedition, I expected turbulent days over the next month and a half.

Our common objective was Pathibhara, a peak on the Indian-Nepalese border, north of Kangchenjunga, that had been climbed only once, in 1993. It seemed that climbing the mountain via the northeast ridge over the Sphinx (a 6,825-meter foresummit) would be an appropriate route for most of the expedition members. Some problems could appear in the upper part, but Rok and I would fix ropes to prepare the route for the others. We were going to climb with camps and fixed ropes in classical Himalayan style, which would enable Rok and I to thoroughly acclimatize.

In eight days we got from Suketar to Pangpema, where we set up base camp under majestic Kangchenjunga. Despite my warnings about the vastness of the glaciers, most expedition members were mentally unprepared for the dimensions of the Himalaya. It quickly became clear that the summit would be difficult to achieve for this team. The first to attempt it, the most experienced member of the expedition, stopped somewhere before the saddle between the Sphinx and Pathibhara. Next it was Rok's and my turn.

Early in the morning we crested the Sphinx. The view was breathtaking. All four peaks of Kangchenjunga greeted us, together with the mighty guardians Siniolchu on the left and Jannu on the right. Kirat Chuli rose like a powerful guard right in front of us, the mountain chain of Jongsang behind. The approach to the saddle before Pathibhara was demanding, and we fixed all 200 meters of our extra rope. The ridge ascended gently for a while, but soon it turned into a saw with sharp ice teeth. I organized protection so the rope would zigzag among the tines. From Pathibhara's northeast summit, we could see that the ridge descended steeply into a deep notch and continued a long way to the top.

It was late afternoon. We had to consider the facts and decide quickly. The rest of the team might reach the main summit if the route were completely equipped with ropes, but this would require material, power, and time we didn't have. Rok and I could continue to the top, but we would have to bivy during the descent and we had neither equipment nor food. We would survive, but we would have to forget Janak. The summit was so close and making a decision so hard. We took the risk and decided to sacrifice Pathibhara for our attempt on Janak. If only success on Janak were guaranteed....

The next day I stood atop the Sphinx again with Marjan, Andrej's father, and Borut Novak. Both were grateful for an ascent to a high summit with such a heavenly view.

△

Our rest at base camp lasted only a day, and soon we were gathering equipment and food on a canvas tarp in front of the tent. We didn't know how Janak would look that season; we

This spectacular leftward ice traverse was the key to breaching the upper headwall. During the descent, the climbers were forced to painstakingly reverse these pitches. *Andrej Stremfelj*

The 1,100-meter southwest pillar of Janak Chuli. The two climbers bivouacked once, by a large crevasse visible beneath the upper headwall. *Andrej Stremfelj*

had been too busy with Pathibhara. But judging by the other faces in the area, we expected to find lots of ice and bare rock, and therefore harder climbing. We had exactly four days to move from Pangpema base to advanced base camp below Janak, climb the face, and descend at least half of it. The weather forecast after that was bad, and we didn't want to endure a storm like I had experienced the previous year.

After moving our camp to a site below Janak, at the end of the Broken Glacier, we rested for a day and then set the alarm for very early, overslept, and then raced to leave in half an hour. We were at the base of the face an hour later. We had expected to advance quickly on the lower slopes, but instead sank into the snow, scratched the ice beneath it, and occasionally found hidden crevasses. Higher we found steps of water ice, which soon turned into a steep ice slope, where we tied in to the rope. After a long pitch that we climbed simultaneously, protected by two or three pitons, we reached the top of a prominent serac band and took a break.

Steep gullies with a difficult passage over a small rock band followed. I placed a belay at the foot of a bigger rock step. Rok masterfully surmounted the first smooth section of the granite barrier, while I tackled the second part, full of steep mixed climbing all the way to the beginning of the central ice slope on the face. We climbed simultaneously up the seemingly endless slope until we finally reached a huge crevasse below the final rock wall. Our moods cleared as we discovered a wide and completely flat ledge, where we put up a tent.

It was a beautiful evening. Lower peaks right in front of us and the higher ones far on the horizon lost the red glow of the setting sun one after another. The cold night came and colored the sky metal-blue. Our stove filled the tent with pleasantly scented steam. We made ourselves modest beds without foam pads and sleeping bags. The night was bearable as long as we cooked. We took turns, snoozing and cooking. Soon after we turned the cooker off, frost began to bite. It would not let us sleep in peace. We shivered and shifted from one side to our backs, from our backs to the other side. Soon we were moving more than sleeping, so we returned to cooking, trying to warm ourselves up. Eventually a gray morning was born.

Veils of humidity dimmed the horizon, but we quickly got ready to leave, and by 6 a.m. I was leading the steep, hard ice slope above the tent. I finished the pitch in rocks under a steep crack. Before starting this pitch, Rok took a look around the corner to see whether it looked any nicer from the other side, but soon he was back. Liebacking, fully exposed, he overcame the crux of the route and pushed on to a belay at the right side of the crucial ice traverse that we had seen from below. This long, narrow ice slope was surprisingly steep at the beginning, with poor ice. Two pitches of traversing and downclimbing took a lot of time and power.

Beyond the traverse we expected some kind of a gully that would lead us behind the headwall to the ridge. What a disappointment! Instead we faced a steep rock wall. But after three pitches of difficult mixed climbing, the face finally gave up. We left the rope under a rock overhang and reached the ridge unbelayed, covered by clouds that had come rolling over from the Tibetan side of the peak. Light snow fell, and the summit seemed far away. The closer we got, the harder it snowed. We both quietly pondered how we would descend in such weather, and so we made our utmost effort to hurry. In fog and heavy snowfall, the sharp ridge suddenly flattened and we waded onto a rather large summit.

My seven-year dream had come true. A tear of joy may have been shed behind my goggles as I hugged Rok. One climber just beginning his career, the other nearing the end of his own. We were the first people on this summit, alone in the middle of the vast Himalaya, yet alone only physically—in fact we were in the thoughts and hearts of many people thousands of miles away. We used the GPS on our satellite phone to determine our position and took a few snapshots. We couldn't see much. I reminded both of us out loud that the story was not yet over, not until we had dropped a thousand meters to the broad plateau of the Broken Glacier.

By evening we had descended as far as our bivouac site. The rope got stuck during the second rappel, but we managed to solve the problem quickly. Again we spent a long time on the traverse, even though we simul-climbed it. We took down the tent and descended into the night. I drilled the last rappel holes into the ice in the morning light. A huge cloud that had appeared somewhere above the Indian plain lifted itself high into the sky and slowly grew toward Jannu, as if attracted by an invisible force from the Himalayan giants. We were so impressed by this play of nature that we forgot where we were for a while.

The first rays of the sun caught us in the middle of the glacial plateau. Janak's face was still in shadow, but the sun brought our phone's batteries back to life. For the first time we could send home the news of our safe return. This was deliverance for our families and the beginning of a new period of suffering for us. Our concentration, so intense for the last two days, slackened fast. Weariness overtook our bodies. The final ascent to our tent at advanced base camp seemed longer and more exhausting than the entire face.

SUMMARY

AREA: Janak Himal, Nepal

ASCENT: Alpine-style first ascent of Janak Chuli (7,041m), by the southwest pillar (1,150m, IV-V, 60°-70° / III 45°-55°), Andrej Stremfelj and Rok Zalokar, May 5-6, 2006. Descent via the route (19 rappels and down-climbing).

Zalokar (left) and Stremfelj take a break during the walk out. *Courtesy of Andrej Stremfelj.*

Translated from the Slovenian by Ana Korenjak.

CHO OYU CONTRADICTIONS

Escaping harsh realities on a single-push new route in the Himalaya.

PAVLE KOZJEK

Chinese soldiers guard their young Tibetan captives at Cho Oyu base camp. *Pavle Kozjek*

I first climbed in the Himalaya more than 20 years ago. In the early 1980s I was a member of large expeditions organized by the Slovenian Mountaineering Association. These opened some hard new routes in classic Himalayan style, using fixed ropes. Now it may seem old-fashioned, but at the time these expeditions were probably the best way to get experience for the following years, when my Himalayan climbing went the other way: alpine style.

From 1986 to 1989 I climbed alpine style on Gasherbrum II, on Dhaulagiri in winter, and on a new route on the south face of Shishapangma, with Andrej Stremfelj. The northeast ridge of Everest without oxygen was another good test for my high-altitude limits. But the Peruvian Andes were the place where I really sharpened my favorite style: to simply climb to the top,

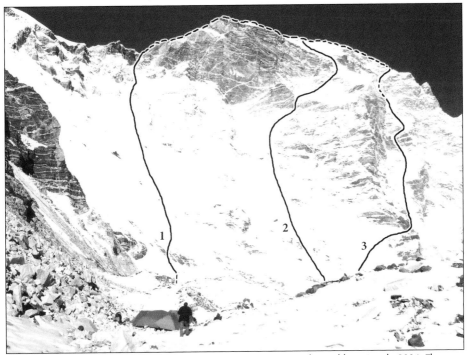

The southwest face of Cho Oyu (8,188m), the sixth-highest mountain in the world. 1. Kozjek, 2006. The route joins the west ridge (Polish Route, 1986) above the southwest face. 2. Yamanoi, 1994. 3. Kurtyka-Loretan-Troillet, 1990. All three routes on the southwest face were established in alpine style. Kozjek's line, the shortest, is the first new route on an 8,000-meter peak to be established solo in a single-day push. *Pavle Kozjek*

as fast as possible, taking only the most essential and lightest equipment. My new routes on Huascarán, Chacraraju, Chopicalqui, and Siula Grande confirmed that this style worked on serious mountains. If one could do this in the Andes, shouldn't it be possible in the highest mountain range as well?

I chose the southwest face of Cho Oyu as the place for this challenge. My idea was to climb alpine style, without bivouacs, in a single push, directly from the base of the two-kilometer-high wall to the top.

△

At the beginning, everything went well. But soon after we left Kathmandu and entered Tibet, health problems reduced our group by two members. On the Tibetan plateau, symptoms of pneumonia or pulmonary edema must be taken very seriously. So only six of us were left: the expedition leader Uroš Samec, young but already experienced leading expeditions to the Himalaya; the senior teammate Emil Tratnik, a member of the epic nine-day ascent of Dhaulagiri's south face in 1981; his son Aljaž, a promising alpinist of the younger generation; Marjan Kovac, my frequent climbing companion in the Andes; and Peter Poljanec from Tolmin, another promising young alpinist.

When we arrived at base camp, most of the other expeditions had already started their work on the mountain. At first it seemed as though there was no room left to pitch our tent.

When we finally found a small open space and began to unload our gear from the yaks, the guide from the neighboring camp shouted, "Move away from there—that place is reserved for my brother's expedition!" A really nice welcome. We decided to stay, and our unpleasant neighbor eventually ignored us.

We acclimatized on the normal route, pitching a tent at Camp I at 6,300 meters and another at Camp II at 7,000 meters. Again there was hardly enough space. Many people were already using oxygen at 7,000; some of them had problems using crampons and ice axes. Some expeditions organized climbing courses in base camp to prepare their clients for the "adventure of their lives." Was this still the Himalaya I knew? The answer came soon.

Four of Kozjek's teammates followed him up the route later the same day. The first pair is seen here entering the narrows that lead to the crux ice pitch. *Marjan Kovac*

The morning of September 30 was just like other base camp mornings except that we were awoken by gunfire. The night before we had played cards late, and I had no real wish to get up. But the shooting continued. What could it be? Hunters? A military exercise? I couldn't think of anything else. I quickly got out of the tent, and something immediately attracted my attention. A long, broken line of people moved across the glacier in the sharp morning light; from where I stood they looked like black dots in the glittering snow. It wouldn't be unusual: A few days back we had noticed people crossing Nangpa La, a traditional route for traders and Tibetan refugees on their way to Nepal. But now the line was longer than we'd ever seen it.

I went back to the tent, but soon I was back out again. A group of armed Chinese soldiers walked among the tents. Then an officer appeared in a spotless uniform with a red epaulet, a golden star, and, surprisingly, cheap sneakers on his feet. Most of the soldiers were very young; they looked friendly and relaxed, without any sign of tension on their faces. Close to them stood a group of children in light jackets, carrying bags like they were on their way to school.

More soldiers came down the path. I took a few more pictures with my zoom lens from the open space between the tents. If nothing else, it was unusual to have such visitors in a base camp. I had a sense that the soldiers might not like to be caught on photos, but there was no real need to hide; the soldiers seemed too preoccupied with other business to care about us. They marched the children slowly toward a large tent under a Chinese flag in the center of the camp.

About an hour later, the soldiers and the group of children, accompanied by some Tibetan adults, passed by my tent again. One soldier carried a Tibetan man on his back, but only for a short time; he soon dropped the man onto the ground, where he lay moaning. He'd obviously been shot in the leg, but after he balanced himself with some ski poles he managed to continue walking. "So, they were shooting at people, not in the air," I realized, shuddering from the truth. Hiding behind our kitchen area, I tried to catch the rest of the scene with my video camera. The group disappeared. A feeling of tension spread across the camp, as if the air had grown heavy. People talked in stifled voices; most seemed to hide in their tents, trying to ignore what was going on. We turned our attention back to packing for the next day's early start.

Late in the afternoon, the camp seemed calm again. More people came out of their tents, talking as usual and preparing to go up the mountain. After lunch we sat for a while in our tent for a lazy game of cards, trying to while away the last hours of daylight before our ascent. Nobody talked except for a few words about the game. Our packs were ready, and time had slowed again, until the sudden words "… the body is there…" broke the peace. The voices were in front of our tent. What body? Where? How? I picked up my binoculars—and there was no doubt. A body lay on Nangpa La, clearly visible 500 or 600 meters from us. Emil started to curse the soldiers, as if the words could change something. Then he stopped and we stood in weary silence. Who could tell us more about what had happened? I found our Nepali cook, who briefed me in a quiet tone, as if he had known the news for a long time: The children I saw were part of a group of Tibetan refugees trying to escape from China; the soldiers shot two people, and a dead girl lay on the path, a bullet in her back.

"Can you repeat your statement?" I asked, pointing my video camera at him. He agreed, although he seemed to hesitate at first. Then he began to speak with carefully chosen words about a "dangerous place for Tibetans." I understood his reticence. He didn't want to jeopardize himself or his family, who probably all live on the money he earns from his expeditions.

My teammates and I slowly drank tea in our mess tent, waiting for night. We had nothing to say. What about tomorrow? No one asked the question. One by one we crept into our tents.

△

In the morning my first view was of Nangpa La. The body was still there: a single black dot on the pass. Why hadn't anyone moved it? Did the soldiers leave it as a warning, to remind witnesses that the same thing could happen to them? Or to demonstrate how little Tibetan lives were worth? I took a final photo, and then I removed the memory card from my camera and locked it into my personal gear barrel. For the climb, I would take a different memory chip; I didn't want to have climbing and killing together. It would be hard enough not to keep the image of the body in the back of my mind over the next few days.

But I didn't feel like giving up the climb. I felt as though I needed to continue, out of a kind of stubbornness and resistance. Would it be of any help if I were to pack up and go home? No. My teammates seemed to feel the same way. There was no discussion between us; they just packed their last things, looking determined to go. It seemed like they also needed to escape from that camp, to be alone with the mountain and have time to think about everything, away from the crowds.

We placed our new camp on the upper part of the glacier, about four hours away from Cho Oyu advanced base camp. From our warm sleeping bags we admired the golden colors that lit up the southwest face, which slowly became red, fading out to a cold blue, then black. The moon rose from behind the ridge of Nangpai Gosum, and again we had light. By morning, though, the moon would be gone and the night would be black. Through the down of the sleeping bag I imagined the bitter cold of ice underneath us.

△

On hard climbing days I usually wake up before the alarm goes off, and I was ready a few minutes before Marjan, Uroš, Emil, and Aljaž, who were all going to attempt the same face I would climb. Marjan and Emil hadn't decided yet which line they would take, while Uroš and Aljaž had chosen the Kurtyka-Triolet-Loretan route in the central part of the face. Only two routes breached the huge face, both climbed in great style by great climbers. How different from the crowds on the normal route on other side of the mountain. I wished good luck to my teammates, still packing the last pieces of their equipment, and set off alone.

The night was warm for the Himalaya, and soon I started to unzip my clothes; I even stuffed my down jacket into my pack. My wind jacket would be enough. If I wanted to make it to the top in a day, I needed to work like a marathon runner. And, as in the last few kilometers of a marathon, the final steps to an 8,000-meter summit are often the hardest.

After about half an hour I found myself under some rock overhangs. My memory of the wall obviously was not perfect, and I probably had turned left from the moraine too soon. The moon was gone, and my headlamp could only cast its light so far. Then a wide snow slope directed me upward. The way was open, and I felt safe under the veil of night. Nobody could see how tiny I was compared to the mighty walls and ridges of the mountain.

I don't know how much time passed before I looked back. I felt that I was moving fast, that I already was high on the face. Four lights appeared behind me, two moving to the right and two following me. So, Emil and Marjan had decided to come the same way. In a way I expected that, and I was glad for the distant company. My crampons scraped upon the icy slope. I breathed the fresh, icy air and felt enfolded in the mysteries of the mountain, far away from the weaknesses of ordinary life.

A few hours later, Nangpai Gosum, a mountain on the southern horizon, glowed metallic blue, then orange, then white. Another sunny day was breaking, just like I needed. When the angle of the snow eased, I dug a small platform to stand upon. I'd been drinking a lot; I was confident that the more than three liters in my thermos bottles would be enough to get me up the mountain and back to one of the camps on the normal route. It was time for another energy gel. I got fed up with the various bars a long time ago. I couldn't forget the one, just below the summit of Everest, that felt like it was getting fatter and fatter in my mouth— I needed about half an hour to finish it. This time all I brought with me, besides my clothing, were my thermoses, six gels, spare gloves, a bivy sack, and a camera. Lightness was the key if I wanted to be really fast.

△

Looking up, I still could not see the exit from the face. I could only hope to find a way up to the west ridge. From our tent below the face, this section had always been in shadow, but we surmised it was steep. Now the wide, icy slope turned into a narrow gully with overhanging walls on both sides. Something like an icefall shimmered at the top of the gully. The closer I got the more sheer it became: vertical ice at 7,200 meters. It wasn't very long, some 10 meters, but I worried there might be powder snow near the top-out, with no placements for my tools.

To the right the rock seemed more reliable. But the gully below me was really steep. "If I fell…." No, in the Himalaya you don't fall. You freeze to death, you get pulmonary edema, you get hit by an avalanche. On Cho Oyu, you might even get shot. But you don't fall.

I looked for holds in the rock, polished by many avalanches. I can focus completely on a single detail when it's really necessary. A tiny edge, a hold for one tooth of a crampon. Step by step I moved up, forgetting the thin air, the strained sound of my breathing, everything outside the moment. Here and there I torqued my axe in thin cracks, but mostly I felt for holds with my bare fingers. It had to have been colder than −20° Celsius, but I felt like my fingers were hot. Carefully I followed frozen granite flakes back toward the left. My front points grated against the rock, but I'm used to that noise. Three more meters, two…and then I was out of rock. The ice hose was beneath me. Once more the route above was open.

As I stood on the west ridge, the view of the normal route and Camp II unfolded. A distant crowd of colorful tents snapped me out of my feeling of solitude and the otherworldly quiet of the mountain. It was another 900 meters to the summit. I took one step and sunk knee-deep into the snow. I searched in vain for solid footing. Only

Kozjek planted a tool at the base of the short crux passage but opted to climb 5.6 rock to the right of the ice. *Pavle Kozjek*

a bit of the last storm's powder had been scoured away. A breakable crust lay on the steeper sections; each time the angle of the slope kicked back, the drifts became deeper. My progress slowed to a crawl. Minutes were slipping into hours. For the first time since starting the climb, I thought I might not make it. At about 7,800 meters, the original west ridge route joins the normal route (the northwest ridge), but the easy ground before this junction was buried beneath an abyss of snow.

One more gel, another thermos emptied. During a break I dreamed about green meadows, warm limestone, a sunset, friends, wine on the beach. Stop! No time for dreaming. Again I pushed through the heavy snow, above the elevation of Camp III. A few more steps and I would reach the normal route. I could already see a climber descending, clinging to a fixed rope. I couldn't see his face beneath the oxygen mask and goggles. He moved down like a robot as he tried to avoid a steeper rocky section. Two Sherpas accompanying him glanced about nervously; they must have been anxious that he was so slow. They should have enough time to make it down, I thought as I watched. I hoped I had enough time, too—I was still going up. Here and there I met more descending climbers, looking exhausted, with hidden faces. No gazes met my own. I'd never experienced a scene like this on a Himalayan mountain. My solitary climb by headlamp that morning seemed to belong to a different mountain, a different realm.

It was already late afternoon when the steep slope rolled back onto the summit plateau. On the hard snow I felt stronger again, but the top was nowhere in sight. At last a small flag appeared; a red oxygen bottle was stuck in the snow. A climber was standing nearby. An icy wind blew from Tibet, and when I took off my gloves for a moment, my fingers went numb. Only the red and golden colors of the evening were warm. A cold battery in my camera produced the last photo of the day.

After a few minutes on top I headed down. Great feelings of joy would come later. Or maybe not at all. The more mountains I climb, the less I know. But this is the world where I feel complete.

△

After two days we were all back in advanced base camp. Aljaž, Emil, Marjan, and Uroš all spent the night in camps on the normal route and reached the summit a day later; all four of them, it turned out, had followed my line on the face. Uroš and Aljaž had encountered bad conditions on the Kurtyka-Triolet-Loretan and traversed back to our new route. All four had climbed the ice hose I avoided; the exit was not as bad as I had thought it would be.

Many expeditions had already left, and some of the rest were packing. In the next two days we did the same. When I got home I sent my photos of the Nangpa La incident to the media, and I was surprised to discover that nobody else had done that. So many people must have seen that drama....

SUMMARY

AREA: Mahalangur Himal, Tibet

ASCENT: New route on the southwest face of 8,188-meter Cho Oyu (Slovenian Route, V 50°-60°, 1,100 meters plus 900 meters of the 1986 Polish Route). Pavle Kozjek climbed the route solo in a single push of 14.5 hours from advanced base camp on October 2, 2006. Four of Kozek's teammates followed him up the same route on October 2 and reached the summit the next day, after camping on the normal route (northwest ridge).

EDITOR'S NOTE: Approximately 75 Tibetans attempted to enter Nepal via Nangpa La on September 30, 2006. One woman, Kelsang Namtso, 17, was shot and killed by Chinese soldiers; a 23-year-old man was badly wounded and may have died later. About 40 Tibetans successfully crossed the border; the remaining survivors were detained. The Chinese news agency reported the soldiers acted in self-defense.

Portions of this story previously appeared in *Alpinist* magazine and are reprinted with permission.

A NOTE ABOUT THE AUTHOR:

Pavle Kozjek, 47, lives in Ljubljana, Slovenia, and works at Statistics Slovenia. He has climbed new routes on Cerro Torre and Shishapangma, as well as a number of hard new routes in Peru, mostly solo and in a single push.

Pavle Kozjek

A TASTE OF
KARAKORAM ICE

Exploring the early-season potential above the Trango Glacier.

DODO KOPOLD

Early-season base camp on the Trango Glacier. The icy north face of Uli Biaho Tower looms over camp. See Climbs and Expeditions for details of the route the Slovakians followed. *Dodo Kopold*

In the Himalayas I don't look for adventure on the classic routes, where you stumble over hundreds of people. I don't look for it even on the routes that have been climbed only a few times. A new line is like a journey without a map, like a question mark at the end of a sentence. You leave for two months with a promise that you will come back alive. You close the door and suddenly you are in another world—in the world of risk, which you try to reduce by your good decisions and a ration of fortune that was given to you. You have two months to fulfill your dreams. The wall you've been observing for three years, looking for an unclimbed line. You study each meter; you think about the individual passages and consider the right tactics. Questions accumulate. A huge avalanche breaks away from the summit ridge. You promised you would not give into the risk; you promised to come back home. But your dream is in front of you.

△

In 2006 we wanted to climb Gasherbrum IV via a new route on the Shining Wall. But the situation with money was worse than we had expected. Fortunately, our motivation to climb in the Karakoram was strong, so we chose Uli Biaho Tower as an alternative. Its unclimbed north face looked to be a fantastic icy line. For this target we had to go earlier, because usually in late season the ice conditions are not good. Ice climbing in the Karakoram was like a new dimension of climbing. We couldn't imagine what would await us.

We arrived at Shipton base camp at the end of May, more than a month earlier than usual. It was snowing a lot and freezing at night, but only in these conditions would we be able to climb Uli Biaho's enormous ice face. In our small team there was a sirdar, cook, kitchen helper, cameraman Palo Pekareík, Gabo Čmárik, and me.

Our idea was to climb the face in perfect style: alpine style, without bolts, and as fast as possible. But snow kept falling at night, and during the day avalanches fell from the walls. We had to wait for a good period of weather to begin our acclimatization climbs.

△

We started climbing our first route, on Hainabrakk East Tower, during the nighttime, in order to avoid avalanches that fell through a steep couloir. This was our second try on this wall, and this time we climbed much faster. At dawn we arrived at the place that we had marked back at base camp with a big exclamation point. We had to rappel 60 meters in a narrow chimney and continue up steep ice to the summit ridge. This was also a main path for avalanches, and the morning one hadn't fallen yet. Our ropes tangled. "That will be...." I started to say to myself, when all of a sudden a huge avalanche roared by a few meters from me and disappeared. That was the one we were waiting for. The way seemed open.

I waited for Gabo to ascend to the belay. "Watch out!" I yelled and cowered against the wall. We hadn't expected that one. We hesitated and discussed whether we should go down. But the way back was closed. We had already pulled the rappel rope, so we had to continue upward. Climbing where the avalanche had fallen only minutes ago, I moved as fast as possible.

In the evening we took refuge in an ice cave, protected from the falling ice. On the second day we reached the summit ridge at 5,375 meters. That was the end of our route; a rock tower blocked the way to the top. The long descent to base camp waited for us.

△

Our next step to perfect acclimatization was the north face of Shipton Spire. Its ice wall had dangerous seracs threatening the lower part of the route and also a hard mixed passage higher up. We began climbing early in the morning, moving fast through an ice chimney and wading through deep, drifted snow on the flats to reach a rocky buttress. We climbed 500 meters through this dangerous terrain, but at 8 a.m., when Gabo arrived at my belay, his face was greenish-red. Sunstroke. We went down. The north face of Shipton is still unclimbed.

△

5,375m

Bivy
Cave

Rappel

The line taken by Dolzag Dihedral on Hainabrakk East Tower (5,650m). *Dodo Kopold*

Third week in base camp. We had acclimatized very well, and we had studied Uli Biaho's minute details. We knew that it was impossible to enter the face by its lower rocky wall and that we had to go instead up a steep ice couloir. But we still had so many questions. How many days would it take? What would the summit ridge be like? What if it collapsed with us on it? Would we find a ledge for a bivy? Would the weather last?

We knew that if we wanted to succeed and come back home, we had to be fast. So we packed only the most essential gear for climbing, high-altitude food for a few days, and energy drinks. No sleeping bag, no reserve clothing.

We left our advanced base camp at 2 a.m., after a short nap. We climbed simultaneously to the col under the north face. The ice was hard, and huge seracs loomed above us. Not good. We climbed as fast as we could, and in four hours we reached the col, 1,000 meters higher. We carefully crossed the bergschrund, and after 200 meters we stood under splendid steep ice. But we were in the way of avalanches and had to move away from there as fast as possible. I climbed first, and when the rope ran out I just yelled to Gabo to climb after me. This tactic was not so safe, but time was the most important thing now.

We had been moving more than 16 hours; we were dehydrated and tired. But there was no ledge, no place suitable for rest, just steep ice and monolithic rock walls. So we hacked at the

Dodo Kopold leads steep ice just below the top of the north face of Uli Biaho. *Gabo Čmárik*

ice to create a small ledge for sitting. We cooked something and took a nap for a while, but we couldn't stay for long. It was cold and we started to slide slowly toward the valley. It was time to continue.

We climbed mostly vertical ice, here and there doing a few moves on rock. The ice was hard, and it was too strenuous to put in screws; our calves were protesting. I looked forward to finishing each pitch and maybe standing on a big belay ledge to take a rest, at least for a while. But there was no ledge. Just two screws in the steep ice for a belay, and above harder and harder ice.

Rasping crampons, axe tips in just a few millimeters of ice. Gabo shouted at me to put in a screw, but I couldn't; I just wanted to finish the pitch. I was fishing for microcams that I had somewhere on my back. The ice was desperately thin, and I climbed a thin crack that I hoped would lead me to the snow ridge.

I made a belay 10 meters under the summit. We didn't dare climb together to the top of the summit cornice, so Gabo went first and when he returned it was my turn. It was 3 p.m. and a lovely day, with a great view of the surrounding mountains. I felt very lucky to have succeeded on the line. The conditions were on the edge of climbability.

Rappelling the route, we arrived totally exhausted at advanced base, 54 hours after leaving it.

SUMMARY

AREA: Trango Valley, Baltoro Region, Pakistan

ASCENTS: Attempt on Hainabrakk East Tower (5,650m), climbed to east ridge at 5,375 meters (Dolzag Dihedral, 750m, VI 6), June 8-9, 2006. Attempt on the north face of Shipton Spire (5,885m); climbed first 500 meters. Alpine-style first ascent of the north face of Uli Biaho Tower (6,109m); the route is called Drastissima (1,900m, ABO VI 6), July 21-23, 2006. All ascents by Gabo Čmárik and Jozef "Dodo" Kopold.

A NOTE ABOUT THE AUTHOR:

Born in 1980, Dodo Kopold lives in Bratislava, Slovakia, and designs outdoor clothing.

THE GENYEN MASSIF

Treading lightly in a sacred range.

MOLLY LOOMIS

The view from base camp, below the Rengo Monastery, showing peaks on the western side of the deep valley that extends northwest from the monastery. The south ridge of Sachun (19,570') is marked. Phurba and Damaru are hidden from view behind the monastery. *Andy Tyson*

Deep in the Shaluli Shan mountains of China lies the Genyen Massif, an area that has been described to us as "the Tetons jacked up on steroids." Dave Anderson, Sarah Hueniken, Andy Tyson, and I have been lured halfway around the world by this description, and we are eager to explore these unclimbed alpine peaks, situated in a remote Tibetan Buddhist stronghold. Although it was first visited by Westerners in the late 1800s, the range has seen just a handful of expeditions, and only Mt. Genyen (20,354'), the area's highest and most sacred peak, has seen the development of technical routes during the past 20 years.

On October 9 we cram into a Jeep driven by our tour operator, a young Chinese guy better versed in American pop culture and vernacular than any of us—Eminem's "8 Mile" is his favorite film. After two long days bouncing in the overloaded vehicle, we arrive in Litang (population 49,126; elevation 13,169 feet), considered by many to be the capital for the Tibetan guerrillas known as Khampas. Although officially outside the Tibetan Autonomous Region (TAR), much of western Sichuan (including Litang and the Genyen Massif) is historically part of Tibet's southeastern Kham region. TAR's boundary, drawn by the Chinese in 1965, quartered off an area much smaller than the historic expanse of Tibetan culture and settlement. Prayer flags, stone buildings with brightly painted eaves and doorways, women in long, black dresses accented with bright color patches, and men riding motorcycles, black ponytails caught in the wind, define the landscape.

Only one road heads south from Litang to Lamaya, the small mountain village where we will hire pack horses for our one-day trek to the Rengo Monastery, located at the base of Mt. Genyen. Nonetheless, it soon becomes painfully apparent that our tour operator cannot remember how to find this road. After multiple false starts, we hire an independent driver and in the late afternoon arrive in Lamaya without incident. We are taken aback by the villagers' sincere interest and generosity; it's refreshing to be in a place where the locals do not yet seem weary, jaded, or demanding of travelers.

We depart the next morning. Two horsemen and seven horses lead us along a well-defined trail up a gently sloping riverbed for approximately 12 miles. Families gather around black tents woven from yak wool, taking a break from the tedious work of digging holes with tin bowls along the trail for the utility poles that will someday bring electricity to the remote village located between Lamaya and the monastery. I keep correcting my direction mid-stride in order to walk clockwise around the large stacks of mani stones along the trail.

Mist settles as we hike higher, the valley narrowing, green moss dripping from the trees, and tall, dark cliffs closing in around us. Through the mist we see the Rengo Monastery guarding the valley from its perch on a southwest-facing hill, a small village blending into the slope below. At the base of the monastery's stupa, I find our tour operator, Dave, Sarah, and two solemn monks sitting on the ground. No one is smiling. Our tour operator is pacing and doing his nicotine-fit thing, ravenously gnawing his fingernails and lower lip. He greets me with, "It's the Italians—the monks are pissed because the Italians climbed Genyen even though the monks told them not to." In the spring of 2006 a team of Italians summited Genyen, the monastery's sacred peak. The Italians were the first climbing team to visit the area since 1988, when a Japanese party successfully climbed Genyen (or Nen-Da, as many of the locals call it). In desperate pantomime, we try to convey that we will not attempt either of the two peaks the monks indicate as sacred: Genyen and a gorgeous granite peak rising directly behind the monastery, a series of five triangles stacked against one another in an ascending pattern.

(According to the Italians, all of their interactions with the monks were positive and they were never told to not climb Mt. Genyen. See "Climbs and Expeditions" for their report.)

After continued pacing and more negotiations, we are permitted to set up a base camp in the meadow below the monastery. Whether it is for spiritual or surveillance reasons, the monks do not want our camp pitched above them.

△

Eager to take advantage of the excellent weather, we immediately prepare to carry loads up to a high camp, our sights set on a Patagonia-esque spire called Sachun. This less than heroic

Andy Tyson follows splitter cracks on the south ridge of Sachun during the first attempt. *Sarah Hueniken*

name translates to the Chicken, belying the peak's formidable east face and steep southern ridge-line, which leads to a crooked little cap of seamless granite set on the summit. Although we would have preferred setting base camp higher to minimize time spent carrying loads, we feel lucky to be welcome in the valley after the tense negotiations with the monks; getting completely turned back didn't feel out of the question.

The next morning we carry loads up-valley, following a gentle trail along a wide, mean-dering riverbed, and ascend a steep slope through dark green rhododendron, golden larch, and boulders speckled with bright red lichen. We return the following day and install a high camp on a moraine at approximately 16,000 feet. Snow patters on the tents all night, so rather than climb we establish an approach route the next day in snow as deep as our thighs.

Although inflicted with some of the worse intestinal gas any of us have ever experienced (thanks to a poorly hydrated dinner), we awake at 3 a.m. to head for Sachun. Sarah and Dave plan to attempt a steep ice line on the east face, while Andy and I focus on the southern ridge's long, smooth rock profile. However, lured by the aesthetic, sunny route, Dave and Sarah join us at the base of the ridge. We spot three of the Italians' fixed lines dangling down the south-eastern face, thick with ice. After summiting Genyen, they had attempted Sachun but were thwarted partway up by weather.

Dave Anderson below Sachun's summit cap. While downclimbing the smooth granite, Anderson fell 30 feet into a snowdrift but was unharmed. *Sarah Hueniken*

Six pitches of mixed terrain up to M5 lead to the ridge proper, where parallel cracks run down the textured granite face. We stare at the sunny face incredulous at our luck—clean, high-quality splitters and temperatures as warm as could be expected for autumn at 19,000 feet. We stuff hands and fingers to climb a full pitch of 5.9 jams. "This is some of the best granite I've ever climbed," yells Dave. But enthusiasm wanes halfway up the next pitch, as we realize we've swiched to rock shoes too soon. We climb through two pitches of offwidth and wider cracks (up to 5.9) choked with snow and ice, our feet growing increasingly wet and cold. We reach the base of what we anticipated to be the crux pitch, and, shaking our limbs for warmth, stare at two cracks slicing the near-vertical face. Dave leads up through 150 feet of exceptional 5.10-plus hands, fingers, and ring-locks. We huff up behind, laughing and groaning at how good this might all feel at sea level. Andy continues up another half pitch, trying to assess how far we are from the top. Unable to determine our position, and pressured by the quickly waning light (this time of year it is dark by 7 p.m.) and the need to establish descent anchors, we begin heading down.

From base camp the next morning we realize in a mixture of relief, satisfaction, and frustration that we had been very close to the summit. Although climbing as a team of four held advantages for the route's initial exploration, we decide a team of two will have a better chance at successfully completing the route. Two days later, after a rest in base camp, Sarah and Dave return to Sachun while Andy and I head up-valley, eager to explore new terrain.

⚐

Better acclimatized, Sarah and Dave make excellent time up to the previous high point and lead through the remaining two and a half pitches, which include a short traverse around to the west in order to gain the final summit cap. This is split into two separate spires, and after climbing the north spire Dave realizes the south spire is the true summit. He climbs an unprotected 25-foot slab (approximately 5.9) to the top, where, unable to build an anchor on the featureless arête, he is forced to retrace his steps. While downclimbing, he breaks a nubbin and plunges 30 feet into a snowdrift, luckily unharmed. Sarah opts for the north spire. Dave and Sarah name the route Dang Ba 'Dren Pa, a Tibetan phrase meaning "to inspire, enthuse, and uplift," in memory of friends Todd Skinner, Karen McNeill, and Sue Nott.

Meanwhile, Andy and I set our sights on a pair of high peaks at the head of the valley, which indeed are reminiscent of mountains back home in the Tetons. Although the area is

The first-ascent lines on Phurba (left, ca 18,650') and Damaru (ca 18,550'). *Andy Tyson*

devoid of climbers' influence, it is not untouched by humans. Walking up-valley, we pass evidence of human life everywhere: spiritual symbols etched into boulders, piles of mani stones, prayer flags adorning trees, boulders, and bushes or hanging from tall poles, chortens, and hillsides decorated with long, tall sticks. Within a short walk from our new high camp at 15,500 feet, we stumble upon what appears to be a meditation chamber: a granite sanctuary hollowed out under a large boulder. Traveling the valley is becoming as much a process of discovery as the climbing has been. The sensation of luck is overwhelming—to be in a place where the feeling of exploration is presented to us in two such distinct but inspiring forms.

By starlight, Andy and I scramble up a slope of talus and snow to the base of what we've nicknamed "The Grand." We work our way up and over, extracting a traverse along the eastern face. Clean crack systems split the faces of enormous, granite blocks just below the ridgeline proper, which proves too knifey and terraced for the quick climbing we are after. We ride à cheval over a series of gendarmes to the final headwall. Dark clouds are moving in quickly, and we debate in the blowing snow about continuing up the estimated three pitches to the top. With the summit in sight we decide to quit wasting time thinking and keep climbing. The rock quality decreases a nd the quantity of snow plastered into the cracks increases. We each tag the circa 18,650-foot summit separately, as the top offers no options for an anchor to accommodate two of us.

Celebrating that night with a big ramen ration, we choose a name for the peak: Phurba, a Tibetan ritual dagger, in reference to the mountain's sharp ridgelines. The route, Naga, we name for the serpent that is often depicted slithering up the phurba's blade. It is certain that the locals have their own name for this peak, but we are unable to obtain local names despite several attempts.

⟁

Back at base camp, we find that a crew of workers from Litang has arrived to help the monastery build a hostel that will house some of the hundreds of pilgrims who arrive each

THE GENYEN VALLEY

Mike Clelland

November for a large festival honoring Genyen. We spend the day helping out, taking turns with rusted tools to work the freshly felled wood. The precision the builders achieve despite the lack of modern tools is impressive. While in Lamaya, we'd seen the village's new school, a concrete building with a bright-red metal roof. Helping roll stones into place for the hostel's foundation, I wonder which type of structure will define Tibetan architecture in years to come.

While the workers break for cigarettes and food, we tour the monastery. Colorful murals of Genyen decorate the entryway, as it is believed that Genyen's body lies beneath the monastery—the mountain embodies his spirit. Tibetan texts describe Genyen as both the faithful servant of the Arahats (disciples of the Buddha Sakyamuni) and as a group of 21 guardian spirits, embodied by the snowy peaks, in charge of protecting the Dharma and the teachings of the Buddha. Onshu, the head monk, ceremoniously unwraps "Genyen's heart" and his "intestines": two polished rocks whose similarity to these organs is uncanny. Towering columns of bright, silky fabric twist from the ceiling down to the floor, and long rows of deserted benches that double as beds, wrapped in saffron-colored cloth, line the main room. We wander through a room housing 1,000 golden Buddhas and another room reserved for the Dalai Lama, complete with a waiting change of clothes.

Due perhaps to its remote setting and location outside of the TAR, the Rengo Monastery was not subjected to the destruction many Tibetan monasteries experienced during the Cultural Revolution; however, it did not emerge completely unaffected. Over 600 years old, the monastery was once home to approximately 275 monks. But during the late 1970s "something" happened (presumably the Cultural Revolution). Now fewer than a dozen monks live there. When we ask through pantomime what happened to the others, Onshu makes a sad expression and gestures with his hands, as if following the contrails of smoke rising into the air.

⛰

Andy and I return to our high camp intent on a peak similar to the Tetons' Teewinot, located just to the northeast of Phurba. It has beautiful southern and northern ridgelines, and a curving couloir splits the east face. Exploring the approach that evening, we find ourselves in the midst of a field of cairns a quarter mile in diameter; towers of three stones cover every inch of available space.

High up in a side valley, east of the main drainage, Dave and Sarah stumble upon a similar cairn field at the base of their new objective, a striking, jagged peak with a highly aesthetic southern ridge. The south-facing side of each cairn is covered in red-orange lichen. The approach takes longer than anticipated, but Dave and Sarah complete five pitches of the southern ridge before turning back.

Back on "Teewinot," Andy and I change plans after two pitches, wary of the extremely loose rock. We traverse into a southeast-facing couloir and simul-climb approximately four

(Top) Unclimbed peaks on the east side of the main valley to the northwest of Rengo Monastery, as seen from Phurba. (Bottom) Peaks to the south of Phurba; Sachun is on the left. *Andy Tyson*

pitches up to 80 degrees; a thin patina of snow and ice is plastered over smooth rock slabs. We then drop into the peak's main east-facing couloir, and our progress immediately slows as we wallow up waist-deep snow over ice until the snow peters out to mixed terrain. Although the climbing is not difficult, the rock quality is very poor; the only reassuring factor is the cold temperature helping to glue the rocks in place. The couloir steepens and the final few pitches present mixed climbing up to M4. We straddle the narrow saddle between the two summits, assessing our options. The summit blocks are only about 25 feet above us, but conditions on both are dismal. The slightly higher southwestern summit presents a large platelike slab balanced at an incline on a tall, crumbling block of rock. A wind slab eight inches thick coats the plate of rock—an ironic "icing on the cake." The other summit looks no better. We are disappointed to turn around so close to the summit, but we acquiesce to the poor conditions and call our high point good.

We call the peak Damaru (until someone can discern the correct name) after the little Tibetan double-headed drums similar in shape to the peak's double summit, and we name our route Kapalika Damaru, the most powerful of all damaru, made with the skull tops of a young boy and girl. The largest of the damaru are used for the "dance of ego-annihilation," a footnote that gives us a good laugh, considering our turnaround so close to the top.

△

One day, kept off the peaks by weather, we take a long hike to the 17,886-foot pass at the head of the valley. We follow a trail through what appears to be a sky-burial site, the spot where traditionally the dead are taken and offered to the birds, a practical way of disposing of bodies in a land of permafrost and limited timber. We walk past wooden paddles (likely placed on the bodies' feet or hands), and clothing and bits of hair hanging in bushes, soon reaching the base of an immense boulder wrapped in prayer flags. We are curious but hesitant, afraid of whom we might offend with our presence. We move on quickly, continuing to curve east toward the pass. The large peak that Sarah and Dave had attempted earlier lines up directly with the boulder, indicating, along with the cairn fields, the likelihood that, although the monks did not state it (perhaps because the peak was not discernible from base camp), the mountain is probably one of the region's sacred sites.

Rockfall punctuates our ascent up the pass as herds of blue sheep (over 200 in total) scramble on the rocks. We pause frequently, collecting small stones inlaid with large, dark-red garnets. By the time we reach the pass the weather has cleared and we are able to observe the peaks and sub-valleys forming the greater Genyen Massif. As we peer over the pass to the east and southeast, the view reveals more snowy pyramids, steep mixed faces, and snaggle-toothed towers—all unclimbed. But the Genyen valley is certainly the region's nexus of snowy alpine routes; the outer-lying edges of the massif, crafted from a different geological recipe, erode into sloping brown hillsides.

Looking out over the endless possibilities, I think about returning someday, a mental list of future objectives already amassed. But a part of me hesitates. The Genyen valley has been and continues to be sacred center to a degree none of us was expecting. It has been a climbing destination for just a fraction of that time. The more I learn about this place, the more I feel I am treading a careful line between sacred and sacrilege, guided by a moral yardstick comprised from individual values like spirituality, ego, and desire—a uniquely mixed concoction lodged in each of our psyches, further complicated by language and cultural barriers.

Over the course of the next few days we attempt other objectives, but storms and poor snow conditions turn us around. Our tour operator orders horses from Lamaya via sat phone. The temperatures have grown noticeably colder, and the larches have turned from gold to dull yellow. The stellar weather has kept us moving at an almost nonstop pace for close to three weeks. Numerous signs, including the possibility of roads being closed by snowfall, point us back to Chengdu. According to our tour operator, the monks say we've been in the region long enough. Although our relations with the monks have been positive, it is difficult to anticipate how they and their community will receive climbers in the future.

Several weeks later we are contacted regarding Charlie Fowler and Chris Boskoff's disappearance on the slopes of Mt. Genyen in November, about a month after our trip. It is an eerie and sad time for us all, in particular for Dave, who had communicated at length with Charlie about traveling and climbing in Kham. Dave puts it well when he writes, "As

Molly Loomis introduces a local monk to one element of modern Western culture. *David Anderson*

climbers, we stand on the shoulders of those that have come before us. We glean knowledge from previous ascents to help increase our chances of success and climb in better style. But the most important information we gain from our climbing heroes does not show up in the topo or the gear list. What they really give us is the courage to step out into the unknown and try." It would be simplistic for us to think that we achieved success in the Genyen Massif alone. Our thoughts and wishes go out to the family and friends of Chris and Charlie.

SUMMARY:

AREA: Genyen Massif, Shaluli Shan, Sichuan Province, China

ASCENTS: First ascent of Sachun (19,570') via the south ridge; the route is named Dang Ba 'Dren Pa (5.10+ A0 M5 70°); Dave Anderson and Sarah Hueniken, October 20, 2006. First ascent of Phurba (ca 18,650') via the east face and south ridge; the route is called Naga (5.8 75°); Molly Loomis and Andy Tyson, October 21, 2006. Loomis and Tyson also climbed the southeast and east face of a peak they called Damaru (ca 18,550'), reaching a point 25 feet below the twin summits.

A NOTE ABOUT THE AUTHOR:

Molly Loomis, 30, writes from her home in Victor, Idaho, where she splits her time working as a mountain guide and as a freelance writer. The team offers enormous thanks for the financial support provided by a W.L. Gore Shipton-Tilman Grant, Montrail, Outdoor Research, and the National Outdoor Leadership School's Instructor Development Fund.

THE CHINESE TIEN SHAN

New routes and great potential in a seldom-visited range.

ANATOLIY DJULIY

The 2,500-meter southern escarpment of Peak Voennih Topografov (Peak of the Army Topographers, 6,873m), with the routes of ascent (black) and descent marked. The route required much traversing, and the team estimates it climbed a total distance of nearly five kilometers. *Anatoliy Djuliy*

The central Tien Shan range in China, south and east of the borders with Kyrgyzstan and Kazakhstan, is a little-known region with many unclimbed peaks from 5,000 meters to almost 6,800 meters high. The first successful mountaineering expedition into this region was likely in 1977, when the Chinese climbed the avalanche-prone southern slopes of Tomur (a.k.a. Peak Pobeda, 7,439m). Other expeditions can be counted on one's fingers: During the 1980s and 1990s, Japanese teams attempted the Chinese route on Tomur and made four attempts to climb 6,637-meter Xuelian Feng, before succeeding in 1990. There were French and Japanese expeditions to Kashkar (6,435m). Other than my own trips, that's about it. The base

The view of Kashkar (6,435m) from a high camp during the traverse of the Vizbor Massif. Anatoliy Djuliy's expedition made the possible first ascent of Kashkar, which had been attempted at least twice, during a 16-day traverse in 2004. To the right is Vizbor West, over which the 2006 expedition traversed as part of its acclimatization climb. *Anatoliy Djuliy*

camps below Khan Tengri and the other peaks by the Inylchek glaciers, north and west of the border, are busy with mountaineers every summer, but the Chinese Tien Shan often goes for years without seeing any climbers.

Teams under my leadership have conducted three expeditions into the region, in 2002, 2004, and 2006. We completed more than 10 traverses of high passes, most of them very complex, and several first ascents. In 2002, we completed a 270-kilometer trek over seven passes, from China to Kyrgyzstan and back. In 2004, we succeeded in a 16-day traverse of Kashkar, likely making that peak's first ascent. Then, in 2006, we traversed the summits of Peak 5,853m and 5,960m, and we completed the objective that had tantalized us since we first saw it in four years earlier: the steep, 2,500-meter-high southern ridge of Peak of the Army Topographers (6,873m).

Dozens of alluring peaks remain unclimbed in this area, but the Chinese Tien Shan is difficult to access for many reasons. There is no tourist infrastructure: no hotels, no porters, few horses for carrying loads. Getting permits for the region takes several months, and some areas may be off-limits. There is no rescue service, so if you have any troubles you are on your own. The weather near Pobeda, the northernmost 7,000-meter peak in the world, can be extremely rough, with hurricane-force winds and snowfalls almost every day. Last season, however, there was extraordinarily little snow, and the result was heavily crevassed glaciers and highly sensitive cornices.

Double cornices encountered during the descent from Peak Vizbor, the team's nine-day warm-up climb.
Anatoliy Djuliy

We flew from Moscow to Urumchi on the 15th of July, and by the evening of the next day, after a two-hour flight, we had reached the city of Aksu, south of the range. In the morning, having bought some fresh food and fuel, we traveled to the village of Talak to begin our approach. The 40-kilometer approach to base camp was problematic. We were abandoned by the leader of our horse caravan, naturally with his animals, and it wasn't until July 24 that our base camp was organized and we could start to implement our plan.

Our base camp was near a short western tributary from the eastern branch of the Chonteren Glacier, at an altitude of about 3,800 meters. This was three to four hours from the south ridge of Peak of the Army Topographers, and it was only about an hour below the 4,500-meter saddle where we planned to end our traverse of Peak 5,853m and Peak 5,960m, which we later named Peak Vizbor West and Peak Vizbor. This massif is to the south of Pobeda's eastern summit, separating the east and west forks of Chonteren Glacier.

Our traverse of the Vizbor Massif covered about 18 kilometers round trip from base camp—10 kilometers from the 4,600-meter saddle at the start to the 4,500-meter col at the far end. The route was more difficult than expected, with passages of ice up to 70 degrees and rock sections up to UIAA IV+ that required many pitches of belaying. We spent nine days on the effort, two or three days longer than we had planned, and reached the summit of Peak 5,853m on July 29 and Peak 5,960m, further to the northeast, the next day. We named the massif in honor of Yury Vizbor, the famous Russian poet, singer, and actor, and were back in base camp by August 2 after a difficult descent along a rocky ridge.

△

We had dragged a guitar to camp with us, and during the next few days of rest, repacking, and weather-enforced relaxation the songs of Yury Vizbor resounded around our camp. Well-acclimatized and rested, we carried a load to the base of the south ridge of Army Topographers on August 6, then left base camp for good the next day, setting up a bivouac at 4,400 meters, directly below the eastern side of the ridge. We had skirted the lower wall by climbing an icefall to the right of a rocky bastion.

Our first challenge was to reach the nearly horizontal ridge crest at about 5,000 meters. This took two days and required 22 pitches of climbing, mostly not very difficult but time-consuming because of powder snow and icy sections. The rock was very sharp, and climbing along a fixed rope I tore my knee—I never thought so much blood could flow out of a knee. During the second day of climbing we reached the ridge top, only to find it was only 60 centimeters wide—no chance for a bivouac there! We continued along the ridge for several difficult pitches, exiting under some impressive rock gendarmes to reach a possible bivy site against a cornice, late in the evening, as snow began to fall. After several hours of work, we managed to level a space just big enough for two tents. It was pitch dark by the time we were done.

Half of the next day, August 10, was spent carrying loads and retrieving the 16 ropes we had fixed below. Then we were able to fix four ropes over rock gendarmes beyond our cornice

Peak of the Army Topographers from the west, seen from the approach to 5,488-meter Chonteren Pass. The Russians climbed the prominent ridge leading straight to the highest summit (second from the foreground). Peak 6,747m rises behind. See the 2003 *AAJ*, p. 405, for a direct view of the steep south face of Peak 6,747m. *Anatoliy Djuliy*

The first camp on the main south ridge of Peak of the Army Topographers, at about 5,050 meters, looking to the south down the Chonteren Glacier. It took two days and 22 pitches to reach this elevation, and the team traversed nearly horizontally for another two days before the ridge headed upward again. *Anatoliy Djuliy*

bivy. We began to understand that this climb was likely to take a lot longer than expected. I had planned for six days of climbing plus six days for the Tien Shan weather. As the climbing was proving slow, we would have to ignore the weather.

In all, it took us three days to traverse the horizontal rib, at an elevation of about 5,100 meters, before the ridge reared upward. This was tedious climbing, difficult with our heavy packs, climbing over and around gendarmes and along the sides of steep cornices and ice slopes. We camped once along the ridge and then found a good bivouac site below a bergschrund underneath the upper wall.

We fixed all of our ropes above this campsite over the next two days, in very poor weather: snow and high winds. The angle was not so steep, but the climbing was delicate and took a lot of time. Apparently, however, all this was insufficient adventure, and therefore on his watch Kolya [Nikolay Dobrjaev] managed to burn the fuel hose on one of the stoves. A trivial event normally, but it could set us back significantly. Have you ever tried to repair a stove in the middle of a mountain ascent? It's an amusing task. Vovka [Vladimir Leonenko] and I took the stove into our tent, and at first we just stared at it stupidly, wondering where to begin. But after three hours, with the help of a file, a bit of a nail, some tape, and superglue from our repair kit, the job was done, everything worked, and once again we had two stoves. Why did we have part of a nail in our repair kit? We had a lot of unexpected things in there. Just a year earlier, with the help of two such nails, we repaired some plastic boots that had fallen apart.

On August 15, our eighth day on the route, we were ready to move our camp upward.

Ascending a fixed line on the crux headwall, between 6,300 and 6,400 meters. The light-colored rock above is the very loose marble band. *Anatoliy Djuliy*

Twenty pitches above the bergschrund bivouac, we found a good bivy site at about 5,800 meters. Despite very bad weather, we kept climbing and fixing ropes, aiming for the steep rock headwall that begins around 6,100 meters. We moved our camp to about 6,010 meters on August 17 and fixed several ropes above.

In sun and terrible cold, we started work on the headwall the next morning. The climbing was very difficult, and Kolya led very slowly using a lot of aid; I was freezing. After two pitches, easier climbing led around a rock tower, and by lunchtime we were already at almost 6,400 meters. We had entered the marble zone, and that marble was something! It was difficult to find a place for a piton, the rock crumbled under our hands and feet, and sometimes it fell off in huge pieces. As I belayed, I twisted and turned away from the falling rocks. All of the climbing on the steep lower wall and through the upper headwall was UIAA V or VI in difficulty. Kolya finally reached the upper edge of the wall, but I didn't want to follow. I was too frozen. We quickly descended to our camp at 6,010 meters. The headwall had been climbed.

In the morning of August 19, sick with laryngitis, Anatoly Gorin announced that he would stay at our bivouac while the remaining four of us continued upward. We took food and gas for two days. By afternoon we had regained the top of the headwall, but the snow-covered marble above was still too difficult for the leader to carry his pack. Finally we reached a snow slope that we hoped would provide an easy route, but the snow was waist-deep and we had to dig a path to some ice below a hanging glacier. Fearful of avalanche conditions, we continued to fix ropes. Finally we gained a snow ledge between some seracs at around 6,480 meters.

After a difficult night with all four of us in a three-man tent, we headed for the top in light snowfall. Climbing in two pairs, we found ice and easy rock until we had to climb one more 100-meter band of unpleasant marble. Easier ground brought us to the snow plateau on top around noon, where we found two rock outcrops, each with notes containing the names of climbers from the Kyrgyz side of the border. We left our names on one of them and began the descent.

The weather had improved somewhat—nearly hurricane-force winds were blowing in, which dispersed the cloudiness. We could see the path to our tent platform below. The tent was buried nearly to its top and slightly damaged. We dug out the tent and built a platform for our second, single-wall tent, where Kolya volunteered to sleep alone. We snuggled in to the two tents, but no one slept. The tent was constantly being lifted up by the wind.

Soon I sensed something wrong with my breathing—it was as though I was suffocating. I realized we probably had been buried and carbon dioxide must be building up inside. I sat up and started to get dressed, and then quickly stuck my head outside. The wind was raging, but I felt better right away. The tent was half buried. After 30 or 40 minutes of digging, I went back inside and the air was noticeably better, but we still couldn't sleep—the devil only knows why not.

Kolya was walking around his solitary cell and digging. After some time, he fell into our tent with the words, "I'm dying!" We explained the symptoms of his "dying" and laughed, saying that we were "dying" as well. Having learned this, Kolya cheered up a bit. We fit him in between us, and right away he fell asleep. Until then he had sat on his haunches all night, afraid he would fall asleep and never wake up.

At first light, we prepared to continue. It was snowing and there was no visibility. Finally we found the pitons we'd left at the top of the headwall and began to rappel. The ropes had iced up, and sometimes this complicated the descent, but, after all, we were headed downward, not upward. Along the way we removed the more or less intact ropes, but we left some 11mm ropes on the lower part of the wall—they were too heavy to lift. At our 6,010-meter camp, Tolya was fine. We had time to go further, but we had neither the strength nor the desire.

In the morning, we considered our options. We had no desire to reverse the horizontal ridge, which might take another three or four days, so after reaching 5,800 meters we decided to head down to the west, despite much uncertainty about this route. During our first observation of the peak, in 2002, we had rejected any possibility of exiting the ridge this way, because of the obvious dangers from avalanches and falling rocks and ice. Well, the uncertainty won out.

Forty meters from our bivouac site we began rappelling. Slings, pitons, ice screws: I lost count of the rappels around the 10th, but it had to have been at least 20 to 22 rappels before we crossed the bergschrund. A lot of garbage was flying, and on one of the ledges I just I hid behind my rucksack as a hail of rocks landed on my pack and helmet. An icy stream of debris flew over the bergschrund without respite—I couldn't imagine where it was all coming from.

As the angle eased, we tied into the rope and downclimbed until we drew near the top of an icefall that plunged 300 to 400 meters to the glacier below us. To the right was a narrow band of ice and seracs along which, possibly, one might pass. To the left, a rocky buttress, but nothing was visible below it. We decided to bivouac on scree atop the buttress, as one is always wiser in the morning than in the evening. Anyway, it had begun snowing again.

The next morning it was sunny and, while we prepared breakfast, I walked out to the left and discovered a wonderful descent route; in the distance I could see an outlet onto the glacier via scree. Had we discovered this path yesterday, we would have started earlier and been onto the glacier before sunrise. Now it was already becoming dangerous, but the sun still hadn't hit the wall above us. Rappelling and frontpointing downward as quickly as we could, we exited the couloir two hours later. It took another two hours to traverse the heavily crevassed icefall, and finally we reached a scree-covered moraine and the descent essentially was over. We prepared a hot dinner—our first during the entire climb—and then descended another two hours to base camp, feeling a sense of deep satisfaction.

Summary:

Area: Tien Shan, China

Ascents: First ascent of the south ridge of 6,873-meter Peak Voennih Topografov (Peak of the Army Topographers), Nikolay Dobrjaev, Anatoliy Djuliy, Aleksey Kirienko, and Vladimir Leonenko, with Anatoly Gorin climbing to 6,100 meters, August 7-24, 2006. The team spent 13 days on the ascent, using seven bivy sites en route and often fixing ropes (as many as 16 at a time) above each site until they moved camp upward; they summited on August 20 and descended to 5,800 meters, then moved onto the south face, west of the ridge, to complete the descent. The same team also made the first ascent of the Vizbor Massif via a nine-day traverse of Peak 5,853m and Peak 5,960m, on the south ridge of Pobeda East, July 25-August 2.

A Note About the Author:

Anatoliy Djuliy lives with his wife and three children in Moscow, where he runs a mobile electric power station company.

This story was compiled from two accounts of the expedition: One written for the AAJ and translated from the Russian by Henry Pickford, and the other published at www.mountain.ru/eng/. Valuable assistance was provided by Otto Chkhetiani.

Otto Chkhetiani

Otto Chkhetiani

Otto Chkhetiani

Tsutomo Ogawa

Unclimbed Tien Shan

Most of the Tien Shan peaks to the east of the Chinese border with Kyrgyzstan and Kazakhstan have never been climbed, attempted, or even seen by mountaineers. Peak 6,571m (opposite page), seen from the southwest, lies due east of Peak of the Army Topographers and is surrounded by rugged 5,000-meter-plus peaks. Peak 6,769m (top, viewed from the upper Tugabed'chi Glacier) is the high point of a massive, marble-topped, east-west ridgeline. Peak 6,342m (middle) rises between the heads of the Kichi-Teren and Tugabed'chi glaciers. Baiyu Feng (bottom, 6,446m), as viewed from the Muzart Pass to the northwest, is the western neighbor of 6,627-meter Xuelian Feng; its northeastern escarpment rises about 2,300 meters above the glacier.

Visit www.americanalpineclub.org/AAJ/ to download a high-resolution panorama of the central Chinese Tien Shan, from the west slopes of Tomur to the mountains east of Peak 6,571m.

INFORMATION ON ICE

Seven years of first ascents and data collection in Antarctica.

DAMIEN GILDEA

Jed Brown sledging toward Mt. Anderson (4,144m), then the highest unclimbed peak in the Sentinel Range. Brown and Damien Gildea climbed Anderson's west face, right of the steep glacier. *Damien Gildea*

I love The Information. I don't know why, I just do; it's the way I am. I also love mountains and climbing, and for 15 years I've felt compelled to give in to this love. Put all these attributes together, turn them loose on the little-known mountains of Antarctica, and you have a passion that is, for me, pretty much all-consuming, for better or worse.

Coming from a dry, flat country (Australia), my alpine climbing started with The Information, and if I'm lucky enough to achieve old age it might end that way. Like a junkie, I long ago sucked dry the innards of the old books, magazines, and journals like this one, needing a fix of the info drug. Facts and figures, names and dates, details and debates—I need it all.

Brown places a GPS unit on the rocky lower summit of Peak 3,368m, above the Embree Glacier. *Damien Gildea*

Nearly 10 years ago, I wrote *The Antarctic Mountaineering Chronology*, which, aside from being the first and only reference book on climbing down south, was pretty much my way of standing up in front of the group and saying, "Hi, my name is Damien and I'm an infoholic." ("Hi, Damien!") Seeing that, and no doubt acting purely out of human compassion, the *AAJ* let me work through my info addiction in its pages, a treatment I repeat annually. This in turn led to a relationship with the Omega Foundation, a not-for-profit body dedicated to supporting scientific, environmental, educational, and literary projects in the Antarctic region. That after nearly a decade of climbing and scientific work in the high mountains of Antarctica the Omega Foundation still confounds people with its extensive support of these projects, with no desire for profit or publicity of any kind, really says more about those people and society in general than it does about the foundation. We think it's a good thing to do, so we do it.

When the foundation first approached me with an offer of support, I immediately saw an opportunity to solve a problem with Mt. Shinn, which sits right next to Mt. Vinson. All the Vinsonites see it from their high camp, but the USGS map gave it no height. I'd already noted this while writing the *Chronology*. Looking back through older records, journals, magazines, and the USGS Gazetteer, I kept coming across references to Shinn being "over 4,800 meters." Given the revision of heights for the highest peaks that had occurred over the years at the USGS, I thought this unlikely. I also thought it inappropriate, if not downright strange, that Shinn might be the continent's third-highest mountain and we didn't know just how high it was. I set out to rectify this.

On my first attempt, in December 2001, Mike Roberts and I were the first climbers up Vinson that season; we went to its summit to acclimatize for a seven-hour sit-in on the summit of Shinn. Because fewer satellites orbit over Antarctica than the more populated parts of the world, it takes a while to collect enough data with a single GPS unit to pinpoint elevation and position. We had to turn back high on the southwest face of Shinn due to slab avalanche danger, and when Mike had to leave I had no partner for a rematch with Shinn, nor for the second part of the plan that year, a 45-kilometer ski north to climb Mt. Anderson, then considered the highest unclimbed mountain in the Sentinel Range. Though we didn't achieve our aims that year, the trip did give me valuable experience climbing in the area, along with the assurance that simply climbing the highest and most popular mountain in an area—Vinson by the regular route, in this case—held no interest for me. I needed something with a bit of the unknown, and preferably with some interesting climbing

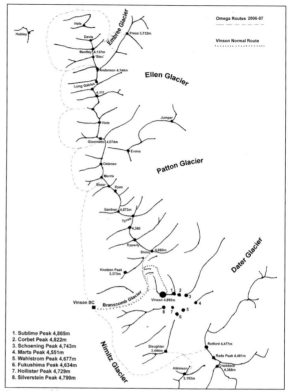

Damien Gildea

involved. Antarctica is a special place, its mountains are treasures, and if you're lucky enough to visit them you should do something special—ideally something meaningful to others as well as to your own ego or website. The place deserves nothing less.

△

I returned the next season with Chilean climber Rodrigo Fica, and we made a safe and successful ascent of Shinn, climbing the steep upper southwest face. Then we sat in a tent just below the summit for seven hours while a GPS unit ran on top. Down at base camp, we processed the data by sending it from our laptop, via Iridium satellite phone, to the Australian government's AUSPOS website. We got a reply within an hour, saying that Shinn was 4,660 meters above sea level. It felt like all our effort had been worth it and that we had actually made a contribution, rather than just doing a climb, as enjoyable as that climb was.

With some variations, this has been our system over the last five seasons. Sending the data home for nearly instantaneous processing allows us to verify that our GPS work was successful while we're still on the continent, where we can redo it if necessary. Coming back is expensive.

The next year, in December 2003, we took a break from inland Antarctica and climbed and measured Mt. Friesland, the highest peak on Livingston Island. Livingston is one of the

South Shetland Islands and sits just off the northwestern tip of the Antarctic Peninsula; it gets some of the world's worst weather. Of our 23 days on the island, 20 were too bad to climb, but we eventually climbed Friesland and established not only that was it the highest point on the island, but also that it was a bit higher than everyone thought, at exactly 1,700 meters.

Our view from Shinn toward Vinson had left something stuck in my brain. All those summits up high on Vinson, near the main one, looked pretty high—how high were they really? Only

Antarctic jug haul: Maria Paz ("Pachi") Ibarra reaches the summit of Peak 3,119m, just to the north of Mt. Viets. *Jed Brown*

one had been climbed, leaving another eight or so unvisited. So Rodrigo, Camilo Rada, and I returned in 2004 and spent over a month at high camp on Vinson, at 3,700 meters. To measure Vinson's summit elevation, we slept on top in –46°C temperatures without sleeping bags, huddling in down suits inside a small tent. We repeated this exercise a month later, finding Vinson to be 4,892 meters—five meters lower than the official height, but within the range given by the USGS.

During the month between our Vinson summits, we made the first ascent of eight of the Vinson subpeaks and the second ascent of another, plus some other climbing. This established that the highest of these subpeaks, Sublime Peak, is only 27 meters lower than the main summit (now officially called Mt. Vinson). While we initially gave, and published, some interim names for these subpeaks, the USGS recently accepted my proposal to name them after the 1966–1967 first ascensionists of Vinson. So now Nick Clinch, Barry Corbet, Eiichi Fukushima, Charles Hollister, Brian Marts, Pete Schoening, Sam Silverstein, and Dick Wahlstrom are all commemorated on the mountain first climbed by them. John Evans and Bill Long already had other significant peaks in the range named for them.

Though our climbing on these virgin subpeaks was never technically difficult, spending so much time up so high there was like walking across another planet. Often we had the whole massif to ourselves and experienced it from several different angles, developing an intimacy with Antarctica's highest mountain that few others have.

△

I always want to climb high, see a bit farther, and then go climb there too. From the summit of Vinson in November 2004, Rodrigo, Camilo, and I looked south to Mt. Craddock. We felt that the unnamed point that we called "Sharp Peak," between Craddock and us, might be higher than Craddock, but eventually we decided it probably wasn't. The next year, in December 2005, Steve Chaplin, Manuel Bugueno, Camilo, and I all climbed a new route on Mt. Craddock and
continued on page 106

UNCLIMBED ANTARCTICA

The Sentinel Range is far from climbed out, as this selection of objectives clearly demonstrates.

The unclimbed south face of Mt. Anderson (4,144m). *Damien Gildea*

The southern aspect of unclimbed Mt. Goldthwait (3,815m), as seen from the Embree Glacier. *Damien Gildea*

The unclimbed, unvisited, and rarely seen north face of Mt. Shinn (4,660m), as seen from the base of the northeast ridge of Mt. Tyree. *Damien Gildea*

The unclimbed north face of Mt. Tyree, Antarctica's second-highest peak (4,852m). The obvious couloir running down to the east is the 1997 French "Grand Couloir" route. The right skyline is the northwest ridge (Corbet-Evans, 1967), the route of the first ascent.

Gildea climbs the mixed wall on the west face of Mt. Anderson. The team was surprised to discover running water and hard water ice on this face deep in the Antarctic interior. *Jed Brown*

saw Sharp Peak from the other direction. We'd gotten it wrong—that peak was clearly higher than everything around us, including us, but we did not have time to get to it. Again, the desire to solve the enigma was irresistible, and so we returned to the area this last season and made the first ascent of the peak now known as Mt. Rutford, finding it to be 4,477 meters—the highest peak of the Craddock Massif and probably the seventh-highest mountain in Antarctica.

Likewise, that previous year, a couple of weeks after climbing Craddock, Steve and I were descending from the summit of Mt. Gardner in the early morning light, and when we looked north along the beautiful raw spine of the northern Sentinels, we saw that a peak on the eastern wall of the Embree Glacier looked higher than we thought it "should," and it looked pretty steep, too. Last season we returned to climb it. It was Mt. Press, a fact we guessed from the map, and it is both steep and beautiful, but we now know for sure, having climbed and measured it, that unlike Rutford it is not really higher than everyone thought.

This year, from the summit of Press, the guys looked farther north and saw more sharp, high virgin peaks that looked good to climb, and no doubt someone will go there and climb them.

Yes, of course, this is a seemingly endless process of desire and consumption, but it has plenty of positives, I believe. It gives more than it takes. We've established new, more accurate heights for most of the high peaks, clarified classification and naming issues, and, in cooperation with the USGS, produced the definitive topographical map for the range. But the process is the thing. Discovery, desire, planning, climbing, knowledge, communication, progression. That's what it's about. Antarctica's highest mountains are among the continent's most significant features, and people now know a lot more about the Sentinel Range than they did before we visited. The Information leads to new climbing, which adds to the mass of The Information, which will in turn lead to more new climbing.

So, for now at least, the list of Antarctica's highest mountains, not including subpeaks, looks like this:

1. Mt. Vinson   4,892m
2. Mt. Tyree   4,852m*
3. Mt. Shinn   4,660m
4. Mt. Gardner   4,573m
5. Mt. Kirkpatrick 4,528m*
6. Mt. Elizabeth   4,480m*
7. Mt. Rutford   4,477m
8. Mt. Craddock   4,368m
9. Peak 4,360m   4,360m*
10. Mt. Epperly   4,359m*

Damien Gildea in icy camouflage on the Gildea Glacier, with the Nimitz Glacier and Bastien Range behind him. Damien Gildea

Along the way, I also have gotten my own little bits of closure. Mt. Anderson had been on my mind since Mike and I weren't able to get to it back in 2001. This last season, after finding a way out of the Embree Glacier, Camilo Rada, Maria Paz Ibarra, Jed Brown, and I sledged south toward Vinson, and in the process made the first ascents of Anderson, Mt. Giovinetto, and Mt. Morris. Climbing Anderson was the highlight—the first ascent of a high, steep, unclimbed peak by an aesthetic route that is not the easiest way up. A week later, Jed, Maria, and Camilo made the first ascent of Giovinetto, and thus brought another form of closure: The last unclimbed mountain in the Sentinel Range over 4,000 meters had been climbed.

There are still dozens and dozens of big, unclimbed faces and ridges in the Sentinel Range, great natural lines in an awesome setting with easy approaches, 24-hour daylight, and pretty good weather. Sure, it's expensive to get there, but plenty of people spend the same or more money to repeat the normal routes on various 8,000-meter peaks. To each his own, of course—it's just a matter of priorities. I know mine.

SUMMARY:

AREA: Sentinel Range, Antarctica

ASCENTS: Jed Brown, Damien Gildea, Maria Paz Ibarra, and Camilo Rada spent more than two months in the Sentinel Range in 2006–2007. Various members of the team made 12 ascents, each of them either the first ascent of a peak or a new route. See Climbs and Expeditions for a complete account of these climbs.

A NOTE ABOUT THE AUTHOR:

Damien Gildea, 38, lives near Goulburn, New South Wales, Australia, where, he says, "I don't work—I'm independently unwealthy, a real self-made pauper, who through shear perseverance cornered the market on sloth." He has done five expeditions to the Sentinel Range.

Denotes heights not measured by the Omega Foundation. Most of these summits would probably be slightly lower than indicated here.

WASHBURN REMEMBERED

Encounters with the man and his photographs.

Bradford Washburn caught in the viewfinder of his Fairchild K-22 camera in 2000. *Thom Pollard*

Henry Bradford Washburn Jr. died on January 10, 2007, after a remarkable life as a mountaineer, cartographer, photographer, and museum director. A full obituary can be found elsewhere in this Journal. Here, climbers recall their own experiences with the man and his extraordinary photographs. To read more Washburn memories or to contribute your own story to a permanent archive, please visit www.americanalpineclub.org/AAJ/.

⌂

Bradford Washburn's photographs of the Alaska Range have given me inspiration for action. His picture of the east face of Hunter showed there was clearly room for a route or two to the right of Diamond Arête, and that motivated Paul Figg and I to begin the adventure we called The Prey. On the summit of Hunter, I got out a copy of Brad's photo of the complex west ridge, brought along to guide our descent. The wind snatched it from my hand, and so began a taxing few days.

These photos are profligate in their affections: Just as you begin to think they are giving their secrets to you alone, as you and your partner hatch plans and trace lines, they tell the whole story to someone else and Light Traveler and Canadian Direct get climbed. Their allure is in their clarity, which brings an air of simplicity—they suggest a sort of order to the chaotic flanks of icy mountains that leads you to think that climbing there will have the same simplicity and clarity. Of course you discover that the reality is different, but then you're already there and the photograph has done its job.

MALCOLM BASS
Thirsk, England

⌂

Bradford Washburn's map of Mt. McKinley revealed a thin, white line to the top of Mt. Huntington: the southeast spur, mostly snow and ice, a simple way to the top. At Washburn's office at the Boston Museum of Science, an aide showed me to the scrapbook volumes of contact prints from the Alaska Range. There might have been more than a dozen volumes, but I could not find a picture of two dangerous-looking icefalls guarding the spur. I had hoped a photo might confirm a way that I thought they could be bypassed.

Washburn found the picture as soon as I pointed to the map. The icefalls were hard to identify as Huntington's because of the tight framing, but were fully revealed in the print. He pecked at the lower one. Anybody who goes in there, he said, deserves to be knocked on the head.

Kent Meneghin, Joe Kaelin, Glenn Randall, and I climbed the southeast spur that summer, in 1978, bypassing the icefalls by gullies and ramps. Two subsequent parties, however, got a closer look.

Jeb Schenck and Dave Holsworth, not knowing our route, climbed the first icefall later that summer. A block of ice the size of Holsworth's head hit him on the shoulder. "We considered ourselves very lucky to have made it," Schenck wrote.

Jeff Thomas, Dave Jay, Scott Woolums, and Jay Kerr reached the second icefall the next year and shunned our route around it. "Being Oregon volcano sloggers and not knowing better, we took the icefall," Thomas wrote. They discovered "a frozen horror" with ice talus at the angle of repose, active overhanging seracs, and terrifying pitches, including a 70-foot tunnel and a 90-degree wall plastered with blobs of unstable snow. They followed our route down.

Last winter, while hitchhiking up to Teton Pass to ski powder, I caught a ride in a car with crampons and cameras in the back. It was lucky Jeb Schenck, and soon we were swapping Huntington stories.

"Worse than the Khumbu," he said of the icefall he had climbed. Sure enough, he and Holsworth also had followed our route down. "One time was more than enough," Schenck said.

Washburn's photographs answered questions that otherwise would have required exploration, and these experiences on Huntington proved it.

ANGUS M. THUERMER JR.
Jackson Hole, Wyoming

⟁

At first, Dougal Haston and I were planning to climb the east face of Denali, because that was the photo Brad had shown us in England, and he was enthusiastic about this unclimbed wall. But when I visited Brad in Boston during my lecture tour of the States in 1976, he showed me a spectacular photo of the south face. We could see that the entire upper section of the wall was still unclimbed, and we knew that this face would be much easier to reach than the east. So we chose the south face instead, climbing it by a new direct line, and Brad would have to continue in his quest to find someone to climb the east face.

DOUG SCOTT
Carlisle, England

⟁

My photograph of a 90-year-old Brad Washburn and his big camera, reproduced on page 106, sums up the timeless energy and enthusiasm he felt for his craft. In 2000, together with Barbara, Brad and I spent two weeks in Alaska. We were filming for a documentary about their adventures, called *Alaskan Reminiscences: 60 Years of Adventure with Bradford and Barbara Washburn*. Brad's 53-pound Fairchild K-22 aerial camera, which he had donated to the University of Alaska at Fairbanks some years before, was under lock and key at a Talkeetna hotel. On display under a glass case, the now legendary camera was carefully guarded by a young assistant to the curator—white gloves and all—under specific instructions not to let anyone touch it, not even Brad. After some choice words that only Brad could so succinctly articulate, the now trembling young man reluctantly unlocked the case, telling us he'd now be leaving for lunch. He expected to see the camera in the case when he returned.

We immediately jumped into our truck, the camera on Brad's lap, and drove straight to the Talkeetna airport. After taking the side door off of a DeHavilland Beaver, Brad hefted that old camera up on his lap and offered a full demonstration of its workings (which I captured on videotape). He demonstrated how he got into position for each shot by belting out commands to the pilot, how he advanced the frames, the whole story. Brad even wore the same clothing that he'd used so many years before, right down to the L.L. Bean hunting boots.

Not a few days later, the day dawned immaculate. Brad and I quickly returned to the airport. Along with our young pilot we took the door off a turbo Cessna and prepared our oxygen masks, a digital video camera, and my medium-format still camera. Locked safely into our seats with climbing ropes and carabiners, we flew all way up and over the summit of Mt. McKinley. Turning from the viewfinder of my own camera, I witnessed the intense stare of Brad's eyes as he scanned the Alaska Range below us.

Some months later, Brad stood in an audio booth for me to record his impressions of McKinley for our documentary. He finished the session by reading one of his favorite poems, "High Flight," by John McGee. The quiver in his voice and a tear in his eye belied the stolid sense of strength that Brad showed in difficult situations:

> *Up, up the long delirious burning blue*
> *I've topped the windswept heights with easy grace*
> *Where never lark or even eagle flew*
> *And while with silent lifting mind*
> *I've trod the high untresspassed sanctity of space*
> *Put out my hand*
> *And touched the face of God.*

THOM POLLARD
North Conway, New Hampshire

Like Brad, I decided to specialize in Alaska and the Yukon, going on expeditions to the far north for 13 consecutive summers. To get ideas for new routes, I pored through Brad's bound volumes of contact prints of the great mountains in the Alaska, Hayes, Wrangell, and St. Elias ranges. Brad kept those volumes on shelves in a kind of walk-in closet, accessible only through his regal top-floor office at the Museum of Science. Though Brad gave me carte blanche to loiter inside that sanctum, for years I felt intimidated by his presence, especially on the two or three occasions when he forgot that I was there and I heard his outer door close before he harangued some negligent employee or schemed up research plans with some famous scientist.

From those furtive hours in the walk-in closet came three of my best and toughest expeditions—to the east ridge of Mt. Deborah, the west face of Mt. Huntington, and the south-east face of Mt. Dickey. As Don Jensen and I first realized on Deborah in 1964, Brad's photos were so sharp, so perfectly exposed, that on the ground we could recognize features as small as six inches in diameter that were clearly shown in the pictures we carried with us.

On Dickey in 1974, a Washburn photo may well have saved our lives. Galen Rowell, Ed Ward, and I were attempting the 5,100-foot precipice of granite, snow, and ice alpine style, with bivy sacks and half bags in lieu of tent camps, carrying all our gear and food in one three-day push—fast and light, in the best Washburn tradition. To make this proposition less than suicidal, before attacking the face we had climbed the easy "back side" of Dickey (first ascended by Brad in 1955) and left a vital cache containing a tent, food, a stove, and sleeping bags near the summit, marked by a tall pole.

On the third day of the climb, a fierce storm engulfed the mountain—heavy snow, 50 mph winds, near-whiteout conditions. We were too high to go down. Foolishly we had brought only one ice axe and one pair of crampons, and the last thousand feet of the route was a bewildering complex of steep ice grooves and flutings interspersed with rotten bands of black schist. I took the axe and crampons and led all day, chopping steps for Ed and Galen, who had

Louis-Philippe Ménard studies an article from the 2001 *American Alpine Journal* while resting during the first ascent of the Canadian Direct route on the south face of Mt. McKinley. Ménard and Maxime Turgeon referred to a Bradford Washburn photo of the face (on the reverse side of the photocopy he's holding) to help find their way up the enormous wall. A similar photo, with the new Canadian route marked, is reproduced in the Climbs and Expeditions section of this *Journal*; the story of their climb begins on page 47. *Maxime Turgeon*

Under the beam of my headlamp, the book between my hands seems like an art piece, totally capturing my attention. Every time I turn a page, it feels like discovering a new world. There are no colors, just a perfect scale of grey that defines every little feature. The Washburn images are so clear that looking at them almost feels like flying over the range. Flipping back and forth through the pages, I keep returning to the same photo. A formation seems to leap out of the picture, contoured on either side by the traces of previous ascents. The line is so obvious: Two perfectly aligned buttresses, one on top of the other, ending right on top of the southeast spur. The lower buttress has never been climbed directly. It almost feels as if the photographer had wanted to underline it....

MAXIME TURGEON
Montréal, Québec, Canada

to use their rock hammers for purchase in lieu of axes.

Protection was almost nonexistent. If one of us slipped and fell, he would likely pull the other two off, and we would take the big ride. It was crucial to our survival that we find the cache near the summit, but I felt that I was heading blindly upward into a maze of bleary white treachery. At regular intervals I pulled out of my pocket the crumpled Washburn photo of our route that I had carried up the mountain and tried to correlate its details with the real world. Yes, amazingly, that serpentine fluting over there, that prong of schist here, showed up on Brad's picture: So I needed to angle a bit farther left.

With ice coating our beards and eyelashes and hypothermia just a careless step away, we struck the summit ridge only a hundred yards from our cache. We pitched the tent, crawled into our dry sleeping bags, and brewed up a victory soup.

DAVID ROBERTS
Cambridge, Massachusetts

Excerpted with permission from an article in the April 2007 issue of National Geographic Adventure *magazine.*

△

On June 5, I set foot for the first time on American soil, a country which is still somewhat legendary for Europeans: legendary for her history, legendary her numerous great men, her progress, her spirit of liberty. And, I say it with complete sincerity, I was not disillusioned by this first contact with the United States; only, at times, I was astonished by people and customs which were new to me. Almost as if in a dream, the great conglomeration of New York and later of Boston returns to mind; and suddenly, quite clearly I see the kind face of Dr. Washburn, who hardly knows his great and unselfish contribution to our expedition: photographs, maps, explanations. He gave essential insight into our undertaking, which, added to facts given to me in Italy by Piero Meciani, gave me, even before arriving, a clear picture of the difficulties which awaited us."

RICCARDO CASSIN, *writing in the 1962* American Alpine Journal *about his
expedition to make the first ascent of Mt. McKinley's south ridge.*

△

In 1972, I and my fellow 17-year-old climbing buds were inspired to read *Bradford on Mount Fairweather*, a book written by him on his first climbing expedition to Alaska, at age 20, to attempt Fairweather's first ascent. We committed ourselves to climbing Fairweather, which still had seen few ascents, via a new route, much to the skepticism of many we talked to. Upon learning of his collection of photos at the Boston Museum of Science, we drove up from New York City to have a look and study route possibilities. We were blown away when Brad, then in his mid-60s, burst into the room to introduce himself, talk to us about the mountain, and enthusiastically suggest lines while pulling out photos. Most importantly, he believed in the high school students in front of him and instilled confidence in our plans.

That was the first of many winter visits during the 1970s to Dr. Washburn's photo library, and each time he made time to sit down with us and add to our enthusiasm for the unclimbed lines we were scoping on McKinley, Foraker, Hunter, and Huntington, while also suggesting, with great authority, additional lines. His passion matched our own, and it was as if, for at least the time we were in his archival room, he was the fifth or fourth or third member of the team.

PETER METCALF
Salt Lake City, Utah

△

I can't claim to have been Bradford Washburn's intimate friend, though we worked together for more than 20 years across an Atlantic divide during my reign as editor of *Crags* and more significantly *High* magazine. In all that time, I never managed to train him into the ways of the electronic modern world, though I tried. I would fax him requesting a photograph and he would phone me up. In later years, I would email him and about a month later he would phone me up. The trouble was that because of the time difference between the U.K. and the east coast of America, he always called when I'd gone to the pub in the evening, so that when I returned home my wife, Jackie, was smiling, having been charmed by this lovely man. Can you believe the man was pushing 90 years old and still able to turn the head of a woman 40 years his junior?

GEOFF BIRTLES
Sheffield, England

△

Like so many, I saw a startling Brad Washburn image, felt the adrenaline surge, and knew, "I've got to climb that mountain!" In my case it was the St. Elias Range's Pinnacle Peak, a mountain of symmetry. Seeing Brad's photograph led me to make nine climbing trips to the St. Elias and also set me on a voyage to find out what had not been climbed in the wild St. Elias landscape. The product of this endeavor was published in the 1992 *Canadian Alpine Journal*. That article was transformed from a sterile list to a best seller because Brad, who knew me not from Adam, spent literally hours on the telephone from Boston to Toronto, helping me choose which of his photographs would illustrate the article. His wonderful black and white photographs, reproduced in the *CAJ*, were the spur to creating new routes all over the St. Elias, including the first ascent of three 4,000-meter-plus St. Elias peaks for my friends and I.

ROGER WALLIS
Toronto, Canada

△

After seeing superb photographs by Bradford Washburn in a mountaineering journal, I realized what a magnificent field of action the McKinely Range would be for an enthusiast of *grande alpinisme*. Immediately I began to dream about the possibility of climbing some of these peaks. As early as 1955 I got in touch with Bradford Washburn, Bob Bates, Fred Beckey, and other American climbers.... In December 1963 I began to actively prepare for the expedition. As always, unforeseen difficulties cropped up, but thanks to Bradford Washburn and Mrs. Helga Bading of Anchorage all the American problems were quickly solved.

LIONEL TERRAY, *writing in the 1965* American Alpine Journal *about his expedition to make the first ascent of Mt. Huntington in Alaska.*

I first met [Washburn] in 1990, when he was a sprightly 80-year-old, lodged at a temporary office in the Royal Geographical Society, waiting to install his huge relief model of Mt Everest for a special London exhibition. "We've spent the whole week trying to get my model out of your darned British customs at Heathrow," he fretted. "They must think it's stuffed full of cocaine or something." The model was released eventually and the only white powder involved was actually some innocent icing sugar dusted over the section joins of his stunningly accurate representation of the world's highest summit.

The model was based on the latest, highly accurate 1:50,000 map of Mt. Everest—a project masterminded by Washburn, using the pinpoint accuracy of aerial photos from a Learjet to complement the ground-slogging surveys of the pre-War British explorers, dating right back to the 1921 Reconnaissance, when Washburn was a young boy in Boston taking his own first pictures on a Brownie box camera, with compositional advice from his mother. Where some cartographers might see photography purely as a surveying tool, he embraced the medium for its own sake, delighting in light and form to produce some of the greatest 20th century landscape photographs. As Jim Enyeart of Eastman House once put it, "Brad Washburn's aerial photographs are exactly what Ansel Adams would have taken if he had used a magic carpet."

In Europe, his aerial shots of the Matterhorn give a whole new understanding to that mountain of a thousand chocolate boxes. Likewise his seminal study of moonrise over the Grandes Jorasses. But, like so many great photographs, the most famous one of all, depicting tiny human figures on the obscure Doldenhorn, was taken by accident. When I asked how it happened, he explained, "It was in 1960 and we were going to get some shots of the Jungfrau. We took off from Interlaken, turned left at Kandersteg, over the Oeschinensee ... then way down to the right I saw these figures on that ridge, so I forgot all about the Jungfrau and said to the pilot, "Jesus Christ, let's get down there."

They did get down there and he got his picture. The exposure is flawless, light and texture scintillating. The tiny silhouettes are just recognizable as humans, giving scale and context to an essentially abstract composition. As with all his great photographs, Washburn uses height to create a whole new dimension, but he doesn't get so high as to flatten the landscape. And, on the basis that big subjects need big negatives, he went for 7-inch by 9-inch frames on a colossal Fairchild K-6 (later upgraded to a K-22) weighing in at 53 pounds—quite a progression from his 12-ounce Kodak Vestpocket! He sat on an empty five-gallon garlic box with a rope tied tightly around his waist and back to the other side of the plane, giving him exactly enough slack to lean right out of the open doorway with the great beast balanced on his lap.

"When you bank it weighs 100 pounds," he boasted gleefully.

"But I thought you said it weighed 53 pounds," I pointed out to him.

"Ah yes, but there's G force," explained the man of science. "That can double or even treble the effective weight."

STEPHEN VENABLES
Bath, England

Excerpted from an article for Geographical *magazine, with permission of the author.*

WASHBURN IN THE *AAJ*

A legacy for mountaineers.

Bradford Washburn's photographs first appeared in the *American Alpine Journal* in 1934 (from Mt. Crillon), and they have graced nearly every edition since. His written contributions to the *AAJ* spanned more than seven decades, starting in 1931 with two notes, covering an unsuccessful attempt on Mt. Fairweather and his election as treasurer of the Harvard Mountaineering Club. Over the decades, his articles traced the arc of a mountaineer's life, beginning with reports on his own attempts and ascents, then sharing his ideas for new routes with younger climbers, and finally looking back with stories about mountain science, geography, and history.

Washburn's most influential articles in the *AAJ* were those from the late 1940s to the late 1960s proposing new routes in Alaska and elsewhere. In 1947, after studying maps and photos, he outlined two new routes on Denali: the "Great West Buttress" and the "Wickersham Ridge." (At the time, Denali had only been climbed three times, always by the Muldrow Glacier.) Four years later, it was Washburn himself who led the first team up the west buttress, which soon became Denali's normal route.

Washburn's articles in the *AAJ* in the 1950s and '60s suggested many other lines on Alaska and the Yukon's great peaks, most of which soon were climbed, including the west ridge of Mt. Hunter, Mt. Huntington, and the northwest ridge of Denali. In the 1963 *AAJ*, he published an article called "Mount McKinley: Proposed East Buttress Routes," which began, "Only three 'major routes' still remain unclimbed on Mount McKinley—Wickersham Wall, the East Face, and the East Buttress." Washburn had previously used the *AAJ*'s bully pulpit to propose routes up the Wickersham Wall, and in 1963 two separate lines on that face as well as the east buttress of Denali were climbed. Of the final unclimbed route, Washburn wrote, "The east face is exceedingly steep, complex, and difficult, and will, I hope, be the subject of one of these analytical articles another year."

Washburn eventually described his ideas for the east face in his final new-route prospectus, originally published in the April 2000 edition of *Rock & Ice* magazine. That article is reprinted here, with the addition of a single paragraph from a Washburn letter. As of the summer of 2007, the east face of Denali remains unclimbed.

DOUGALD MACDONALD

DENALI'S EAST FACE

By Bradford Washburn

Once, many years ago, the lower icefall insulating Denali's east face was traversed as part of a summit bid via Thayer Basin. In 1998, determined to solo that mighty and aloof virgin, Eigerwand ascensionist Tom Bubendorfer studied the icefall thoroughly, then

Bradford Washburn's proposed route up the east face of Mt. McKinley. This photo, Neg. #5816, was taken in July 1966, and ice formations on the face are likely to have changed. © *Bradford Washburn, Courtesy Panopticon Gallery, Boston, MA.*

prudently backed off, the route being too isolated for a reasonable solo ascent. But this is the sort of face that eventually gets climbed, no matter how difficult or dangerous.

The east face rises 9,000 feet above the Traileika Glacier to its 17,425-foot crest—still 3,000 feet below Denali's summit and two and a half miles east of Denali Pass. To reach its base requires an 11-mile hike from McGonagall Pass, which means a 30-mile trek from Denali Park Highway, or 40 miles from Kantishna Airport. Although the utterly crevasseless Traileika Glacier would permit a DC-10 to land at base camp, the National Park Service prohibits all aircraft landings in the area. Air drops—free-fall or by parachute—are likewise a no-no. In short, the east face is very, very remote.

I suggest a simple end-run around the Park Services regulations: Hire a competent sled-dog driver to haul a big cache of food and fuel from Kantishna to an excellent position for a base camp on the West Fork of the Traileika at an altitude of about 7,500-8,000 feet. This could be done early enough in the spring to be certain that the McKinley River is still frozen solid enough for sledge traffic to cross it safely and easily.

Given its position and magnitude, Denali's east face is likely to fall to a party of four climbing in two, closely related teams or to a single powerful pair. The icefall danger at the start is no worse than the Khumbu, which, though dramatic and dangerous, is traversed by hundreds of Himalayan climbers each year. The route's upper part, characterized by steep granite and ice, looks climbable and thrilling. The primary obstacle making the east face so treacherous is avalanches.

Before setting foot on the east face, climbers would be wise to spend *at least a week* studying its avalanche patterns. Most of the activity seems to originate from three small hanging glaciers, situated above the route and to its left, at about 15,000 feet. Does debris really cross the route? How frequently? After a big slough, is there a "safe" period before the next avalanche hits, or is the route cursed by a steady trickle of little falls the whole time?

The best place to study the avalanche behavior is at an 8,000-foot base camp at the head of the Traileika Glacier. There, hopeful climbers can train powerful binoculars on the proposed line until it's known exactly when, where, and how frequently the avalanches occur.

The weather on the northeastern side of Denali is much less violent than its western and southern aspects. However, less direct sunlight and rare storms can make the east face a much colder place than elsewhere. If I were to try this route, I'd leave Kantishna in mid-June and make the climb in early to mid-July.

Assuming a feasible route still negotiates the lower icefall, climbers will find a marvelous advanced base camp location at 11,000 feet, thus reducing the altitude gain of the most difficult part of the climb to about 5,000 feet. What climbers should do at the 17,425-foot crest of the east face poses its own questions. Should climbers deposit in advance, by way of the west buttress, a substantial cache of food, fuel, and even a tent, for a summit bid? Or is a speedy descent via Thayer Basin a better proposition? Then again, should climbers make a hurried retreat down Denali Pass, or simply downclimb the route on the same day as the ascent? Only one thing is certain: An attempt should only be made in excellent weather. The race is on!

This article originally appeared in Rock & Ice *No. 99 (April 2000) and is reprinted with permission of* Rock & Ice *and Barabara Washburn.*

THE FRONT LINES OF CLIMATE CHANGE

Mountaineers are the world's witnesses to glacial decline.

JOE STOCK

The Easton Glacier on Mt. Baker in Washington shows all the signs of a glacier in retreat: moraine-coated valley floor, gently sloped terminus, and little snow cover on the lower two-thirds of the glacier. *Joe Stock*

Thirty miles into the Neacolas, clouds spread over the Blockade Glacier and reduced our visibility to zero. We groped along in the murk, making slow progress toward a series of passes that would get us to Glacier Fork. A rock outcrop appeared just ahead of us, even though our altimeters still placed us far out in the middle of the glacier. Annoyed, we rechecked the altimeters, compared them to the GPS reading, and passed around the 1958 1:63,360-scale USGS map. Was our navigation that far off?

Dylan Taylor, Andrew Wexler, and I were aiming for Lake Clark and a first ski traverse of the entire Neacola Mountains in Alaska. After endless crosschecking of our tools, we isolated the source of our confusion: a consistent difference between the altitude shown by our altimeters and the 1958 map altitude. Since the map was made 48 years earlier, the glacier had lost over 100 feet of altitude. The rock outcrop was shown on the map, but, based on our altitude, we thought we were still a couple of miles away from it.

△

Mountaineers and alpine climbers frequently encounter the effects of climate change. Not all the changes are negative: In the Neacolas, shrinking glaciers made ski touring easier. With less snow surviving the summer months, the glacial conveyor belt has slowed and fewer crevasses form. In many places, however, melting glaciers means harder or more dangerous climbs. Many approaches to alpine climbs now are moraine bashes instead of easy glacier walks, and climbing up and down moraine walls is sometimes the most dangerous part of a trip. Blocks of seasonal snow cascade off glacier-polished slabs. Rocks previously frozen for hundreds of years plunge toward our flimsy helmets.

Classic routes are gone—at least in their old prime seasons. The Black Ice Couloir on the Grand Teton is a smear of dirt by August. The Diamond Ice Couloir on Mt. Kenya depends on rare melt-freeze cycles to form. The legendary White Spider on the Eiger must be climbed in the old "off season." Perhaps only a generation will still see the snows of Kilimanjaro. The glaciers of Montana, Wyoming, Colorado, and California are hiding under piles of moraine. Remaining ice faces are often composed of unpleasantly hard ice above gaping bergschrunds.

Most Americans hear a lot about climate change, but their conversation on the subject may be spurred only by a heat wave or a balmy winter; their interest soon dies and they go on with their lives. The situation is different for those of us who play and work on glaciers. We have climate change shoved in our faces on every trip.

△

Glaciers are products of climate and are sensitive to changes in weather. By looking at a glacier and its surrounding basin, we can see the climatic trend. Large valley glaciers, like the Kahiltna Glacier on Denali, respond to climatic shifts in 100 to 200 years. Because of their length—the Kahiltna is 45 miles long—it takes at least 100 years before warming or a lower precipitation trend causes a measurable negative mass balance, or net ice loss. On the other hand, small mountain glaciers, like those in the Cascades, are more responsive to climate. Within a couple of decades, changes in weather show up as negative mass balance.

In September 2006, I guided the Easton Glacier on Mt. Baker in Washington; this glacier is climbed by hundreds each year, and has a serious negative mass balance. Within 15 minutes of seeing the Easton, my clients were asking about climate change. The glacier's illness was obvious. Ground moraine coated the valley floor where the glacier had flowed less than 50 years ago. Along the glacier margins we saw bathtub rings where the glacier once had scoured the rock and since has melted down. These trimlines now frame the sides of most modern glaciers. Several kilometers up the valley, we saw the withering end of the glacier. As if wheelchair-accessible, the snout was a smooth ramp of dirty ice instead of the vertical or bulbous front typical of a healthy glacier. Higher, bare ice stretched up the mountain, with only the top quarter of the glacier covered in snow. Near the top I saw the dividing line between the old snow (firn) and new snow from the previous winter. This line, known as the equilibrium line altitude, or ELA, should be only about halfway up a glacier if the glacier is to survive. Input must equal output.

Not all glaciers are shrinking. The Taku Glacier near Juneau is a 57-mile-long, 261-square-mile beast that has been fattening along its full length for over 30 years. The warming climate has shifted its accumulation area into the zone ideal for maximum snowfall. Forests are still being crushed by the Taku's advancing front. However, virtually all of the rest of North America's glaciers are not enjoying the same benefits.

As the Roosevelt Glacier on Mt. Baker retreats, the lateral moraine is no longer supported by the ice and slumps downward, leaving trimlines along the glacier's edge. *Joe Stock*

Any scientific debate about global warming ended quickly. Global warming is fact—the temperature has been rising since the Little Ice Age ended 150 years ago. The debate has been to what degree humans are involved. With the report by the Intergovernmental Panel on Climate Change released in March 2007, that debate is now over. Scientists now agree with 90 percent certainty that the majority of the average global temperature increase in recent decades can be attributed to human causes. Carbon emissions are to blame. We know from polar ice cores that temperature follows atmospheric carbon dioxide level, and carbon dioxide has risen dramatically above pre-industrial levels.

Although the tide of public opinion seems to be turning and action to reduce carbon dioxide emissions now seems more likely than it did a decade ago, pressure must be maintained on policymakers to take speedy and effective action if the trend of shrinking glaciers is to be halted. With our unique understanding of glaciers based on years of climbing and camping on them, mountaineers can influence people through our first-hand accounts of what we know about global warming. It is our responsibility to share our experiences in order to help save the mountain environment that we love.

Sharing your data, photos, and stories is the key. Nonclimbers want to hear news from the mountains. Tell your stories. Blow up your photos. Write a story for your local paper. You don't have to be a scientist. Just tell them what you see. I include a five-minute section on climate change in my Alaska ski mountaineering slide show that is seen by hundreds each year.

While traipsing around the mountains, document what you see. Take photos of the end of glaciers showing the surrounding rock outcrops for reference points, and try to do this each year for comparison. Take photos of glaciers from vantage points that show the complete length of the ice. (Try taking your photos in late summer when most of the seasonal snow has melted.) Then compare the glacier to the map and to similar photos taken years earlier. If you don't have old photos, take a macro photo of the area on a map, with pointers showing the before and after locations of the glacier's terminus.

Glaciers lose most of their mass through thinning, and an easy way to measure this ice loss is by taking GPS elevations to compare with your USGS 1:24,000 or 1:63,360-scale maps. Handheld GPS units are not very accurate, but even approximate data is better than none. Using this technique, I found average glacier elevation loss of 70 feet over 10 locations across the Neacola Mountains. Keith Daellenbach measured an average elevation loss of 33 feet across

The receding terminus of Mt. Baker's Coleman Glacier is a far cry from the steep, swelling snout of a healthy glacier. *Joe Stock*

the Juneau Icefield, an area that includes the Taku Glacier, the United States' healthiest glacier. These very simple data sets are great for slide shows and kids' science classes.

Another way to measure ice loss is to take a GPS waypoint at the glacier terminus. Then compare that location to the map you're using. I recently compared my April 2007 GPS reading of the Eklutna Glacier terminus near Anchorage to the 1994 USGS map and discovered that the Eklutna terminus had retreated an entire mile in this 13-year period.

Mountain guides have a unique opportunity to share the message about climate change with others, especially in talking with clients during trips and in presentations about our adventures to the public. Teaching others about climate change is an important part of your job. Your clients are interested and respect your knowledge. Be prepared to answer their questions.

As mountaineers, we also contribute to climate change, and we have a responsibility to mitigate our impacts. Our biggest negative contribution occurs while getting into the hills. We burn hundreds of gallons of gas each year, and this, in turn, sends hundreds of pounds of carbon into the atmosphere. Traveling to and from a recent Tordrillo ski traverse, for example, we flew 450 total miles in a Cessna airplane, burning over 100 gallons of gas. To help offset those greenhouse gas emissions, we purchased Denali Green Tags (www.denaligreentags. org). The money we spent to purchase these tags goes toward developing wind energy, arguably the cleanest renewable energy available.

To promote Green Tags among climbers, a group of us in Anchorage is working on an initiative called Climb Green (www.climbgreen.org). We aim to have the cost of Green Tags incorporated into one's ticket price to fly into Alaskan mountains. For example, when booking a ticket with an air taxi to fly into the Ruth Gorge, Denali Green Tags will be included in the ticket cost.

Glaciers can't just grab a thicker blanket of snow from the closet, and we can't grab another planet. Glaciers are pointing their thawing fingers right at us mountaineers. Let's step up and be ambassadors for the mountains.

A NOTE ABOUT THE AUTHOR:

Joe Stock works as a mountain guide, hydrologist, writer, and photographer. He lives in Anchorage with his wife, Cathy.

THE ALPINE CONSERVATION PARTNERSHIP

A global initiative to protect and restore alpine ecosystems.

ALTON C. BYERS, PH.D.

Relentless harvesting of shrub juniper and dwarf rhododendron by lodges during the past 10 years has had severe impacts on the alpine ecosystems of the upper Hinku Khola valley in Makalu-Barun National Park and Buffer Zone, Nepal. In May 2007, however, lodge owners agreed to ban the harvesting of juniper following a meeting with the Mountain Institute and national park representatives. *Alton Byers*

Alpine ecosystems, gateways to the world's highest summits, are among the world's most beautiful and important landscapes. They are characterized by low-growing shrubs, cushion plants, and grasslands adapted to the harsh, high-altitude climate between the upper treeline and permanent snowline. Covering just three percent of the Earth's surface, they contain over 10,000 species of plants, the highest biodiversity per unit area of any ecosystem in the world. They are also critically important to millions of people in the lowlands as sources of fresh water for drinking, agriculture, and hydropower.

Compared to rainforests, oceans, and coastal regions, however, alpine environments throughout the world have been neglected by the international conservation community, possibly because of their remoteness, high altitudes, harsh climates, and extremely difficult travel and working conditions. They are nevertheless exceptionally fragile ecosystems, characterized by young and thin soils, slow plant growth cycles, and a lack of resiliency, where even minor forms of disturbance can take decades to heal.

During the past 30 years, devastating but often insidious human and domestic-animal impacts have occurred throughout the world's alpine ecosystems. Alpine environments are being rapidly transformed into high-altitude wastelands by overgrazing, overharvesting of fuelwood, uncontrolled lodge construction, and other impacts. In response, in early 2007 the American Alpine Club (AAC) and the Mountain Institute (TMI) launched a pioneering project designed to reverse these trends: the Alpine Conservation Partnership (ACP).

◬

This project's genesis dates back to 1984, when I spent a year living in Khumjung village in Nepal, measuring soil erosion and studying landscape change between Namche Bazaar and Dingboche. Surprisingly, I found that most hill slopes below 4,000 meters were stable, but those above 4,000 meters were losing tons of soil to erosion, for reasons that I didn't entirely understand. In 1995, I replicated hundreds of historic photographs and found that, while there were more trees in 1995 than in 1961, more than 50 percent of the shrub juniper in the Dingboche region had been removed.

In 2001, we followed up this work by conducting the first detailed study of contemporary human impacts in the upper Imja Khola and Gokyo valleys of Sagarmatha (Mt. Everest) National Park in Nepal. We found that the typical tourist lodge, of which there are dozens throughout the alpine zone, had dozens of cords of shrub juniper stacked outside, each piece typically taking 175 years to grow to a diameter of only 2 centimeters. Up to 50 percent of the typical groundcover plot we sampled was bare during times when a continuous cover of herbs and grasses should have been found.

In addition to demonstrating their awareness of these growing problems, the local Sherpa voiced a strong desire to take action to protect and restore their fragile alpine ecosystems. They specifically recommended a community-based project that would give them the chance to educate all stakeholders about these problems, including climbers, trekkers, development agencies, and lodge owners. They also hoped to introduce alternative fuel and energy sources and to establish exclosures, similar to those constructed near Namche Bazaar by the Himalayan Trust, that would allow the land to heal itself.

The Everest Alpine Conservation and Restoration Project officially launched in Nepal in 2003 with a $21,000 start-up grant from the AAC that was subsequently matched by over $100,000 from conservation organizations (e.g., the National Geographic Society), governments (e.g., the U.S. Agency for International Development), foundations, and private individuals.

Since its formation, the Everest project has:
- Established the Khumbu Alpine Conservation Council (KACC), the world's first alpine NGO committed to protecting and restoring high-altitude ecosystems
- Saved more that 80,000 kilograms of fragile shrub juniper per year that was formerly used for fuelwood
- Banned the burning of shrub juniper as incense at the Everest base camp
- Established a kerosene and stove depot as alternative fuel for tourists and lodges
- Restored a porters' rest house in Lobuche to provide shelter, warmth, and cooking facilities, thereby decreasing porter dependence on local shrubs for fuelwood
- Developed new curricula for local schools
- Begun actively restoring devegetated hill slopes by building high-altitude nurseries and cattle-proof demonstration exclosures.

In February 2006, the KACC received a $50,000 capacity-building grant from the United Nations Development Programme/Nepal that will strengthen its ability to sustain the Everest project. And in January 2007, the Alpine Conservation Partnership was officially launched with a $150,000 grant from the Argosy Foundation. Now the ACP will begin expanding the conservation success in the Everest region to alpine regions worldwide.

△

Over the next 10 years, the community-based models of alpine conservation developed in the Everest region will be adapted, modified, and applied to priority alpine ecosystems throughout the world that include the Gokyo and Thami valleys in Sagarmatha National Park (an expansion of the existing activities); Mera Peak in Makalu-Barun National Park (TMI conducted a detailed survey of this heavily impacted area in May 2007); Huascarán National Park, Peru (activities in the Ishinca and Pisco valleys are scheduled to commence in June-July 2007); and the Baltoro and Biafo glacier regions, Pakistan. Patagonia Inc. recently provided a generous grant to the project that will assist the Patagonia National Park authorities in Argentina with the conservation of heavily impacted backcountry sites there. Phase II (2012–2017) could expand the project even more, with prospective work sites including the Wind River Range, Wyoming; Aconcagua National Park, Argentina; Kilimanjaro National Park, Tanzania; Mt. Kenya National Park, Kenya; and Belukha Nature Park, Russian Altai.

The continued refinement of the Everest model will represent a major contribution to the field of high-altitude conservation and adventure tourism management in general. For example, while recent research suggests that the impacts of poor alpine ecosystem management are nearly identical worldwide, it is clear that the causes will differ on a case-by-case basis, thus demanding a scientific understanding of the real threats before prescribing solutions. Linking conservation with real improvements in local people's livelihoods, and building their capacity to manage and sustain conservation/livelihood projects themselves, will be critical to achieving the long-term objectives of the project.

Additional benefits and opportunities related to the project could include internships for young AAC members to work with the various alpine conservation and restoration projects; "green guide" training for climbing guides throughout the mountain world; workshops on themes such as conservation-linked mountaineering expeditions and high-altitude sanitation technology; and the development of new partnerships among scientific, educational, and conservation organizations, international mountaineering clubs, and the private sector.

In summary, the Alpine Conservation Partnership represents an unprecedented opportunity for the AAC, TMI, and other partners to play a lead role in the hands-on conservation of the world's fragile and rapidly deteriorating alpine ecosystems. Our goal is to leave a legacy that will be unmatched in the history of conservation projects initiated by mountaineers.

A NOTE ABOUT THE AUTHOR:

Alton C. Byers, Ph.D., is director of the Research and Education Program at the Mountain Institute (www.mountain.org). In February 2006, he received the AAC's David Brower Conservation Award. In March 2007, he received the Sir Edmund Hillary Mountain Legacy Medal for "remarkable service in conservation of culture and nature in remote mountainous regions."

LE PIOLET D'OR

Whither prizes for alpinism?

Marko Prezelj addresses the audience, translator Anthony Moinet, and journalist Gilles Chappaz, on stage at the 16th annual Piolet d'Or ceremony in Grenoble, France. Prezelj's climbing partner, Boris Lorencic, is at left. The story of their climb begins on page 14 of this *Journal*. *Philippe Descamps*

Arguments over the wisdom of attempting to honor the "best climb of the year" came to a head before and after the 16th Piolet d'Or ceremony in Grenoble, France, on January 26, 2007. The Piolet d'Or is sponsored by the French magazine *Montagnes*, with the winner chosen each year by a jury of climbers and journalists. In recent years, several nominated teams of climbers have declined to participate in the awards program, arguing that such awards run counter to the spirit of alpinism, and that comparing ascents of different styles is impossible. In late 2006, the Groupe de Haute Montagne (GHM), a cofounder of the Piolet d'Or program, said it would no longer cooperate with *Montagnes* on the awards.

Nonetheless, the 16th annual Piolet d'Or awards proceeded, and the jury chose to honor Boris Lorencic and Marko Prezelj for their first ascent of the northwest pillar of 7,326-meter Chomolhari, on the border of Tibet and Bhutan. (Prezelj's account of this climb begins on page 14 of this *Journal*.) Prezelj, who received the very first Piolet d'Or, in 1991, and has been nominated a total of four times for the prize, spoke out against the awards at the 2007 ceremony in Grenoble; afterward, at the request of *Montagnes*, he wrote an essay opposing such prizes, which he disseminated widely, generating much discussion. *Montagnes* responded with an editorial stating its arguments for maintaining the award and promising to revise the program with critics' concerns in mind. As of June 2007, the magazine had not yet announced its plans for the 17th Piolet d'Or.

Because we feel that this discussion touches on many issues vital to today's climbers— Why do we climb? What is the meaning of success? Is climbing a "sport" with winners and losers?—and because most of the past winners of the Piolet d'Or have written articles for the *AAJ* about their ascents, we present both Prezelj's original essay and the *Montagnes* editorial for your consideration.

GLADIATORS AND CLOWNS D'OR

Marko Prezelj
February 2007

Several people criticized me for participating in the Piolet d'Or ceremony this year. None of them were in Grenoble. Joining this circus gave me the opportunity to present my opinion about the award publicly. Time will tell if doing so was a mistake.

I don't believe in awards for alpinism, much less trophies or titles presented by the public or the media. At the ceremony I could see and feel the competitive spirit created and fueled by the event's organizers. Most of the climbers readily accepted this mood without understanding that they had been pushed into an arena where spectators thrive on drama, where winner and loser are judged.

It is not possible to judge another person's climb objectively. Each ascent contains untold stories, influenced by expectations and illusions that develop long before setting foot on the mountain. In alpinism, even the most personal judgments are extremely subjective. When we return from the mountains we remember moments differently than they were—there and then—when we had to make decisions under the pressure of many factors.

Comparing different climbs is not possible without some kind of personal involvement, and even then it is difficult. Last year I climbed in Alaska, Patagonia, and Tibet. I cannot decide which expedition was the most...the "most what," in fact?

To illustrate this, I asked (during the first part of ceremony) the father of several children to decide which one was the best and which was the worst? He could not answer.

I might choose which wine, food, song, book, or movie I like the most in a certain moment, but a jury cannot decide which is the best, worst, or "most" for everyone in one year. If a jury chooses a single winner, it automatically implies a loser, which is the essence of competition. And first place means there is a second, third, and last place. Is the last-place climb truly the worst, or were the winners simply more adept at the manipulation game? Did they exaggerate the "beauty" of their ascent more effectively or market themselves better to the jury?

The idea of inspirational gatherings of climbers is positive, but I cannot support the absurd idea of those same climbers "competing" at alpinism. At the Piolet d'Or ceremony, I said the trophy is not important to me because the choice of a winner is subjective, like singing and beauty contests, and commercial influence on the event is obvious and definite. My broken English prevented me from being clear.

But the story of the Piolet d'Or makes it clear that comparing climbs (and the protagonists and their ideals) is nonsense, especially doing so for one calendar year. If comparison is impossible, what are the media and sponsors presenting and promoting, and why? Are they doing it for increased sales, or for *fame* maybe?

In Slovenia, where I come from, fame has a woman's name: Slava. Old people used to say, "Slava je kurba" ("fame is a bitch"); one day she is sleeping with one, and the next day with another. Fame is a cheap trap set by the media in which the complacent are quickly caught and exploited, realizing too late that trust and honor do not live in the same house as notoriety. The public doesn't truly care about climbers, who are links in an incestuous chain binding sick hunger for attention to media that promote or criticize according to their interests. The Piolet d'Or shows that organizers know and count on the cruel fact that they will always find plenty of desperate, passionate gladiators and clowns to role-play in the fame game. The more interesting question is: Is it a reality show or a soap opera?

If the romantic idea of the Piolet d'Or will survive in the future it must evolve into a simple gathering where climbers can exchange ideas and share their dreams, illusions, and realities. Perhaps they might even climb together—with no one cast as winner or loser. I ask the media and the promoters to stop forcing the competitive spirit into alpinism, and to start respecting alpinists, their human differences, and the creative ideas that make alpinism a complicated and rewarding experience.

I apologize if I have offended anyone who is addicted to Miss Fame; she gets around, so watch out for STDs. And finally: Alpinists are bullets, and the media is a rifle. Where is the target?

ELITE

Philippe Descamps
April 2007

At long last, the debate on the Piolet d'Or is open! Thanks to Marko Prezelj's provocative statements, our mountaineering community has started to exchange points of view and to ask itself questions about the award's meaning. From the organizers' point of view, certain statements could seem a little bit unfair or even out of place. But to understand the passionate stances, one must understand the issues at the heart of the debate, which is far from being simplistic. While everybody agrees on the dangers of an excessively competitive spirit, there is also a broad consensus on the impor-

From left: Pavle Kozjek, the "people's choice" winner for his single-push new route on Cho Oyu; Marko Prezelj; and Boris Lorencic, holding the golden ice axe. *Philippe Descamps*

tance of providing a space where great mountaineers can meet together and with the public. It's now only a question of finding the right formula, the right balance.

Far from fostering a spirit of healthy emulation, the logic of pure competition is not only bad for mountaineering as a whole, it is also dangerous for mountaineers individually. Distracted by financial objectives, mountaineers are encouraged to overstretch their capacity, to make use of performance-boosting substances, and to take inconsiderate risks. An excessive competitive spirit fosters a feeling of superiority, which in turn develops into arrogance and creates a hierarchical vision of the community.

Within the mountaineering community, the race for celebrity didn't wait for the Piolet d'Or. The media hierarchies set up in the '70s and '80s were mostly determined by the talent of the various press agents. By becoming international, by attempting to formulate objective criteria—however imperfect—and by taking an ethical stance, the juries of the Piolet d'Or have over the years managed to defend a certain style of mountaineering. None of those who were awarded the Piolet d'Or over the last 16 years were undeserving, even if their exploits sometimes had very little in common. The juries' decisions were coherent with the defense of a certain style of mountaineering, which has had a lasting influence on the evolution of mentalities in many countries. If the staging of the award ceremony probably needs to be revisited, the show of the past few years has at least had the merit of showing that mountaineering needs spokespersons more than it needs champions.

The real challenge for the members of the mountaineering elite is to open up to the world, to meet each other, and to share their experiences with the public. Since the fall of the Berlin Wall, we know that the greatest arsenals are of no use if their only purpose is to protect those who despise the values that they pretend they are defending. We know since Vilfredo Pareto [the French-Italian sociologist and economist] that history is a "cemetery of aristocracies." Clubs are for a fossilized elite who have lost all contact with reality.

The experience of these last years has proven that if they stay within the boundaries of their professional objectives and don't try to overstep their competence, specialized journalists have an important part to play in the evolution of mountaineering. Their job is to check on the information at its source, to cross-reference the information, if possible, with information from other sources, and to make the information understandable by putting it into perspective. It's not about objectivity—there is no such thing—but about a subjective point of view trying to embrace the largest number of objective facts possible. That is the art of critique. It has nothing to do with the art of propaganda, which is all about passing things off for what they are not.

If the question today is whether we should rethink the Piolet d'Or or scrap it, one has to start from what it is today: a prize that is known throughout the world and which helps promote mountaineering and its universal values. Whom does it profit? Mountaineers and mountaineering as a whole. All ideas are welcome. The discussion is open. We will make the selection criteria more explicit and give mountaineers a bigger say in the outcome, by giving the competing teams an opportunity to vote for their favorite climb (their own excluded). We also intend to break away from [being] a French event by taking a more international approach, in order to better promote the specificity and the meaning of the different nations' approach to mountaineering. The competition is open again for mountaineers and for all men of good will.

This editorial originally appeared in Montagnes *No. 316. Translated from the French by Anthony Moinet.*

CLIMBS AND EXPEDITIONS

2007

Accounts from the various climbs and expeditions of the world are listed geographically. We generally bias from north to south and from west to east within the noted countries, but the priority is on a logical flow from one mountain range to the next. We begin our coverage with the Contiguous United States and move to Alaska in order for the climbs in Alaska's Wrangell Mountains to segue into the St. Elias climbs in Canada.

We encourage all climbers to submit accounts of notable activity, especially long new routes (generally defined as U.S. commitment Grade IV—full-day climbs—or longer). Please submit reports as early as possible (see Submissions Guidelines at www.AmericanAlpineClub.org/AAJ).

For conversions of meters to feet, multiply by 3.28; for feet to meters, multiply by 0.30.

Unless otherwise noted, all reports are from the 2006 calendar year.

NORTH AMERICA
CONTIGUOUS UNITED STATES

Washington

CASCADE RANGE

Washington, summary of activity. [Note: In addition to mention in this summary, several of the bigger routes have individual reports, below—Ed.] The Cascades saw a fairly typical year of new route activity, with notable winter ascents, ski descents, and summer ascents. Backcountry ski descents continue to grow in popularity, 2006 highlights being Ross Peritore's descent of the Triple Couloir on Dragontail Peak, and Sky Sjue's descent of the Kautz Headwall on Mt. Rainier. Sjue teamed up with numerous partners to make notable descents on Mt. Logan, Mt. Stuart, and West McMillan Spire. A new traverse, over 30 miles, given the current access conditions, was pioneered in the Twin Sister Range.

The 2006-7 winter's smaller-than-typical windows of cold temps and high pressure limited access to a lot of winter alpine climbs, but some great lines were done. Arguably the biggest climb of the winter was the Northeast Face (IV WI4+ M3) of Three Fingers Peak by Dave Burdick and John Frieh. New routes continue to be established within an hour's drive of Seattle, including Spindrift Daze (III AI3+) on Abiel Peak, by Kurt Hicks, Matt Cusack, and Bob Masasi, and the Conlin-Gullberg Route (III WI3+ M4), by Dave Conlin and Scott Gullberg, on the north face of Kent Peak. Wayne Wallace and Gary Yngve climbed the hardest new ice route on Snow Creek Wall, the North Dihedral Direct–Swing and a Prayer (300m, IV WI5 M6R).

Alpine ascents during 2006 demonstrated that potential still exists even at popular alpine areas. In the Alpine Lakes Wilderness, Dragontail Peak gained a new route on its northwest face, Dragonscar (2,500', IV 5.11R), by Max Hasson and Jens Holsten. At Washington Pass, Ross Peritore and Tony Bentley established the Direct West Face (8 pitches, III/IV 5.10+) on Pernod Spire. Mark Allen, Joel Kauffman, and Tom Smith established Mojo Rising (6 pitches, III 5.11 A1), a direct line on the northwest face of South Early Winters Spire.

Perhaps the most remarkable lines were climbed by Wayne Wallace, Mike Layton, and Eric Wolfe in the Picket Range. In mid-August Wallace and Layton made the first ascent of the Haunted Wall on Spectre Peak (2,100', IV 5.9+). Photos of this wall had led to years of attempts and speculation. Layton returned to the area with Eric Wolfe to make the first ascent of Plan 9 on The Blob (16 pitches, IV 5.10). But the most lauded climb of 2006 was Wayne Wallace's epic solo first ascent of Mongo Ridge (VI 5.10-), a mile-long line on West Fury Peak with 4,000' of elevation gain.

The *Northwest Mountaineering Journal* is an annual online presentation, of the accomplishments of climbers and skiers, and documents the history of our travels in the mountains from the North Cascades to Mt. Hood. *NWMJ* issues are typically published in late summer, covering activity from April 1 to March 31, and can be found at www.nwmj.org.

CHRIS SIMMONS AND ALASDAIR TURNER, *Northwest Mountaineering Journal, AAC*

Twin Sister High Route. An easily accessible alpine training ground during the 1980s, the Twin Sister Range on the western edge of the Mt. Baker Wilderness is now isolated behind miles of private and gated logging lands. From May 12-14 Mark Allen, Dr. Greg Balco, Paul Kimbrough, and I made the first known ski traverse (V class 4 AI1 50°) of the entire range, going from south to north: Step Sister Peak to North Twin Sister Peak. The first day involved whiteout navigation in the morning and ski descents of the north faces of Last Sister Peak (5,562') and Saddle Slab Peak (5,802'), as well as a traverse along the east side of the range beneath Nancy, Barbara, and Trisolace peaks, and across the third largest glacier/ice field in the range, which we christened the Ripple Glacier.

On day two we crossed to the west side of the range at Saddle Slabs, skied the North Face of Cinderella (6,480'), and watched Mark ski the proudest line of the trip—the South Couloir of Little Sister Peak (6,600'). Crossing a series of cols past Hayden and Skookum peaks led to the technical crux: crossing the range for the third time to gain the Sisters Glacier just south of South Twin Sister Peak. What we expected to be a simple mixed and steep snow climb proved to be 40m of 4th-class rock followed by 100+m of 50° ice and mixed rock. Our thin rack (one hex, two cams, four stoppers) and short 8mm ropes (one 20m, one 30m) meant that we had to pitch it out on the rock and haul packs and skis, then Mark and Paul simul-climbed on one rope while Greg and I simul-climbed on the other. When we reached the ridge at sunset, we were surprised to find not a simple ski descent, but 100+m of rappelling. Double-rope rappels and down-climbing shenanigans led to a final fixed 40m single-strand rappel with a knot pass. We started setting up camp at 2:00 a.m.

Day three was incredibly hot, and we were incredibly tired. Looking up, we realized we had crossed the ridge several hundred meters farther south than we intended and had rappelled down the tallest aspect of a buttress we tagged Mirage Peak. Reconnaissance proved that our intended ascent would have required a 5th class pitch; our actual line was the best possible. The loss of our ropes and two cams in the rappels meant that our intended climbs and descents of South and North Twin Sister Peaks had to be scrubbed, so we spent the day skiing the Sisters Glacier, crossing back to the west and hiking out the last five miles to the car.

We actually traveled for 30 hours over three days, covered 26 miles, gained 12,000', descended 14,000', skied every single permanent snowfield/ice field/glacier (except for the Twin Glacier) according to the USGS map, and made significant descents across the range.

Special thanks to John Scurlock for his aerial photography.

CHRIS SIMMONS, *AAC*

Spectre Peak, Haunted Wall. Wayne Wallace and I braved the round trip 50 miles of hiking and 20,000' of elevation gain to climb the south face of Spectre Peak in the Northern Pickets in August. This is in one of the most remote places in the Lower 48, and a hauntingly beautiful area. We accessed the mountain via Easy Ridge, over a col right of Challenger's summit, and a few miles down to a camp below Phantom Peak's south face.

The Haunted Wall on Spectre Peak. No other routes are known to exist in this photo. *John Scurlock*

The 2,100' of climbing was solid, but devoid of cracks for protection. Our route, the Haunted Wall (IV 5.9+), starts in the center of Spectre's south face. Runout climbing for ~800' turns into a deep, spooky chimney inside the mountain (completely enclosed at times!), then continues to the great gendarme on the prominent, towered south ridge. One rappel gets you into the notch—and fully committed—then exposed face climbing up and right of a giant offwidth leads to a long ridge traverse to the summit. Downclimbing snow on the other side of the mountain took us to an amazing series of ledges to skier's right, around Spectre back to the south face.

MIKE LAYTON

Mt. Fury, West Peak, Mongo Ridge. It started by our looking, again, at a stupid map. The coolest USGS quadrangle in the Lower 48 is, by far, the Challenger map. It contains both the Northern and Southern Picket Ranges, with long, serrated ridges and enormous vertical relief rising from remote valleys. "Mongo Ridge," as it was pre-named by local enthusiast John Roper, is the South Buttress of the West Peak of Mt. Fury. The map reveals a mile-long, 4,000' vertical rise,

The enormous Mongo Ridge (skyline) on the West Peak of Mt. Fury. Mike Layton in the foreground, during the pair's Haunted Wall trip. *Wayne Wallace*

interrupted again and again by towering monoliths and gendarmes.

Mike Layton and I gaped at it while climbing the Haunted Wall on the west face of neighboring Spectre Peak, and agreed that it was a monster of grim fantasy. I even ventured that it might never be climbed, for a number of reasons. For one, all of the possible approach routes appeared to entail several days of strenuous bushwhacking. But the key hit me one night, pre-sleep: instead of approaching up the hell known as Goodell Creek, climb East Fury and descend to the ridge! I would just need to climb a major mountain to reach the start of an even more major climb.

I tried for a couple of days to find a qualified partner. Finally, I could take it no longer. Colin Haley's slide show about a first ascent on Mt. Moffit in Alaska [see Jed Brown's feature earlier in this *Journal*] set my blood on fire. When I got home from the show, I packed and left at 4 a.m. the next day, Thursday, August 24.

My plan was to power the 60+-pound load to the top of East Fury in two brutal days, meaning I had to get through the brush of Access Creek on day one. A bee sting on the left eyelid, the usual brush, and a violent, several-hour thunderstorm reintroduced me to the gauntlet of adversity and special pain available during approaches in this range. But Friday night I slept atop East Fury, feeling utterly spent.

Despite my wishes to stop it, the planet spun around, and again I awoke to face the solar onslaught. Morning light revealed a relatively easy way down to what felt like my ultimate doom: a route you would only see in the greater ranges of the world, and one to scare the boldest of explorers. As I began my descent, my iPod played the ominous words of the Talking Heads: "And you may ask yourself: My God, What have I done?"

It quickly became apparent that it was going to be tough just cresting the ridge. After several pitches I gained a somewhat clean ridgeline, which never failed to entertain me over the next two days. On the ridge, as I set the first of a dozen rappels, I knew each subsequent descent would render retreat increasingly difficult, dramatically increasing the commitment level.

After my fourth rappel, a full-length double rappel, I reached the base of a pinnacle that could itself be a major summit. The traverse rightward across the face led to a shallow yet steep prow. Although I was going unroped as much as possible to save time, it was time to break out the hardware. Up I climbed again and again until I ran out of rope, each time returning down the rope to retrieve anchors and pack. The knobby arête offered steep and exposed climbing. A 5.10 pitch made me hope it was the most difficult section of the massive route. Hundreds of tough feet later I finally balanced atop an incredible perch.

Rappelling down the other side of these pinnacles was now becoming an awesome routine. The backside of pinnacle #3 was so steep that I dangled in space much of the way down.

Pinnacle #4 was also hard going. I was again unroped, and as I did another scary traverse left, cramps mutated my hands into grotesque arthritic shapes. As the climbing continued, the rock again proved to be of fantastic quality and solidity.

As the afternoon wore on, time seemed to tick quicker, and I grappled with a difficult knife-edge horizontal traverse. Evening rapidly approached as I neared the final obstacle. A dreaming John Roper had already named this pinnacle the "Pole of Remoteness," figuring that it had to be the hardest place to reach in the 48 states. I wasn't going to argue. I looked ahead for a way up and, even more, a flat place to sleep, but neither was apparent from below. It was the only pinnacle that allowed me an easy way around it; graciously I accepted a narrow ledge system to the right instead of the 5.11 headwall straight above. I reached the deep up-hill notch and found it an accommodating 5.7.

Although I found the way to its summit easily enough, I had an eerie feeling that something might happen, that attaining the summit of the "Pole of Remoteness" would extract a price. With no solid rappel anchors, I slung a loose block as a handrail/rappel line. As I descended, a rock severed the rope. Fortunately, I still had the second line.

As the sun set, I made a dash for somewhere to camp. Now climbing into the 13th hour, I spotted a small glacier clinging to the south side of the upper ridge. The moat between it and the rock would provide shelter. As I drifted off to sleep, I reflected on the hard climbing of the day, grateful to live in a state that could still provide this kind of adventure.

In the morning 500' of elevation remained to the summit of West Fury. The way eased off to class 4. Tired, but not about to let down my guard, I stood atop West Fury at 10:00 a.m.

No wonder the Picket Range is so revered. In my few trips here I have renewed my enjoyment of the sport and my appreciation for the truly wild.

The journey was still far from over. I forgot how complicated it is getting from one Fury to the next. It involved more rappelling and tons of ridgeineering. All that was left from East Fury was to retrace the long glacier and ridges to Luna Col. There I went down in a heap of pain. Spending my last night there, I rehydrated, ate, and cried when a sad song played on the player.

Some final stray thoughts: I believe the nature of sport pushes the player to reach for more and continually improve. Everyone who safely does so will see the personal accomplishment that my friend Erik Wolfe describes as "the trip you never fully come back from." Enjoy the mountains and help keep them wild.

WAYNE WALLACE

The Blob, Plan 9. In August, Erik Wolfe and I battled our way into the remote Crescent Creek Basin of the Southern Pickets to climb the south face (IV 5.10) of The Blob (a.k.a. The Rake). Our route, the only one on the face, took a prominent, clean, and steep buttress on the left side of the face, climbing excellent rock with plenty of protection opportunities. The climb follows the center of the ridge to a series of massive gendarmes. It tops out on the first, traverses left just below the second, and tops out on the summit. We then traversed the long summit ridge east, across the spine of the peak, to the notch between the Blob and Terror. Two rappels reached the col, from where we down-climbed back to camp.

A full report with photos can be found at www.cascade-climbers.com

MIKE LAYTON

The Blob, showing Layton and Wolfe's Plan 9 (and descent). *Erik Wolfe*

Erik Wolfe cruising on Plan 9. *Mike Layton*

Mt. Buckner, Complete Southeast Ridge. On my first climb of Goode Mountain two years ago, the striking southeast ridge of Mt. Buckner caught my eye, but I was sure that such an obvious line must have been climbed decades before. After climbing Goode again in 2006, I researched Buckner and found that the ridge remained unclimbed. From the east this ridge contrasts sharply with the halves of the Buckner Glacier, which it divides. Through the climbers' grapevine, I learned that Gordy Skoog had been eyeing this climb since before I was born. We were soon in e-mail contact and planning our attempt. Gordy and I met for the first time at our rendezvous below the Buckner Glacier on August 5, Gordy having come in from the west side of the Cascades, and I from the hamlet of Stehekin to the east. We began the ridge at the bottom of the glacier and soloed several hundred feet of 4th and low 5th class to the end of the lower ridge. This natural break gives access to the last snow and bivouac spot along the route, the high point of a 1980s attempt. On the morning of the 6th we started up the steep ridge crest, apprehensive of gendarmes that we knew lie ahead. The rock was often loose and licheny, although none of the climbing felt dangerously run-out. Steep 5.8 crack climbing led to the top of one of the towers, from which we rappelled off the backside. We bypassed the summit of another tower on the left, via enjoyable, blocky climbing. We soon returned to the crest and, after a few more pitches, reached the summit (IV 5.8). The second day's climbing had taken 12 hours, and we were rewarded with a beautiful scenic sunset during the 3rd class descent into upper Horseshoe Basin.

BLAKE HERRINGTON

Bonanza Peak, Northwest Ridge. Tim Halder and I climbed Washington's highest non-volcanic peak (9,511') via a new route (V 5.8), following a traverse from the northwest. On August 19 we left the Agnes Creek trail at Swamp Creek and climbed Needle Peak via the north ridge. We carried over Needle and made the first ascents, via low 5th class, of the north and south Anonymity Towers (*Cascade Alpine Guide*, p. 232). In late afternoon we climbed the Dark Glacier and summited Dark Peak as the sun set. Early on the 20th, after a memorable belay-jacket bivy atop the glacier, we began climbing toward Bonanza Peak. The route follows an obvious high ridge crest that connects Dark Peak to the massive bulk of Bonanza. Climbing along the crest is wild and variable in quality, and this is not a good route to begin during unsettled weather, as you'd have to retrace your steps to retreat. Ten hours of climbing brought us to Bonanza's west summit. The tin-can summit register had two entries, from 1952 and 2003. From here we ran the knife-edge ridge to the main summit, passing some exciting *a cheval* moves and solid 5.8 climbing on the last two pitches. An evening descent down the heavily crevassed Mary Greene Glacier route ended our technical difficulties just as darkness fell.

BLAKE HERRINGTON

Halder and Herrington's Northwest Ridge route (right-hand line) on Bonanza Peak, with descent down the Mary Green Glacier. *John Scurlock*

Three Fingers, North Peak, Northeast Face. On February 3, 2007, John Frieh and I climbed a new route (IV WI4+ M3) on the northeast face of Three Fingers. We approached up the Squire Creek valley to the basin under the east face in early morning. A steep gully breaches the cliffy cirque in the center of the basin. We traversed to where the climb began in a narrow gully on the right side of the face. A short pitch of WI3 led to easier climbing for several hundred feet. We exited the gully on the left wall, via an easy pitch of ice that led to a bowl under a headwall. The next three pitches ascend the 600' tier of water ice. The first of these is the crux, giving a sustained pitch of WI4+. For the second and third pitches we continued up the right side of the flow for long ropelengths of WI3+ and WI4. Above the headwall is a snow bowl that we traversed to a gully leading down from the north summit. We climbed the gully to the ridge crest, then followed a short mixed chimney and a rimed-up ramp to the summit of the North Peak. After a short bit on top we descended the north face to the Craig Lakes basin, and back into the valley below the face.

The North Peak of Three Fingers, showing the Northeast Face (Burdick-Frieh, 2007), the only route visible in this image. *John Scurlock*

DAVE BURDICK

Dragontail Peak, Dragonscar. Blessed with easy fall access to the Stuart Range, Jens Holsten and I managed a new route on the northwest face of Dragontail Peak on September 6. Starting to the west of the Boving Route, on the opposite end of the broad slab, we climbed two pitches off the glacier to the top of a small pillar. From this comfortable perch I watched Jens cruise up a beautiful stretch of crack and face climbing. The next pitch would not go so smoothly. Faced with several equally intimidating options, we were left with the crux of the route by a grueling process of elimination: a strenuous bulge through microwave-size blocks and off-size jams. One more long pitch brought us to low-angle terraces. Relieved, we took off our climbing shoes and put away the rope. Unsure of the

Jens Holsten leading pitch 3 (higher circle), with Max Hasson belaying, on the pair's new route, Dragonscar. *Nick Pope*

Jens Holsten finishing the second pitch on Dragonscar.
Max Hasson

route to the top, we wound our way through a thousand or more feet of fun alpine scrambling to the west ridge, then continued with a short hike to the summit. We dubbed the route Dragonscar (2,500', IV 5.11R) after the golden patch of exfoliation, easily spied from the lake below, that we climbed through.

MAX HASSON, *AAC*

Boola Boola Buttress, Black Velvet. On our fall's first foray into the obscure and unknown, on August 16 Jens Holsten and I explored the exceedingly featured granite of Boola Boola Buttress. Unable to locate the 1984 Jim Yoder route, due to a vague and confusing description, we just started climbing. We aimed for a large left-facing corner that dominates the right side of the buttress, but deemed this feature too thin and ascended cracks to its right, just west of Michael Layton's route, Thank You, Baby Jesus. The first pitch may or may not have been virgin territory, but the rest of our path most certainly was. We found clean rock down low, culminating in a spicy dihedral on the fourth pitch, and then several ropelengths of loose scrambling. Finally we surmounted the upper headwall in two exciting pitches and topped out onto the Dragontail Plateau just as a storm approached. 1,500', IV 5.10+R.

MAX HASSON, *AAC*

Mt. McClellan, Granite Mountain, and Pernod Spire, various new routes. On the east face of Mt. McClellan, in the Enchantments near Leavenworth, Rolf Larson and I climbed a new route in July. The Madcap Laughs (IV 5.10+ C1) starts with four pitches on clean rock at the toe of the lower buttress (5.8). Several hundred feet of 4th and 5th class gain the upper pillar. From the notch three steep pitches right of the arête gain the summit blocks (5.10, with a C1 move freed on second). Downclimb west then follow the goats to the north.

Larson and I made the first ascent of The Central Pillar (IV 5.10+ C1) on the north face of Granite Mountain in the Stuart Range (also near Leavenworth), in August. Begin just right of the central pillar's toe, turn the lower roof on its left and continue up the buttress, remaining close to its arête for five 5.10 pitches with one C1 offwidth move (second freed at 5.11-). Stay on the knife-edge arête (5.9) for one long pitch. Several hundred feet of 4th and 5th class gain the summit. Walk off southwest.

Also in August, on the west face of Pernod Spire (Washington Pass), for Peter Hirst's birthday, he, Rolf Larson, and I established Birthday Party (IV 5.10+ C2.) From right center on the lower northwest face, follow the obvious weakness up and left for two pitches (5.8 and 5.10) to the beautiful crack midway up. Climb this crack (5.10). Continue up the steep, clean face (5.10). Trudge up to the spire and climb its apron (4th and 5th). Climb two steep furry pitches (5.10+ C2 and 5.9) directly up to the knife-edge. Follow the knife east to just below the summit blocks. Bail to the gully (like we did) or take the original West Face (Nelson) finish. In hindsight we should have summited, via the last pitch of the West Face line, and rapped east as per that original line. Instead we rapped the West Face, scurried down, went north through Sandy Gap, and rapped the lower northwest face...highly discouraged, as our descent blows.

DANIEL J. CAPPELLINI, *AAC*

California

YOSEMITE VALLEY

El Capitan, Lost in Translation. Seven years ago I was inspired by Leo Houlding to find a line on El Cap and do it in perfect alpine style, from the ground to the top, free in a day. I tried this many times, but we got shut down every time. On El Capitan granite, it takes only 6' of blank rock and a 30-pitch rock climb turns to an aid line.

I scoped Lost in Translation for years and always wondered why people hadn't climbed it. It's not a big route like the Salathe, El Corazon, or the Nose, but it was a chance to accomplish a dream to put up a new free line ground-up, something that was never done before on El Capitan. I met Nico Favresse when he was working on one of the coolest free routes in Yosemite: Lappat (5.13a/b R) on Yosemite Falls wall. Nico climbed the route without placing any bolts. We talked a few times about new free lines, and then we decided to go for it on the right side of El Cap.

We scoped the line, and a perfect corner stood out. It looked from the ground that it would go free, but we thought there must be a reason why no one had free-climbed it. But our instinct kept us on track, so we decided to have fun and see where we would get, ground-up.

On August 30 at 8 a.m. we started climbing. We had a big free rack and a few pitons, copperheads, and a bolt kit. We didn't have bivy gear, only three gallons of water, and a few Power Bars. After eight pitches, a majority of them around 5.10/5.10+R, we reached the base of the big corner. We were surprised everything had gone free, with only 300' of the climb left to discover. The corner was grassy, and we couldn't see what was under the grass. It looked like people had attempted the corner before, because there were a few lead bolts and rap anchors. As the light went down we decided to stay and wait for morning. We spent the night on a small ledge dreaming of what could be under the grass. We were only two pitches from the top.

On September 1, after 10 minutes of cleaning, we knew the line would go. After cleaning holds and freeing moves, we estimate the pitch to be 5.12b/c stemming. After that the climbing eased up and allowed us to top out around 12. The dream became reality. Lost in Translation (1,200', 10 pitches, 5.12b/c R).

On September 8 we climbed the route in seven hours.

From Ninov's website, WWW.STONEMONKEYS.NET

El Capitan, Atlantis; Porcelain Wall, House of Cards. In the fall of 2005, just left of Block Party (which I established in spring '05), I completed my second new line on El Capitan, in the alcove area of the southeast face, naming it Atlantis (VI 5.9 A4). I fixed the first two pitches to the top of the alcove over two days in early October, and then committed for another 18 days alone on the face. This route shares a few pitches with Tempest but turned out to be 75% independent, requiring 74 hand-drilled holes for belays and leading, with no drilled bat hooks. One of the cruxes came on pitch six, under the Great White Shark feature of the South Seas route. Extensive hooking up and left, with a marginal tied-off Arrow for pro, led into the continuous crack system of the route Space. I followed this route for three easier pitches until I broke off on new terrain for most of the remainder of the route. Two-thirds of the way up the wall, I came upon possibly the last major ledge on El Cap that had never been touched. This feature, Bobo Ledge, gave me somewhere to stand and sit other than my portaledge, after 13 days in aiders. Another 60+m pitch led up to the left side of the luxurious Island In The Sky, a very comfy natural ledge on the Pacific Ocean route. Climbing off this ledge I headed up the left side of the Black Tower on my way to the long-awaited summit.

Then, in spring 2006, I turned my focus to the Porcelain Wall. I headed up on another solo mission, looking for unclimbed terrain to scare myself on. Luckily I found it, 100m right of the only other route on the absurdly steep central headwall section. In 1995 Eric Kohl went to this face alone to climb a direct line right up the middle of this not-so-well-known Valley gem. But after fixing the first four pitches, he teamed up with Pete Takeda for the ascent. In similar unintended style, I fixed the first four pitches solo until my good friend Matt Meinzer showed up and wanted in. The first four pitches went very well and completely natural, but up higher remained a few stretches of blank rock, which I knew would be easier to drill through with someone to share the workload. After we regained the highpoint up my three fixed lines, we continued on for 10 more days to the summit of this beautifully colored wall. Our route, House of Cards (VI 5.9 A4+), was characterized by difficult climbing through large roofs and flakes with some rivet ladders to connect delicate features. In the early 90s a section of the wall, about 200' around, fell off, leaving the adjacent rock expanding and dangerous. We hand-drilled 114 holes, including a few into pitch 10's death flake, until I could see what I was attaching myself to. We topped out after 11 days.

DAVID TURNER, *Sacramento, California, AAC*

SIERRA NEVADA

Incredible Hulk, free activity. True to form, Dave Nettle called me in the midst of a heavy Sierra winter. As I often hear from him, "I just want to put a bug in your ear." But no bug was needed. When Dave calls, people listen.

We cruised snow most of the way up, getting to the Hulk as early as we could: early June. On day one we reached the headwall corner that forms the right-hand border of the Hulk headwall, which each of us had spied from Dave and Peter Croft's route, Venturi Effect. Yet another clean and steep corner up high. The end of the corner required bolts for free climbing, and as Dave is the human hammer, we rapidly dulled our bits. The next day we simply tidied up the first four pitches.

We returned a few weeks later, joined by Truckee resident Donald Otten. The three of us freed the pitches to the high point. Then, after a bit of aiding, cleaning, and working, we freed the upper pitches, which connect to the second-to-last Venturi Effect headwall pitch.

We put together approximately five new pitches along with seven pitches from other routes to complete the line, Tradewinds (IV/V 5.11+). It's really a piecing together of various routes to form a direct, fairly sustained, high-quality free route.

After climbing on the Hulk you won't want to quit, and neither did I. I came back with Jonny Copp, of Boulder, a few weeks later to check out other good-looking lines. We went light and brought no drill. We managed to aid/free four more new pitches between Tradewinds and Venturi Effect but were thwarted midway. We achieved the bivy ledge at about one-third height and got in another pitch-and-a-half before our vision faded into seams and flakes.

I returned again in August with Brent Obinger to free the four lower pitches. We added a few bolts to straighten out the second pitch, which is one of the few true face pitches I have climbed on the feature. The third and fourth pitches each have high-quality steep and varied cracks.

Even with the drill we couldn't piece the line together up high, as it was fraught with large loose blocks and incipient cracks. Nevertheless there is now yet another high quality, four-pitch, 5.12- variant start to a number of Hulk routes, as this line goes directly to the "midway ledge" from which many other routes join and depart.

NILS DAVIS

Balloon Dome, various ascents. The Crucible (IV 5.11 A1). Dave Nettle and I started this route in late October 2005 and retreated from the bivy ledge atop pitch five, due to an early winter storm. Chris LaBounty, Neal Harder, and I completed the remaining pitches during the fol-

The upper half of Balloon Dome. Left to right: Northeast Face via Leaning Tower (IV 5.8 A3, Beckey-Cundiff-Hackett, 1971; Free Dike Variation 5.11+, Harder-LaBounty-Thau, 2006), Northwest Ramp (5.10, Harder-LaBounty-Thau, 2006), Northwest Face (5.9 A3, Black-Graber, 1974). Not shown: Netherworld (somewhere right of the Beckey route, but exact line unknown, Jones-Jones, 2005) and, out-of-view to the left, the East Face (5.8) and Boku-Muru (5.9). *Chris LaBounty*

Chris LaBounty belaying Neal Harder on the 5.9+ fourth pitch of Beckey's Leaning Tower en route to the Free Dike Variation. *Brandon Thau*

lowing June in extreme heat. The route follows a natural line from the San Joaquin River up to the bushy ledge that divides Balloon Dome in half. This line follows a prominent drainage originating from the middle section of the dome, hence slippery rock from pitch three onward. The climb starts in a left-facing dihedral that is below and right of two parallel, splitter, wide cracks three pitches up. The route then follows the left parallel crack (5.11 fuzzy off-width). Super-slick rock leads up to the base of a right-facing dihedral, which is on the skyline when viewing the route from the river. This dihedral is a mixture of thin A1 and 5.11a climbing for 180'. One more 200' pitch ends the technical climbing, and 3rd and 4th class bushwhacking is required to get to the base of the upper dome.

Northwest Ramp (5.10). This route follows the prominent right-leaning ramp up the northwest face of upper Balloon Dome. Four 200' pitches reach the end of the ramp, then two-and-a-half more lead up steep dihedrals to the summit. Chris LaBounty, Neal Harder and I completed this in June.

Beckey's Leaning Tower Route – Free Dike Variation (IV 5.11+). This follows the excellent Fred Beckey route to the top of the spire that leans against the east face of upper Balloon Dome. From the top of the spire, rappel 50' and belay in the notch from two bolts. Instead of climbing the A3 cracks above the notch, follow the dike that heads left and clip one bolt. Gain the intersecting dike that heads right and clip seven more bolts to the belay (5.11+). Two more pitches lead to the top. Chris LaBounty, Neal Harder, and I completed this in June.

BRANDON THAU

Mt. Clarence King, with the new Northeast Ridge route, its approach gully, and the previously climbed East Ridge indicated. *Misha Logvinov, www.verglasphoto.com*

Mt. Clarence King, Northeast Ridge. Pavel Kovar and I discovered and completed the first ascent of one of the few remaining unclimbed technical ridges on a major Sierra Nevada mountain, the northeast ridge of Mt. Clarence King in Sequoia and Kings Canyon National Park. We attempted this route during two separate three-day efforts in September. The final attempt, between September 15-17, involved nearly 30 miles of hiking over three high passes, 10,000'+ of vertical gain, one and

Pavel Kovar simul-climbing about halfway up the Northeast Ridge, with the summit of Mt. Clarence King in the background. *Misha Logvinov, www.verglasphoto.com*

a half days of technical climbing, and a cold bivouac on the summit ridge. On the approach from the east side of the Sierra, we experienced winds exceeding 50 mph and unusual cold for the time of year. The night before the climb, our thermometer registered 14°F. Fortunately, the weather improved, and we were able to continue. While on the ridge, we belayed 16 pitches and simul-climbed/soloed more than a half of the route. After approximately one mile of technical terrain, the northeast ridge merges with the previously climbed east ridge and follows it to the top of the mountain.

After running out of daylight and enduring a cold bivouac near the summit, we descended the regular route to our base camp in Sixty Lake Basin, walked 13 miles back to the Onion Valley trailhead, and drove home for seven hours, thus staying *mostly* awake for 48 hours straight.

The route features a lot of sustained and exposed ridge traversing and is rated IV+ 5.7.

MISHA LOGVINOV

Upper Castle Rocks, various ascents. Dave Nettle joined me, in May 2005, on my first excursion to Upper Castle Rocks in Sequoia National Park. We knew of only two routes in the area: The Gargoyle (5.10 A1), on South Guard, and the Beckey Route (5.8 A2) on Amphitheater Dome. After figuring out where the Gargoyle route started, we freed its 10' A1 tension traverse, at 5.10. The rock was not as clean as Castle Rock Spire or the Fin. Contrary to the Sequoia-Kings Canyon guide, The Gargoyle starts at the top of a 4th/5th class, right-leaning ramp that starts at the base of the north gully. The next day we climbed The South Arête on the Little Spire (5.11-). Our route follows the broken south ridge for three long pitches to the base of the Little Spire summit block. Two fantastic pitches lead up overhanging and well-protected face climbing to the pointed summit. The exposed belay and arête climbing on the second pitch are spectacular.

In June 2006 Chris LaBounty, Neal Harder, and I climbed three new routes. Axes of Evil (5.11) starts at the lone pine tree at the base of the South Guard/Ax gully. It follows face features for three pitches, before entering the gully for four more pitches. Golden Axe (5.11a A0) follows the only weakness on the improbable south face of the Ax. This six-pitch route starts at the base of the Ax/Amphitheater Dome gully and follows the left leg of the obvious "wishbone" crack system. We did not free the section between the third and fourth bolt on the fourth pitch, but it will likely go free. Lastly, we did an enjoyable two-pitch route near camp (point 9,081' southeast of Castle Rocks). It follows the obvious chicken-headed pillar that lies against the southeast face of the dome. One tricky 5.10 bolt-protected move guards the summit and a nice view of Sequoia.

BRANDON THAU

Polemonium Pillar, and the southwest side of Mt. Russell on the far right, home to multiple routes. *David Harden*

Polemonium Pillar. Approaching Mt. Russell from the Whitney-Russell col, while dropping down toward Russell's towering west face, the climber is stunned by the beautiful cracks, corners, and arêtes that make up the south and west sides of the mountain. Often overlooked is the thousand-foot-high south face that drops down from the ridgeline extending off of the long west ridge of Mt. Russell. In July Micha Miller and I climbed a route up a series of left-facing corners in the center of this face. It tops out just right of the sharp prow that forms a high point on long west ridge. To descend we traversed toward Russell and dropped down the west couloir. We named both the formation and the route Polemonium Pillar (IV 5.10b).

Most of the climbing was in the 5.9 range, with a shallow, flared crack on the third pitch providing the crux. Insecure jams and questionable pro made things interesting. Lovely blossoms of Sky Pilot (*Polemonium*) scattered on the ledges give the route its name.

DAVID HARDEN, *AAC*

Mt. Whitney, …Lost. Our climb was spectacular and, compared to our expectations, epic. Not counting 8,000' vertical of carrying loads in the first 24 hours. Not counting getting snowed off

...Lost (not showing the scramble to the summit), the only climb on the entire southwest quadrant of Mt. Whitney. *Doug Robinson*

The venerable Doug Robinson, ...Lost, pitch two. *Michael Thomas*

the Fishhook Arête, our training climb. Not counting our tarp shelter ripping in half in the middle of the night, exposing us to a four-inch snowfall dump at 12,000'. And not to mention venturing the first moves onto the entire southwest quadrant of a fairly popular peak. No, the real epic didn't even start until Michael Thomas and I roped up at 8 a.m. on October 3, taking a middle arête among many choices. We re-climbed the nine pitches we had done before dark two years ago, including two 5.9 sections.

Then we tried to weasel around the headwall, but it forced us back to front and center. Straight up was steep and delicate and likely 5.10, but it was a relief that protection showed up. Soon after, it got dark. But the moon was nearly full, sparkling off the white granite in beautiful and climbable ways. Several hours later, a best-guess choice led us into moon shadow and under a nasty-looking block. Couldn't tell what was holding it up over our heads. In the midst of delicate climbing around it, my foot slipped and my headlamp popped off and sailed down the gully. Fortunately, that kept us from trying to further climb under that block's eerie tonnage. We found another way. To make a long story short, after 20 pitches we unroped at 2:30 a.m. It was so cold, with a biting wind blowing at 30+ mph, that with all our clothes on and walking uphill we could not stay warm. Summit at 4:00 a.m.; a three-hour nap in the stone shelter on top.

Our first ascent so much longer than expected, we called the route "... Lost." Lost for years on the backside of Whitney. Lost our way several times, as on the crux headwall and up under the threatening block. Lost a headlamp. However, "Not all who wander are lost" (J.R.R. Tolkien).

DOUG ROBINSON, *AAC*

The Whitney Cirque: east faces of Third, Day, and Keeler needles and Mt. Whitney. *Renan Ozturk*

Day Needle, new variation and Whitney Cirque linkup. In late July Jake "The Snake" Whitaker and I climbed a new direct free variation to the East Face of Day Needle in the Mt. Whitney cirque. Prior to our climb I had already learned about Jake's horrendous epic on his initial onsight solo attempt of this line. He and his free-soloing companion had collaborated in their gusto, only to get trapped in a formidable alcove a third of the way up. After yelling for a rescue produced only useless helicopters, Jake committed to the insecure downclimb to rescue his petrified partner.

Under this suspicious pretext I agree to climb with Jake for the first time and take part in his emotional cleansing. This time, however, I was happy we could use a 100' 9mm rope, some wires, and a set of Camalots, to #3. Above the previous high point I encountered a burly 5.10 off-fists crack, which I protected by placing RPs in a seam behind my back as Jake simuled below me. Above, Jake onsighted the crux, a brilliant 5.11 overhanging hand-and-finger crack on a golden headwall, close to the 14,000' summit, thereby completing his catharsis.

A week later Jake and I returned to the Whitney Cirque and completed a one-day free linkup of some major faces that form the iconic California skyline. With our 100' piece of cord we first repeated our Day Needle free variation (V 5.11), then downclimbed the classic East Face (III 5.7) of Mt. Whitney, looped back into Keeler Needle's Harding Route (V 5.10c, onsight for me), then glissaded a snowfield and onsighted the Western Front (IV 5.10c) on Mt. Russell. During our scramble off Russell, we watched a huge lenticular of fire smoke overcome the highest point in the contiguous U.S. As the setting sun descended through this anomaly, it cast a rare neon red, day's-end alpenglow, capping our adventure.

RENAN OZTURK, *AAC*

Keeler Needle, The Strassman Route. Yup. Eight days. Constant work, no rests. And that's why I ran out of food and water. Not to mention that this was completely unknown terrain. I am not 20 years old anymore.

What would motivate a 46 year-old guy to solo a new route on a remote backcountry wall, when he knows what's involved? As any woman knows, four things motivate men: money, sex, food, and ego. I would be deprived of the first three on the list, so it must be that seventh deadly sin of pride. And there's more—a race, a friendly 20-year competition to see who would be the first to climb all nine east faces of the Whitney Crest. I won and became President of the East Face Club. Five of those climbs were by first ascents. If I could now do a first ascent on each face, I would become Lord Overseer of the East Face Club.

So in September I hiked in to the east face of Keeler Needle with a light pack and food for three days that could be stretched to six. I'd left gear and ropes fixed from an earlier solo attempt that floundered after two pitches. I planned to reach my high point in a single day. But I was terribly out of shape, and the altitude didn't help. By the time I reached the snowfield at Keeler's base it was well past dark and well past my bedtime. With my only sleeping bag on the wall, I had to keep moving. The snowfield was frozen solid, and I had no ice axe or crampons. I inched upward through the night, arriving at the base with near frostbitten fingers, as the first light of dawn bathed me in warmth.

After a brief nap, I reached my high point and immediately ran into an overhang, followed by a perfect little ledge and another overhang. This one looked malicious, so I found the finger ledge of contentment that allowed me to traverse right into another crack system. It looked like it might end on a bivy ledge. I threw myself at the continuously wide crack, climbing high above my last piece, only to realize that what looked like a ledge above wasn't a ledge at all. Dejected, I descended back to the ledge where I started.

The next morning I moved back into the original crack and found an exquisite hand crack in superb granite. I also found pitons and slings from climbers who had gone the wrong way on the Harding Route or were descending it. Afternoon thunder, rain, and hail spurred me upward to a magnificent ledge and the promise of low-angle scrambling. But more haul-bag hassles ate up my time. The scrambling would have to wait until tomorrow.

I could see a beautiful corner with perfect double hand-jam crack leading to the massive ledge that juts out in the middle of Keeler Needle. From the ledge easy ramps led to a slightly-less-than-vertical wall of fins. As I descended back to the big ledge, I looked up and wondered how I would fare tomorrow on a horror show that I dubbed the "Miserable Pitch." A spectacular sunset treated me. My position on the ledge had me in the exact center of a giant half-sphere formed by Whitney and the

The Strassman Route on Keeler Needle. Several other routes climb this face. *Michael Strassman*

Whitney Needles. It was as if I was looking out from the inside of a crystal ball. This is why we climb in the mountains.

The next day, I attacked the Miserable Pitch. The rock quality changed to scaly loose flakes and flaring, hard-to-protect seams. I had been going on half rations and the food was nearly gone. I had maybe one swig of water left. During the entire climb I had a mental jukebox playing songs in my head. But now the jukebox had stopped. I was starting to lose it. Fatigued and confused I kept messing up simple yet essential tasks. Then I looked up at the next pitch: downward-pointing loose flakes on a deteriorating overhanging wall.

I wanted to tell someone of my predicament. What would I say? I certainly didn't want a rescue. I knew I could make it to the top. I dialed my friend Alice. "Hi this is Mike. I have no food or water. I probably will not summit until Saturday. Maybe you can convince Timmy to hike in and help carry out the gear." She cut me off. "I'm not going to be responsible for convincing him." The cell phone died.

Four days climbing Keeler Needle alone, and I was out of food and water. With much effort, and to avoid the demonic face above me, I spent the rest of the afternoon getting to a ledge that I remembered from the Harding Route. But when I finally got the haul bag and myself over to it, it wasn't the ledge at all. On this ledge I slept with my feet dangling and the continuous feeling that I would roll off the ledge into the black night.

Come morning, I got moving early. My attitude had changed. Goddamn it, I said to myself, I am going to attack that crack. It turned out to be far tamer than it looked. Above, I climbed a long continuous corner right on the edge of the south and east faces. I climbed past sunset, past exhaustion.

The next morning became the next afternoon, and I didn't feel up for climbing. But I was very close to the ledges that might get me out early. I started climbing. The next part was easy and enjoyable. I reached the ledges, but lack of food and water was playing tricks on me. I heard voices. It turned out to be hikers on Day Needle. I called out, "I've had no food or water for two days. Do you think you could help me?"

I had reached the end of my rope. The ledge system was a longer than I thought. I untied and free soloed. A thousand feet later I was on the talus field of Keeler's west slope. I ran down to the trail as the sun balanced on the horizon. There was a quart of water, some energy bars and salami and cheese. I burst into tears. I arrived back just as true darkness fell over the Whitney Needles and began hauling the bag to my sleeping spot. Of course it got stuck.

In the morning I packed the bag for a big impact: 2,000' to the snowfields below. Then I climbed to the top and yelled to people on the trail that I needed more food and water. I used a hiker's cell phone to stop any rescue attempts, and a ranger I met on the trail made an official call, but the helicopter still came. I was afraid it would land on Mt. Whitney and hand me a bill.

When the hikers heard my story, I became a bit of a celebrity. Beautiful women offered me their gorp and others wanted to know the answer to that one question: how do you go to the bathroom? Someone offered to carry my climbing gear down, and suddenly I was alone again. I staggered down the trail and back to town with a beard, burnt lips, sore muscles, hands that wouldn't close, and numb fingertips. A friend asked, "Did you learn anything?"

I learned that I could do it.

MICHAEL STRASSMAN

Mt. Chamberlain, I Fink Therefore I Am. Having long been fascinated with reports and photos of Mt. Chamberlain, deep behind the Sierra Crest, I finally made the trip in July. Ever ready for adventure, the energizer bunny himself, Jonny Copp of Boulder, was my partner.

Jonny and I rendezvoused in the sleepy town of Lone Pine. He had flown to L.A. to visit family, and I dropped down from Bishop. The forecast was grim. As we organized and drove up the Whitney Portal road, the clouds conspired and swirled in blackness above the crest.

With a late afternoon start, we reached Trail Camp well after dark. As with most of my Sierra ventures, we were underequipped, with one bivy sack and no tent. It rained on us all night.

We set off the next morning damp in the fog and cold, but it's the Sierra, how bad can it be? It rained most of the way over to the camp in the Crabtree Lakes area at the base of the wall. The afternoon cleared a bit and gave us time to scope our options. The dry evening allowed us to discover bouldering reminiscent of Tuolumne Meadows.

Not sure, because of the weather, if we would climb, we were pleasantly surprised when the clouds held off just long enough for us to piece together an entirely independent eight-pitch line up the right side of the northeast face.

This line starts in a shallow corner system, fairly indistinct among the rows of these along the base of the wall. The third pitch is a scramble over a large ledge and shares a belay with the

Mt. Chamberlain: (1) Asleep at the Wheel (V 5.11+, Haden-Pennings, 2001). (2) East Pillar (V 5.11a, Brugger-DeKlerk, 1992). (3) I Fink Therefore I Am (V 5.11- A1, Copp-Davis, 2006). (4) Breaking Point (V 5.11, Nettle-Zanto), a free variation (another is Hot Damn, V 5.10d, Binder-Brennan, 1995) to the original Northeast Face (V 5.10 A2, Fiddler-Harrington, 1980). The unnamed face on the left, reputed to have bad rock, has no routes. On the North Pillar, Barracuda (5.10, Nettle-Thau, 2006; foreshortened inset photo by *Brandon Thau*) begins from the snowpatch just up and right of the letters "NP," while the 1979 Farrell-Rowell (V 5.10; not shown) climbs a continuous chimney/crack system to the left. *Nils Davis*

top of the fourth pitch of Dave Nettle's route, Breaking Point. The following pitches climb the obvious diagonal crack system splitting the face proper. The first is marked by a quartzite-like ramp; the next holds the only aid (should go free with more cleaning and possibly a bolt or two) on the route and is also the most spectacular: a 180' crack-switching splitter up a broad wall. From there, it's back to ramps and corners.

I Fink Therefore I Am, although not the quality of the Hulk or the Valley, is a quality, fun, and direct V 5.11- A1 in a beautiful and pristine setting.

NILS DAVIS

Mt. Chamberlain, Barracuda. On July 12 Dave Nettle and Brandon Thau established Barracuda (9 pitches, 5.10) to the right of the Rowell route on the North Pillar. The route is reportedly complicated to describe, and a report was unavailable at press time.

Idaho

Baron Falls Tower, Carpal Tunnel. John Frieh and I headed out to Idaho's best-kept secret, the Sawtooth Range, in mid-August with the intent of spending four days climbing some of the excellent established routes in the area. We forwent the usual routes and crowds on the Elephant's Perch and hiked back toward Warbonnet Peak. Our plan of attempting an established route changed when we got lost at 3:00 a.m. on the approach to our planned climb. Lucky for us, fortune favors the foolish, and once the sun came up John and I spotted a sweet line on the southwest face of Baron Falls Tower. We named the route Carpal Tunnel due to the finger-intensive crux, as well as the most impressive inset dike either of us has ever seen, running roughly parallel to the route approximately 100 yards to its right. We stretched out (and then some) our 70m rope on each pitch, which allowed us to complete the route in six pitches; future parties should expect additional pitches if they do not use a 70m rope, as well as simul-climb.

Carpal Tunnel on the southwest face of Baron Falls Tower. *John Frieh*

The route parallels the dike for the first four pitches and then joins it at the top of pitch four, where you climb under a chockstone, wedged in the dike, that is as large as a bus. Pitch five climbs wedged blocks to gain the top of the chockstone. The rock was exceptional, minus a brief section of kitty litter.

From the summit descend east via two single-rope raps to a ridge that connects Baron Falls Tower to Point 9,211'. Once across the ridge, traverse south around Point 9,263'. Cross over to the south ridge of Point 9,211' and locate a gully system that diagonals northeast across the face. Downclimb this gully until, halfway down, a different gully, trending southeast, appears. This gully requires one single-rope rappel and a lot of downclimbing.

Carpal Tunnel checked in at IV 5.11- A0 and was as good as anything on the Elephant's Perch. The icing on the cake? We returned just in time to enjoy Idaho's other best-kept secret, Josh Ritter, who played a free show at the Red Fish Lake Lodge.

BRYAN SCHMITZ

Utah

ZION NATIONAL PARK

Thunderbird Wall, first free ascent. Michael Anderson and Rob Pizem made the first free ascent, with variations, of one of Zion's biggest routes, the Thunderbird Wall (16 pitches, VI 5.13- R). Both climbers led or followed every pitch free over May 31-June 1. Anderson's recent free climbing efforts in Zion have resulted in ten FFAs of grade IV or longer routes, most of them grade V or VI. See Anderson's feature earlier in this *Journal.*

John Frieh beneath the greyhound-sized chockstone on Carpal Tunnel. *Bryan Schmitz*

Touchstone Wall, first free ascent. The free climbing season in Zion started off with a bang, as Rob Pizem and I freed the last holdout of the trinity of classic Zion big walls. Moonlight Buttress fell in 1992, Spaceshot in 2005, and finally the Touchstone Wall in 2006. Touchstone was a reluctant project for me, despite prodding from various sources, not the least of which was Rob. I had scoured the wall with binoculars and couldn't see a free route. The last straw came from Zion pioneer Jeff Lowe, who implored me to "take care of" Touchstone. My priorities changed.

We tried the route over a January weekend, but were stymied by the brutally thin second pitch. We returned in February to explore a promising face climbing variation to the right of pitch two, which we established from the ground up. Rob placed two bolts from aid slings, but the second bolt was a spinner. From that position, I free-climbed 15' to a stance to tap in the third bolt. This was hairy. The wall's angle and small holds made the hand drilling tenuous. Meanwhile, there was a bad bolt below, followed by a ledge. I only managed a few taps of the hammer before I felt compelled to down climb to a rest and repeat.

The next day, February 12, we made our attempt. Rob led the 5.13a fist pitch easily. I followed, but struggled with the crux, a lingering effect of the lead bolting the day before. I took pitch two, but failed on my first two attempts. I was demoralized; convinced that the fatigue from the previous day was leading to failure. In desperation, I finally linked the 5.13b crux on my third try. I traversed left to rejoin the route and barely executed the 5.12a moves over the roof to a no-hands-rest. Rob followed the pitch on his first try, letting out a few screams, which thrilled the tourists assembled below.

The 5.12d third pitch was a change of pace, as the route transitions from viciously thin face climbing to a steep finger crack. Fortunately, I redpointed it first try, as the sun was sapping our strength. Rob soon followed, and from there we blasted to the summit. Our fatigue made some of the more "trivial" pitches feel harder than they should, but we held on nevertheless. We summited (1,000', 8 pitches, IV 5.13b) and descended by 5:30 p.m., seven hours after we had started, and just in time to make the 10-hour drive back to Colorado for work on Monday morning.

MICHAEL ANDERSON, *AAC*

The Birthday Bash; Free Lhasa; and The Monkeys Always Send, Dude. In late winter Cedar Wright and I opened three new free climbs in Zion National Park in an "onsight in a day" style. These adventures were preceded by a gut-wrenching journey to Kashmir in which we assisted with earthquake relief in a Himalayan war zone. After flying back to Salt Lake our efforts began with a team-free repeat of the quality route Wind, Sand, and Stars in Kolob Canyon, in which we endured a frigid night atop 8,000' Paria Point. During the shiver-bivy it became clear that our experiences in Kashmir had amplified our threshold for suffering, friendship, and above all our appreciation for the rich climbing lifestyle we lead.

With this in mind we drove into Zion proper and spied an unclimbed line, to the right of Monkey Finger, ending in a dramatic roof. We started up a crack system, clipping old Olevsky-drilled angles, and continued by tip-tapping up poorly protected metallic patina. The last pitch was freed on top-rope by headlamp and is still awaits a lead. It climbs changing corners past a 00 TCU offset, an undercling out the roof, and finishes on a headwall splitter that requires wild moves to link face features above RPs and small cams. The Monkeys Always Send, Dude (900', 5.11+R C2 or 5.12).

Next, lured by a beautiful Eric Draper photo featuring a clean 500' continuous headwall splitter, we embarked to climb Mt. Kinesava roughly via Lhasa (5.11 A1, Anker-Quinn, 1990). We would follow the first few and last few pitches of the original line. After successfully freeing the lower pendi-point and encountering a wild tunnel pitch in the middle of the wall, we were shocked to find that the giant virgin splitter above was a monster offwidth—the dreaded Tatonka Knuk! Cedar began by leading a 200' varied wide crack, pushing single cams for extended sections to a perfect ledge. This set me up for the crux grovel, consisting of four-inch enduro hand stacks, capped by an exposed squeeze through a roof. The ankle gobies and bloodshed from this pitch, coupled with the three rounds of antibiotics I took in Kashmir, won me my very own systemic infection in my right leg. The Free Lhasa (1,300', 5.11+).

"Ahhh, Keflex, the breakfast of champions," I muttered as I squeezed puss out of my ankle and racked for our third new route in the Zion area. It followed the obvious continuous system just left of the route Free or Burn and the great arch formation to its right. Cedar lead the crux second pitch, on his birthday, after two hours of work and a 40' whipper that scarred his forehead. The Birthday Bash (700', 5.12c).

I don't think the people of Kashmir could ever image a place like Zion or our dirtbag climbing lifestyle. In the end we are compassionate for those who suffer, and grateful for our experiences on the dreamy sandstone.

RENAN OZTURK, *AAC*

Peak 6,482', The Reach Around; and Peak 6,482', and Slow and Delirious. In spring 2005 two routes were started on Peak 6,482', unnamed but known in the local climbing community as G-1. G-1 is short for Mt. Greer, named in honor of the Greer brothers after their successful attempt on the west face in 2005. G-1 is located east of the Nature Center in Zion Canyon, two major peaks south of Bridge Mountain. Slow and Delirious and the lower half of The Reach Around follow a major weakness up the middle of the central buttress leading to the main summit.

The best access to G-1 is by following the Watchman Trail in its entirety. The popular part of the trail ends at a viewpoint above the first and lower cliff band. From the viewpoint continue east past the sign that reads "No Trail Maintenance Beyond This Point." This historic part of the trail takes you within 500' of the start of the routes. The Reach Around (IV 5.10+ A0) is the first known route from the main canyon side of the peak and was put up by the Greer brothers, Brody and Jared, in early spring 2005, over two days with a heavy bender in

The west face of Peak 6,482' (a.k.a. G-1), showing its only routes: The Reach Around (left) and Slow and Delirious. *Bryan Bird*

between. On day one of their ascent Carl Oswald and I, after a serious effort at the bar, climbed the first six pitches of Slow and Delirious (not to be confused with fast and furious), while the Greers were establishing the first 300' of The Reach Around. Carl and I ran out of gas by late afternoon and descended the first chimney/gully north of the top of the tower on pitch six. After one rappel we downclimbed 400', drilled an anchor, and rappelled down to find our friends' fixed lines on The Reach Around.

The Greers finished their route the following day. The Reach Around begins roughly in the middle of the peak, 50' left of Slow and Delirious on the right side of a 100'-tall square buttress with large ponderosa pines on top. TRA starts with a low-angle crack that faces south (the rest of the route faces west). It then follows vertical cracks that lead into the major gully on the north side of the main summit ridge. Nearly halfway up the peak the route breaks left into the major gully and curls around to the summit.

A year or so later I returned with Joe French. We began by following the previously attempted Slow and Delirious line. The first pitch begins in a finger crack in a right-facing corner with a sharp roof 30' off the ground. We followed cracks up the center of the ridge. This route offers many options from its abundant ledges. We tried to follow the cleanest path of least resistance. That path turned out to be a good blend of quality cracks, corners, and chimneys, along with bits of typical Zion choss. Three pitches from the top we moved left off the main ridge, across the first chimney/gully system north of the summit, to the next buttress between that gully and The Reach Around gully. Joe and I climbed 14 pitches up to 5.10+ (5.7R) on this enjoyable route. We descended The Reach Around, which required much downclimbing and route-finding to locate the rappels. Our adventure went at IV 5.10+R and took 11-12 hours car-to-car.

BRYAN BIRD

Gatekeeper Wall, Gatekeeper Crack. In October Dave Jones, Chris Owens, and I established this route on the Gatekeeper Wall, which is the first formation lower than and east of the Watchman. We started up the canyon where the NPS has their shuttle bus storage facility. Our route follows a thin crack system that starts 35' right of the Locksmith Dihedral. The first pitch uses a few points of aid past a chockstone to gain a loose section of sandy talus behind a 200' finger-like exfoliated flake. On the second pitch Dave followed a broken crack system on great rock to a small stance. That night we visited the emergency room, because Chris had lacerated his fingers when a 200-pound block rolled over them. He was now resigned to jugging, organizing belays, and heckling the leaders. The next day, on the third pitch,

Brian Smoot jugging the excellent fourth pitch of Gatekeeper Crack. *Dave Jones*

I followed the cracks, overhanging there, to a sling belay. Dave led the beautiful fourth pitch (C2), which mostly ascended a thin face crack for 165' to a welcome ledge, which was big enough for one person to lie down on. After a short jog right, I led through an improbable and exciting roof, with ledge-fall potential, to an exposed belay beneath the final steep headwall crack. The good rock quality continued on the last pitch, which ended at one of the best top-outs any of us had ever done. We were excited about the quality of the climbing. We rapped the route using 60m ropes. We only placed five pitons on the climb. Otherwise every pitch, all of which had at least some aid, went clean at C1 or C2. I recommend this aid route (V 5.10 A2) because it's not too hard, has a clean, aesthetic crack system, and is away from the crowds.

BRIAN SMOOT

GATEKEEPER WALL

A Locksmith Dihedral IV 5.11 C1
B Gatekeeper Crack V 5.10 A2

Gatekeeper Wall. *Brian Smoot*

Montana

Pensive Tower, Gloomy Ruminations. Over a gorgeous Labor Day weekend, Bryan Schmitz, Neil Kauffman, and I ventured into the West Fork of Rock Creek in the Beartooth Mountains and completed a new route on Pensive Tower. The tower's west face is bordered on each edge by aesthetic ribs, and the Kennedy-McCarty ascends the left-hand, northern rib. Our route, Gloomy Ruminations (IV 5.10) follows the right-hand rib for eight pitches, most of which were between 60m and 70m long.

We surmounted the lowest band of loose red rock via a right-leaning dihedral near the left edge of the face. Hike right across a scree field to the broken notch below the upper rib. Another blocky, easy pitch leads to the rib proper. From here, the quality of the rock and route improve greatly. Three distinct steps, separated by spacious belay ledges, form the rib. Surmount the first step via a slanting dihedral system just right of the rib crest (5.9). Both the second and third steps tackle vague corner systems just left of the crest. The rib ends in a notch of dark rock below the upper headwall. Pitch six (5.8) ascends short, stacked corners to easier terrain. The crux pitch passes several difficulties, including a tight chimney with a huge hollow flake. The final pitch takes a difficult dihedral (5.9+). Several hundred feet of 3rd and 4th class terrain leads to the summit.

TREVOR BOWMAN

Wyoming

GRAND TETON NATIONAL PARK

Mt. Moran, South Buttress Prow to top of buttress. On a cool, crisp autumn day in September, Hans Johnstone, Greg Collins, and I paddled across Leigh Lake in the dawn's early light. We hiked from the outlet of Leigh Canyon to the base of Mt. Moran's towering South Buttress and did the standard entrance pitch onto the higher of the two large ramps at the base of the South Buttress. We scrambled and soloed up the ramp to its western edge and its junction with the South Buttress route. Once here we roped up again and ran the belay to the large east-facing dihedral on the prow of the buttress. Greg led a long 5.10 pitch high into this dihedral. Hans then led a short, cryptic traverse and run-out face pitch that established us below the overhanging crack in the dihedral's left wall. This pitch fell to me. Amazingly, the pitch went free and with little cleaning, though I fell at the crux, an overhanging, lichenous, rattly finger lock. Once it was a bit cleaner, and with sausages for fingers, Greg free-climbed the pitch following it. One of the best crack pitches in the Tetons, it seemed in the 5.12b range. It overhangs perhaps 20' to 30' in its 100'. A short pitch, with a traverse left, finished our time in the dihedral and put us in position for a 5.11- finish that exits at the apex of the prow, and joins the exit to the South Buttress Direct. From here it is possible to escape east to a series of rappels that lead to the base of the buttress, or continue up 2,500' of easy 5th class to the summit. All of us, having done the shin-splinting slab-paddle to the summit, opted for the rappels. We have left to a future party the integral ascent of the line to the summit.

BEAN BOWERS, *AAC*

Mt. Owen, North Ridge, first winter ascent. My partner, local innkeeper Hans Johnstone, and I, a guide, completed the first winter ascent of the North Ridge of Mt. Owen on March 18, 2007. One of the longest rock climbs in Grand Teton National Park, the route took us a very long day, 18 hours from car to summit. We circumnavigated the peak, first climbing the Koven Couloir, then descending the Briggs Ski Diagonal route and crossing the Run Don't Walk Couloir before ascending the 1,000m route and descending the Koven to Glacier Gulch.

GREG COLLINS, *AAC*

Grand Teton, Squeeze Box to junction with Hossack-MacGowan. On February 6, 2007 Hans Johnstone and I climbed Squeeze Box (1,000', IV M7 A0), a new route [climbed to easy snow near the intersection with the Hossack-MacGowan Couloir—Ed.] on the north face of the Grand Teton. The line lies between Shea's Chute and the Alex Lowe Memorial Route and ascends a weakness up a beautiful granite buttress. I spotted the line during a flurry of activity with various partners in October 2004, which gave us the best ice conditions in the Tetons in years. Brian Harder and I attempted the line on January 28, 2007, climbing about halfway up while excavating considerable snow from the cracks, before retreating due to approaching darkness. With clear weather and high pressure continuing, I was excited to make another attempt.

Hans and I began skiing from the Taggart-Bradley trailhead at 4 a.m. and began the more technical climbing up and onto the north face five hours later. The climbing was challenging and interesting, with technical difficulties up to M7 (5.10 rock equivalent). A challenging squeeze chimney, too narrow to climb facing in, offered little in the way of climbable ice and had me grunting and thrashing. Above was a beautiful ice gully, which brought us to the black chimney. For the next two ropelengths we climbed steep rock with axes and crampons. The second-to-last pitch involved a tension traverse across smooth slabs to reach another set of bottomed-out seams with minuscule and insecure features. In spots protection was difficult, but the route unfolded nicely, as we were treated to alpenglow on Teewinot. With great desire to complete the route, I darted up the last pitch by headlamp. Given the insecure nature of the climbing, success was never guaranteed. We rappelled the route and downclimbed across the Teton Glacier to our skis.

After switching boots and packing up, we made sweet turns on good snow down the glacier. Lower, the descent became a nightmare when we started breaking through the crust into soft and unconsolidated snow, often resulting in face-plants followed by my pack smacking the back of my head. After one of these episodes at the bottom of Glacier Gulch, while excavating myself I was excited to discover wolf tracks.

With mixed climbing techniques and skills increasing, there are countless opportunities for other new routes on the north face of the Grand Teton and throughout the range.

STEPHEN KOCH

WIND RIVER MOUNTAINS

Wind Rivers, various ascents. In the Cirque of the Towers, the south face of Wolf's Head—specifically the striking crack left of the Beckey South Face route, splitting the upper half of the face and leading up to Darth Vader tower—recently caught the attention of several talented climbers.

In fall 2005 Dave Anderson and Jamie Selda established Canus (III 5.11c), which climbs the first three pitches (5.10c, 5.11c, 5.10d) of this new crack before traversing off right (but still left of the Beckey Route) into two more excellent crack pitches (5.10d, 5.10b) to the ridgecrest.

In July Greg Collins and Kent McBride started with the first two pitches of the Beckey route, then climbed a hard traversing face pitch (5.12d), placing three bolts and two pins on lead, to gain the upper crack. The upper pitches were thin hands and fingers, 5.11a and 5.11b/c. They fixed rap anchors on the descent, which can be made with a single 70m rope. Their route, White Buffalo (260m, III 5.12d), is the hardest reported route in the Winds.

Anderson writes: "The link up of the two routes—tentatively called the White Wolf—would be, in my opinion, the 'Astroman of the Winds.' It is a little shorter than Astroman, but with an enduro-like corner, a tough squeeze/offwidth pitch, a hard boulder pitch (that can be aided/pendulumed through), and other fine jam cracks up high, it is a great climb. The rock is good overall, but a wire brush might be recommended gear for the first two pitches until they get climbed more."

Anderson also did the Cirque of the Towers Traverse (16 miles of trail, plus four miles of 3rd, 4th, and 5th class climbing, up to 5.9) in 13:25 car-to-car, and climbed Gannet Peak in 8:20 from Green River Lakes, 17 hours for the 36-mile round trip. Each time is about an hour-and-a-half faster than the previous record.

In mid-August on the fin-like feature of Ambush Peak's far-right northeast face, Renan Ozturk and Cedar Wright climbed what they think to be a new route, Attack of the Killer Clowns (5.11+ R). The route climbs past bail 'biners, steep cracks, and intimidating overhangs. At one point, some 800' up on sketchy 5.11 flakes, Wright was "shocked yet thankful" to find an old quarter-inch bolt inscribed "Banditos." Just above, he yarded past a blank slab on a fixed bashie, and the pair continued to the top. Unsatisfied due to their 5' of aid, they rapped 600' back down and found steep climbing to the left of the Banditos passage; this comprised the crux pitch and led to the summit.

A couple of days prior, the pair headed toward Ambush's intimidating and chossy-looking Northeast Face route (Arsenault-Young, 1971), originally rated 5.8 A4. Though unclear whether they climbed the exact line of the 1971 route, they made a one-day free ascent at 5.10+ R/X and, reports Wright, were "ecstatic to find that the climbing was actually superb, following a solid streak of glacier-polished rock through what appeared from below to be a sea of choss."

Also climbing a possible new route on Ambush in mid-August were Jonny Copp and Matt Segal. They climbed a route farther left than Ozturk and Wright's possible new line, starting with several easy pitches up a gully and continuing on steeper terrain (up to 5.11) for another eight pitches to the summit. They found a bail anchor low down but no further traces higher up—and atop a 5.11+ pitch that dead-ended they left their own bail anchor, rapped to a ledge, and found another way. Copp reports fun, roofy, and spicy climbing with circuitous routefinding, and notes that many excellent climbers have been active in the Winds over the years and not recorded their ascents in the climbing media. *Wind River Mountains* guidebook author Joe Kelsey reports, for example, that he's received information on nine new routes on Ambush, most unreported elsewhere, since the second edition of his book. "It's hard to say if it was new or not. It's definitely adventure climbing though, regardless," says Copp.

Colorado

ROCKY MOUNTAIN NATIONAL PARK

Longs Peak, Lower East Face, Endless Summer; Lower Chasm View Wall, The Invisible Wall, first free ascent. On July 31 Chip Chace and I completed Endless Summer (300m, V- 5.12- (5.11R)) on the Lower East Face of Longs Peak. This was the first free climb of the Nassewand, as it was called in the 1960s, the 1,000' Yosemite-like wall to the left of the Diagonal. During the late 1960s many attempts were made on this wall by the likes of Michael Covington, Wayne Goss, and Larry Dalke, but no one found a way through the giant wet arches of the lower part. The wall was abandoned and sat untouched for almost 20 years.

In 1987 interest in the Nassewand rekindled with two different parties completing aid lines up the wall. Jim Beyer, rope-soloing, found a dry, elegant start just left of the wet arches and forged a line up to Broadway that he called Antinuclear Tide. Also that summer Dan McGee and Layton Kor climbed a similar line, Question Mark Wall, which finished in a wet, vegetated crack. The next year Greg Davis and Todd Bibler began searching for a free climb up the Nassewand. By the time they walked away from the wall two years later they had established two lines that crossed at mid-height, each ending about 140' below Broadway. They named one

Chip Chace freeing the 5.11 third pitch of The Invisible Wall. The climb's crux pitch, the hanging crescent, arcs above and left. The wall rising in the upper left is the Diamond. *Roger Briggs*

line Slippery People and the other Endless Summer. Word got out that the left-hand start to the right-hand finish had all the best pitches, on dry rock, and this worthy six-pitch line received sporadic ascents during the 1990s.

In 2003 Chace and I climbed this line and added a connecting pitch from the right-hand high point to the left-hand high point. We were impressed by the superb quality of almost every pitch and the high standard of the climbing that Davis and Bibler had done. After reaching the high point, it occurred to me that the final 140' of blank marble up to Broadway might go free with a few bolts. The idea haunted me until the fall of 2005, when Chip and I rappelled off Broadway to have a close look. I came away believing it would go free, but wanted to remain within the stylistic limit of two bolts. We returned in early summer and rappelled down to place two protection bolts and fix a micro-cam. Then in late July we completed the line to Broadway. We chose the name Endless Summer as a tribute to the efforts and vision of Greg Davis and Todd Bibler 16 years earlier. This is one of the finest climbs in Rocky Mountain National Park.

Unreported from summer 2004, Chace and I did the first free ascent of The Invisible Wall (200m, IV 5.12-), a little-known Kor aid route from 1965 on the Lower Chasm View Wall of Longs. The climb has superb rock throughout and several remarkable features. Two moderate approach pitches from the right lead to the heart of the climb, three elegant and challenging pitches. The first of these is a prominent gold corner that disappears after 130', just short of an amazing hanging crescent. The next pitch is the crux and moves left under the hanging crescent, ending at the base of a final clean corner system. A final moderate pitch to the left ends on Broadway, where descent can be made via five rappels down Babys R Us.

When we climbed it there was nothing fixed and no sign of previous passage. We left it the way we found it and hoped that it would remain in this condition. However, when we repeated the climb the next summer, hoping to add a direct start and finish, we found two fixed pitons, and 50' of beautiful vegetation had been torn out of the final corner pitch. Despite the heavy hand of another party, this is a worthwhile climb, with lots of great climbing packed into six excellent pitches.

ROGER BRIGGS

BLACK CANYON OF THE GUNNISON NATIONAL PARK

Various activity. In late May I completed my long-term project of linking The Free Nose (V+ 5.12) and Tague Yer Time (V+ 5.12), all free, in a day, leading every pitch. I began with The Free Nose and finished with Tague Yer Time, completing the link-up in 13.5 hours from North Rim to South Rim. I'm indebted to Phil Gruber and Jed Wareham-Morris (they belayed and jugged for speed) and Erinn Kelly for their generous support. In November Zack Smith and I made the first ground-up ascent of Leonard Coyne and Mick Haffner's 827 GO! (V 5.13-). Although probably slightly easier than its reported grade, the climb is without doubt a wild addition to the North Chasm View Wall and a testament to the pioneering vision and creativity of one of the Black's greatest climbers, Leonard Coyne. Unreported from 2005 is the addition by Kent Wheeler (and ?) of Stand Up Comic (IV 5.11) to the Comic Relief Buttress. The climb is of excellent quality and, like many Wheeler routes, has already become popular. Information on these climbs is available from the North Rim Ranger Station.

JOSH WHARTON, *AAC*

The Blacksmiths. The steep wall between Cheap Shot and Dry Hard has been the scene of aborted aid attempts due to loose rock and massive roofs. In fall 2005 and spring 2006, Jared Ogden and I tried to find a free variation, but were unable to force the line. In May we ended up climbing the first five pitches of the Earl Wiggins sketch-fest Dry Hard, and then traversed left above the roofs into a steep, airy position halfway up the wall. From there we did six new pitches on gently overhanging, high-quality rock to the rim. Four of the new pitches are 5.12, and it is the steepest bit of rock we've yet found while free climbing in the Canyon. The Blacksmiths (1,600', 5.12).

TOPHER DONAHUE, *AAC*

Sistine Reality. The fourth lead was mine: the first and most prominent roof. Jonny Copp handed me the rack, raised his eyebrows, and wished me luck. As I entered the hollowed chamber beneath it, the sky and ground disappeared. I no longer could tell which way was up, only out. I was inside an enclosed box a few hundred feet above the ivy-choked gully. I reached for the first jam and it was solid, deep hands. Perfect. Twelve feet later, when I pulled the lip, I trembled and fumbled with every piece of gear that I wedged into the scaly, bone-white rock. This was only my second time on the intimidating pegmatite of the Black. My confidence grew as I continued on the flaring thin-hands corner above, particles of granola-like rock crunching beneath my rubber soles. I built an anchor and glanced over my shoulder to the inner canyon. The sky had turned black, the wind roared, and an ominous rumble sounded on the horizon. Jonny arrived, and we quickly escaped, sprinting to the car amid thunder and laughter.

Jonny took off for Alaska, and I headed home to Missouri, but we promised to return at our next opportunity. This chance didn't happen until two years later, in April 2006, although the Gothic was often on my mind. The scrappy riverside limestone in my home state offered perfect training.

Four pitches up at the belay, white dust collected in my lap. I pretended not to notice the incoming snow; maybe we could sneak by without the weather knowing we were there. We carried on. I followed the fifth pitch admiring various sections of offwidth, perfect hands, a clean slab, and eventually a broken roof. The stone looked as though it had been burning in a fire for the past hundred years, scalloped and fire red. The crux pitches beneath us, we sped up the remaining 700' of highly featured rock, connecting clean faces, deep cracks, and sharp dihedrals. The white stuff came and went, and we summited in a heavenly orange and violet sunset.

Our route begins a few hundred yards left of Kor's Route on the west face of Gothic Pillar. Approach by passing Exclamation Point, passing two gullies, and descending the third. Where it cliffs out, rap or traverse left to the next gully, descend it for 20 minutes, pass beneath a huge chockstone and continue to a large white boulder on the left. The route starts here, with the fourth pitch roof crack visible above.

On our initial attempt, I'd just returned from Rome, where I'd seen Michelangelo's Sistine Chapel painting. Inspired by the ceilings on the route, we titled our own masterpiece Sistine Reality (IV 5.11+, no bolts, no pins, no lassoes, no big whoop).

JEREMY COLLINS, Kansas City, Missouri, AAC

SAN JUAN MOUNTAINS

Peak 13,134', Ski Line. In late October I recruited Dave Ahrens to help me finish a project I started years ago, the north face of Peak 13,134' in the northern San Juans. The face can be clearly seen from Dallas Divide, and I had made several attempts with different partners over the past few years. The most serious attempt was with the late Johnny Soderstrom in October 2004. The route more or less follows a left-angling ramp directly through the center of the rocky north face.

Ski Line on Peak 13,134'. *Jared Vilhauer*

After a fairly short approach, the route starts with a couple of hundred feet of 50° snow. As you near what seems to be a dead end in the couloir, a beautiful cascade of water ice comes into view to the left and is the entrance to the face. We soloed the first 100' pitch of WI3 and kicked steps up more 50° snow. After a few more steps of low-angle ice, we reached the high point of the 2004 attempt. Johnny and I had tried to follow the obvious weakness by continuing left on snow but were turned around by deep snow on slab rock. This time Dave and I left the snow and took the direct route up mixed terrain. The climbing was typical San Juan mixed climbing, solid in places, incredibly loose in others, and almost always run out. After three long pitches of good climbing, including an exciting, airy 5.8 traverse, we reached the final rock headwall. We ascended a chimney, which provided a good finish to the route, with good dry-tooling and stemming. This pitch resembled the last pitch of Birdbrain Boulevard, but at 13,000', and Dave especially enjoyed following it in the dark without a headlamp. After another 100' of snow we reached the summit in the dark, with whiteout conditions and a few lightning bolts.

While we took a break on the summit, the weather cleared enough that we could see our planned descent route. We traversed just below the south ridge and descended a bowl between Peak 13,134' and Peak 13,252'. After wandering in the forest, we found our way back to the car at Dallas Creek, labeled "Box Factory" on a map. There was no sign of previous ascent on the face and none of the locals have heard of prior climbs. The route is worthy of more ascents if conditions are right, with firm snow. The route would be hard to retreat from, though, with a lack of features for rap/belay anchors. Most of our anchors consisted of ice tools in moss and snow-seat belays. With the conditions we had, the difficulty of the 1,600' route was WI3 M5 5.8R.

JARED VILHAUER, *AAC*

North Carolina

Whitesides Mountain, Children of the Sun. Mark Ilgner and I had been working on a new line on Whitesides Mountain for two years. We finally completed it in December. The route climbs the left side of the headwall section, beginning between Ship of Fools and The Promised Land. It begins with three beautiful pitches of vertical or near-vertical face climbing (5.11d, 5.12a, 5.12b/c, each 110') mostly protected by bolts. Pitches four (5.10d, 130', mostly traversing) and five (5.11d, 100'), however, are almost completely protected traditionally. Pitch four follows a horizontal crack while pitch five follows a right-arching dihedral. The sixth pitch (5.12 A1, 90') climbs through the upper overhanging section of the wall and is protected by bolts. Here we encountered a blank section too difficult for us to free. Two more pitches of easier-grade climbing (5.10 and 5.5, 100' each) finish the route.

This route is absolutely amazing and requires both sport and trad skills to master. The face climbing is thin, intricate and requires much attention to balance and body position. The trad pitches follow spectacular features in extremely exposed positions. The sixth, crux, pitch has about 15' of aid on bolts, just waiting for a talented climber to free.

ARNO ILGNER, *AAC*

Alaska

ALASKA RANGE

Geographical note: While the well-known peaks in Denali National Park are often called "The Alaska Range," these peaks form just one part of the immense Alaska Range, which contains many significant subranges, including the Hayes and Delta ranges, and the Revelation, Kichatna, and Tordrillo Mountains.

HAYES RANGE

Mt. Moffit, Entropy Wall. In the Eastern Hayes Range, from July 10-13, Jed Brown and Colin Haley established the Entropy Wall (2,300m, VI 5.9 A2 WI4+) on Mt. Moffit (3,969m). Their route ascends Moffit's north face, one of the largest faces in North America. See Brown's feature earlier in this *Journal*.

DENALI NATIONAL PARK

Denali National Park and Preserve, summary. Our season was significantly impacted this year by the death of two friends, Karen McNeill and Sue Nott, who were lost on Mt. Foraker. Karen and Sue had both befriended many of the Talkeetna staff and were well known in the climbing world as accomplished alpinists. Both of their families flew to Alaska during the search effort, as did many of their friends. It was a trying time for all. We will probably never know what happened or where they are located on Mt. Foraker. We also lost Mr. Kim, a South Korean climber who died of a sudden medical illness while descending the fixed lines on Denali [Note: The official name of the mountain is Mt. McKinley, but most climbers and locals use the native name, Denali. The two names are often used interchangeably—Ed.]. The Kim family also came to Talkeetna to thank the guides, mountaineering rangers, volunteers, and the Talkeetna staff for their help.

Temperatures in the Alaska Range seemed closer to the norm in 2006, as the firn line did not reach as high as the 7,200' Kahiltna Basecamp. During the prior season, warm temperatures resulted in considerable snowmelt at these lower elevations.

The U.S. Army High Altitude Rescue Team (HART) was able to support our camp insertions this year (and end-of-season extractions) at 7,200' and 14,200'. We hope to work with this invaluable team next season, though in the event they are redeployed to Iraq we wish them a safe journey. (*The above paragraphs from South District Ranger Daryl Miller.*)

Overall, it was a quiet season, with lower than average numbers on Denali and only

The most accurate forecast going... *Marko Prezelj*

five notable new routes climbed. The age-old dilemma about what constitutes a new route is always an issue. Is it a new route if the climbers did not go to the summit? Climbers can decide for themselves.

In another noteworthy expedition, a three-member Russian party replicated the circuitous route Dr. Frederick Cook claimed to have taken to the top of Denali back in 1906. Commencing May 19 at the Don Sheldon Amphitheater on the east side of Denali, Oleg Banar, Victor Afanasiev, and Valery Bagov ascended Traleika Col, descended the Traleika Glacier to the West Fork, moved up the West Fork, then ascended a line on the south face of Mt. Carpé. The threesome then traversed the ridge crest from Mt. Carpé to Mt. Koven, and on to Karstens Ridge. Continuing to the summit via the Harper Glacier, the Russian team reached the top on June 2, 14 days later. *(The above two paragraphs from Mountaineering Ranger Joe Reichert.)*

As detailed in the Mountaineering Summary (available at the web address below), 46 patients/climbers received NPS medical assistance, including 17 evacuations. Cases ranged from serious falls, cardiac events, altitude illness (including HAPE and HACE) and cold injury, to a pulled hammy.

Likewise, NPS staff and volunteers performed a variety of other on-mountain duties, including search missions, rescues, patrols, and education, and even a call for assistance from a team with a panic-stricken member (followed, the next day, by a call from the same team, this time needing route-finding help).

Quick Statistics—Mt. McKinley:
- *1,154 climbers attempted Mt. McKinley, with 50% reaching the summit. 1,053 attempted via the West Buttress, with 52% summiting. (28 climbers attempted Mt. Foraker. None summited.)*
- *Average trip length: 17.8 days. Average trip length for groups that summited: 18.5 days.*
- *Busiest summit day: May 29, 50 summits. Summit breakdown by month: June (315), May (199), July (67).*
- *Average climber age: 37.*
- *Women constituted only 7.1% of climbers, down from 11% in 2005.*
- *38 nations were represented on Mt. McKinley this season, including U.S. (719 climbers), Canada (67), Japan (60), U.K. (44), Spain (33).*
For more information, go to: www.nps.gov/dena/planyourvisit/mountaineering.htm

Summarized from the DENALI NATIONAL PARK &
PRESERVE ANNUAL MOUNTAINEERING SUMMARY

The south face of Mt. McKinley. (1) Cassin Ridge (Cassin-Airoldi-Alippi-Canali-Perego-Zucchi, 1961), sun-shade line. To the left is the southwest face. (2) Slovak Route (Adam-Korl-Krizo, 1984). (3) Japanese Direct (Kimura-Senda-Tsuneto-Watanabe-Yamaura, 1977; finishes on (5)). (4) Canadian Direct (Ménard-Turgeon, 2006; finishes on (5) with high point (c)). (5) American Direct (Eberl-Laba-Seidman-Thompson, 1967). (6) Haston-Scott (1976; starts on (5)). (7) Milan Krissak Memorial (Bakos-Johnson-Orolin-Petrik, 1980). (8) Southeast Spur (Cochrane-Everett, 1962). ©Bradford Washburn, courtesy Panopticon Gallery, Boston, MA

Mt. McKinley, Canadian Direct. On the south face of Mt. McKinley, from May 28-30, the prolific young Quebec climbers Louis-Philippe Ménard and Maxime Turgeon established The Canadian Direct (8,000'/4,000' new, Alaska Grade 6, 5.9 M6 AI4), in 58 hours from 'schrund to summit ridge. See Turgeon's feature earlier in this *Journal.*

Mt. Foraker, McNeill-Nott Memorial to French Ridge. From May 12-14, Will Mayo and Maxime Turgeon climbed 5,200' of difficult new terrain, up to WI5+ M6R A0, on the south face of Mt. Foraker to the junction with the 1976 French Ridge route. Their climbing took 40 hours, plus 10 hours for the descent. See Mayo's feature earlier in this *Journal.*

Mt. Foraker, first winter solo. On day 39 of my expedition, I stood atop Mt. Foraker. It was March 10, 2007, at 5:03 p.m. The temperature was -50°F, with 20-30 knot winds, making a wind chill of almost -100°F. I only stayed for 10 minutes, but this was the culmination of four years of attempts to solo Foraker in winter.

My journey began in the summer of 1995, when I climbed Denali and dreamed of climbing solo in the winter. My dream became a quest to climb each of the three highest summits in the Alaska Range (Denali, Foraker, Hunter) in winter. After 10 winters of climbing, I had stood atop Denali in winter, and Mt. Foraker twice just a few days after the spring equinox.

On January 31 I flew into the Kahiltna Glacier with Paul of Talkeetna Air Taxi and unloaded 300 pounds of gear. The next day I started ferrying my gear to the beginning of the Southeast Ridge (6,700'), and then to Camp 1 at approximately 8,100'. On day 4, my 14' aluminum safety poles were put to the test when I stepped in a hidden crevasse and the poles and skis stopped me from a serious fall.

Above Camp 1, the climbing became more technical and on several occasions I had to fix my two 200' ropes. It took me eight days to make five trips to Camp 2 (9,780') and build a snow cave, where I was established by day 19. From Camp 2 the views of McKinley, Hunter, and the rest of the Alaska Range were fantastic. The winds began to pick up. I was stuck in my snow cave for five days, until I could start moving to Camp 3 at 11,300'. It took me four trips in a six-day period to ferry my gear to a point just below Camp 3. In the first week of March, I continued making carries toward Camp 4 (High Camp, 13,400'); this took me six days. It was good to finally be at High Camp with my supplies. High winds keep me at camp for the next three days (days 36-38) as lenticular clouds formed over Mts. McKinley, Foraker, and Hunter. I sat, watching and waiting. On March 10 lenticulars still formed on McKinley and Hunter but not Foraker. I will try!

I first encountered a steep, knife-edge ridge with an overhanging cornice. I had to stay back from the cornice, but high enough not to cause an avalanche. Next, I came to a tricky, time-consuming crevassed area. The rest of the way to the summit was hard ice and snow, and I had to watch my step so I would not slip.

At last, after 9 hours 15 minutes of climbing, I reached the 17,400' summit. I only stayed 10 minutes in the -100°F wind chill. It was late, and my glasses were fogging. With this and the flat light, it seemed too dangerous to try to cross the crevassed area and the knife-edge ridge. After descending for three hours, I made an emergency snow cave at 14,500'. It took me 3½ hours to dig the cave. I spent a cold night without a sleeping bag at -20°F.

I woke to a calmer day and descended to High Camp, but by afternoon the winds had picked back up, so I spent another three days there. It took me another nine days to descend to my old base camp on the Kahiltna Glacier, which I reached on day 52, March 23.

The wind had made the landing area extremely rough, so I had to ferry my gear three miles to a protected area on the Southeast Fork of the Kahiltna (standard base camp for McKinley climbers). On March 28 Paul arrived and flew me back to Talkeetna. After a long, hot shower, I ate two double cheeseburgers, two house salads and two orders of french fries. I topped this off with two desserts at Latitude 62. [Editor's note: Kuriaki normally weighs 130 pounds.]

MASATOSHI KURIAKI, *Japan*

Various ascents. In June I was a climbing instructor with a Slovenian army expedition of eight members. It was an interesting experience, despite unstable weather and challenging conditions. The North Couloir on Hunter's Mini Moonflower, the upper part of the West Rib to the summit of Denali (in seven hours, for acclimatization), the Cassin Ridge (22 hours to the summit; the last 15 hours in snowfall and strong winds), and a free, on-sight ascent (17 hours) of the Cobra Pillar on Mt. Barrill were the climbs where I was trying to have some fun. All members summited Denali, and two members skied from the summit.

On the Cassin Matej Bizjak and I started the climb with three young Slovenians (Matej Kladnik, Tine Cuder, and Rok Blagus), who decided to descend after about one-third of the route due to a strong snow storm. Kladnik returned about 10 days later to solo the route.

MARKO PREZELJ, *Slovenia*

Mt. Huntington, first winter ascent. On March 10, 2007, Jed Brown (Fairbanks) and I flew from Talkeetna to the Tokositna Glacier below Mt. Huntington. On March 12 we climbed to the summit of Huntington via the West Face Couloir (Nettle-Quirk) and descended via the same route, in just under 15 hours roundtrip from camp. 'Schrund-to-'shrund was probably about 13:30 roundtrip. We believe this might have been the first ascent of Huntington during the winter season. [This was also the fastest known ascent of Huntington—Ed.] Although many teams descend from the top of the ice ramp, we found it to only be halfway to the summit in terms of time and effort. Conditions and weather were excellent, although the temperatures were cold; we both frost-nipped a few digits. After a few days contemplating other objectives, we gave in to the cold nights and flew out on March 16.

COLIN HALEY, *AAC*

Peak 7,400', South Ridge. Micha Miller and I spent two weeks in May in the Ruth Gorge, where we climbed a few things and failed on a few more. We left our camp under Mt. Dickey one morning hoping to get on something that wasn't too committing, as the weather was marginal at best. We climbed the broad couloir that leads to the low point on the ridge between Peak 7,400' and London Bridge. An attempt to stay on the crest of Peak 7,400' was soon thwarted by unstable cornices, so we dropped 300' or so into the basin to the east. From there we worked our way back up to the ridge at a notch just south of the summit. Three pitches of mixed snow and rock (up to 5.7) put us on top of the peak.

As far as we know, and according to our research, the route on Peak 7,400' had not been done before. But it's a pretty obvious and straightforward route, so it is quite possible someone had done it and never reported it.

DAVID HARDEN, *AAC*

Mt. Grosvenor, The Warrior's Way, and Mt. Johnson, The Escalator, third ascent. In 2005 Eamonn Walsh and I climbed two new routes on Mt. Grosvenor in the lower Ruth Gorge, which also were the mountain's second and third ascents (*AAJ* 2006). The best line we saw, however, was an obvious yet unclimbed ramp directly splitting the 4,400' east face. Poor weather that season prevented an attempt.

When we returned a year later, two weeks of heavy snowfall ensued.

Mt. Grosvenor's east face. The Warrior's Way (Walsh-Westman, 2006) takes the huge crescent corner in the center. Once Were Warriors (Walsh-Westman, 2005) starts in a barely visible cleft beginning halfway up the gully on the right. For a broader view and more routes, see *AAJ 2006* p. 186. *Mark Westman*

Mark Westman on The Warrior's Way. *Eamonn Walsh*

March had been bitterly cold and returning Gorge teams reported virtually no ice, but the new snow would work to our advantage.

Strong high pressure arrived, and on April 14 we arose at 2 a.m. to an astonishing aurora display over the Gorge. By headlamp we departed under a biting north wind and temperatures well below zero. We entered the huge cleft in the center of the east face, climbing to where it steepens into a continuous ramp soaring to the left skyline. Eamonn began a long lead block as the sky lightened, and we ascended many pitches of rolling, 55-70° terrain with occasional steeper sections. The climbing was fast and pleasant but usually runout. The ramp—a major drainage—was plastered with compressed snow ("s'nice") and scant patches of real ice. Rock protection was equally scarce in the compact granite, and we frequently simul-climbed to utilize the occasional ice for belay anchors.

Our seventh pitch began with our first rock anchor: solid pitons, which were necessary and comforting. Eamonn cool-headedly unlocked this serious pitch, taking long and uncertain runouts on insecure M5 terrain, cleaning rotten snow from crumbly granite slabs.

A snow bowl briefly interrupted the ramp, before its unrelenting continuation. Immediately we encountered the second crux, a steep and unprotectable 30m slab coated with a half inch of rotten and hollow s'nice. Eamonn boldly sent this insecure pitch entirely without protection, running a full ropelength before finding a good crack for a belay.

Moderate pitches, with the occasional vertical step, followed, before the ramp abruptly ended in a snow bowl beneath intimidating black cliffs and wild snow mushrooms.

The exit to the summit ridge had appeared uncertain when viewed from the Gorge, and was equally enigmatic once we were there. Floundering in a meter of unconsolidated snow, I began leading a physical block of pitches on the fluted wall to our left. I surmounted a short rock step with an awkward bulge, using one point of tension to clean snow from the overhang.

A short mixed runnel gave way to two ropelengths of trenching through steep, exposed flut-ings. After tunneling through a cornice onto the east spur of the mountain, I led a traverse beneath the spur to a steep mixed step and more excavating up a narrow arête. Thoroughly soaked, I belayed from pitons and brought Eamonn up for the final lead. A steep mixed chim-ney, some digging, and we suddenly emerged onto level terrain and an intersection with our South Face route of 2005.

We left the pack and traversed the final ridge to stand on top, 15 hours after leaving the base, at 8 p.m. It was frigid, still, and the setting sun turned the sky amazing shades of red and purple.

While descending, I released an 18" slab above the Church-Grosvenor col, but was able to jump off as it slid away. We continued down without further incident. After 19½ hours away, we happily returned to our camp. We named our new line The Warrior's Way (4,400', V AI4 M5R A0) [photo on p. 186, *AAJ 2006*]. Of the three routes we have established on this peak, this was the most demanding and aesthetic.

Two days later, high pressure holding, we made the third ascent of The Escalator (4,400', III 5.5 AI3) on Mt. Johnson. This route is surprisingly moderate and very enjoyable. Mostly soloing or simul-climbing, we reached the summit after eight hours, descended the dangerous Johnson-Grosvenor gully, and reached camp as the weather window collapsed. Twelve hours round trip.

MARK WESTMAN, *Talkeetna, Alaska, AAC*

The east face of the Broken Tooth, showing Walsh and Westman's impressive "new bail." *Paul Roderick, Talkeetna Air Taxi*

Broken Tooth, east couloir to summit ridge (new bail). In early May, after our Ruth trip [see above], Eamonn Walsh and I arrived on the Coffee Glacier to investigate an unclimbed couloir on the east face of the Broken Tooth. Climbers had eyed this route for years; Paul Roderick's gorgeous aerial photo sealed our enthusiasm.

We established an advanced camp in the small basin beneath the route and began climbing at 4 a.m. the next morning, May 10. Easy snow for 1,000' led into the narrow slot, which met a formidable headwall. A vertical slot chimney broke the left side but looked unappealing and hard to protect. To the right, a flow of s'nice coated a very steep cor-ner. Eamonn chose this course and began leading; the corner started moderately enough but soon reared up to dead vertical and continued that way for a considerable distance. The frothy, semi-detached ice yielded marginal screw placements and made for a heady pitch. Above a good belay stance, an easy slot emptied us into a 70m snow bowl.

The next section had looked questionable from camp, but to our surprise a beautiful, narrow ice hose split the right side of the rock band above us. Inside we found some of the most aesthetic climbing imaginable: 600' of perfect ice in a shoulder-width slot, averaging 60-70°, interrupted occasionally by short, steeper steps. This feature opened into a broad snow couloir, where we climbed together for several ropelengths.

An intimidating headwall of steep rock plastered with huge, threatening snow mushrooms now loomed above us. It looked doubtful. I belayed as high as possible, then Eamonn lead up the left side of a steep slab into an awkward chimney. An A0 exit move led to M5 mixed terrain and a belay high on the right side of the narrowing corridor. Continuing straight up seemed hopeless, but to the right a narrow passage not visible from below looked promising. It would prove to be the key to the route. Eamonn entered the slot and soon encountered a short but difficult crux (M6), pulling a small roof onto a nearly blank slab above. Steep ice in a narrow runnel exited to snow slopes, leading to a breathtaking perch on the wildly exposed summit ridge, and an inspiring view of the awesome walls of the Bear Tooth and Moose's Tooth.

The summit was shouting distance away and perhaps 150' above us. However, a monolithic gendarme on the ridge, which we had noted in photos, formed an imposing barrier. It severely overhung both sides of the ridge, and climbing it directly looked improbable. A committing rappel to the west might offer a way around it, but there were many unknowns associated with this course. We opted out, leaving this problem for the next party to solve. A dozen rappels, interspersed with downclimbing, brought us back to the glacier after a 16-hour round trip.

This sort of "significant failure," which is common in alpine climbing, has popularized the term "First Failure" or "New Bail" with a number of Alaskan climbers. It distinguishes completed climbs from strong efforts that terminated, for whatever reason, at the "end of the technical difficulties," or at a definable geographic feature. Call the effort what you may, but our goal here was the summit, not the summit ridge. As such, we leave the naming of this route to the party that finishes it; until then it remains, simply, the east couloir, or its local nickname, "Root Canal" (3,300', V AI5+R M6).

Mark Westman leading into the spectacular ice hose in the center of the Broken Tooth's east couloir. *Eamonn Walsh*

MARK WESTMAN, *Talkeetna, Alaska, AAC*

Before the Dawn on the Broken Tooth, rising from the Buckskin Glacier. *Katsutaka Yokoyama*

Broken Tooth, Before the Dawn; Mt. Hunter, Deprivation, third ascent. In April the Giri-Giri Boys (Fumitaka Ichimura, Tatsuro Yamada, Yuki Satoh, and I) tried various lines around the Buckskin Glacier. Tatsuro and Yuki tried the east side of the Moose's Tooth (10,355') twice. Although they couldn't reach the summit, it looked like a good line, a good try. Fumitaka and I tried the east face of the Bear Tooth (10,070') first. But we were totally defeated by various difficulties. For the next two weeks we waited for a period of good weather and good conditions. The north face [perhaps northwest] of the Broken Tooth (9,050') was not as distinguished as its neighbors, but tasteful in its own way. Fumitaka and I targeted a weakness on that wall.

On April 26, after a one-and-a-half hour approach, we went up corn snow toward the first ice runnel and started climbing at 5:30 a.m. The first pitch was the crux: dry-tooling in a mostly good, thin crack (M6). After that, we contin-

Fumitaka Ichimura firing the crux first pitch of Before the Dawn. *Katsutaka Yokoyama*

ued up a left-hand narrow runnel to escape the main ice, which was too exposed, thin, and unstable. The wall's complexity made it difficult for us to find the correct line, so we linked up various weaknesses, including steep, thin ice and mixed (M5+ WI4+R). At the snow slope, about two-thirds up the wall, two obvious chimney systems appeared to lead to the summit. We chose the right-hand one, and after one ice pitch in this chimney, traversed right to a snow band, where we dug out a bivy ledge.

Fumitaka Ichimura leading pitch 5, beginning with a downclimb off the belay before climbing the ice above. *Katsutaka Yokoyama*

The next day we climbed a loose chimney (5.9) and traversed again to a right-hand ridge (M5). Some troublesome rock, covered with soft snow, led us to a final ice field (70°) and the summit at 1 p.m. It was snowing with poor visibility, so we started our descent. On the way down we found so many places for natural anchors—rock horns and V-threads—that the 19 rappels were relatively easy. We returned to the Buckskin Glacier after 38 hours roundtrip. Our route, Before the Dawn (1,000m, 23 pitches, Alaska Grade 5, 5.9 WI4+ M6), follows obvious snow and ice systems in the center of the north face. The climbing was not too difficult, with relatively stable rock and ice climbing. I suppose this route could someday become a classic.

We then flew to the Kahiltna Glacier and completed Deprivation (6,000', Alaska Grade 6, ED+ 90°, Backes-Twight 1994) on the North Buttress of Mt. Hunter (14,570'). We did it in 72 hours roundtrip, with the West Ridge descent. Once on the wall, the climbing conditions were not as bad as some people said or as I could imagine. Deprivation follows a natural line of weakness, and the whole route was fun.

KATSUTAKA YOKOYAMA, *Japan*

KICHATNA SPIRES

Various activity. Jen Olson (Canmore, Alberta) and I (Vancouver, B.C.) arrived in Talkeetna on May 23. That same day Paul Roderick of Talkeetna Air Taxi flew us to the Cul-de-Sac Glacier in the heart of the Kichatna Spires. The weather gods were with us then, but we would pay our dues eventually.

Paul planted us directly below our main objective: the southwest face of Sunrise Spire, which rises for 800m above the glacier. The face is divided into four buttresses by three distinctive weaknesses. We intended to attempt a crack system on the better rock to the right of the rightmost weakness, following Klemen Mali's 2002 attempt. Surrounding us on all sides were the impressive faces of the Citadel, the Steeple, the intimidating north face of Kichatna, Mt. Jeffers, the Dark Tower, and Cemetery Spire.

For the next two weeks we woke to blue skies every morning. We climbed Sunrise Spire via the Southeast Couloir, which we hoped would be our descent option from the southwest face. On the southwest face we fixed 150m of rope and made a summit bid.

The rock we encountered on Sunrise was friable and gritty. The 200m that formed the steepest part of our climb were charac-

Jen Olson on Pitch 5 of the Sunrise Spire attempt. *Katherine Fraser*

The southwest face of Sunrise Spire, showing the Fraser-Olson attempt. Rumors of a Russian line up a pillar on the left side of the face, where old fixed ropes remain, could not be confirmed. *Katherine Fraser*

terized by loose, flaky rock and seamed-out cracks. The aiding and climbing above our fixed lines (which we threw off, intending to get them later since we planned to descend the east side) was tenuous and engaging. Past the steep buttress we had anticipated less demanding terrain. However, we encountered burly pitches of rock that could be described as kitty litter. A strenuous 60m icy, overhanging offwidth capped our day in the dwindling 1 a.m. light. We huddled together for a couple of hours of frozen head-nodding. In the morning we climbed another snowy offwidth, to a heartbreaking 50m below the summit ridge, before bailing the way we had come and retrieving our fixed ropes. The decision to retreat was especially hard, as we knew descending the couloir on the backside would be far less demanding than rappelling the entire face.

After several rest days we climbed 450m of new ground on Cemetery Spire, following an obvious couloir that diagonally splits the west face. We were stopped, though, 50m below the summit by a lack of wide gear. Two days later we climbed Peak 7,270', beside Mt. Jeffers, by a Grade II route and called Paul for a ride out of Dodge.

The weather gods decided we'd had too much high pressure. The skies closed in, and the winds picked up. We waited eight days by eating, drinking, reading, and going crazy, before

Paul was able to come and pick us up, 23 days after dropping us off, for breakfast at the Road-house Grill in Talkeetna. We came out to the tragic news of the disappearance and deaths of Karen McNeill and Sue Nott. If we had forgotten amidst our own drama, this reminded us that the most important part of going out is not getting to the top, but coming home.

We thank the Mugs Stump Award for the generous support.

KATHERINE FRASER, *Canada*

NEACOLA MOUNTAINS

Neacola Mountains, first full-length ski traverse. Next time you're in Anchorage on a sunny evening, go downtown to Fourth Street and have a pint at Simon and Seafort's Grill. As you hydrate, look through the picture windows across Cook Inlet. The big mountains you're seeing are the Tordrillos. At their left end is Mt. Spurr, with a tiny pompom of steam venting from the summit. Below the left side of Mt. Spurr is Lake Chakachamna, visible as a large break in the mountains. Farther left, beyond Lake Chakachamna, the Neacolas stretch southwest for 81 miles to the Tlikakila River and Lake Clark.

On April 6 Doug Brewer of Alaska Air West in Nikiski flew us to 5,000' on the Glacier Fork where we cached 150 lbs of booze and food. Doug then shuttled us to the east end of Lake Chakachamna. With six days of food and a 1:250,000-scale map, we headed back to our cache, across the high névés of the McArthur, Blockade, and Tanaina glaciers. Once at our cache, we base-camped on the Glacier Fork, Neacola Glacier, and North Fork for 10 days, fighting constant storms, skiing deep powder and couloirs including the likely first descent of The Gorilla Finger (2,600' vertical) off the west side of the North Fork Glacier at 4,150'. The final five days we toured onto the Tlikakila River via the Kijik River, Portage Lake, and Otter Lake, making another likely first descent of a couloir we dubbed Immortal Technique (3,000' vertical). The final 15 miles were alder 'shwacking on grizzly trails to Lake Clark. On April 27 Doug fetched us in his DeHavilland Beaver on a gravel bar.

We found the Neacola Mountains to be a heavily glaciated version of the North Cascades, with granite peaks rising to 9,000'. Along our tour, we compared 10 WAAS GPS elevations to 1958 1:63,360 USGS maps and found an average elevation drop of 70'. Our Neacola traverse was about 100 miles and 20,000 vertical feet. We skied 57,000 total vertical feet.

JOE STOCK, *AAC,* ANDREW WEXLER, *and* DYLAN TAYLOR, *AAC*

CHUGACH MOUNTAINS

Pt. 6,000' of Mt. Yukla, Gank'd and Slayed. Often the crux of climbing in Alaska is finding a partner with the same goals and ambitions. Things came together for John Kelley and me in the second week of February, 2007, and we headed out to the northwest face of Mt. Yukla (7,535') with a new grade V route in our sights. We approached from Eagle River's Icicle Creek and topped out on the 6,000' subpeak that is roughly 0.75 mile northeast of Yukla's true summit.

An unclimbed left-trending ramp, a narrow chimney (climbed by Kelley and Varney [pp. 193-194, including photo, *AAJ 2006*]) and a right-trending snow-and-ice couloir make up three forks, just to the right from the toe of the Icicle Glacier.

We left our base camp at treeline early in the morning and soloed roughly 700' of third-class terrain up to WI3. We had originally intended to attempt the left-trending ramp, but ultimately decided upon the coveted ice-and-snow couloir. I took the first lead up a WI3 ramp and encountered a rock headwall with a previous party's rappel anchor. Several moves up (mostly 5.9-ish laybacks), I encountered downsloping rock and poor feet. After struggling for an hour in vain, I lowered, and John gave it a try. He attempted to free it, but decided it would have to be aided. Using pins and a few birdbeaks (one of which popped out on him under bodyweight), he surmounted the obstruction and continued up, on virgin terrain, through a narrow snow chimney. I led the next pitch, which started in the snow chimney, then stepped up and over some WI3-4 steps. Higher up I was left scratching and picking at veggies. I went right at a fork and the rock blanked out, forcing me to tediously downclimb 10' and take the left chimney. With only a Spectre hammered into some frozen moss, I manned up and made my way through the rest of the pitch, which went at M6. We then had our first bivy on a small, protected ledge.

John led the next pitch in the morning, up and over a dicey dihedral to a right-trending corner system, then traversed a steep snow slope up to a rock outcrop. With the packs being hauled, I jugged up the ropes. On the way up my tool became dislodged from my harness and dropped off the face. Luckily John had a third tool and we were able to continue. Several pitches of WI3 and steep snow traverses put us at the bottom of the crux ice pitch. John led an intimidating 80' smear with thin protection and long runouts. He made a few impressive moves and then dominated his way through the crux, which went at WI6 due to its thin condition, runout, and a 15' overhanging section under a powder snow mushroom. We traversed over a steep snow slope that would be atrocious in the wrong conditions and dug a snow cave for our second night on the face.

In the morning we packed our soaking wet bags and climbed one more WI3 pitch, to put us on top of our route. We unroped and hiked up and over Pt. 6,000', then descended the Icicle Glacier from the standard Northeast Ridge route.

This was John's third new route on Yukla within the past year (see *AAJ 2006*) and my second attempt overall. Our route, Gank'd and Slayed, went at 2,800', V WI6 M6 A2.

CLINT HELANDER, *AAC*

Abercrombie Mountain, Southwest Face. For a few years Abercrombie Mountain (2,120m) had been in the back of my mind, for a time when conditions were decent and I had a good partner. Its southwest face starts at only 640m, presenting an unclimbed 1,480m face only a few hours' ski from the road. Alpine climbing is normally out of the question in Valdez due to the huge snow depth, but Valdez had just experienced six weeks with almost no precipitation and very high winds. Hence, while the Heli-ski hopefuls sulked about Valdez, Colin Haley and I skied up the Valdez Glacier to the top of the Second Bench on March 19, 2007. The NOAA forecast called for "a major change in the weather pattern" to show up on March 21, so we knew we would be racing the weather. We left camp under clear skies at 6:40 on March 20 and climbed steps of water ice and mixed terrain to around WI4- and 5.4b. Almost halfway up the face, there is a large snow bench on which one could casually stroll off the face. We knew we had to move a couple of gully systems to the right, but indecision and poor visibility caused us to go farther than we wanted. This caused us to hit the north ridge sooner than we would have liked.

Abercrombie Mountain's Southwest Face (Brown-Haley) route. *Jed Brown*

We reached the summit at 15:00 in a whiteout and began the descent. Four hours later we were back in camp, coaxing enough water out of our dying gas cylinder for a ramen each. We were pleased that we had gone high class and brought Maruchan rather than Top for this important recovery meal. Although we wore harnesses and carried a rope and some rack, we never took it out of the pack. Good training, I guess. The next day, we skied out just before the snow began in earnest.

Colin Haley cruising on Abercrombie Mountain. Haley and Jed Brown continued up the ice above and just right, never breaking out the rope on their 1,480m new route. *Jed Brown*

We believe this to be the first ascent of the face. It offered enjoyable climbing, and the rock quality was better than usual for the Chugach. There are at least half a dozen good-looking lines remaining. Most would go at about the same grade, with perhaps one or two harder pitches. There were also a few nice waterfalls in the area, probably all unclimbed, for a time when the avalanche conditions are low. For more photos see http://59A2.org

JED BROWN, *AAC*

Pk. 3,596', a.k.a. the Brackish Bitch, showing the Varney-Hoyt route. The dot marks their portaledge camp. Three other routes are rumored to exist on this face. *Josh Varney*

PRINCE WILLIAM SOUND

Pk. 3,596' (Brackish Bitch), Varney-Hoyt. Over 21 days in August, Andy Hoyt and I, both of Girdwood, Alaska, put up a new line on Pk. 3,596', a.k.a. the Brackish Bitch, at the head of Deep Water Bay, approximately 40 boat miles from the Whittier harbor. Heavy rains characterized our trip; the four days after we arrived were the only consecutive days of sun. Furthermore, the cracks were

Andy Hoyt leading during a rare spell of clear weather. Inset: more typical conditions on the Brackish Bitch. *Josh Varney*

consistently filled with moss and dirt if they were narrower than four inches. Our free-climbing shoes never left the tent. Having to clean the cracks slowed us drastically, forcing us to set up a portaledge one-third of the way up the wall, from where we fixed down to the base. After we made multiple attempts to push above our camp, the second-to-last day of our trip dawned clear, and we raced up our fixed lines and pushed to the top in 20 hours camp-to-camp. The climbing was all direct aid, with a few free sections to connect crack systems. We rappelled the route in 16 raps, with some ledge scrambling between. We rated the 900m Varney-Hoyt route V 5.6 A3.

Special thanks to Andy Morrison of Alaska Backcountry Access, LLC, for providing affordable and safe boat rides. I highly recommend him for any future expeditions to the region. He is based out of Girdwood and can be reached at www.girdwoodactivity.com or 1-800-783-300.

JOSH VARNEY

NUTZOTIN MOUNTAINS

Peak 8,500'+, possible first ascent. On July 27 Don Welty of Wrangell Mountain Air flew me to the Horsfeld Airstrip along Beaver Creek, near the Canadian border at the northeastern boundary of Wrangell-St. Elias National Park. My objective was a solo high mountain traverse of the Nutzotin Mountains from Horsfeld to Chisana and then on to Nabesna. However, the weather did not cooperate.

It was raining hard when we landed at Horsfeld, and a local outfitter, Dick Petersen, invited me down to his camp. The area streams are known for their grayling fishing, and it was a great chance to talk with Dick, who provided a wealth of knowledge about the local mountains. I finally packed up and headed off across the tundra, encountering a lone wolf as I ascended Klein Creek later that afternoon in drizzling rain.

It took 2½ days reach the small glacier atop Klein Creek. I set up camp at roughly 6,200' near a cluster of small lakes and checked out the 8,200' pass that accesses the upper Carl Creek Glacier. Then I traversed south to access a short snow/ice ramp leading up the east side of Peak 8,500'+, which borders the south side of the pass. A few hundred feet of climbing saw me on the summit.

I had hoped to spend several days in this high camp and climb several of the higher peaks. However, the weather changed that night and it rained and snowed for a couple of days, forcing me to abandon my original plans. I retraced my steps down Klein Creek and then hiked up the Beaver Creek drainage.

Although I only got in one climb during my ten-day solo adventure, it was a joy to be alone in the wilderness again. I try to keep up on the climbing history in the Wrangell-St. Elias region, and this may have been the first ascent of the peak. Dick Petersen has climbed a handful of the peaks in this region, and two other peaks to the east were climbed by a couple in 1972. However, a lot of climbs and adventures in Alaska go unreported.

DANNY KOST, *Alaska Section, AAC*

ALASKA COAST MOUNTAINS

Peak 7,030' (Mt. Bearzi) and Peak 6,230'. In July Carl Dietrich and Kale Sommer made the third ascent of Peak 7,030', located six miles northwest of Devil's Thumb in the Stikine Icefield, via a new route from the east. From the Burkett Glacier, the pair traversed Peak 6,230' (likely FA) and up the east ridge of 7,030', then reversed the ascent (with a bivy en route).

Unreported from 2002, two local climbers made the second ascent of 7,030'. From the Witches' Cauldron the pair climbed up the mixed southeast aspect. Due to storm and ensuing hazard on the ascent route, they traversed the summit and descended the original northern route (Balog-Clark-Ippolito, 1979), with a bivy on the way down to the long walk back. The ascensionists, family, and friends have chosen to refer to Peak 7,030' as Mt. Bearzi, in memory of the late Mike Bearzi.

DIETER KLOSE, *Alaska*

Canada

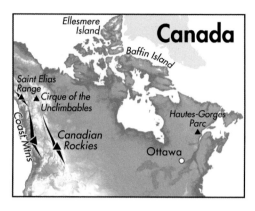

St. Elias Range

*Kluane National Park and Reserve, moun-
taineering summary.* Weather in the Kluane
Icefields during the 2006 climbing season
was predictably unpredictable. As a result
of sustained storms and snowfall, the
Mt. Logan massif in particular saw fewer
climbing parties than usual in recent years.
A total of 86 persons participated in 29
mountaineering expeditions. This accounted for 1,535 person-days in the icefields of Kluane
National Park and Reserve.

Expeditions are usually concentrated in the Mt. Logan area. However only nine parties
made it to the massif, with all but one expedition attempting the standard King Trench route. The
East Ridge was attempted by one group, but it was unsuccessful due to lack of snow. The mountain allowed only two expeditions to successfully reach its main summit. Uncooperative weather
for aircraft and foot travel was the main factor in the low number of successful expeditions.

Other mountains that received climbing activity included Pinnacle Peak, Mt. Wood,
Mt. Walsh, Mt. Steele, Mt. Queen Mary, and McArthur Peak. There were three ski-touring
expeditions into the Icefields.

Of note was an Alpine Club of Canada 2006 Centennial Camp, which was held in the
vicinity of Donjek Mountain. The group of approximately 10 established their camp on the
Eclipse Glacier and spent two weeks exploring various routes in the area. Successful ascents
were made on Mts. Walsh, and Badham, and other peaks. The last major ACC expedition was
organized in 1966 in the Steele Glacier area.

No major search and rescue operations occurred in the icefields during the climbing season.

Mountaineering in the Icefield Ranges of Kluane National Park is an inherently dangerous
activity, but with proper preparation and planning most groups have very positive experiences
and return with memories that last a lifetime.

Registration is mandatory for all overnight activity in Kluane National Park and Reserve.
Anyone interested in mountaineering should contact:

Mountaineering Warden, Kluane National Park and Reserve, Box 5495, Haines Jct., Yukon,
Y0B 1L0, CANADA. Phone 867 634 7279; Fax 867 634 7277; e-mail Kluane_info@pch.gc.ca. For
a mountaineering application package, visit the Parks Canada web site: www.pc.gc.ca/kluane

KLUANE NATIONAL PARK AND RESERVE

South Walsh, first ascent; Mt. Walsh, Southeast Ridge; other ascents. On May 28 Graham
Rowbotham and I reached the pointed summit of South Walsh (4,223m). This was the highest
unclimbed peak in the St. Elias range and, as claimed in *AAJ 2006* (p.199), in North America.
Prior to our visit the complex south side of the Walsh massif seems to have been untouched*
apart from minor Peak 3,450m, climbed in 2005.

Mt. Walsh (W) and the previously unclimbed South Walsh (SW) from the southwest, showing all visible routes: (1) Mt. Walsh, West Face to Southwest Ridge (ridge reached from a bowl on the left-hand, or west, side, not visible in this image; Clarke-Sowinski, 1996). (2) South Walsh, Southwest Ridge (Knott-Rowbotham, 2006). (3) Mt. Walsh, Southeast Ridge (Knott-Rowbotham, 2006), obscured from view by the foreground skyline ridge except for where it climbs over Pt. 4,227m (also previously unclimbed), which pokes up just below the numeral 3. *Paul Knott*

Twelve days before, Andy Williams flew us in from frozen Kluane Lake to 2,855m on the upper Donjek Glacier. As Andy flew off, our attention was drawn to the striking cirque formed by Mt. Walsh and South Walsh. The generous plastering of fresh snow quickly convinced us to attempt South Walsh by its southwest ridge rather than one of the possible routes on the west face. On our first attempt we retreated from 3,900m due to wind. Our second, successful, attempt is described here.

After skirting the avalanche-prone entry slopes, we weaved around rotten rock and waded 'schrund-infested snow to a spacious campsite at 3,700m. Above, we traversed a sharp corniced arête, before being forced onto the south face to avoid rime-encrusted rock towers. On the face we relied on a thin covering of sugary snow over shattered quartz-veined limestone. There were no belays. In our search for a viable route we traversed into a series of couloirs, crossing buttresses where the snow allowed. Luckily it was cold enough that the snow did not deteriorate, even in the direct afternoon sun. We escaped by trenching up steep wind deposits to a ledge below a huge triangular ice cornice.

Buffeted by a gale on the summit of South Walsh, we descended to the plateau connecting the massif. Since there was no effective shelter from the relentless maelstrom, we dug in the tent but found ourselves compressed overnight by deposited snow. The next day we traversed the long ridge over Pt. 4,227m (also unclimbed) to the main summit of Mt. Walsh (4,507m), via its previously unclimbed southeast ridge. Below the final wind-scoured slopes we found a sheltered, sunny bivy-schrund in which we could revive the stove and our dehydrated bodies. From the summit we descended the West Ridge, the route taken on the 1941 first ascent (called the northwest ridge in *AAJ 1942*, p.348). In doing so we completed the first full tra-

Graham Rowbotham on day two, traversing into the couloir on the south face of South Walsh. *Paul Knott*

verse of the massif. After a more congenial night near the base of the ridge, we waded through a heavily crevassed bowl to reach the Walsh-Steele col. The postholing back to our stashed snowshoes was mild by St. Elias standards, as there was a wind crust on the glacier.

Earlier, on May 18, we had made the first ascent of Jekden South, a ca 3,745m summit west of our base camp, climbing via the shallow, snowy east rib. On our return flight to Kluane Lake, the controls were taken by Donjek Upton, son of Phil Upton, who flew climbers and scientists here from 1960-84. We found we had been lucky to complete our climb: the unsettled weather had disrupted the plans of practically every other party. We would like to acknowledge financial support from the British Mountaineering Council and UK Sport.

PAUL KNOTT, *New Zealand*

Knott adds: While researching the ascents of Mt. Walsh, I found the following route, which was not reported in the *AAJ*. *CAJ 1997* includes an account of a route climbed by Dan Clarke and Mark Sowinski on what they called the "South Face of Mt. Walsh" (pp. 34-37). Based on their description and annotated photo, the location of their route might be more precisely described as the southwest ridge of Mt. Walsh, reached at 3,800m via west-facing slopes. The route shares no ground with our traverse from South Walsh. Including ours, there are now four recorded routes to the main summit of Mt. Walsh (4,507m): West Ridge (1941), West Face to Southwest Ridge (1996), Northwest Ridge (1997), and Southeast Ridge (2006).

Eclipse Glacier area, various ascents. One of the Alpine Club of Canada's centennial activities was a ski mountaineering camp in the Icefield Ranges of the St. Elias Mountains, Yukon. The early June camp had 16 members, and we climbed 12 mountains surrounding the Eclipse Glacier and also made an ascent of Mt. Walsh. An interesting event was 12 hours of torrential rain at 2,840m (9,500') at our base camp. Rain in the St. Elias has become more common in recent years, and one needs to be prepared.

Four of the climbs were first ascents, and four were new routes. A "guidebook" (57 pages, 11" x 8", 36 colored photographs, and a colored 1:50,000 map) to the general Donjek area is available by contacting me (roger.wallis@sympatico.ca).

The party consisted of Bob Bolin (RB), Paul Geddes (PG), Jim Given (JG), Willa Harasym (WH), Klaus Haring (KH), Jan Ijsakkers (JI), Jessica Logher (JL), John Myles (JM), Peter Oxtoby (PO), John Rasch (JR), Uta Schuler (US), Helen Sovdat (HS), Tim Styles (TS), Bill Walker (WW), Ted Wood (EW), and I (RW).

First Ascents of Mountains:
(1) Pt. 3,340m (South Donjek Group); June 1, PO, TS, via southwest ridge
(2) Pt. 3,300m; June 6, HS, TS, PG, JI, JM, JR, US, WW, EW, via west face
(3) Pt. 3,460m; June 8, HS, TS, PG, JI, JM, JR, US, WW, EW, RB, WH, via south ridge
(4) Pt. 3,500m; June 8, party as above, via west ridge from Pt. 3460m

New Routes:
(1) Pt. 3,540m, 2nd ascent of mountain; June 6, HS, TS, PG, JI, JR, US, WW, EW, from Pt. 3300m via south face
(2) Eclipse Peak/Pt. 3,620m, 2nd ascent; June 9, HS, TS, JI, JR, WE, RB, up snow/ice ridge on east face to reach south ridge, which was followed to summit
(3) Donjek 4/Pt. 3,700m ("East Donjek Group"), 3rd ascent; June 12, TS, PG, JR, via the Eclipse Glacier/East Donjek Glacier col, then traverse below and around Donjek 3/Pt. 3,650m on its northwest side to reach the southwest slopes of Pt. 3,700m
(4) Island Peak/Pt. 3,420m, 4th(?) ascent; June 13, RW, JR, JG, via west face, descent southwest face

ROGER WALLIS, *Canada, ACC, AAC*

COAST MOUNTAINS

Coast Mountains, remote areas summary. Summer 2006 was warm and dry in the Coast Mountains, but fewer adventurous parties took advantage of the fine conditions than usual.

As always, the Waddington Range was the primary focus. In mid-May Simon Richardson and Don Serl spent a sunny week in and around Remote Glacier in the far northwestern corner of the range, where they got up a new seven-pitch easy mixed gully route on the east face of Remote Mtn. (3,038m).

In July Benoit Montfort and four other French climbers flew to the Waddington-Combatant col. They quickly established two new routes on Mt. Combatant (3,756m), one of which featured climbing to 5.11c. Details are not available.

Pat Callis and Dan Davis joined long-time "Coasties" Mickey Schurr and Peter Renz near the Isolation Peaks. Their chief innovation was the pleasant mid-5th class rock on the prominent West Ridge of Shiverick (2,625m).

Ade Miller and Simeon Warner had a productive visit to the Radiant Glacier in mid-August, including the first complete ascent of the Buszowski-Kippan route (1,250m, ED1 60°) to the summit of Serra 3 (3,642m). They bivied on the hanging glacier after 17 pitches the first day, then a second time at the Tellot rim after 13 pitches the second day. Their return to base camp via the Shand-McCormick col was much more complicated and technical than "guidebook conditions" suggested. They followed this with a new narrow couloir line on Mt. Shand (3,096m). The Madness of "King" George (250m, WI3) lies immediately left of the

Pegasus Peak: (1) Northwest Face (500m, 5.9/10 65°, Harng-Mason, 2006). (2) Southwest Face/West Buttress (Class 3, Firey-Knudson-Renz-Rose-deSaussure-Schurr, 1980). (3) South Ridge (FA route, Class 3-4, Culbert-Woodsworth, 1964). *Jesse Mason*

Shand-McCormick col. Finally, they completed the previously tried 200m southwest ridge on Unicorn Mtn. (2,909m), which required a tension traverse to bypass a blank slab and a shoulder stand to overcome a short overhanging offwidth.

Tom Gray, Seth Hobby, and Ian Wolfe climbed a new line on the south face of Tellot Spire Number One between the Central Dihedral and the indicated line of the Fabische-Waters. A left-facing dihedral to half-height led to a beautiful right-facing corner/ramp, then a chimney broke them out onto the southeast face about two-thirds of the way to the summit. There were two short aid sections; the route was graded D 5.9 A1.

The only other innovation in the Waddington Range this summer took place during a NOLS outing. Chris Agnew, Ben Lester, Ben Liebenskind, and Gaelen Kelly climbed the longest buttress in the center of the west face of the previously virgin southernmost Arabesque Peak (ca 3,030m). They encountered five short pitches to about 5.6, with good rock in the first half and easier, looser terrain above (One Boot Route, PD).

Elsewhere in the Coast Mountains, the unusual hot spot for activity proved to be the seldom-visited west side of Chilko Lake, 80km southeast of Waddington. A DAV party traveled all the way from Dresden to climb the namesake Mt. Dresden (2,656m) in celebration of the 800th anniversary of their city's founding. They made first ascents of a couple of other summits in the area and proposed names to "round out" commemoration of all the ships involved in the 1914 Battle of Coronel off the coast of Chile. They also climbed the standard route up the highest peak in the region, Mt. Good Hope (3,242m).

Fourteen-year-old Brandon Schupp also climbed Good Hope as part of his self-inaugurated campaign to raise money to combat childhood cancer. About $100,000 was raised; good going, Brandon!

Robert Nugent, Graham Rowbotham, and Don Serl base-camped at Glasgow Lakes (1,708m), northeast of Good Hope. Their climbs included an easy new line on Kese (3,059m) via the scree and snow of the west face to the upper north ridge. They completed it with a long traverse across the upper west face, to avoid towers high on the ridge. After a move by boat to Farrow Creek, Nugent and Rowbotham succeeded on the impressive Mt. Merriam (3,099m) by its east ridge, still the only route on this great peak. This was perhaps only the third ascent, and the bushiness of the approaches has undoubtedly increased considerably since Malcolm Goddard and Kese made the first ascent as a formidable 16-hour day trip from Chilko Lake (1,175m) in 1911.

Chris Barner and Paul Rydeen returned to their favorite stomping grounds, the Klattasine and Mantle areas 40km southeast of Waddington. During their outings they found a fine new route on the north ridge of a twin-summited peak of just under 2,400m high at the head of the valley (Peak 2,328m(?), 7 pitches, 5.7-5.8).

Steve Harng, Jesse Mason, and Jordan Peters spent a productive week and a half in August in the Pantheon Range, 25km north of Waddington, establishing three new lines. After a short route on the southeast face of the Cyclops, Harng and Mason climbed the middle buttress on the east face of Fenris (2,859m, 250m, 8 pitches, AD low-5th) and then the outstanding route of the trip, and one of the Coast Mountains' summer highlights, the steep northwest face of Pegasus Peak (2,805m). The pair followed a compact rock ramp for 10 pitches, then a chimney, to gain a snowy exit gully (500m, 13 pitches, TD? 5.9/10 65°, 13 hours). On the descent of the south face, they bivied, regaining camp the following afternoon.

DON SERL, *Canada, ACC, AAC*

Southwest British Columbia (southern Coast Mountains and Canadian Cascades). 2006 was a relatively slow year in southwest British Columbia, with few new routes to report compared to previous years. In part this reflects the ending of the spurt of interest shown after the publication of the *Alpine Select* guidebook in 2001. A renewed interest in destinations farther afield, whether the Waddington Range, South America, or the Karakoram, has also reduced the number of local climbers putting up routes in the local mountains.

In April, shortly after the end of calendar winter, Tyler Linn and Nick Elson skied into Wedgemount Lake in Garibaldi Park and dispatched a prominent couloir on the north side of Lesser Wedge Mountain, which gave six pitches of climbing (III WI3 M4). This may have been the only new alpine route of the spring.

The summer saw several high-standard lines climbed and one very notable repeat. In the Anderson River Range, Craig McGee was active on Les Cornes. First, with Colin Moorhead, he climbed a direct start to the classic Barley-Cheesemond-Lacey-Lomax Springbok Arête (IV 5.10c) that avoids the rotten lower ramp pitches of that route. The new direct climb gives six full-length pitches of steep, solid climbing before continuing up the crux upper pitches of the original route, for a good IV 5.11. Craig later returned with Brad White and Jason Kruk to climb a route up the east face, between Springbok and the Lumberjack Wall. A 13-pitch 5.11 was the result, which the climbers, in the Darryl Hatten tradition, named Sprung Cocks Erect. SCE crosses the Springbok ramp low, then climbs straight up. Meanwhile, on the adjacent Steinbok Peak, Sonnie Trotter, Jon Walsh, and Will Stanhope made the first known repeat of the Edwards-Spagnut (V, sandbag 5.10+, 1 point of aid) in the same style as the original ascent, using one rest point. Sonnie was also in the news for his successful free ascent of Cobra Crack on Squamish, a "last great problem" and contender for "World's Hardest Trad Route"; it goes at 5.14-something, depending on one's finger size.

In the Chilliwack Valley area, Shaun Neufeld and Drew Brayshaw climbed a steep pillar on the south side of the false summit of Mount Rexford on their second attempt, to give a six-pitch grade III 5.11+. The second pitch crux, a 30m long, immaculate finger crack, is probably the standout on this route. In the adjacent Cheam Range, a party of four from Chilliwack (Lorne, Allan, and Vivian Bleakney, with Dan Sluess) ventured onto the north face of Mt. Cheam in August, to climb a new route, the prominent northwest ridge. Cheam's north face, which rises over 2,000m above the Fraser River, is a mixture of steep West Coast jungle and loose metamorphic rubble that is somewhat repulsive in summer but attractive under winter conditions. The climb was completed in one long day, at a low technical standard but a high commitment level (AD IV low-5th class); a winter ascent remains as a challenge.

Only one new route was reported from the fall, as dry conditions resulted in temporary travel bans on some logging roads, limiting backcountry access. In mid-September Jesse Mason and Drew Brayshaw established a fine route on Old Settler's southwest face, between the established routes Contact Zone and Duck a l'Orange. The new climb begins up the latter route, before moving right partway up the first pitch to gain a slender buttress. Black September goes at IV 5.10- and was named on the night descent, as Jesse had forgotten his headlamp.

DREW BRAYSHAW, *Canada, AAC*

Isolation Peak 1, first ascent; Mt. Shiverick, West Ridge. Mike King flew Pat Callis, Dan Davis, Mickey Schurr, and me into a camp between Isolation Peak 7 and Peak 2,488m on the Isolation-Malamute Glacier Divide on July 23. We climbed these peaks that afternoon. There were no signs of visitors since Glen Cannon and I climbed them in July 1998. Then we approached

Mt. Shiverick from the northwest, with the Shiverick Glacier in the foreground. The 1947 first ascent (Putnam-Shiverick) climbed the north ridge (left skyline). The 2006 team (Callis-Davis-Renz-Schurr) climbed the west ridge (right skyline), likely the second ascent of the mountain. *Peter Renz*

from the Sunrise Glacier, the same camp Steve Harng, Jordan Peters, and Ben Stanton used in 2005 to climb the South Buttress on Isolation Peak 2 (*AAJ 2006*, p. 207).

On the 24th we made the first ascent of Isolation Peak 1 via snow slopes, then scrambling, from the north. We dropped south, circling Isolation Peaks 1 through 7 back to camp. On the 25th Mickey and I climbed the south ridge of "Map Sepia" of Don Serl's *Waddington Guide*. This bump is a topographic control point, with remnants of a ranging mast, probably brought in by helicopter, near its summit. The peak named Sepia by Jim Bullard, Sterling Hendricks, Don Hubbard, Ken Karcher, and Jane Showacre in 1953 is Isolation Peak 6, not the Sepia Mountain of the map. The photographs of the 2005 and 2006 parties let Serl nail down the numbering of these peaks for future editions of his guidebook.

On the 26th we climbed Mt. Shiverick (2,625m) by its west ridge (right-hand ridge in the photo; moderate fifth class and a new route). Bill Putnam and Charlie Shiverick made the first ascent of Shiverick on July 17, 1947 by the north (left-hand) ridge. They were in their early 20s; we are in our late 60s. Ours was probably the second ascent. Serl's *Guide* suggested that the south side of Shiverick might offer a nice route. Snow gullies beckoned, and we descended them to the Malamute Glacier, then plodded up to camp. It was kicking steps down, rather than the glissading we had hoped for, but scenic. Shiverick is hardly a big climb, but it's a rather nice area for recreational climbing, and the fact that it can be done by geezers might inspire those who are not supermen.

Rest days, a climb of McCowan, and a ramble along the Isolation Peaks ridge rounded out the trip, until July 30. This is an area with ideal camping, routes at many levels, and unrealized possibilities. We recommend it highly.

PETER RENZ, *AAC*

PURCELL MOUNTAINS

BUGABOOS

Bugaboos, various ascents. On Eastpost Spire in August, Aleksey Shuruyev, Elizabeth Whitcher (age 17), Sam Adelman (age 17), and Andrew Freeman put up two new routes that, combined, would make a logical seven-pitch outing up the center of the south face. The lower route, Gabriel's Face, climbs two pitches (5.8 and 5.10) on the lower wall (where some other two pitch routes exist on the left side) and ends at a big walk-down ledge. Their second route, Afternoon Delight, begins on the ledge, slightly down from the end of Gabriel's Face and 15' left of a prominent left-facing dihedral. Afternoon Delight's five pitches go at 5.7, 5.8, 5.8, 5.9, and 5.7.

After the above climbs Shuruyev and Whitcher tried a new line on the east face of Snowpatch Spire, between the regular and Beckey-Mather routes, but retreated after eight pitches (up to 5.10). They were two or three easy pitches from the summit when Shuruyev broke a hold and fell 30', resulting in a broken ankle, a forced bivy, and a helicopter rescue.

To rehab his dislocated hip, Janez Ales underwent an impressive physical therapy regiment, soloing eight routes, including Sunshine (Snowpatch Spire), the Beckey-Chouinard (South Howser Tower), and All Along the Watchtower (North Howser Tower). In accordance with the preventive mindset of rehab, Ales self-belayed all non-scrambling sections.

North Howser Tower continues to receive considerable attention, and from September 7-8 on the 1,000m west face Ulysse Richard and Manuel Quiroga freed Seventh Rifle, at 5.11b. The pair reportedly encountered much loose rock and wet/icy chimneys. This was initially thought to be the FFA, but it appears that Mike Tschipper and Ward Robinson freed it in ca 1986, thinking it to be around 5.10c.

Dave Russel and Chris Harkness climbed North Howser's west face over eight days in July, enduring a blizzard, rockfall, being hit by lightning, and running out of food, while thinking they were on a new route. However, Harkness reports, "after further study [including talking with Hugh Burton], I feel like we may have mostly repeated The Warrior (34 pitches, VI 5.9 A3, Burton-Sutton, 1973). After gaining the large snowy bivy ledge, we followed a crack system to the right of the main dihedral. We climbed up, then right across a ramp, and then straight up 500' of 5.9/A3 crack systems and flakes, before connecting with the dihedral."

Of note to future parties, the pair established a rap route down their ascent line, with the first rappel being two bolts on the far left side of the ridge, just before it cliffs out. Some raps, especially the eighth, are over 60m.

Also on the west face of North Howser, Bean Bowers and the indefatigable Dave Nettle not only blitzed All Along the Watchtower (34 pitches, VI 5.10 A2 or 5.12-) in 11 hours, but Bowers freed all of the climb (on lead, follow, or solo on easy sections). This is likely the first time the route has been freed in a day.

On South Howser and the Minaret a couple of days later, Bowers, Nettle, and Chris Swetland did a new free linkup that they called Bad Italian Hair. Beginning with Bad Hair Day (V 5.12-) via a new 5.10 start, they then joined the Italian Pillar (V 5.11+) and continued to near the top of South Howser from where, on easy terrain, they descended in high winds.

South Howser Tower, Serge Overkill. In mid-August, Steve Su and I tried to make the most of a week off of work and a 10-day spell of perfect weather. After ticking off a couple of Bugaboo classics, we hiked over from the Applebee Campground to scope out a new line near The Seventh Rifle on North Howser Tower. Nothing caught our eye, so we backtracked to the South

South Howser Tower, showing: (1) Serge Overkill (Menitove-Su, 2006). (2) Catalonian Route (Burgada-Cabau-Masana-Wenciesko, 1983). (3) Soul Cinders (Martino-Ozturk, 2003). Where (1) and (2) join, (2) might be slightly left for two pitches. The classic Beckey-Chouinard (1961) roughly climbs just beyond the left skyline, and The Minaret is the detached tower on the right. This foreshortened view hides some low-angle terrain near the top of the tower. *Steve Su*

Tower and found a line near the Catalonian Route. (Note: if approaching the west side of North Howser from Applebee Campground, one can shave 2-3 hours by going through East Creek and rapping down from the south.) By the time we got started, it was 2:00 p.m. We were equipped to spend the night on the wall, so we plodded upward undeterred by the prospect of sharing a sleeping bag on a pizza-box-sized ledge, which is what happened.

The route followed a 5th-class ramp system, which we soloed, into a gully where Soul Cinders continues up. Before getting committed to the gully, we cut left onto a wall with incipient thin cracks (5.11a) and continued up, probably sharing some of the Catalonian Route (we weren't certain of its exact location in this section). We then followed a continuous crack system that led to a large ledge shared by the Catalonian Route. From the ledges we followed the leftmost crack system, which was 50' left of the Catalonian Route. Most of the climb follows hand-and-finger cracks (5.9-5.10+). The upper portion has good rock, but the rock on the lower portion is mediocre. Along the way we found very old rap slings. Marc Piché (author of *Bugaboo Rock*) seemed to think that these were from someone retreating off Lost in the Towers. Although we bivied once on Serge Overkill (V 5.11-), it would not have been necessary had we started at a reasonable hour. A competent party could climb this route in one day.

ARI MENITOVE

The Minaret, Reinhold Pussycat; Flattop Peak, Sibling Rivalry. On July 28 Bruce Miller and I completed the first ascent of the west face of The Minaret in 18 hours round trip from the East Creek Basin. Reinhold Pussycat (V 5.10+ A2) follows a natural crack system from bottom to top, including a prominent right-facing dihedral, offering 600m of steep and mostly solid granite. This beautiful and obvious line had been attempted several times over the last 20 years but never finished.

Chris Weidner on Reinhold Pussycat. *Bruce Miller*

On August 2, in marginal weather, Bruce and I made the first ascent of the southwest ridge of Flattop Peak. We gained the col between Flattop and Crossed Fish Peak via 55° ice and snow, then followed the ridge, usually staying to the right, over two unnamed, unclimbed summits to the top. We encountered mostly low 5th class climbing, with a couple of pitches of steep 5.8 below the summit of Flattop. We highly recommend this alpine ridge, which can easily be done with mountain boots and a light rack in a short day from a camp in East Creek. We dubbed the route Sibling Rivalry (III 5.8), naming the lower subsummit "Uli Tooth" and the higher "Satchel Spire."

CHRIS WEIDNER, AAC

Bugaboo Spire, Divine Intervention; Snowpatch Spire, Bugaburl; Pigeon Spire, FFA of Cleopatra's Alley. On August 1 I joined Chris Brazeau for a trip to the Bugaboos. Our first objective was an incomplete aid line to the right of the Midnight Route, in the obvious corner system between that route and the Harvey-Roach on the east face of Bugaboo Spire. Stepping onto the face at noon, Chris quickly established us on the terrace below the impressive stepped corner system. The first corner proved to be an amazing pitch with sustained stemming and laybacking enlivened with several roof cruxes. Chris rocked up with his gap-tooth grin, utterly stoked, then I encouraged him to follow the line of weakness which just dragged us toward the Harvey-Roach. Chris reversed a few moves and cranked out an intimidating undercling, getting us back on the plumb line. A few joyful whoops escaped Chris's usually reticent lips as he discovered a perfect golden finger splitter that led to a comfy belay perch.

The next pitch proved key to the route, and from the belay things didn't look promising. It was getting late, 5:00 p.m., so I tentatively started up, figuring I would just be checking it out for our next attempt. I worked through a section of incipient seams by welding a couple of blades, which we left in place for future ascents. Regaining the main corner, we started to question our crack-of-noon strategy, but with several cruxes below us, it would be a shame to retreat now. The rest of the climb went quickly, with sustained 5.10 leading to a high point on the Northeast Ridge route. We took a minute to shake hands, give a bro hug, and languish in the endorphin shower that comes from such an intense experience. We couldn't believe that we'd left camp at 11:30 and somehow established a 300m+ 5.11 classic with no falls or A0 bullshit. A close call on the descent involved me and a large block that barely missed shearing Chris off the wall. This inspired the route's name, Divine Intervention. Its excellent sustained climbing, close proximity to camp, and sunny exposure will hopefully make it a popular classic. We experienced no loose rock or the legendary stonefall that has tarnished the east face's reputation, probably because we weren't directly below the famed Northeast Ridge with its climber-induced hazards.

The next day we woke late and had a leisurely breakfast. I was a little sore from the tumble, but my psyche wasn't the slightest bit sore, and Chris is perpetually psyched. So after our second cup, we racked up with the intent of a new line on the west face of Snowpatch: the screamingly obvious corner system between the North Summit Direct and the Tower Arête. Our late start put us at the base of the wall just before noon. After a couple of surprisingly tricky pitches on the visionary Gibson-Rohn line we veered off. Above was an unappealing, wet, 5.9ish chimney sort of thing, to the left an intimidating right-leaning corner reminiscent of Astroman's fabled Enduro Corner. The rock climber I truly am won out over the alpinist I'm truly not, so up the corner I went. The overhanging, leaning nature of the corner, coupled with body-pumping technicalities, made me oblivious to the fact that it had started snowing. I set up a hanging belay sheltered from the storm and cunningly short of a mean-looking offwidth. It was obvious that we had to go down, as the storm was full-on, the Howsers had vanished, and everything was soaked. But rapping and cleaning the pitch looked more involved than Chris seconding. By the time Chris was halfway it had stopped snowing, and by the time he reached the anchor it was sunny and the rock had dried. No reason to bail now. After three more big 5.11 pitches, Chris pulled onto the summit ridge in the last scrap of twilight, leaving me to clean by headlamp. As we traversed the ridge under the stars, looking down the east face, the lights of camp seemed far away. Our methodical descent saw us sipping Scotch in camp at 2 a.m. We dubbed the route Bugaburl (6 big pitches, 5.11d) due to the burly Yosemite-style crack climbing.

Determined to get an alpine start, we actually walked out of camp around 5 a.m. Our inadequate footwear made for an exciting steep snow slope leading to the base of the 12-pitch route Cleopatra's Alley on the east face of Pigeon. The lower portion of the face had some of the best moderate rock climbing we have ever experienced, zigzagging finger and hand cracks on perfect white granite. The headwall finally stopped our dreamy simul-climb, and Chris confidently eliminated the pendulum of the first aid section with some committing face moves. The next aid pitch was mine, and after some aiding and gardening, I pulled the rope and barely squeaked-out the redpoint of this amazing tips splitter. The remaining four pitches were excellent, and the 60m "alley pitch" seemed particularly undergraded at 5.10. I belayed Chris up the final knife-edge to Pigeon's summit, completing the FFA (5.12a). The warm evening sun, benevolent high winds, and classic position made this perhaps the defining sublime moment of my climbing career. Chris was also stoked. Descending the west ridge gave us the bonus of an east-to-west traverse of the peak. A perfect day.

The rest of our trip was less successful but included a valiant attempt at freeing the west face of Central Howser, a four-day "rest day" in Golden, the good company of a couple of ex-Lake Louise millwright skids, and an official noise complaint filed against us and our offensive music. For me this trip was a dream come true.

COLIN MOORHEAD, *Canada*

CANADIAN ROCKIES

Summary. [Note: In addition to mention in this summary, several of the bigger routes have individual reports, below—Ed.] Following a string of hot, dry summers, routes that were once climbable year-round in the Canadian Rockies have been increasingly reduced to unattractive and frequently dangerous chutes of dry slabs and rubble. The upside is that, perhaps as a consequence of milder winters, seasonal ice occasionally forms and resuscitates them. While many of what used to be classic summer alpine adventures can no longer be recommended in that season, they can still offer excellent climbing, but now in winter and spring.

In May, having found surprisingly excellent ice conditions on Shooting Gallery and the Andromeda Strain in the weeks prior, Scott Semple and Raphael Slawinski climbed a new route on the northeast face of Mt. Andromeda. The Doctor, The Tourist, His Crampon, and Their Banana (V M7) follows a faint crease some 100m left of the Andromeda Strain, but with significantly more difficult and sustained climbing than that route.

In the summer Chris Brazeau soloed the well iced-up Grand Central Couloir (V WI5). Over the years the GCC had seen a number of solo ascents, but Brazeau upped the ante by climbing the route without rope or harness. Later the same month he soloed the rock buttress of the Greenwood-Jones (V 5.9) on the north face of Mt. Temple in the same style. Risky? Perhaps, but climbing does not get much purer.

In early September Brazeau teamed with Jon Walsh to provide the highlight of the season, when the two, on their first try, created a new route (VI 5.11 M6) on the north face of Mt. Alberta. To put their achievement in perspective, until last summer the 1972 Lowe-Glidden route was the only route on the north face, and it has likely not been repeated in the past 15 years.

Another George Lowe route, the Lowe-Hannibal (VI 5.11a) on the north face of Mt. Geikie, saw two ascents the past summer, making it a trade route by Canadian Rockies standards. The first of these ascents, by Steve Holeczi and Mike Verwey, was all the more noteworthy as both climbers free-climbed the route. A 2001 ascent by Eric Dumerac, Jeff Nazarchuk, and Slawinski had freed all but two points of aid on the route at 5.11a. But that team climbed with only the leader free-climbing and the two seconds jumaring. Holeczi and Verwey, in addition to removing the remaining aid on the route, considerably improved the style of ascent, climbing on a big north face the way one would on the local crag of Mt. Yamnuska.

For whatever reason (perhaps the abundance of roadside ice?) the alpine winter of 2006-07 was rather quiet. The only climb of note was the first winter ascent of the classic Humble Horse (IV WI4 5.7) on the north face of Mt. Diadem. In late February 2007 Greg Tkaczuk and Eamonn Walsh climbed and rappelled the route in very cold conditions from a bivouac at the base. The ice on this once-popular route had largely disappeared in the late 1990s, leading to speculation that the climb was gone for good. Tkaczuk and Walsh's ascent showed that the route may still be enjoyed as an alpine ice climb, though perhaps no longer in summer and fall.

As mentioned above, the 2006-07 ice season was an exceptional one. The famous venues of the Terminator and Stanley headwalls were lean, but areas like the Ghost and Waiparous valleys in the front ranges, and Mt. Wilson on the Icefields Parkway more than made up for it. Some beautiful ephemeral lines appeared in unusual places, a couple of which were even climbed. On Mt. Wilson, Verwey took advantage of the exceptional conditions and boldly soloed Malice in Wonderland (500m, M5+ WI5+), a linkup of the classic Ice Nine and the obscure Eh Spring Chicken Named Logan, with original variations along the way. At the southern end of the range, in rarely visited Waterton National Park, Slawinski and Walsh filled in a few blanks with remote first ascents. Probably the best of these was Walk the Line (500m, WI4+) on the north face of Mt. Lineham, climbed in tandem with Kelly Cordes and Scott DeCapio. This beautiful, quiet area holds potential for new ice and mini-alpine routes, especially if one is willing to venture into the backcountry.

Last but definitely not least, Will Gadd finished a long-standing project on the south face of Mt. Yamnuska. Yamabushi (ca 300m, 5.13a) is the hardest multi-pitch rock route yet done in the Canadian Rockies. Gadd started bolting it eight years ago, primarily bottom-up but with some pitches established top-down. Progress was slow until this past fall when, assisted by a variety of partners, Gadd finished bolting and cleaning the spectacularly steep line. Taking advantage of sunny October weather, he then worked the moves, until finally linking all eight pitches without falling, in a continuous push.

RAPHAEL SLAWINSKI, *Alberta, AAC*

Mt. Alberta, Brazeau-Walsh. On September 6 Jon Walsh and I forded the frigid waters of the Sunwapta River with a bit of food, lots of fancy-wrapped processed sugar/caffeine products, and high hopes for good conditions on the remote and seldom visited north face of Mt. Alberta.

After a few hours of fitful sleep in Lloyd Mackay hut, we woke at midnight to brew coffee and oats. A full moon greeted us as we made our way to the rappels to the base of the face. However, the moon snuck behind the bulk of the mountain and, despite Jonny Red having rapped to the base before (and sketching out the same way due to poor conditions), we missed the rappel line, lightened our already skimpy rack, and increased our doubts. What are we doing here? Why can't we just sport climb in the sun? Or drink coffee in the sun, for that matter?

Mt. Alberta's coveted nordwand: (1) Swigert-Tenney, 1985. (2) Lowe-Glidden, 1972. (3) Brazeau-Walsh, 2006. (4) Blanchard-Elzinga, 1990 (arises from other side, out of view, to gain the northwest ridge). *Jon Walsh*

But with dawn comes fresh thoughts and psyche, as we get our first look at the face, which appears to be in perfect shape. There's a weakness to the right of the Lowe-Glidden 1972 route (nice work boys!) that jumps out at us, and we have no need to discuss it. What a magnificent day! Not a cloud in the sky, a pristine mountain environment, glaciers rolling down to valley bottom, seldom-seen and even less-visited alpine meadows and lakes, and not another soul for days. It feels so good to be here it's a little disconcerting.

I take a load off on the glacier as JR charges on, thinking (rightly, it turns out) that we won't be sitting down for a while. By the time I catch up he's racked and 15' off the deck, trailing a rope. Fired up! We simul the first few pitches to the big icefield, then put the ropes away and … what luck! The ice is perfect for one-swing sticks, and we move quickly to the base

Chris Brazeau on the headwall, onsighting the 5.11 crux. *Jon Walsh*

of the headwall. We rope up again and are engaged, swapping leads and finding perfect conditions: a fine balance of iced-up cracks and good pick placements, warm enough for hands-on rock climbing but cold enough to keep the ice from delamming. What luck! How many factors had to come together to make for these conditions, and for us to be here at this moment? These thoughts roll around in my mind, tumbling with my doubts and fears as we slowly move upward. I don our one pair of rock shoes for a couple of pitches. Jon follows in his boots

Chris Brazeau following the second pitch of the headwall on the Brazeau-Walsh. *Jon Walsh*

and crampons; the aiders and ascenders stay in the pack. What luck! We top out on the summit icefield in the last rays of the day, only a few easy ice pitches to go. The fears and doubts ebb but leave that exhilarating buzz that will linger for days. Hugs on top, followed by some chocolate and a green tea brew. Jon finally gets to sit down after 21 hours on the go. The hazy sky dims the full moon, but the views of the Columbia Icefields are incredible and inspire talk of future adventures. All we have to do now is get down one UGLY chossy descent, and watch the breaking of another new day as we stumble back to the hut 30 hours after leaving it. How lucky we felt that everything came together and we were able to journey to the mountain, and on. Brazeau-Walsh (1,000m, 5.11 M6).

CHRIS BRAZEAU, *Canada*

Mt. Andromeda, DTCB. Mt. Andromeda graces countless postcards and coffee-table books, and, more to the point, is the climbing centerpiece of the Columbia Icefields. Andromeda is a university of alpine climbing. Over the years, as I worked my way through its routes, starting with the sweeping Skyladder through the "hard" classic Andromeda Strain, the mountain has taught me well, though at times (such when I whipped off of slush that passed for ice on Shooting Gallery) it could be a stern professor.

Having climbed most of the established routes more than once, I began looking beyond the red lines in the guidebook. If you squint at the photo in *Selected Alpine Climbs*, a possibility,

From left to right: DTCB (Semple-Slawinski, 2006), Andromeda Strain (Blanchard-Cheesmond-Friesen, 1983; direct variation Glovach-McKay, 1989), M31 (Babanov-Slawinski, 2005). *Raphael Slawinski*

Scott Semple, still with two crampons, on the first pitch of DTCB.
Raphael Slawinski

the faint crease of a corner system, can be imagined left of the A-Strain. In spring, with the mountain well iced up, this unlikely line seemed ripe for an attempt.

Scott Semple and I got an inauspicious start, having overslept the alarm and woken with dawn illuminating the sky. But we had nothing better to do, so we wolfed down bananas and Danishes, piled into the car, and drove the remaining half-hour to the trailhead. The morning was disconcertingly warm, the snow on the moraines barely frozen. As the sun rose Andromeda's northeast face came alive with noisy wet sloughs, fortunately well right of our intended line. We simul-climbed the lower portion, past the avalanche cone, up brittle ice and to the base of the rock.

Dr. Slawinski wishing for a banana and a Danish on the crux of DTCB. *Scott Semple*

At first a chossy crack had me looking for a way to traverse around the difficulty, but straight up was the way to go. Stuffing in cams, hooking loose chockstones, and grunting to make sure I had Scott's attention at the belay—it was steep, dammit!—I was pleased to find a hidden runnel of thick ice lurking above. The first pitch set the pattern for the rest of the route: the stream of more (or less) thick ice down the corner system would be interrupted once or twice every pitch by steep dry-tooling. Our magic line kept going, twisting and turning and blocked by overhangs, so we could never see farther than half a pitch ahead.

As afternoon wore on, we secretly hoped for moderate ground. Instead, we found ourselves below yet another corner, with a dripping, slabby rock wall. But a delicate front-point shuffle, made more interesting for Scott by a broken crampon, opened the door, and soon we stood lashed to a small rock outcrop, looking up in dismay at a massively overhanging cornice. It seemed to grow the closer we got to it, assuming monstrous proportions. It took us over a ropelength of crawling beneath the cresting wave of snow before we were able to escape from the face. The gentle south slopes were already in shadow, though Bryce, Forbes, the Lyells, and a hundred other white peaks still glowed in the setting sun. We snapped a few photos, took a deep breath, and headed down. The Doctor, The Tourist, His Crampon, and Their Banana (700m, V M7).

RAPHAEL SLAWINSKI, *Alberta, AAC*

NEWFOUNDLAND

Blow-Me-Down Wall, Lucifer's Lighthouse. Towering nearly 1,300' above Devil's Bay on the south coast of Newfoundland, the solid white granite of Blow-Me-Down offers some of the best sea cliff climbing in North America. Accessible only by boat, the bottom half of the wall is just shy of vertical while the top half steepens considerably and is capped by three intimidating roofs that guard the summit. Justen Sjong and I lived at the base of the cliff for three weeks in September, the first 10 days of which we shared with friend and photographer Celin Serbo.

Lucifer's Lighthouse on the main Blow-Me-Down Wall. Some half-dozen additional routes climb to the top of this wall. *Chris Weidner*

Justen Sjong on the 5.11c 7th pitch of Lucifer's Lighthouse. *Celin Serbo*

We adopted a top-down approach to routefinding, since this would be the most efficient way to establish a high-quality full-length free route. On our first day, we hiked 45 minutes from our camp to the summit and rapped through fog and rain over the roofs, deciphering a free passage. Sunshine prevailed for the next two days, as we repeated the process, top-roping difficult sections where possible.

On September 13 clear skies abruptly segued into one of the most powerful storms the south coast has seen in the last half-century: Hurricane Florence. Fortunately the three of us, along with a young duo from Maine, were rescued from our primitive campsite by Kim and Charles Courtney, the friendly couple who had ferried us to the cliff three days earlier. We settled into their dilapidated cabin for two nights in nearby Rencontre West, an abandoned fishing village, while the hurricane raged. Just a few miles to the west a house was ripped off its foundation, broken in two, and blown into the sea.

Florence dissipated as quickly as she arrived, and we returned to Blow-Me-Down on calm waters, under sunny skies. We took advantage of each daylight hour with renewed urgency, by spending as much time as possible on the wall. We placed a dozen bolts and pins for lead protection and another dozen at anchors before redpointing individual pitches.

Celin began his journey home as four grueling days of non-stop rain plagued the coast, leaving Justen and I to fester in our sodden tents. On the first cloudless day we were like pent-up dogs, squirming to climb. We allowed our route to dry for a few hours, then acquiesced to our impatience and gave it a redpoint attempt starting at 1:30 p.m. We climbed nine of the route's 12 pitches before an arctic wind and total darkness stopped us cold three pitches from the top.

The following day was forecast to be the driest of the next five, and our time was running out. Weary but determined to finish our project, we began at 10:30 a.m. in sunny, windy conditions. Each pitch felt more difficult than the day before, but we managed a no-falls ascent in nine hours, topping out at dusk, just as lighthouses were becoming visible on the horizon, reminding us that we were not alone. Lucifer's Lighthouse (V 5.12c) is the most difficult free climb on Blow-Me-Down, offering everything from hard crack and face pitches to overhanging corners and arêtes. Our final day in Devil's Bay dawned clear and warm, but after breakfast we could only muster enough energy to collapse onto the granite floor of our cooking area and relax.

CHRIS WEIDNER, *AAC*

Terry Winkler on the summit of Pt. 1,528m, a sub-peak of Pt. 1,547m. *Greg Horne*

CANADIAN ARCTIC

Bylot Island, ski traverse and ascents. Starting April 13 and finishing May 9, Louise Jarry, Terry Winkler, and I made an unsupported crossing of Bylot Island, 237kms, with ascents in the Byam Martin Mountains of Sirmilik National Park. The original plan had been to begin at the northwest tip of the island. After a day and a bit of travel by snowmobile using Pond Inlet out-fitter Polar Sea Adventures, we turned back short of our intended drop-off point due to rough sea ice, poor visibility, wind chill, and concern about polar bear encounters. Instead we began from Tay Bay on the west coast of Bylot. This was the starting point of a summer traverse by Kelly, Lamont, et al. in 1977 (see *AAJ 1978*).

We ascended Inussualuk Glacier to its head and crossed a 1,270 m pass, the first of 19 we would eventually cross. Although clear, temperatures of -20°C plus considerable wind chill made it prudent to take a couple of layover days early in the trip. Once over the first pass, on average we traversed one or two passes per day as we traveled southeast. On April 21 we ascended our first peak, Pt. 1,506m, a fine glaciated pyramid just north of Pass #7. In the after-noon and evening of April 23 we ascended Angilaaq Mountain (1,944m), the highest peak of Bylot, via its southwest spur and south ridge, enjoying clear views to both the north and south coasts of the island.

We camped April 26 near the pass that Bill Tilman probably used during his 1963 north-to-south foot crossing of the island. An enjoyable descent down the middle portion of the Ser-milik Glacier led to an ascent of Pass #13 and travel down glacier E-67 (Glacier Inventory Area 46201). We also climbed Pt. 1,718m by its south ridge. Next we crossed the steepest and most avalanche-prone pass (#14) of the trip, a divide between glaciers E-67 and A-41, in whiteout conditions. From May 1 to 8, as we traveled east over glaciated terrain, we ascended seven more peaks: Unnamed 1,547m (NW and W ridges), Unnamed 1,537m (SE and E ridges), Pt. 1,321m (GPS 1,350m, W ridge), Mt. Qitdlarssuaq (1,180m, N slopes), Pt. 1,085m (GPS 1,090m, NNE ridge), Pt. 901m (SW ridge), Mt. St. Hans (808m, N slopes). Five of these were probably first ascents. From Button Point an evening snowmobile ride returned us to Pond Inlet.

GREG HORNE, *Canada, ACC*

Greenland

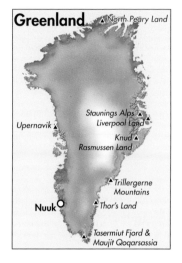

Milne Land, circumnavigation; Hergenlitop, Sleeping Giant.
During August Dan Jones, Ben Lawes, and I circumnavigated Milne Land and explored this part of Scoresby Sund, the largest fjord system in the world. At N 71° the fjord is covered with ice for much of the year, and due to the remoteness and difficult, expensive access, little climbing has been done.

We flew to Constable Point and collected our previously shipped kayaks from Ittoqqortoormiit, close to the settlement of Scoresby Sund. The supply boat reaches this area only once a year, if it can penetrate the ice. We chartered a boat for about £850 and after a five-hour journey were dropped off at the southeast corner of Milne Land. Campsites on this side of the island are sparse and small.

Wonderful unclimbed granite on the north coast of Milne Land, Scoresby Sund. *Olly Sanders*

We set off west with about 24 days food, fuel, the normal camping kit, and climbing gear. It was tight in the boat. The island is ca 300km in circumference, and we would have to paddle back to Scoresby Sund. Our trip was unsupported, and we had no means of outside contact bar the EPIRB, which at best is hit and miss. The weather was excellent after the first three days and toward the end, when it got cold and the fjord began to fill with ice. Paddling conditions were generally good, with only a couple of windy days and a fair bit of ice off the western shore.

As we paddled around the western end of the island we spotted a peak called Hergenlitop, which had a steep south face and fairly easy access from the sea. We picked a line up the center of the face and climbed it in seven 55m pitches of difficult rock, followed by four pitches of easier terrain to the summit. The rock was good most of the way, our main problem being harassment by peregrines. We named the climb Sleeping Giant (300m, British XS) and climbed many excellent pitches of British 5a/5b. There is room for harder lines. As we continued along the north coast we saw fantastic granite peaks soaring above the sea and holding vast potential for exploration. However, we had limited food and a long way to go, so we had to push on.

It took six days to paddle from Milne Land to Ittoqqortoormiit, where we arrived with only one day's food left and having run out of fuel a week previously. The journey was 500km, and we encountered just three other people. We didn't encounter any live polar bears, which are common to this region, but did find evidence of them having been shot. We thank the Winston Churchill Memorial Trust for its assistance.

OLLY SANDERS, *U.K.*

Milne Land, probable first ascents. Between May 8-16 David Cook and Simon Turner, *guided* by me, climbed seven peaks on Milne Land. We were taken to the island from Constable Point by Skidoo, across the sea ice of Scoresby Sund, but had to be helicoptered out because of melt. We established base camp 10km from the coast on the Charcot Glacier, east of the icecap. Subsequently, we placed an advanced base higher up the glacier. The peaks we climbed were generally straightforward ski ascents.

The south face of Hergenlitop at the western end of Milne Land, showing the line of Sleeping Giant (300m, British XS 5b). *Olly Sanders*

PEAK	LATITUDE	LONGITUDE	ELEVATION
1	N70° 43' 22.5"	W26° 00' 30.2"	1,254m
2	N70° 42' 39.0"	W26° 08' 08.2"	1,607m
3	N70° 44' 59.7"	W26° 05' 12.5"	1,383m
4	N70° 44' 04.5"	W26° 12' 54.4"	1,606m
5	N70° 42' 44.9"	W26° 09' 31.3"	1,666m
6	N70° 43' 11.5"	W26° 10' 17.7"	1,667m
7	N70° 45' 52.1"	W26° 08' 35.2"	1,770m

PHIL POOLE, *U.K.*

Editor's note: This is the area visited by a Tangent expedition from May 13 to June 2, 2005. That expedition, led by Barry Roberts, made 20 first ascents, mostly on sksi. Roberts also reached the snout of the Charcot by a seven-hour, 150km journey across sea ice from Constable Point but was flown out by Twin Otter. Poole was also guiding for Tangent Expeditions, but how his peaks relate to those climbed by Roberts is not known.

Milne Land, first ascents. During the summer of 2005 I led an exploratory trekking trip to the Arabetoppe region of southeast Milne Land. From July 22 to August 5, 2006 I was back, leading another trekking group to the western end of this large island, deep inside Scoresby Sund. We made a number of easy first ascents in the vicinity of N 70° 25', W 27° 49'. The trip involved uncomfortable access by open boat through heavy pack ice for more than 200km. We also encountered musk ox and were involved in a narwhal hunt on the return journey

JIM GREGSON, *Alpine Club*

West of Knud Rasmussen Land, first ascents. A Brathay Exploration Group (U.K.) expedition, comprising Peter Clutton-Brock, Miles Doughty, Anna Griffith, Gavin Henderson, Thomas Moorcroft, Andrew and James Watson, and Paul Williams (leader), climbed five peaks in a previously unvisited area of East Greenland well inland from Knud Rasmussen Land. Peak altitudes ranged from 1,950m to 2,350m. Difficulties ranged from Alpine F to D; they ascended two peaks on skis, Because temperatures were as high as +19°C and on occasion never dipped below freezing at night, the snow pack never properly consolidated. The team had a secondary aim of lichen research, and sent samples collected from rocky outcrops to world authorities at the University of Copenhagen. The expedition was on the ice cap from July 17 to August 7, losing five days to bad weather.

LINDSAY GRIFFIN, *Mountain INFO Editor, CLIMB Magazine*

Knud Rasmussen Land, Sortebrae Mountains, first ascents. On May 27, 2006, a Twin Otter ski-plane transferred my group from Isafjordur in Iceland to N 69° 05.016', W 27° 38.879' on a tributary glacier feeding into the main Borggraven system. These glaciers lie east and northeast of the Ejnar Mikkelsens Fjeld and Borgtinderne massifs, ca 90km east of Gunnbjornsfjeld and the Watkins Bjerge.

On departure, the plane lifted out another British group, led by Rosie Goolden, which over the previous 20 days had made a number of ascents close to the fringe of the inland ice. My own group comprised Geoff Bonney, Julian Davey, Kate Keohane, Sandy Gregson (all U.K.), Bill Cunningham (U.S.), and I as leader. With a pick-up proposed for June 16, we had 20 days for exploration and climbing.

During the first four days we skied to a number of cols to spy out the terrain and also made two first ascents: Triangle Peak (2,340m, N 69° 07', W 27° 31') and Surprise Peak (2,405m, N 69° 04', W 27° 34'), the surprise being a deep crevasse hindering our passage to the gendarmed and corniced final crest.

On June 1 we transferred to a new campsite, downstream at the junction with a more easterly branch glacier. This promised access to other peaks, although it was obvious that dangerous icefalls, which we were unwilling to risk, protected some of the higher mountains. We skied up Devil's Dome (2,151m) to inspect approach routes, and in subsequent outings made first ascents of Stegosaurus 4 (2,285m, N 69° 03', W 27° 32'), Nipple (2,189m, N 69°01', W 27° 33'), Snow Castle (ca 2,105m, N 69° 04', W 27° 32') and Stegosaurus 7 (The Fin, 2,276m, N 69° 03', W 27° 32'). These climbs were predominantly on snow and steep ice, with sections of narrow, exposed arête. All rock encountered was fairly rotten basalt.

We also turned around on a few other attempts because of poor snow or storms. (The weather was more fickle than on any of my previous 10 Arctic expeditions.) Meanwhile Julian and Kate explored on ski a little farther west. The area holds impressive unclimbed peaks, but there will be considerable risk involved in reaching some of the summits.

JIM GREGSON, *Alpine Club*

Mt. Currahee (2,612m) in the Gronau Nunatakker, showing the line of the first ascent (solid) and descent (dotted). The route was completed in a round trip of 28 hours at AD with a bivouac on the ridge at (B). *Hauke Engel*

Gronau Nunatakker, first ascents. In August three undergraduates from Oxford University, Chris Abbott, Ben Spencer, and I, flew by ski-equipped plane to a glacier in the Gronau Nunatakker Range and made first ascents in largely unexplored territory. Traveling on skis and pulling sledges, we crossed 90km of terrain in the region separating the main Greenland Icecap from the Watkins Mountains. Since the range has not been mapped, we navigated using GPS, compass, and aerial photographs taken in the 1970s.

Hauke Engel pulking toward unnamed and unclimbed peaks during the final stages of the Oxford University expedition to the Gronau Nunatakker. *Hauke Engel collection*

Crossing 30m-wide crevasses, experiencing 24 hours of daylight, and absorbing the otherworldly beauty of the hostile landscape made the trip worthwhile in itself. But we did not forget our primary objective, and three-and-a-half weeks of snow and ice climbing resulted in 12 first ascents graded between F and AD.

The first climb, a prominent snow-and-basalt pyramid we named Mt. Currahee, proved to be the most demanding ascent of the trip, involving steep ice, an impromptu bivouac just below the summit, and an extremely difficult bergschrund. We deemed the 28-hour climb a perfect introduction to Arctic mountaineering. We made other notable ascents in an unexplored range just west of the huge Christian IV Glacier. We named this range the Oxford Nunatakker and climbed six of the seven peaks, small nunataks, at F and PD.

We experienced a variety of weather patterns on the icecap, with high pressure systems giving way to clinging fog and even rain, as the temperature rose to +7°C. Toward the end of the trip, as the Arctic summer began to draw to a close, heavy snowfall produced several tent-bound days and much lower temperatures. The thermometer dropped below –20°C during our last few days, and strong winds forced us to abandon one exposed climb.

After 13 months of planning, preparation, training, and, above all, fund-raising, we agreed that the expedition had been everything we had dreamed of and more. It certainly spawned plans for the future.

The following table gives GPS locations of our camps as we skied through the area, and previously virgin mountains (with grades) we climbed.

NAME	DATE	NORTH	WEST	ALTITUDE
Camp 1 (Drop-off point)	08/06/06	69°35'58"	29°49'37"	2,103m
Mt. Currahee (AD)	08/08/06	69°35'33"	29°55'01"	2,612m
Camp 2	08/10/06	69°36'23"	29°32'03"	2,609m
Abbottsbjerg (ski ascent)	08/11/06	69°36'09"	29°38'38"	2,609m
Camp 3	08/11/06	69°35'10"	29°24'14"	2,556m
Mt. Brasenose (F)	08/12/06	69°33'27"	29°17'48"	2,562m
Byrnesfjeld (F)	08/12/06	69°34'25"	29°17'33"	2,628m
Helenasbjerg (F)	08/12/06	69°34'32"	29°14'46"	2,603m
Camp 4	08/12/06	69°33'59"	29°18'42"	2,490m
Camp 5	08/13/06	69°30'45"	29°15'01"	2,382m
Hannahsbjerg (F)	08/13/06	69°30'55"	29°14'08"	2,520m
Schwerdtfegersbjerg (PD)	08/14/06	69°30'09"	29°11'04"	2,479m
Qureshisbjerg (F)	08/15/06	69°30'26"	29°15'55"	2,517m
Camp 6	08/16/06	69°27'33"	28°50'01"	2,215m
Charlottesbjerg (F)	08/19/06	69°26'55"	28°51'15"	2,444m
Camp 7	08/19/06	69°24'19"	28°40'11"	2,522m
Elizabethsbjerg (F)	08/20/06	69°19'54"	28°30'08"	2,602m
Camp 8	08/20/06	69°19'25"	28°30'20"	2,465m
Camp 9	08/21/06	69°12'39"	28°22'47"	2,019m
Mt. Ward (PD)	08/22/06	69°12'34"	28°27'44"	2,550m
Camp 10	08/23/06	69°09'08"	28°24'50"	1,913m
Sarah's Spur (F)	08/25/06	69°08'13"	28°26'12"	1,975m

HAUKE ENGEL, *U.K.*

Gunnbjornsfjeld region first ascents. A Royal Navy expedition comprising Tim Brookes, Guy Buckingham, Belinda Fear, Al Grieg, Derek Scott, and Barrie Whitehead traveled 160km and climbed 14 peaks in the Watkins Mountains. These included Greenland's highest, Gunnbjornsfjeld (3,694m); Cone (a.k.a. Qaqqag Johnson, 3,669m) the third highest; and the seventh highest (possibly Deception Dome, 3526m), as well as four previously unclimbed peaks of ca

3,000m. Ascents of the third and seventh highest mountains were believed to be by new routes. The team spent three weeks in the region and reports temperatures down to –47°C.

LINDSAY GRIFFIN, *Mountain INFO Editor, CLIMB Magazine*

Kangerdlugssuaq South, first ascents. From July 22 to August 18, 2005, Dave Swinburne and I climbed 16 new peaks within three previously unvisited glacier systems that descend from the fringes of the ice cap southeast of the Hutchinson Plateau. We shared a Twin Otter from Isaffordur, Iceland, with another group, but, after setting a GPS location and date for the pick-up, we loaded pulks and headed off on our own, leaving the other group to explore the immediate area.

Our routine was simple. We would typically spend three or four days in one location, climb, and move on to another destination. The vagueness of our two A4 satellite photos from NASA, at a scale of 1:150,000, encouraged us to choose peaks and routes that we found attractive, as and when they appeared. There is insufficient detail on the images to allow for prior planning, and a small pair of binoculars proved useful on the ground. Each day we would spot new goals in the distance, and each time we moved camp we would see new objectives around the next buttress or above a col. First ascents primarily involved broken granite ridges and, invariably, sections of unstable granular snow. Some of the granite was superb, and friction in "big boots" was excellent. All the routes were between F and AD+ in difficulty. One route we climbed toward the end of the trip was particularly good: a rock rib, a sharp undulating snow ridge, a tower that required a committing rappel, and then a series of cracks up a clean vertical wall. We graded this enjoyable route AD/AD+, with pitches of UIAA IV (Pk. 2,501m in the list below). Altitudes and GPS coordinates of our new peaks were as follows: Pk. 2,208m (N 68° 10', W 33° 52'), Pk. 2,215m (N 68° 10', W 33° 51'), Pk. 2,195m (N 68° 09', W 33° 49'), Pk. 2,142m (N 68° 09', W 33° 43'), Pk. 2,042m (N 68° 11', W 33° 45'), Pk. 2,122m (N 68° 15', W 33° 35'), Pk. 2,037m (N 68° 18', W 33° 38'), Pk. 2,222m (N 68° 18', W 33° 41'), Pk. 2,224m (N 68° 18', W

Stuart Howard positioned just below the top of Pk. 2,195m in the Kangerdlugssuaq South region of East Greenland. This summit gave a simple mixed climb of PD standard. The view north shows a multitude of peaks, many of which remain unclimbed. *Stuart Howard collection*

33° 50'), Pk. 2,155m (N 68° 20', W 33° 42'), Pk. 2,501m (N 68° 19', W 33° 53'), Pk. 2,518m (N 68° 19', W 33° 52'), Pk. 2,260m (M 68° 20', W 33° 46'), Pk. 2,437m (N 68° 21', W 33° 48'), Pk. 2,401m (N 68° 15', W 34° 08'), and Pk. 2,277m (N 68° 08', W 33° 46').

We enjoyed excellent weather throughout the trip, but when we eventually met with the other group for the return flight to Iceland, we were stuck for two days in poor visibility, before the pilot could land.

Opportunities abound in this region, and to wake every day with clear skies and pleasant temperatures almost made us feel guilty. Alpinism involves suffering? The trip was pure pleasure.

STUART HOWARD, *U.K.*

Schweizerland, Mt. Forel, Pepe e Isabel; Perfeknunatak, Al Tran-tran. 4V X-trem is a project that involves climbing virgin or rarely visited mountains in extreme areas. The first phase took place from May 21-June 10, when a team from Madrid, Curro González, Vicente Holgado, Raúl Lora, and I, flew to Kulusuk and then took a 45-minute helicopter flight to the Bjorne Glacier. From there we traveled 6km in four hours to a campsite at 2,250m in the Mt. Forel region.

Forel (3,391m) stands on the northern edge of Schweizerland, where

Perfeknunatak in the Mt. Forel region showing the line of Al Tran-tran (V/3 F6a M4). It is not clear whether this peak had been climbed before the Spanish ascent, or has a different name. *Gerard van den Berg*

Mt. Forel (3,391m) showing the line of Pepe e Isabel (900m, V/3+ UIAA V+ 75°) on the southeast ridge. *Gerard van den Berg*

the coastal mountains meet the inland ice cap. It is the second highest peak in Greenland outside the Gunnbjornsfjeld region and may not have been climbed more than a dozen or so times. Despite temperatures estimated to be –40°C on the summits, we climbed two routes that we believe to be new.

After walking three hours to a second camp below Forel, we climbed its southeast ridge. We named the 900m route (1,500m of climbing) Pepe e Isabel. The first half was primarily rock, with difficulties up to UIAA V+, and occasional sections of ice to 75°. Above, the route continued on snow and ice, through a serac barrier, to the summit cap. The ascent took 12 hours, and the overall grade of the ice/mixed terrain was V/3+. We descended, slowly, in 10 hours, by downclimbing and 11 rappels, from Abalakovs and rock anchors. We believe this to be the first Spanish ascent of Mt. Forel.

Curro and Raúl then climbed a peak called Perfeknunatak. We recorded a GPS measurement of 3,544m for the summit of Forel and 3,400m for Perfeknunatak. We are unclear as to whether the peak had been climbed previously. Perfeknunatak gave a harder though shorter climb, which Curro and Raúl christened Al Tran-tran (V/3 F6a M4). The ascent proved dangerous at the bottom, due to large quantities of snow. Higher, they crossed a steep, exposed arête, then snow ramps and several vertical rock walls. Including the descent by a relatively easy route, the climbers spent eight hours on the mountain.

Gerard van den Berg, *Spain*

Schweizerland, Pk. 3,200m, first ascent. An 11-member Indian expedition, led by former naval officer and Everest summiter Satyabrata Dam, arrived in Kulusuk on July 1. They were helicoptered, with two local ski guides, Leifur and Fritjon, reputedly amongst the most experienced in the region, to the Hans Glacier. Pulling sleds weighing 100kg, the team skied north to the Mt Forel area, where they climbed a 3,200m peak that the guides assured them was previously virgin. They named it India Peak and were able to reach the summit on ski. They then traveled farther north in a large loop before returning to the coast at the base of the Hans Glacier.

Lindsay Griffin, *Mountain INFO Editor, CLIMB Magazine*

Schweizerland, Asta Nunaat. The drill finally hums. "On belay," comes the shout from above. Our rain-soaked drill, chilled by the polar wind, has reached operating temperature again. However, by the time we reach the next hanging stance, the drill has refrozen. A fall at this point would have deadly consequences. A glance over the gaping emptiness at the glacier below, the fields of rubble that lead down to the fjord, and the fjord itself,

Roger Schäli during the first ascent of Tartaruga (18 pitches, 7b A2) on the rock spire of Asta Nunaat. The glacier in the picture appears to have no name. Its snout can be reached from the fjord via the village of Tinitequilaq on Greenland's east coast. *Roger Schäli collection*

Asta Nunaat in Schweizerland showing the line of the first ascent, Tartaruga (18 pitches, 7b A2, Fichtner-Schäli-Hainz, 2006). *Roger Schäli collection*

covered in icebergs, is sobering. Our only means of transport back to civilization is by small, shaky fishing boat, and sometimes these cannot penetrate the fjord due to ice. In any case we are unable to make radio contact with them from here, and it would take days on foot to reach the nearest Inuit village.

Andi Fichtner, Christoph Hainz, and I flew to Kulusuk with Iceland Air and traveled four hours by boat to the village of Tinitequilaq. From there it took seven hours up an unnamed glacier to reach base camp. We had information from a friend in South Tyrol, who had married a local girl. From mid-July to mid-August we climbed a previously unnamed rock peak. Despite considerable bad weather with heavy rain, we completed a fine crack system up the compact west face. We have named the mountain Asta Nunaat and called our route Tartaruga (18 pitches, 7b A2).

Roger Schäli, Switzerland

Schweizerland, first ascents. In late June the Cambridge University East Greenland Expedition set off for Schweizerland. Our destination was an area of 20km by 40km situated to east of the Knud Rasmussen Glacier, just south of the Arctic Circle. Over five weeks James Dynes, Lachy Low, Steve Mounsey, and I aimed to put up new routes and make first ascents of peaks up to 1,600m. Several ski-touring parties had visited the area, but we found no evidence of climbing expeditions prior to ours.

The Danish Polar Center has recently changed its regulations, and a permit is no longer required to visit this area. We reached Kulusuk by scheduled flight, our unwillingness to pay excess baggage or freight costs resulting in each man wearing 15kg of gear on the plane, a strat-

One of the four base camps established by the Cambridge University expedition to Schweizerland in 2006. The team climbed the two peaks in the background, linked by an almost horizontal ridge. *Mark Reid*

The area of Schweizerland east of the Knud Rasmussen Glacier. Most of the peaks visible remain unclimbed. *Mark Reid*

egy that miraculously worked. We chartered Inuit-owned boats to transport us to near the snout of the vast Knud Rasmussen Glacier, from which we spent five days ferrying 500kg of equipment and supplies to the snowline. Once we reached snowline, overland travel became more efficient; we hauled everything in pulks.

We spent the next few weeks making alpine-style first ascents up to AD, operating from four base camps during the course of the expedition. We do not recommend a few of these routes, due to horrendously loose rock. The worst incident, which made for a particularly spicy day, involved a falling boulder the size of a washing machine severing a rope. We lost about two weeks of climbing to appalling weather, mostly relentless rain and poor visibility, but by the time the boat arrived to pick us up, we had made eight first ascents. We also climbed a mountain at the edge of the expedition area but found a cairn and an empty sardine tin. A label displaying "Produce of West Germany" indicated that we had been beaten to this summit by a few decades. On our way out we removed not only our own trash but also huge amounts left by a recent French expedition to the lower Knud Rasmussen.

The east coast of Greenland still offers incredible new-route potential in a stunning location. It is hard to imagine any climber not being excited by the sight of hundreds of jagged peaks, many of which await first ascents, jutting out from a vast network of glaciers. We felt we had barely scratched the surface, and our departure day came far too soon.

Our list of peaks, with GPS coordinates is as follows: Mt. Reid (931m, PD, N 66° 4.465', W 36° 8.717'); Mt. Mounsey (1,001m, AD, N 66° 4.085', W 36° 8.300'); Lachy's Jaws (1,117m, AD, N 66° 6.459', W 36° 7.988'); Mt. Dynes (1,242m, PD, N 66° 7.461', W 36° 2.970'); Sara's Left (1,110m, PD, N 66° 11.485', W 36° 3.920'); Lesser Guf (1,152m, PD, 66° 10.843', W 36° 7.979'); Greater Guf (1,231m, AD-, N 66° 10.445', W 36° 7.210'); Mt. Sardine (1,326m, PD-, N 66° 16.436', W 36° 5.947'); 6am Peak (1,589m, AD, N 66° 14.890', W 35° 58.924'). All but Sardine were first ascents.

MARK REID, *U.K.*

SOUTH GREENLAND

Pamiagdluk Island, Dinas Not, The Jams, the Jams; Dinas Not, Niviarsiaraq Qaamasunik Nujalit. In 2005 we repeated routes on the 1,340m Baron and added two new routes to Dinas Not, a 100-110m crag on the slopes below the Baron, closer to the fjord. Prior to our visit Dinas Not had just one route, Life of Riley, climbed in 2004 (100m, two pitches, British E2 5c, Tim Riley-Louise Wilkinson). We climbed toward the left side of the face. On July 1 we created The Jams, the Jams (110m, British E2 5b) and returned on the 27th to climb an independent second pitch up the big corner to the left, which we named Niviarsiaraq Qaamasunik Nujalit (the Golden Haired Girl, E2 5c). We also repeated some of the 2004 British routes on the lower Southeast Face of the Baronet, which we found to be of excellent quality. However, we witnessed a huge rockfall down the big gully that lies between 21st Century Arctic Fox and The Cams! The Cams! We believe the lower section of the latter route, put up in 2004 by Leanne Callaghan and Glenda

The southeast face of the Baronet on Pamiagdluk Island, showing the current state of play. (1) The Cams, The Cams (E2 5c, seven pitches, Callaghan-Huxter, 2004). (2) 21st Century Arctic Fox (E5 6b or E4 6a and A1, six pitches, Neill-Wilkinson, 2004). (3) Supercrack of Greenland (E3 5c, four pitches, Callaghan-Huxter, 2004). (4) Little Foxy (E3 6a, one pitch, Briggs, 2001, but repeated several times since). (5) Banana Crack attempt (E3 5c and A1, 10 pitches, Neill-Riley-Wilkinson, 2004). (R) marks the starting point of the huge rock fall in 2005, which descended the gully below and may well have seriously damaged route 1. *Tony Whitehouse*

Huxter (300m, seven pitches, E2 5c), may have suffered terminal damage.

SARAH AND TONY WHITEHOUSE, *U.K.*

Mexico

COAHUILA

Pico Candela, new routes. [Located north of Monterrey off Highway 1 and split by the border between Coahuila and Nuevo León, but accessed from Coahuila, this obvious 1,000' granite spire has received numerous shorter routes recently, bringing the total to more than 25. Alex Catlin, who has established most of the routes, reports on two longer routes.]

On the south face in April, Ralph Vega, Rick Rivera, and I put up Where There Is A Whip There Is A Way, six pitches, all 100' (5.8, 5.6, 5.10b, 5.10a, 5.8, 5.9). Start at the clean black hand crack. The second pitch is better started on the left. The 3rd pitch has an awkward offwidth move. Then climb right, to the crack in the roof. Belay in the chimney. Pitch 4 takes the right crack to a large ledge. Pitch 5 goes to the top of the next buttress. Pitch 6 goes straight up.

In November, also on the south face, Rick Rivera and I established Fortune Favors the Stupid (5.10a, 5.12a, 5.11b, 5.12b, 5.9, 5.9). Start in a deep gully. Chimney up and left past five bolts and a set of anchors to a better belay. Climb the steep left-leaning dihedral past four bolts until you can cut back right (bolt) and then straight up past three more bolts. Climb up and left past a single bolt to the clean orange dihedral. Climb the corner past three bolts and thin stoppers to an obvious ledge on top of the pillar. Climb left past bolts (tricky stopper placement after first bolt), then work back right out the roof. Clip over the lip and continue straight up to anchors. Pitch 5 wanders up the face past two bolts to a huge ledge. Pitch 6 passes a bolt and continues to a ledge with trees. From the highest ledge rap the east crack to Dog Food Coffee (a 135' 5.10c up an obvious black streak).

Guerrero de Luz, on the 550m Neptuno wall. *Luis Carlos García Ayala*

ALEX CATLIN

NUEVO LEÓN

Neptuno, Guerrero de Luz. I saw this south-facing wall in 2000, but we couldn't reach it because we couldn't get a permit to cross private land. This time, with my friends Artemia and Odin, I drove from our home in Jilotzingo, taking nine hours to reach Santa Catarina, Nuevo León, and another 10 minutes to reach La Huasteca National Park. We drove 25km of dirt road from the entrance to Santa Juliana Canyon to the 550m big wall known to local climbers as Neptuno.

At Gerardo we met Omar and Juliana Tellez de Luna, the owners of Ranch Santa Juliana, and explained our objective. They asked us for personal information and IDs, in case something happened when we were climbing, then gave us a permit to cross their land.

We started climbing on December 31, spending the next three days bolting the first four pitches and stashing water, food, and gear on the last pitch. Then we left to recharge the drill batteries, and Artemia left for México City.

Javier Israel Odin Pérez Arias and I returned to the wall, jugging the fixed ropes, climbed another pitch, did more fixing, and rappelled to the our first bivy, atop pitch 4.

On day 2, in windy, sunny weather, we climbed two 50m pitches. On day 3, in continuing cold and wind, we moved the bivy to pitch 7, 350m from the ground. We bolted the first part of pitch 8 and rappelled to the bivy in scary thunderstorms. On day 4 we finished bolting the 8th pitch and the first 30m of the pitch 9. The weather was again windy on day 5, when we finished bolting pitches 9, 10, and 11 and reached the top at 3:30 p.m. I can only explain the view as magnificent: on one side the city of Monterrey, on the other the beautiful La Huasteca Park. We rappelled to pitch 7, where we spent our last night on the wall. On day 6 (January 5, 2007) we stuffed everything in the pig and rappelled to the ground, reaching the base at noon, ready for a celebratory beer.

Our line ascends the middle of the wall on good limestone with big holds, gets progressively harder in 550m of climbing, and was bolted ground-up, with 140 bolts (including bolted belays with rap rings). We called it Guerrero de Luz (V 5.12- A0). This is the first route on the wall. It could be repeated in a day with just helmets, 20 quickdraws, and two 60m ropes. But you must get a permit from the family Tellez de Luna of the Santa Juliana Ranch. Contact them through La Huasteca Park.

LUIS CARLOS GARCÍA AYALA, *Mexico*

Marisol Monterrubio getting burly in an offwidth on Via Lactea. *Oriol Anglada*

DURANGO

Peñon Blanco, Via Lactea. Oriol Anglada (Catalonia) and Marisol Monterrubio (Mexico) opened Via Lactea (270m, 7 pitches, 5.12c [5.12a C2 obl.]) on the south face of Peñon Blanco, near Yerbanis in the high desert of Durango. The route ascends the middle of the smooth central portion of the face, between the routes Lluvia de Estrellas and Irritilas, and is likely the 10th route on the wall. Via Lactea starts with a 5.7 slab (bolts) beside a large boulder, and climbs slabs, thin face, cracks from finger to offwidth, and a chimney. The pair equipped and then freed the route over three days in November, hand-drilling 37 bolts (including belays) ground-up. They recommend a double set of Friends to #3, one #4 Camalot, TCUs, a set of nuts, and micronuts, 12 quickdraws, and double 60m ropes. Rappel the route. More information can be found at www.xpmexico.com –> Roca-Guias –> Durango-Peñon Blanco.

COMPILED FROM EMAILS WITH THE CLIMBERS

Looking down into Sumidero Canyon and the 500m high wall with Hombres del Pañuelo Rojo marked. The approach from the river starts at the arrow, and the shorter aid line to the right was climbed to access the large cave. *Calvin Smith*

Chiapas

Sumidero Canyon, showing Hombres del Pañuelo Rojo. No other routes exist in this area, but the climbers weren't the first to be there: they found ceramic artifacts and corn grinding stones on a ledge 200m above the river. *Calvin Smith*

Sumidero Canyon, Hombres del Pañuelo Rojo. This majestic canyon forms part of the Sumidero Canyon National Park, located near the capital city of Tuxtla Gutierrez in the southern state of Chiapas. In February 1999 a local nonprofit climbing club, Grupo Escala Montanismo y Exploracion A.C., was founded in the state. From 2000 to 2006 this small group began putting up sport, trad, and mixed climbs in two prominent limestone areas near the city: Copoya and the Sumidero Canyon. The group has created more than 50 quality limestone routes throughout the state, including the most important project to date: the first complete big wall ascent in Sumidero Canyon.

The expedition occurred from January 8-23, with climbers Alejandro Rene Gomez Aldama, Jose Manuel Gomez Aldama, Carlos Miguel Hererra Tapia, and I. Other expedition members included Mauricio Lopez Nafate (base camp), Valentina Gomez Orantes, Cintya Hartman, Carlos Sevilla (lookout, communication, and media coverage), Kalet Zarate, Tomas Torres, Aventura Vertical magazine (photographers and film crew), and Grupo Espeleologico Jaguar (logistical support).

We named the route Hombres del Pañuelo Rojo (Men of the Red Handkerchief) in honor of the group of explorers who made the first successful trip (hiking, rafting, and canyoneering) through the canyon in 1960. This original event received significant media attention on both state and national levels, because the group was made up of locals and because several other groups, national and international, had failed at previous attempts. Also, the silhouette of the wall appears in the state's coat of arms and has been a local historic symbol since 1535. A surprising bonus was the discovery of archeological remains on a ledge near our base camp (200m above the river!).

In spring 2005 we chose this 500m vertical-to-overhanging face because of its apparent rock quality, lack of plant growth, relative shade, and the existence of potential bivouac ledges. We made outings prior to the official expedition date, to establish and stock base camp and to climb and fix ropes on the opening pitches. We topped on January 23 at 4:30 p.m., after 14 days on the wall and 600m of climbing. We used both aid and free-climbing techniques and protected the route on lead with bolts, hooks, cams, and an array of passive gear. We estimate the rating as 5.11 A1; a complete free ascent would surely add at least another number to the grade. Special precautions should be taken during future ascents, as there is still an enormous amount of loose rock. For detailed route information, e-mail grupoescala@yahoo.com. Web Links: www.grupoescalachiapas.com and www.montanismo.org.mx

Calvin A. Smith, *Grupo Escala Chiapas*

Peru

CORDILLERA BLANCA

Pucahirca Oeste, attempt. In late June John Miller and I set out for the Pucahirca group, assisted by a Mountain Fellowship Grant from the AAC. After acclimatizing in the Ishinca Valley, we were unable to establish a new line on the north face of Pucahirca Oeste (6,039 m) [some sources call this peak Pucahirca Sur], due to deteriorating snow and ice conditions.

The approach was our first challenge. We could make the three- to four-day trek with burros from Hualcayán to the north of Santa Cruz and Alpamayo, then down to Laguna Sajuna, or we could take a 10-hour bus ride over the range to Pomabamba. From Pomabamba a five-hour taxi ride to base camp still would await, if a taxi willing to negotiate the journey could be found. We decided to make the four-day trek, but a stomach bug sent me back to Caraz. After recovering, I took the bus to Pomabamba and a taxi as far as one would take me toward base camp, which left me 30km to cover by foot.

The unclimbed chimney on the remote northwest face of Pucahirca Central (6,014m), visible just left of center and guarded by a complex icefall approach as well as hazards from above. The peak's right skyline is the upper Southwest Arête route (Dionisi-Fecchio-Ghigo-Marchese, 1961), reached from the opposite side. From this side of the mountain, a 1980 Italian team led by Mario Curnis (Azzoni-Bianchetti-Bonicelli-Curnis-Fassa-Rota-Scarpelini-Nava-Testa) climbed the west face to a few meters below the summit before retreating in bad conditions. *John Miller*

We scoured John's telephoto pictures for the best lines in the cirque. Two interesting, unclimbed lines attracted us. A breathtaking ice chimney over 1,000' long split the middle of the northwest face of Pucahirca Central (6,014m). This intimidating line looked to have a horrific approach up the icefall. It would be quite an accomplishment, if global warming does not do away with it. The other line linked various promising features up the middle of the north face of Pucahirca Oeste. This was our line.

We camped on the glacier below the north face of Pucahirca Oeste. Some of the features that seemed in good condition just a few days before had deteriorated in the sun, and we watched debris fall directly down our intended line.

We made a high camp on the glacier and made an attempt that night. However, we moved slowly on the low rock buttress, which was less than optimal and steeper than expected. Combined with the fear of unfavorable conditions ahead, we turned back. The next morning we realized the wisdom of our decision when we watched an awesome avalanche sweep near our intended line.

ASA FIRESTONE, *AAC*

Taulliraju, El Centelleo. Riding a bike for three days from Carhuaz (2,650m) to Punta Olimpica/ Pasaje de Ulta (4,890m) sounded like a fast, simple method of acclimatization. Two hours after Matej Flis, Tadej Golob, and I departed, though, I realized once more there are no shortcuts in alpinism.

Our objective was an alpine-style ascent up the unclimbed center of Taulliraju's south face. Aware of the difficulties before us, we brought all kinds of gear, but by daybreak on the first pitch, it was clear that we wouldn't be able to make our way over the powder-covered granite.

Thus we pared down our equipment for the GMHM Route (400m, TD+ WI4+ M4, Gleizes-Gryska-Prom, 1987), which we hoped to use to access the start of the east face, where we would attempt a new line. The GMHM Route surprised us with a variety of conditions. At nightfall we bivied on a comfortable shelf on the top of the buttress. The following day we continued along the Guides' Route (800m, TD+, Balmat-Fabre-Monaci-Thivierge, 1978) to the east face [Cordillera Blanca scholar and *AAJ* correspondent Antonio Gómez Bohórquez notes that this portion of the route is erroneously attributed to the 1978 Chamonix guides. Credit belongs to the 1976 Japanese team of Mizobuchi-Nagashino-Yoda.] half a pitch to the right of the Monasterio-Richey 2002 attempt (as we found out later). I started up the first two pitches wearing crampons, but after two falls, I changed to climbing shoes. The granite was first class, only briefly blemished by some huge, loose flakes. On the last pitch, powder again covered the rock, and it was nearly impossible to set belays.

The sun had already set behind Alpamayo as we stood on the summit (5,830m) on May 29, having completed El Centelleo (700m, VI 6b M6+). A glance down the Guides' Route wasn't promising, so we instead rappeled the east face, which appeared mushroom-free. At the end of the first rappel, I practically fell into an ice cave; it proved to be the best shelter we could find.

After we spent an uncomfortable night, the next rappel led to an established anchor. The following rappels were made in a similar manner to the base of the mountain. Looking over the photos back in base camp, we found we'd descended the Monasterio-Richey attempt.

GREGA LACEN, *Slovenia (reprinted/adapted from* ALPINIST, *issue #18, www.alpinist.com)*

Huandoy Sur, correction. The route on the northeast face, climbed by Canadians A. Sole and G. Spohr, in June 1979, repeated by Spaniards M. Ábrego, J. Muru, and G. Plaza, in May 1980, and by Slovene P. Kozjek in August 1995 (*AAJ 2003*, p. 306, *AAJ 2002* p. 300, and *AAJ 1996*, pp. 215-216), was climbed in 1978 by the French expedition of F. Tomas, D. Julien, R. Mizrahi, R. Müsnch, G. Vionnet-Fuasset, and H. Lüdi.

ANTONIO GÓMEZ BOHÓRQUEZ (A.K.A. SEVI BOHÓRQUEZ), *Andesinfo, Spain*

Tocllaraju (possible new route); La Esfinge; Huandoy Sur, new route to summit ridge. I went to Peru in early June, headed straight to Huaraz, the "Chamonix of South America," and spent three months climbing in the Cordillera Blanca.

After acclimatizing on four smaller peaks, I went to the Ishinca Valley, where Evan Sloan, of Boulder, Colorado, and I climbed the left side of the west face of Tocllaraju, staying well left of the normal route. Our route consisted of about nine pitches of mostly ice and snow averaging 60°-70°, with a short overhanging s'nice pitch to get out of the ever-widening bergschrund. This possible new route/variation (many variations and lines have been climbed on this face and are hard to tell apart) ended 100m below the summit, from where we followed the standard route (Northwest Ridge) to the top. We climbed the line in a 20-hour round-trip from base camp in perfect typical Peruvian weather.

I then moved on to La Esfinge in mid-July with a Californian friend, Matt Meinzer (also of Sacramento), intending to seek out a new line on the east or southeast face. We scoped both faces in search of a natural new line, and decided upon the steep central orange-and-red wall 100m right of the original east face route. As we started climbing, Matt got increasingly sick and after two pitches was forced to descend. Since solo big-wall climbing is my passion, I wasn't hesitant to continue, but was saddened to see Matt have to bail. In the six days I was on the face, I was subject to snow and high winds almost every night but had beautiful daytime conditions. The climb went well, with only seven holes, hand-drilled on pitches four and five. The route is about 650m long and almost completely independent, topping out on the last few easy pitches of Lobo Estepario. [Antonio Gómez Bohórquez, the *AAJ*'s Cordillera Blanca expert, notes that, actually, Turner's line joins the upper half of the 1999 French route, Papas Rellenas (Cruaud-Devernay-Peyronnard-Plaze).]

After La Esfinge I wanted to climb another challenging alpine route, so I headed to the Llanganuco Valley and Huandoy Sur's southwest buttress, which borders the immense 1,000m south face granite wall. My style was simple: To climb fast and light, alone on a new route. I hiked to camp with a light pack, after catching an afternoon bus from Huaraz. After a nap I headed up with no rope, stove, or bivy gear on the mixed spur that separates the south face from the Southwest Buttress route. My route turned out to be harder and steeper than it had looked through the clouds the previous evening, having continuous mixed climbing with steep unconsolidated snow. After 700m, I came upon the final crux, an overhanging cornice below the ridge. Unable to go around it and too high to turn back, I had to wallow up it, using every technique possible. I crested the summit ridge at dawn, after climbing for six-and-a-half hours from the 'schrund, just in time to see the summit area before a storm hit. I hurriedly continued until it was impossible to see. I knew I was about 100m vertical from the elusive summit, but was unsure if I could continue and make it back without bivy gear. With the last drink of my water and half an energy bar, I raced down the Southwest Buttress and eventually found my tracks on the glacier. I was back in Huaraz 28 hours after leaving. I was happy with the climbing, but disappointed that the last few easy meters eluded me. With so many beautiful mountains here, I will surely come back. I thank the AAC for its generous support with a Mountain Fellowship Grant.

DAVE TURNER, *AAC*

Simone Pedeferri on pitch 10 of Qui Io Vado Ancora. *Fabio Palma*

Chaupi Huanca, Qui Io Vado Ancora (to junction with Caravaca Jubilar). Italian Ragni di Lecco climbers Simone Pedeferri (leader, age 34), Andrea Pavan (26), and I (41) explored the granite walls of Peru's Quebrada Rurec, where on July 12 we made the first ascent of Qui Io Vado Ancora (7c max, 7a oblig with two pitches of A1), on Chaupi Huanca [a.k.a. Punta Numa, but the native (Quechua) name is correct and preferred. Also see note on naming, *AAJ 2006*, p. 241]. We named the route for the song "Here I Go Again" (Whitesnake, 1987), because it explains well why we are so alone chasing our passions. Thanks to David Coverdale, the singer, and Adrian Vandenberg, solo guitar, for that song! We love free-climbing, and free-climbing at high altitude is for us a dream.

We arrived in the Rurec Valley on July 1 and left on the 12th. The valley is 12km of easy, lovely walking from the village of Olleros, which is 30 minutes from Huaraz. The route starts 20 minutes from the bottom of the valley, at 4,050m.

The route is 15 pitches long (540m), starting 50m right of the Spanish route, Caravaca Jubilar (5.11 A4). We freed all the pitches except the 10th (because it's dirty; with a day of cleaning it could became maximum 6c) and the 14th (too cold that day, but it could be a fantastic 7c). We suggest one set of Friends, from the small yellow, and doubles in sizes 1, 2, 3. The Friends are mainly useful/necessary from pitch 10 onward. Some micronuts could be used on the slab pitches. Ratings of the 15 pitches are V, V+, 6b, 7a, 7a+, 7a, 6b+, 7b, 7a+, 6b A1, 6c, V, 6c+, 7a A1, 7a. The last pitch ends, at 4,600m, with a fantastic crack that needs Friends #4 and #5 (minimum #3).

The route is mainly slab climbing, often with distant protection. Pitches 4, 5, and 6 are exposed; there are bolts, but falling is not an option! Runouts are as long as 12m, with 6c/7a mandatory, compounded by the facts that before 11 a.m it's too cold and dark arrives at 6 p.m. However, belays are easily established, so it's not a problem to stop and come down during the evening. It would be a worthy goal to try to on-sight the route in a day and to free the 14th pitch—surely possible for a strong team. The climbing is not physical but often very technical.

We finished the route in seven days, in stable weather, with only three days of cold wind and one day of snow. Some pitches are really nice; maybe the best are the last three. From the exit it is possible to try to reach the top of Chaupi Huanca by Caravaca Jubilar, maybe freeing its dihedral, but we didn't have enough time. There are other possibilities, though not easy, and the granite has few cracks.

Our route represents part of the "Liberi in Libera" project, a sort of exploratory journey to celebrate the 60th anniversary of the Ragni di Lecco association.

FABIO PALMA, *Ragni di Lecco, Italy*

Cashan Este, Southwest Ridge. An Andes [commercial group] expedition, led by Martin Akhurst, was in the Cordillera Blanca in June. Between June 23-25 they made an ascent of Cashan Este (5,716m) by the southwest ridge (from the col with Shacsha). Apparently this route had not been recorded—the route of the first ascent in 1948 lies on the southwest glacier and west ridge. The group climbed from a base camp in the Quebrada Rurec, with higher camps at 4,700m and 5,000m. After a half-day scouting and trail-breaking, Peruvian guide Damian Aurelio, with David Galloway and Ray Tennant, reached the summit at 12 noon on June 25. The grade was about Alpine AD; the route involved complicated route-finding through crevasses and a steep pitch to gain the summit.

JOHN BIGGAR, *U.K.*

Huantsan Norte, The Wayqui Way. Rolando Morales Flores, Beto Pinto Toledo, Michel Bernuy Qiuto, and I (all International Federation of Mountain Guides aspirants from the Casa de Guias in Huaraz, Peru) entered the Rajucolta Valley on July 11 and set up base camp on the west side of Huantsan, at 5,175m. The next day we climbed the west face of the col north of Huantsan Norte (6,113m), with only a half-liter of fuel, food for two days, two sleeping bags, two mattresses, five Friends, seven Stoppers, five ice screws, and six pitons. We climbed in pairs, 3m apart, sharing a rope on the exit pitch. We started with 240m of a new route. The first pitch contained mixed climbing on thin ice patches over rock, with hard-won protection, followed by two pitches of vertical ice and snow up to 90°. The fourth pitch had vertical ice and mixed climbing over rock slabs and 4m of vertical rock and ice that allowed us to exit the face.

We dug a snow cave and waited for morning to make a summit bid, but bad weather kept us cave-bound, and we ate the remaining food. On day 4 we left our bivy at 2 a.m. and started the Northwest Ridge with just a liter of water and two Power Bars for the four of us. We climbed 10 runout pitches, using only deadmen as anchors. The most difficult part required crossing from the west face of the ridge to the east face, over cornices and mushrooms. At 6:34 a.m. in perfect conditions, we became the first all-Peruvian team to reach the summit of Huantsan Norte. Fourteen rappels later, down the northeast face, leaving seven snow stakes, four pitons, and all the cordelettes we had, we reached the glacier and our bivy at 5:30 p.m. Our supplies exhausted, we kept going, and at 11:30 p.m., after 21 hours on the move, we feasted on the remaining food in base camp and drank from a nearby a water hole, having finished our almost-epic ascent of the The Wayqui Way (850m, TD+ WI4 M4 90°; in Quechua, *wayqui* means "brothers").

CHRISTIAN ANDREAS STOLL DAVILA, *Peru (adapted from www.alpinist.com)*

Huantsan Sur, Death or Glory. The northeast buttress of Huantsan Sur is approached from the east side of the range. Unlike the heavily frequented west side, the east is another world. A four-hour bus drive dropped us in the quiet town of Chavin. Word spread that weird western-climber types wanted horses for load-carrying, and, with bartering done, the next day Matt Helliker and I completed the six-hour walk to base camp in the very secluded Quebrada Alhuina.

Quebrada Alhuina is a cul-de-sac, headed by Nevado Rurec (5,700m), Huantsan Sur (5,919m), Huantsan Oeste (6,270m), and the formidable main Huantsan (6,395m). At the time there were only two routes in the whole valley. Our intended line, a splitter couloir between the main peak and Oeste was not to be, given the unsettled weather. To the left of the couloir, Huantsan Sur stood, with ridges and buttresses, a totally independent peak, pointed and stunning and in much better condition. After we waited the snow out for several days, it stopped, and we went for a walk with packed bags.

On June 25 we left base camp (4,400m) at 8:30 a.m., reaching the moraine beneath the face at 10 a.m. Deliberation on route lines and gear faff took another two hours, but at midday we finally began our line, the central northeast buttress, starting at 5,000m. The buttress can be split into thirds. First is rock, of a kind: 200 crumbling meters offering V-diff climbing with a pack and big boots. Brushing the holds before crimping was de rigour. Knocking, pulling, and testing before committing was essential. With no trustworthy placements for gear, we soloed, keeping

Huantsan Sur (5,919m) with Death or Glory climbing the northeast buttress (roughly the right skyline). The east face is unclimbed. The left-hand skyline might be the 1980 Polish route (Berlinski-Walkosz-Wiltosinksi-Zyzak), as part of their Huantsan Sur and Oeste traverse, but details are unclear. *Matt Helliker*

Death or Glory, on Huantsan Sur. *Matt Helliker*

Matt Helliker climbing the crumbling 200m lower rock portion on his and Nick Bullock's new route, Death or Glory. *Nick Bullock*

close as the shale, gravel, and tiles flew.

At the top of the rock section we donned crampons and axes and roped up. This middle section proved the most testing, as we sneaked and sprinted, passing beneath, on top of, around, and through countless overhanging, cracked, and creaking monster seracs. Massive umbrellas of wind-blown, icicle-encrusted overhangs loomed atop the runnels in the afternoon sun. Speed and luck were our friends. At 5:30 p.m. we made a bivouac on rock to the left of a gully, near a massive umbrella at 5,500m. A serac high on the face calved in the night, debris hit us, and we cowered.

Leaving the bivouac at 7 a.m. the 26th, we climbed beneath a massive umbrella with free-hanging icicles as thick as telegraph poles, eventually exiting on the left. From here, concerned about falling debris, we pitched it out for 60m. We traversed rightward across a snow slope lumped with television-sized ice blocks from the sleep-depriving serac. 60m. A 75° ice runnel led right of another ice umbrella, to an exit through a keyhole and a poor belay on rock atop a fluting. The Keyhole Pitch, 70m. After searching left to no avail, we found a mixed runnel connecting the middle section to the summit snowfield. It was a left-rising traverse, crossing several flutings and dropping into a deep and hidden ice gully. The Link Pitch, 70m. With nervous anticipation we followed the deep ice gully, but luck was with us, and it opened onto the summit snowfield. 70m. On the final section, the 60° summit snow slope, we moved together for the last 170m, hitting the left ridge just below the top and summiting at 3 p.m.

The descent was a fraught and torrid affair, with one bivouac beneath the massive umbrella of ice at 5,600m. We rappelled the snow and ice and downclimbed the rock section. We reached the base at 1 p.m. on the 27th and base camp at 3 p.m. The weather broke the next day.

We have purposely omitted technical grades from this description, as the grades bear no relevance to the commitment needed to complete this route.

NICK BULLOCK, *U.K.*

CORDILLERA HUAYHUASH

Rondoy, attempt to summit ridge cornices. Aritza Monasterio (Basque-Peruvian) and I (Basque) made this ascent in continuous style (30 hours bivouac-to-bivouac) on June 26. [Editor's note: Saez de Urabain considers it a new route, calling it Bagabiltza (900m, WI5). They climbed the

Rondoy (5,870m), showing from left to right: Northwest Face (Carrington-Rouse, 1977; to north summit), Southwest Face (Becik-Porvaznik, 1982), and the 2006 Monasterio-Saez de Urabain attempt. *Mikel Saez de Urabain*

huge, west-facing, Y-shaped ice funnel to the right of the 1982 Southwest Face route, ending just below the summit ridge cornices.] The approach can be quite complicated, due to the enormous, fractured glacier. First we climbed to the "Ghost Col," then descended and bivied under the west face of Jirishanca, and the following day continued descending until reaching the snow cone at the start of our route.

We started climbing technical ground in *piolet traction*, because of favorable ice conditions. These conditions were produced by intense snowfall and the consequent shedding of this snow, conditions best at the beginning of the season. We only used ice screws for protection. The route is obvious, with a good perspective from Lake Jahuacocha. A great cone of snow indicated the beginning of the wall, and protruding vertical ice then put us in a lower-angle zone, where we progressed quickly until reaching the crux of the climb: a 250m wall of vertical ice with overhanging sections. Passing that section we reached the final zone, a wide, low-angle wall of ice with infinite runnels. The climbing continued in terrain featuring challenging snow mushrooms. The face is capped by an enormous, unstable cornice that crowns all of Rondoy. After assessing the risks we finished there and rappelled our line of ascent, using V-threads. I dare to say that the route is high quality and very beautiful.

MIKEL SAEZ DE URABAIN, *Basque (translated by Thad Eggen)*

Siula Antecima, Mis Amigos. In August Italians Silvano Arrigoni, Lorenzo Festorazzi, Eugenio Galbani, and Franco Melesi made the first ascent of what they have called Siula Antecima, the ca 5,550m rocky summit that stands immediately in front of the northeast face of Siula Grande (6,344m). The team approached via Laguna Carhuacocha and Laguna Siula, above which rises the obvious rocky spur forming the northeast ridge of Antecima. After establishing a high camp at the bottom of the spur (4,750m), they climbed the first steep pitch on the August 3, during less-than-perfect weather, and completed the initial 250m (the major rock difficulties) the following day, leaving three ropes fixed before returning to camp for the night. On the 5th they set off lightly equipped, carrying just rock gear and one bivouac sack per pair. After the initial difficulties (UIAA VII), a couloir (III-V) led to easier ground, which they climbed in eight pitches of IV and IV+. They made a cold, sleepless bivouac on a terrace at mid-height on the ridge.

Mis Amigos, the likely first ascent line on Siula Antecima, and the team's long descent through the complex glacier. The northeast face of Siula Grande towers above. *Lorenzo Festorazzi*

Leaving at 7 a.m. on the 6th, the four continued on generally easier rock to the difficult summit snow ridge. After an awkward mushroom (A1), four pitches along the crest led to the top of the peak, which they reached at 5 p.m. They started their descent immediately, rappelling straight down the north flank to the Siula Glacier, which they reached in the middle of the night after 11 rappels. They then had to climb up and around a rock spur to the north in order to traverse to the Yerupaja Southeast Glacier, finally reaching the moraine at 9 a.m. The same day, they descended to Carhuacocha and by midday had arrived at base camp. The 800m, 33-pitch Mis Amigos is generally on brilliant, compact rock, which is often difficult to protect (pegs useful).

LINDSAY GRIFFIN, *Mountain INFO Editor, CLIMB magazine*

Nevado Quesillo, Northeast Face; Nevado Carnicero, attempt. Carlos Buhler and I planned a 17-day trip into the east side of the Cordillera Huayhuash, with hopes of climbing Yerupaja as the final objective. After an acclimatization period in the Cordillera Blanca, on July 9 we drove to the village of Queropalca and spent two days walking to our base camp in a quiet valley above Laguna Carnicero. Following two rest/organizational days we hiked past Laguna Suerococha to gain the glacier beneath the northeast face of Nevado Quesillo (5,600m; also named Jurau F on the 2004 Cordillera Huayhuash map). We made camp halfway up the glacier. Underestimating our day's objective, we did not leave our tent until 7 a.m. on July 14. Ascending the glacier we gained the bottom of the rock face by traversing left onto a ledge system. I led the first pitch, starting in a corner and followed by a chimney (UIAA V-) for 30m. Carlos led the second pitch (70m) of steep loose rock (UIAA V), stopping just short of the snow face above. From here we climbed three 70m pitches of 55-75° snow and ice to the summit ridge and followed an airy 70m pitch to the summit. We descended making five 70m rappels down the right side of the face, including a scary free rappel after dark down a wet chimney. We arrived at our tent about 9 p.m., feeling that this easy-looking new route (350m, D+ V- AI3 55-75°) took longer than it should have.

After a few days' rest we attempted a new route on the steep, 660m east face of Carnicero (5,960m). Retracing our tracks up to the glacier below Nevado Quesillo, we made a long tra-

verse right across the glacier to a campsite on a ridge below Jurau D. We planned to climb with light packs and no bivouac gear, hoping to get up and down in 24 hours. Departing at midnight we traversed the glacier to the bottom of the east face and climbed together up the first 70m of the central gully system. At a fork in the gully we started belaying. I led the first 70m pitch up the right-hand gully, involving many steps of 80° AI4. Carlos led another similar 70m pitch. Then I led two pitches of bulletproof, blue ice averaging 60-70°. At the top of this gully system Carlos led to the right, up 70-80° mixed ground (AI4/4+), to gain the easier-looking snow slopes in the middle of the face by 9 a.m. Here we were disappointed to find soft snow from the sun and rocks beginning to fall. We climbed two more 70m pitches before taking cover under an overhang from the rockfall. At 3:30 p.m. when the face finally quieted down, without bivouac gear and still only halfway up, we rappelled, since we had lost so much time.

The Buhler-Johnson attempt on the unclimbed east face of Carnicero (5,960m). *Brad Johnson*

BRAD JOHNSON, *AAC*

The Northeast Face (Buhler-Johnson, 2006), and line of descent, on Nevado Quesillo (5,600m). The skyline on the right is the 1964 North Ridge (Lindauer-Salger). *Brad Johnson*

CORDILLERA VILCANOTA

San Braullo, West Glacier; Alccachaya, South Ridge; Quimsachata Este, Via de las Vizcachas.
In July and August I led an Andes expedition group in the southern half of the Vilcanota.
We traveled to the mountains via the city of Cuzco and the village of Tinqui, then trekked
through the northern Vilcanota past Laguna Sibinacocha. The expedition finished by trekking
out through the remote southern Vilcanota to the town of Corani.

On August 4, from a camp by the Rio Mates, J. Bull, T. Frawley, N. Little, B. Woods, and
I ascended the West Glacier of San Braullo (ca 5,674m by GPS). It was a straightforward snow
and ice route at about Alpine PD.

The following day L. Biggar and I, and clients J. Bull and T. Frawley, made a first ascent
of the long South Ridge of Alccachaya (5,780m; also known as Intermedio), which is the most
prominent peak in this part of the range. This gave a long day at about Alpine AD, on a mixture of rock followed by a fine snow arête. We descended the northeast face.

Finally, on August 7, in sunny weather, the group climbed a fine granite slab followed
by a short ridge on the northeast side of Quimsachata Este (ca 5,370m by GPS), grade about
UIAA III or IV. L. Biggar led the route, Via de las Vizcachas, while J. Bull, T. Frawley, B. Woods,
and I seconded. We were preceded up the easier lower slab by several vizcachas!

During the expedition various members also climbed other peaks, including Tacusiri
(5,350m), Jatunñaño Punta (5,812m), and Quimsachata Oeste (5,400m).

JOHN BIGGAR, *U.K.*

Colque Cruz I, I Am Dynamite; Peak Bethia, possible first ascent. On August 2 Alistair Gurney
and I made the first ascent of the southwest face of Colque Cruz I (6,102m) in Peru's remote
Cordillera Vilcanota. Our route up the icy 650m face, I Am Dynamite, weighed in at TD+ (AI4
M4 60°).

Our expedition began as a nightmare. Arriving in Lima a day before me, Alistair had all
of his equipment stolen at gunpoint on his way from the airport to our hostel. Several days later
we'd finally hired enough gear to get the trip back on track. Progress was derailed again when

I Am Dynamite, the only route on the southwest face of Colque Cruz I (6,102m). *Lindsay Griffin*

Alistair Gurney getting by on borrowed gear, halfway up the previously unclimbed southwest face of Colque Cruz I. *Rufus Duits*

I contracted AMS, twice: first in Cuzco, then—after a seven-hour bus journey southwest to Tinqui and a two-day trek with our commendable horseman, Fransisco—at base camp, necessitating a swift retreat to Cuzco.

Returning healthy to our Yanacocha basecamp, we made an acclimatization ascent on the nearby Carhuaco Punco massif, climbing its most southwesterly subsidiary peak via its short, snowy southeast face (AD 60°). We christened it Peak Bethia, though unsure whether it was virgin, and estimated a height of about 5,400m.

We then made a circuitous two-day approach to the southwest face of Colque Cruz I, across massive moraines and a crevassed glacier. Leaving a bivouac below the face at 3 a.m. on August 2, we reached the summit at 2:15 p.m. and in another three hours rappelled the route from Abalakovs. The route began roughly in the summit fall line, followed the vague couloir up the middle of the face, trended rightward through a mixed section at three-quarters height, and finished straight up, meeting the south ridge where a couple of steep, deep snow pitches led to the summit.

After a third night out below the face, we followed our tracks back down the glacier. In one section they had been obliterated by an icefall from a nearby face. Proceeding cautiously I promptly fell through the freshly settled snow and found myself hanging on the rope 15m below the glacier surface, 5m from the bottom of a crevasse. Alistair had done well to hold my fall. I prussiked out and we completed the grueling trek back across the moraines to base camp without further incident.

However, Alistair's borrowed boots had decimated his feet, which were numb, swollen, and a sinister grey. We descended as quickly as possible, and tests in Cuzco determined that they would recover without surgery.

Colque Cruz I was first climbed in 1953 by an Austro-German expedition that included Heinrich Harrer. Its southwest face was the objective of several expeditions before us. In 1983 a British team, whose base camp was attacked and robbed by bandits, abandoned their plans in bad weather; in 2003 Amy Bullard and Peter Carse descended in a storm from 5,900m; in 2004 heavy snowfall stopped Slovenian and British expeditions from making attempts; in June 2006 an American team decided that our line was out of condition.

Alistair and I gratefully acknowledge the generous financial support of the BMC, UK Sport, and Fore-Wood.

RUFUS DUITS, *U.K.*

Cayangate, Satan's Legs; Nevado Chumpe, Three Chumps on Chumpe. On June 11 Mark Hesse, Chris Alstrin, and I walked into the Cordillera Vilcanota. Within the first week we climbed the northwest face of Nevado Chumpe (6,106m; a.k.a. Jatunriti), descending the northeast side, to acclimatize on a route we referred to as Three Chumps on Chumpe (550m, IV 75°). We then focused on the beautiful 1,100m east ridge of Nevado Cayangate (6,110m; indigenous name Nevado Collpa Anata). [Many peaks in this region have several names—Ed.]

On the afternoon of the winter solstice we walked up-glacier toward the base of Cayangate, as clouds began to build in the north. When the alarm sounded, clouds rose toward us from the valley floor and descended from the ridge; verglas shone on the rock in the last light of the waning moon. We retreated to our base camp, and hail arrived with us. The next three days brought persistently poor weather.

Although we only had three days before the caballeros returned with their horses, we walked back to the base of the route on June 25. Arriving beneath the red granite ridge at 10 a.m., we simul-climbed the initial 200m of 5.8 and 5.9 in the sun, beneath a brilliant sky. Our joy continued into the early afternoon when high clouds closed together, and we entered a long section of excellent mixed climbing that took us to our first bivy. The first pitch of the next morning had the poorest rock quality and protection of the route, but it also provided stellar exposure and sun, for which we were grateful after the long night. Following another six pitches of surprisingly continuous 5.9, we reached the snow high on Cayangate's shoulder and began traversing up the east face, unroped beneath large hanging seracs and sometimes climbing short water-ice pitches to skirt crevasses and rock bands. The afternoon was a blur of white as clouds descended again, and we struggled through them until we summited in a whiteout around 5:00 p.m. We descended to the

Satan's Legs, likely the only route on the east side of Nevado Cayangate (6,110m). *Mark Hesse*

Mark Hesse on the crux pitch 16, day 2 on Satan's Legs, Nevado Cayangate (6,110m). Nevado Pico Tres (6,093m) rises in the background. *Chris Alstrin*

col on the north side of Cayangate and bivied just below the curve of the pass. There we suffered a night of unrelenting winds, as the temperature buried itself in the negatives.

It took almost the entire next day for us to rappel the heavily crevassed glacier that flows down from the col and to make it through an additional 300m of rock rappels to the base of the ridge. We arrived in camp at dusk to the warm smiles of the caballeros. The next morning we began our walk back to the village of Tinqui. We named the route Satan's Legs (1,100m, VI 5.9 M5+ WI4 65°, July 24-26) thinking of that powerful red granite ridge, and in consideration of Virgil and Dante's climb out of The Inferno by Lucifer's legs into the Southern Hemisphere, toward Paradise.

ANDREW FROST, *AAC*

CORDILLERA ORIENTAL

Huarancayo South, first ascent. Tony Barton returned [*AAJ 2006*, pp. 249-250] to the rarely visited and still partially unexplored subrange of Cordillera Huagaruncho, but unusually poor weather thwarted ambitions. With Andy Houseman he made the first ascent of Huarancayo South (5,150m) via the southeast ridge and southeast slopes. Starting from a base camp at 4,200m, the British pair found the only technical climbing was limited to four mixed pitches near the summit and rated the ascent PD. They then established a high camp at ca 4,800m below the unclimbed southwest ridge of Huagaruncho Chico (ca 5,445m; photo in May 2006 *INFO*) but bad weather and unstable snow conditions forced a retreat. The mountains were well covered with new snow, and there were only six days of good weather in the two weeks they were at base camp. Returning from their high camp on June 28, they found that base camp had been raided, with the theft of food and the camp stove. This and continuing poor weather forced a conclusion to the expedition.

LINDSAY GRIFFIN, *Mountain INFO Editor, CLIMB magazine*

Venezuela

Acopán Tepui, north pillar, Purgatory. Victory in Venezuela: Stefan Glowacz endures "Purgatory" in Jungle Paradise. Folding canoes, machetes, and climbing shoes were the keys to success for a team led by Stefan Glowacz to the Gran Sabana rain forest in December. Result: A first ascent on the vertical walls of Acopán Tepui (2,200m).

Pemón—the "true human beings"—this is what the native Indians who live in the green thicket lining the rivers of Gran Sabana in eastern Venezuela call themselves. To these "true human beings" the Tepui flattop-mountains, rising from the high plateau on the border to Guyana, are the dwellings of the gods. To reach their residence, Stefan Glowacz (41), Holger Heuber (44), Kurt Albert (53), and Ivan Calderón (30) had to suffer through their personal 20-pitch Purgatory (700m, 5.12) on the north face of Acopán Tepui.

The climbers were accompanied on their trip by photographer Klaus Fengler (43), cameraman Jochen Schmoll (34), and expedition doctor Tilo Marschke (35). In a jam-packed all-terrain-vehicle the team negotiated the three-day journey from Caracas to the Indian settlement of Karuai. Here their equipment was stowed into three folding canoes. In their hopelessly overloaded boats Glowacz and his friends paddled down the Rio Karuai until they reached the Indian settlement of Yunék at the foot of Acopán Tepui.

From their base camp they cleared a trail through the dense rainforest to the north face, soaring up to the summit plateau in a sweep of overhanging rock. "Never have I seen such a crazy wall!" exclaimed veteran Kurt Albert, looking back on a climbing career of some 40 years.

They approached the projected line in pairs. Taking turns, the teams Glowacz-Heuber and Albert-Calderón pushed their route up the wall. Although the lower section had looked compact from the distance, it turned out to be extremely loose. Glowacz: "You could scratch out a hole with your finger!" The overhanging middle part of the face also had its "character-building" qualities, while the

The north pillar of Acopán Tepui, showing Purgatory (white line) and the Dempster-Libecki variation (stroked line). *Klaus Fengler*

headwall offered stupendous "dream climbing." On the lower half of the wall the team used fixed ropes to facilitate the hauling of supplies. (They removed everything on their descent.) Higher, the climbers stuck it out in "Purgatory" and refrained from seeking relief down on terra firma. The climbing proved extremely athletic, the difficulties continuous between 5.11 and 5.12. They equipped all belays two bolts. They used mostly Friends and nuts to protect the pitches. Glowacz: "Despite the roofs and overhangs, the route always follows a natural line."

After going through "Purgatory," the team again took to the boats and paddled to the Uonkén airstrip, where they were picked up by a single-engine Cessna. With their first ascent, Glowacz, Heuber, Albert, and Calderón were the first mortals to scale the north pillar of Acopán Tepui. Purgatory is the third route on this extended massif. In 2002 Helmut Gargitter, Walter Obergolser, Toni Obojes, Pauli Trenkwalder, Ivan Calderón, and Renato Botte pioneered the 10-pitch Jardinieros de Grandes Paretes (5.11) on the south face. In 2003 the British couple John and Anne Arran, with Alfredo Rangél, stomached the 21-pitch Pizza, Chocolate y Cerveza (5.12+) on the southeast face.

MAYR NELL PUBLIC RELATIONS, *Germany*

Mike Libecki heading to work on steep sandstone, jugging pitch 7 on Acopán Tepui. *Kyle Dempster*

Acopán Tepui, north pillar, Dempster-Libecki variation. Mike Libecki and I left home in Salt Lake City on December 28 clad in shorts and flip-flops, with a foot of fresh snow on the ground. Three days later, after reciting the Rosary in Spanish, our pilot gunned the chartered Cessna, we rumbled into the sky, and my stomach dropped. Meandering rivers and streams snaked through the heavily forested jungle, thousand-foot water-falls seemingly dropped from nowhere, miles of rolling grasslands with silica content glistened in the intense equatorial sunshine and gave rise to stunningly broad red and black sandstone plateaus. I pictured Brachiosauri eating leaves from the high canopy, raptors racing across the open grassland in pursuit of their next meal, a T-rex stalking his next victim, and Archaeopteryxes flying alongside our Cessna. The Gran Sabana was a dinosaur's world.

Our plane circled around the village of Yune-ken, and I watched its residents emerge from their homes. [Editor's note: This is the village spelled "Yunék" in the above report, although the teams used different approaches. This village has also been spelled "Yunek Ken."] Consisting of 10 or so grass-roofed, mud-walled homes, no electricity, and a population of around 40, Yune-ken contributed to the prehistoric atmosphere. As intently as the villagers eyed us with our 300 pounds of stuff, my eyes fixated on their beautiful land, pristine culture, and innocent existence. Leonardo, Yune-ken's chief, accepted our gifts—soccer balls, clothing, school supplies, and especially the Juicy Fruit—with smiles, oohs, and ahhs.

Less than two hours later Libecki, our hired porters, and I were hiking the four miles to our first camp at the jungle's edge. We shook hands, exchanged smiles, and relayed that in "dos semanas" (two weeks) we would need their help again. The porters, some wearing rubber boots and some barefoot, headed back to Yune-ken.

The next day we hiked for two miles on a relatively well-defined trail through the jungle, paralleling the Acopán massif. Later in the day we fixed the initial jungle pitches to reach the base of the wall. The five pitches of jungle madness consisted of slippery footholds, slimy tree braches, numerous spiders, thick vegetation, and our scraped limbs. Eventually we arrived at the base of the wall.

A bolt: 15' off the ground and 8" from a bomber cam placement! The gear, ropes, and portaledge that Libecki had left four years prior were gone. Rumors we had heard in Yune-ken of European climbers in the area were true. We both wondered: Did they summit? Is this a sport climb? Where are we? What the hell? Not to mention that we didn't have the mandatory portaledge and extra ropes. We rappelled back down the jungle lines and walked the two miles back to camp.

In one day we shuttled all of our stuff up to the base of the wall, established camp, and climbed the first pitch. Mike gave me the honor of getting us started. A beautiful 5.10+ finger/hand crack out a medium-sized roof finished with 100' of easier ground. I fell in love with the Venezuelan sandstone. It was getting dark so I fixed and rappelled to the ground. That evening, out of the corner of my eye, I noticed a small black scorpion swinging his battle axe and sprinting toward my exposed thigh. "Kill it!" Mike shouted. One step ahead, I retaliated with the bottom of my flip-flop.

The next two days of fixing involved more close encounters with various arachnids and a better example of the shitty rock quality remaining above. We were disappointed to see random bolts to the left of the natural line we were following. It seemed that for each of our pitches, the sport climbers would veer left up impressively steep face climbing, drill a two bolt sub-anchor, and then cut back right to the natural line, where Libecki had drilled anchors four years prior. After four pitches we entered terrain new to us, but it was not virgin. Bolts were spaced in the most random places, with fresh rock dust and chalk guiding the path. Our psyche was blown. The extreme steepness of the wall made it mandatory for us to leave fixed ropes on many pitches, but since we only brought five we would have to figure something else out.

Back in Yune-ken we had seen a villager carrying a butchered chunk of rope. We walked down, and after some disturbing Spanglish that only an American would be proud of, we eventually borrowed several sections of rope and Libecki's portaledge.

Fueled by curiosity about the mysterious world atop the cliff, we climbed the remaining nine pitches in five days. 5.11 free climbing, coupled with A2 moves on frighteningly horrific rock, was the norm. When we could avoid the bolted madness, we did, but subsequently found ourselves following the Europeans' line, with the exception of the last two pitches. The jungle experience and a new climbing partner were the highlights on my Venezuelan foray. Blue and gray tarantulas hid in cracks, beautiful green and yellow parakeets awoke us in the mornings, mysterious screaming came from the jungle canopy a thousand feet below. Spectacular plants with exposed root systems grew straight out the rock, and beautiful, several-thousand-foot waterfalls streamed down the panorama in most directions.

The summit was not what we had expected. The top was a blackened, boulder-strewn world with intricate flowers hiding in cracks and crevices, and we felt like we'd put our heads in an oven. We hung out for an hour, took in the magnificent sights, and rappelled back toward our families in Utah. On our descent we removed all of our gear from the wall, as well as a fixed rope abandoned by the European team, and as many of their littered candy wrappers as we could realistically get.

Going on a trip with Mike Libecki is a privileged experience, and the opportunity to climb with him in Venezuela was a learning experience that I will never forget. His positive philosophy and dominating love for life are inspiring and encouraging. As a University of Utah student my ability to participate in this Venezuelan adventure would not have been possible without gracious funding from the American Alpine Club's Mountaineering Fellowship Grant. Thanks to everyone at the Club, especially the old dogs, for all your generous contributions directed at enhancing the sport and safety of climbing.

KYLE DEMPSTER, *AAC*

Guyana

Roraima, Cutting the Line. Our expedition to the Pakaraima Mountains in the southwestern corner of Guyana had two objectives: to establish a new route on the east face of Mt. Roraima; and to set up solar power in the village of Wayalayeng, a small Amerindian community where

we would begin our trek to the mountain. Our team included climbers Greg Child, Jared Ogden, and me, as well as filmmakers Scott Simper, Rob Raker, and Angus Yates. Biologist Bruce Means also accompanied us. This was my second expedition to Mt. Roraima with Jared; in 2003 we established a new route on the Prow (an overhanging north-facing buttress) called The Scorpion Wall. We arrived in Wayalayeng by bush plane and helicopter on November 7. Before heading off on the 40+-mile trek to the mountain, we helped install two solar panels on the roof of Wayalayeng's one-room school house. The panels were soon generating electricity, and it was exciting to watch the Amerindians' reaction when we turned on a light for the first time ever in their village. More importantly, the power would be used to operate a high-powered VHF radio with which they could communicate with the outside world.

The trek from Wayalayeng to the base of the Mt. Roraima took us five days.

Greg Child leading the first non-vegetated pitch (5.11) on Cutting the Line, while Jared Ogden belays and filmmaker Rob Raker jugs. *Mark Synnott*

About 20 Amerindians accompanied us, leading the way through the pristine rainforest and helping carry our equipment. We saw a lot of wildlife along the way, including a fer de lance, one of the deadliest snakes in the Amazon. In 2003 we climbed a section of the cliff about 200' to the left of the 1973 British Route, which takes a line more or less straight up the Prow. Both routes start on a high ledge accessed by a steep vegetated ridge. This time we traversed left for several hundred feet below the east face to a point below an obvious big red dihedral that started about 300' up the wall. Getting to the dihedral was a nightmare, as the bottom section of the cliff was nearly crackless and covered in thick vegetation. It took two days to get past this section, but once we did the cliff suddenly became severely overhanging, and we found ourselves climbing some of the most beautiful rock imaginable. We managed to climb the next six pitches almost completely free, with the hardest bit going at about 5.12a.

After fixing four ropes, we set up a portaledge camp 700' up the wall, beneath a massive roof. From this camp we fixed a few more pitches, before making a bid for the summit on Thanksgiving Day. The last pitch nearly shut us down, as it was almost completely blank and wove its way between two waterfalls. After seven-and-a-half hours, Jared topped out just as it got dark. While Greg followed, I was left to jug a free-hanging dynamic rope that was running through a waterfall. I thought I could just punch it, but after a few feet the water was pummeling me so hard I literally started to drown. Greg saw my predicament and managed to swing out and pull my rope into the wall. Our climb ended on a small ledge 15' below the rim. We could have scrambled unroped to the rim, but, as it was dark and pouring rain, we headed down instead, removing everything except 100' of rope that got irretrievably stuck. The route was 10 pitches and ca 1,500' high. We named it Cutting the Line (VI 5.12a A2+ J5), in honor of our Amerindian friends, without whom we could not have succeeded.

MARK SYNNOTT, *AAC*

Bolivia

General information. Unseasonably early snowfall arrived late in the climbing season, substantially increasing the avalanche risk. Local guides say the climbing season is moving earlier each year. Last year the weather was almost continuously bad throughout September. The political situation is always an important consideration in planning a trip to Bolivia's cordilleras. The February democratic elections saw unprecedented turnout and results. For the first time Bolivia elected an indigenous leader from a nontraditional party as president. Evo Morales from the MAS Party (Movimiento Al Socialismo [Movement Toward Socialism]) won by a clear majority, surprising commentators and observers. The victory has given rise to a populist-socialist government, with strong ideological affiliations to Venezuela and Cuba, and has been a resounding rejection of the United States' influence in Bolivian politics. Morales' spectacular ascendancy from poverty to power brought initial stability to the nation. The frequent political demonstrations and strikes that in previous years paralyzed the nation were not a problem during the May-September climbing season, but political tensions have again surfaced, and a struggle for autonomy in the Eastern Provinces may lead to serious unrest in the years to come. Despite the stability during the climbing season, visitor numbers were below those in previous years. This may have been due to an unfair and often misleading press coverage given to Morales's government.

ERIK MONASTERIO, *Bolivia/New Zealand*

CORDILLERA APOLOBAMBA

Palomani Sur, first ascent, and various new terrain. Climbing on equal terms with Bolivian guide Pedro Quispe, Charlie Netherton attempted an integral traverse of the Palomani Tranca group in the northern Apolobamba. They approached this rarely visited area with porters from the road at Paso de Pelechuco, hoping to establish a base camp at Laguna Chucuyo Grande. However, after six hours' walk the porters stopped at a smaller lake to the south. The climbers later discovered a 4x4 mining road that runs from Apacheta Pampa to a roadhead only one hour from their camp.

Short on time, they climbed without a reconnaissance directly up a rock band east of their camp (200m, III [UIAA rock]), followed by a pitch up a frozen waterfall (WI3) to a hanging valley and the toe of the glacier southwest of the group. Here they pitched a tent and climbed a loose rocky peak up to the left that they thought was the most southerly of the group. The next day, September 4, they packed the tent, climbed the snout of the glacier (200m, up to 50°) and headed up the plateau beyond. Two tiny rock steps on the southeast ridge led to the previously unclimbed Palomani Sur (estimated to be between 5,500m and 5,600m), which they traversed at II-III with a rappel on the far side down steep, loose terrain. Continuing north they traversed another rock summit on the crest over tricky, loose snow before reaching the first of three summits (all of more or less the same altitude, though the middle is considered the highest) that make up Palomani Tranca Central. This they climbed via 100m of 50° snow on the southeast face. Continuing more eastward, they reached a foresummit of Palomani Tranca Main (5,638m), which was 50m away horizontally. They could see that to the north of the main peak the ridge continued down at 45°, with steep steps of loose rock to the col between Tranca Main and Palomani Grande (5,723m). From the foresummit they forewent the nasty traverse over loose rock and instead headed southeast onto a glacier, from which they followed scree slopes back to base camp. They rated their two-day outing Alpine D.

CHARLIE NETHERTON, *U.K., and* LINDSAY GRIFFIN, *Mountain INFO Editor, CLIMB magazine*

CORDILLERA REAL

Pico Schulze, southwest face; Punta 5,505m. Three new routes were added to the southwest face of Pico Schulze (5,943m), a fine fluted snow-and-ice pyramid northwest of Illampu (6,368m) in the northern Real. These may be the first new routes on the face since the first one, 34 years ago.

In July young Catalonian climbers Pau Gomez, Faust Punsola, and David Sanabria established a new route on the right side of the face leading to the 5,850m col between Schulze and Huayna Illampu. Starting on the 22nd from Laguna Glacier (5,038m; southwest of the mountain), they reached a point just 60m below the col and bivouacked. The next day they gained the col. They did not continue to the summit but descended the far side and made their way north down to Aguas Calientes, returning to their camp at Laguna Glacier on the 24th. They rated their 400m route TD+ WI5- M5.

Later a French Alpine Club expedition of young female alpinists, accompanied by two guides, based themselves at Laguna Glacier. On August 11 Perrine "Perinnou" Marceron and Elisabeth Revol, with Arnaud Guillaume, climbed the couloir immediately left of the Schulze's 1973 Original Route to gain the upper northwest ridge. The 11-pitch route lies immediately right of a prominent spur on the left side of the face. It gains ca 550m vertical and was graded TD- (80° and F4+). Four days later Toni Clarasso, with Perrine Marceron and Juliette Géhard, climbed the couloir on the left flank of the spur. Starting off in excellent weather, the team found steep and well-frozen snow, giving relatively easy climbing almost to the top of the couloir. However, the last section was deep, unstable, and impossible to protect. As the weather seemed to be deteriorating, the team made a rapid escape down the ridge. This was fortunate, as the storm, when it arrived, was severe. The new couloir was also ca 550m vertical and graded D+.

The French party put up two routes on Punta 5,505m, a subsidiary summit of Schultze. The climbs took parallel ice smears that flowed from the left edge of a large serac barrier down through the rock barrier below. After reaching the hanging glacier, the climbers followed gentle slopes to a final steeper snow face and the summit. The right-hand smear was continuous and more pronounced, climbing five pitches to the glacier (200m, M4 WI4+). Guillaume, Marceron, and Rivol climbed it on August 9. The smear to the left first led to a shoulder before angling back right, through a section of pure rocky terrain, to the glacier. Clarasso and Perinne Favier climbed this (200m, F3c M5 WI4+) on the 18th.

LINDSAY GRIFFIN, *Mountain INFO Editor, CLIMB magazine*

Northern and Central Cordillera Real, various new routes. Nick Flyvbjerg (New Zealand) and Erik Monasterio spent six weeks exploring the central and northern Real. They first visited the Chekapa (Chikapa) Valley, east of the Negruni and north of the Condoriri massifs, where during a visit in October 2005 bad weather thwarted any climbing. These mountains are sometimes referred to as the Chekapa or Lico Group. The pair approached via a six-hour jeep ride along the road to Laguna Jankho Khota and over the Mollo Pass (5,100m) to Mina Fabulosa. Monasterio had climbed in the region west of Mollo Pass 10 years ago and was staggered by the amount of glacial recession, which made the area almost unrecognizable.

On July 26 they climbed a new route on Cerro Choque Santuro (5,160m on the Guzman Cordova map Cordillera de la Paz – Central). They made a straightforward crossing of the Chekapa Jahuira River and climbed south to the base of the peak. Several poor-quality bolted rock routes have been developed in this vicinity. Their 350m route started up a rocky vegetated gully on the right side of the north face. Three 60m pitches, with difficulties up to 5+ (French), led to easier ground and the crest of the loose, blocky northwest ridge/face. Easy unroped scrambling led to the prominent summit obelisk, which they surmounted by a pitch of 5+. It is unclear whether this summit had been reached previously.

After this ascent the pair moved south up the valley and camped at the foot of Cerro Chekapa (5,460m). On the 28th they climbed a central gully on Cerro Chekapa West (5,418m) that led to the north-northwest face at ca 5,100m. The climbing above, at first unroped up straightforward terrain (4), became increasingly difficult and loose. They roped for three final elegant pitches to the summit (6a max).

Peaks on the west side of the Ancohuma massif: Ancohuma (6,427m), Pico Gotico (5,750m), Rumi Mallku (5,982m). (1) approach to Northwest Ridge of Ancohuma. (2) Via del Arco (Ducret-Monasterio, 2002). (3) Long Laguna Glacier (Monasterio-Monasterio, 1998). (3a) Fly the Crack (Flyvbjerg-Monasterio, 2006). (4) Northwest Face (Flyvbjerg-Monasterio, 2006). On RM, the northeast (left) and west (right) ridges are both easy scrambles made by guided parties in 2006. *Erik Monasterio*

Although these two routes were certainly new, Rudi Knott's 1969 Bavarian expedition made the first ascents of seven summits in this group of peaks, mainly from the south. The summits' identities are unclear, but as Knott's base camp was just south of the three Chekapa summits, it is likely all were climbed.

Moving to the northern Real, on August 5 Flyvbjerg and Monasterio made the first ascent of the northwest face of Punta ca 5,982m (DAV Cordillera Real – North, 1:50,000), a striking rock peak southwest of Ancohuma, above Laguna Glacier. Starting from a camp at 5,500m, the pair climbed unroped up the loose lower walls to reach the start of a compact gully at 5,850m. Two steep pitches on sound granite (6a+) led to unstable blocks and the summit. The peak had been previously climbed in May by two teams headed by Bolivian guides José Callisaya and Gonzalo Jaimes. These teams climbed the easy west and northeast ridges, meeting on the summit and walking down the south face to the Ancohuma Glacier. As the two ridges look like the outstretched wings of a condor, they christened the peak Rumi Mallku (Condor of Stone).

On August 7-8 Flyvbjerg and Monasterio added a third route to the rock peak known as Pico Gotico (5,750m on the DAV map). This monolithic rock west of Ancohuma was named after the shape of its north and south ridges, which resemble the incomplete arches of Gothic cathedrals. Monasterio made the first ascent in 1998 with his brother Grigota, via Long Laguna Glacier (6c A2), up the right side of the 500m west face, one of the highest-altitude technical rock routes in the country. He returned in 2002 with Marie Ducret to climb the left side of the face and join the upper northwest ridge (Via del Arco, 6c A2).

On the afternoon of the 7th Flyvbjerg and Monasterio added a direct start, 100m to the right, to Long Laguna Glacier. The first pitch (6b+) climbed over resonating blocks, with marginal protection and fatal ground-fall potential. The second pitch trended left to a point where they discovered a bolt belay. They fixed these pitches and re-ascended the following day, when a third pitch trending right over easy ground brought the pair to another bolt belay and the original crux of the Long Laguna Glacier route. Flyvbjerg led, taking three hours to climb the 50m, 4cm-wide crack, with two off-width sections, over a succession of roofs. A comprehensive rack and three in-situ bolts allowed him to climb the pitch free, at 6c. Flyvbjerg, an accomplished technical climber, described the "killer crack" as the most challenging alpine rock pitch he'd experienced. The upper face appears to have suffered rockfall, but four more pitches (6b max), first right and then left of the original route, led to the top of the face and a foresummit at 5,600m, where a boulder ridge rises to the main summit. However, the climbers descended the foresummit. Fly the Crack (6c) took 14 hours and required multiple midsize cams.

The June 2003 INFO [in *CLIMB* magazine, U.K.] documented controversy and confusion surrounding an attempted second ascent of Long Laguna Glacier in 2000 by the Spanish climber Cecelia Buil and the Australian guide Jeff Sandifort. Buil believed she was attempting a new route (though the original topo had been available in Sorata prior to the attempt, and Sandifort appears to have known of the route's existence). After Monasterio heard rumors that bolts had been added to his route, a flurry of e-mails between Buil and him failed to clarify the issue. Buil, upset by the allegations, apologized but steadfastly maintained she placed no bolts on the original route; just two belay bolts and a couple for rappel anchors. (The pair terminated their ascent at the top of the crux pitch.) Finding three bolts at key sections on the crux crack confirmed that a serious breach of ethics had taken place. For Monasterio, whose country it is, the use of drilling equipment on high-mountain terrain is taboo; he champions the preservation of adventure in Bolivia's high mountains. Monasterio notes that any breach of such principles is regrettable but is of particular concern when it takes so long to clarify the facts.

In late August Monasterio and Flyvbjerg added a second route to the steep slabs of the east face of Pk. 24, a.k.a. Punta Badile, probably becoming the first party to climb this face in its entirety from the ground up. From a camp at 5,000m they reached the foot of the southeast pillar, which was taken by 1994 Lehmpfuhl-Rauch-Schöffel route, Don't Take the Long Way Home (650m, 6b). The 2006 pair climbed the gully to the right, which slants up to the foot of the magnificent mahogany-colored granite wall that forms the upper section of the east face. Forty meters up the gully they climbed up and right over steep blocks (4+), followed by two pitches of 5+, to reach the big terrace below the upper wall. They then climbed chimneys, cracks, and corners for six pitches, at sustained 6a to 6b+, to arrive on the summit ridge in a whiteout. Three long rappels took the team back to the main terrace. The route, which took 14 hours, required a full rack and an assortment of pegs. The pair notes that this face offers considerable potential for future development.

Robert Rauch (Germany), with Thomas Lehmpfuhl and Florian Schöffel, created controversy in 1998 with his ascent of Paititi on the east face of Pk. 24. After climbing a new route on the west face at III+, the team rappelled 160m down the east face to an arbitrary point in the middle of the wall, placing 23 bolts as they descended. They then climbed back up the line at 7a, creating the hardest technical alpine rock climb in the Real at the time. The "route," which lies to the left of the 2006 line, remains understandably unrepeated. The obvious challenge now is to start from the foot of the peak with the Flyvbjerg-Monasterio line and climb the initial steep smooth section of the upper wall to link with the start of Paititi.

ERIK MONASTERIO, *Bolivia/New Zealand, and*
LINDSAY GRIFFIN, *Mountain INFO Editor, CLIMB magazine*

Chearoco south summit, East Pillar. On May 19-20, Denis Levaillant and Alain Mesili climbed the East Pillar of the south summit of Chearoco (6,127m or 6,014m). This is possibly the first route climbed on the vast east face of this remote triple-summited massif, located southeast of the Illampu-Ancohuma group in the central Cordillera Real. The pillar itself is 550m high and gave difficulties of 5+ (French) on good granite, with sections of mixed at 75° (M5) and 80° ice. From the pillar's top, another 150m up a delicate, narrow, and classically Andean ridge, with unconsolidated snow, dramatic cornices, and no worthwhile protection, led to the summit. The pair climbed the TD+ route from a camp at 5,200m three hours' walk from the face.

This central area of the Real, with adjacent peaks such as Cazalda (5,650m), Kelluani (a.k.a. Quelluani, 5,912m), and Chachacomani (6,074m), is the least explored of the range, and the exact lines of routes on the big peaks are not well documented. Despite a handful of ascents from the west and south flanks, Chearoco is infrequently climbed, and the east face holds many possibilities.

LINDSAY GRIFFIN, *Mountain INFO Editor, CLIMB magazine*

Illimani, Phajsi Face, Inti Face, and Puerta del Sol; Pico Layca Khollu, Acalanto. In June Fumitaka Ichimura, Tatsuro Yamada, Yuki Satoh, and I established four new routes on the south face of Illimani (6,439m), the highest mountain in Bolivia's Cordillera Real.

In late May, after one-and-a-half months of climbing in Alaska, we flew to La Paz and went to Illimani's normal route to acclimatize. Then we returned to La Paz to rest and prepare for three weeks of climbing. We approached Mesa Khala (4,700m) with six horses and four porters. Although there we had trouble with the porters, we made our base camp the day we departed.

On June 14 Yamada and Satoh gained Illimani's south peak (main summit) by a new route, Phajsi Face (1,200m, TD+ WI4+). The line followed an obvious ice line straight up to the upper snow slope in the center of the south face. Eight technical pitches and a 500m-long snow slope led to the easy summit ridge. They descended the West Ridge (normal route) to its base (Puente Roto, 4,400m), then had a long walk back to base camp.

Acalanto (Ichimura-Yokoyama, 2006), on the 950m south face of Pico Layca Khollu (6,159m). The controversial Alain Mesili (with Bruce Card, 1978), claimed the right-slanting corner high on the face, but inconsistencies surround his claim. *Katsutaka Yokoyama*

Pico Layca Khollu (6,159m) is a small satellite peak on the far southeastern end of the Illimani massif. [Frenchman Charles Wiener, with two local helpers, made the peak's first ascent in May 1877 and called it Pico de Paris—Ed.] But its south face was not so small and was vertical. There was a line straight up toward the summit in the center of the face. It was connected by thin ice and so beautiful. Ichimura and I started climbing at 3:00 a.m. on June 14, getting through the lower part before dawn. The upper part rose vertically, and the rock was loose. Pitch 13 was the crux (WI5R), thin and unstable with overhangs,

The south face of Illimani (6,439m): (1) Puerta del Sol (Ichimura-Yokoyama, 2006). (2) Inti Face (Satoh-Yamada, 2006, no summit). (3) Phajsi Face (Satoh-Yamada, 2006). (4) Disputed route claimed by Mesili (with Jaeger, 1972). (5) Nada es Seguro (Hendricks-Hendricks-McNeill, 2001). The Southwest Ridge (Dowbenka-Ziegenhardt, 1983) follows the left skyline. The original South Face (Jacquier-Mesili, 1978) climbs a gully just out of the frame to the right. Also not shown: Gabarrou solo (1988). *Katsutaka Yokoyama*

but the crux section was not as long as I expected. The long, sustained 15th pitch led to the summit ridge. We stood on the summit at 4:00 p.m. and descended the opposite side of the peak, walking on the glacier and reaching 5,600m by sunset. The next morning, after a short

Fumitaka Ichimura leading the crux pitch of Puerta del Sol on Illimani. *Katsutaka Yokoyama*

walk on the ridge, we rappelled the west side of the ridge, four rappels landing us just above our base camp. We named our route Acalanto (950m, ED1 WI5R).

On June 22 Yamada and Satoh opened an alternate start, just to the left of the Phajsi Face, naming it the Inti Face (600m, TD+ WI5). Its six pitches were steeper and more beautiful than the original ones. They rappelled from halfway up, where their route meets the Phajsi Face at the snowfield. "Phajsi" and "Inti" mean "moon" and "sun" in the Aymara language.

On the same day Ichimura and I set our next target as the straight-up ice gully just left of Yamada and Satoh's line. The first gully was easy (WI3), though it was hard to find the correct line. We then climbed thin ice and mixed terrain in the dark. By daybreak we started the crux pitch, 50m of continuous 90° thin ice with poor protection (WI5R). Then we followed a comfortable ice runnel for two pitches. Just below the upper snow slope there was no ice, so we dry-tooled (M5). The slope led to the summit ridge. We reached the summit at 1 p.m. and reversed our route, downclimbing and making over 10 rappels. Near the bottom I was hit by rockfall and injured my left leg, though it was not fractured. We got off the wall and reached ABC by sunset.

We climbed this route nearly at the summer solstice. In the ruins of Tiwanaku, near La Paz, there is a gate called Puerta del Sol, meaning "gate of the sun"; at summer solstice the sun rises just above this gate. Since the line we climbed rose toward the summit like the sun, we named the route Puerta del Sol (1,200m, ED1 WI5R M5).

KATSUTAKA YOKOYAMA, *Japan*

Editor's note: Confusion exists regarding possible routes on the south face of Illimani. The controversial French climber, guide, and guidebook author Alain Mesili claims a 1972 route (TD WI4 and 5.5) just right of center (see photo) with the late, prolific Frenchman Nicolas Jaeger. Although Mesili has pioneered many impressive (confirmed) routes, repeated inconsistencies and contradictions, often from his partners, have recently clouded many of his claims. Serious doubts surround the supposed 1972 line. Also on this face, in 1988 renowned French alpinist Patrick Gabarrou soloed a route but its location is unknown.

CORDILLERA QUIMSA CRUZ

Cerro Sofia, west face and correction. [Page 275 of the 2005 *AAJ* reports a possible new route on the west face of Cerro Sofia (5,720m) by British climbers Matt Freear, Sarah Griffin, Tim Moss, and Ted Saunders—Ed.] On April 25, 2002, I teamed with the Dutch Gustaaf and Marjan Wijnands and climbed the west face of Cerro Sofia (we thought it might face southwest). We started from our high camp on the glacier at 5 a.m. and reached the ridge at 12 p.m. We chose a line on the far right of the face, close to the rocks. Gustaaf rated the climb as AD+/D-, with the following details for individual pitches: pitches 1-5, 50-55° (hard snow and ice); pitch 6, 65° (hard snow); pitch 7, 70° (hard snow and ice). We traversed to the summit, wanting to descend the north-northwest ridge. However, this ridge, though shown on our map, was nonexistent, and in bad weather we descended the way we came. The roundtrip took us 14 hours.

PHILIPP KLINGEL, *Germany*

Argentina and Chile

NORTHERN ANDES, ARGENTINA

Cerro Mirador del Pissis, Northwest Ridge. On November 22 I soloed a new route on Cerro Mirador del Pissis (5,415m). I left base camp at 9:15 a.m. and after walking the normal access route to Pissis I gained the northwest ridge of Cerro Mirador del Pissis, reaching its summit at 2 p.m. with a superb view of the massive volcano, Pissis. In deteriorating weather I descended to the north, via the only other route on the mountain. I was so hungry that I reached Pissis base camp in only one hour. The next day, in a light snowfall that grew harder by the minute, we descended to Fiambalá in dark clouds.

MARCELO SCANU, *Buenos Aires, Argentina*

Mt. Pissis, Southwest Face and first winter ascent; Cerro Veladero, West Route and first winter ascent. On September 16 Guillermo Glass, Rolando Linzing, and I reached the summit of Mt. Pissis (6,882m), the second highest mountain in the Andes, for the first time in winter. We also filmed a documentary in HDV format about the climb, directed by Glass. Our crew of 11 Argentineans followed a new access route from the south, but the vehicles were soon

Cerro Veladero (6,436m), showing the 2006 new route from the west, pioneered on the mountain's first winter ascent. *Guillermo Almaraz*

stopped by deep snow. We three mountaineers walked and skied on, totally self-sufficient, for about 50km across mainly unexplored land, following the course of the Salado River, to the base of the mountain. Carrying filming equipment, we experienced very windy and cold conditions, which made setting up camp a daily ordeal. We found unfrozen water only twice during the nine-day expedition. Finally, we climbed a new route, near no existing routes, up the massive southwest face of Pissis. Our route ascended 40-45° snow to a col and then a ridge, during a day when the temperature reached almost -40°C.

   Also on September 16, after starting from a camp near the vehicles [22km from the start, with camps at 4,220m, 4,602m, 5,075m, and 5,547m], Guillermo Almaraz, Eduardo Namur, and Nicolás Pantaleón made the first winter ascent of Cerro Veladero (6,436m), climbing by a new route from the west. The first winter ascent of Aconcagua (6,959m) was made in 1953, and of Ojos del Salado (6,879m) in 1989. Mt. Pissis rises in one of the earth's most virgin regions, fortunately included in a government Natural Protected Area.

DARIO BRACALI, *Argentina, AAC*

Agujas Máxima, with South American Aphrodisiac on main summit (left) and Percolator Addicts on the north peak. *Menno Boermans, www.mennoboermans.eu*

CENTRAL ANDES, CHILE

Cordón Granito, various new routes. Ice avalanches roared into the big gorge looming in front of our base camp. The immense Cipreses Glacier, which forms one of the largest ice plateaus of the Andes outside Patagonia, forces its way through this 100m-wide gorge. Worried, we studied the gorge and its flanking walls. We had to find a way through, in order to reach the glacier plateau above, where virgin rock awaited.

Five days earlier, in December 2005, we landed in Santiago, bought food for five people for three weeks and arranged a 4x4 jeep ride to the entrance of the Cipreses Valley. We were a party of young Dutch climbers (Ruben van Walen, Michiel van de Ent, Michiel Engelsman, Menno Boermans, and I), eager to venture beyond the well-known Alps. Chased by armed mine guards, we reached the entrance of the Rio de los Cipreses National Park, where we arranged for mules and two gauchos to transport our loads into the valley. It took two days of trekking, river crossing, river jumping, and swamp walking to reach the end the valley, where we established base camp. The gauchos and their animals left and would return within three weeks.

Immediately we scoped possibilities for reaching the upper glacier plateau. Our only navigational helps were prints from Google Earth and photos taken by the Chilean expedition (thanks to Jose Ignacio Morales) the previous year. With luck we discovered a series of ledges on the right side of the gorge, which led us directly onto the glacier with only one rappel and almost no objective danger. We named this passage Dutch Alley. We spent the following days ferrying loads to the glacier, made an exploratory trip over the glacier plateau from an intermediate camp, and finally made our camp high on the upper glacier. This camp was opposite the Agujas de Palomo (see *AAJ 2006*, pp. 260-261) and beneath a small group of granite peaks that we called the Agujas Máxima. Immediately we started climbing, using only natural protection. On the Agujas de Palomo we established one route of average-quality rock up the west corner of Punta 3,970m: A Steady Diet of Nothing (200m, not to the summit, UIAA VII-). We then attempted the next peak directly south, failing to summit due to dangerously loose rock. We called our route House of Cards (150m, V+). Although disappointed, we turned our attention to the pillars and faces of the Agujas Máxima, immediately above our camp. Here we found perfect granite and established South American Aphrodisiac (250m, UIAA VII) on the east pillar of the main summit (3,980m) and Percolator Addicts (300m, VII+) on the east pillar of the north summit (3,960m).

Since establishing camp took longer than planned, we had few climbing days left. We also ran out of food, so we headed back after three weeks. But not before we climbed (hiked) the Volcan el Palomo (4,850m), which dominated the view from camp. We reached the summit by crossing a little pass through a row of peaks running north from the Agujas de Palomo, then continuing by moderate slopes of scree and snow. We were probably the first party to the summit from the northwest. At base camp we welcomed the gauchos on the arranged day, and with only one energy bar per person started the one-day, 55km trip back to the park entrance, as images of beer and burgers dragged us back to the relative luxury of the small farming village.

EELCO FRANZ, *Netherlands*

CENTRAL ANDES, ARGENTINA

Ansilta Range, first enchainment and general access note. The beautiful Ansilta Range lies near Mercedario. It consists of seven peaks, numbered 1 to 7 north-to-south. Ansilta Número 1 is a little higher than 5,400m on the new IGM map, the second and highest is 5,886m, the third 5,557m, the seventh is glaciated and 5,780m, while the others are not as high, the smallest being 5,116m. Its first ascents were made in the 1960s

In the 1980s I had the idea of enchaining them, but the idea was not carried out until December 2005 by Alfredo Cevallos and Federico Sacchi. They made a 27km enchainment, from the base of #7 to the summit of #1, in just under four days, climbing 6,105m overall and descending 5,800m. They made first ascents of the south faces of #5 and #6 and the third ascent of the Schiller Glacier on #7.

On a note of general importance to climbers in the San Juan province, a new cyanide-using gold mine is restricting climber access. Specifically, the Canadian company Barrick is not allowing climbers access to the Valle del Cura. I, and many climbers have had problems with them. What are they hiding?

MARCELO SCANU, *Buenos Aires, Argentina*

NORTHERN PATAGONIA, CHILE

COCHAMÓ

Cerro Trinidad, home to more than 15 routes, as seen from the refuge in Cochamó Valley and showing the new German route, Water Music. *Jens Richter*

Cerro Trinidad, Water Music. Cerro Trinidad dominates the Cochamó Valley. A German team, supported by British climbers Tony and Sarah Whitehouse, put up a new free-climbing route in the center of the big, challenging northwest face of Cerro Trinidad. The 950m route was completed on February 23. Led by

Ruediger Helling on Water Music's 3rd pitch (5.10c), a double crack system leading to the first crux, a 12m traverse on thin edges to the challenging corner system on the right. *Jens Richter*

Ruediger Helling and Jens Richter from Dresden, the team negotiated 18 pitches, most of them 60m long, up to 5.12d, with one short A1 passage.

Reaching the valley's walls requires walking through jungle, often without a trail, route-finding skills, and a machete.

Most lines in this region need extensive gardening, but the German's route was steep enough to prove an exception. They brought Portaledges and

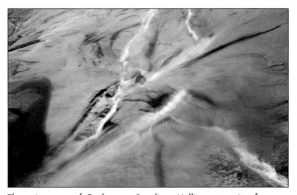

The rainstorms of Cochamo...Ruediger Helling retreating from an early attempt that gave the route its name. *Jens Richter*

bivy gear, but, due to unusually poor February weather, with lots of rain and even snow, progress was difficult, and they fixed ropes and worked individual pitches. Heavy rains can make climbing a drenching experience, with cracks becoming waterfalls within minutes, making rain-proof clothing a joke and even the descent a challenge. On one such day, after climbing a delicate slab in a slight rain and rappelling mostly in a water-pipe, the climbers named the route Water Music.

Water Music takes an impressive line directly up the "nose," sharing the first two pitches of the Ides of March, a 1998 5.11 A3+ British route, but continuing straight up where Ides trends right. It crosses Ides again in the middle part of the face, where the only aid pitch is situated, a 10m section of blank wall with thin edges that might go free at a really high grade. The route has 96 bolts, 36 of them at the belays, many others protecting flared cracks and steep face sections. It offers perfect granite, with cracks from thin fingers to off-width, slabs, face-climbing, and great exposure. Aside from the first and last pitches, the climbing is 5.10 or harder, mostly 5.11 with some 5.12 pitches. American Daniel Seeliger, who runs the refuge, called it one of the best and most demanding free-climbing lines in Cochamó Valley.

RUEDIGER HELLING, *Germany, and* LINDSAY GRIFFIN, *Mountain INFO Editor, CLIMB magazine*

El Escudo, Icaro y la Luna and Pulso; Milton Adams Wall, Martes 13. Icaro y la Luna and Pulso are on El Escudo (The Shield) in the Amphitheater area, beside Cerro Walwalun (a.k.a. Cerro Noemi), on the backside of El Monstruo [see map, *AAJ 2006,* p. 264, and www.cochamo.com/rock climbing]. Approach by a five-hour hike from the refugio along a difficult-to-follow trail and a streambed. At the streambed's end sits a 10m boulder, where it's possible to bivouac. From the boulder it's five minutes to the routes.

Pulso (left) and Icaro y la Luna, the only routes on El Escudo. Cerro Walwalun (a.k.a. Cerro Noemi) has one route, 100 Ans de Solitude (800m, ED- 6b A2+), by a French team in 2002. Out of view, several impressive walls form the left side of this cirque. *Martin Waldhör*

Icaro y la Luna (5.10c) climbs 11 pitches of finger cracks, hand cracks, chimneys, and faces, some of the best climbing in the valley. Martin Waldhoer and I opened it ground-up over January 28-29, 2007, using a rack of Friends, a #4 Camalot, and a set of stoppers and microstoppers, as well as hand-drilling a few bolts.

The free route Pulso (5.10c) made Cochamó history as the first 100% Chilean route in the valley. It climbs 12 pitches of crack, grooves, ramps, and chimneys, sharing its first three pitches with Icaro y la Luna. Icaro then goes right and Pulso left. Chileans Paulina Trujillo, Luis Pavez, and I opened the route ground-up on February 8, 2007, using bolts and the same rack as Pulso.

Martes 13 (5.10b) is the first route on a previously unexplored wall that we named Milton Adams. The wall is close to, and clearly seen from, the refugio. The approach hike from there takes about seven hours. The trail is not hard to follow, until the last 20%. The route has 11 pitches and some easy scrambling. It starts with four pitches in a groove, followed by a scramble. The last six pitches are mostly crack climbing with a short chimney, 55m of off-width on pitch 10, and an easy pitch to the summit. José Dattoli Palominos, Sebastián Moreno, and I opened it ground-up from March 12-13 with some bolts, a rack of Friends, Camalots up to #4, and a set of stoppers and microstoppers. We recommend taking Camalots #5 and #6.

MICHAEL SÁNCHEZ ADAMS, *Chile (translated by Daniel Seeliger and Silvina Verdún)*

SOUTHERN PATAGONIA, ARGENTINA

CHALTEN MASSIF

Chalten massif, summary. Several changes have taken effect in the Fitz Roy and Cerro Torre massifs, in the northern part of Los Glaciares National Park. Due to the increase in visitors, from a few hundred in the early 1980s to 20,000 in 1998 and 45,000 in 2005, the area has suffered severe environmental degradation. As a result, starting in September 2007, horses will no longer be allowed. This new regulation will have a direct impact on climbers, who, for the last couple of decades, have relied on horses to carry their gear to their base camps. Climbers planning to visit the area should come prepared to carry their gear and food.

Climbers should also note that the "climber's hut" at Campo De Agostini, a rustic structure made of logs and nylon that was built in 1987, then quadrupled in size in 1994, has been taken down. The huts in the Rio Blanco base camp will be taken down in the near future. The Park intends to enforce a policy that allows no structures of any kind other than a tent.

In the last few years a large percentage of climbers have been basing themselves in El Chalten and hiking directly into the mountains when the weather improves. This approach lengthens their journey by a mere two hours and helps focus the environmental impact in the town itself. It also gives better access to the many crags near town and allows climbers to check Internet weather forecasts, which in the last few years have become increasingly reliable.

All other regulations will remain unchanged. Climbers visiting the area have to register in the Park's office upon arriving in Chalten. Climber registration is mandatory, but free.

In climbing news, controversy erupted when American climbers Josh Wharton and Zack Smith disclosed their intention to chop the bolts on Cerro Torre's southeast ridge, a.k.a. the Compressor Route. Cesare Maestri placed these bolts during his 1970 attempt. Some argue that the bolts have historical value and should therefore be left in-place. Others argue that the bolts are mostly unnecessary—avoiding natural features instead of connecting them—that they detract from the experience, and should therefore go.

By the end of February 2007, most climbers qualified the season's weather as marginal. However, two young Swiss climbers, Cyrille Berthod and Simon Anthamatten, both 23, managed a slew of impressive repeats in a short time. The two Swiss climbed most of the major peaks in the Fitz Roy chain, including Poincenot, Fitz Roy, de la S, Guillaumet, and rarely repeated lines on Saint Exupery (the Super-Trek variation to Chiaro Di Luna), Innominata (Corallo), and Mermoz (Red Pillar). They also climbed the Compressor Route on Cerro Torre in just 11 hours from the Niponino camp. "We would have never summited on such a marginal weather day if not for all the bolts, but we did not get as much pleasure reaching the top of Cerro Torre as we did on other summits in the area," they explained, alluding to the bolt controversy. Anthamatten and Berthod also climbed El Mocho and Torre de la Media Luna, two small summits near the base of Cerro Torre. After climbing Fitz Roy via the Franco-Argentine Route, they attempted the Kearney-Knight variation to the Casarotto route on Fitz Roy's Goretta Pillar, but descended upon reaching the top of the pillar. On Cerro Torre, El Mocho, de la S, Saint Exupery, and Innominata they were joined by Anthamatten's brother, Samuel, and on the Franco-Argentine and Casarotto by Swiss Jvan Tresch.

ROLANDO GARIBOTTI, *Club Andino Bariloche, AAC*

Cerro Torre, A la Recherche du Temps Perdu and the Ragni di Lecco route. In early January, taking 32 hours base-to-summit and two days round-trip from their bivy, Kelly Cordes and Colin Haley made the first link-up of A la Recherche du Temps Perdu (800m to Col of Hope, no summit, Marsigny-Parkin, 1994), on the south face of Cerro Torre, with the upper 600m of the Ragni di Lecco route (Chiappa-Conti-Ferrari-Negri, 1974) on the west face and west ridge. See Haley's feature article earlier in this *Journal*.

Cerro Torre, Southeast Ridge, attempt by fair means. In early February 2007 Josh Wharton and I emptied our bank accounts and traveled south. Our goal was to climb the Southeast Ridge (Compressor Route) of Cerro Torre in the best style we could imagine. This meant climbing in a single push and, more importantly, avoiding as many of Maestri's 400 bolts as we could. After a week and a half of typical Patagonian weather, we started up our objective, leaving high camp at 8 p.m.—a proper alpine start. We toiled up fresh snow and then climbed the lower crack pitches through the night. Just as the sun rose we stopped and brewed up where the "Monumental Bolt Traverse" makes an illogical rightward traverse across blank stone. Above us, right on the crest of the arête, was a vertical splitter seam. Unfortunately, it was covered in places with a meter of atmospheric ice, too unstable to climb directly. For several hours Josh aided around it, onto the south face, eventually doing a wild pendulum onto the "Ice Amoeba" and then hacked through it to ascend the crack. Two more pitches of perfect rock, with occasional 5.10 runouts, led back onto the Compressor Route. In 1968, two years before Maestri, a strong British/Argentine team attempted this same line, retreating after the aid seam. In 1999 the successful Patagonian climber Ermanno Salvaterra established the excellent face pitches higher, though ultimately retreating.

After a few classic moderate mixed pitches through the Ice Towers we came to the second major bolt ladder. We continued to the right of this, then up a wildly overhanging crack that terminated in unclimbable s'nice mushrooms. The sun came around and started melting the unstable features. It was 3 p.m., and the weather was perfect, plenty of time to descend a pitch and go up the bolt ladders to the summit. After a brief discussion we placed a cam and began our rappels to the ground. At one of the belays we stopped. Without moving my feet I could touch eight bolts. Many were next to hand cracks. We pulled a cat's claw from the pack and for the first time in our lives attempted to remove a bolt, to see if it would be possible to return Cerro Torre to its original state. After several minutes it barely budged. We returned to town. Some climbers slandered and threatened us for our 10-minute experiment and barely mentioned our attempt on the ridge. Many were afraid of the idea, while others were excited by the possibility.

Five days later we got another chance on the ridge. This time it was a lot colder, and sometimes on the lower cracks I was forced to stop and warm my hands, even in direct sun. The "Ice Amoeba" aid pitch went a lot faster, and Josh did an amazing job sticking the delicate and scary slab moves in huge wind gusts. This round we went left at the second bolt ladder and entered a deep chimney system that we had scoped before. The 60m pitch was 50' deep into the bowels of Cerro Torre, 3' wide, and filled with bullet blue ice. If this pitch were at a crag, it would be world famous. We got spit out right at the belay of the headwall, where the bolts began again.

Our original goal was to make it to this point without clipping a bolt, which we did. Looking up at the headwall it was obvious it would go further without the bolts. The weather was drastically worsening throughout the day. Wind repeatedly body-slammed us against the wall while we organized the rack. Below we could see several parties descending.

The first pitch went without bolts, with a combination of small gear, free-climbing, and hooking large flakes. In less-icy conditions this pitch would probably go at 5.9 or 5.10. The variations we made below the headwall felt natural and warranted, but here it felt ridiculous to be placing sketchy gear mere inches from bolts. Eventually I started clipping the bolts. Instead of feeling thankful that they allowed me to continue, I felt angry that the climbing on the headwall was ruined. I clipped a hundred bolts, sometimes a foot apart. Occasionally it was faster to free-climb around them, even wearing boots and gloves. All around us were difficult yet climbable features. We arrived just below the fixed compressor, where the rock blanked out, and the bolts were finally justified. The last pitch is referred to as the Bridwell Pitch, because he re-established this section on the second ascent with copperheads, dowels, and hooks, after Maestri chopped his own bolts. [The 1979 Brewer-Bridwell ascent was actually the first to summit Cerro Torre via this line, and to even complete the rock headwall. On his infamous 1970 climb, Maestri chopped his own bolts on this final section as he rappelled from his highpoint, which was on vertical ground just below the top of the rock headwall—Ed.] This perfect line on one of the most iconic alpine peaks in the world could be climbed with 60' of holes instead of hundreds of holes.

At the top of the headwall the full force of the storm hit us. The final snow mushroom can be WI6, but this year it was a 50' steep hike. Nevertheless, we decided to keep our fingers and toes and, like Maestri and many climbers before us, didn't continue. Twenty-four hours after leaving, we escaped the wind in our cave at advanced base camp.

Politics aside, the variant we did produced some amazing, varied climbing at a reasonable grade. Maybe the bolts will be left to fall out on their own, and our intended statement will fall on deaf ears. Or maybe, next season, when a team climbs the Southeast Ridge of Cerro Torre and someone asks them down in a café, "Did you climb the mushroom?" they will also ask, "So, how many bolts did you clip?"

ZACK SMITH

Cuatro Dedos, Fingerlicious; Domo Blanco, La Suerte Sangrienta. Chris Brazeau and I arrived in Patagonia on January 11, 2007, and teamed with Crystal Davis-Robbins. Within a week we had climbed two new routes, on Aguja Cuatro Dedos and Domo Blanco.

On January 13 the window was forecast to be short, so we went for a smaller tower by Torre Glacier standards, Cuatro Dedos. We walked past 10 or more other beautiful towers on the approach, which was probably why Cuatro Dedos had only a couple of ascents. A prominent northeasterly buttress that led directly to the summit had been on my mind for a few years, and finally it was time to attempt it.

When the alarm went off at 2 a.m., the wind blew so hard that we reset our watches for four. At four we reset them to seven. Coffee and a casual breakfast ensued, as conditions remained cold and windy. At 9:30 we took the gear for a walk, just in case. We meandered up the glacier scoping the options. Sure enough, around noon the wind died, and the sky cleared. Little did we know then, but most climbers in the valley had started much earlier, bailed from their objectives, and returned to camp. By 1 p.m. we were roping up for the first of two mixed pitches, followed by 11 clean pitches of mostly finger cracks, mixed with lots of face climb-

Cuatro Dedos: (1) Tres Dedos Traverse (TD+ 6b, Bonapace-Ponholzer, 1990). (2) East Face (TD 5+ A0, Bonapace-Ponholzer, 1990). (3) La Suerte Sangrienta (650m, 5.11d A1 M4, Brazeau-DavisRobbins-Walsh, 2007). Domo Blanco: (4) South Ridge (Bonapace-Dünser-Ponholzer,1993). (5) Fingerlicious (500m, 5.11b/c M4, Brazeau-DavisRobbins-Walsh, 2007). *Jon Walsh*

ing and cryptic route finding. The climbing was sustained at 5.10 and 5.11, with pitches averaging about 50m in length. We climbed the route, Fingerlicious (500m, 5.11b/c M4), in three blocks with the seconds following with jumars. We on-sighted every pitch, and each got a share of cruxy leads. The summit was a surreal experience under a calm, starry sky at 3:30 a.m. After a half-hour of enjoying the moonlit views of the Hielo Sur and the surrounding spires, we rappelled the route and made it back to camp in a 25-hour roundtrip. It was likely the second or third ascent of the peak, and via a virgin wall.

Merely a flesh wound. Crystal Davis-Robbins about to start up Domo Blanco after an encounter with a flying rock on the approach to what would become La Suerte Sangrienta ("Bloody Luck"). *Jon Walsh*

The next window again looked small, but this time, January 18, we started in the dark for Cuatro Dedos's neighbor, Domo Blanco. Like Cuatro Dedos, Domo Blanco was ripe for new routes, and its east face was unclimbed. The glacier travel to get to there likely had something to do with it, but we found our way through the maze of crevasses and began climbing just after it got light. Unfortunately, the sun hit the mixed approach gully just as we started

Chris Brazeau sending a 5.11+ pitch on La Suerte Sangrienta. *Jon Walsh*

Jon Walsh on the new route, Fingerlicious, on Cuatro Dedos. Cerro Torre is just visible in the background. *Chris Brazeau*

up it, and rockfall started immediately. Just before making it through the danger zone, Crystal took a rock to the forehead. At first there was lots of blood, and as she got to the anchor, another rock pegged her square in the head, splitting her helmet in two. She and Chris quickly continued another 30m to my anchor, where it was safe and we could access our situation. Going down would have been the most dangerous thing to do and Crystal, although shaken, felt fine and was psyched to continue. Had we been an hour earlier, the gully would likely have been safe. A few easy pitches above the gully brought us to the inspiring headwall and three difficult pitches of perfect splitters. The most notable features included a corner with 30m of overhanging ringlocks and short section of sideways off-width climbing, all on superb granite. These two pitches required a few moves of clean aid but would likely have been 5.12 free. The hardest pitch free-climbed was about 5.11d. A few more rock pitches brought us to the aesthetic ice face/ramp leading to the summit. We rappelled to climber's right of our ascent route and made it back to camp in 24 hours. La Suerte Sangrienta ("Bloody Luck") (650m, 5.11d A1 M4).

Jon Walsh, *Canada*

Fitz Roy, Los Ultimos Dias del Paraiso. Grega Lacen and I stared on the north face, on the left side of the obvious snow ledge below and right of Tehuelche. The first seven pitches were quite hard, with sandy rock and loose flakes. We free-climbed up to 6c (French), with aid moves (A2) in icy cracks. I think we were somewhere near a 1984 French attempt. We saw rap stations close to our line, and I assume our predecessors were climbing more or less in the big corner/chimney system. It was full of ice, so we climbed more on the right-hand slabs and joined the system after five or six

Grega Lacen down low, leading pitch 7 of Los Ultimos Dias del Paraiso. Inset shows Lacen on the summit in a Patagonian tempest. Jakofcic had climbed Fitz Roy twice before, but in the storm he needed an hour to find the summit. *Tomaz Jakofcic*

pitches. Our original plan was to climb the big corner left of the Afanasieff Route on the upper part of the face, but ice and bad weather most of the day slowed us, and when we saw that the corner looked super-loose, we headed for the Afanasieff. We joined it on the big tower below its hardest part. This section had better rock, but again a lot of ice and harder climbing than we expected (10 pitches, 6a A2). We continued climbing through the night and reached the ridge at dawn. It was too windy there, so we brewed a bit higher. We had no topo for Afanasieff (I don't think one even exists), so we had route-finding problems, especially since we were in clouds half of the day. As we went higher it became clear that the shortest, safest way down was over the summit, so we pushed on and summited at 10 p.m. in a raging storm (same as Afanasieff). So far everything was okay, and we were enjoying the climb despite bad weather, but on the summit things were different. I had been there twice before but still needed an hour to find the right summit and the way down in such bad visibility. On the way down, 100m below the summit, I broke my fucking aluminum crampon. The slope was super-hard, so Grega made bigger steps for my left foot, and I grabbed them with my left hand. Finally we reached the point where the Franco-Argentine rappels should began, but conditions were crazy. Snow, strong winds, and bigger and bigger spindrifts. We could not see anything. We rapped a full ropelength a few times but couldn't find anchors and jumared back up. We tried to dig a small ledge on which to wait for dawn, but it was Sisyphean work, because avalanches covered it in seconds. So we stood like soldiers for the rest of the night. We covered ourselves with our bivy bag and tried to cook, but because of the wind we were surfing more than cooking. Anyway, at dawn we found the raps and things began to run smoothly. Over Paso Guillamet we descended to Piedra and on to El Chalten.

We did 600m of a new route/variation (6c A2), before continuing by the Afanasieff Route to the summit. We needed 38 hours of nonstop climbing to summit, and 72, without sleeping, for the whole story. We named the route Los Ultimos Dias del Paraiso and dedicated it to our friend Ozbej Povsod, who died last year.

TOMAZ JAKOFCIC, *Slovenia*

Desmochada, Puerta Blanca. On February 7 Mario Walder (Austria) and I hiked in from Campo Bridwell to Niponino, the camp directly below El Mocho. In unstable weather we waited another day and only hiked to the base of the route to check everything out.

At 6 a.m. on the 9th we hiked to the base of the Desmochada's west face. Our route starts at the left end of the face and follows the obvious ramp system to the beginning of the snow and ice couloir that separates de la Silla from Desmochada. From the narrow col atop the couloir, the route follows the north buttress (the descent route from the Bridwell line, El Condor) directly to the summit.

We climbed the first 300m of easy low-angle ramps to the start of roped climbing, on a beautiful, grey pillar of the best granite. After six pitches we gained easy terrain and continued to the big ramp. Seven wild pitches brought us to the couloir between de la Silla and Desmochada. The couloir, with 40-50° snow and ice, is not hard, and we reached col—the "Puerta Blanca"—where we spent the night.

The next morning we climbed the 250m buttress that leads directly to the summit. First, two pitches of mixed climbing in iced-up cracks, then four pitches of beautiful and pleasant climbing, and at 12 noon we reached the top of Desmochada. After many rappels we reached our tent at Niponino in late afternoon and returned to Campo Bridwell the next morning.

We climbed the route without previous exploring, fully alpine style. Most of the route had been climbed during previous attempts, but, as far as we know, nobody had reached the summit by this route. Because of the snowfall in the days just before our ascent, some of the wall was iced-up and made for difficult climbing. Due to the cold and icy conditions we didn't redpoint all the pitches.

Although not hard technically, the route is highly alpine, challenging, and long (1,300m, 5.10 A0). It is exposed to objective dangers, especially low. Due to its ever-changing terrain, the climbing demands experience, logistically and tactically. To repeat the route, we recommend bringing Camalots 0-4, a full set of stoppers, three ice screws, crampons, and ice axes. A small set of pitons might help, though they aren't essential. Aside from the rappel stations, there is no fixed gear on the route.

ALEXANDER HUBER, *Germany*

Poincenot, El Sacrificio del Raton. At its best, alpinism challenges not the heights of distant mountain ranges, but the limits of human cognition, our ability to dream, create, and remember a reality that perhaps never existed anywhere but in our minds.

December, 2006: For 40 days and 40 nights, the west wind blew and a solemn curtain of gray clouds obscured the granite spires of Patagonia. Climbers came and left empty-handed, some without ever having seen the summits of the Fitz Roy range. We drank coffee and bouldered, drank beer and danced. The Bridwell Hut was torn down, and mice snuck into our tents and food bags. A rash of injuries sidelined many friends: a pulled back, a sprained wrist, a tweaked knee. A quiet desperation stirred through the base camps and the town of El Chalten.

Rumors of good weather circulated, but nothing materialized. Something had to be done. Some small act of defiance, some symbolic show of fortitude. One rain-soaked afternoon I discovered that a particularly plump mouse had begun nesting in the stuff sack that served as my underwear drawer—I stunned him with an overhand toss of Peter's paperback copy of *Shogun*, tossed him outside the tent, and finished him off with a blow from our cooking stone. We

Poincenot from the southwest: (1) Fonrouge-Rosasco (1968), original start unknown but likely on left. (1a) Leoni-Salvaterra start (1994). (2) Southern Cross (Copp-Taylor, 2002), bottom hidden from view. (3) El Sacrificio del Raton (Sharratt-Wilkinson, 2007). (4) Judgment Day (Gerberding-Smith, 1992). (5) attempt ("Historia Interminable," Cobo-Murcia, 1987). (6) Whillans Route (Cochrane-Whillans, 1962), with (6a) alternate finish (unknown, 1980s). *Freddie Wilkinson*

The soft-spoken hardman Dave Sharratt, off on a short-fix lead on El Sacrificio del Raton. *Freddie Wilkinson*

hung his bloodied, stiff body by the tail outside our tent as an offering to the Torre Gods.

And, miraculously, the weather improved. In early January 2007 Dave Sharratt and I, with a half-dozen other parties, raced up the valley toward high camp. Dave and I were on our second Patagonian campaign together. He is tall, thoughtful, and a remarkable technical climber—different from me in all respects. But perhaps differences, rather than similarities, make partnerships successful. Our chosen climb was a crack system on the south face of Poincenot, to the left of Jay Smith and Steve Gerberding's Judgment Day (1992). We began climbing at 6 a.m. from the Niponino bivy, summited at 2 p.m. the following day, and descended via a combination of the Fonrouge and Southern Cross routes, arriving back at our tent by 3 a.m. that same night. Unfortunately, the crack system we climbed, aesthetic and alluring from afar, ended up being a bit gravelly and went at a rather ignoble 5.11 A1, with plenty of scrappy groveling. We named our climb El Sacrificio del Raton. Sorely missed was our friend Peter Kamitses, who was sidelined by a wrist injury but nonetheless held down the fort at high camp while we were climbing, guided us back through the moraine by flashing his headlamp, and had a big dinner of tortellini waiting for us. The memory of my two friends' faces, illuminated by headlamp in the dead of night, with the stars and summits of Patagonia twinkling overhead, will remain long after the other details of our climb are slowly, inevitably, erased.

FREDDIE WILKINSON, *AAC*

Aguja de la S, The Art of War. With rumors of a weather window opening, Crystal Davis-Robbins, a 24-year-old also from the Durango area, and I frantically schlepped loads to our high camp at Niponino. A few Canadians, not as influenced by the bad weather as we were, had just attempted a new route up the unclimbed south face of de la S. They reported a "super steep overhanging headwall, with several splitter crack systems." This was all we needed to hear. From the east de la S is much shorter, as the north ridge can be climbed in four pitches, but from the west (which gives access to the south face) the peak starts far lower. The upper headwall on the unclimbed south face of de la S forms a tidal-wave-like feature, vertical to overhanging on every pitch.

On the morning of February 11 I took the first block: four or five 70m pitches up the perfect splitter buttress. Starting with good moderate pitches, mostly 5.10 and maybe a 5.9, I reached a techy thin 5.12a face and crack pitch. This led me directly into a thin, mossy corner with sparse gear and ledge-fall potential. I aided it (A2), but if the crack was cleaned it would probably be 5.12b or c. Crystal then led a splitter 5.11 that gained the ridge, joining The Thaw's not Houlding Wright (1,300m, 5.10, Houlding-Thaw-Wright, 2004) for two pitches, to the ledge system below the tidal wave feature.

We struggled to find continuous free systems on the south face and were close to giving up, when Crystal eyed a wonderful dihedral. She led a 90m simul-climb through this corner to reach the burly portion of the headwall, where she did amazing onsights. The burliest was a continuous, slightly overhanging wide crack (#4 Camalots) that Crystal onsighted at 5.12-.

Our situation was beginning to deteriorate, despite the good climbing. Darkness approached, and the good weather started to close. Rapping the overhanging headwall with our small rack was not a pleasant thought. I took over the lead, and began French-freeing through overhanging rotten chimneys and pouring-wet crack systems. Melting snow from the summit slopes drips like rain through the upper roofs. Soon I found myself soaked and shivering violently, as I'd left my shell in the pack. It seemed that every pitch we thought would get us up would yield another soaking pitch.

Crystal Davis-Robbins hiking 5.11 splitters, sin problema, to gain the west ridge on The Art of War. *Ryan Nelson*

We kept pushing through the night, and I finally climbed past the last roof and onto the summit slopes. It was still dark and, freezing in a cold wind, we attempted to find shelter until daylight but could not find relief from the wind. In deteriorating weather we began climbing for the true summit at dawn. We reached the summit only to realize that one of Crystal's boots had come unclipped from her harness and fallen off during her lead. The storm was now in full force. She rapped back down and found it at the base of the last pitch.

Our descent was a nightmare; I will never forget the fury of the Patagonian winds. We only had four pitches to descend to reach the snow gully that would lead back to camp, but we were being literally blown off our feet, even when rappelling, and could hardly move down the face. On our first rappel our rope became desperately stuck and took us several hours to

Crystal Davis-Robbins and Ryan Nelson's 2007 route, The Art of War (1,000m, V 5.12-A2), on the south face of Aguja de la S. The Thaw's not Houlding Wright (1,300m, 5.10, Houlding-Thaw-Wright, 2004) climbs the sunlit west face. *Ryan Nelson*

retrieve, possibly due to our exhaustion. We began downclimbing, then tried rappelling again, but our rope became too stuck to retrieve (several days later we retrieved it), and climbing up was not an option. Luckily we had enough rope to fix to get us to a ledge and the snow slopes below. The hardest part was now behind us as we stumbled down the gully to our base camp, reaching it 34 hours after leaving, thirsty, hungry, and happy to be alive. We ate chocolates, soup, and cheese, happy as clams to have pulled it off. The Art of War (1,000m, V 5.12- A2).

RYAN NELSON, *AAC*

SOUTHERN PATAGONIA, CHILE

TORRES DEL PAINE NATIONAL PARK

Agujas Walicho and Kenko, first ascents. In early March 2007 Chileans Tomas Marusic (from Punta Arenas), Jaime Sapunar (from Puerto Natales), and I climbed two towers between Cerro Blanco Sur and Cordon Olguin in the northwest corner of the Torres del Paine National Park. We accessed this area via the "circuit trail," from the Refugio Grey to the Paso John Garner. The last valley before the pass gives the best access to the towers we climbed. The other valleys are very steep, and one would have to climb loose sedimentary rock to get to the base of the granite formations. The valley does not offer protected places for a high camp, so we camped in the forest not far from the circuit trail. From there it took us four hours to reach a small glacier below our objectives, a series of unclimbed and unnamed granite towers.

On our first day we took equipment to the base and fixed three pitches on the west face of one of the towers. The second day we climbed a further four pitches to reach the summit (300m, III 5.10+ A1). We named the tower Walicho, a word in the native Tehuelche tongue that

Kenko and Walicho as seen from the west, approaching Paso Garner. The towers to the left are unnamed and likely unclimbed. *Andre de la Barca*

means wizard. This is the first formation anywhere in Paine to have a native-tongue name. We placed one bolt and one pin at each belay. The rock quality was not particularly good.

Tomas hurt his knee and had to go back to Punta Arenas. Jaime and I then climbed a steep, pointy tower just left of Aguja Walicho. On March 14 we bivied one hour from the base, and the next day we climbed an easy but exposed snow couloir on the left side of the west face for about 1,000' (50-65°). After seven pitches, near the end of the couloir, we climbed onto the granite and climbed a further three pitches to the summit (450m, III 5.10). We named this second tower Aguja Kenko.

ANDRE DE LA BARCA, *Puerto Natales, Chile (translated by Rolando Garibotti)*

Cerro Cota 2000, Osa ma non Troppo. It's the same old story…an evening with friends, a couple of photos, a few beers, and then, while driving home, talk about those photos. The next day the four of us were talking about it. Why not go for it?

So in less than two days we're in Patagonia. In our thoughts, at least. The woman behind the counter at the travel agency reminds us of our age and suggests more exotic destinations. All of us have reached 40 and one of us 50. A quick glance at the brochure with sun-blessed beaches and curves and…we remain faithful to our belief. The roaring 40's are off: Michele Cagol, Rolando Larcher, Elio Orlandi, and I.

How things change. We were preoccupied with the rock faces, about what awaited us, about the cold and the storms. But now the true difficulties are about leaving home and families, partners, and children, who must wait out our self-centeredness and vertical projects. But we're lucky: they understand, and we depart serene and highly charged.

The east face of Cerro Cota 2000, from left to right: Osa ma non Troppo (700m, 7b A2+, Cagol-Larcher-Leoni-Orlandi, 2007), The Keyhole Route (700m, VI 5.10 A4, Heaton-Reichert, 1997), Italian Route (500m to base of shale band, 6b A3, Canzan-Moreolo-Pancierre-Raccamello-Valmassoi, 1993). *Rolando Garibotti*

CUMBRE

⑯ 35 mt / 5c / A2

⑮ 50 mt / 6a+ / A1

⑭ 60 mt / A2 / 6b

DANGER !!!

⑬ 30 mt / 6b

⑫ 65 mt / 6c / A2

⑪ 30 mt A2 / 5c
LOOSE

CHANGING
DIHEDRAL 7a
obb.
⑩ 35 mt / 7b

SMALL
SPIRE
⑨ 60 mt / 6c

⑧ 20 mt / 5c

2° VIVAC
(GOOD
BIVI)
⑦ 65 mt / 6c +

⑥ 50 mt / 6b / A1

⑤ 25 mt / 6b / A2

④ 55 mt / 6b+ / A2

1° VIVAC
③ 30 mt / A2 / 6b

② 40 mt / 7a

① 50 mt / 6c +

START

Osa ma non Troppo topo. *Elio Orlandi*

And how Patagonia has changed! No more never-ending approach walks, several days with oxen or horses transporting everything to base camp. Now there are porters, and in less than a day we're at the head of our dream valley, in the heart of the French Valley.

Torres del Paine National Park is one of the world's foremost trekking destinations, resulting in an incredible influx of people: 120,000 during the time we were there, compared to months of complete solitude at the end of the 1980s and start of the 1990s. So what has become of the legendary, austere Patagonia described by so many as a hellish land with a merciless climate? All we need is a bit of imagination and, walking just that little bit farther, we rediscover the treasured austerity. Just off the tourist's beaten track one can still breathe a land of rucksacks and glacial moraines, of yoyoing up and down due to the harsh climate, of victories and of giving up, of unique moments shared with the best of friends.

Seven days after departing we come to grips with the oceanic granite of Cerro Cota 2000's east face. It resembles El Capitan, but it's almost unknown and been breached by only two other routes. A rock face, a group of friends, and a vertical 700m face. Not even an outline of a terrace or small snow-filled ledge.

On January 21, 2007 we're on the wall with portaledges. We haul food, 40 liters of water, and lots of equipment. Morning sun gives way to afternoon showers, then to storms with lightning—almost unheard of in Patagonia—high winds, and, finally, peace and quiet in the evening. We fall asleep 400m up, snug and content. That night and the next day it rains so hard that, after 24 hours of continuous downpour, it was like sleeping in a swimming pool. Immediate evacuation! We're soaked to the bone and frozen solid, and we need to dry our sleeping bags and clothes. But if tourists walk for hours in this downpour and these high winds, then surely veterans like us shouldn't complain? We shift around here and there, and a day-and-a-half later the sun returns.

The best present ever: two hours of morning sun that dries us out. Then, like true hard men depicted in magazines, we start to climb again. We kick off at 11 a.m., up the first two pitches of the day. They are the best of the line, difficult and beautiful, worth all the sacrifice of the expedition. We relish a superb 50m flake, pitch nine, in just T-shirts and find a tiny but comfortable belay. The demanding, surprising tenth pitch is the crux. We called it the Changing Dihedral, and it led from a series of corners to a beautiful direct pitch on the right. From below this featureless, overhanging changeover looked like a contender for aid, but we freed it with a bit of courage and hard obligatory climbing. The route then continues up dreamlike granite, and after six days of climbing capsule-style in sun, rain, wind, and mist we reached the top. No conquest, but a sweet taste to savour. A series of hugs and smiles, plenty of photos, the shared success of such a climb. Only the name was missing. We called it Osa ma non Troppo (700m, 7b [7a obl.] A2+), roughly translated as "dare, but don't exaggerate."

Recommended gear: one set of wires, two sets of Camalots to #4, triples from 0.5 to 2, two sets of microfriends. We equipped all belays and left all pegs we placed in situ. At the seventh belay two or three people can bivy without a portaledge. We freed 85% of this beautiful, interesting route, which is in the lee of the wind. With lucky weather and drier cracks, we think the route can be climbed free, except for the third pitch. We highly recommend a repeat.

FABIO LEONI, *Italian Alpine Club*

Trono Blanco, Hoja de Rosa; Cuerno Norte, Dentelle de Roche; Cerro Catedral, Escoba de Dios, second ascent. In late February and March 2007 a team from the Equipe National de Jeunes Alpinistes (ENJA) visited the Valle del Frances in the heart of the Paine Massif.

In late February, Julien Dussere, Jehan-Roland Guillot, Rémi Vignon, and I climbed a new route on Trono Blanco (2,170 m), in the northern edge of the cirque. Our route climbs a series of easy slabs (4+) on the west face to reach a col at the base of Trono Blanco's south face, north of Aleta de Tiburon, from where it tackles a steep granite headwall (180m, 6c A1), followed by 500m of mixed terrain, to reach the summit (55° M5). On our first attempt we climbed an easy snow couloir (55°) on the east face to reach the col, but this approach, although easier, proved too dangerous (rockfall). Earlier in the season, with more snow, the east couloir should be the approach

Cuerno Norte's northwest face, from left to right: Caveman (Thomas-Turner, 1992; approximate line) and Dentelle de Roche (Dusserre-Guillot-Mounier-Salle-Vignon, 2007). *Rolando Garibotti*

Trono Blanco from the southwest, showing Hoja de Rosa. On the left is Cerro Mellizo Oeste, on the right Aleta de Tiburon. *Rolando Garibotti*

route of choice. We summited on February 24 and first down-climbed along the west ridge, then rappelled the line of ascent. It should be possible to climb the route in one day from a bivy near the base. The climb took three days: one day to explore the east couloir and fix two ropes on the headwall, a second day to find the alternate access to the col from the west and fix a few more pitches on the headwall, and a third day to climb to the summit and descend. We had fairly unstable weather throughout those days, with strong winds. We named our route Hoja de Rosa (1,000m, ED-).

Between March 1 and 9 Clément Mounier, Jehan-Roland Guillot, Rémi Vignon, Julien Dusserre, and I opened Dentelle de Roche on Cuerno Norte's northwest face, just right of Caveman, which was the only route on this side of the mountain. We climbed 14 pitches (700m) up to 7a, with a few short sections of A1 and A2. Most of the pitches are enjoyable, with high-quality climbing, except pitch 11, which follows a series of big flakes and is quite runout. The face is directly exposed to the wind, which on some days blew 100mph. In light of this we used fixed ropes. We stopped upon reaching the schist band up high and did not continue to the summit.

On the east face of Cerro Catedral, Jean Burgun, Victor Estrangin, Pierre Labbre, Erwan Madoré, and Jérôme Para made the second ascent of La Escoba de Dios (Catto-Fowler-Gallagher-Kendall, 1992). This 24 pitch, 950m route has difficulties up to 6b and A4. It took six days to fix ropes up to pitch 13, after which they rested for six days due to bad weather. After jumaring the 500m of fixed ropes, they installed a portaledge camp, but bad weather forced them to return to the ground after fixing just three more pitches. After two more days of forced rest they regained their high point, and the following day all five climbers climbed the remaining seven pitches and reached the summit. During the descent they spent one more night, taking the time to retrieve the ropes and all other gear. They describe the route as being magnificent, complex, and demanding but with a lot of enjoyable, beautiful climbing.

FREDERIC SALLE, *ENJA, Pyrenees, France (translated by Rolando Garibotti)*

Torre Sur, southeast buttress, attempt. It was Stuart McAleese and my 15th day climbing on the face. The December winds regularly gusted 100mph. The climbing, 800m above the glacier, was becoming markedly easier. Our summit was tantalizingly close. One good day and only 300m of 35° snow led to the summit, and a month's hard effort would be worth it.

[Editor's note: The McAleese-Turner highpoint is in a prominent diagonal dike below the intersection with the route Hoth (Amelunxen-Easton, 2000). From where Hoth enters the dike above, Hoth climbs two pitches of mostly rock (5.8 WI3), then bulletproof snow and ice, then two more pitches of rock (5.9 and 5.6) to gain the summit. McAlesse and Turner called their efforts "The Good, the Bad, and the Ugly,"

Torre Sur, home to only four complete routes. Its highly sought, unclimbed south face is left of the sun/shade southeast buttress, which shows the 2006 Turner-McAleese attempt and Hoth (Amelunxen-Easton, 2000). Other strong attempts on the storied buttress include a ca 1998 Swiss team that survived a major epic (blown hook, big whipper, torn-off finger, broken femur) and a 1980s attempt by a South African team (Andre Vercueil and partners) that also endured a memorable retreat after climbing to just above the prominent roof halfway up Hoth. To the right En el Ojo del Huaracán (Piola-Sprungli, 1992) and Self Right to Suicide (Belczynski-Kowalski-Wiwatowski, 2004) climb the sunlit east face. The standard North Ridge (Aiazzi-Aste-Casati-Nusdeo-Taldo, 1963) climbs just beyond the tower's right skyline, and the Southwest Buttress (Bagattoli-Cagol-Espen-Leoni, 1987) roughly follows the left skyline. Torre Central, the tower to the right, has more than a dozen routes. *Rodrigo Diaz*

and several sources, including Turner's website, referred to it as a new route. We asked Turner's opinion on whether they consider it an attempt or a new route: "On the route which we claimed as not complete...."]

Stuart clipped into the top belay and looked down. The weather had worsened. It was time to bail to our bivy 500m below. As we descended, the funneled winds between the South Tower (Torre Sur) and Paine Chico gusted to 150mph. We hung like puppets, swinging horizontally in the gusts. During the

Stuart McAleese enjoying a refreshing moment in the sun on Torre Sur. *Twid Turner*

short respite between gusts, rappelling was only possible by pulling ourselves down the iced-up ropes. Every two minutes our eyelashes would weld together. Breathing into the wind was difficult, we had to look away. Finally we reached the bottom of our ropes, 100m from our bivy kit. A simple snow climb now was a terrifying crawl. Eventually we swung off our anchors inside a bag of Gore-Tex, covered in snow; we now knew we would survive.

The southeast face of the South Tower of Paine is still unclimbed. The kilometer-wide and at least kilometer-high wall has no obvious linking lines leading to the summit. A 200m grey belt of compact granite halfway up the face truncates cracks. Our chosen line wandered up the right-hand side of the face, left of the excellent Canadian route Hoth. It linked hanging grooves and cracks, providing hard aid, mostly on hooks. During our climb (800m, E2 A3+) we encountered only eight hours of good weather in four weeks. It was constantly windy and often snowing. We resigned ourselves to aid climbing, as exposing flesh and wearing rock boots would bring certain frostbite. Every day on the face we clad ourselves in every stitch of clothing we had. It was like Scotland in winter, we kept repeating, so we had to keep going!

Climbing capsule-style, we had stretched our ropes 600m up from our bivy, 200m above the glacier. Our climbing equipment remained high above. Stuck in our bivy we had no choice but to wait for four days during a massive storm. The fifth day was our last chance to descend; otherwise we would miss our flights home. We had no choice but to battle back up to our kit at the top of the lines, rescue sufficient gear and ropes, and make our escape. (We ended up leaving 150m of static rope but returned 200m of rope borrowed from local climbers and brought home the rest. We also took out all trash, including rubbish gathered in a full day's work at Bader Camp.) Descending to a hanging snowpatch I triggered a sizable avalanche. Back on the glacier we waded out to our advanced camp and started home. We had barely survived the mountain and Patagonia weather. We were happy with our efforts but saddened not to summit. The route in perfect weather would go free, but its location generally means cold and wind.

MIKE "TWID" TURNER, *U.K.*

Torre Central, Golazo, second ascent, and first BASE jump. Tim Akhmedkhanov, Igor Pekhterev, and leader Arkadiy Seregin (all from Russia), with Sergiy Kovalov from the Ukraine, arrived in Puerto Natales on January 9, 2007, and five days later started fixing the initial pitches of Golazo (1,200m, VI 5.10 A4+, Schneider, 1999 [with Christian Santelices to pitch 12]).

On January 20 they reached the big ledge atop pitch nine and established two portaledges. After fixing pitch 10 (A3+) the following day, they were forced down by a storm. On January 24 they were back on the wall with 150 liters of water. They also took 12 ropes and fixed them all. It took six days to climb the next three pitches. Pitches 14-21 were A2 or A2+ and were climbed somewhat faster. While the first 15 pitches had two bolts at each belay, above there was only one, so the team added a second bolt to all higher stances. On February 2 Akhedkahnov and Pekhterev led pitches 20 and 21, and then Kovalov and Seregin joined them and continued to the summit. By 8 p.m. it was snowing but the climbing was relatively straightforward, despite icy rock. At 11:20 p.m. all four stood triumphantly on the summit. By 6 a.m. on February 3 they had regained the portaledges. A big storm began two hours later as they were descending the lower part of the wall, but by 4 p.m. all were safely on the glacier. Seregin feels that this route is definitely harder than Reticent Wall on El Capitan and that Schneider is a real hero. "He did a hard job. I'm going to send him a bottle of our good Russian vodka."

Other recent activity on the Central Tower includes the area's first BASE jump, a 1400m flight down the east face (plus some tracking out) by Russian Valery Rozov on February 24. To reach the top he climbed the Bonington-Whillans route (700m, V 5.11 A2) in two days with Russian Big Walls Project hardmen Odintsov, Ruchkin, Provalov, and Kachkov.

Adapted from WWW.ALPINIST.COM, *originally by* LINDSAY GRIFFIN

Antarctica

ELLSWORTH MOUNTAINS
—SENTINEL RANGE

Vinson, summary of the 2006-7 season.
There were 100 ascents of Vinson (4,892m)
out of 130 attempts. This success rate of
only 77% is statistically the worst on record
and contrasts strongly with 2005-6, which
had the most summit successes with 149
out of the 153 attempts. Failure to summit
last season was mainly due to bad weather,
particularly in the first few weeks, but there
is also a consensus that Vinson clients are
becoming progressively less competent and less experienced. Some are now simply not up to
the ascent, especially in less than ideal weather. As in previous years, several poor decisions by
guided groups led to situations that really should be avoidable on this mountain. The weather
was almost never really bad but was regularly quite poor. Usually one can expect several spells
of very good weather lasting around five days or more. However, these never happened and
good weather rarely lasted longer than two days. Two guided groups required assistance, one as
a result of a crevasse fall and associated hypothermia and frostbite, and the other for a case of
pulmonary edema. The seracs on the southwest face of Shinn were again active, calving onto or
near the Normal route in the cwm below the Vinson headwall on at least three separate occasions. A serac at the top of the headwall itself also fell early in the season, disintegrating down
the middle of the slope to the left of the ascent route.

The total number of individual ascents of the continent's highest summit is now 1090.
This does not include repeat ascents: Dave Hahn, for example, has climbed it on 25 occasions,
so the total number of ascents must be well over 1,100.

DAMIEN GILDEA, *Australia, AAC*

Sentinel Range, various first ascents and GPS Work.
During the season I led my fifth expedition to the
Sentinel Range, and as on previous trips the aim
was to climb and re-survey a number of the highest peaks, in order to increase and refine the geographical knowledge of Antarctica's highest mountains. The main objectives for this season were the
first ascent of Mt. Rutford, a newly designated high
peak to the south of the Vinson Massif, followed
by climbing from the Embree Glacier at the very
northern end of the range. After this we hoped to
climb the remaining two virgin 4,000m peaks.

Eiichi Fukushima, John Evans, Sam Silverstein, and
Brian Marts back at Vinson base camp in December
2006 to celebrate the 40th anniversary of their first
ascent of Vinson. *Damien Gildea*

Peaks at the northern end of the Sentinel Range. From left to right: Bentley (4,137m), Sisu (ca 4,050m), Anderson (4,144m). Marked is the route taken by the Omega expedition on the first ascent of Anderson via the west face. In the lower section the solid line marks the route followed by Brown and Gildea, while the dashed line is that taken by Paz Ibarra and Rada. Sisu and Bentley were climbed in 1998 by Patrick Degerman and Veikka Gustafsson. They followed the left side of the snow/ice slope between Bentley and Anderson, then traversed Sisu to reach Bentley. *Damien Gildea*

On November 26 we skied south from Vinson base camp with sleds containing food and fuel for 12 days. After reconnoitering two possible routes down to the Nimitz Glacier, we followed our third option, passing across the Cairns and Tulaczyk Glaciers, through two easy cols, and down into the Zapol Glacier. From here, the icefall leading down to the Nimitz was straightforward, requiring just a short section near the bottom, where we lowered sleds. From here we skied around to the Nimitz and up to the base of the Gildea Glacier. We camped here for four days in poor weather, unable to see our route up through the crevasses of the Gildea. On December 1 we finally made our way east up the glacier for 11km to camp at ca 2,450m near the foot of the north ridge of Mt. Atkinson.

During the afternoon of December 3, we made the second ascent of Atkinson, Jed Brown and I needing just a couple of hours to climb an easy line that slanted up the north face to the north ridge. We left the GPS on the summit in high winds. Camilo Rada and Maria Paz Ibarra ('Pachi') followed us a few hours later, taking a more direct line up the ridge and retrieving the GPS, which later showed that Atkinson is 3,192m, over 100m lower than previously thought. The first ascent of Atkinson was by Robert Anderson and Joseph Blackburn in December 1992.

After three days bad weather we headed for Mt. Slaughter. This peak was first climbed in 1998 by Guy Cotter and Terry Gardiner via a couloir on the north side. The south side is less steep, though all the ridges require some classic, moderate technical climbing. Jed and I took different lines up the south face, but mine ended at a difficult section on the east ridge, so I was forced to down climb and traverse across to Jed's line in the center of the face. The climbing was never difficult but steepened toward to the top, following some shallow gullies and rock ribs. Pachi and Camilo followed the line later that day. Slaughter was previously thought to be around 3,600m but proved to be 3,444m.

The Craddock Massif in Antarctica's Sentinel Range, viewed from the west. (A) Rutford (4,477m), (B) Bugueno Pinnacle, (C) Rada (4,402m), and (D) Craddock (4,368m). (1) Jed Brown, solo (December 9, 2006), first ascent of the mountain. Repeated by Paz Ibarra and Rada. (2) Chaplin-Gildea (December 7, 2005), new route and second overall ascent of the mountain. Repeated the next day by Bugueno and Rada. *Damien Gildea*

After another day of strong, cold southerly winds, we set off for the west face of Mt. Rutford on December 9. I soon realized I had not suitably refueled or recovered sufficiently after my overly-long ascent of Slaughter, and was not feeling as strong as I would like. I turned back after crossing the bergschrund, while Jed powered on, climbing 2,000m of mostly snow and ice in four and a half hours to make the first ascent in perfect weather. Camilo and Pachi repeated the line, meeting Jed on the way down after he had also walked across to the small virgin point of Bugueno Pinnacle.

Rutford is the highest point of the newly designated Craddock Massif. We had seen this high, sharp point numerous times during our ascents of Vinson in previous years, and while we initially thought it might be higher than Craddock to its south, we eventually decided not. However, after making the second ascent of Craddock in December 2005 and gaining a new perspective on the topography, we realized that this sharp point *was* higher than Mt. Craddock and everything else in the massif of which Craddock was a part. In the process of producing our new topo map of the range, I discussed this issue with the USGS and they decided that the whole big feature would be named the Craddock Massif. The highest point would be named Mt. Rutford, after Robert Rutford, a U.S. glaciologist who did a lot of significant work in the area. Rutford is 4,477m, making it the sixth or seventh highest mountain in Antarctica, depending on the accuracy of Mt. Elizabeth's published height of 4,480m.

Having extended our stay, we were now out of food, so had to leave immediately. Through cold weather and low visibility we made a 14-hour ski journey back to Vinson base camp and spent the next two days resting. On December 14, Jed soloed a 1,500m new route on the main west face of Vinson. Conjugant Gradients, which lies between Jay Smith's Linear Accelerator to the left and the Dave Morton–Todd Passey route Purple Haze to the right, wanders up the easy rock and snow of the lower face before climbing more rock as the face

Situated south of Ostenso, Mt. Morris was first climbed and measured (3,793m) in January 2007. Brown, Paz Ibarra, and Rada's southwest face is marked. *Damien Gildea*

steepens. It eventually gains an obvious short couloir high on the face, visible from the Branscomb Glacier. Jed followed this couloir, topping out near Branscomb Peak around seven hours after leaving base camp. He then walked across to the main summit of Vinson, reaching it just before midnight and was back in camp six hours later.

As we all wanted to maintain our acclimatization, the same day Camilo and Pachi headed off for a single push up Mt. Shinn and I went to look at lines at the left end of Vinson's west face. In perfect sunny weather I reached Low Camp in two hours and spent a cold night there alone. Late the next day I climbed a minor new route on the rock rib that splits the face above Low Camp. The route was 1,000m of mostly steep snow, easy ice and, higher, fun rock climbing. It is a more direct, mostly independent, version of the route climbed by Spaniards Miguel Angel Vidal and Maria Jesus Lago in 2004. I reached the top of the face in high winds after about four hours climbing, spent some time checking out the new VHF radio repeater installed there, then descended by the steep snow slope at the far northern end of the west face. This slope, which narrows to a fin higher up, has previously been mooted as a possible alternative to the regular Vinson route, which takes the cwm and "headwall" just to the north. I believe the upper slope is probably too steep for most modern Vinson clients, particularly in descent, though given the increasing objective danger of the normal line, some strong groups may want to consider it. The slope is shorter than the normal route, possibly less windy and enables you to place high camp an hour or more above the traditional site at Goodge Col.

Meanwhile, Camilo and Pachi had climbed a new route on the southwest face of Shinn (4,660m), which they named Soleil de Media Noche (Midnight Sun). Their route gained the lower left side of the face, across from the old site of C2, and climbed through a narrow mixed couloir that required a rope in places. This led to somewhat easier ground, which they traversed up and right, frontpointing unroped, to gain the big obvious shoulder reached on the Normal route up Shinn. They followed this to the top, completing only the third route on Antarctica's third highest mountain and the first not to have the advantage of going from Vinson's High Camp on Goodge Col.

Back at base camp we were able to spend some time with the guys from the 1966 expedition, who had returned to celebrate the 40th anniversary of their first ascent of Vinson. We then loaded our sleds with 30 days of food and fuel, and took a spectacular flight 50km north along the range to land on the beautiful Embree Glacier. Only two teams had visited the main part of this glacier before, making some minor ascents and attempting Mt. Bentley. Camped in the upper cirque at 2,450m, we spent the next five days in poor weather, placing the GPS on some nearby minor rocky points and going for short skis up and down the glacier. Christmas Day turned out nice and we made the first ascent of a small peak on the southern wall of the cirque. This wall is a long ridge running northeast from Mt. Anderson toward Mt. Press and contains a number of small peaks. We thought the one we headed for was the highest, going on photos taken from far to the south in previous years. However, once on top we found this was incorrect and at least two other tops were higher than ours. The route was straightforward, up a ramp into a couloir of soft snow and then onto a very corniced hanging summit. The GPS was placed slightly to the south on a lower rock outcrop, which was found to have an altitude of 3,368m.

After two days of bad weather, during which we retreated from the base of Mt. Todd, the 29th was better, so Jed and I set off in the afternoon for Mt. Bentley. The northeast ridge had been almost climbed by Wally Berg and Bob Elias in 1999 but they stopped a short distance from the summit. Climbing unroped up independent vague lines atop the ridge, we wove around and over several rock patches, until gaining the easy-angled rocky wall beneath the summit. Here Jed stayed more to the right on mixed ground, reaching the summit well before me: I went to the left on bad steep snow. The summit ridge is quite narrow and corniced, and I found it challenging in the strengthening winds. Pachi and Camilo waited until next evening before repeating the climb and retrieving the GPS in perfect weather. Bentley later proved to be 4,137m, only 8m lower than its official USGS height.

Pachi, Camilo, and Jed celebrated New Year's Eve with an ascent of the beautiful Mt. Press, northeast of our camp, climbing the west spur to south ridge. We had seen Press the year before, while descending Gardner and thought it looked much higher than its altitude on the map of 3,760m. In fact our GPS data showed it is actually lower at 3,732m.

Jed spent the first day of 2007 narrowly avoiding being taken for a ride on a slab avalanche he triggered on the west face of Mt. Todd after we retreated from crappy conditions on the west ridge. We abandoned Todd and on January 3, packed the sleds and skied northwest to a col that we hoped that would lead us out of the Embree. The west side surprised me by being steeper than we imagined, so we spent an hour or two lowering the sleds 150m straight down the slope to a small cirque, its floor a sea of sastrugi. A couple of hours hauling brought us out of the cirque into more open terrain, where we camped the night in beautiful weather.

Over the next two days we took our time covering 18km of rolling sastrugi to reach the cwm west of Mt. Anderson. Anderson is the highest and southernmost peak of a massif that has Bentley to the north and a peak unofficially named Sisu in the middle. With Rutford climbed, Anderson was now the highest unclimbed mountain in the Sentinel Range and a long-held objective of mine. Patrick Degerman and Veikka Gustafsson had climbed Bentley and Sisu in January 1998, using the left side of the steep snow and ice slope between Sisu and Anderson. We considered using this slope to gain the north ridge of Anderson, but found it considerably threatened by a huge serac in the middle. We had also become increasingly wor-

Looking north at Shinn (4,660m) from a point near Goodge Col, the pass between Vinson and Shinn. Marked is Soleil de Media Noche on the southwest face (Paz Ibarra–Rada, December 2006). The Normal route follows the gentle snow slopes from the col around to the shoulder on the left where it joins the marked route. *Damien Gildea*

ried about the avalanche danger on particular slopes with certain aspects. On the flight in we had spied a couloir cutting through the west face, reaching a notch on the west ridge. Jed proposed this route as a safer and more aesthetic alternative to the north ridge and eventually I agreed, though somewhat worried about the possibility of being turned back high on the route by difficulties we couldn't see from below.

My fears turned out to be groundless and we climbed the route on January 8. The lower mixed face was ca 800m high, after which ca 450m up the easy slanting couloir took us to the notch. We roped up for the face above, but the climbing was straightforward: there were pitches on good positive rock, interspersed with easy mixed ground and sections of terrible snow. Jed bypassed the biggest and steepest rock step via a sneaky back alley requiring just one rock move. The actual summit was a short steep pinnacle atop a knife-edge ridge and required a few body lengths of easy rock climbing. We were on the summit at 4 a.m. after 13 hours of climbing.

We descended by a mix of rappelling and down-climbing, meeting Camilo and Pachi on the way up. We had a chat about the route and they decided to take an easier option up the ice slope, bypassing much of the lower mixed wall and making things a bit quicker. This day, January 9, was the hottest I have experienced in eight Antarctic expeditions over the last six years. While we were initially surprised to discover hard water ice on the lower mixed wall, we later realized this whole wall literally runs with water on hot days: you could actually hear it from a distance, running under and between rocks. This wall, which is really the north face of the west ridge, catches a lot of sun during the hottest part of the day, yet is sheltered from much of the wind.

After resting on the 10th, we left camp late on the 11th in bad weather and sledged for several hours before camping northwest of Mt. Viets. The next day Camilo, Jed, and Pachi placed the GPS on the USGS satellite point nearby and also on the summit of a small peak between Viets and Pk. 4,111m that turned out to be 3,119m high. The next day we sledged further south and into the valley west of Mt. Giovinetto, the last unclimbed 4,000m peak in the range. Here we spent six days in poor weather, waiting to climb.

On the 20th the weather was perfect, so we set off for the west face. I soon found snow conditions were far from ideal, and with a worsening knee problem retreated low on the face while Jed continued. He reached the summit without problem and even walked some way south along the ridge to be sure he was on the highest point. Pachi and Camilo repeated the route in the early hours of the next morning and were back by midday on the 21st. The measured height was 4,074m and all the mountains above 4,000m in the Sentinel Range have now been climbed.

Running short of time, we left camp later that evening and sledged around into the cirque beneath Mt. Morris. Although less than 4,000m, Morris is a good-looking peak with no easy way up. Late on the 22nd Camilo, Pachi, and Jed set off in poor weather, climbing an obvious shallow couloir on the southwest face. They reached the summit around midnight, after climbing through continuous bad weather. The descent proved as long as the climb, but all were back in camp later the following morning. The measured height was 3,793m.

We began skiing out at 2 a.m, the following day in cold and windy weather with poor visibility. We spent around eight and a half hours traveling 22km, much of it ploughing through fresh snow sometimes 30cm deep. This was the greatest accumulation of snowfall—not just drift—I have ever seen in the range. After safely descending the steep slope down on to the Branscomb, we hauled up the last section and reached Vinson base camp at 10:30 a.m. on the 24th. That night we were collected by Twin Otter and after my customary five-day wait at Patriot Hills, we flew out to Chile in the early hours of January 30. The expedition had achieved all its main objectives in term of GPS work and climbing, making 12 ascents, all of which were either first ascents of peaks or new routes.

DAMIEN GILDEA, *Australia, AAC*

QUEEN MAUD LAND

Fenriskjeften mountains, Ulvetanna, north face, and other ascents; Holtedahl mountains, six first ascents. Stein-Ivar Gravdal, Trond Hilde, Ivar Tollefsen, and I visited the Orvin mountains in Queen Maud Land from November 2 through December 10. In the magnificent Fenriskjeften mountains we climbed the north face of ca 2,960m Ulvetanna (ca 960m, 21 pitches, 5.10 A4) in 16 days, November 5-20. We climbed in capsule style, fixing the first four pitches from a tented camp on the ground, before moving onto the face and establishing three portaledge camps on our way

On the northwest ridge of Store Gruvletind (2,254m), Holtedahl mountains, during the first ascent. *Stein-Ivar Gravdal*

to the summit. The climb follows a thin line slightly to the left of the center of the wall, ca 150m left of the other, more obvious, line attempted in 1994 by Thomas Cosgriff and Trond Hilde, who only got four pitches (150m) up before aborting.

The north face of Ulvetanna (ca 2,960m) showing the line of the Norwegian Route (ca 960m, 21 pitches, 5.10 A4, Caspersen-Gravdal-Hilde-Tollefsen). The face was attempted in 1994 by a line a little further right. *Stein-Ivar Gravdal*

We had a wonderful time on the face. Climbing in capsule style with portaledges and plenty of food was quite comfortable. The climbing was ecstatically good and totally surpassed all our expectations. In general the rock in this area is heavily frost weathered, giving it a coarse and flaky structure. From earlier experiences we were expecting shitty rock and a lot of squeeze chimneys and offwidths. However, our line followed thin formations on surprisingly good rock, and the amount of natural skyhooking and delicate nailing was a positive surprise. The most difficult pitches were in the lower half of the wall. For comfort and

The Ulvetanna group from the northeast. The dominant peak on the right is Ulvetanna (ca 2,960m, first climbed in 1994 by Norwegians via the northwest face. The north face, climbed in 2006, is sunlit). To the left are Hel (2,335m, Norwegians in 1994), Stetind (2,558m, climbed in 2001 first by a multi-national and then a Spanish team, and again in 2006 by Norwegians), Kinntanna (2,724m, climbed by Norwegians in 1994 and again by multi-national and Spanish teams in 2001), Holsttind (2,577m, climbed by Norwegians in 1994 and again by a multi-national team in 2001) and, peeping up just behind it, the upper part of Holtanna (2,650m, climbed by a multi-national team in 2000). Peaks of the Filchnerfjella are visible in the distance. *Stein-Ivar Gravdal*

aid we placed a total of five expansion bolts on the pitches, 40 on belays (by hand drill of course), and drilled 25 bat-hooks. We felt that this was an acceptable style for such a seemingly compact wall. We experienced mainly good weather, apart from one 48-hour snowstorm (60cm on the ground) that we sat through in our portaledges halfway up the face. Temperatures averaged –20°C.

All in all, the route has great climbing, the line is very aesthetic, and the face and mountain is in a class of its own in this area—all the right ingredients to make it a future classic.

After the climb we skied 30km with pulks and light climbing gear eastwards to the Holte-

The camp below Kubbestolen (2,079m), which the Norwegians climbed via an ice gully behind the large pinnacle and relatively straightforward mixed terrain above. The rock formation near the left edge of the picture is Andersnuten, climbed in 2005 by Mike Libecki and dubbed the Ship's Prow. Kubbestolen was first climbed in 2000 by a Swiss couple. *Stein-Ivar Gravdal*

dahl Mountains, where we did what we believe to be six first ascents. We found no traces of previous activity. The only person we know to have been in this area is Mike Libecki, who climbed two summits there the previous season (Windmill Spire and Andersnuten). The six climbs we did all had major and distinct summits: Store Gruvletind (2,254m); Kubbestolen (2,079m), and four nameless summits of ca 2,200m along the Vinten-Johansen ridge. All the ascents involved fairly easy climbing (max 5.10), with only shorter sections requiring the use of a rope. After this we skied a further 30km east and climbed the freestanding Sandneshatten (2,200m) in the same style—in one day and only roping up for a short section. We then skied back to Fenriskjeften and the Ulvetanna region, where we did some smaller climbs, including a route on the west face of Stetind (ca 2,500m), first ascended in 2001 by André Georges and Alain Hubert.

ROBERT CASPERSEN, *Norway*

Editor's note: The Holtedahl mountains were probably first visited by a climbing party in 1999-2000. Cestmir Lukes and Irene Oehninger ascended six peaks including Kubbestolen, which they climbed via the west face. In January 2001 a Spanish party made the second ascent of Stetind (2,558m quoted) via a route on the west face. The first ascent, earlier the same month, was made via a south to north traverse. See AAJ 2001, pp. 316-319.

Oman

Western Hajar, various first ascents.
Following our visit to Oman
reported in *AAJ 2006*, pp. 295-
296, Geoff Hornby and I returned
to the Western Hajar in January
2007. As before, our aim was to
climb new alpine-style routes on
the textured limestone faces of
Jabal Kawr and Jabal Misht. First
we returned to the shaded north
face of Jabal M'Seeb that we had
enjoyed in 2005. Black Gold made
an excellent start to the trip and a
second route on the face (400m,
D+ UIAA V). Following this, we
scrambled through a boulder
choke to the hidden cirque of
Nadan village—one of the few in
Oman still inaccessible by road—
hoping to climb above the cirque.
However, we turned back the next
morning in threatening weather.

The northeast face of Jabel Asait in Oman's Western Hajar. Marked
are just a few of the recent additions. (1) Sunshine Pillar (245m, D
V, Knott-Walsh, 2007). (2) Nora Batty (335m, TD- V, Hornby-Knott,
2007). (3) Shamsa (445m, D+ V, Hornby-Sammut-Turnbull, 2004)
takes a more or less parallel line to 4. (4) Arch Wall (385m, TD- V+,
Hornby-Knott, 2004). Between 2 and 3 lie routes such as Alone in
Space (450m, TD- V+/VI-, Davison, solo, 2002), Two's Company
(470m, D+ V/V+, Hornby-Sammut) and Three's a Crowd (475m,
D V+, Honrby-Sammut, 2002). Right of 4 lie Sackgasse (350m, TD-
VI-, Mayr-Oberhauser-Reischauer-Zinner, 2004) and the Albert
Precht solo, Straight Up (500m, D V+, Precht, 2001). The right arête
is taken by Internationale (500m, TD+, Brachmayer-Hafner-Hornby-
Oelz-Precht, 2001). *Paul Knott*

Moving to the north side of
the Kawr massif, we scrambled to
the left end of Jabal Asait's northeast face and climbed Nora Batty
(335m, TD- V), which was named
after a bat cave we judiciously
avoided. As we became happier
about the weather, we turned our
attention to the more committing Jabal Misht, where we had in
mind a line up the gray walls left
of our 2005 route Palestine (800m
TD- V+) on the southeast pillar.
Jerusalem turned out to be another good line, also TD- and 800m.

Oman guru Geoff Hornby on pitch three of Jerusalem (800m, TD-),
southeast pillar of Jabal Misht. *Paul Knott*

Geoff left for the U.K., and
I returned to Jabal M'Seeb with John Walsh. We found a sustained line that follows the dark
walls right of Black Gold; we named it Black Magic (510m, TD- V+). The next day we moved
to Jabal Asait, where we climbed a line left of Nora Batty, finding several excellent pitches on
some of the best rock of the trip to make Sunshine Pillar (245m, D V).

The east face of Jabal Misht (2,090m), one of Oman's finest high mountain rock climbing venues. The face has a strong British history and a selection of routes are marked. British grades are used throughout. (1) English Arête (1,200m, E4 6a, Davison-Oberhauser, 2002). (2) Icarus (1,100m, E4 5c, Littlejohn-Sustad, 2001). (3) The Empty Quarter (1,000m, E2 5a, Chaudhry-Eastwood-Ramsden, 2000). (4) Eastern Promise (1,000m, E2 5c, Nonis-Ramsden, 1999). (5) Intifada (1,000m, E1/E2 5b, Hornby-Wallis, 2001). (6) Southeast Pillar (800m, HVS 5a/5b, Howard-McDonald, 1988). (7) Jerusalem (800m, VS 4c, Hornby-Knott, 2005). (8) Palestine (800m, VS 4c, Hornby-Knott, 2007). *Paul Knott*

It was a pleasure to climb these long mountain routes without having to deal with mountain weather and access (boulder chokes, long talus slopes, and possible flash floods aside). As always the people in the mountains were hospitable, and we found the country safe. In the city the passions we witnessed were due to Oman reaching the semi-final of the Gulf Cup soccer. We met no other climbers during the trip, though during the season, parties from Russia, France, and the U.K. made ascents on Jabal Misht. Oman-based climbers are also developing the potential for shorter, often bolted routes in various wadis. In the mountains almost all climbing to date has adhered to traditional ethics, using natural gear.

PAUL KNOTT, *New Zealand*

Jordan

WADI RUM

April 2006-April 2007, summary. In April 2006 regulars Walter Haupolter and Albert Precht visited the west side of Jebel Rum and with friends put up three routes: Silver Fox (6a), Pensionier's Tango (6a+), and Jordan Express (6b). These routes were 250-300m high, were climbed in traditional style, and finish on the shoulder of Frustration Dome, north of Sheikh

From left to right, the 500m east and southeast faces of South and North Nassrani, in Wadi Rum. Muezzin is visible as the large crack line toward the right side of the southeast face of North Nassrani. The new American-Canadian route, Dar al Salaam (5.13a) crosses Muezzin to finish up the smooth wall right of Muezzin's final crack. La Guerre Sainte climbs the left side of the same face, finishing up the prominent black water stripe. *Tony Howard*

Hamdan's Siq. During the same month O. Didou, P. Jammeson, and P. Voignier put up Misery and the Banana Skin (5+, 200m) on El K'Seir and two new lines in Barrah Canyon: a single 6b+ pitch left of the classic Merlin's Wand and a 6b pitch right of Siege of Jericho. Also, they suggest that the classic pitch of Little Gem in Rakabat Canyon is nearer 7a.

The two 600m west faces of North (left) and South Nassrani, with the smaller Draif al Murragh to the right. The big new French route (18 pitches, 6c A1, Guillaume-Ravier, 2006) climbs the west face of North Nassrani. *Tony Howard*

More new routes appeared in Wadi Rum during October. On challenging terrain in the Barrah Canyon, Thomas Senf and Rolf Weber put up Ehe Auf Zeit on Jebel Abu Judaidah. They climbed the 16-pitch route using traditional protection throughout. Pitches 7-15 follow an obvious line up mostly perfect rock at a grade of 5b+ to 6c. The same team added Sex (w)as Well on Abu Judaidah's north gendarme, also in the Canyon. This six-pitch route, with a crux of 6b, mostly follows cracks in good rock but has serious moves on the difficult pitches. Two days later they climbed Ritter der Kokosnuss (6b, seven pitches) on

Tony Howard on the upper slab of The Haj, Suweibit Gharbia, Wadi Rum, during the first ascent. In November 2006 Italians added another route to the left on the same face, a nine-pitch traditionally protected climb at UIAA VII A1. *Di Taylor/Tony Howard collection*

Abu Aina Towers, finishing on the final two pitches of the Edwards' classic, Lionheart. They report it to be "a classic line on good rock." The following day, still hungry for rock, they almost completed Coitus Interruptus on Vulcanics Tower. The pair climbed three pitches of 6b and 6b+, commenting that they were "too fat for the last pitch." This didn't stop them from making a six-pitch route two days later on Draif al Muragh's east face; Model TV is 6b+ A0 and "a nice line on good rock."

In November an American-Swiss team added a couple of single pitch climbs (both 6a) on the 30m-high granite rock just above Rum village. Two more were put up on sandstone near the Kharazeh rock bridge, northeast of Rum towards the highway. Both were 6a, and for some reason bolts were added afterwards. This team also added two more single-pitch routes "near Obeid's Bedouin Camp at Disi village," again northeast of Rum.

Italians Gianluca Bellin and Andrea Cozzini were in the area during November and added the nine-pitch L'Alba di Fabio to the south face of Suweibit Gharbia, left of the classic line of The Haj. They used traditional protection throughout, grading two hard pitches UIAA VII A1 and VI A0. The two report the climb to be "a beautiful and varied route on good rock."

In early December two French Pyreneans Arnaud Guillaume and Christian Ravier, moved onto Haupolter-and-Precht territory, climbing the 600m West Face of North Nassrani over three days. Their 18-pitch route was sustained at 6a and 6a+, with crux pitches just below the summit at 6c and 6b A1. They left nine pitons and 13 bolts in place. The pair then added another route to the Dark Tower on Jebel Rum's east face, between existing classics Mira Khoury and Black Magic. The new five-pitch line had a crux of 6c+.

Over the winter Britains Hugh Cotton and Robert Durran added Southern Star to the south face of Jebel Suweibit, east of The Haj. They reported this seven-pitch route to be excellent and on good rock, with good protection. The pair gave it a U.K. grade of E2 5b, equating the crux to 6a+. They repeated a number of classics over the Christmas period but found "the weather unusually cold, the worst for 12 years." They were caught out on the Traverse of Jebel Rum, a great Bedouin classic, spending two days snowed in under an overhang. At the same time two Italians suffered from "rain, hail and cold," which provided "scary climbing" on the 300m slabs of Orange Sunshine (British VS or French 5) on Jebel Burdah.

The next big route appeared in March 2007, when the American-Canadian team of Aaron Black, Ben Firth, Jean Gamalovsky, Chris Kalous, and Heidi Wirtz put up Dar al Salaam on the southeast face of North Nassrani. This is on the same wall as the Arnaud Petit bolted route, La Guerre Sainte (7b, 12 pitches), which the team repeated. Their new eight-pitch line crosses Muezzin from left to right and gives "sustained climbing on excellent rock with an unbelievable final pitch." The last four pitches go at 5.10a, 5.10b, 5.12a, and 5.13a (or 5.12/A0). Approximately 60 bolts were placed on this 320m route, though none interfere with the neighboring Muezzin. Kalous redpointed the top pitch on his last day, but the climb is yet to have a continuous free ascent.

Finally, a little note on action elsewhere in Jordan. Climbers have found numerous crags along the length of the Jordan Rift Valley, of granite, basalt, sandstone, conglomerate, and limestone. Some routes are even below sea level (the Dead Sea is 400m below sea level). Though Di Taylor and I have discovered some of the cliffs, the main protagonists are the French, in particular the guide Wilf Colonna and friends. (Wilf spends around six months of each year in Jordan.) Most routes are about 20m high, but a few are between two and nine pitches. Some have been equipped, and it is inevitable that there will be more development.

There are also superb treks and canyons throughout Jordan, though there are dangers: three people were killed in a flash flood during April, in one of the canyons leading to the Dead Sea. Information will be found in *Jordan—Walks, Treks, Caves, Climbs and Canyons* (by Di Taylor and Tony Howard) and *Canyons in the Jordan Rift Valley* (Itai Haviv). Also see *Treks and Climbs in Wadi Rum* (Tony Howard) for routes in Rum. This guide had been out of print for over a year, but a fourth edition was published in May 2007. This recent edition contains most of the Rum classics, and although no new climbs have been added, there is new information on access, and a copy of the Rum Protected Area Guidelines for Safety and Environmental Awareness for Climbers and Trekkers.

TONY HOWARD, *U.K.*

Africa

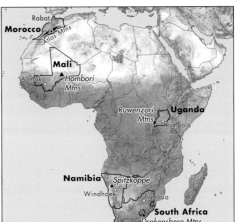

MOROCCO

TAGHIA

Tagoujimt n' Tsouiant, La Bas. Climbing has been a wonderful vehicle for seeing and enjoying some of the planet's less-known nooks and corners. There are experiences that leave one gratified and richer from the journey. The Atlas Mountain village of Taghia is three hours' walk from road, electricity, plumbing, and phone. During our month in Taghia we, a group of climbers steered by Cloe Erickson, established a multipitch 5.12 route, but that wasn't all. The union between North Face and Global Giving means that the former includes a charitable component in each trip we propose. So as well as climbing, we built a new roof for the only school in this remote village (materials portaged to town by mule) and attempted to bolster local trails with handrails. Conrad Anker, Kris Erickson, Renan Ozturk, Heidi Wirtz, and I climbed La Bas (5.12b) on Tagoujimt n' Tsouiant; the route name

is a local expression meaning "no harm." Our new line had 12 pitches of bolted 5.10 to 5.12, leading to several meters of easier, traditionally protected terrain, which we simul-climbed to reach the top of the 800m cliff. On October 3 we redpointed it ground-up with no falls. Others with us in Taghia included Roman Gackowski, Josh Helling, Jeff Hollenbaugh, Ken Sauls, and Jim Surette.

Many European climbers have visited the Taghia Cirque over the past 20 years but new-route activity has increased recently. From our climb we could see the school roof and watch goats being herded through steep trails recently reinforced with chain and rebar. No more drips in the school room, hopefully no more fatal tumbles from precarious trails, and together with a fine new route, these made for a fine experience.

KEVIN THAW

The line of La Bas (5.12b) on Tagoujimt n' Tsouiant, Taghia. Fantasia (7b+/7c) takes a parallel line to the left of the large rectangular alcove (see *AAJ 2006*, p. 303). *Kevin Thaw*

Oujdad, north face and west spur. A Spanish team added a fine line while we busied ourselves with La Bas. In September Luis Alfonso, Dani Martin, and Javi Saez put up Los Ratones Coloraos on the north face of Oujdad. The 400m route has 12 main pitches, finishing right of Whisky Berebere, and from the top of the wall it is possible to scramble to the summit (French 2 and 3) and descend the normal route. The climb is vertical, technical, and sustained (6c+, 6b+ obl) on generally sound but smooth rock with little friction. It is fully bolted, so future ascensionists need carry only 15 quick draws. According to the Spanish topo, it's not one of the best routes at Taghia, but it's still pretty good.

KEVIN THAW

Various new routes and repeat ascents. From March 31 to April 24 the Freewall Team of the German Alpine Club visited the limestone walls of Taghia. After two years of successful training, where they learned the fundamental climbing tricks, from aid to sport-climbing to bouldering, and from body-weight placements to double dynos, Daniel Gebel, Christoph Gotschke, Markus Grieshammer, Paul Sass, Benno Wagner, and I as trainer put up five new routes up to 8a+/5.13c. We also repeated classic routes up to 7c. All targets and expectations were fulfilled. Two new 500m routes with multiple 7th grade pitches would rank among the five best multi-pitch limestone routes I know in Europe.

The north face of Taoujdad showing from left to right: D'Antonion und die 3 Musketiere (16 pitches, 7c+), Riviere Purpur (16 pitches, 7b+), and Fata Morgana (15 pitches, 7c). The five-pitch Mastermind (7c+) lies just to the right of Fata Morgana. *Toni Lamprecht*

The team was lucky in its choice of new-route lines up the walls around the small village of Taghia and enjoyed three weeks of largely good weather throughout the stay. The walls lie in the middle of a dreamlike climbing valley, where time is slow and the potential for pioneering is awesome. However, one accident showed the seriousness of our climbing trip. After repeating a few hard classic routes, the team focused on first ascents on the north face of Taoujdad. This 600m-high wall has scope for beautiful hard lines and is just 30 minutes walk from the small Berber village of Taghia, with its 300 inhabitants. The village is only accessible by 4WD and a four-hour walk through an amazing gorge. It is situated in a beautiful green valley at ca 2,000m. The tranquility and hospitality of the local people are inspiring, and the surrounding peaks, which rise to 3,000m, complete a wonderful ambience. Most climbs lie between 20 minutes and three hours from the village.

During the first ascent of Fata Morgana (7c) on the north face of Taoujdad, Taghia. *Toni Lamprecht*

From April 3-7 Gebel and Gotschke climbed a new route that they named Fata Morgana (500m, 15 pitches, 7c), finishing on Riviere Purpur. On April 13 they made a one-day ascent. From April 4-9 Grieshammer, Lamprecht, Sass, and Wagner climbed D'Antonion und die 3 Musketiere (520m, 16 pitches, 7c+) This route was climbed in a day on April 16, again using Riviere Purpur for the finish. Gebel, Gotschke, and Lamprecht created Mastermind (150m, five pitches, 7c+) on April 12 and 14, with a one-day ascent being made on the 16th. Gebel made the first ascent of Fire Inside (8a) on April 18, and Gebel and Wagner made the first ascent of Muy Benno (8a+) on the 20th.

We also repeated Jamiro (11 pitches, 7a variation, Grieshammer-Wagner, April 3), Riviere Purpur (16 pitches, 7b+, Grieshammer-Wagner, April 4), Fata Morgana (the first 10 pitches by Gotschke and Lamprecht, April 13; all 15 pitches including the Riviere Purpur finish by Gebel and Sass, April 19), Fantasia (11 pitches to the rappel anchors, 7b+, Sass-Wagner, April 14), La Mano de la Maroc (13 pitches, 7b+, Sass-Wagner-Lamprecht, April 17), and Le Zebta (eight pitches, 7b+, Gebel-Gotschke, April 17).

TONI LAMPRECHT, *German Alpine Club*

MALI

Hand of Fatima, Suri Tondo, north summit. In February Eliza Kubarska and I, from Poland, arrived beneath the famous sandstone towers known as the Hand of Fatima. Our main objectives were a new route on one of the main towers that make up the Hand and look for new

The northeast face of Suri Tondo, Mali, showing the line of Krolestwo Sepa (Royaume de Vautour; 7b, 6b+ obl). *David Kaszlikowski*

High above an African dust storm, David Kaszlikowski climbs a pitch of 7a+ on the northeast face of Suri Tondo during the first ascent of Krolestwo Sepa (7b, 6b+ obl). *David Kaszlikowski collection*

possibilities in lesser-known areas. As the best time for climbing in this region ends in February, when temperatures rise considerably (on one day we experienced 56° C), we were the only climbers in the area.

Our presence was only possible thanks to Salvador Campillo and his family, especially his wife Miriam Dicko and her son Yaye, who run the climbing campsite in Daari village. Together with friendly Moussa they arranged frequent water supplies. Dehydration is the main concern in desert climbing, and each day we approached the climb with eight liters of water.

After a reconnaissance we realized that the big northeast face of Suri Tondo only had two routes. The line we decided to try seemed to be compact and relatively long, so we weren't sure if we had enough ropes and bolts; we came prepared only to try something short.

Our original idea was to climb through the immense roofs high in the center of the wall. However, the higher we got, the more we realized that the rock in these roofs was loose, and huge blocks might collapse if we climbed on them. We decided to slant right and bypass the

The massifs of Barkoussou and Kissim, which form part of Mali's Hombori Mountains, are more or less unexplored by climbers. *David Kaszlikowski*

overhangs on a solid part of the face. In doing so we found excellent rock. In fact there is only one place on the route where the rock is dubious, at the level of the big roofs. A ledge there looked dangerous to me. It could have formed a good hold, but we decided not to touch it and instead found a more bouldery alternative.

While we were climbing, the infamous Saharan wind, the Harmattan, started to blow, covering everything with a thick layer of dust, from fixed lines on the wall to filters inside my camera bag. After a few days of this wind, vision decreased to 100m. The only advantage of the dry Harmattan is that it lowers the temperature.

After six days we finished the line. Before the redpoint ascent we removed ropes and installed independent rappel anchors. This descent is probably the easiest way to rappel from Suri Tondo's north summit. We redpointed our line on March 15, naming it Krolestwo Sepa or Royaume de Vautour (Vulture Kingdom, 450m, 7b, 6b+ obl). Our line is partly equipped with bolts, but some crack sections required traditionally placed protection in the form of Friends. During the climb we watched, and were watched by, huge vultures (and *marabouts*, local Muslim hermits), which sometimes flew only 5m from us. The birds didn't seem to be bothered by our presence and luckily we didn't climb through their nests.

After repeating some established routes on the Hand of Fatima, we drove around the main massifs that make up the Hombori Mountains. The potential for new routes seems almost infinite: hundreds of kilometers of unclimbed walls 200m to 300m high. Massifs such as Sarniere, Dyounde Plateau, the cliffs above Boni village, and many remote towers await future ascensionists.

DAVID KASZLIKOWSKI, *Poland*

Marisol Monterrubio following the first pitch (7b) of Lunar Eclipse on the north face of Suri Tondo's south summit. *Oriol Anglada*

Hand of Fatima, Suri Tondo, south summit, north face. It was mid-March and necessary to climb in the shade. Any wall facing the sun was too extreme. There were only two existing lines on the section of the north face of Suri Tondo's south summit, where we fancied putting up a new route: Black Mamba (320m, 7a+, 6c+ obl, Faucheur-Pellissier-Petit, 2005) and Le Cri (320m, 7a+, 6b obl, Baillargé-Pellissier-Savary, 2005). Our initial idea had been to establish a new route on the 400m north face of Hombori Tondo 10km away, where in its almost 1km length there are few routes and only one big route in the center of the wall, Futuroscope (400m, 12 pitches, 7c+, Albrieuz-Faucheur-Pellissier-Perrillat-Petit, 2005). Other parts of the wall have beautiful lines that connect faces, dihedrals, and roofs. But first we concentrated on Suri Tondo.

The lower half of our new route, Lunar Eclipse, took longer to open than the rest, since there was little protection, slowing our ascent. The excellent compact rock was like nothing we had seen, though the climbing was similar to the Ordesa in northern Spain but with older rock. The rock was sharp, with many features for handholds and footholds.

Our route combines technical face-climbing with arêtes, dihedrals, roofs, and a short but stout offwidth. Pitch one climbs a 7a face and short technical corners to a good belay (7b). Pitch two, which forms the long crux, features two cracks leading to a strenuous and technical overhang. There are 7c+ moves between bolts, but this pitch can be climbed at 7b+ and C2 (two moves). We were unable to complete the whole pitch without rest points. On pitch three are great moves but also a run-out section between the second and third bolts (7a). Pitch four is 6a and involves climbing on top of a moving gendarme, while pitch five presents another long crux section: a 7a+ slab and a roof crack, followed by an offwidth, layback, and final section of 7a+. A redpoint of this pitch is 7b+. Pitches six and seven are 6b+ and 6c+, respectively, while pitch eight is another memorable ropelength on good rock at 7a+. A shorter but equally memorable ninth pitch (6c) leads to a big ledge, where, just to the right, we joined the second-to-last pitch of Le Cri. We rappelled from here using 8mm bolts, back-clipping when descending pitch five, which is overhanging.

Lunar Eclipse is equipped with 35 8mm bolts but also requires a set or a set and a half of camming devices up to Camalot 4, with 4.5 or 5 useful for the offwidth. We highly recommend Lunar Eclipse (the name comes from the total eclipse that occurred during early March). Pitches two and five were done with rest points, so it still awaits a truly free ascent.

It is now the fifth route on this side of the formation. In addition to the two mentioned above, there are Grains of Time, near the left edge of the wall (toward the north summit) and BMW, around toward the west face.

ORIOL ANGLADA *and* MARISOL MONTERRUBIO, *Spain (translated by Chris Barlow)*

Hombori Mountains, Débéré, Erosion Solare; Yéyéné, Passagio Dogon; Suri Tondo, north summit, northeast face. The year 2006 marked the 60th anniversary of the formation of the famous Italian climbing club, Ragni di Lecco (Lecco Spiders). Five members visited the Hombori region in December as part of the celebrations. In three weeks of climbing Cesare Bugada, Giovanni Ongaro, Simone Pedeferri, Adriano Selva, and Marco Vago repeated a number of existing routes in the region, before going on to put up three of their own. On the south face of Débéré in the Grimari, Bugada and Ongaro teamed with regular Belgian visitor B. Marnette, Salvador Campillo, and his 16-year-old son Yaye to produce Erosion Solare (270m, 6 pitches, 6b, 6a obl). Descent is by 60m rappels down the route. Campillo is a Spanish-Catalan who has lived in Mali for more than 20 years with his locally born wife and son. They stay there during the six "winter" months; in summer they move back to Spain.

In the last 24 years Campillo has put up a number of routes on the Hand of Fatima and surrounding walls. He is undoubtedly the person with the greatest knowledge of this area, and there is no one better to show you the innumerable possibilities for climbing, and the dangers that hide behind its great charm.

Ongaro and Selva made the first ascent of Passaggio Dogon on Yéyéné (300m, eight pitches, 7b, run-out 6b obl) and equipped a bolted rappel route. On the northeast face of the north summit of Suri Tondo, all five Italians put up Danza Tribale (500m, 13 pitches, 7b, 6b+ obl). From the top they descended by making one rappel down the Polish route, Royaume de Vautour [reported above], after which they traversed a ledge and rappelled their own route with 60m ropes. One notable repeat of an established route was Selva's free solo of Kaga Tondo's north pillar (600m, 5+, Desveaux-Girard-Pujos-Tugaye, 1979). He completed this great West African classic in three hours, carrying ropes in a rucksack so that he could rappel the far side.

The team also spent three days traveling in a 4WD, examining numerous walls 200m-500m high, all beautiful and composed of compact sandstone. Dehydration and intestinal disease are common afflictions, and Vago noted that climbing in this region is as severe and harsh as Patagonia, though for different reasons.

FABIO PALMA, *Italy*

MADAGASCAR

TSARANORO MASSIF

Tsaranoro Be, east face, Short Cut; Tsaranoro Kely, Bravo les Filles, second and third free ascents. Our four-person team arrived on September 18 in the Madagascar capital of Antanariva. From there we traveled to the Andringitra National Park 800km to the south. Situated here is the famous granite massif of Tsaranoro, and we spent almost a month climbing in this area. The team comprised Harald Berger and Florian Scheimpflug from Austria, and Tomáš Sobotka and I from the Czech Republic. For half the time we were accompanied by the photographer, Herman Erber, and his wife.

Our main aim was a new route, which we wanted to achieve in the same style that we would use on our own home sandstone, i.e. ground-up. We first focused on the largest wall in

The east face of Tsaranoro Be, Andringitra National Park, showing the line of Short Cut (800m, 7c+). Gondwanaland (7c) follows a line based on the black water stripe to the right, while the big corner system to the left is Vazimba (7a). *Ondra Benes*

Ondra Benes climbing pitch seven (7a+) of the new 800m route Short Cut (7c+) on Tsaranoro Be, Madagascar. *Tomas Sobotka/ Ondra Benes collection*

the group, the 800m east face of Tsaranoro Be. A black water stripe falls the whole height of the face; it was a super line, and we immediately started to work on it. After five days of climbing, fixing ropes, jumaring, and drilling, we reached the top, having equipped the 16 pitches with a total of 140 bolts. The majority of the climbing was 7a or more, with the crux pitch at 7c+. The rock in this area is large-grained granite; that although most of the faces offer holds, there is no classic crack climbing.

After a rest we made a redpoint attempt. Climbing all the pitches in one day was exhausting, as the sustained difficulty presented virtually no possibility for rests. We also had to climb as quickly as we could, because the heat made our feet painful in climbing shoes. After 10.5 hours on September 30, Tomas and I made the first redpoint ascent, leaving the second redpoint for Hari and Floe to complete on a later day. We named the climb Short Cut.

We spent rest days climbing other routes and taking photographs or film for a video. Floe and Tomas made an on-sight ascent of Always the Sun (450m, eight pitches, 7c+, 7b+ obl, Farquar-Mayers-Turner-Thomas, 1999, with Steve Mayers the only one to lead the runout crux pitch at the top of the wall) on the north face of Karambony. This was the third ascent, the second having taken place shortly before [see below].

In the meantime Hari and I had started work on Bravo les Filles (500m, 13 pitches, 5.13 A0, Feagin-Hill-Rodden-Pyke, 1999) on Tsaranoro Kely. On the first ascent Lynn Hill had only been able to climb the crux eighth pitch with rest points, but it was finally free-climbed in 2004 by the Spanish Pou brothers at 8b (5.13d). After three days of practice, both Hari and I led the route free in a day for the second and third free ascents.

The rest of our time we spent at Diego Suarez (Atsiranana) in the north of the island. This is a city of beautiful women, beaches, and limestone climbing on the mainland and nearby small islands. We recommend a visit and believe you will enjoy Madagascar as much us we did.

ONDRA BENES, *Czech Republic*

Editor's note: Both Benes and Berger were in good form before this visit with 23-year-old Benes having just made a rare repeat of Beat Kammerlander's masterpiece, Silbergeier (six pitches, 8b+) on the Fourth Kirchlispitze in the Ratikon, Switzerland. At much the same time Berger completed the first free ascent of an old sportingly bolted project, Antihydral (six pitches, 8b), on the wall just to its left. But three-time World Cup ice champion Hari Berger was killed on December 20 while ice climbing near his home in Salzburg.

Karambony, north face, Always the Sun, second ascent; Tsaranoro Be, Gondwanaland, rebolting; various other ascents. The Tsaranoro massif offers world-class free big-wall routes from 5.9 to 5.13, in a country that is one of the planet's poorest, yet is full of the happiest, warmest people we have ever met. In September our group, comprising Anne and John Arran, Giles Cornah, Jerry Gore, and Gaz Parry made a visit. On our first day in Andringitra National Park we all climbed Out of Africa (580m, 7a). This proved a tough intro, with 14 pitches of superb granite slabs offering the best flakes, chickenheads, and big-crystal climbing any of us had ever experienced. Not to be missed if you are a 5.11 climber.

Next up was the British extreme, Always the Sun. Put up in 1999 by Grant Farquar, Steve Meyers, Louise Thomas, and Twid Turner, it offers eight pitches up to 7c+ on a 400m smooth granite face with "better-than-gritstone" friction. An "on-form" Gaz onsighted all the hard pitches, commenting, "Imagine climbing a 7c+ route with no handholds!" A typical day of climbing would involve 10+ pitches and leave our arms strong, our skin in tatters, and our feet on fire. Footwork is the key in Tsaranoro. With the team accustomed to the rock, we picked off the hot ticks. Gaz and John made an onsight ascent of Rain Boto (420m, 10 pitches, 7b+). The entire team made an ascent of Le Crabe aux Pinces d'Or (320m, 11 pitches, 7b+), with both Gaz and John onsighting the crux pitches. Gaz and John made an ascent of Bravo Les Filles (600m, 15 pitches, 8b). However, they were unable to free the crux, a boulder-problem pitch that is very hard and out of character with the rest of the route. With a bit of cleaning and a slight change in line, this pitch might go free at around 7c/7c+, and in John's opinion be much better for it.

Gondwanaland (800m, 7c, 7a+ obl) is one of the massif's longest, most demanding routes, a true directissima up Tsaranoro Be, the biggest wall in the area. Cited as one of the hardest big-wall routes in Africa, it offers 20 pitches up to 7c, including a killer midsection comprising eight continuous pitches of 7a/7b on expanding flakes with numerous runouts up to 10m between bolts. The climb, put up in 1997 by Botte, Cola, Egger, Gargitter, Obrist, Trendwalker, and Zanesco, uses hand-drilled 6mm and 8mm steel bolts that are now rusty. Recently it has been thought of as a chop route, and even Leo Houlding decided against it when he visited in 2003.

Gondwanaland was Jerry's primary motivation for climbing in Madagascar, and he persuaded us others that it was ours too. We climbed the route, rebolting every belay but replacing only the handful of protection bolts we didn't trust. We thus effectively "reopened" this amazing line, without adding bolts or otherwise changing the route. Over five days Jerry went up with various partners and rebolted the first 10 pitches with 10mm stainless (now *de rigeur* in the Tsaranoro massif, because the area is subject to continuous rainfall during the rainy season, which starts at the end of October). We got gear and rope established up to the grassland bivouac ledge at half-height.

In two teams, each taking two days, we climbed the entire route. Gaz, Giles, and Jerry climbed as a threesome, rebolting the upper section as we went (again, only belays and the occasional protection bolt), followed by John and Anne, who shared leads, climbing every pitch onsight or redpoint. The route is now physically and psychologically safer. The belays will not fail, and most of the unreplaced bolts are quite adequate. (They improve the higher you climb; one or two of the original protection bolts low on the wall may still be dubious.) Gondwana-land felt like the Bachar-Yerian on Medlicott, but five times as long.

Runouts up to 10m are one aspect of the Tsaranoro that makes the climbing committing, exciting and, despite bolt protection, more akin to trad than sport climbing. It is essential to have good edging boots that are both comfortable and good on "holdless" pitches, where there is a continual emphasis on the feet. Forget wires, Friends, and pitons, this place is all about friction slabs, crystal-pinching, and expanding flakes: "braile" climbing.

The last week of the trip was centered around Diego Suarez, party capital of Madagascar. Wild dance action with beautiful Malgash girls, sea-view accommodation, and amazing spear-fish food were all in plentiful supply. We also reveled in the high-quality single-pitch routes at the northern tip of Madagascar, on the mainland at Montagne Des Francais and on the tiny islands of Nosy Anjombalova and Nosy Andantsara. The most notable achievements included John's flash ascent of the second hardest route on the islands, Tafo Masina (8a, the route's fourth ascent) and Gaz's ascent (first redpoint) of Madagascar's hardest route Les Nuafrages Du Rhum (8b+). Gaz's successful send of Les Nuafrages on the last day, as the sun's fireball dropped into the ocean, was the perfect end to the perfect climbing trip.

The person to contact when planning a visit to the Tsaranoro Massif, and to arrange accommodation in the park, is Gilles Gauthier (Gondwana Explorer, B.P. 5133, 101 Antanana-rivo, Madagascar, madamax@madamax.com or bourdon-to@wanadoo.mg).

To climb on the islands at the northern tip of Madagascar, contact Mathieu and Trina (Newsea Roc Madagascar, Agence spécialisée dans le sport d'aventure, Gestion de Camps d'Escalade, 26 rue Colbert BP 541, Diego Suarez, Madagascar, www.newsearoc.com).

JERRY GORE, FRANCE, *and* JOHN ARRAN, *U.K.*

Jerry Gore runs Alpbase.com from the Ecrins Massif in the heart of the southern French Alps. He provides affordable mountain courses and low-cost self-catering chalets, apartments, and other accommodation for climbers, walkers, skiers and mountain bikers. The company also provides detailed fact sheets on ice and sport climbing, alpinism and free big wall routes, so clients won't waste their holiday trying to find the good stuff. jerry@alpbase.com and www.alpbase.com

The east face of Mitsinjoarivo, Andringitra National Park, showing Another Tour in Merry-go-round (330m, 7b+). *Alberto Zucchetti*

Mitsinjoarivo, east face. In September Sandro Borini, Paolo Stoppini, Daniele Zinetti, and I put up a new route on the east face of Mitsinjoarivo. It proved to be a magnificent route with varied climbing. We equipped all eight pitches with 8mm stainless steel bolts, plus maillon rapides at the belays. We christened our 330m route Another Tour in Merry-go-round. The crux fourth pitch is 7b+, the fifth pitch is 7b, the second and sixth 7a+, and the remaining are all 6a and above. There are obligatory 6c+ moves. From the top of the eighth pitch it is a simple 50m walk to the summit. All but Zinetti are mountain guides

On the first ascent of Another Tour in Merry-go-round (7b+), Andringitra National Park. *Alberto Zucchetti*

from Italy, and every year we trek and climb in the mountains of Madagascar and the islands off the coast of Diego Suarez. Contact Via Cantone Sopra, 16 Rocca Pietra (VC), 13010 Italy (alzucc@yahoo.it).

ALBERTO ZUCCHETTI, *Italy*

Norway

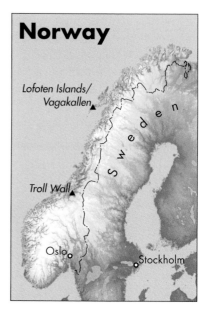

TROMSØ REGION

Kvaloya Island, Blamannen, Frost. From February 21-26, 2007 Anne Grete Nebell and I climbed a new route on the north face of Blamannen, near Tromso. The face is steep, with a big-wall feel, though it is no more than 400m high. We spent six days climbing the nine-pitch route, during mostly beautiful but cold winter weather. The grade is M5 A3.

Our route, Frost, lies immediately right of our 1998 summer line Pishtaco (eight pitches, A2 and Norwegian 6); it is the route farthest right on the wall.

The first five-and-a-half pitches required aid, on mostly excellent rock. The climbing was interesting, with discontinuous icy cracks, though reasonably well protected. We spent time linking features but did so with minimal drilling: a bat-hook move past a dangerous flake and a bolt at the belay, both on the first pitch. The last three-and-a-half pitches ascend less steep terrain, and we climbed them largely free. However, they proved the scariest part of the route. The final 50m or so coincides with Pishtaco.

We camped at the base of the wall while we fixed the first two pitches and then climbed capsule-style. We estimated the temperature to be –15°C, which feels pretty cold so close to the sea. Even at this time of year the days are long enough in northern Norway that it is possible to climb from 7 a.m. to 5 p.m.

BJARTE BØ, *Norway*

Editor's note: Blamannen now offers about nine steep and generally well protected aid routes 10 or so pitches long on generally compact, solid granite. Two of these have been free-climbed. A report on the first free ascent of Arctandria appears in AAJ 2006, pp. 318-319.

The north face of Blamannen, near Tromso. Marked is the line Frost (ca 400m, M5 A3, Bo-Nebell, 2007). There are now around nine routes on this face, mostly aid climbs. *Bjarte Bo*

LOFOTEN

Austvagoy, Alkoholvegen, Prohibition and Drink it Up. Four young Slovak climbers, Andrej Harsany (21), Jan Harsany (16), Peter Nesticky (20) and Marcel Zemko (19) visited the Lofoten Islands from June 19 to July 15. On June 29 they put up two new routes on Alkoholvegen (the Alcohol Wall), northwest of Kallevatnet on the main island of Austvagoy. The crag is home to the popular nine-pitch climb Rom and Cola (5.8, Bjornstad-Bjornstad-Meyer, 1977).

Andrej Harsany on the first ascent of Drink it Up (7 pitches, UIAA VII) on Alkoholvegen. *Peter Nesticky*

Climbing in excellent weather on the previously untouched left part of the face, Jan Harsany and Zemko did Prohibition (UIAA VI+). This route is seven pitches long, with excellent crack climbing on perfect granite. Andrej Harsany and Nesticky did Drink it Up, a seven-pitch route at UIAA VII. The first two pitches coincide with Rom and Cola, but the new route continues directly up the 100m dihedral above.

During their stay on the island they also climbed the established routes Forside (5.8, five

Jan Harsany on the classic Vestpillaren (13 pitches, 5.10a/b) on Preston. *Andrej Harsany*

pitches), on the famous 150m granite pinnacle of Svolveargeita (the Svolvaer Goat above the city of Svolvaer); Mygga (Mosquito), the middle pillar on Vagakallen (5.8), climbed by the team in six pitches; and the classic Vestpillaren with the direct start (5.10a/b, 13 pitches), on Preston.

VLADO LINEK, *Slovak Mountaineering Union, Slovakia*

ROMSDAL

Trollvegen (Troll Wall), Suser gjennom Harryland, first quasi-winter and third overall ascent. Rolf Bae, Sigurd Felde, Trym A. Sæland, and I wanted to try a winter ascent of the Franskeruta on the Troll Wall, but poor weather and resulting avalanche danger made this impossible. Instead we opted for Suser gjennom Harryland, which is steep, with compact rock, and lies on the far left side of the wall. Except for a couple of pitches, where the rock is poor, this is probably the safest climb on Trollvegen. Suser gjennom Harryland (18 pitches, Norwegian 6 and A3, Hagen-Ostbo, 1996) ends about half way up the east pillar of Trollvegen, and unlike other routes on the wall, where you walk down from the summit, it has a rappel descent. This is significant in winter, as the roads are closed. However, the route has quite a few traverses on overhanging rock, and to facilitate our descent we brought 6mm rope to fix on the two overhanging sections that involved the most traversing. We were also able to link pitches on the topo, for example rappelling from pitch 12 to 10.

We spent 11 days on the climb from March 15-25, 2007 with portaledge camps at the start of pitches six and eleven. The most difficult pitches involved largely sky- and bat-hooking, which was sometimes hard due to snow/ice on the rock. We also had to deal with poor visibility, due to spindrift and bad weather. In fact, the weather was poor at first, and we had to stay one whole day inside our ledges. However, despite snow, spindrift, and wind, we kept climbing, and for the second half of the climb the weather was good. We estimated temperatures to be between –5 and –10°C the whole time.

Activity on Trollvegen is limited these days, due to rockfall. In the summer of 2006 three teams (including Trym and I) climbed the Swedish route and a Russian team is thought to have climbed the French route.

SIGURD BACKE, *Norway*

Editor's note: In July 2006 Russians Pavel Fedorov, David Gindiya, Grigory Kochetkov, Maxime Nechitayio, and Denis Savelyev attempted what they thought was Baltica (1,300m, VI 5.10 A3 , Odintsov-Potanikin, 1997) immediately right of Suser gjennom Harryland. However, near the top of the initial steep wall leading to the east pillar they reported being unable to find the continuation and eventually finished on the 1965 Norwegian route. Local climbers observed the Russians actually on the line of Suser gjennom Harryland and not Baltica. However, they were unable to talk with the Russians after the ascent.

The name of the route comes from a line in a song by a Norwegian group called the Dum Dum Boys and approximately translates as "cruising through redneck country."

Russia

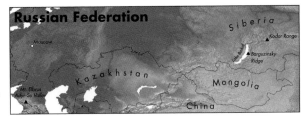

CENTRAL CAUCASUS

Chatyn-tau, north face, first winter ascent. Probably the most notable achievement in the Caucasus was the first winter ascent of the main north face of Chatyn-tau (4,368m), via the feature known as the Rhombus. Chatyn-tau stands just north of the famous double-summited Ushba.

The first recorded winter ascent of Chatyn took place in February 1984, when Boris Barulin, Anatoliy Moshnikov (leader), Sergey Kalmikov, and Victor Sazanov followed the Moshnikov Route over the summit of Pik Trud (Russian 5B). In February 1994 a team from the Elbrus Mountain Rescue Service put up a new route at 5B on the far right side of the north-northwest face, close to the Ushba Pass. Twelve years later Andrei Kazakov, Sergey Nilov, and Victor Volodin started up the north face but were forced down by bad weather, leaving their portaledge and other equipment on the wall. One month later, in March, they were back, but on their third day, again in bad weather, their portaledge broke, and they retreated.

Nilov got together another team and arrived in the Caucasus at the end of December with Dmitry Golovchenko, Sergey Kutkin, and Sergey Michailov. Temperatures at their base camp dropped to –19°C and it took five days to shuttle gear to the foot of the face through deep snow. At the end of the second day of the climb Michailov became ill, and the team retreated again, leaving their gear at the foot of the face. All but Nilov were now nearing the end of their holiday time, so Nilov made calls to enlist new volunteers. Sergey Doronin and Evgeny Korol arrived, and the three-man team left on January 17, 2007, for Nilov's fourth attempt. The team progressed up the Myshliaev Route (6A) on the Rhombus, fixing their five ropes above the ledge before moving up.

The team made progress mostly by aid climbing. Advancing was difficult, and erecting the portaledge in wind and night temperatures of –30°C proved a struggle. At several points on the way they found little notes, left in tins as waymarks by previous ascensionists. On the 25th they left the portaledge and climbed to the exit of this couloir over a large roof. Above, they reached a corniced ridge and were quickly on the summit, which they gained at 11 a.m.

ANNA PIUNOVA, *www.mountain.ru, Russia*

SIBERIA

ALTAI RANGE

Pik Vector, first ascent. From March 7-23 Aleksey Avdienko, Maxim Brits, Vitaly Ivanov (leader), and Igor Slobodchikov made the first ascent of Pik 3,716m in the Mushtuajri valley not far from the highest peak in the range, Belukha (4,506m). The team climbed the middle of the northwest face in capsule style, using portaledges. They named the peak Vector. Their route, graded 6B, is probably the hardest yet established in the Altai.

PAUL KNOTT, *New Zealand, and* ANNA PIUNOVA, *www.mountain.ru, Russia*

Afghanistan

Wakhan Corridor, Koh-e-Bardar (6,078m), previously unreported first ascent. In late spring 2005 Mark Jenkins and I spent two-and-a-half weeks in the Wakhan Corridor, traveling its entire length with Greg Mortenson to visit schools that Mortenson is constructing through his organization, the Central Asia Institute. We used a Toyota 4WD that barely got us through some major river crossings but managed to reach Sarhad at the road head in the Wakhan, where there is a nearly constructed school that will hold 250 students. We also met huge quantities of snow due to unusually heavy falls the previous winter. Despite this we managed to make what may be the first ascent of any previously unclimbed peak in the country (certainly above 6,000m) since the Soviet invasion in 1979.

With the blessing of our trusted guide and interpreter, Sarfraz Khan, we pitched base camp in the one-hut village of Purwakshan (3,156m) on April 30. The next morning we hiked and later post-holed up the steep Purwakshan Valley to the north, entering the craggy peaks of the High Pamir. We spent the night of May 1 at 4,427m and the following day reached our high camp at 4,842m on a glacial moraine. Koh-e-Bardar's elegant, scimitar-shaped south ridge was our obvious choice. To take advantage of night-frozen snow, we left camp at 12:45 a.m. on May 3 and gained the ridge by soloing a 50-60° snow slope. The ridge itself was spectacular, moderate climbing with an exciting knife-edge. A short AI 3 section led onto the crevassed summit glacier and waist-deep post-holing. We clambered atop the summit block at 6:45 a.m. and soaked in the stunning views of the Hindu Kush and the Wahkan's High Big Pamir. Descent was via an icefall to the west of the ridge. In honor of the integrity and tenacity of our guide, we named our route Sarfraz Ridge.

DOUGLAS CHABOT, *AAC*

The girls at one of Greg Mortenson's Central Asia Institute schools in the Wakhan Corridor, and Doug Chabot on the summit of Koh-e-Bardar, with views to the High Big Pamir's mostly unclimbed summits. *Mark Jenkins*

Kyrgyzstan

PAMIR ALAI

KARAVSHIN

Ak-su valley, Pamir Pyramid, west face. The Anglo-German team of Daniel Danzer, Jens and Michael Richter, Markus Stofer, and Sarah and Tony Whitehouse climbed a new route on Pik 3,700m, the pyramid that stands immediately west of the Russian Tower. This summit has become know as the Pamir Pyramid, though it is not clear whether the name was originally given to this formation or to the smaller pointed summit below the northwest face of the Russian Tower.

The team arrived early, reaching base camp in the Ak-su valley at the start of July, and had mixed weather throughout their stay. Their new route, Russendisko, lies well left of center and left of all known lines on the triangular, slabby, west face. It has 10 pitches at 7a, 6c obl. The crux eighth pitch comes just below the second overlap high on the face. From the top a few

The west faces of the Pamir Pyramid (3,700m) and, above, the Russian Tower (a.k.a Pik Slesov, 4,240m). Only a few of the existing routes are shown. (1) Semiletkin Route (6B). (2) Klenov Route (6B, 1993). (3) Peristroika Crack (7a A2, 1991, 7b 1995). (4) Russendisko (7a, 6c obl, 2006). (5) Reluctant Chief (British E3 5c, 1999). (6) Missing Mountain (6b, 1998). (7) The Hostage (E5 6a, 1999). (8) The Last Laugh (E5 6a, 1999). The big face right of (8) is the Wall of Dykes. *Tony Whitehouse collection*

High on Perestroika Crack (18 pitches, 7b) on the west face of the Russian Tower (a.k.a Pik Slesov, 4,240m). The route starts on a shoulder below and just to the right of the climber. This shoulder is the top of the Pamir Pyramid (3,700m). Way below is the Ak-su valley. *Tony Whitehouse*

During the ascent of Russendisko (10 pitches, 7a, 6c obl) on the west face of Pamir Pyramid (3,700m), Ak-su valley. *Tony Whitehouse collection*

easier pitches up right lead to the start of Perestroika Crack, or a short rappel down the wall to the left leads to scree slopes and an easy descent.

The original route on this face, Trento Passi nella Meta del Cielo (18 pitches, 6c+/7a), which was climbed in 1996 by Italians Marco Borghetti, Roberto Invernizzi, and Stefano Righetti, took a fairly direct line up the center, right of the prominent rock scar. In 1998 Sonja Brambati, Eraldo Meraldi, and Paolo Vitali added Missing Mountain (580m, 14 pitches, 6b), a route toward the right side of the face, finishing on the last pitch or two of the 1996 route. In 1999 Ian Parnell and Mark Pretty climbed The Reluctant Chief (530m, E3 5c) just to the right of the 1996 route, while Anne and John Arran climbed The Hostage (550m, E5 6a), which starts toward the right side of the face, crosses leftward through Missing Mountain and parallels it until moving right for the final three pitches. The same year Mark Baker and Chris Forrest climbed a series of corners around to the right, to give Mr. Chippendale (550m, E2). In 2005 Niall Grimes and Donie O'Sullivan thought they were on an unclimbed line left of The Reluctant Chief but met bolt belays and probably made a variant start to the 1996 Italian route.

The main objective of our Anglo-German expedition was a free ascent of the brilliant Peristroika Crack (7a A2, Faivre-Gentet-Givet-Roche, 1991; 7a+/7b, with one pitch of aid, by Francois Pallandre in 1993; all free at 7b/5.12 by Greg Child and Lynn Hill, 1995) on the west face of the Russian Tower (a.k.a. Pik Slesov, 4,240m). We fixed ropes, and most members of the party eventually completed the ascent, the best effort being a continuous 9:40 ascent by the Richter brothers. We climbed the route in 18 pitches, with the crux on the 12th pitch.

SARAH AND TONY WHITEHOUSE, *U.K.*

Kara-su valley, Asan, Alperien Route, variant finish. Through friends in China who had contacts with local Kyrgyz, I acquired permission to visit an area in Uzbekistan. I got the idea from photos taken from a helicopter by an Austrian friend. Our goal was to reconnoiter and then climb some of these granite formations. The backup plan would be the Karavshin. When we reached the Uzbek region, our hopes were quickly shot down. My brother Andy and I looked

The ca 900m northwest face of Asan (4,230m) in the Kara-su valley, Karavshin. To the left is the broad-summited Pik 1,000 Years of Russian Christianity (4,507m), whereas the rocky peak to the right with a left-slanting snow couloir is sometimes confusingly referred to as Aksu (4,925m). (1) Pogorelov Route (6A, 1986). (2) Moros finish (6A, 1986). The dotted lines show the Australian party's variants on the first free ascent via the Moros finish. (3) Odessa (Moglia) Route (6B, 2004). (4) Gorbenko Route (6A, 1986). (5) Russiaev Route (6B, 1988). The dotted lines show The Hammer and Sickle (2006). (6) Timofeev Route (6A, 1988). (7) Odessa (Pugachev-Maksimenya) Route (2004). (8) Alperien Route (5B, 1986). The dotted line is the Libecki variant. *Lukasz Depta*

at valleys close to those I had seen in the photos and saw finger-like spires encased like children in a family of snowy peaks, but access was impossible in the time we had available. With all the river crossings and bushwhacking, it would have taken a few weeks just to get our gear to a base camp. I still felt blessed: it would be an area for future adventure in a virgin amusement park of climbing.

So we proceeded with a back-up plan. We headed to the Karavshin and spent four days scouting the area, while indulging in boiled goat, horse milk, and pungent yogurt curds. We were accompanied by beautiful local people, through a landscape that fueled enthusiasm and appreciation for life. This was when our first bout of sickness began. If you've walked from sunup to sundown while "it" is coming out both ends, you'll know the agony. Antibiotics had to be unleashed like warriors to kill demons ravaging our digestive systems. Five weeks later, at the beginning of September and after another dream trip of culture, reconnaissance, and climbing mayhem, the antibiotics were still being sent in for battle. I had to go through four courses to sustain vertical progress.

In our weakened state we scoped beautiful, enticing granite towers and slabs in two valleys, but, once we got up on a ridge and looked down into the Kara-su valley, where Asan and Usan emanate grand majesty, we could not resist temptation. We set up base camp with our sights on the 900m golden-granite northwest face of Asan.

We battled intestinal aliens while climbing easy pitches to a big ledge 250m up. That's where the spiciest part of the route began. Four consistent ropelengths of off-width challenged

Andy Libecki high on the Alperien Route on the northwest face of Asan (4,230m). *Mike Libecki*

my old skills, learned when I was living in Yosemite. Nothing better than being 25m above the belay, walking a fully spread cam that is probably only good enough to hold itself. Although my brother had jumared before, he'd never had to deal alone with logistics. I led all the pitches; he belayed, cleaned, and dealt with hauling issues for the first time.

On two pitches we found ancient rivets and remnants that could have been hemp rope. Once we got higher, we traversed left to splitters. From this point the climb appeared to be on untouched stone. There was some basic A2 coral digging, but two of the pitches were among the best 5.11s I have experienced. We fixed six pitches, then took a few rest days through rainy weather. We still had around 450m to go to the top.

We started just before dawn, taking only one liter of water each. After 20 hours we found a nice ledge, where we each ate two inches of summer sausage, curled up in fetal positions, and shivered like cartoon characters until dawn. We had no bivouac gear, and the temperature was below 0°C. Next day we made the summit a few hours after the sun reached us. When we reached the top, where we took pictures in our Year of the Dog masks, we had been gone 35 hours from our high point.

It was clear that trying to rappel the route would be too risky. Ropes would inevitably get stuck and pull loose flakes onto us. Late that night, 15 hours after we had reached the top, we found ourselves in a gully that led to the valley floor. From the summit we'd made 17 new rappel stations down an untouched section of the wall on the side of the mountain opposite to that we'd climbed. I was in a paranoid state for the entire time. I knew if we got our ropes stuck, we were basically fucked. It was Russian Roulette every time we pulled the ropes. From our high point it had taken us 50 hours to summit and get down. Our climb had 21 pitches and rated 5.11 A2.

MIKE LIBECKI, *AAC*

Editor's note: the line climbed by the Libecki brothers appears to follow the classic 1986 Alperien Route (Russian 5B) on the right pillar of the northwest face. Above half-height, where the original route continues directly up to the crest of the southwest ridge, the pair moved left onto the wall and climbed a variant between the Alperien and the 1988 Timofeev Route, gaining the southwest ridge nearer the summit.

Kara-su valley, Asan, northwest face, The Hammer and Sickle and a free ascent of an existing aid line. During July and August, a team of four Australian climbers, Steve Anderton, Julian Bell, David Gliddon and Kent Jensen, spent 40 days living and climbing on the huge northwest face of Asan (4,230m). While climbing lines on the wall, we raised money for the charity Project Dare. Members of the public pledged cash, based on the number of hours the team spent on the wall. For the duration of our climbing period we were supported by three Australian climbers and two locals, who tirelessly brought food and water to a camp a few pitches up the face.

The approach, in an ex-Soviet truck via the dusty town of Osh, was incredibly taxing. The team faced endless roadblocks by gun-toting soldiers demanding bribes. These ranged from money to vodka and cigarettes. A washed out road extended the approach and caused the team to spend three days on horseback before arriving at base camp. However, a clever maneuver by an interpreter avoided the $10 per day protection fee administered by a wandering contingent from the Kyrgyz army.

The ca 900m northwest face of Asan (4,230m) seen from Yellow Wall. On the right is the highest peak in the region, Pik Piramidalniy (5,509m). Marked are the three routes climbed by visiting parties in 2006. (1) A combination of the 1986 Pogorelov Route and 1986 Moros finish climbed free at 5.11d by an Australian team. (2) The Hammer and Sickle (VII A4 5.11, Bell-Gliddon). (3) The 1986 Alperien Route (5B) with a variation finish climbed by the Libecki brothers. *Dave Gliddon*

The four of us initially summited the wall in a relaxed style, taking 16 days and using plenty of fixed rope. Our climb was rated A3+ 5.10+ and we established a rappel route with the aim of free climbing and filming the line. To our surprise, it was not an original route, as we discovered an array of decrepit Soviet hardware [apart from a more direct start and a couple of variation pitches along the way, the line was the same as the 1986 Pogorelov Route, with

Steve Anderton free climbing pitch 10 (5.11b) of the 1986 Pogorelov Route on the northwest face of Asan. This is the second pitch above Camp 3 on top of the pillar. *Dave Gliddon*

the 1986 Moros finish, 6A—Ed.]. The climb featured excellent bivouac ledges every 200m, with each able to accommodate at least five people. Portaledges were only used for comfort and convenience.

After a few days' rest at our advanced base camp on a vast, comfortable ledge at 150m, we began free climbing and filming the route. To our surprise we managed to free most pitches first try. The climbing was of excellent quality, with soaring cracks and plentiful features. The solid pinkish granite sucked up natural gear and only nine protection bolts were used during the entire climb. After nine or so pitches the angle increased, giving six steep, wildly exposed pitches of 5.11+ crack and face climbing. After a rest at the luxurious Camp 4, we traversed right and climbed another 10 or so pitches of mainly 5.10-5.11 to the summit.

The resulting climb is a superb 25-pitch (many 60m in length) line at 5.11d. The quality is excellent, the rock good and the bolted belays provide a continuous rappel line. With fantastic bivouac ledges and a sustained level of difficulty, this is surely one of the best, moderate, big wall free routes in the world. Oh, and did I mention that it hardly rained and the temperature hovered around 25°C?

Later, over eight long days, Julian Bell and David Gliddon climbed a steeper line on the face to the right. The Hammer and Sickle (VII A4 5.11) was completed in capsule style, featured a 30m pendulum, and had two huge roofs, including a 70m A3+ arch that I felt was the greatest pitch of my life. The route featured substantial sections of hooking and copperheading up a very steep section of the wall [the route uses a few of the lower pitches of the 1988 6B Russiaev Route, before a pendulum left leads to the left slanting arch. Higher, it rejoins the Russiaev for two more pitches. Where the original route swings left, a direct line is followed to the summit ridge]. The route gave around 1,300m of climbing and a small video of the ascent can be found on YouTube at: http://youtube.com/watch?v=SUWSx2x9FgE

Our base camp manager, Glen Foley, and Kyrgyz climber "crazy" Alex climbed a line up Yellow Wall on the opposite side of the valley. Over three days they retrieved bullet-riddled gear and a portaledge abandoned by the Caldwell-Dickey-Rodden-Smith party in 2000, when they were kidnapped. In the last week of the expedition Steve Anderton went back to the summit of Asan with "crazy" Alex, and on our 40th day jumped from the top in a wingsuit.

JULIAN BELL, *Australia*

The line of the new Polish route, Czarna Wolga (29 roped pitches and ca 1,700m of climbing, 7a), on the northwest face of Kotina (4,521m), Kara-su valley. *Jan Kuczera*

Kara-su valley, Kotina, northwest face, Czarna Wolga. There are many problems to overcome if you go to the Karavshin. It's possible to hire an agent to prepare everything, but we couldn't, as we didn't have the money. Nevertheless, at the beginning of August we reached the Kara-su, the western of the region's two main valleys. The five climbers in our group split into two teams: Łukasz Depta and Wojciech Kozub as one and Artur Magiera, Jerzy Stefa ski, and I as the other. Artur, though, was ill at the start of the trip and didn't take part in the initial climbing.

To get the feel of the rock, we first chose the Diagonal Route, the most logical line up the Yellow Wall (3,800m). We climbed this 500m line at 6a+, but moved simultaneously up half of it because of the low level of difficulty. Artur and Wojciech later also climbed this line.

Next Jerzy and I climbed the Timofeev route on the 900m northwest

On the first ascent of Czarna Wolga (ca 1,700m of climbing, 7a) on the northwest face of Kotina (4,521m). *Jan Kuczera*

face of Asan (4,230m). This route was established in 1988 at Russian 6B, but it subsequently became popular and was downgraded to 6A. Because our ropes were only 50m long, we had problems on some pitches, which were up to 60m long. The difficulties were 7a and A3, on solid rock except in the upper section, which was friable and wet. We made two uncomfortable bivouacs and arrived on the summit of Asan during our third day, having made the ascent in alpine style.

Our next objective was the beautiful, huge northwest face of Kotina (4,521m). We first rested for six days in order to heal finger wounds, then Artur, Jerzy, and I set off alpine style. We estimated that it would take us three days to climb the face, but in fact we completed it in half that time. The entire route gave nice climbing on solid rock. Up to two-thirds height the face offered mainly slab climbing, up to 6a, but the line through the steeper headwall above followed cracks and corners, which we found harder and graded 7a. We used mostly nuts, Friends, and occasional pitons and placed no bolts. After one-and-a-half days we were on the summit. However, an unpleasant descent was still to come. After eight hours of rappelling, downclimbing, and walking to the east, we arrived in the Ak-su valley, from where it was another three hours walk back to our base camp. We finally arrived at our tents at midnight. We named our route Czarna Wolga (1,500m of climbing plus 200m up the summit ridge, 29 pitches all climbed onsight, 7a). The name roughly translates as "Black Volga," in reference to the infamous Soviet car associated with the KGB.

Artur, Jerzy, and I now wanted to try the awesome west face of Pik 4,810m. Our plan was to repeat the Rusayew route, graded Russian 6A, but we weren't prepared for the 10-15m ice wall that guarded access to the foot of the face; without ice gear we were unable to set foot on the wall. Meanwhile, the other two members of our team, Łukasz and Wojciech, completed a new route on a nameless peak opposite Asan [see report below].

It was now September, and temperatures were getting lower and the wind stronger. We made two other attempts, one on Asan and the second on Yellow Wall, but due to poor weather, tactical mistakes, and a certain lack of motivation, we decided to go home.

JAN KUCZERA, *Poland*

Kara-su valley, nameless tower, Opposite to Asan. Our plan was to repeat existing routes but also climb new ones in the Kara-su valley. For our new route we chose the east face of the nameless tower directly opposite Asan; its altitude is ca 4,000m. We met a Kyrgyzstan climber named Alexiej who told us this yellow granite wall was unclimbed. Stable sunny weather helped us achieve our goal.

We scoped the face from the ground and saw a possible line up a system of corners and chimneys in the central section of the face. We sketched topographic details, to make route-

The new Polish line, Opposite to Asan (6a, 700m), on the east face of a ca 4,000m rock formation on the opposite side of the Kara-su valley to Asan. *Lukasz Depta*

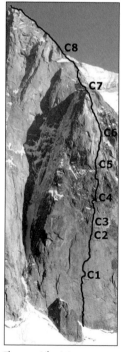

The new Ukrainian route up the right side of the north face of Rocky Ak-su (a.k.a Aksu North, 5,217m). *Anna Piunova collection*

finding easier once we were on the wall, and with this topo of a nonexistent route and some aid gear we set off at daybreak.

From the start we were pleasantly surprised by the quality of the granite and hoped it would continue. We climbed the great corner by a system of elegant cracks. A little roof appeared above, and it seemed likely we would need to use aid, but we found that it went free. The pitch above, however, turned out to be the hardest of the route, though perfect Friend placements assured good protection for this 40m dihedral.

By now the sun was leaving the wall. We exited the great corner and followed a system of shallow chimneys, while watching shadows creep slowly up the west face of Asan. Chasing darkness but still on excellent rock, we came to the end of the difficulties and avoided an unpleasant bivouac on the harsh vertical wall, reaching the summit at twilight.

Although it was a frosty night, it seemed better to stay than lose our way in the dark. The sparkling lights of the other climbers on Asan disappeared, to be replaced by familiar constellations appearing from behind the ridge. Cuddled inside a rescue blanket, we fell into a restless slumber. Next day we returned to the valley and paid our respects to shepherds in a wooden shelter, before making our way back to base camp. We named our route, logically, Opposite to Asan (700m, 17 pitches, French 6a, sustained at V and V+, 150m of easier II-IV). We also repeated the classic Alperien Route (Russian 5B) on the west face of Asan, taking one-and-a-half days to make a redpoint ascent at 6c+.

LUKASZ DEPTA, *Poland*

Liayliak Valley, Rocky Ak-su, north face, Odessa Route. In July and August Ukrainians V. Cheban, A. Lavrinenko, T. Tsushko, and V. Mogila (leader) climbed a new 6A route up the right side of the north face of Rocky Ak-su (a.k.a. Aksu North, 5,217m). The route starts on the steep wall between the original line on Aksu, the 1982 Troshchinenko route (6A), and, to the right, the 1988 Pershin route (6B) and its more direct variant, the Klenov route (6B, 1996). After broken ground above the first buttress, the new route cuts through the Pershin route to take a line more toward the right edge of the second pillar. Above, it follows the Pershin and then the Troshchinenko up the long but easier ridge above to the summit.

The Odessa Route is 1,700m long, with technical difficulties up to A4. Eight camps were required on the face. With the exception of a 30m section below Camp 4 (at the top of the first buttress), the first 20 pitches (as far as Camp 6, midway up the second pillar) were new. The remaining 22 pitches to the summit coincided with the Pershin and/or Troshchinenko. The climbers left all pitons in place, and the ascent was awarded second place in the Alpinism category of the CIS championships.

PAUL KNOTT, *New Zealand, and* ANNA PIUNOVA, *www.mountain.ru, Russia*

PAMIR

Zaalayskiy Range, Pik Ekishak, first ascent; Pik Molly, northwest ridge; Zarya Vostoka and Kurumdy West, attempts. Our Madteam/X-plore Expedition of Raúl Andrés, Olga Ariño, Irene Artuñedo, Enric Canosa, Albert Falcó, Daniel Guimaraens, Julio Masip David Oliveras, Jordi Sidera, David Taurà, Quim Valentí, and Gerard Van der Berg visited the eastern Zaalayskiy Khrebet, close to the borders with Tajikistan and China.

This is a rarely visited region of the Pamir, the northern flanks of which have been explored by only four or five expeditions to date. There were no other climbers in the range while we were there, and we found the solitude and vast potential for exploration amazing. However, we were not able to make major ascents, due to the poor weather and poor mountaineering conditions. Summer 2006 featured rain every afternoon and high temperatures (a minimum of −1°C at 4,200m). There was no frost at night, the snow was always soft, there were avalanches and rockfall day and night, and the rock we encountered was of poor quality. We established base camp at 3,550m, an

Ekishak (5,155m) showing the route of the first ascent up the southeast couloir to northeast ridge (PD+). *David Taurà*

The north face of Zarya Vostoka (a.k.a. Eastern Sunrise Peak, 6,349m) in the Zaalayskiy Range of the eastern Pamir. The line of the first ascent by a four-person Kyrgyz team in 2000 follows a hidden ridge to gain the snow rib in the center of the lower face. It then climbs straight up the uniform snow face above to reach the summit ridge left of the highest point. The lower, flat-topped peak to the right contains two summits both marked as 5,998m. *David Taurà*

Pik Tarka (5,368m) on the east side of the Kurumdy Glacier. A Spanish expedition made an attempt on Pik 5,262m to the northeast of Tarka, climbing a 45° couloir on the west flank of its north ridge. They crossed a small top, which they named Aguja Eiger (4,812m), before reaching a high point of ca 5,000m. *David Taurà*

Climbing the easy couloir on the southeast face of Ekishak (5,155m) in the Zaalayskiy Range to make the first ascent. *David Taurà*

advanced base on the western bank of the Kurumdy Glacier at 3,950m, a second advanced base alongside the upper eastern bank of the glacier at 4,200m, and placed a high camp on the east side of Golova Orla (5,441m) at 4,650m. From this high camp we attempted the northeast ridge of Golova but failed short of the summit. A British-Russian team climbed this peak via the northwest ridge by in 2000.

Falcó and I did make the first ascent, on August 1, of an easy route to the summit of a 5,155m peak on the long ridge connecting Golova Orla and Shining Peak. We climbed a couloir on the southeast face, which in the last 200m steepened from 50-65°, to break through a cornice onto the northeast ridge at a 5,030m col. We continued up the crest on poor rock (II) to the summit. As the top was composed of two horns, we named the peak Ekishak (Kyrgyz for "two horns") and our route Chocolate Ice (700m, PD+). Artuñedo and Oliveras repeated the route two days later.

From our first advanced base we climbed the east flank of Shining Peak (4,789m) at PD, a peak first climbed by the mixed north ridge by a British expedition in 1999. From our second advanced camp we climbed the northwest ridge of Pik Molly (4,748m), a peak also first climbed by the 1999 British expedition via a rather dangerous snow face. Our 600m ridge (Dancing in the Moonlight) was AD, largely rocky (II/III), with some snow and ice ramps of 55°.

The highest peak in the ring of mountains immediately east of our advanced bases on the Kurumdy is Pik Tarka (5,368m). We attempted Pik 5,262m to its northeast, first by walking up a side glacier to ca 4,300m, then climbing an open couloir/snow slope of 45° on the west flank of the north ridge. Turning right at the top, we crossed a small point that we named Aguja Eiger (4,812m) and continued up the ridge above (60° maximum, mixed), until forced to retreat by bad weather at just over 5,000m.

We tried to climb Zarya Vostoka (a.k.a. Eastern Sunrise Peak, 6,349m,) via the north ridge-north face, the route of the first ascent in August 2000 by the Kyrgyz team of Leonid Fishkis, Aleksandr Novik, Daniil Popov, and Natalya Zotova. This team reached the crest of the ridge via a snow couloir on the west flank. We climbed to the left, on the west face of a point on the ridge we named Aguja Jularg (4,890m). Our route to this small summit we named Chiquita cuesta Chacho (410m, D 65° M3). We then continued up the ridge and onto the broad slopes of the north face of Zarya Vostoka, reaching a height of 5,400m before deep, unconsolidated snow forced us back.

The other big peak we tried was Kurumdy West (6,545m), from our high camp east of Golova Orla. We only reached a low col, having experienced dangerous rock fall. We retreated from 5,000m. The main summit of Kurumdy (6,613m) was climbed in 1932 from the south: the west peak is still unclimbed.

DAVID TAURÀ, *Spain*

WESTERN KOKSHAAL-TOO

Navlikin and Malitskovo glaciers, first ascents. At the start of September our ISM expedition made the now-familiar trip via Naryn to the Kokshaal-Too and established base camp at the delightful lake below the west side of the Navlikin Glacier. The team comprised Ulrik Andersen, Ben Box, James Bruton, Joanne da Silva, Greg Paul, Todd Siemers, Nick Wheatley, and guides Adrian Nelhams, Vladimir Komissarov, and I.

On our first full day all of us walked five hours up the glacier to reconnoiter objectives and acclimatize. After this the weather closed in, and it snowed heavily for 24 hours, putting 30cm of snow at base camp and considerably more at higher altitudes. Once the weather cleared, we made an exploratory trip to the Malitskovo Glacier immediately east, which revealed a cluster of excellent unclimbed peaks. After a "council of war," one team led by me attempted Pik 5,611m, the peak next to Pik Byeliy (a.k.a. Grand Poohbah, 5,697m) at the head of the Navlikin, while two other teams led by Nelhams and Komissarov attempted peaks around the Malitskovo.

It took two days for da Silva, Box, Bruton, and I to establish a camp at 4,650m below Pik 5,611m, but we were then pinned down for the next three days by evil weather. Most slopes were then even more heavily laden and avalanche-prone than before. We climbed to ca 4,850m but turned back when the depth of unstable snow reached the handles of trekking poles. At night wind gusts were like express trains, but we had a bombproof tent (Bruton's Hillenberg). On the plus side, da Silva taught us to play Bridge, which gave some in-tent entertainment. A tent fire also enlivened proceedings. Finally, there was a brief clearing, and we climbed a small

Looking south up the western branch of the Malitskovo Glacier. On the left is Pt. 4,996m (dubbed Pik Kanashay), which was climbed via the north ridge facing the camera to a point ca 300m from the summit. The big peak in the far distance is Byeliy (a.k.a. Grand Poohbah, 5,697m), a well-defended summit that awaits an ascent. *Pat Littlejohn*

peak above camp (Pt. Argon, 4,880m), before heading down when food ran out. On the way back to base we had a fantastic day, making the first traverse of Macciato Peak (4,656m), nine hours of fine mountaineering along a sharp crest.

Meanwhile, the other teams had been attempting five peaks above the Malitskovo Glacier. Here the weather was much better, it being lower and farther north. Byeliy seems to hold its own weather system and often be in a storm cloud when everything lower is clear. Andersen, Komissarov, and Paul climbed Pik Ascha (4,717m) and the more distant Pik Novey (4,760m). Nelhams, Siemers, and Wheatley then joined them for an ascent of Pik Berum (4,812m).

The dominant peak of this glacier is the superb, fin-like Pik 4,996m. Nelhams, Siemers, and Wheatley climbed the east flank of this, and then followed the sharp north ridge to a ca 4,940m forepeak just short of the summit, where they were stopped by lack of time and 300m of dangerously corniced ridge ahead. They propose the name Pik Kanashay (Queen). Finally, Andersen, Nelhams, and Paul reached 4,900m on Pik 4,975m but turned back because of avalanche danger. The expedition was felt to be excellent and memorable, despite not achieving the major objective of Byeliy.

PAT LITTLEJOHN, *Alpine Club*

BORKOLDOY RANGE

Southwest Borkoldoy, Piks 4,608m, 4,778m, 4,661m, 4,705m, and Damdjjegs, first ascents; At Bashi region, first ascents. We traveled to Kyrghzstan in September for a month's climbing. After a few days acclimatizing in the Ala Archa National Park, we headed for the Borkoldoy, just north of the Kokshaal-Too in the southeast of the country. This proved to be a two-day journey on deteriorating tracks, where we met Pat Littlejohn and members of an ISM expedition. Following their generous advice, we went to a previously unvisited valley in the southwestern corner of the range.

We established base camp, just beyond the valley's narrow entrance, at 3,300m. Our first day involved climbing a steep ridge above the south side of the valley, which we followed for three hours to a prominent whaleback plateau marked with a distinctive set of gullies in the shape of a chicken's foot. The flat glaciated plateau led onto a narrow snowy ridge, with a line of sharp peaks linking to the highest summits above the valley.

On this day we were limited to an ascent of the first of these, a sharp peak that we called the Chicken's Head, marked 4,608m on the map.

Subsequently, we made an advanced base 8km farther up the widening valley at a delightful spot (ca 3,800m) near the foot of the main glaciers. The following day we climbed the distinctive snow peak on the south side of the valley, the main summit on the ridge farther on from the Chicken's Head. A long, snow slope led to a sting in the tail: a steep snow-covered ice slope (AD) leading to the shapely summit. Our maps gave the height as 4,778m and we named it Hamish's Peak. There were fantastic views in all directions, especially to the south toward the mountains of the Kokshaal-Too.

The north side of the valley was our next target. While the southern slopes are mainly snow-free and covered with vast piles of scree, the northern slopes are entirely snow-covered, with glaciers spilling down from summit ridges. Steep scree-scrambling (or scree-stumbling) brought us to steep, loose, rocky slopes. These gave two pitches of III to a summit of 4,661m, which we named the Bear's Paw. From here we had extensive views over the Borkoldoy Range, looking down onto the main wide valley running from the western edge of the range right into the center. We romped along the narrow ridge, ascending steep little summits. At one point, ca 4,500m, we encountered large animal tracks. Their size (as big as size 10 boots) convinced us they were bear tracks. Eventually, Misha, our Russian camp manager, declared he'd had enough of our seemingly insatiable progress, so we made a long scree descent.

The next day we headed up-valley in deteriorating weather to a distinctive long, hump-shaped mountain splitting the valley in two, with large glaciers on either side. It turned out to be farther away than we estimated and provided a demanding slog up the ridge and onto the 4,705m summit, where a cairn and large wooden posts clearly revealed we weren't the first. Puzzled by the size and weight of these posts, we later asked Vladimir Komissarov, who suggested they may have been deposited by the military in the days of border tensions. As they were most likely dropped by helicopter, perhaps we could claim the first ascent on foot.

After a rest day due to heavy snow, we walked into the cwm south of our camp and, crossing to the southeast corner, went up straightforward snow slopes, with a few small crevasses, to a summit named Pik Damdjjegs (4,690m). Clear weather revealed farther peaks and ridges still waiting for ascents. None of the peaks was significantly higher than any other, so the highest is probably be no more than 4,800m. Placing a camp farther up the valley, either on the moraine or on the glacier would give more reasonable days.

Leaving the valley, we moved farther west to the At Bashi Range, making the first full exploration of the gorge and valley above the village of Akalla. Our Russian-built UAZ 4x4 van took us high into the valley, where we placed a camp at 2,885m. However, we underestimated the size of the mountains and failed to put our camp high enough to ascend any of the peaks we were after.

On our first excursion we explored a hanging valley, heading for distinctive sharp summits at its head. Poor snow led to a retreat at 3,780m, after a small slab avalanche gave a clear warning.

We will be returning to some unfinished business. The following day we scrambled up the ridge east of our camp, only to find deep snow over large blocks, which limited us to a prominent top at 4,100m. One kilometer farther more distinctive peaks appeared to rise to ca 4,400m.

Attempting to improve our chances, we bivouacked the following night at 3,350m on the far side of the valley, hoping the extra height and an early start would allow us to reach a more satisfying summit. Deceptively large distances and hidden drops took us to an attractive sharp ridge that provided enjoyable scrambling reminiscent of the North Ridge of Tryfan in North Wales. However, fatigue limited progress to a height of ca 4,200m at a prominent top, the ridge continuing to a distinctive summit at ca 4,600m.

We thank Igor Prasolov, Dmitry Sosedov, and Micha Suhorukov from ITMC for their devoted, unstinting support: Dima for ascending his first 4,500m peak, Micha for letting himself be towed along an apparently unending and bear-infested ridge by two crazy English guys, and Igor for his inimitable approach to driving and keeping us safe for the month.

DAVE MOLESWORTH *and* MARK WEEDING, *U.K.*

Editor's note: the At Bashi (Horse's Head) is a range of limestone peaks immediately north of the Kyzyl Asker group at the west end of the Western Kokshaal-Too. There are no peaks above 5,000m and no record of any climbing until 2002, when it was visited by an ISM expedition. An adjacent area was visited the same year by another British expedition (see AAJ 2003, pp. 352-353, which includes a sketch map of the At Bashi).

TIEN SHAN

Ak-Shirak, seven first ascents, first south-to-north crossing. By daylight the river flood plain of moraine debris stretched away to where distant peaks shone whitely. The skis and sledges lay forlorn at the roadside, where we had been unceremoniously dumped in pitch darkness the night before. The drivers had caused a five-hour delay in reaching our destination by getting the truck stuck in thawing river ice. Those same drivers had assured us that no vehicle track led up the Kara Suy valley. We were looking at one now. There was no option but to break camp and follow this track.

Looking from the northwest over a ruined meteorological station toward the peaks of the Ak-Shirak, Tien Shan. From left to right: Piks Eagles, Koyon, Kargo, Chasovoi, and Kyrgysia. *Dave Wynne-Jones*

The upper reaches of the Petrov Glacier, an unexplored part of the Ak-Shirak Range. *Dave Wynne-Jones*

Our seven-member team, comprising Derek Buckle, Alistair Cairns, John Goodwin, Lizzy Hawker, Anna Seale, Mike Sharp, and I as leader, traveled by 4WD from Bishkek via the Barskoon Gorge and Suek Pass (4,000m) to Kara Suy village, where a border-zone permit was required. We then moved on to the Kara Suy valley, up which we expected to continue by vehicle on a dirt track, seen during our 2003 reconnaissance.

After four days of sledging on gravel and river ice, with a few double carries, we camped at the snout of the Kara Suy Glacier. The Mer de Glace in the Mont Blanc Massif of France carries a wealth of associations, but this sea of ice had more and bigger waves than any of us had seen from Ecuador to Antarctica. Navigating to a high camp, from which we could access several peaks, we found ourselves above the waves at 4,200m.

We sited our camp (N 41° 48.560', E 78° 13.815', 4,193m GPS) on the flank of an icefall, beneath a ridge coming down from Kyrgysia (4,954m), the highest peak in the northern half of the Ak-Shirak. After making a first ascent of Pik Chasovoi ("Sentinel," 4,765m) in a near white-out, then scouting the route to Kyrgysia Pass in a bitter wind that froze fingers and cameras, we climbed the south spur of Kyrgysia. From the summit we enjoyed panoramic views of the Ak-Shirak Range and the extensive peaks of the Tien Shan beyond. The ski descent to camp was superb.

Over the next few days we climbed the exposed Pik Karga ("Raven," 4,831m) and the superb viewpoint of Pik Anna (4,658m), skinning to within 100m of the summits before donning crampons. Then, on a less auspicious day, we moved camp to the glacial watershed and made three further first ascents.

A glacier bay to the northwest gave access to two of them. Skirting the steep north face of Pt. 4,865.9m, with its tottering seracs, we gained the north col and found a good line up its steep north ridge. On the way up we were surprised by tracks that could only have been those of a hare, so the summit had to be Pik Koyon ("Hare" in Kyrgyz). Returning to the col, I led off up the south ridge of the second peak, rising through a series of ice bowls to a fine, narrow summit ridge. Hunched brooding above the gold mine far below, we Eagle Ski Club members named our summit Eagle's Peak (4,822m).

We climbed our final summit, east of camp, in flurries of snow, first ascending an easy snow dome, then, when it looked as though a nearby rocky pinnacle could be higher, along a mixed ridge to that summit. Scrambling along granite blocks reminiscent of Chamonix, we reached a turret with "twin cannons" pointing to the sky. We took turns bridging up between these rocks to a precarious summit, which I christened Snow Cannon (4,720m at both summits).

We had been on the traverse for 15 days, and it was time to ski out. An unknown glacier system on the far side of a pass provided an easy descent for the laden pulks. We glided through stunning scenery to the foot of the Petrov Glacier, where we finally camped on the fine gravel shores of Lake Petrov. But there was a sting in the tail. The lake ice would not bear our weight, so we were forced to carry heavy rucksacks and drag our pulks along the increasingly chaotic moraine banks on the southern shore of the lake to reach the road.

We had completed the first south–north traverse of the Ak-Shirak Range, a distance of ca 50km on foot and ski, during a trip lasting from April 29 to May 21. En route we made seven first ascents of summits from 4,600m to 4,954m, all at a standard of around PD. We thank the Mount Everest Foundation, British Mountaineering Council (UK Sport), and the Eagles Ski Club for their support.

DAVE WYNNE-JONES, *Alpine Club*

This 900m face is only a small part of the huge north face of Pik Karakolski (5,280m) in the Terskey Ala–Too. Most of the north face is seriously threatened by serac fall. The two new Slovenian routes are marked: (1) Frappuccino Kirgizzo (TD+ V/5+) and (2) Expresso (TD+ V/5). The rock rib between these routes is The Snake, a Russian route (Belousov) from 1978. *Andre Magajne*

Karakol region, Pik Slonenok, north face; Pik Karakolski, north face; Dzhigit, north face. The Terskey Ala–Too runs for 300km along the southern edge of Lake Issyk Kul. Its highest summits are located by the Karakol Valley. The range used to be a venue for mountaineering championships in the former Soviet Union, but the Soviets weren't so keen on climbing ice and escaped onto rock faces wherever possible. Today there are many incredible virgin ice lines.

The range is also well known for rapid changes in weather. Although the majority of the annual precipitation falls at the end of spring, and the weather in July and August is considered relatively stable, frequent thunderstorms with snowfall are common during summer. September is the most stable month but is cold, with short days. The town of Karakol is the starting point for climbs in the Karakol Valley, with relatively good 4WD roads leading into the massif.

I first visited the area in 2004, trekking around Karakol and admiring the 1,500m north face of Pik Karakolski (5,280m), which became the main objective for Simon Slejko and me in 2005. However, bad weather forced us to change plans; large quantities of fresh snow on the north faces of Pik Karakolski and Dzhigit (5,170m) forced us to acknowledge that climbing would be too dangerous. When the skies finally cleared, we decided to go for a consolation prize, the north face of Pik Slonenok (4,728m). This gave a potentially classic ice route, with 700m of good névé, vertical steps, and an exposed, corniced summit ridge. The climb took nine hours on August 7. We required a further four hours to downclimb and rappel the Normal Route. We named the new line Amor Therapeutica and graded it TD+ (V/5).

Unfinished business saw my return in 2006. This time Simon and I were accompanied by Andrej Erceg and Dejan Miskovic. On our first acclimatization trips we found that, even in the Tien Shan, global warming has changed proud ice faces into a burial ground for seracs. But ice conditions on Pik Karakolski and Dzhigit seemed good, and we turned our attention to our first goal, the north face of Karakolski.

We traveled light, not taking a tent or making food dumps above base camp. A few minutes after midnight on August 11 we started up the obvious 900m snaking couloir on Karakolski's north face. We found excellent 60–75° ice and climbed unroped, except for the last 100m, which were quasi-vertical. We descended the Normal Route on the west ridge over tricky ground, reaching base camp that evening. We named our route Expresso (900m, TD+ V/5).

The final section of Frappuccino Kirgizzo (TD+) on the north face of Pik Karakolski (5,280m) before it reaches the broad glacier terrace below the summit slopes. The pointed Dzhigit (5,170m) is visible in the background. *Andrej Erceg/Andre Magajne collection*

The next day Andrej and Dejan climbed a parallel line to the left on the same face, a long icefield cut by two vertical ice steps, each one pitch long. Toward the top they worked right to finish at more or less the same point as we did. Around midday they joined the west ridge, which Dejan followed to the summit. The pair bivouacked on the On Tor glacier and returned to base camp on the 13th. They named their route Frappuccino Kirgizzo (900m, TD+ V/5+). The same day Simon and I inspected the north face of Dhizgit and were amazed by the number of continuous ice runnels on the right side of the wall. However, access to the headwall appeared to be threatened by a 300m-high serac barrier.

The north face of Slonenok in the Terskey Ala–Too, showing the line of Amor Therapeutica (700m, TD+ V/5). The normal route up this peak, which lies between Karakolski and Dzhigit, is the east ridge (left skyline), although the easiest route is via the dangerous hanging glacier to the right and the long corniced west ridge. The rock pillars on either side of Amor Therapeutica were climbed in 1978 and 1984. *Andre Magajne*

The weather now became unstable for the rest of the trip, but on the 22nd all four of us left a relatively comfortable bivouac at On Tor Pass and started up a huge couloir, which promised a relatively safe passage through the far right side of the serac barrier on Dhizgit's north face. By early morning we had made an exit from this ice trap, had a short break on the mid-height snowfield, and begun the steep headwall. Although the entire runnel on the headwall is steep, major difficulties were presented at mid-height by a 60m vertical corner with unconsolidated snow and poor protection. In the upper section the weather rapidly deteriorated, and climbing became a run for life through spindrift avalanches. After almost 17 hours of nonstop climbing, we reached the corniced ridge, dug a small ledge, and survived an uncomfortable freezing bivouac. In the morning we climbed the final few meters to the summit, where in excellent weather we enjoyed breathtaking views over countless peaks, many of them still unclimbed. We descended the Normal Route. We named our route Tretje oko (The Third Eye; 1,200m, ED2 VI/6).

ANDREJ MAGAJNE, *Slovenia*

TENGRI TAG

Pik Pogrebetskogo, northwest face. From August 10-16 the Krasnoyarsk team of Vladimir Arhipov, Sergey Cherezov, Vladimir Gunko, Andrey Litvinov, Alexander Mikhalitsin (leader), and Alexander Yanushevich made the long-awaited first ascent of the northwest face of Pik Pogrebetskogo (6,487m) at the head of the South Inylchek glacier. This mountain appears to have been climbed only once before, in 1980 via the west ridge. Its name commemorates the first ascensionist of nearby Khan Tengri, M Pogrebetskiy. The face consists of an initial 1,000m-high snow-and-ice slope, topped by an 800m rock wall. It was first attempted in 1984 by a team from Moscow, again in 1989 by Krasnoyarsk climbers, and subsequently in 1991 by a team from Irkutsk. All were defeated, as was an attempt by four strong British climbers in 1994, and the face gained the reputation of being the last virgin high-altitude wall in the former Soviet Union.

On the recent ascent the team found serious difficulties on the upper rock wall, reached the summit in the early afternoon on the 16th, and then began rappelling the route. However, part way down the weather deteriorated, and heavy snowfall made the lower section dangerous from avalanches. They continued through the night of the 17th and by midday on the 18th were safely back at base camp. The overall grade was 6A.

PAUL KNOTT, *New Zealand, and* ANNA PIUNOVA, *www.mountain.ru, Russia*

Tajikistan

FANSKIE MOUNTAINS

Chimtarga, west face. From August 4-7 the four-man team of Gladysheve, Igolkin, Kondrashov, and Soldatov (leader) climbed a new route up the center of the west face of Chimtarga (5,489m), the highest peak in the Fanskie mountains, a beautiful alpine range northwest of Dushanbe at the western end of the Pamir Alai.

ANNA PIUNOVA, *www.mountain.ru, Russia*

SHAKHDARA RANGE

Piks 5,635m, Litovskiy North, Karl Marx, Nikoladsye, Ovalnaya, Nikoladsye South, possible first ascents and new routes. The Shakhdara Mountains are the southernmost range of the Pamir. They lie in Tajikistan's semi-autonomous *oblast* of Gorno Badakhshan, immediately north of the Afghanistan border. The range has three distinct areas, separated from one another by passes. The highest peak is Karl Marx (6,736m), which lies in the Eastern Shakhdara. The highest peaks in the Western and Central ranges are Pik Mayakovskiy (6,096m) and Pik Vorujenik Sil (6,138m), respectively.

Pik Karl Marx (6,736m) showing the line on the west face to southwest ridge to west ridge climbed by a British party as part of a west-east traverse of the mountain. The peak was first climbed in 1946 by Abalakov via the west ridge (4B). The black spot marks the British camp at 6,384m. *Phil Wickens*

During the Soviet era many of the peaks were ascended from large organized camps, notably in the Zugvand and Shaboy valleys. These ascents were well documented in the Russian Mountaineering Classification tables, and many were via extremely hard routes. Ascents outside these camps were poorly recorded and often not included in the tables, the only record being cairns, or a note in a tin left on the summit of an apparently unclimbed mountain. The area has rarely been visited since Soviet times, due to the Tajik civil war, which lasted from 1992 to 1997. However, since 1999 Tajikistan has become both safer and political more stable, making expeditions to this fascinating little-known area again feasible.

I was asked by the committee of the Alpine Club to organize an expedition to coincide with the formation of its Climbing Fund, which had been established to assist members, particularly younger members, with expeditions to lesser-known areas. I had kept the Shakhdara Mountains in the back of my mind, and this was the perfect opportunity to visit.

The journey from the Tajik capital, Dushanbe, along rough roads that cross high hills, before following the river Oxus, must be one of the greatest road journeys in the world. Cutting through breathtaking scenery it follows the Tajikistan-Afghanistan border to the regional capital of Ishkashim. From here a rough road took us along the barren Wakhan Corridor to the village of Iniv, perched above the Oxus and close to the start of a faint mule track that leads northward into the Nishgar Valley. We followed this track steeply up the hillside, before dropping to a pleasant flat, grassy pasture, on which we sited our base camp.

Soon after arrival the whole team headed into the Western Nishgar Valley, which proved ideal for initial exploration and acclimatization. Despite unsettled weather Steve Hunt, Tim Sparrow, and Alex Rickards ascended the northwest flank of Pik 5,635m (initially nicknamed

Rick Allan nearing the summit of the north ridge of Pik Ovalnaya (5,935m). *Phil Wickens*

Rick Allan on the summit of Pik Sosedniy (5,928m). Behind him, across the upper Central Nishgar Glacier, is Pik Ovalnaya (5,935m), showing the British line of ascent up the east flank and north ridge. The peak was probably first climbed via this line in 1961 by a pair from Leningrad University and may not have been repeated before last year. In the distance are peaks of the Afghan Hindu Kush. *Phil Wickens*

"Peak of the Glorious Committee of the 150th Anniversary of the Alpine Club" but later shortened to "Great Game Peak"), which gave straightforward snow climbing followed by a narrow ridge (PD, 500m, possible first ascent). Two days later Derek Buckle and Kai Green climbed the southeast face of Pik Litovskiy North (5,905m) via a very direct and increasingly steep snow and ice line (750m, D, possible new route).

Access to Pik Karl Marx (6,736m) from the Nishgar Valley is guarded by steep, loose slopes, which we nicknamed "the beast." These led to the Central and East Nishgar Glaciers. The team split here, with Hunt, Sparrow, and Rickards working a route through the seracs of the East Nishgar Glacier to place a camp directly below the end of the south ridge of Karl Marx. They passed this to the east, ascending a small tributary glacier in a deeply cut valley, then its steep headwall, to reach the Marx–Nikoladsye col (6,200m). Above, steepening slopes led to the snowy upper south ridge and finally the summit (900m, PD+, possible new route). After a rest day at their high camp they climbed diagonally up the west face of Pik Nikoladsye to reach a col at 6,150m, from where they continued up the rocky north ridge, past three exposed steps, to the summit at 6,340m (500m, AD+, possible new route).

Meanwhile, Rick Allen and I had placed a camp next to a small glacial lake at 5,345m on the relatively benign Central Nishgar Glacier. After climbing Pik Sosedniy (5,928m) by its easy northeast ridge (600m, PD) we started up the west face of Pik Karl Marx. An 800m snow slope led to a broad shoulder and campsite at 6,348m, from where we could see Hunt, Sparrow, and Rickards reaching the summit. The following day was cloudy with light snowfall, but we were able to make use of brief clearings to follow the southwest ridge to the summit blocks. A delicate traverse on steep, loose and poorly iced rocks led rightward to the top of the south ridge, which we followed easily to the small rocky summit (1,200m, AD).

We made a straightforward descent in poor visibility down the south ridge and southeast flank, following the line, and occasionally the footprints, of Hunt, Sparrow, and Rickards, whom we met at their upper camp. This exact traverse may not have been completed before.

The following morning we descended the East Nishgar Glacier and icefall, re-ascended the Central Nishgar to retrieve a food depot, and the next day climbed the east face and north ridge of Pik Ovalnaya (5,935m). This gave a very enjoyable climb along a wonderfully exposed ridge, with numerous short steps of perfect water-ice, which we reversed from the summit and then continued over the north top (5,808m) to reach the Ovalnaya-Sosedniy col. From there we returned to our camp at 5,345m. Our route was D- and may not have been climbed before.

At camp we met Buckle and Green, who were back from their ascents of Pik Sosedniy via the northeast ridge and Pik Karl Marx via the west face and southwest ridge (1,200m, AD-). They had climbed the latter after aborting an attempt on the west ridge at 5,840m due to poor rock and deteriorating weather. The next day this pair repeated our route up Pik Ovalnaya.

With time running short but energy in abundance, Hunt, Sparrow, and Rickards set off from base camp to investigate the Far East Nishgar Glacier, which lies below the impressive unclimbed west face of Pik Tajikistan (6,585m). From a large plateau at 5,360m they followed the glacier to its head and then traversed, from north to south (AD and a possible new route), Pik Nikoladsye South (6,265m), returning to base a few hours before the mule drivers arrived. They were just in time for a final celebration of chocolate-garlic gateau and a selection of fine whiskies.

The Shakhdara Mountains have potential for many new routes, though most would be on poor rock. All our ascents were carried out from August 13-27, when the weather was generally unstable, with thick cloud but very little precipitation or wind. More snow and ice lines may be in condition slightly earlier, but remaining winter snow could make access difficult. We thank the Mount Everest Foundation, British Mountaineering Council (U.K. Sport), and the Alpine Club for their support.

PHIL WICKENS, *Alpine Club*

Pakistan

Overview. This year 91 applications were received by the Pakistan authorities for permits to climb various peaks. Of these, 78 applicants were granted permission to climb their peaks of choice, including 10 applicants who were granted permission to climb two peaks each. Ten expeditions were unable to gain permission to climb peaks situated in the Hindu Kush, as these objectives were considered too close to troubled Afghanistan. Peaks situated close to the war zone of the Siachen Glacier were similarly affected. Three expeditions later withdrew their applications.

Of 88 attempts on 22 peaks, 40 succeeded in putting 199 climbers on the summit of eight peaks. Eighteen out of 21 expeditions attempting Gasherbrum II in the year of its golden jubilee were successful, with 126 climbers reaching the summit. Seven expeditions went to K2, but only two were successful, putting four climbers on the summit. These included the Japanese Yuka Komatsu, who at 23 years and 10 months is the youngest female to climb the mountain, and Tatsuya Aoki, who at 21 years and 10 months became the youngest person. Four Russians were caught in an avalanche at 8,350m and disappeared.

Fourteen teams went to Broad Peak, of which six were successful in putting a total of 21 members on top. Only three expeditions and a total of nine climbers out of the seven expeditions to Gasherbrum I reached the summit. On Nanga Parbat three of the six teams were successful, though only four climbers summited. Eight teams tried the normal route on the now popular Spantik. Six were successful, and 30 climbers reached the top. Parties climbed both Latok II and III. The rest of the expeditions, which included those to Baintha Brakk, Batura II, Chogolisa, Diran, Gasherbrum IV, K7, Khunyang Chhish, Latok I, Masherbrum, Passu Peak, Rakaposhi, and Shispare were unsuccessful [though a number of these attempts are reported below].

SAAD TARIQ SIDDIQI, *Honorary Secretary, Alpine Club of Pakistan*

HIMALAYA

NANGA PARBAT RANGE

Nanga Parbat, attempted first winter ascent. A strong, primarily Polish expedition failed to make the first winter ascent of any 8,000m peak in Pakistan, when fierce winds forced it to abandon an attempt on Nanga Parbat (8,125m) in January 2007. Led by the world's most accomplished high-altitude winter mountaineer, Krzysztof Wielicki, the expedition attempted the southeast (Rupal) side of the mountain via the Schell Route, which broadly follows the spur forming the left edge of the Rupal Face till it reaches the vicinity of the Mazeno Col at 6,940m, below the final section of Nanga Parbat's west-southwest ridge.

The team established base camp on December 9 at 3,500m and Camp 1 a few days later at 5,100m. There was far more snow than expected, and the climbers planned a traditional approach, fixing 3,000m of rope and placing well-stocked camps. They established Camp 2 on December 23 at 6,100m in temperatures below –30°C. Wielicki, who turned 57 during the expedition, pushed out ropes to 6,800m in early January, and Przemyslaw Lozinski and Robert Szymczak later established Camp 3 there. However, severe winds prevented further progress, and on January 17 the decision was made to abandon the mountain.

There have been several genuine (i.e. calendar) winter attempts on Nanga Parbat, the best to date by another Polish expedition on the Damir Face. On February 11, 1997, Krzysztof Pankiewiez and Zbigniew Trzmiel retreated just 250m below the summit with severe frostbite.

LINDSAY GRIFFIN, *Mountain INFO, CLIMB Magazine*

Deosai Plains ski crossing. Thomas Niederlein, Norbert Trommler, and I arrived in Pakistan in mid-March, with plans to circumnavigate Nanga Parbat on skis, crossing the Shontar Pass into Kashmir and the Barai Pass toward Chilas.

Just before donning our skis, we were stopped by the army at Rattu in the Astore Valley. Despite the fact that we had a permit to enter the Pakistan-controlled sector of Kashmir, permission issued by the Kashmir Tourist Department, the army stopped us and warned us not to try traveling illegally; they would inform their check posts close to the border of our existence. Too bad!

We changed our plans to try a crossing of the Deosai Plains (east of Nanga Parbat, south of the Indus) from Astore toward Skardu. We would have to do so without a map, without any prior knowledge of the area, but with a rough idea of the route to take. An old jeep took us into the valley leading to Chilam until the snow was 30cm deep. From that point, at an altitude of ca 2,600m, we skied. We didn't use pulks but carried 20kg rucksacks, which got 700 grams lighter each day.

That afternoon we skied along the snow-covered road for 16 km. The locals were friendly and invited us into their houses for the night. However, worried about catching fleas, we preferred to camp. The next day we traveled another three kilometers to Chilam, at 3,400m, where we had to pay a four-dollar fee to enter the Deosai National Park. Here we went into the wilderness.

It's hard to imagine how people live here in winter. Snow closes the road by the end of October and does not clear till the start of April. In early spring there is more than a meter of snow, and some of the villagers move around on ski.

From Chilam our route climbed steadily to 4,300m Chhachor Pass. In summer there is a jeep road, but in winter it is a great mountain area, with nice peaks that would be suitable to climb on ski. We didn't, because we had no idea how long it would take to get to Skardu and hurried on our way. From the pass the descent to Sheosar Lake was easy but too gentle for skiing fun. On the subsequent four days we crossed the Deosai Plains, at an average altitude of 4,100m. We didn't follow the summer track, close to the rivers, but made a more interesting route by crossing ridges and saddles, resulting in at least two fantastic powder runs. Crossing rivers was not a problem, because the entire Deosai Plains were covered by two meters of snow, creating solid bridges. The temperature varied from below -20°C on clear nights to about 0°C on cloudy days. Half the time we were able to collect fresh water by digging deep holes through the snow.

The last day, a ski descent of the Satpara Valley, was the best. We mostly kept on, or close to, the jeep track, which has been dug out of the steep valley walls. We were able to ski 10km to an altitude of 3,200m, then had to walk another 10km up to the village of Satpara. This time we did not refuse the invitations from friendly people, enjoying a fresh meal and a night's sleep in a room. And not a single flea! Next morning a jeep took us to Skardu.

There have been reported ski journeys at the Satpara end of the Plains, but most skiers have used a helicopter for access. In 2006 a freestyle skiing and kite event, organized by the Pakistan Tourist Development Company, took place a few days before we arrived. Normally they erect a comfortable base camp at the point where the Deosai Plains begin and ski up surrounding mountains in day trips. We could find no reports of a previous ski crossing of the Plains, and locals at Chilam said no one had done it before. But of course no reports doesn't necessarily mean that it's never been done. What is certain is that the whole area between Skardu and Astore has great potential for ski mountaineering.

CHRISTIAN WALTER, *Alpine Club of Saxony*

KARAKORAM

BATURA MUZTAGH

The upper Baltar Glacier in the Batura Muztagh. (A) Pt. 6,250m and (B) Dariyo Sar (a.k.a. Biril Gai Chhok, 6,350m), which lie on the crest of the long ridge running south from unclimbed Beka Brakai Chhok (6,940m) on the Batura watershed. (1) Southeast face (1,000m, 70°, Ferrari, solo, 2005). (2) East face (1,200m, 70°, Corona-Ferrari, 2005). (C) marks the bivouacs before each route. *Ivo Ferrari*

Dariyo Sar, first ascent; Pt. 6,250m, first ascent. Unreported from 2005 are the first ascents of two peaks on the Baltar Glacier. After an unsuccessful attempt to reach the northwest spur of Rakaposhi as part of a larger Italian expedition, Renzo Corona and Ivo Ferrari traveled up the Baltar Glacier and made the first ascent of the impressive 6,350m Dariyo Sar (a.k.a. Biril Gai Chhok). This peak lies on the west rim of the upper Baltar, between the north and west branches of the glacier, and on the crest of the long ridge running south from unclimbed Beka Brakai Chhok (6,940m) on the Batura watershed. There had been no previous serious attempt on this peak, though in 1998 it was the goal of a British expedition that met with poor snow. The two Italians climbed the 1,200m east face (70° maximum), a great sweep of snow and ice, over two days, August 14 and 15. A few days later Ferrari made the first ascent of the unnamed 6,250m peak immediately to the south. Over August 17 and 18 he climbed the 1,000m southeast face, with maximum steepness of 70°.

LINDSAY GRIFFIN, *Mountain INFO, CLIMB Magazine*

The south side of the Batura group. (A) Batura II (7,762m, unclimbed). (B) Batura I West (7,775m, unclimbed). (C) Batura I East (7,785m, first ascent in 1976 by Germans via the large sunlit snow slope). (D) Batura V (7,531m, first ascent in 1983 by Poles). (E) Batura VI (7,462m, first ascent in 1983 by Poles). *Peter Thompson*

Batura II, attempt; Yashuk Glacier, Nadin Sar, Jehangir Sar, Caboom Sar, and Mamu Sar, first ascents. In early summer Markus Walter (Germany) and I made another attempt on Batura II (7,762m), considered by some the highest unclimbed peak in the world. Unseasonable rains at the beginning of June caused much snow-shoveling, even in base camp beside the Muchuar Glacier, and heavy going in deep snow on the mountain. When good weather came, it was very good, and we

Markus Walter climbing above Batokshi Col (5,930m) on the south face of the Batura group with Hachindar Chhish (6,870m) behind. *Bruce Normand*

made rapid headway to Camp 1 at 5,200m and Camp 2 in the Batokshi Col at 5,900m. We stocked Camp 2 with considerable food and equipment. We quickly established Camp 3 at 6,600m, but beyond we foundered. Our intended route through the summit headwall was washed by spindrift avalanches, hard to protect, difficult to exit, and led to dangerously unconsolidated summit slopes. The alternative, crossing the increasingly serac-threatened slope beneath and going around Batura I to approach from the north side, was possible only by following the foot of the headwall. Here we were forced to abandon our efforts in knee-deep powder on 45° slopes. We had to concede that this was not the year for Batura II.

After clearing the mountain and base camp, we decided to use the two remaining weeks for a rapid sortie into the Yashkuk Glacier basin on the north side of the Batura Range, reached from the Chapursan valley. The Yashkuk Glacier is smooth and straight and rock-covered for its 20km length between the snout and the confluence of the East and West Yashkuk glaciers. These diametrically opposed forks are both predominantly ice-covered, ca 5km long, and ringed by 6,000m peaks. The basin has been visited only twice: in 2001 by solo Japanese explorer Shigeru Masuyama and in 2005 by a Russian team under Lev Ioffe. Moving with difficulty on late-summer open glaciers, Masuyama and his Pakistani sirdar, Sarfraz Khan, were nonetheless able to climb a 5,800m outlier of Zod Khon Peak at the extreme southwest corner of the West Yashkuk catchment. The Russian climbers attempted the northwest face of Pamri Sar (7,016m), reached from the end of the East Yashkuk, but were driven back from the summit of Pt. 6,923m by bad weather, after surmounting the climbing difficulties [see below].

Our mini-expedition reached an idyllic site for base camp at Pamri (4,040m) in two short days from Aliabad, the trekking portion of the approach requiring six hours on a grazing trail, following the true left side of the glacier. After waiting out two days of bad weather, we were treated to eight days of sunny skies and high temperatures. We therefore formulated the ambitious plan of an in-situ reconnaissance and alpine-style ascents of three unclimbed 6,000m peaks, one in each of the three major branches of the Yashkuk. We were entirely successful.

First came Nadin Sar (6,211m), the dominant peak of the upper Chapursan and located directly west of Pamri. On the first day we ascended a straightforward glacier, curving beneath the east face to attain a high camp at 5,400m. The following day we climbed snow slopes alongside the northeast ridge to the summit crest, finishing in deep, unconsolidated powder. The next

Nadin Sar (6,211m) seen from the southwest ridge of Jehangir Sar (5,800m). The route climbed from the lower left, beneath the large snow face, to meet the northeast ridge (facing the camera) above the sharp, rocky section. Near the top it passed to the right of the leftward-slanting collection of rocks and through a small notch in the ridge, reaching the summit by the west side of the north ridge. *Bruce Normand*

The elegant snow peak of Yeti Sar (6,189m) as seen from Mamu Sar. Yeti Sar was first climbed in 1988 by Dieter Rulker and Markus Walter from the far side. The peaks in the left distance are Zod Khon Sar (6,080m, left, unclimbed) and Kutshkulin Sar (6,074m, climbed twice; by Germans in 1998 and British in 1999). The mountain in the right background is one of the Koz Sar group. *Bruce Normand*

morning saw a brief ascent of an outlying 5,800m summit, named Jehangir Sar after our faithful sirdar, cook, and friend in base camp. This gave us valuable views over the Yashkuk basin.

After a night in base camp, we set off for the next peak on the list, the shapely Caboom Sar (6,186m), located directly opposite Pamri and best approached from the south via the East Yashkuk. The approach to this glacier fork is a long but simple exercise, and we placed our first camp at 4,600m. In another long day we climbed southeast-facing snow slopes to attain the corniced east ridge, finding firm conditions except for the last 300 vertical meters. Views from this strategically placed peak are dominated by the northwest faces of Pamri Sar and Kampire Dior but include the full West Yashkuk basin.

The last summit of the trilogy was a granite peak known only as Pt. 6,096m, It is hidden at the back of the West Yashkuk cirque, where we placed a camp at 4,700m. The peak is accessible only by a broken side glacier, which we navigated before dawn, finding easy going as far as the col between 6,096m and Sax Sar (6240m, climbed from the opposite side by Walter and colleagues in 1998; *AAJ 2000*, pp. 323-325). A fine viewpoint (5,780m), clearing the col by some 100m on both sides, provided excellent views in all directions. From this upper basin we reached the summit by a snow/ice couloir through the east face, where unconsolidated conditions necessitated several hundred meters of belaying. We chose to name the peak Mamu Sar as a tribute to climbing colleague Mamu (Uncle) Guenter Jung, lost on Nanga Parbat in 2004.

BRUCE NORMAND, *U.K.*

Kampire Dior group, Pk. 6,928m, previously unreported attempt. Pk. 6,928m lies on the main east-west watershed separating the Yashkuk and Batura glacier basins, about 5km to the east of the major summit in this region, Kampire Dior (7,143m). The north side of the water-

Unclimbed Pk. 6,928m on the Yashkuk-Batura watershed showing the line up the northwest spur to north ridge attempted by the Russians in 2005. Camps 2 and 3 are marked and the summit is the rocky high point visible. *Lev Ioffe*

shed ridge is steep, crowned with cornices, and regularly swept by avalanches, leaving room for few possible lines. In particular, all routes leading directly to Kampire Dior, to Kampire Dior II to the east of it, and to the lower peaks to the west seem to be extremely dangerous. Farther east the main ridge turns left (north) for a few kilometers before curving east again. In this section it eases and features a small subsidiary ridge that leads down to the northeast branch of the Yashkuk Glacier.

Approach is made simple by a jeep road that goes up the Chapursan valley. When not washed away by mudslides, this road goes all the way to Afghanistan and is used by local people to reach Afghan and even Tadjik markets.

The goal of our 2005 expedition, which comprised Dima Berezin, Lena and Misha Lebedev, Alexei Panchenko, Yura Soyfer, and I, was to explore the region and to ascend, if possible, one of its peaks. We arrived in Islamabad on July 13, and our trek began from the bridge on the jeep road.

A week of reconnaissance convinced us that the far corner of the northeast branch of the Yashkuk Glacier provided the only objectively safe route to the main ridge, so we focused on it. The technical part of the route started from the upper cwm of this northeast branch, which is separated from the main glacier by an icefall.

We established Camp I above the icefall on July 21. Above, our route crossed the glacier toward the foot of the side ridge and climbed the crest right of seracs (80° maximum). We fixed 200m of rope on this section and on the 31st established Camp 2 in the middle part of the

The Russian Camp 2 in the middle of the northwest spur of unclimbed Pk. 6,928m above the Yashuk glacier basin. The view is looking southwest. (A) Kampire Dior II (6,572m). (B) Kampire Dior (7,143m). (C) Kampire Dior North (6,856m). (D) East Yashkuk Glacier. *Lev Ioffe*

ridge. At that point the weather deteriorated, heavy snowfalls made the route dangerous, and we had to wait until August 6 before making our next attempt.

The ridge above Camp 2 is not steep; it terminates at a 400m-high snow/ice wall that leads to the crest of the main ridge. We fixed another 200m of rope on this wall and reached the crest on the 9th. Huge cornices overhung the Batura (east) side, so we were forced to dig our tent platform for Camp 3 out of the slope 50m down the west flank. The next day, we explored the ridge above, but a day later further progress was blocked by the next spell of the bad weather, which brought a lot of fresh snow and new avalanches on all slopes. We descended to base camp on August 12.

LEV IOFFE, *New Jersey*

HISPAR MUZTAGH

Shimshal White Horn, second complete ascent. Alexandra and Mattias Robl and Markus Tannheimer made an ascent of Shimshal White Horn (6,303m) that is apparently only the second complete ascent to the highest point of the mountain. As reported in *AAJ 2006*, p. 352, the mountain was climbed in 1999 by an international party by the east spur of the northeast ridge from a base camp at Parigoz on the Yazghil Glacier. One member believed he had reached the summit on July 19 and believed his ascent to be the first of this shapely snow and ice pyramid south of Shimshal village (but see below). This climber reached his high point in a white out, and subsequent to the 2006 ascent and photos provided by the Germans he realized there was a point perhaps 30m higher 200m farther along the ridge toward the southwest. This higher top is the one the German trio claims to have reached, so making the first complete ascent of the mountain from the east. The first ascent was in fact made by a British expedition in 1986, see below.

The team acclimatized by making ascents of several smaller peaks in the region, some of which may have been previously unvisited. On July 11, from a high camp at 4,450m, Tannheimer and Mattias Robl climbed the 5,366m east summit of Chu Kurrti Dast. The ascent took only a few hours and reportedly featured ice up to 85°. Three days later both Robls made the ascent of the 5,700m west summit with a short section of vertical ice. From the 16th to 18th the team made ascents of both the east (5,730m) and west (5,685m) summits of Yeer Gattak (a.k.a. Sunrise Peak), relatively easy climbing but with a 70° section. The west summit had been reached previously.

On the 21st they established a base camp at 4,500m in the Yazghil Valley below the White Horn and the following day a high camp at 5,200m. Starting at 1 a.m. both Robls and Tannheimer climbed the steep 750m north-facing ice wall leading to the high col on the east spur, at a point where it starts to rise to the junction with the northeast ridge. This shortcuts the line taken in 1999, which started well to the east, reaching the crest of the east spur via the north flank, before traversing the rounded snow dome below the col; in 1999 the team thought the ice wall looked too dodgy. Despite an 85° section, they moved unroped and speedily, reaching the col at 5 a.m. From here they climbed near the crest until 150m from the top, where they traversed almost horizontally across the left flank, well below the crest, before climbing to the summit directly. They reached the far (southwest) summit at 9:30 a.m., after climbing four pitches of ice up to 70° and rock to UIAA III. (The first ascensionist of this route rated the difficulties as AD, with snow and ice to 50°.) Unfortunately, members of this expedition declined to write a report for the *Journal* if a historical record of climbing on the mountain was also to be published. This report is based on an account published on Mattias Robl's website and in the German magazine *Klettern*.

LINDSAY GRIFFIN, *Mountain INFO, CLIMB Magazine*

Shimshal White Horn, attempt; Madhil Sar, probable first ascent; Haigutum East, first ascent; Khani Basi Sar, attempt; Gorhil Sar first ascent. Peter Thompson and I visited three regions during the summer: Shimshal, Hispar, and Chapursan. In Shimshal we were accompanied by fellow U.K. mountaineers Ben Cheek and Gregory Nunn. We attempted six peaks, reaching the summits of four. Nearly all climbing was on snow and ice.

The unclimbed north face of Shimshal Whitehorn (6,303m). The left skyline is the northeast ridge, the upper section of which was climbed in 1999 and again in 2006. The right skyline is the north ridge, currently unclimbed despite attempts in 2005 and 2006. The face itself is probably more than 1,200m high. *Lee Harrison*

Looking up the final section of the unclimbed north ridge of Shimshal Whitehorn (6,303m) from close to the exit (ca 5,600m) of the 2005 French couloir. The right skyline is the upper northwest ridge, the route followed on the first ascent in 1986. The left skyline is the northeast ridge, climbed on its east flank in 1999 and 2006. *Lee Harrison collection*

We spent June and July in the Shimshal region, first acclimatizing on Yazghil Sar (5,964m). Ben, Peter, and I then made three unsuccessful attempts on Shimshal White Horn (6,303m) from a 4,400m base camp and higher bivouac at 4,600m on the Adver Glacier. Our intended route was the north ridge, gained by a couloir (D, 50°, 800m) well to the right of the true north face. This couloir had been climbed in 2005 by a French team. Our first attempt was thwarted by bad weather that began soon after we started climbing. Poor visibility led us mistakenly to follow a smaller branch couloir that reached a dead end after 300m. We made a second attempt two days later. After quickly climbing the first 700m of couloir, we were subjected to rockfall. Ben was struck on the thigh and injured. We retreated, a determined Ben lowering himself on two axes.

Five days later Peter and I tried again. Following the left side of the couloir toward the top, to avoid further rockfall, we encountered poor ice conditions. With limited ice protection we were forced to make a tricky traverse to the col. Exhausted from our efforts, we bivouacked a short distance up the ridge, at 5,600m. The following morning the weather was again bad, and we again

The Hispar Wall. The north faces of peaks in the Bal Chhish Range overlooking the upper Hispar Glacier. (A) Pt. ca 5,700m, (B) Gloster Peak (ca 5,962m) and (C) Haigutum East (5,783m). Marked is the line followed on the first ascent of Haigutum East: north face and northeast spur (D) Harrison-Thompson, 2006. *Peter Thompson*

retreated. However, there was time for a quick ascent [possibly the first, but see entry below on Shifki-tin Sar] of Madhil Sar (ca 5,700m), a small summit 100m above and northwest of the col.

During July and August Peter and I spent two weeks at or above a base camp at Hagure Shangali Cham (4,570m), on the north side of the Hispar Glacier. Not long after we established camp, we made the first ascent of Haigutum East (5,783m) in the Bal Chhish Range on the south side of

Peaks of the Khurdopin group northwest of Hispar La. From left to right: Tahu Ratum (6,651m), Pk. ca 6,100m and Pk. 6,305m. The impressive Tahu Ratum has received only one ascent. In 1977 a Japanese expedition climbed the southwest ridge, which forms the right side of the vertical rock wall of the west face. *Lee Harrison*

the Hispar Glacier. The ascent took two days. Route-finding through the numerous crevasses and seracs that litter the mountain was a challenge, and poor snow conditions prevailed. Our route involved an easy traverse across the north face to a bivouac at 5,200m, from where we climbed a northeastern spur. The route warranted Alpine D, with the main difficulties occurring higher up.

Toward the end of August we made a six-day excursion to the Lupgar Mountains of Chapursan. We established base camp at 4,700m on the edge of a glacial side valley to the east of Lupgar Pir Pass. We subsequently climbed Gorhil Sar (5,800m, altimeter reading) in a single day from a bivouac east of the mountain. We first reached a 5,200m col left of the north face and from here ascended the east ridge (30-50°) to make the first ascent. During the climb we found snow conditions to be excellent and made rapid progress. However, on the descent we dropped directly to the glacial floor, as rapidly softening snow deterred us from traversing back to our bivouac site. As we again carried no rope, we had to downclimb, rather than rappel, the 55-60° hard, sugary ice immediately below the col. Our route up Gorhil Sar was around Alpine AD+ but felt harder given the ill-equipped nature of the descent.

LEE HARRISON, *UK*

Editor's note: The 2005 French attempt on the north ridge was reported in AAJ *2006, pp. 351-352. In it the valley used on the approach is referred to as Goz. However, Harrison has always known this as the Adver Valley, confirmed by the Shimshali guide and four-time 8,000m peak summiter Qudrat Ali. Adver Sar is a local name for the Shimshal White Horn. A popular trekking guide also refers to the stream below the glacier as Adver. In the* AAJ *2006 report we also noted that the peak was probably first climbed in 1999. Further research has dated the first ascent to a much earlier date; see below.*

Shimshal White Horn, history. In 1984 Dick Renshaw and Stephen Venables, taking advantage of new trekking regulations allowing visits with minimal formalities to high points up to 6,000m in designated areas, explored the lower Malangutti Glacier. They concentrated their efforts on a cwm above the east side of the glacier, at the back of which rose a beautiful snow pyramid, "which for want of a local name we chose to call Shimshal Weisshorn" [White Horn on modern maps]. After acclimatizing on Corner Peak (ca 5,600m) at the end of the long northwest ridge of the White Horn, which forms the southern rim of the cwm, and a 5,200m peak on the long north ridge directly above Shimshal, the pair attempted the knife-edge north ridge from the cwm but were thwarted at the start by 30 hours of continuous snowfall. They estimated the height of the peak to be around 6,400m.

In 1986 Shimsal White Horn became the objective of a British team comprising Paul Allison, Chris Clark, John Burslem, Paul Metcalfe, and Dave Robbins, who discovered the local name "Adver Sar." This team approached via the lower Malangutti and established a base camp at just under 4,000m on the true left bank of the cwm that lies northwest of the summit. They climbed an ice face to the west col and from there more easily up the northwest ridge to the summit, which they reached on August 16 after a bold four-day alpine-style ascent. Prior to this they had acclimatized by making the first ascent of a 5,700-5,800m peak on the north ridge that they believe was called Shifkitin Sar. This peak had been attempted just before their visit by an Irish team, which attempted the north ridge but aborted just past a 5,300m subsidiary summit. They refer to the glacier cwm as the Madhil, and it may be that Shifkitin Sar is one of the four summits also referred to as the Madhil Sar peaks (see report above by Lee Harrison). The trip ended in tragedy, when Metcalfe developed cerebral edema at 5,900m, and then at a point just below 5,500m, with the glacier and safety in sight, a rappel anchor failed and Clark and Robbins fell 200m. While Clark sustained serious injuries, Robbins was killed instantly.

Clark has downloaded and processed space shuttle data, which gives the summit's location as E 75° 16.30' E, N 36° 22.06' and altitude as 6,555m. However, shuttle data is notoriously unreliable for snow-covered surfaces, because of problems with radar backscatter, so the altitude likely lies in the range 6,400m to 6,555m (though the reports on the German ascent and British attempt above quote a lower height of 6,303m). There are also unconfirmed reports that one or more Japanese climbers were killed in an avalanche, attempting the mountain at a later date from the Malangutti Glacier. What has been confirmed is that Japanese visited the Madhil Glacier in 1988 after an aborted attempt on the north face of Distaghil Sar. They climbed the most northerly of the four Madhil peaks (ca 5,670m) and nearly reached the top of the most westerly (ca 5,200m) but did not attempt the highest of the group. The 2005 French team, which in 2005 attempted the north ridge of Shimshal White Horn from the Adver Glacier, descended the west flank to the cwm (Madhil Glacier) mentioned above and then down through what they described as seriously crevassed terrain to the Malangutti glacier.

PAUL ALLISON and LINDSAY GRIFFIN, U.K.

Khunyang Chhish, South Ridge, attempt. Kazuo Tobita, 60, returned to the Karakoram to attempt an ascent of Khunyang Chhish (7,852m), a mountain he has inspected six times and tried to climb four times. From May to July, with five other Japanese, he attempted the unrepeated south ridge. The south ridge was climbed in August 1971, for the first ascent of the mountain, by Andrzej Heinrich, Jan Stryczynski, Ryszard Szafirski, and the doyen of Polish climbing, Andrej Zawada. This very long ascent is considered to have marked the start of Polish domination of high-altitude climbing in the Karakoram and Hindu Kush during the 1970s and early 1980s. The Japanese placed an upper base camp at 4,800m at the start of the south ridge, Camp 1 on June 27 at 5,600m, and reached 5,900m before giving up in bad weather. Avalanche danger was high, due to the potential for cornice collapse on the ridge.

Tobita has now attempted the mountain from the Yazghil glacier to the north, from the northwest via the upper Yazghil glacier twice, and via the long and technically demanding west ridge.

TAMOTSU NAKAMURA and the Japanese Alpine News

Khunyang Chhish East, attempt. Vince Anderson and I had a tough go of it in the Hispar region of Pakistan, mostly due to bad weather. However, we still managed to get to within 300m of the summit of Khunyang Chhish East, which at 7,400m is one of the highest unclimbed peaks in the world.

Our route to base camp was not easy; four separate road washouts set us back in both time and budget. Then, once at the roadhead, we had to deal with the problem of unseasoned porters. Compared to porters for hire to more popular expedition destinations in Pakistan, those here were relatively inexperienced and therefore high maintenance, with a lot of extraneous demands. And they charged roughly double the going rates found on the Baltoro or in the Nanga Parbat region. This caused an instant swelling of our budget to more than 120 percent of our funds. I can't blame them for wanting more money; it's hard work. But a day's carry cost us $50 per load, which is almost U.S. wages.

Arriving at base camp with three friends, Chris, Ian, and Katharine, we first attempted to acclimatize on a 6,000m peak above base camp but came up short due to bad weather. Vince and I then tried to acclimatize on Ice Cake Peak, a 6,500m snowy tower on the long south ridge of Khunyang Chhish itself. After two weeks of attempts we had only reached 5,900m, hampered by weather and wind, which left much of the route dangerously avalanche-prone and kept us well clear of the summit.

With less than 10 days remaining, we decided to go for it and try to climb Khunyang Chhish East. We weren't properly acclimatized but were simply running out of time. With a decent if not perfect weather forecast, we started up on September 10. The climb up the south-

Looking up the Pumari Chhish Glacier at (A) Khunyang Chhish South (a.k.a. Tent Peak, ca 7,600m, unclimbed). (B) Khunyang Chhish (7,852m, two ascents). (D) Khunyang Chhish East (7,400m, unclimbed). (E) Pumari Chhish (7,492m, one ascent). (F) Pumari Chhish South (7,350m, unclimbed). (1) is the line attempted by the Americans in 2006 with their bivouacs marked, C1 (5,900m), C2 (6,400m), C3 (6,700m), and (H) the high point at 7,100m. The dotted lines show the route taken by the Poles in 2003, where different from the Americans. Their high point was the American C2 at 6,400m. (2) South Ridge. *Lee Harrison*

west face went relatively smoothly, as all but one pitch was easy, or at least easier than I thought it would be. Although an earlier attempt had reported climbing up to M7 midway up the face, we had better (colder) conditions and were able to simul-climb or solo on good firm ice and névé the entire way to our second bivouac. At the M7 section we went a bit farther left and found 60-80° ice, eight to 10cm thick. The next day the most difficult climbing of the ascent came immediately: one pitch of M6+, followed by another of M6, and then progressively easier ground as we climbed toward our third and highest bivouac. We had surpassed the previous team's high point and made our top bivouac 600m below the summit. The weather was clear but windy.

The next morning was brilliantly clear but incredibly cold, and we headed out as soon as the sun came up. We took six hours to climb the next 300m, reaching the top of the face at around 2 p.m. Here we were stopped on the crest by a steep step that we could just not avoid. To the right was a massive cornice; to the left was steep, blank rock. Vince tried for some time to figure a way to climb directly up the edge between snow and rock, but with no real gear, bad rock, strong, cold winds, and tired bodies, we turned around. In hindsight we agreed that lack of acclimatization contributed to the retreat. We were both really cold (and it got colder on the ridge), and I wasn't able to keep down food or liquid. I have no regrets about turning around, as I have a feeling that had we continued, something bad would have come of it.

The next day we did about 10 rappels to regain our second bivouac. Then it started to snow really hard. After about an hour (of wishful thinking), we called a halt to our descent and repitched the tent on the tiny site. A sleepless, stressful bivouac followed. It continued to snow hard all night, and we had to dig ourselves out once per hour. It was the worst bivouac I've had since that night on the summit of North Twin a few years ago with Marko Prezelj.

At 5 a.m. it cleared, so we quickly crammed our sodden gear into our packs and started to rappel. It was a good thing, too, because by the time we were stepping off the face eight hours and many, many rappels later, it was starting to snow again.

STEVE HOUSE, *AAC*

Editor's note: In 2003 an experienced three-man Polish team comprising Janusz Golab, Stanislaw Pie-cuch, and Grzegorz Skorek climbed unroped up the 2,500m southwest face for ca 1,000m, then pitched more sustained ground, Skorek leading a very thin ice/mixed pitch at M7, with little or no protection, to 6,700m. Temperatures were high, snow conditions were bad, and after their third bivouac the weather began to look ominous. They retreated.

Prior to their visit the mountain had been attempted by a 10-man Korean team. Their original aim may have been the south ridge, but they were unable to make inroads, and it appears they turned to the long south ridge of Khunyang Chhish Main, presumably hoping to traverse over or around Khunyang Chhish South to the east summit. They climbed as far as the Ice Cake before retreating.

SHUIJERAB GROUP

Wulio-I-Sar (6,050m), first ascent. Mathieu Paley, a French professional photographer based in Hong Kong, has spent a considerable amount of time in the Karakoram over the last three to four years working for NGOs. He and I are passionate about British exploration in the northern areas of the Karakoram (the travels of Younghusband, Conway, Shipton, et al). We are also interested in the history of Shimshal's remote population. The aim of our two-man trip was to explore the Braldu Valley near the Chinese border and make the first ascent of an easy peak named Wulio-I-Sar (a.k.a. Chikar Sar, 6,050m).

This involved a walk of five days from Shimshal village to our base camp. We reached the spot known as Wulio, which lies below the south face of Wulio-I-Sar, and walked up a narrow valley to the start of the glacier at 5,000m. Here we spent the night under a large boulder on the moraine. The next morning, August 8, we began at 4:30 a.m. We avoided seracs by slanting right up the south face to a small col and then up through an easy crevassed area to reach the east ridge. We gained its crest at ca 5,800m and followed it easily to the summit. This was Paley's first-ever mountain. It took six-and-a-half hours from the moraine and was Alpine F. We had no altimeter and have taken the height from Nelles Map Sheet 2.

For over two weeks we explored the lower reaches of the Braldu Valley and an old salt mine located at place known as Darband, near the Chinese border. The former mining activity may have justified the existence of an old route across the Lukpe La (5,620m), connecting the Braldu to Askole in Baltistan. This Lukpe La (maybe first identified by Younghusband, then Schomberg in 1934) is the fifth pass that was originally identified by early British explorers (after the Turkestan Pass, Saltoro Pass, and West and East Muztagh passes). In a cave we discovered a burial site and skeleton, which leads us to believe that this deserted area was formerly inhabited by travelers and salt workers.

BRUNO COLLARD, *France*

RAKAPOSHI RANGE

Garumbar Glacier, Uyumrung Sar, second ascent. Four friends and I aimed to explore the Garumbar Glacier, the first tributary to the south of the main Hispar Glacier. We hadn't seen any pictures of this valley, nor had any information, and were curious about the northeast face of Spantik, which rises from the head of the glacier. Unfortunately, its 3,000m of rocky and, in places, vertical face was threatened by big hanging seracs on every side. So we looked at several neighboring 6,000m peaks and eventually climbed one, which we named Uyum Rum Chhish after the name of the yak pastures with small lakes that lie at the base of the mountain's east ridge.

Our base camp was situated at 4,000m [*Uyumrung*], six to eight hours walk from Hispar Village. It was a convenient site, grassy, covered with flowers, and with water flowing down from a collection of towering rock pinnacles. The rock on these 500m vertical walls looked to be sound granite [*one of the 300m faces was climbed by a British party at E1/E2; see below*], but the same could not be said of our mountain. Rocky outcrops there were composed of a layered and sandy material, unsuitable for protection with pitons and stoppers.

We climbed the east ridge, placing a tent at 5,000m. From there we climbed the mountain in a single push, in a 23-hour roundtrip. It wasn't very difficult, but neither was it easy. Heavy corniced ridges led to domes of deep snow, hidden crevasses, and bergschrunds. The finish led over a complicated cake of seracs, with some technical ice climbing. We arrived

Approaching the summit seracs on the east ridge of Uyumrung Sar (ca 5,900m) during the second ascent. *Kike De Pablo*

on the summit, which we felt was over 6,000m, in light snow. From there we rappelled from a stake. We then downclimbed and rappelled from Abalalovs and snow bollards to reach the tent. Three of us began the climb: Fernando Rubio, Iñaki Ruiz Peribañez, and I. However, Rubio stayed in the tent, and only Ruiz and I reached the summit.

At ca 5,500m on the east ridge of Uyumrung Sar during the second ascent. Below is the Garumbar Glacier, with unnamed and unclimbed peaks forming its eastern rim. *Kike De Pablo*

The peak we climbed is the one immediately left of Spantik as you contemplate the classic view of the Golden Pillar from the west, so it might be possible that our mountain already has a name. In any case it was super to be climbing in a largely unknown area packed with elegant 6,000m summits having no names and no existing routes.

We spent 25 days at or above base camp in July and reached Hispar village by jeep in nine hours from Karimabad. We first traveled to Nagar on a tarmac road, then along difficult tracks and dangerous bridges.

KIKE DE PABLO, *Spain*

Editor's note: At the time the Spanish climbers were unaware of a previous visit by a four-man British expedition. In 1994 Brian Davison, Bill Church, Tony Parks, and Dave Wilkinson reached the Garumbar Glacier, camped at Uyumrung (4,000m) and at 4,800m on the lower east ridge of what they christened Uyumrung Sar. They inspected the route above to 5,000m, where it got steep, then returned to base camp. Returning a few days later, they avoided the rotten rock step above 5,000m, via a couloir on the left, and camped at 5,700m, before it got too hot. The following day they continued to what appeared to be an impenetrable serac barrier guarding the summit. They made a long traverse left to gain the south ridge, up which they climbed easily to the top. They estimated the altitude of this summit, which lay approximately two kilometers north-northeast of Spantik, as ca 5,900m.

CHOGOLUNGMA GROUP

Twin Peak I. Previously unreported was a 2005 visit to the Kero-Lungma Glacier by a small British expedition comprising Bill Church, Pete Holden, and Colin Morton. During July and August they planned to explore the northeast branch and climb some of the biggest peaks at its head but were only able to make the probable first ascent of Twin Peak I (ca 5,500m on maps), which they felt was more like 5,800m. On several occasions they were forced to retreat from high camps on Twin Peak II (ca 5,450m) and Pt 6,123m by poor weather and dangerous conditions. They warn future expeditions that indicated heights vary from one map to another and rarely agreed with their own findings.

The Kero-Lungma flows southeast from the Nushak La, an old pass linking the valley to the Hispar Glacier. No peaks appear to have been climbed from the Kero-Lungma before 1996, when the valley was visited by a four-man British expedition that included Bill Church. The British in 1996 climbed three peaks, including Redakh Brakk (ca 6,000m) on the Hispar watershed. [See *AAJ 1997*, pp. 313-315.]

LINDSAY GRIFFIN, *Mountain INFO, CLIMB Magazine*

PANMAH MUZTAGH

Baintha Brakk, southeast ridge, attempt; Choktoi Spire, probable first ascent. In early June Paul McSorley and we arrived at a 4,400m base camp on the Choktoi Glacier, intent on climbing the southeast ridge of Baintha Brakk (a.k.a. The Ogre, 7,285m). McSorley's luggage, though, including climbing gear, had gone missing during the flight, and he decided to return home. Over the next two weeks, between heavy snowfalls, we ferried gear plus food and fuel up the glacier to the base of The Ogre at 5,000m.

The icefalls and avalanche slopes above, leading to the 5,650m col between the Ogre and Ogre II, proved to be very active during the day, so we spent the next four nights sketching our way through this difficult ground. Despite fixing our four ropes to help ferry the gear, it proved grueling work for unacclimatized bodies. Each night we'd carry three loads each as far as we could and retreat to the Choktoi before the mountains became alive and the snow too soft to

Seen from the east, Baintha Brakk II (a.k.a. Ogre II, 6,960m, left) and Baintha Brakk (a.k.a. The Ogre, 7,285m), separated by the 5,650m col. (2) is the southeast ridge of the Ogre, a much-attempted line, showing the 6,850m Relph-Walsh high point (H) in 2006. (1) The northwest ridge climbed by Koreans in 1983, the only ascent to date of Ogre II. *Jon Walsh*

Jeff Relph climbing to the 5,650m col at the foot of the Ogre's southeast ridge. *Jon Walsh*

The ca 5,900m Choktoi Spire above the upper Choktoi Glacier. The route of the first ascent took the curving snow couloir right of center, and then the skyline rock ridge on the left to reach the doublepronged summit. *Jeff Relph*

bear our weight. Around June 20 we established an advanced base, stocked with 10 days of food and fuel, on the col.

We spent three days on the col resting and acclimatizing. Then, after fixing two ropes above the col, we set out for an alpinestyle attempt on the ridge, taking two ropes, four days of food, and no tent. We climbed the 700m rock buttress that forms the first section of the route in one day. It gave excellent free-climbing on beautiful red granite, except for the 10m bolt ladder installed by a previous party. Sustained at 5.7, the hardest sections were around 5.10a and, where it was mixed, M5. Route-finding was easy due to three sets of old fixed ropes and other junk, shamefully left in place on earlier attempts. Above the buttress four rope lengths of ice/mixed led to a long horizontal band of 60° ice. Here we hacked ice from an abandoned portaledge at 6,350m to make a bivouac site. During the next day, in unsettled weather, we traversed right several hundred meters along the band to a better bivouac site below an overhang.

Despite a drop in pressure, the next morning dawned clear, and we set off for a lightweight push to the summit. A few more insecure pitches along the traverse led to a serac band guarding the upper snowfields. Excellent mixed and overhanging ice climbing led through the barrier to another traverse system (45-50°) leading back toward the south face. Bad weather arrived a little after midday. The westerly wind became increasingly strong, and the summit soon disappeared in cloud. Rationalizing that a night out in a storm at this altitude could prove fatal, we bailed from a height of 6,850m. The next day we arrived back at the col in full-blown storm, having been able to use old anchors from previous trips for most of our rappels. Spindrift and small avalanches became incessant, and we lost most of a rope. We continued down from the col when the storm briefly subsided and were back in base camp on the 30th.

When good weather returned, we had no more than a week left, not enough time for a second attempt. So we tried an attractive nunatak at the head of the glacier; it rose almost 1,000m on its south side and was around 5,900m in altitude. We dubbed it Choktoi Spire and chose a west-facing couloir leading to the southeast ridge. Leaving just after midnight on July

Jeff Relph near the summit of Choktoi Spire (ca 5,900m), with the upper Choktoi Glacier and Biacherahi Towers (North, ca 5,850m; Central, ca 5,700m; South, ca 5,700m) behind. *Jon Walsh*

5, we reached the top of the 600m couloir (average angle of 50°) shortly after daybreak, then continued up the 200m rock ridge above in six pitches of excellent climbing up to 5.10. A short overhanging face just below the summit required a tension move from a piton. With rock shoes it would have gone free at mid-5.11.

We had planned to be down the couloir before the sun struck it, but we were an hour late. While downclimbing in the early after-noon, Relph was hit by a falling rock, which dented his helmet, split his forehead, and broke his sunglasses and his nose. Glass in his left eye compounded the damage. He hur-ried down to the glacier, where eight Steri-strips were applied to hold the skin together. It certainly could have been worse. We named the 800m route Pain is a Privilege and graded it 5.10 A2 (one point). During our 35 days at or above base camp and five out of the seven days on the approach, besides their local staff we never saw another person.

JEFF RELPH *and* JON WALSH, *AAC*

Editor's note: The southeast ridge of the Ogre has been attempted on numerous occasions, often with fixed ropes, and remains one of the great prizes of the Karakoram. The best attempt to date was by the American team of Mike Colombo, Tom Nonis, Steve Potter, Mimi Stone, and Brinton Young, who in 1991 climbed the 700m rock buttress free at around 5.9, apart from two points of aid on old bolts. Higher, the team attempted to traverse the snow band and mixed ground leftward to the base of the granite tower forming the main summit. However, they were stopped by a huge overhanging cleft of rotten rock, which they felt would require time-consuming aid. Instead they tried to climb to the virgin ca 7,150m east summit, hoping that when they reached the ridge, they could follow it to the main top. A storm forced them down from 7,120m. A subsequent notable attempt took place in 1996, when a British team reached 6,900m. They fixed some of the route but removed their gear and a significant amount left by previous expeditions. The portaledge is thought to have been abandoned by a German team.

HAR Pinnacle, Corn Beef Chili Pasta à la Wahab; Pt. 5,500m, G-Strings and Plastic Boots, not to summit; Latok I, north face and north ridge, attempts; Sus Galinas. On August 12 Louis-Philippe Menard and I set up base camp on the Choktoi Glacier, beside Damian and Willie

Benegas, who were there for a third attempt on the often-tried north ridge of Latok I (7,145m). During the flight transfer in London British Airways lost one of our bags, which contained all of my partner's essential equipment, including boots, gloves, and down jacket. Fortunately, in the Skardu bazaar we managed to buy some replacements, dating from the 1980s.

On the second day after our arrival we went for a route on HAR Pinnacle (5,600m), across the glacier from Latok I. The peak had been climbed once before, by the south ridge. [John Bouchard and Mark Richey made the ascent in 1997, by 300m of easy mixed gullies followed by 11 pitches of rock up to 5.10b. They estimated the altitude to be around 5,700m and named the summit after the initials of their three base camp staff.] After bivouacking at the base, we opted for a crack system that split the west face. We found nice climbing, with pitches up to 5.10 on good granite. There were splitter hand and finger cracks and a stellar view of Latok and the Biacherahi towers. After less than 12 hours we were

The west face of HAR Pinnacle (ca 5,600m) on the Choktoi Glacier, showing (1) Corn Beef Chili Pasta à la Wahab (600m, 5.10, Menard-Turgeon, 2006). (2) South Face (ca 600m, 5.10b, Bouchard-Richey, 1997). *Maxime Turgeon*

back on the glacier, having completed Corn Beef Chili Pasta à la Wahab (600m, 5.10), named after the good meal our cook prepared when we returned to camp.

After three days of bad weather, we went for a mixed route on Pt. 5,500m, on the east ridge of Latok III. By the end of the day we were a few pitches below the summit ridge. Then it began to get epic. First a huge disk-shaped block missed one of us by a foot during a traverse. The thing was spinning vertically like a saw blade and could have easily cut someone in two. Three pitches later, with us in a steep groove, the slope below the col avalanched and passed right over L-P's head. It flushed twice again by the time we both reached the belay. That's the advantage of steep terrain, even if it pulls on the arms. The next pitch was by far the worst we have climbed in the mountains: a one-meter roof of loose blocks with a waterfall at the lip. When we finally got over it, we were soaked but had finally reached the col. We started to downclimb immediately and returned to camp at 10 p.m., after zigzagging through a nightmare of an icefall. We missed the first ascent of the peak by 150m but got off alive. We decided to give the route a name, just for ourselves and to preserve the "good" memories, and not forgetting L-P's new footwear: G-Strings

The untrodden summit of Pt. 5,500m on the east ridge of Latok III, showing G-Strings and Plastic Boots (900m, M7, Menard-Turgeon, 2006) on the North Flank. The climbers reached a notch in the summit ridge ca 150m from the top but immediately descended the far side of the peak. *Maxime Turgeon*

Louis-Philippe Menard on the lower section of the north ridge of Latok I, with the summit far above. *Maxime Turgeon*

and Plastic Boots (900m, M7).

On August 19 at 4 a.m. we left for our main goal: the north face of Latok I. Even as we were sticking the first ice pick over the bergschrund, we realized fragments of ice were falling down the wall, across its whole width. When we looked up, we were hit in the face. We managed four desperate pitches on steep unconsolidated slush and then called it a day. Seracs twice swept the base of the wall, and we ran down the approach slope with our tails between our legs.

It was obviously too warm to climb the face. With only two weeks left, our only chance to summit Latok I was to be the 26th team attempting to complete those final unclimbed meters of the north ridge. We wanted to climb alpine-style, without fixed ropes or jumars, but to do this we decided to climb the first 700m with fuel, food, and bivouac equipment, leave it at a comfortable site at 5,300m, then descend to base, rest, and climb back up with the remaining gear. There was no way we were going to climb 5.10 rock with 20+kg sacks on our backs. On the 26th the initial 700m rock section went smoothly, and we slept at 5,300m to improve our acclimatization.

We waited out continuous snowfall in base camp for two-and-a-half days before a good weather forecast, sent to the Benegas brothers from Argentina, allowed us to try again. The rock was covered with fresh snow, and we had to mixed-climb sections. We were forced to bivouac without sleeping bags 100m below our previous high point. The next day we reached it, dug out the gear, put up the tent, and slept.

Thirty-six hours later the terrain was buried under two meters of fresh snow. Seven hours later we regained the glacier and swam five kilometers to base camp. Just before the porters arrived we climbed an easy rock ridge above base camp. It was not a big route but was just what we needed to regain our spirits. We walked down the couloir to the right and were back in camp three hours after leaving. We called the route Sus Galinas (250m, 5.8), in memory of the Benegas brothers' chickens, which almost got back to Askole after a month's stay in base camp but eventually succumbed to our hunger. I thank the Mugs Stump Award and other sponsors for their support on our first Himalayan experience.

MAXIME TURGEON, *Canada*

Latok I, north ridge, attempt; Tony Tower, Releasing Bad Energy. Damian and Willie Benegas were again on the Choktoi for an attempt on the north ridge of Latok I. They arrived in base camp on July 22 and found conditions on the face to be the best they had seen, with mostly dry rock and clean granite cracks where on their previous two attempts, they had climbed under huge snow towers and avalanche gullies. In contrast the weather was probably the worst they had encountered in the area. Their first attempt, in early August, reached 5,200m. Here a storm pinned them in the tent for four days before they were able to escape.

Their second attempt began on August 13. On the initial rock buttress, they climbed a few new variations up to 5.10a, but while leading the fourth pitch Willie pulled off a huge block, which chopped the rope and went straight toward his brother, belaying below. It broke in two just above Damian's head, and only a watermelon-size fragment dealt him a glancing blow, ripping his jacket. The brothers continued and that day climbed almost 1,000m from base camp. The next day they continued for seven pitches to the second shoulder, finding the climbing enjoyable and safe, a big change from 2005, when they were climbing under huge threatening snow mushrooms. The altitude was around 5,500m.

The next morning it was snowing hard, and by the 16th the easy 4th- and 5th-class rock above looked like a 55° powder ski run. On the 17th they made a difficult and dangerous rappel descent, keeping near the crest of the rock buttress in the lower section to minimize the danger of flanking avalanches. On a couple of rappels, ropes irretrievably jammed and had to be cut. They reached base at 10 p.m.

On August 19, four days before leaving for Skardu, the pair climbed a short new rock route on Tony Tower, which they called Releasing Bad Energy (six pitches, 5.10a). They have proposed to the Alpine Club of Pakistan that in 2007 they initiate a Karakoram Climbing School to teach Pakistan climbers to become high-altitude guides and to bring them closer to the standards of safety and professionalism characteristic of Nepalese Sherpas.

FROM EXPEDITION DISPATCHES ON THE NORTH FACE WEBSITE

Latok V, first ascent; Latok II, south ridge, first alpine-style ascent. Doug Chabot, Mark Richey, and I arrived at base camp on the Baintha Lukpar Glacier on July 28, with the intent of climbing the west face of Latok III. We arrived at the end of an extended period of hot weather, which had melted much of the ice from the face, causing considerable rockfall. During acclimatization we made what we believe is the first ascent of Latok V (6,190m). [See note below on Latok nomenclature.] On August 4 we ascended the glacier to the col between Latok V and Latok IV and then up the east face to the south ridge. We continued along the crest of the ridge to a bivouac at 6,000m. On August 5 we reached the summit and descended to our bivouac, then back to base camp the following day.

Observations of rockfall on the west face of Latok III made during acclimatization trips up the glacier caused us to change our objective to the south ridge of Latok II (7,103m). At the time we did not know this route had been followed by a 17-person Italian expedition, to make the first ascent of the peak in 1977. We made a reconnaissance of the route on August 14 and discovered fixed rope and trash left from 1977. On August 19 we started up the south ridge and climbed to above a large gap in the ridge that would force us out onto a glacier to the left. A serac barrier threatens this glacier, and by midday it was too hot to venture in that direction, so we stopped at 5,500m to wait for cooler early-morning temperatures. On August 20 we crossed the glacier and climbed an ice face on the opposite side. This led to a point above the seracs where we could recross the glacier to the south ridge. We then climbed an ice face and chimneys to our second bivouac, at 6,400m.

On our third day we climbed through several rock bands to a snow ridge, where we placed a high camp at 6,700m. On August 21 the weather started to deteriorate, and we reached the summit in a storm. We took two more days to descend to base camp.

After Latok II we waited to do more climbing, but poor weather and lots of new snow prevented us from doing anything else.

STEVE SWENSON, *AAC*

Editors note: This was the second ascent of the Italian route (summit reached on August 28, 1977 by Ezio Alimonta, Toni Masé, and Renato Valentini, after the expedition had fixed 2,600m of rope) and the fourth of the summit.

Latok Group, clarification. During the summer Mark Richey, Steve Swenson, and I spent six weeks on the Baintha Lukpar Glacier, a branch of the Biafo Glacier, climbing Latoks II and V. Having copies of *AAJ 1998* and *2000* with us, it became apparent there were significant errors and inconsistencies in the photos, maps, and accounts of the locations of Latoks IV and V. The accompanying photo shows the five Latoks correctly labeled. This will hopefully put to rest the confusion.

For correction sake, in *AAJ 1998*, p. 321, a sketch is incorrectly labeled. The peak captioned Latok IV is actually Latok V, the smallest of the group. Latok IV is not represented in the drawing but would be to the right of Latok V.

In *AAJ 2000*, pp. 333-334 there are also misrepresentations in regards to Alexander Huber's account of Latok IV and Omiya and Tsuchida's attempt on Latok V. Omiya and Tuschida did, in fact, attempt Latok V, the height of which they reported as 6,190m. This height corresponds closely to our altimeter reading on the first ascent. We also found a picket with Japanese markings, further buttressing their claims. Their account in the *AAJ* is correct, and the editor's note was wrong. Furthermore, Alex and Thomas Huber climbed the lower of two obvious summits on Latok IV (6,456m). The photo by Omiya on p. 333 incorrectly labels Latok V as Latok IV, thus the Huber's line is not in the photograph.

So the sketch in *AAJ 1998* is wrong, the photo in *AAJ 2000* is incorrectly labeled, and the editor's note about Omiya and Tsuchida's attempt is mistaken.

DOUG CHABOT, *AAC*

Latok III, third ascent. No doubt influenced by the inclusion of the route in the seminal book, *Himalayan Alpine Style*, Alvaro Novellon and Oscar Perez of Spain made the third ascent of the southwest ridge of 6,949m Latok III, also the third ascent of the mountain. The first ascent was

The Latok group and Baintha Lukpar Glacier from the west. (LII) Latok II (7,103m): the south ridge was repeated in alpine style in 2006. (LI) Latok I (7,145m). (LIII) Latok III (6,949m): the southwest ridge (right skyline) was repeated in alpine style during 2006. (LV) Latok V (6,190m): first ascent in 2006 by an American team via the col between V and IV, the east face, and upper south ridge. (LIV) Latok IV (6,456m). *Doug Chabot*

made in 1979 by a Japanese expedition, which approached from the Baintha Lukpar Glacier and made a three-week siege of the ridge, climbing mostly on the right flank and using 1,600m of fixed rope. From the glacier the route has a vertical interval of 2,300m, though it is the upper 1,700m on the ridge itself that provides the main difficulties. The crux proved to be a steep rock barrier high on the mountain, giving difficulties of UIAA VI+ and A2. In 1988 three Italians repeated the route, with seven bivouacs, in a self-supported push, helped in places by old Japanese rope. They needed three more days to regain base camp.

Novellon and Perez first climbed to the shoulder (5,300m) at the base of the ridge, where they deposited food and equipment. After they regained this point in seven hours climbing from base camp on July 21, they set off for the summit the next day in alpine style. On the 22nd they connected runnels, couloirs, and snowfields to arrive at the base of the steep barrier, having found the initial ground easier than expected and making fast progress. The second day, after an uncomfortable bivouac, they started late and climbed the step, using aid in places and making several variants, because cracks were chocked with ice. (The whole route was in icy condition.) On the third day, after another poor bivouac, at 6,500m, they left most of their gear, overcame three pitches of rock and mixed terrain, made more difficult by fatigue and lack of acclimatization, and arrived at the summit snowfield. They unroped and continued to the top, only 12 days after arriving at base camp. They rested for a day at their top bivouac and made it back to base in a roundtrip of seven days, exhausted but having removed all their equipment. They used no fixed ropes, though they did use anchors from the Japanese expedition for rappelling, making theirs the first ascent of the mountain in alpine style.

LINDSAY GRIFFIN, *Mountain INFO, CLIMB Magazine*

BALTORO MUZTAGH

ULI BIAHO AND TRANGO GROUPS

Uli Biaho Tower, north face; Hainabrakk East Tower and Shipton Spire, attempts. From July 21 to 23 Slovakians Gabo Čmárik and Jozef "Dodo" Kopold made the first ascent of the north face of the spectacular 6,109m Uli Biaho Tower. They climbed the 1,900m route, named Drastissima, in a 54-hour roundtrip that involved hard, thin ice climbing rated VI/6. The pair used the dangerous 800m couloir originally climbed in 1979 by first ascensionists Bill Forrest, Ron Kauk, John Roskelly, and Kim Schmitz, before tackling the steep icy face right of the Americans' east pillar. Prior to this, the two had climbed a prominent couloir to the left of the central pillar on 5,650m Hainabrakk East Tower, completing the 1,000m line, named Dolzag Dihedral (VI/6), to the east ridge. They attempted to continue to the summit but were stopped by a steep rock tower on the crest 300m below the top. An attempt on the unclimbed north face of 5,885m Shipton Spire was thwarted after 500m when Cmarik became ill from sunstroke. Kopold's account appears earlier in the *Journal.*

The unclimbed north face of Shipton Spire (5,885m). Čmárik and Kopold hoped to climb into the large hanging couloir from the right but were forced to retreat when Čmárik became ill with sunstroke. The big pillar on the left forms the right side of the southeast face and is taken by the route Prisoners of the Shipton, climbed to within 80m of the summit (the last 14 pitches via Ship of Fools) in 2005 by Koller and Linek (UIAA VIII A3 WI5+). *Dodo Kopold*

Cat's Ears Spire, second ascent, partial new route. Eric DeCaria Michael Schaefer, and I planned to climb something on Uli Biaho, but on our first night during the approach, just two hours out from Askole, Michael became seriously ill. We first thought it was the usual sort of illness caused by contaminated food and decided the best thing was to continue at Michael's pace.

After 15 miles in nearly as many hours we arrived at Jola, the first of two stages on our route to Trango base camp. The next morning Michael was feeling a little better, so we decided to

Eric DeCaria on the first ascent of Super Cat of the Karakoram (ca 1,000m, VI 5.11+R A1) on Cat's Ears Spire (ca 5,550m). *Micah Dash*

continue. Again moving at Michael's pace, we pushed on to Paju, where we rested for a day so Michael could regain strength before we moved up to base camp.

Two days later we were on our way again and eventually reached base camp, ate dinner, and went to sleep. At 1:30 a.m., 12 hours after our arrival, Michael came to my tent in significant respiratory distress. After contacting a doctor in the United States by satellite phone, we decided to stay put and hope that Michael would recover, now that we were in a cleaner mountain environment. It was to no avail; 48 hours after our arrival I was on the phone again, speaking with the Pakistani Army and initiating a helicopter evacuation. There was no avoiding the fact that Michael was extremely sick. By 3 p.m. of our third day on the Trango Glacier, two Puma helicopters arrived, and I handed Michael off to a Pakistani Army crew. An overwhelming sense of sadness came over me; I knew Michael was going to miss out on the adventure of a lifetime. As it turned out, the decision to evacuate him was a good one. His x-rays upon arrival in Skardu showed one lung nearly full of fluid and the other on its way. This was most likely due to a bacterial infection exacerbated by the altitude.

Given our position and the prevailing good weather, it seemed a good idea to climb what was closest, so by noon the next day Eric and I were five pitches up Cat's Ears Spire. To climb as fast as possible, we left behind sleeping bags and brought little more than two Clif bars and one packet of noodles per person per day. We led in blocks of three or four pitches, with the second jumaring while carrying the pack.

The first night saw us in a small cave 12 pitches up. The pitches we climbed that day were independent of the route taken by the first ascensionists [Americans Jonny Copp and Mike Pennings in 2000 via the 1,000m route Freebird, VI 5.11d A1]. We'd encountered difficulties up to 5.11+ on serious terrain. As we eased into our bivouac that night, we gazed across the valley at Great Trango and Trango Tower, thinking that for a rock climber, this must be one of the most spectacular views in the world.

On the morning of the second day Eric and I crossed from the top of the first buttress to the base of the main wall and spent several hours trying to find a new line. However, our options were limited. In order to climb the wall above in the style we wanted, i.e., no bolts or pins and as free as possible, we unknowingly found ourselves on the first ascent route. Eric led off on difficult run-out terrain, free-climbing his entire first block. I took the lead a few pitches later. The climbing was wide, burly, sustained, and at times loose, leaving me with what I call "that A5 feeling." On July 30, after two and a half days of climbing, we found ourselves on the needle-like summit of Cat's Ears Spire (ca 5,550m) in a snowstorm. We each led and down-climbed the tiny summit block, becoming the second team to stand on it. We called our partial new route, which had 23 pitches, Super Cat of the Karakoram (1,000m, VI 5.11+R A1).

This expedition was supported by an AAC Lyman Spitzer Grant.

MICAH DASH, *AAC*

Shipton Spire, Women and Chalk, second ascent and first to summit; Trango Tower, Eternal Flame, not to summit; Trango II, second known ascent; Little Shipton, first ascent. In mid-July a five-man expedition from the Austrian Tyrol, comprising Matthias Auer, Karl Dung, Ambros Sailer, and us, spent 40 days on the Trango glacier. We established two possible new routes and repeated a string of existing routes, notably the second ascent of Women and Chalk on Shipton Spire (5,885m).

Looking southeast over the Trango Glacier to the Trango Group. (A) The ridge leading to Trango I (6,363m). (B) Trango II (6,327m). (C) Trango Monk (5,850m). (D) Trango Tower (6,251m). (E) Little Trango (5,450m). (F) Great Trango Northeast. (G) Great Trango (6,286m). (H) Great Trango Southwest (6,250m). (I) Trango Castle (5,735m). (J) Garden Peak. (K) Garda Peak (ca 4,700m). (L) Severance First Tower. (M) Ibex Peak (ca 4,200m). (N) Sadu Peak (ca 4,400m). (O) Base Camp Slabs. (P) The approach gully used to reach Trango Tower and the normal route on Great Trango. (1) West Couloir (ca 1,700m, 55° M5, first known ascent by Auer and Dung, 2006). (2) The start of Severance Ridge, which leads toward the summit of Trango II (ca 1,600m, VI 5.11 A2 AI3 M5, no summit, Clearwater-Frimer-Johnson, 2005). (3) The start of Azeem Ridge, which more or less follows the right skyline of Great Trango (2,250m, 5.11R/X A2 M6, Cordes-Wharton, 2004). *Dodo Kopold*

Difficulties ease considerably in the upper section, and Bole terminated his route on the crest. From here eight pitches of predominantly mixed climbing via Ship of Fools lead to the summit.

Although we were the first to climb the route to the summit, we congratulate "Bubu" Bole for his performance. Climbing such an uncompromising line from the ground up in 13 days commands respect, especially since he onsighted every pitch.

Almost all belays are equipped with two bolts, and there are in-situ pegs. However, repeating the route in complete alpine style may prove difficult, as there are no good bivouac sites in the lower section and collecting water is difficult.

Little Shipton (ca 5,400m) showing the line of the first ascent up the east face and northeast ridge: Winds of Change (550m, 7a+, Auer-Scheiber, 2006). *Hansjörg Auer collection*

The two of us also made a two-day alpine-style ascent of Eternal Flame on Trango Tower, to the top of the pillar and junction with the British route (28 pitches) but didn't continue to the summit. We climbed the approach couloir above Trango base camp in the morning, continued up the eight pitches to Sun Terrace in the afternoon, and after a bivouac reached our high point in eight hours the following day, negotiating the rock difficulties at 7b and A2.

Elsewhere, Matthias and Karl attempted The Flame via the American route, Under Fire (5.10+X A3 M5 AI 4), climbed by Brian McMahon and Josh Wharton in 2002. However, bad conditions prevented them from reaching the summit. They then climbed the normal route on Great Trango and later made the second known ascent of Trango II (6,327m). Starting early on August 19 and traveling light, the pair climbed the huge couloir on the southwest flank that falls from just north of the summit to the Trango Glacier close to Shipton base camp. At two-thirds height they headed up right through a mixed section to the final summit ice field (55° and M5). The last four pitches proved to be the crux. They reached the summit at 2 p.m. and rappelled and downclimbed their line of ascent partway, before bivouacking for the night. Next morning they made it back to base camp.

[Editor's note: Trango II was climbed in 1995 by Antonio Aquerreta, Ferman Izco, and Mikel Zabalza, via the broad snowy southeast ridge above Trango Monk. Jonathan Clearwater, Jeremy Frimer, and Sam Johnson nearly reached the summit in 2005 after their ascent of the Severance or southwest ridge. It seems likely there could have been other ascents. It is believed the couloir used by the Austrians has been climbed for at least part of its length before.]

Lastly we two made the first ascent of a ca 5,400m tower dubbed Little Shipton. This is the triangular wall to the right of, and just beyond, Shipton Spire. Despite the uninviting appearance of the east face, we found perfect steep rock. The central part of the wall overhangs, and lack of cracks forced us to start toward the right side. After four pitches we traversed right (crux, 7a+, 1 bolt), to focus on crack systems on the ridge. One crack followed another, and after some wonderfully enjoyable pitches (mostly 6b) we reached the highest point. We rappelled the route using mostly flakes and blocks but placing four bolts. We climbed the 550m, 14-pitch Winds of Change (7a+) alpine style in six hours.

HANSJÖRG AUER *and* THOMAS SCHEIBER, *Austria*

Trango Tower (6,251m) from Great Trango, showing only the routes mentioned in reports. (A) Southeast Ridge of Trango II. (B) Trango Monk (5,850m). (1) West Pillar (1,100m, VI 6c A4, Dedale-Schaffter-Fauquet-Piola, 1987). (2) Eternal Flame (1,000m, 7c+ A0, Albert-Guillich-Stiegler-Sykora, 1989). (3) Slovenian Route (1,000m, 7a+, Cankar-Knez-Srot, 1987). Routes 2 and 3 separate at the Sun Terrace, the original start to Eternal Flame, below the Terrace, is now threatened by rockfall and no longer used. *Andrej Grmosek*

Uli Byapjun; Uli Biaho Great Spire, first ascent; Base Camp Slabs, Piranski zaliv; Trango Tower, Eternal Flame, one-day ascent. Many climbers say that late summer weather in Karakoram is more suitable for rock climbing, so our group chose that time to visit the Trango Glacier. We were nine: a "girls' party" of Tina Di Batista, Tanja Grmovšek, and Aleksandra Voglar; "youngsters" Matjaž Jeran, Matevž Kunšič, and brothers Nejc and Aleš Česen; and "veterans" Silvo Karo and I. However, once at base camp, changeable weather prevailed for most of our 25-day stay. The only two totally cloudless were August 19 and 20, with a week of continuous rain and snow at the start of September. The second week of September was warmer and more stable.

Instead of acclimatizing by walking up and down the big couloir leading to Trango Tower, Silvo and I climbed smaller peaks. On August 17 we ran across the Trango Glacier to an unnamed, unclimbed peak in the Uli Biaho group. We climbed Warming up Ridge (450m but 700m of climbing, 6b) in six hours, gaining the crest from the couloir to the right. We reached the ca 4,800m summit and named it Uli Byapjun. We were back at base camp in time for dinner.

After a day's rest we headed back to the Uli Biaho group. We reached the bottom of a big couloir below the unclimbed Uli Biaho Great Spire, a 5,594m summit to the southeast of Uli Biaho Tower, and climbed through the afternoon. After a bivouac we started from a col to the south of the peak early in the morning of August 20. We climbed a northeast-facing wall to the crest of the south ridge and followed this to the rocky summit. The route Three Hundred Eggs (600m but 800m of climbing, 6b+) took eight hours and was named after our request for more food from our cook. We were back in base camp for a late dinner the same day.

We took one rest day and on the 23rd stood on the summit of Great Trango (6,286m) with Sandra, Tanja, and Tina. We followed the normal route in changeable weather. Our acclimatization plan now achieved, after a rest we were ready for bigger things. However, the weather was not obliging, so we continued cragging on slabs and walls above base camp, repeating the recent Belgian route, Oceano Trango. The best of our base camp climbs was the first ascent of Piranski zaliv (650m but 800m of climbing, 7a obl. R), which we completed in eight hours on the 31st. This route lies on a face that we refer to as Base Camp Slabs (4,700m, the formation climbed by Oceano Trango). None of our ascents required bolts, and we used pitons for a few rappels only. However, a few days later we decided to clean vegetated cracks and exfoliated granite on Piranski zaliv to make a better route. In doing so we added a bolt to one of the cruxes, an unprotected slab, leaving the other 7a R crux in its original form.

Time was running out, and the high summits were plastered with snow, but we got a nice weather forecast for the last few days of our stay. A fast, one-day attempt on the legendary Eternal Flame on Trango Tower (6,251m) was the only interesting goal, as the route is steep and sunny. On September 8 at 4 a.m. we started climbing from the south col. I led the first half of the route, and Silvo jumared the harder pitches, climbing easier ground with the small sack. At 8 a.m. we arrived on the shoulder and met the rest of our group, who had started the previous day. Sandra, Tanja, and Tina were also headed for Eternal Flame, while Matevž, Matjaž, Ales, and Nejc were going for the Slovenian Route. While overtaking the girls on the first few pitches above the shoulder, I used some aid but climbed the rest of my leader block free. We switched leads on the small ledge atop pitch 19 and by 2 p.m. were at the big ledge just six pitches below the top of the rock wall. There, a snow shower with icy winds froze us, and we stopped climbing for half an hour. After the storm, we made slower progress, mostly aiding due to the cold and the pitches being harder. At 9 p.m., after two hours climbing in moonlight, we reached the point 150m below the summit where mixed terrain starts. We thought the rest would go quickly, but there was a lot of snow and mixed climbing up to M5. We were tired and with only one set of ice gear, the second had to climb the snow pitches in a pair of lightweight sneakers. We reached the summit a little before midnight, rating the 1,000m route VI 7b A2 M5. Rappelling through the night without incident, we regained the col at 4 a.m. Our 24-hour roundtrip marathon reminded us of a similar, long single push on Cerro Torre in 2005, where we climbed the 1,700m partial new route, Sitting Start, in a 32-hour round trip. Although that climb was far longer, Eternal Flame is at a much higher altitude and has more free-climbing. The next day we left for home.

ANDREJ GRMOVSEK, *Slovenia*

Editor's note: Prior to this year the only alpine-style ascent of Eternal Flame to the summit of Trango Tower was made over three days in 2004 by Slovenians Tomaz Jakofcic, Klemen Mali, and Miha Valic.

Trango Tower, Eternal Flame, all-female ascent; Garda Peak, Karakoram Khush, first free ascent. The female part of the Slovenian expedition reported above comprised Tina Di Batista, Aleksandra Voglar, and I. We definitely provided the spice to the male-dominated climbing society in Trango base camp.

We came to Pakistan open-minded, though with many ideas, but our goals changed as fast as the Pakistan weather. Our first objective, repeating in alpine style the Slovak route, Mystical Denmo, on Hainabrakk East, changed after we watched rockfall bombard the approach gully daily. We crossed off our second goal, an alpine-style repeat of Inshallah on Shipton Spire, after hearing a report from Americans that part of the route above pitch nine had fallen down. So our next goal became the Slovenian Route on Trango Tower in alpine style. After discussion with members of our expedition who wanted to free-climb the route, we realized that we couldn't all climb at the same time. So we opted for an alpine-style ascent of Eternal Flame. This plan we stuck to right to the summit.

Tanja Grmovsek, belayed by Tina Di Batista, on the initial section of Eternal Flame, above Sun Terrace. *Andrej Grmovsek*

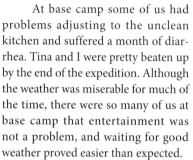

From left to right: Aleksandra Voglar, Tina Di Batista, and Tanja Grmovsek on the Trango Glacier. The three Slovenians made the first all-female ascent of Trango Tower, via an alpine-style ascent of Eternal Flame. *Andrej Grmovsek*

At base camp some of us had problems adjusting to the unclean kitchen and suffered a month of diarrhea. Tina and I were pretty beaten up by the end of the expedition. Although the weather was miserable for much of the time, there were so many of us at base camp that entertainment was not a problem, and waiting for good weather proved easier than expected.

To acclimatize we twice walked up and down the long approach gully to Trango Tower, then we climbed Great Trango Tower (6,287m) by the normal American route on the north flank (ice and snow to 80°, though mainly 40-60°). We reached the summit on August 23.

We also climbed Karakoram Khush (graded 6b A0 by first ascensionists Jakafcic, Mali, and Valic in 2004) on Garda Peak (ca 4,700m), where we did a free variation to the first pitch at 6a/b (50m). On the 26th we climbed the whole route free (6a/b, 300m). On the 29th we repeated the pleasant Oceano Trango, feeling it to be 6a+, and then continued for two additional pitches to the top of the tower above, christened Pinocchio. This provided a logical conclusion to the route with a 55m pitch at 5 and a 60m pitch at easy 6a. Bad weather intervened again, and when it finally turned for the better, we had only six days left before our intended departure for home.

Our goal now was a fast and light alpine-style ascent of Eternal Flame. We wanted to reach the summit and more important, come back safe and happy. We climbed as a party of three, with the leader going light and the other two bringing up the gear. We took just two sleeping bags, a stove, one ice axe, and one pair of crampons. The two backpacks were heavy to begin with and felt heavier the higher we climbed. We led in blocks, while the second and third climbers jumared. We climbed most of the lower section to Sun Terrace free, as we did with the snow and mixed pitches leading to the summit. The rest of the route we climbed mainly on aid due to the cold, though there were sections of obligatory free climbing.

Starting from the south col, we took three days to completing the first all-female ascent of the tower. The weather on the first day was poor, but on the second, as we climbed above Sun Terrace, it improved. We bivouacked on the "big ledge" atop pitch 23, where we shivered through the night on a spot just big enough for one person. Not looking carefully enough at the topo, we mistakenly climbed the variation to pitches 20 and 21 put up by the Pou brothers in 2005. This year it was completely dry.

Our third day began with nice weather, but an increasingly strong wind soon chilled us to the bone. At 9 p.m. on September 9 we stood on the summit, screaming with joy while admiring the moonlit scenery. After climbing such a route I was standing on top of Trango Tower with smiling and crying women around me. We regained Sun Terrace at 2 a.m. after loosing a rope, stuck on a rappel. Back at base camp the following night we packed our gear, ready for porters to carry out the following morning. We were only able to really rest once we'd reached Skardu.

For us the ascent of Eternal Flame was challenging from the very beginning, and we walked a thin line between going up and going down. We were tired and cold and frostbit fingers and toes, but each of us kept silent and did her job. We climbed the 1,000m route at 6c A2 M5. It was hard, but it was worth it.

TANJA GRMOVSEK, *Slovenia*

Trango Tower, West Pillar, second ascent. A Swiss team comprising Francesco Pellanda, Giovanni Quirici, and Christophe Steck made the second ascent of the 1987 Dedale-Schaffter-Fauquet-Piola route on the west pillar of Trango Tower (6,251m), a demanding 1,100m line originally graded VI 6c A4. This route involves amounts of hard aid, as confirmed by the experienced Spanish big wall climber, Alfredo Mandinabeita, who attempted the route, solo, to half-height in 2004. The Swiss were attempting to free climb the route and, after a lot of work, reached the summit on August 2 using aid only on pitches 13 (A4), 15 (A3), and 16 (A3). They estimate the 13th pitch would go free at around 8a.

LINDSAY GRIFFIN, *Mountain INFO, CLIMB Magazine*

Trango Group, various new routes; tower northwest of Garda Peak, first ascent; Trango Tower, attempts. Two Polish teams operated separately from the Trango Glacier during August and September. One comprised Maciej Ciesielski, Wawrzyniec Zakrzewski, and I. At first the weather was bad, and it wasn't until August 31 that we could climb our first route: Oceano Trango (300m, 5.10a), a warm-up on the slabs above base camp. [This route was put up in July 2006 by the Belgian team of Christophe Bingham, Sanne Bostels, Jasper de Coninck, Stijn Dekeyser, An Laenen, and Hans Marien, who compared it to routes in northern Italy's Mello Valley.] More rain and snow intervened until September 5, when improving weather allowed us to open a new line on an unclimbed tower left (northwest) of Garda Peak. The route was 540m long and went at on-sight at 5.11c, with one move of A0: a pendulum from a muddy crack to a crack on the left. We baptized the virgin summit Garden Peak, not only due to the rich vegetation on the face but also as a sort of tribute to nearby Garda Peak. The route, named PIA after the national airlines, offers fine climbing on mostly good rock. It should make a good warm-up for teams coming to the Trango area with more challenging goals. We used 70m ropes, and some pitches are quite long. After reaching the top we rappelled once down the summit ridge, then descended 20-30m to the northwest. We then made four long rappels into a gully, which led down easily to the glacier.

On the 17th the three of us climbed a new route that solves the problem presented by the central section of the southwest face of Sadu Peak. We climbed Pretty Close onsight at 5.10d. It is the third route on this face, the others being the original Sadu [350m, 5.11b, Antoine and Sandrine de Choudens, 2003], and Piyar, Piyar [Love, Love, 350m, 5.11a, Jakofcic-Mali-Valic,

2004]. Our line to the right is longer than the previous two, but with 430m of climbing is still a route for a long afternoon, rather than a full alpine day. The rock is good, and some of the pitches are really nice. We named the route after our near miss on Trango Tower and the fact that the approach from base camp to the foot of this wall is a mere 15m. We descended by a gully to the left. This proved inconvenient, and we should probably have kept to the left ridge, more or less following the line of Sadu.

A day later, as a farewell to the Karakoram, we climbed a variation start to Severance Ridge on 6,327m Trango II. This provides a separate route on the First Tower. [The 1,600m Severance Ridge was first climbed in 2005 by Jonathan Clearwater, Sam Johnson, and Jeremy Frimer in 63 pitches at VI 5.11 A2 AI3 M5; see *AAJ 2006* pp. 353-356.] We finished our 670m route just below the top of the First Tower, at a point where only a short section of easy scrambling remained. Our variant climbed at least 200m of new ground, including a 5.11a pitch climbed onsight and a 12a pitch AF (All Free: all the moves were climbed free but rest points were taken). Higher, but before the route joins the original line, there were difficulties between 5.10d and 5.11b, with a short section of C1 (we used no pitons on our routes). After the variant joins the original line of Severance Ridge, the difficulties did not exceed 5.10a/b (with a single point of A0). We called the variant Let's Go Home, and it was one of the most demanding rock climbs we have done. The rock quality was the best of the three new routes we climbed and almost as good as that found on Trango Tower. Protection is good, but, as on neighboring routes, in places cracks are a bit vegetated.

The second Polish team comprised Adam Pieprzycki and Marcin Szczotka. They kicked off by repeating Oceano Trango (as did every team visiting the Trango Glacier this season). On September 5 they repeated Karakoram Khush on Garda Peak, probably following the variation taken a few days previously by the Slovenian women [see above]. In 2004 the first ascensionists used aid points (A0), but now the 300m route goes free at 5.10d, with many variations possible in the upper section.

On September 14 they repeated the original line up the First Tower of Severance Ridge (at the time they didn't realize the ridge had been climbed). The two probably climbed variations to the first three or four pitches but reached the true top of the tower after a 700m climb at 5.11d and A0. From the top they descended easy ground to the south for 150m and then made seven rappels to the gully.

On the 17th they climbed a route on the slabby tower left of Sadu Peak: Escape from the Freedom (300m, 5.10d). They are not sure whether this peak had been climbed before, but if it has not, they propose the name Ibex Peak. Two days later the pair started up a pillar on the Second Tower of Severance Ridge. The line lies on the right flank of the ridge and was terminated 50-80m below the top, as the remaining ground would have probably required hard aid. The unfinished route was named Elusive Summits (650m of climbing, 5.11a/b A0).

JAKUB RADZIEJOWSKI, *Poland*

Trango Tower, free ascent; Trango Monk, second ascent. After an unsuccessful expedition to the Trango group in 2004 with 26-year-old Matevž Kunšič, I decided to return to the wonderful people and mountains of Baltistan. Matevž and I were joined by the brothers Aleš (23) and Nejc (21) Česen (the sons of Tomo Česen) and with another five Slovenian climbers [see above] we hit the road to the best golden granite I have ever seen. Our goal was an alpine-style ascent of

Trango Tower, but, more important, we wanted to climb it free.

From our first visit to the Karakoram we learned that the most stable weather is in September. On August 19, after four days in base camp, we summited Great Trango Tower (6,286m), for all of us our first peak above 6,000m. No one had problems, and the view was absolutely magnificent. As expected, it provided a great opportunity to check out the Slovenian route on Trango Tower. The next day we climbed Garda Peak (4,700m) via Karakoram Khush (300m, 6b A0),

Nejc Cesen on Pitch 17 (7a+) of the Slovenian Route, Trango Tower, during an all-free ascent. The big snowy shoulder, generally referred to as Sun Terrace, is visible below. *Matjaž Jeran*

but the weather then became unstable for two weeks. We did shorter climbs above base camp and nice bouldering. On one of the sunny days the Česen brothers repeated the American Route (250m, 5.9) on Little Trango (5,450m). [The first ascent of this tower was made in 2000 by McMahon and Wharton, who rated their route 5.10+.]

On September 7, after a few days of fine weather, we climbed onto the biggest rock needle in the world. It was cloudy and windy, but we managed to free climb, the second also following free with a seven-kilo rucksack, as not everything fit into our 70-liter haul bags. After nine pitches we reached the spacious Sun Terrace and met the three Slovenian girls climbing Eternal Flame. The next day we were graced with more sun, though it was still quite chilly. We had a great time jamming excellent 5.12 splitters and reached a good series of ledges at 5,900m. We had climbed 11 pitches and had a clear night, with a full moon rising from behind Gasherbrum IV. It was hard to believe our eyes.

On the 9th we continued up icy 5.11+ pitches before they melted. The best pitch of the day was a 50m, overhanging 5.11 crack with enormous jugs. It led to easier ground, and at 5:30 p.m. the four of us stood on top of the Tower. Aleš and I had free-climbed every centimeter from the start. Although I felt happy standing on top, I was also sad, because I realized the best climbing of my life was over. We rappelled Eternal Flame, meeting the girls, who summited later that day. They joined us in the middle of the night on Sun Terrace, where we all bivouacked. In the morning we sat in the sun, drinking coffee and enjoying being tired. We climbed the Slovenian route (1,000m, 5.12), in alpine style, and the three girls had made an alpine-style ascent of Eternal Flame.

After three days rest we decided to repeat Trango Monk (5,850m). September 14 should have been a sunny day, but it was already cloudy and cold when we started at 7 a.m. Matevž was experiencing problems with one of his feet so did not join us. The first six pitches, mostly mixed, with lots of fresh snow, were led by Aleš in crampons.

I led the next four. There was a bit of sunshine and, wearing rock shoes, I found the 5.11 offwidth easier than what we had done, so was happy with my block. Nejc had the hardest job, leading through a strong wind into the cold darkness, to take us to the summit at 9 p.m. The descent was a horror story in the wind; ropes jammed many times, and we were lucky to save two 35m lengths from our two 60m ropes. It took us six hours to reach the ground and another two before we could drink hot tea in base camp.

MATJAŽ JERAN, *Slovenia*

BALTORO MUZTAGH – OTHER

Baltoro Cathedrals, Reflexes Nocturns. A large Catalan team comprising Antonio Bayones, Oscar Cadiach, Ramon Canyellas, Elias Coll, Pilar Rossinyol, Albert Segura, and Toti Vales climbed a big new rock route on the Baltoro Cathedrals. These are a complex collection of rocky spires overlooking the Baltoro Glacier and rising above the east bank of the lower Dunge Glacier opposite the Trango Group. The expedition took place from June 20

The Cathedrals rise above the Baltoro Glacier with the entrance to the Dunge Glacier and the Trango group to the left. *Peter Thompson*

to July 16. The new route, which they named Reflexes Nocturns (1,500m, 7a), consists of four sections. In the first difficulties are moderate, with plenty of 4 but a crux of 6b. Above, 300m of scrambling and easy climbing lead to the upper section of the wall, where difficulties increase. The crux 7a pitch is situated near the top. The top of the wall is at ca 5,500m. From there, 300m of scrambling lead to the ca 5,800m summit. The climbers made three camps on the route.

It is unclear which summit the Catalans reached, but the Cathedrals have been the objective of several expeditions, the first recorded climb being by Jim Beyer, who in 1989 soloed a 54-pitch line off the Dunge Glacier to the summit of Thunmo (5,866m), which lies south of Cathedral Spire. His impressive 13-day ascent was graded VII 5.10d A4+.

Lindsay Griffin, Mountain INFO, CLIMB MAGAZINE

Peak 5,607m, northwest face, attempt. Our small expedition arrived at base camp on July 22, hoping to make the first free ascent of Lobsang Spire (5,707m) by a new route on the south face. After a reconnaissance, we abandoned this plan, feeling the route would need different logistics from those we wished to employ. There is an alpine super-route alternative, but it would require more snow than was present. Instead, we turned to our second objective, an unnamed 5,607m peak opposite the spire that had been attempted by Germans in 2000. After crossing the unstable glacier and approaching via a loose couloir, we made two attempts on the northwest face, finding the granite to be generally excellent. On our first attempt we climbed 12 pitches from scrambling to British E4 6a, using only removable protection, passing the German high point, before a sleepless night without sleeping bags in freezing rain sent us packing. On our second attempt, this time with sleeping bags, we reached the same point. It snowed heavily. We estimate we were only four pitches from the summit when we retreated.

When leaving for Skardu, we found it something of a task convincing our guide that we had to thoroughly clean our base camp and that we needed an extra porter to carry the rubbish out. Both on the way in and out we were shocked at the attitude among parties to leave rubbish for camp staff to clear up, and we felt that the camp site at Paiju, while having generally good facilities, with toilets and water systems provided by the UNDP, was being poorly maintained by local staff.

ANNE and JOHN ARRAN, *Alpine Club*

Editor's note: The following report concerns events on Broad Peak's normal route. It is included to raise awareness of the selfless deeds performed by Egocheaga and Morawski, despite the fact that such actions should be standard in the mountains, not the exception.

It may be apposite here to quote from the 2002 Tyrol Declaration on Best Practice in Mountain Sports, where in section six, under Emergencies, there is a statement: "If any person we meet – regardless if it is a fellow climber, a porter, or another local inhabitant – needs help, we must do everything in our power to provide qualified support as quickly as possible. There is no 'morality-free zone' in climbing." Or Doug Scott, writing in the 2006 Alpine Journal: "We are all capable of heroic deeds…. It is just that sometimes we lose the plot and are only reminded of our obligations after returning. By then a visit to the summit will forever be a hollow victory if we fail another in need."

On July 5 Sepp Bachmair and Peter Ressmann, from our 10-member Austro-German expedition, climbed in a single push from base camp to Camp 3, catching up with our leader, Markus Kronthaler. Together they left for the summit at 11:30 p.m. Climbing behind a strong Spanish group and two other climbers, they arrived at the 7,800m col between the central and main summits at 12:30 p.m. on July 6. Continuing ahead of his partners, Ressmann reached the main summit at 6 p.m. Three Spanish also summited earlier that afternoon, among them Dr. Jorge Egocheaga, who made a speed ascent (21 hours roundtrip between base camp and summit). On the descent Ressmann met his partners, who had decided to bivouac in a crevasse at 7,950m. Ressmann continued down to his ski cache at 7,500m and skied down to Camp 3 by moonlight, arriving at 11:45 p.m. The next day he skied to the base of the mountain. Previously, the highest ski descent from Broad Peak had been from 7,000m in 1994 by Hans Kammerlander. Ressmann believes it may be possible to ski the whole route from the main summit, though a short section below the col is often rocky and would have to be rappelled.

After their bivouac Bachmair and Kronthaler continued slowly, not reaching the main summit until 3-3:30 p.m. on July 7. On the way down Kronthaler's strength gave out halfway between the top and the foresummit. Through the night Bachmair tried to support, drag, and even carry his partner but to no avail. Kronthaler died of dehydration and exhaustion at 6 a.m. on July 8. Bachmair continued his descent to the notch, where he came across a Polish-Slovakian rope. One Pole, Piotr Morawski, gave up his summit bid and accompanied Bachmair down to Camp 3. (Morawski reached the summit solo the next day.) Above Camp 3 they were met by Jorge Egocheaga, who, despite his speed ascent two days earlier, had immediately offered to climb back up again and help. He nursed Bachmair during the night and, with two Argentineans, accompanied him down to base camp on July 9.

Our expedition extends heartfelt thanks to Dr. Jorge Egocheaga and Piotr Morawski for their extraordinary efforts in helping Sepp Bachmair. The support we received from them and every other expedition on the mountain will be a lasting memory and was notably different from the selfish acts seen on Everest in the spring of 2006.

JOCHEN HEMMLEB, *German Alpine Club (DAV)*

MASHERBRUM RANGE

Masherbrum, northeast face, attempt. In late June a strong Russian expedition under the noted leader of the Russian Big Walls Project, Alexander Odintsov, set up base camp on the Yermanendu Glacier for an attempt on the futuristic northeast face of Masherbrum (7,855m). This face is as impressive and as hard as the north face of Jannu, climbed by the Russian team in 2004. It is 3,000m high, and the crux will undoubtedly be the near-vertical yellow rock band starting around 7,000m. A reconnaissance in 2005 led the Russians to believe the wall would be very difficult but possible. However, it failed to reveal the objective dangers.

Immediately after arrival at base camp, Odintsov became seriously ill with hepatitis and had to be evacuated by helicopter. Later Michel Michailov was injured falling into a crevasse. Alexander Ruchkin, who was the first to summit Jannu in 2004, took over as leader and, having decided that the lower northeast face was severely threatened by avalanche and serac fall, switched to an approach via the north ridge to the right. The weather was unhelpful, and work on the route had to be carried out at night or during early morning. Eventually they established an advanced base on the ridge at 5,800m. However, after repeated snowfalls, Ruchkin realized that there was no safe way forward, and they abandoned the objective in mid-July. Interviewed later, the climbers stated they had no intention of returning, leaving this awesome project for the next generation.

The north ridge itself is a superb and elegant goal that has been attempted three times. Japanese tried it in 1975 but retreated from 5,500m, when they found the start too threatened by serac fall. Another Japanese expedition started up in 1985 but, finding the upper glacier dangerous, made a long traverse right to the northwest ridge and climbed it to the summit. A strong American-Slovenian team tried the face in 2003 but retreated in dangerous avalanche conditions from 5,900m

LINDSAY GRIFFIN, *Mountain INFO, CLIMB Magazine*

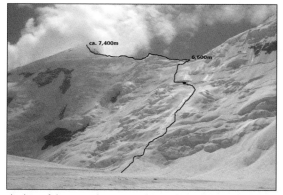

The line of the Spanish route up the northwest face to southwest ridge of Chogolisa (7,665m). The face is over 1,000m high and a camp was placed half way up, with a second on the col at 6,600m. The climbers retreated in bad weather from 7,400m. *Carles Figueras Torrent*

Trinity Peak, northwest ridge, attempt; Chogolisa, northwest face of southwest ridge, attempt. Two days after leaving Hushe village on July 16, we established our base camp at a pleasant site called Xhuspang (4,680m) on the northwest side of the East Gondogoro Glacier. We spent several days acclimatizing around and above this camp, then, due to poor snow conditions caused by the hot summer of 2006, we decided not to attempt the impressive west face of Laila Peak. Instead, Pep Permañé and I devoted our efforts to the northwest ridge of Trinity Peak (a.k.a. Tasa Peak or Tasa Burakha), a ridge leading to the southwest summit (6,614m). On July 24 and 25 we climbed alpine-style 1,700m up the ridge, the first day on excellent granite to grade IV and the second day mixed climbing, first on snow, then ice. However, 300m below the summit, snow conditions deteriorated so badly that we retreated. The descent involved 25 rappels to Gondogoro Glacier. [The southwest summit was reached in 1978 by a Japanese expedition, which sieged the northwest ridge, not realizing that the ca 6,700m central summit was higher. It was reached in 1988 by British climbers Nicolas Hellen and Julius Grainger, either by the same route or the southwest ridge. —Ed.]

On July 29 we crossed the Gondogoro La and established an advanced base camp at Ali Camp on the west side of Vigne Glacier. On July 30 and 31, Jordi "Barraca" Bosch, Ramon Estiu, Pep Permañé, and I climbed the 1,100m northwest face of the southwest ridge of Chogolisa (7,665m), by a route to the right of the line followed in 1986 by the British team that traversed both summits. On the first day we pitched our two tiny tents at 6,000m. The next day we continued to the 6,600m col on the southwest ridge between Chogolisa and Prupuo Barakha [the Kaberi Col, reached from the Kaberi Glacier on the far side in 1975 by Edi Koblmuller's expedition, which made the first ascent of the southwest, highest summit of Chogolisa.] Just below the col we had to climb a serac, where we left a fixed rope. By the afternoon of that second day we were back at Ali Camp. On August 2, Barraca, Estiu, and Permañé reclimbed the face to the col, where they pitched a tent. The next day they found the ridge ahead to be corniced with deep snow. Estiu stopped at 7,100m, but Permañé and Barraca went on without rucksacks until above 7,400m, a point where all difficulties had been overcome. It was snowing and was late, so they did not to push on to the summit. They returned to the tent and the next day reached Ali Camp.

CARLES FIGUERAS TORRENT, *Spain.*

Editor's note: A British expedition was on Chogolisa at the same time, having had their permit to Noshaq in the Hindu Kush denied shortly before leaving for Pakistan. They were behind the Spanish but found the route dangerous. One evening a colossal serac fell down the entire face along the line of ascent. The Spanish had just finished climbing through this section, and the British felt they were lucky to escape disaster. After a week of bad weather at base camp, the British returned and climbed a steep 400m ice line to a col on the northwest ridge, above which they made a cache on a flat section of the crest at 6,000m. They hoped to return and follow the ridge to the summit, but daily snowfalls of 15cm prevented further attempts.

CHARAKUSA VALLEY

Charakusa Region, corrections. The following information relates to the Italian expeditions operating above the Chogolisa Glacier in 2004 (*AAJ 2005*) and 2005 (*AAJ 2006*). Pointed Peak (5,400m), climbed by Giordani, Maspes, and Paoletto in 2004 by the northwest face and west ridge (where on the upper crest they found indications that the peak had been visited), was first climbed, by the same route, in 1989 by George Armstrong and George Szuca. They also climbed the peak immediately to the west, from the col between the two, naming it Parantha Peak (ca 5,300m). The same two also made the first ascent of what the Italians refer to as Sheep Peak (ca 6,000m), climbed by Barmasse and Giordani in 2004. Armstrong and Szuca climbed it twice, via the north couloir (climbed by the Italians) and the south couloir. They refer to the whole mountain as the Dru. Completing their productive expedition, they also climbed 5,800m Tower Peak and ca 6,000m Pata Kha. At the same time John Ashdown and David Scott Maxwell added another route to Raven's Pyramid (ca 5,300m), first climbed by the south face by Mick Hardwick and Pat Littlejohn in 1987. The new route climbed the west face and south-west ridge over three days, to give 1,000m and 41 pitches of excellent climbing up to British 5c. Ashdown and Maxwell rappelled the route. Note that Pt. 5,500m, with the Italian route Fast and Furious, is the peak immediately east of Crested Peak (5,560m). The first expedition, likely the first people to visit the Chogolisa Glacier, comprised 13 Japanese and their local staff, who traveled to its head in 1977 and made the first ascent of Pruppoo Brakk (6,867m).

Another British party, operating from the Charakusa Glacier in 1989, made the first ascent of Rona Peak (5,800m) and Fiona Peak (5,900-6,000m) from the south, as well as another peak of ca 6,000m. Fiona Peak seems to be the same summit reached from the north by the Italian Hervé Barmasse in 2005. On the Japanese Pruppoo Brakk expedition map, it is referred to as Karupa Peak. See below for details of the first ascent of Farol West.

LINDSAY GRIFFIN, *Mountain INFO, CLIMB Magazine*

Farol Peak, first ascent. The first ascent of the highest summit of Farol Peak, Farol West (6,370m) was made in 1991 by British climbers Neil Wilson and me. We climbed the 1,000m south face at Scottish III, reaching the summit at 3 a.m. We began rappelling the route from there, leaving a snow stake. In the photo in *AAJ 2006*, p. 373, our route climbs the hanging glacier between the west and central tops, until just above the large serac formation in the "narrows." From there we slanted steeply up left directly to the summit. While based on the Charakusa, we also made the second ascent of Sulo Peak (ca 5,900m).

IAN STEWART, *U.K.*

NANGMA VALLEY

Logmun Tower, north face, Inshallah Mi Primo. Logmun Tower stands close to the standard base camp in the Nangma Valley. It is the middle of three impressive north-facing granite towers that have also been referred to as Roungkhanchan (or Roun Khan Chan, peak of many graves) I, II and III or the Green Wall. [The north face of Roungkhanchan I (ca 4,600m) was climbed, probably for the first time, in 2004 by three Italians to give Troubles, Cough, and Fever (14 pitches, 6b+ A1, *AAJ 2005*, p. 363). The sheer north side of the middle tower was also climbed in 2004 by Frenchmen Frédéric Hasbani and Marco Vanpé. Their 600m route climbed directly up the north face, finishing with a few pitches on the east face. They named the sustained but never extreme route Zen and the Art of Motorcycle Maintenance (VI 6b+ A3). The French referred to this tower as Roungkhanchan III. Its height is ca 4,700m. —Ed.]

Our three-man Basque-Aragonese expedition was one of the first to arrive in Pakistan during 2006 and reached base camp at 3,900m in the Nangma Valley on June 5. We were Dani Ascaso, Gorka Díaz, and I. We had no fixed plans, except to try one of those arêtes that you see in the photos and make you say, "That's the line!" However, our dream was shattered when continuous rockfall showed the reality to be different. During acclimatization we inspected many walls and eventually decided on the Logmun Tower. The only information we had was of the

French route. We looked for other possible lines, and in another attractive crack system discovered signs of previous passage. We now think there were two or three established routes on this wall before our arrival. [Two routes were climbed by Americans in 2001, prior to an unsuccessful attempt on Shingu Charpa, see below]. In the end we opted for the elegant north pillar, direct and attractive. Steep crack systems promised long sections of free climbing.

We took 13 days to climb the wall. We spent the first four fixing four pitches (200m) and establishing a portaledge camp. We then climbed capsule style from June 18-26, with Camp 2 at 450m and Camp 3 at 570m. The climbing was sustained without being extreme. The weather was good throughout this period, but we only took food and water for five days, and moving camp required a whole day. However, the day after we finished our water, we came across a snowpatch, which prevented us from having to descend. From the ground we'd

The north pillar of Logmun Tower (a.k.a. Roungkhanchan III, ca 4,700m) showing (1) Inshallah Mi Primo (850m of climbing, 6a A3, Ascaso-Díaz-Larrañaga, 2006). (2) Dirt Box (20 pitches, VI 5.10 A3, Davis-Offenbacher, 2001). In 2001 McCray and Warren climbed a route that (1) likely shares in parts. *Jonatán Larrañaga*

underestimated the size of the face. The pillar gets little sun, but near the top we made two pendulums to gain the northeast face, which we felt offered faster ground to the top and also got more sun. We hauled our equipment to the top of pitch 16, left it, and climbed the 17th and final pitch at night. From the top we made a three-hour descent on foot to base camp.

After eating and sleeping for two days, we went to retrieve gear and the following day went to the summit, rescued our gear, and brought everything back to base camp. We named the route Inshallah Mi Primo (850m of climbing, A3 6a), in honor of our cook at base camp.

Most of the cracks were dirty, but during our ascent we found traces of previous passage: bolt belays halfway up pitch two and 10m to the left of the third pitch, another bolt on pitch six, and other material on pitches 10, 11, and 12, though nothing above. However, from this evidence we still believe much of our climb was new.

JONATÁN LARRAÑAGA, *Spain*.

Logmun Tower, Dirt Box, previously unreported. In 2001, before making an attempt on the north ridge of Shingu Charpa, Nils Davis, Brian McCray, Brenton Warren, and I climbed two routes on the Logmun Tower. The Davis-Offenbacher route, Dirt Box, took four-and-a-half days to complete after we fixed the first two pitches. The climbing was steep, and almost all the cracks filled with dirt. We could have climbed the route much faster, free-climbing most of it up to 5.11+, had the cracks been Yosemite clean. The route was around 20 pitches long, with the crux, A3 hooking, halfway up. We placed one rivet at a belay before the hand drill broke and thereafter only placed a few pitons. We spent four nights in a portaledge under clear skies, and when we launched the haul bags from a ledge two pitches below the top, the bags took two bounces before falling free to the ground. From the top of the tower a fantastic knife-edge ridge led back to terra firma. The grade was VI 5.10 A3.

McCray and Warren climbed to the top of pitch two of this route and then broke out left. In their middle section, they followed a long, and striking offwidth that was clearly visible from base camp and appears close to the Spanish route [reported above].

TODD OFFENBACHER, *AAC*

The 1,550m north ridge of Shingu Charpa (5,600m). The line of the Cordes-Wharton attempt is marked, finishing after 45 pitches, all free up to 5.11+, some 60m below and 150m away from the summit. (R) is the start of the "escape ramp" that slants up right to meet the ridge at one-third height. The first ascent of this summit in the Nangma Valley was made in 2000 by three Koreans, who climbed the prominent snow couloir to the right, then angled back left up the west face (5.11 A2) to the top. *Kelly Cordes*

Shingu Charpa, north ridge, attempt. Huge controversy has surrounded the claim by three Ukrainians to have made the coveted first ascent of the formidably long north ridge of Shingu Charpa (a.k.a. Great Tower, 5,600m). Igor Chaplinsky, Andrey Rodiontsev, and Orest Verbitsky arrived at base camp (3,900m) in the Nangma Valley and acclimatized by spending 10 days circumnavigating the mountain, to check out possible descent routes. They found the peak impressive on all sides and realized they would have to rappel the route, an estimated 1,550m high. At first they claimed to have begun their final alpine-style attempt from the base of the ridge on July 20. However, when later tackled by the magazine *Alpinist*, Chaplinsky acknowledged that on their first attempt they had indeed started from the foot, but after the first day Verbitsky was injured in the eye, and they retreated by descending an easy ramp/ gully that slants across the east face to reach the crest of the ridge at 4,650m, one-third of the way up the route. This ramp has been used by several parties, either to gain or escape from the ridge.

On their second, final attempt the Ukrainians used this ramp to short-cut their ascent. They reported continuing to the summit in a five-day push. The trio seems to have climbed at least 58 pitches to the top of the rock, at 5,400m, above which a difficult, dangerous snowy ridge, with snow mushrooms and menacing cornices, and hard ice and difficult mixed climbing up to M5, led to the summit. Chaplinsky reported finding that on the way down, one of these large formations, beneath which they had traversed on the ascent, had fallen off in the intervening time. Later they stated publicly that they climbed the route completely free at 7a or 7a+ and placed no bolts on the ascent, though three or four for rappel anchors. The team was nominated for the Piolet d'Or. But did they really climb the route free and did they really reach the summit? Kelly Cordes takes up the story.

Day three on the north ridge of Shingu Charpa (5,600m). Kelly Cordes starting up the 40th pitch. There are still a few more difficult pitches before reaching the summit ridge. *Josh Wharton*

Shingu Charpa, north ridge, attempts and deception. In July, sitting in the gorgeous Nangma Valley base camp, I hacked up nasty chunks of something laced with blood, stricken with who-knows-what. My ultra-strong and ultra-capable partner, Josh Wharton, paced away the time until I recovered enough to try again.

We'd made an attempt that failed when I fell sick one-third of the way up Shingu Charpa's 1,550m north ridge, a stunning-looking and highly sought line for which we received generous, greatly appreciated support from the Lyman Spitzer and Polartec Challenge grants. Unfortunately, the route largely consisted of vegetation, closed cracks, serious runouts, mud, and loose blocks. We retreated via a descent gully that comes in from the east to meet the ridge. A team of three Ukrainians (Igor Chaplinsky, Andrey Rodiontsev, and Orest Verbitsky) had failed on an earlier attempt and retreated down this gully. As I blew our weather window recovering, we watched them return to retry the route, skipping the bottom third of the route by coming up the descent gully and continuing up the north ridge. We lost sight of them as they turned the summit ridge onto the side facing the village of Kande.

After a week out, they returned to camp triumphant, and we offered them our sincere congratulations. They were friendly and kind, with Orest remaining mostly silent, Andrey speaking a little, and Igor talking a lot, eager to tell us about their success. Despite our personal disappointment, we were happy for them. So it goes.

A couple of weeks of rain followed. Near the end of our trip we got a brief window and punched it. We again started from the very bottom, because we wanted climb the whole thing. Josh and I climbed 45 pitches in three days and spent a fourth descending (Aug 18-21), all free/ clean on lead to 5.11+ (second jugging with the pack). We shivered through the nights due to our weight-obsessed-no-bivy-gear idea, which made sense in the sun at base camp. It was real climbing from beginning to end, with the technical crux coming in the middle, as we expected (thus Josh's leader block). The route offered little in the way of good climbing and the piles of garbage left by the Ukrainians didn't help (we carried off some of their mess). But the positioning was spectacular, the views immaculate, and the feeling of freedom wonderful. Like it always is.

Early afternoon on day three, we realized the inadequacy of our setup; the white stuff up high was solid ice, not snow. With ultralight boots for the leader, sneakers for the second, strap-on aluminum crampons for both, and one-and-a-half ice axes, it felt too dangerous. In retrospect, perhaps we could have made it work, but what the hell, the thing had already been climbed. So we thought. Maybe we'd have pushed harder, maybe not. I don't know. The cliché we strive for, to climb for only ourselves, dictates that our decisions should be our own. Indeed they should, and so we made our call to bail some 60m vertical and perhaps 150m horizontal from the summit. No excuses, we failed.

As we left Kande, the villagers, who have an unobstructed view of the peak, were certain that the Ukrainians did not summit either. We brushed it off, trusting the word of the Ukrainians.

I like to think that the mountains and the travel—especially to places like this, where people live impoverished lifestyles yet overflow with human warmth and kindness—bring humility and perspective. Someone would truly have to lack integrity to lie about something like climbing.

Once home, I e-mailed the Ukrainians to again offer congratulations. Only "the legendary" (as one Eastern journalist called him) Igor Chaplinsky responded, gregarious as usual and reminding us: "Please accept my regrets that you haven't made it to the top. As I have already told you in the base camp the most difficult and unexpected part of the route is the one closer to the top."

Indeed, often the top is the hardest, and we didn't make it. Neither did they.

Igor Chaplinsky ceased contact when I politely asked about his "all free" reports on websites and his first-hand account in *Alpinist* magazine. I thought it odd because, in base camp when he made that claim, Rodiontsev promptly corrected him, saying they aided 50m or 100m, which seemed clear to us while watching through binoculars. Plus, I saw a photo on a Russian website, clearly showing the leader standing in aiders. Also, in photos and reports Chaplinsky consistently drew a continuous route line from the bottom, omitting mention of their final-go shortcut. Huh? That's a third of the route. WTF? It had us curious, but what could we say without sounding like whiners?

Additional questions emerged, but I optimistically dismissed them to the language barrier. In camp Igor Chaplinsky had proudly proclaimed "no bolts!" But Josh and I wondered about the shiny bolts we saw high on the route, higher than anyone but the Ukrainians are known to have reached. Then, in one of Chaplinsky's write-ups he mentioned placing bolts. Huh (again)? Also, in photos he sent me, he drew their line ending beyond the summit, at a far-side sub-summit. From some angles, if you haven't done your homework, it looks like the real summit. Chaplinsky was probably just in a hurry and sketched it in quickly. Whatever. It felt like Josh and I were saying that a lot.

Igor Chaplinsky and Andrey Rodiontsev attended the Piolet d'Or ceremony. Their nomination seemed surprising, considering their shortcut. But maybe nobody knew, since Chaplinsky wasn't up front about it and drew a continuous line on all the posted photos. But anyway, the PdO? Whatever (again.) Cool, go for it guys, have fun.

Orest, the young guy who we sensed was the team's rope gun, couldn't take it anymore and finally came clean. He didn't go to the PdO ceremony, saying he stayed home because they had not reached the summit, stopping 100m below and—contrary to the hype—that they therefore "had no moral right to be among the nominees." While he could have been honest a bit earlier, once the ball gets rolling, especially with him being the youngster alongside two older and "respected" climbers, this couldn't have been easy.

In contrast to his initial demeanor, Igor Chaplinsky stopped replying to, at the least, www.mountain.ru, *Montagnes*, *Alpinist*, and *Climb* magazines, and the *AAJ*. I hope they enjoyed their 50 grams of fame before Orest had the courage to speak up. History tends to forget the corrections, the after-the-fact details, favoring the now-sexy hype. So it goes, good for them. The north ridge of Shingu Charpa remains unclimbed.

Yes, I know, it's just climbing. And so I have to wonder: If you can't even be honest about this, then what else in life do you lie about?

KELLY CORDES, *AAC*

Changi Tower, attempt. Previously unreported from 2005 is the ascent, but not to the summit, of a previously unclimbed line up the east pillar of one of the formations that makes up the Changi Tower. Jordi Comas from Barcelona, Oriol Ribas, and I from Andorra reached the Nangma Valley in July 2005. In the 24 days that we were in the valley, there was much rain and snow, and it was only possible to climb on 10. After placing a camp near the base of the wall, we fixed 200m of rope and then made a second camp at the foot of the upper pillar. We spent six nights on the face to complete our 12-pitch climb. However, we didn't reach the summit. On the last day we were hit by a savage storm when only 50m below the top and were forced to descend. We grade the route TD+ 6b A2.

XAVI BONATTI, *Andorra*

The incomplete Andorran-Spanish route (TD+ 6b A2) on the east pillar of an unnamed rock formation that forms part of the Changi Tower massif, Nangma Valley. *Xavi Bonatti*

India

HIMALAYA

Overview. Climbing activity in the Indian Himalaya has decreased. The number of both foreign and national expeditions was reduced. Fewer peaks are being attempted, especially the more challenging peaks and routes. One important deterrent is the unrealistic fee structure and regulations set by state governments. Activity was at an especially reduced level in Uttarakhand (formerly Uttaranchal) and Sikkim.

In contrast, trekking in the Indian Himalaya has grown by leaps and bounds, and more Indians than ever are now enjoying the mountains. This increase has brought about concerns about environmental protection, though the impact of trekkers is negligible compared to the damage caused by pilgrims, security forces, and the local population. Locals have been introduced to modern packaging; paper wrapping has been replaced by aluminum foil. Together with global warming and glacial retreat, many aspects of human impact need to be examined by the government.

Thirty-seven foreign expeditions visited the Indian Himalaya during 2006, nearly all to the states of Jammu and Kashmir, Uttarakhand, and Himachal Pradesh. The majority were either commercially organized to easy routine peaks, or teams tackling popular high mountains. Six expeditions climbed Stok Kangri (officially, that is), two went for Dzo Jongo, and two for Kang Yissey. The Nun Kun massif was visited by four expeditions, while Shivling and Satopanth received three teams each. Difficult routes were attempted or climbed on Kedar Dome, Meru, and Changabang. Nineteen expeditions visited Uttarakhand, where the ever-popular Gangotri area attracted 13 groups and Kumaun the remaining six. Two teams visited Himachal Pradesh and one the East Karakoram. The low success rate can generally attributed to poor weather; the general unpredictability of the Himalayan weather is becoming a major concern in climbing circles.

Each year the number of Indian climbers visiting their own mountains is decreasing. The trend of attempting routine peaks such as Kalanag, Rudugaira, Hanuman Tibba, Deo Tibba, Chhamser, and Lungser Kangri has been replaced by an emphasis on altitude. Kamet, the third highest mountain on Indian soil, was attempted twice; Satopanth, the mighty 7,000er in the Gangotri, four times; and Nun once. However, some climbers did attempt difficult peaks. In addition to expeditions mentioned elsewhere in this report, Rajsekhar Ghosh's 12-member team from West Bengal made the third ascent of Nanda Khat (6,611m), and Debasis Biswas's 10-member team, also from West Bengal, made the fourth ascent of neighboring Panwali Dwar (6,663m). In the Rupshu valley, J.S. Gulia and a 20-member school expedition claim a first ascent of an easy 6,000er (either 6,250m or 6,440m; details are lacking). Another West Bengal team, under Samir Sengupta, climbed Kullu Pumori (6,553m) on the Bara Shigri, while Kajal

Dasgupta's 12-member team (again from West Bengal) climbed Manirang (6,593m) on the Kinnaur–Spiti divide. Indian teams also attempted Purbi Dunagiri and Shivling. Twenty-six expeditions visited Himachal Pradesh, and, despite additional peak fees imposed by the state government, 20 expeditions visited Uttarakhand. Ladakh and its surroundings received six expeditions, but all to routine peaks.

HARISH KAPADIA, *Honorary Editor, The Himalayan Journal*

EAST KARAKORAM

Junction Peak, ascent; Singhi Kangri, south face, attempt. An Indian Army expedition led by Col Ashok Abbey visited the Siachen Glacier from August 31 to October 7. Moving relatively swiftly up the glacier, the expedition established base camp on September 12 at the "Oasis," the junction of the Siachen and Teram Shehr glaciers. Climbers immediately set about making an ascent of Junction Peak (6,350m), a fine vantage point first climbed in 1912 by American Fanny Bullock-Workman and her Italian guides. The team established Camp 1 at 5,320m on the 14th and began opening a route on the west face. They eventually reached the summit a little after 1 p.m. on the 18th, after an eight-and-a-half-hour ascent from the final camp. The ascent, only the third of Junction Peak, was made in avalanche-prone conditions.

Junction Peak (6,350m) above the Siachen Glacier. The first ascent of this fine vantage point was made in 1912 by Fanny Bullock-Workman and her Italian guides. In 2006, Indians made the third ascent via slopes facing the camera. *Harish Kapadia*

The expedition then made only the second-ever attempt to climb 7,202m Singhi Kangri near the head of the Siachen on the border with China. They established a new base camp on September 16 at 5,100m and Camp 1 at 6,325m on the 21st, having climbed the west face. It appeared that the hardest part of the climb was over, and they deemed only one more camp necessary before making a summit attempt on both Singhi Kangri and Pt. 6,850m. However, poor weather and dangerous snow conditions prevented further progress, and they abandoned the route on the 29th.

Singhi Kangri was climbed in 1976 by a Japanese expedition, in what was a remarkable climb. The Japanese, under the leadership of Haruo Sato, approached up the Bilafond Glacier in what is now Pakistan, crossed the Bilafond La and descended the Lolofond Glacier to the Siachen. They then moved up the Siachen to attempt the south face of Singhi Kangri, but finding it too difficult, crossed another pass (Staghar La) in the wall dividing the Siachen from the Staghar Glacier in China. They established their Camp 2 (an advanced base) on the Staghar and from there climbed the northwest ridge to the summit with two further camps. The expedition left Kaphlu in Pakistan on June 9 with 137 porters, and the first summit party, Masafumi Katayama, Junichi Imai, and Shohei Takahashi, only reached the top on August 8.

Singhi Kangri (7,202m) at the head of the Siachen Glacier seen from the west. The Indian Army expedition climbed the west flank to gain the south face, the triangular, sunlit snow face on the far right. They were thwarted at over 6,300m by bad weather. The peak has only been climbed once, in 1976 from the far side. *Harish Kapadia*

After their 2006 attempt, members of the Indian Army expedition reached the Sia La (leading over to the Kondus Glacier) at the western tip of the Siachen and also walked up Peak 36 Glacier to inspect the northeast faces of Saltoro Kangri I (7,746m) and II (7,705m) for a possible future attempt. The lower of the two summits is currently one of the highest unclimbed peaks in the world. A serious attempt on the Saltoros could not be mounted in 2006 because of the on-going Siachen war, but hopefully the climbs by the Army indicate relaxation regarding access permits in the future.

HARISH KAPADIA, *Honorary Editor, The Himalayan Journal*

Plateau Peak, attempt. A 15-member Indo-Italian expedition attempted unclimbed Plateau Peak (7,310m), which lies southwest of Saser Kangri I (7,672m) in the Saser group. Jointly led by M.S. Gomese and Marco Meazzini, the team established base camp at 4,700m and an advanced base at 5,400m on the Central South Phukpoche Glacier. During August they equipped the slopes leading to the crest of the west ridge with ropes and food dumps, but bad weather prevented progress above 5,800m.

HARISH KAPADIA, *Honorary Editor, The Himalayan Journal*

ZANSKAR

Kang Yissay, possible new route. It is reported that on July 17 Spanish climber Santiago Sagaste soloed what is believed to be a new route on the northeast face of this very popular 6,400m mountain above the Nimaling Plains in Zanskar. We have no further details, so it is impossible to know how the route relates to other lines on this side of the mountain.

JOSEP PAYTUBI *and the* SERVEI GENERAL D'INFORMACIO DE MUNTANYA, *Spain*

HIMACHAL PRADESH

MIYAR VALLEY

Goya Peak, first ascent. Our small multinational team of Jeremy Frimer (Canada), Sarah Hart (Canada), Michel van der Spek (The Netherlands) and I made two first ascents of alpine rock climbs in the Miyar Valley. We established base camp at the usual spot near the entrance to the

Dali (a.k.a. Thunder) Glacier and first spent time acclimatizing and reconnoitering a peak on the far (west) side of the main valley. We dubbed this "Himashanca" because of its resemblance to the famous Jirishanca in Peru's Cordillera Huayhuash. However, we found the approach to the attractive north face problematic, due to heavy crevassing, and an inspection of the valleys to the south shed no light on a possible descent, were we to reach the summit. Instead, we returned to base camp, unaware that Catalans Oriol Baro and Oscar Cacho had climbed this 5,930m mountain in 2005, via a 950m route on the north face (Antiparques, TD M6 60°, see *AAJ 2006*, pp. 382-384).

Michel van der Spek climbing above the Miyar Valley during the first ascent of Goya Peak (600m, D- 5.9). The main valley descends southeast towards the 6,000m Gangstang Group in the far distance, before turning right and eventually dropping to Udaipur on the Chenab River. *Oliver Metherell*

On September 23 van der Spek and I made the first ascent of a peak near base camp, directly above the north bank of the Dali glacier and between Lammergeier Peak (5,300m) and Pt 4,916m. Lammergeier is a fine pointed spire first climbed in 2004 by a British expedition (*AAJ 2005*, p. 367). After several roped pitches up the southwest ridge, the third pitch crux being 5.9, we untied and climbed easier terrain to the ca 5,300m summit, which we named Goya Peak. We reached the top, where we built a small cairn, at 3 p.m. We graded our 600m route Alpine D-. We reversed the route, downclimbing and making four rappels, arriving back at base camp after nightfall.

OLIVER METHERELL, *UK*

Pt. 5,650m, Gateway Ridge, not to summit; Jangpar Glacier, reconnaissance. Hanging to the east of the greater Miyar Valley, the Chhudong (a.k.a. Tawa) Valley is predominantly flat, save for a slabby cliff situated just before the Chhudong Glacier. On September 14 Michel van der Spek (Netherlands) and I made an alpine-style first ascent of the 1,100m ridge that rises north from just below the glacier. The climbing was on what I believe to be metamorphosed granite, characterized by consistently solid rock, with many face features but few cracks.

We began just below the glacier, gaining the ridge by a 4th-class left-trending chimney/ramp. After crossing a snow gully, we climbed an easy 5th-class ridge before cutting left onto a second ramp. The sun rose as we roped up. After climbing one pitch to gain the upper crest, we simul-climbed for several pitches, before increasing difficulties slowed our progress. While inclined at moderate angles, the ridge's challenge lay in its narrow and, in places, hammer-head crest. We climbed five pitches (to 5.9R), before traversing onto the right flank, where

The south face of Pt. 5,650m above the entrance to the Chhudong Glacier, Miyar Valley. (1) Gateway Ridge (1,100m, TD- 5.9/5.10- R, no summit). (2) The descent route. *Jeremy Frimer*

we again found the terrain suitable for simul-climbing. We reached a notch in the summit ridge at 1 p.m. and climbed the final crest toward the top. After 100m of climbing to 5.10-R, we terminated our ascent 50m from the summit, so as to leave enough daylight to contend with our chosen descent ridge, which we could see was far narrower than we had anticipated.

After several raps and stuck ropes, we simul-climbed an 80m traverse across a hanging slab to a notch. Here the descent ridge became particularly difficult, so we rappelled onto a hanging scree field on the south side of the crest, which gave access to the upper section of the ramp by which we had gained our ascent route. We named our climb Gateway Ridge (1,100m, TD- 5.9/5.10-R).

After recuperating in base camp, Michel, Sarah Hart (Canada), and I visited the relatively unexplored Jangpar Glacier. Brits had visited this valley early in 2004 (see *AAJ 2005*, p. 367), where they encountered much snow, which expedited the approach but hindered climbing efforts. Our visit was probably the first during the usual autumn climbing season. While we can confirm that there is much in the way of alpine and big-wall potential on granite or metamorphosed granite, the challenges of approaching these climbs should not be understated. We found the camping situation in the rubble-filled valley and its arid swales to be abysmal, and noticed that icefalls, extending from wall to wall, barred reasonable access to the majority of peaks. The challenge and expense in climbing these walls would undoubtedly be in the approach.

JEREMY FRIMER, *Canada*

Tamadonog, Doomed to Miyar; Geruda Peak, first ascent. The Tharanga, the local population of the lower Miyar Valley, are mainly shepherds and farmers. They gladly help expeditions visiting their valley and were of great assistance to our second Polish trip to the area.

From the beginning we had difficulty reaching base camp. Our first obstacle was a broken bridge on the way from Manali to Tingrad. Travel beyond became impossible in our off-road vehicle, so we had to carry our baggage across a footbridge and on the far side arrange a second truck to Tingrad. There we encountered another unpleasant surprise. We could not use horses to transport our gear, as I did in 2005. The bridge at Chaling was broken, and we had to hire porters to carry our 300kg of equipment. After five hours of negotiations we brought down the price by 50 percent and hired 11 men. We left Tingrad the next morning and arrived at base camp two days later, after a walk of 30km.

During the first three days the weather was unkind,but despite the rain we thought we ought to try something. To acclimatize, Przemek Wojcik and I went to the northwest face of Tamadonog (ca 5,245m; the name given by local porters) overlooking the Takdung (a.k.a. Nameless) Glacier valley. We set up advanced base at 4,240m. The next day, after looking at the face for the best line, we started climbing, covering 500m, mainly in cracks, until the weather broke. We had a cold camp that night, and the next day, August 14, climbed the remaining 500m of easier terrain, largely up an arête, to the summit. Our 1,000m new route, Doomed to Miyar, took 31 hours, with a crux of VIII- and every pitch climbed onsight. We think this peak was climbed by a Spanish party in 2005, and ours was probably the second ascent.

The west face of Geruda Peak (ca 5,640m) above the Chhudong Glacier, Miyar Valley, showing the line of the first ascent (900m, VII+ AO 50-60°). The peak was attempted by Italians in 2005 by the steep, leftward-slanting ramp above the snow gully toward the left side of the face. *Michal Krol*

Bad weather kept us in base camp until the 21st, when we set off up the Tawa Glacier. It took two days to establish an advanced base at 4,860m, at the site used by Italians in 2005 (Francesco Camilucci and friends, see *AAJ 2006*, pp. 384-385). Our main goal of the expedition had been the unclimbed east pillar of Three Peaks Mountain, but after a reconnaissance we decided that the chimney system forming the obvious line was too brittle and dan-

Michal Krol leading a grade VII (UIAA) crack on the first ascent of Doomed to Miyar, northwest face of Tamadonog (ca 5,245m), Miyar Valley. *Przemek Wojcik*

The northwest face of Tamadonog above the lower Takdung (a.k.a Nameless) Glacier with the line of the Polish route, Doomed to Miyar (1,000m, UIAA VIII-). Above the initial 500m wall shown, another 500m of easier terrain up a ridge above leads to the summit. *Michal Krol*

gerous. On the 27th the weather finally improved, so we decided to go for the virgin summit immediately right of Lotus Peak (climbed by David Kaszlikowski and me in 2005). This summit was also attempted in 2005 by Massimo Marcheggiani and Massimo Natalini, who completed a route, Million Indian Stars, to the top of a tower. To this tower they assigned an altitude of 5,650m, though it was obviously much lower.

Our route started up the west face to the right of the couloir used on the 2005 attempt. After a 250m ice/mixed gully, we negotiated a further 250m of relatively friable but easy rock. Above came the steep headwall forming the second half of the climb. Vertical cracks and chimneys led to a point three pitches below the summit, where the weather broke. We continued with some difficulty through snow and rain, but the conditions meant I was forced to climb the last pitch using aid. Our 900m route took 21 hours and led to the summit of what we have christened Geruda Peak (ca 5,640m). Difficulties were VII+ A0 50-60°.

Our two friends Michal Apollo and Marek Zoladek made an ascent of Masala Peak (ca 5,650m) via an 800m route of WI4. All our routes were climbed alpine style, without bolts.

MICHAL KROL, *Poland*

CHANDRA VALLEY

Pt. 4,600m, Stressful Rain, attempt. Gianni Cilia and I planned to visit the Miyar Valley to try the big west-facing wall of Three Peaks Mountain (the unclimbed 6,000+m peak at the head of the Dali Glacier), which I tried in 2003. However, flooding of the Miyar River damaged bridges in the valley, making it impossible to reach the normal base camp site. We changed plans and returned along the Chandra Valley, past the turn-off leading to the Rohtang Pass and on for a little way in the direction of Batal and the Kunzum La. This journey took six hours in an off-road vehicle.

On August 4, before reaching a point on the road lying due north of 6,221m Indrasan, we moved south and established a base camp. Here we located a steep rock wall leading to a tower with an altitude of ca 4,600m. On the 8th we set up an advanced base below the wall, but the

Pt. 4,600m (dubbed Ezio Bartolomei Tower) above the Chandra Valley, showing the line of Stressful Rain (1,450m of climbing, 6c, not to summit). C1 and C2 mark the camps, and B the bivouac where Roberto Iannilli spent a week entirely alone. *Roberto Iannilli*

weather turned bad and prevented climbing until the 11th, when we climbed 15 pitches (600m) up the face to a ledge and good bivouac site. On the 14th, after another spell of rain, we climbed another 11 pitches and left fixed rope before returning to the bivouac. At this point Gianni started to feel weak and unwell.

I stayed at the bivouac site alone, sitting out bad weather, until on the 22nd I was able to solo up to the ridge that would lead to the summit. However, I was eventually forced to retreat, unable to negotiate complex slabs. On the 25th I tried again, this time in a more direct line. After 1,450m of climbing from the foot of the wall, I reached the end of the major technical difficulties, where an easy rock ridge rose left for 200-300m to the summit. Typically, the weather was bad again, and as time was running out, I descended. After spending a week at the bivouac alone, I'd added another seven pitches (310m of climbing).

Although we didn't reach the summit, we have called the peak Ezio Bartolomei Tower and the unfinished route, Stressful Rain. Apart from one bolt, we used only traditional removable protection in our 33 pitches. There were two pitches of 6c and many between 5+ and 6b.

ROBERTO IANNILLI, *Italy*

GANGOTRI

Meru South, west face/northwest ridge to below summit, BASE jump of northeast face; Meru Central, second ascent, west face/southeast ridge. May 23 saw the completion of a six-year project to climb to and perform a wingsuit BASE jump from the "highest-altitude cliff in the world," by my wife Heather Swan and I.

Combining alpinism and BASE jumping (BASE climbing or Paralpinism) goes back to 1990, when Jean-Marc Boivin leaped from the Grand Capucin in the Mt. Blanc Range, having made the second winter ascent of the route O Sole Mio, on the east face. In 1992 Nic Feteris and I set an altitude record for BASE jumping when we leaped from Great Trango Tower, after climbing the northwest ridge. In the last 10 years a new generation of hard climbers, like Dean Potter, Leo Houlding, Valery Rozov, and the Blanc-Gras brothers have extended their interaction with wilderness by combining climbing and BASE jumping.

Inspired to join me and challenge my world record, Heather spent six years learning to rock climb, mountaineer, skydive, BASE jump, wingsuit skydive and wingsuit BASE jump. In 2001 her

Looking southeast from the summit of Meru Central to Meru South (6,660m). The arrow points to Glenn Singleman and Heather Swan at ca 6,600m on the northwest ridge. They are preparing for their successful wingsuit BASE jump of the wall to the left, which they completed on May 23 for a new world altitude record. *Glenn Singleman collection*

attempt to BASE climb the Great Trango Tower failed due to avalanche danger and 9/11, though she did reach the summit.

In addition to Heather and me, our 2006 expedition included James Freeman (BASE jumper), Malcolm Haskins (lead climber), Michael Hill (climber), and Tove Petterson (climbing camerawoman). Samgyal, Mingma, Norbu, and Tinless Sherpa helped us. The amount of gear required for the jump and filming necessitated a multi-camp, fixed-line approach to the climb. The top section of the northeast face of Meru South is vertical for 800m, an aesthetic line to BASE jump. Meru South (6,660m) has been climbed only once, in 1980 by a strong Japanese team led by Kenshiro Ohtaki, via the southeast ridge.

Our route ascended the west face. Due to heavy late winter snow it took 16 days to establish base camp on the upper Kirti glacier at 5,300m. The upper Kirti is an impressive box canyon, bounded by Thalay Sagar and Kirti Stambh to the west, Bhrigupanth to the northwest, and Meru to the northeast. The west face of Meru has two large rock buttresses separated by a wide snow/ice field. There are future possibilities for high-altitude, big-wall routes on granite. However, our team focussed on the alpine route in the center, though we had difficulty finding information or photos of this side of Meru.

A straightforward gully led to Camp 1 at 5,550m, atop a small spur, below and to the side of an imposing serac band. The route to Camp 2 avoided this serac band and crossed an exposed snowfield. We chopped a ledge at 5,880m, beneath a rock buttress that leads to Meru Central. Just above Camp 2 James Freeman was struck with altitude illness and had to descend rapidly. He ground-launched his canopy and traveled the 580m to base camp in four minutes, where his symptoms soon cleared.

Camp 3 was at 6,200m atop another serac band. The route above was steep, and spindrift avalanches were constant. We built two snow caves that became our home for nine days. With its narrow, fan-like shape, Meru South attracts high winds that blast and harden the upper slopes. We fixed 11 pitches above Camp 3 before topping out at the col between Meru Central and Meru South. This took six days, due to a combination of bad weather and hard, 50–70° ice. From the col we fixed a rope to the summit of Meru Central (6,310m), which became a base for camera operations. [Malcolm Haskins and Michael Hill first reached the summit on May 17. On the 23rd Haskins, Petterson, and four Sherpas reached the top to film the jump—Ed.]

To access the top of the wall on Meru South we climbed three more pitches above the col.

At an altitude of 6,604m, we dug out a 50cm-wide ledge above the vertigo-inducing northeast face. For three days our team climbed from Camp 3 to the exit point, hoping to jump. However, low cloud over the Meru Glacier obscured the landing area. Finally, on May 23, after waiting at the exit point for five hours, we had a brief opening in the clouds. Heather and I jumped at 2:15 p.m. Our wingsuits took about four and a half seconds to inflate, after which we rapidly accelerated away from the wall. We took 45 seconds to fly about one kilometer down the Meru Glacier, passing Meru Central, before opening our parachutes near the bottom of the southwest pillar of Shivling. The jump set a new world record for altitude BASE jumping and wingsuit BASE.

Although our team spent 23 days on the mountain, the route could probably be climbed in lightweight style in less than a week. We graded the route alpine 3+ (North American Alpine III WI2 5.5). For more information or a copy of the documentary film, visit www.baseclimb.com.

GLENN SINGLEMAN, *Australia*

Meru Central, northeast face, variation. Yasuhiro Hanatani, Hiroyoshi Manome, Yasushi Okada, and I planned to climb Meru Central (6,310m) by the oft-tried line of the Shark's Fin or northeast pillar. We had attempted the route in 2004 but retreated above 6,000m, when Hanatani took a fall and broke both legs.

Last year our team reached Tapovan base camp on September 1 and established an advanced base at 4,800m, from where we hoped to attempt the line in capsule style. We placed our first camp at 5,300m, close to the rock ridge that forms the left edge of the lower snowfield, but were pinned down for days by bad weather. Deciding that the Shark's Fin would be consequently out of condition, we instead opted to slant right across the lower snowfield. Starting on September 24, we took only three ropes and six ice screws, and climbed more or less in alpine style. We climbed onto the ridge taken by the original Babanov route on the face, Shangri La, via three difficult pitches of loose rock. From here we followed the Babanov line, bivouacking, without sleeping bags, at 5,800m, just under the cornice of the summit ridge at a little over 6,200m. On the morning of September 26, we pulled onto the northwest ridge and quickly reached the summit at 7:30 in a bitterly cold wind. This appears to be the third ascent of the peak, the second having been made by Australians earlier in the year. We returned to our 5,300m camp the same day, rappelling mainly from Abalakovs. We graded the route 5.10a M5 WI3 75°.

MAKOTO KURODA, *Japan*

Meru Central, northeast face, variation. On September 17 Marek Holecek and I reached base camp at Tapovan, with the intention of climbing the Shark's Fin on Meru Central (6,310m). From the 18th to the 23rd we acclimatized and bouldered. On the 24th we transported our equipment to the base of the northeast face of Meru, crossing a 5,200m col. The next day we started on a capsule style-ascent, taking one portaledge, 200m of rope for fixing, the usual climbing hardware, and a few bolts. The following day we established our first camp, on the left edge of the lower snowfield at 5,250m. On the 28th, after moving our equipment up to the top left corner of the snowfield, we made our second camp at 5,650m, at the point where the snowfield joins the rock ridge. By October 2 we'd climbed 200m up the rock ridge and made our third portaledge camp at 5,900m, more or less at the base of the Shark's Fin itself. The next

The northeast face of Meru Central (6,310m) with (1) the route climbed by the Czechs Holecek and Kreisinger for the fourth ascent of the mountain (7a M5 80°): (C) marks the site of their camps. (2) The Czech attempt on the Shark's Fin. (3) The original route, Shangri La, climbed by Babanov in 2001 (5c/6a A1/A2 M5 75°). The 2006 Japanese ascent, the third of the mountain, starts up 1 to above the first camp, where it slants right up the snowfield to reach the snow arête just left of the point marked 3. From here it continues up the Babanov route to the summit (5.10a M5 WI3 75°). *Jan Kreisinger*

day we climbed a chimney encased with snow and ice, then traversed into the corner toward the left edge of the headwall. We reached our high point on this line the next day, after having spent nine days on the face. It had been hard work, we were tired, and I was beginning to have health problems.

We returned to Camp 3 and the following day continued up a different line. With Marek in the lead, we climbed a steep rock step to reach the snowfield on the right side of the headwall and returned again to camp. On the 6th we went for the summit, making a rising traverse across the steep upper snowfield to join the last section of the Babanov route (the original route to the summit of Meru Central, climbed by the Russian Valeri Babanov, solo, in 2001.) This proved dangerous. Snow conditions were bad, with no possibility to arrange protection. Once we connected with the Babanov route, we found ourselves on good snow/ice and after seven long pitches reached the crest of the northwest ridge. From here we continued easily up the crest for 70m to the summit.

We spent that night in a bivouac sack just beneath the crest and the following morning made it back to our portaledge at Camp 3. By mid-afternoon on the 9th we were down to the base of the wall and continued to Tapovan, reaching it that evening. We spent 13 days on the wall, placing two bolts and climbing 2,000m, with difficulties up to 7a M5 and 80°.

JAN KREISINGER, *Czech Republic*

Editor's Note: The compelling line of the Shark's Fin has repulsed numerous first-rate climbers. The best attempt so far has probably been that of Nick Bullock, Jules Cartwright, and Jamie Fisher, who in 1997 climbed to ca 6,100m on the left side of the prow before retreating.

Shivling, northeast face direct, attempt. An eight-member expedition from the Corean Alpine Club made an attempt on the unclimbed direct route up the northeast face of Shivling (6,543m). The climbing proved to be steep, with avalanche danger, but more serious was the rockfall. Team members survived several injuries, before eventually deciding to abandon the attempt at 6,000m.

HARISH KAPADIA, *Honorary Editor, The Himalayan Journal,*
and PETER JENSON-CHOI, *Corean Alpine Club*

Editor's note: In 1986 an Italian trio climbed toward the left side of the face, cutting through the left edge of the steep rock headwall to reach the upper section of the east ridge. A direct line through the main headwall to the summit is perhaps the most obvious line still to be climbed on the mountain.

Thalay Sagar, north face, central couloir with new finish. In September 1998 Koreans Choi Seung-chul, Kim Hyun-jin, and Shin Sang-man, whose previous experience included a new route on the Norwegian Pillar of Great Trango and the summit of Nanga Parbat, spent just three days on a direct route up the central couloir of the north face. Having made their last bivouac at 6,700m, the three climbed through the black shale band and into the final chimneys. Watched by friends at base camp, they took six hours to climb the chimney system to the final snow slopes. Reaching the summit from this point looked short and easy, and the base camp observers expected to see the three continue swiftly to the top of the mountain. However, at that moment the top became

The north face of Thalay Sagar (6,904m) showing the line of Period For Friends (ca 1,400m, 5.8 A3 M5 WI5), a variation finish to the 1997 Australian-New Zealand route up the central couloir. *Lee Young-jun collection*

enveloped by cloud. The observers were unable to see anything of the summit area for over an hour and were perturbed, when the cloud lifted, to see no trace of the climbers. Just after sunrise on the following day one of the team spotted an object at the base of the mountain. Inspection found the bodies of the three Koreans still roped together, having fallen the length of the face. Since then, the north face of Thalay Sagar has aroused grave sentiments in the hearts and souls of the Korean climbing community.

In 2006 Kim Hyeong-seop recruited 23 Korean climbers to partake in the NEPA-sponsored Thalay Sagar North Face Expedition. Members of the Seoul Alpine Rescue team formed the majority of this group. They arrived at base camp on August 1 and began climbing immediately after a memorial service on August 5 for their lost comrades. They pitched a nine-man tent at 4,900m as an advanced base, from which both Jogin and Thalay Sagar (6,904m) are accessible via a Y-shaped couloir. To acclimatize for Thalay Sagar, the group intended to climb the normal route on Jogin I (6,465m). However, their maps were confusing, and by mistake they first summited Jogin III (6,116m).

On August 11 Camp 1 on Jogin III was established at 5,500m. On the 14th Gu Eun-su, Yu Sang-beom, and Yun Yeo-chun reached the summit. They soon realized that they had actually climbed Jogin III and not the intended easier mountain, so on the 17th Kim Hyung-su, Yeo Byeong-eun, Yeom Dong-woo, and a Korean Broadcasting Station team summited Jogin I in just 15 hours from advanced base. By the 18th other members of the expedition had established Camp 1 at 5,400m below Thalay Sagar's north face.

The following day Gu and Yu pushed the route up to Camp 2 at 5,600m. The weather remained clear for three days, during which time all members helped haul gear and provisions to Camp 2. Heavy snow fell on the 27th, but Gu and his teammates pushed on to 6,400m, despite deteriorating conditions. Continuing snowfall forced all climbers down to base camp, and on the 30th Camp 2 was completely buried. Climbers spent the next five days excavating fixed rope and tents at Camp 2 from beneath at least two meters of snow.

It was not possible to start climbing again until September 5. At 11 a.m. on the 7th, Gu and Yu fixed rope up to the start of the steep shale band—the Black Tower—and bivouacked at

Yook Geun-ho ferrying loads to Camp 2 on the north face of Thalay Sagar. The central couloir can be seen high above and to his left. *Lee Young-jun collection*

6,800m. The following morning they aided their way to a point just 30m short of the top of the Black Tower, fixing more rope as they climbed. They rappelled from this point and regained their previous bivouac site, spending a second night there. The climbing that day had involved sections of A3. Starting again at 10 a.m. on the 9th, Gu and Yu completed the final 30m of the Tower and the snow slopes above, reaching the summit at 1:15 p.m.

Gu Eun-su named the new route Period For Friends, dedicated to his three friends lost in 1998. The grade of the 1,400m route is 5.8 A3 M5 WI5.

LEE YOUNG-JUN, *Corean Alpine Club (translated by Peter Jensen-Choi)*

Yu Sang-bum aiding through the initial section of the Black Tower, north face of Thalay Sagar, during the variation finish to the central couloir. *Lee Young-jun collection*

Editor's note: The Korean expedition appears to have followed the 1997 Australian-New Zealand route up the central couloir to the start of the shale band but then moved right and climbed perhaps a more direct continuation, either through or close to the obvious depression/gully that splits that part of the face. The NEPA-sponsored team is reported to be about the 10th Korean expedition to attempt the north face; the total number of attempts by teams of all nationalities is about double that number.

GARHWAL

Arwa Spires, north face, Fior di Vite, attempt. Three Spanish climbers, Rubén de Francisco, José Miguel Herrera, and Santiago Millán, attempted to make the second ascent of Fior di Vite on the north face of the central summit of the 6,193m Arwa Spires. Fior di Vite was climbed in 2002 by Swiss guides Stephan Harvey, Bruno Hasler, and Roger Schali. It follows the central couloir on the Spires until forced to break out right and gain a large snowfield high on the adjacent rock wall. Working up to the right edge of this face, the Swiss then climbed four aid pitches and easier terrain to the summit. The grade of their 800m line was 80° VI+ and A2.

As did previous parties to this area, the Spanish team lost much time on the approach, largely due to unreliable porters. The anticipated two-day walk to base camp took nine. During this period, though, they climbed an unnamed, probably virgin 5,500m summit for acclimatization. Above base camp poor snow cover on the glacier leading to the face delayed their progress further. Eventually they made several forays onto the route and fixed 500m of rope, after some long, unprotected leads up steep mushy snow. Toward the end of May they made their final attempt, but Herrera was ill and forced to descend, leaving the other two to continue with all the gear. High temperatures, wet conditions, and unstable weather forced them down from about two-thirds height on the face, before they had come to grips with the upper rock wall.

LINDSAY GRIFFIN, *Mountain INFO, CLIMB Magazine*

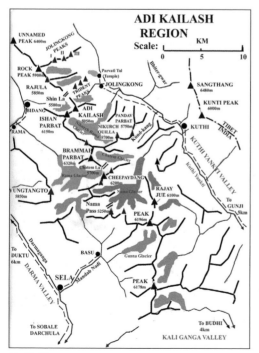

Martin Moran

KUMAUN

Eastern Kumaun, Adi Kailash Range, Ishan Parbat, first ascent. In September an Indo-British-German party visited the Adi Kailash Range, which lie between the Darma and Kuthi Yankti valleys to the east of the Panchchuli massif.

Access to foreigners was restricted, and no climbing was recorded, until 2002, when I, a British guide, led a team to attempt the sacred summit of Adi Kailash and trek through the major passes of the range: the Shin La (5,500m) and Nama Pass (5,250m). Adi Kailash (Old Kailash, seat of Lord Shiva, 5,950m) is also known as Little Kailash, as it bears a resemblance to holy Mt. Kailash, 100km north in Tibet. Our 2002 party attempted the north face but was turned back by avalanche danger 130m below the summit.

In 2004 a British party led by Andy Perkins and Martin Welch approached

Looking southeast from Ishan Parbat to the unclimbed Nikurch Rama or Brammah Parbat (6,320m), the highest peak in the Adi Kailash Range. *Martin Welsh*

Adi Kailash from the southeast and found a relatively easy way to the summit up the southwest ridge (AD), stopping 10m below the highest point in respect of the peak's sacred status. They established the summit height as ca 5,950m, lower than indicated on local maps, and discovered an unnamed, higher, parent peak to the west. In addition they photographed an impressive range of 6,000m peaks to the south.

Martin Welch and I returned in 2006 with a team of five climbers, to attempt the highest peak in the massif, known to local villagers as Brammah Parbat (a.k.a. Nikurch Rama) and surveyed at 6,321m. However, the State Government of Uttarakhand (formerly Uttaranchal) would only allow permission to attempt Adi Kailash and refused access for any approach from the northwest, which gives the best chance of success on Brammah Parbat.

We trekked into the region via the Kali Ganga Valley and established base camp at Kuthi village (3,850m) in the Kuthi Yankti Valley. From there, we made the first ascent of a snow peak 1km southwest of, and higher than, Adi Kailash. We approached from the southeast and climbed the south face

Ishan Parbat (6,100m) in the Adi Kailash Range seen from the southeast. A primarily British party made the first ascent via the south face and east ridge (right skyline) at AD. *Mike Freeman*

to the east ridge at AD (one rock pitch and snow/ice to 60°). Welch, Mike Freeman, James Gibb, Mangal Singh, Stephan Rink, John Venier, and I reached the summit on September 30. We have proposed the name Ishan Parbat (6,100m), Ishan being one of the many names of Lord Shiva, who dwelt by Jolingkong Lake below Adi Kailash, before moving to Mt. Kailash in Tibet.

We also reconnoitered the Nama Valley, which runs south from Kuthi. Here lie several beautiful virgin peaks, in particular Rajay Jue (Horse Peak, 6,100m) and Cheepaydang (Peacock Peak, 6,200m). We ascended an unnamed glacier to the 900m southeast face of Brammah Parbat, where we identified several potential TD/TD+ mixed lines. I soloed to the 5,700m col between Brammah Parbat and Cheepaydang at AD. The glacier has been named Chatem and the high pass the Chatem La.

Despite great potential for alpine routes of all levels of difficulty, exploration of the range remains difficult as long as the Uttarakhand State Government adheres to its rule of only giving permits for listed peaks. Although groups may be blocked from climbing activity, trekking groups can explore the area, if they obtain Restricted Areas Visas and Inner Line permits.

MARTIN MORAN, *Alpine Club*

SIKKIM

Kabru North, probable third ascent. It is reported that on April 27 an Indian expedition from the Himalayan Mountaineering Institute, under its acting principal K.S. Dhami climbed Kabru North (7,338m). They established base camp at Dzongri (4,500m) on April 14 and opened the mainly on skis through the Kabru Dome Glacier. The upper section proved difficult, and the team fixed ropes almost to the summit. This is the third recorded ascent, and the expedition appears to have followed the same route as the first ascensionists (1936) and second (1994), who finished on the southeast ridge above Kabru Dome. One member skied down from ca 7,000m.

LINDSAY GRIFFIN, *Mountain INFO, Climb Magazine*

Re-opening of the Nathu La to trade. During the summer China and India re-opened a historic trade route that had been closed for almost half a century. The Nathu La, at over 4,000m on the border of Sikkim and Tibet, was part of an old Silk Route. At present it is only open to traders from Sikkim and Tibet, with a special pass being issued. Two markets have been created on each side of the border, and, although goods can continue farther into both countries, the traders themselves cannot continue to Lhasa or Gangtok.

Things, however, are likely to change. There is talk of tourists being able to drive across the Nathu La to Lhasa. The Chinese are extending the Lhasa train to Xigaze, nearer to Sikkim, and that too will change things. Motorbike enthusiasts are planning to drive on this road through Indian government patronage.

The opening of the Nathu La has implications for mountaineers, as there is also talk of allowing climbing on peaks that lie on both sides of the Chumbi Valley, with permission from Bhutan in the east and India (Sikkim) in the west. Relations between China and India are improving regarding borders, and restrictions on trekking and climbing in Arunachal Pradesh are likely to ease. Only local rules and steep fees may cause problems.

HARISH KAPADIA, *Honorary Editor, The Himalayan Journal*

Sikkim, mountaineering associations, regulations, fees, and permitted peaks. The Sikkim Amateur Mountaineering Association (SAMA) was founded in 2001 and recognized by the Sikkim Home Department in 2003. It is a small but growing association that aims to promote mountaineering and provide training for local people, as well as protecting the mountain environment. It advises the Home Department on issues concerning access to the mountains and the opening of more peaks for local people and visitors. In addition, it runs training programs for the Sikkim government. We found its assistance invaluable in arranging mountaineering permits with the Home Department and for undertaking the logistics of getting us to base camp. Its members include experienced mountaineers who are competent instructors. The current president is Kunzang Gyatso Bhutia (kunzong_gtk@yahoo.com); the vice president and treasurer is Sagar Rai (southspur@yahoo.co.in). Sikkim Holiday Tours and Treks works closely with SAMA and is a reliable tour operator (www.sikkim-holidays.com; sikkim_holidays@yahoo.com).

Visitors to Sikkim are required to have an Inner Line permit. Indian missions abroad are authorized to issue a 15-day permit, which can be stamped in your passport when you obtain your visa. It is also possible to get a 15-day permit from the Sikkim Tourist Office in Delhi, Kolkata, or Siliguri. A permit will be issued on the spot if you present copies of passport and visa details, along with two passport-sized photos. Moreover, if you arrive at Rangpo, the state border, without an Inner Line permit, the Tourism Officer stationed there can issue a permit, valid for 15-days, allowing you to enter the state. In Gangtok you can extend the permit for two further 15-day periods.

Climbing in the Chaunrikiang Valley means entering the Kangchenjunga National Park. Foreigners are required to register at the park headquarters in Yuksum and pay a fee: 250R for the first six days in the park and 50R per day thereafter. Within the park are basic wooden shelters, providing floor space, at the main overnight rest spots on the trail and also tent sites. A caretaker resides at each campsite and collects the fees: 50R per person per night at the shelters or 30R per night to pitch a tent.

The Home Department of Sikkim has designated five newly opened Alpine Peaks to encourage small expeditions. They are:

West Sikkim:
Frey Peak 5,830m (Chaunrikiang Valley)
Tinchenkang 6,010m (Thansing Valley)
Jopuno 5,936m (Thansing Valley)
North Sikkim:
Lama Wangden 5,868m (Lachen)
Brumkhangse 5,635m (Yumthang)

The peak fee is relatively modest at $350 US for a team of four. The regulations for climbing these peaks can be found at http://sikkim.gov.in. Go to Government and click on Old Gazettes. Then click on 2006, and the gazettes for that year will appear in a PDF document (http://sikkim.gov.in/asp/Miscc/sikkim_govtgazettes/GAZ/GAZ2006/GAZ2006.pdf). Go to page 90 and the gazette dated March 29, 2006, which contains application forms, guidance notes, and fee schedules.

It should also be noted that under the Places of Worship (Special Provisions) Act 1991 and the State Government's Notification No.59.Home/98 dated 26.10.1998, certain peaks are classified as sacred, and the "scaling of the sacred peaks" is banned. These peaks include Kangchenjunga, main, south, and west summits; Narsing; Kabru (a.k.a Gabur Gangtsen), north and south summits and Kabru Dome (but see the report earlier about a recent ascent of Kabru North by an Indian expedition); Pandim; Simvo; Goecha Peak; Fork Peak; Paohunli; and Siniolchu.

ROGER PAYNE, *Switzerland*

ARUNACHAL PRADESH

Dibang Valley, retracing Bailey and Morshead's journey to the Yonggap La. Few trekkers and explorers have been deep into the Arunachal valleys, due to difficulties and restrictions. The Dibang Valley in eastern Arunachal Pradesh is deep and thickly wooded. Tibet lies to the north and east, while to the west is the Tsangpo Valley. In the past three years we have visited the neighboring valleys of Kameng, Subansiri, and Tsangpo. In late 2006 we traveled farther east to the Dibang.

The Yonggap La is a pass on the northern border (the McMahon Line). Both this and the adjoining Andra La lead to the Tibetan region of Chimdro. Almost due north of the Andra La stands Kundu Potrang, one of the three holiest mountains in Tibetan religion (the others being Kailash and Takpa Shiri), which the pundit Kinthup had reached on a pilgrimage during his search for the place where the Tsangpo flows into India. Now that the Chinese have restored religious freedom, many Tibetan pilgrims visit this area and perform circumambulations. Ian Baker has reached this peak from the Tibetan side (see his book *The Heart of the World*). The first forays into the Dibang were British punitive expeditions, but the first explorers to reach the passes at its head were the British army officers Bailey and Morshead. In the spring of 1913 they were unsuccessful in crossing the Andra La but did traverse the Yonggap in pouring rain. In Tibet they traveled west towards the Tsangpo Gorge and after a long journey through forbidding terrain, eventually reached Bhutan, from which they gained the Indian plains. Their survey work during the arduous journey formed a basis upon which Sir Henry McMahon drew his famous line in 1914, demarcating India and Tibet. (This border is still disputed by China, which claims the entire region of Arunachal. The dispute was one of the reasons for the 1962 Indo-China war.)

On November 10th, our team of Capt. Sandeep Dhankar, Lt. Gen. (Retired), R.K. Nanavatty, Vijay Kothari, Rajendra Wani, and I reached Anini at the head of the Dibang Valley, intent on following Bailey's route to the Yonggap La. Via the Mathun Valley and Mipi we reached Basam, where our difficulties began. The trail continued northwest above the Yonggap River through thick jungle, with steep ascents and descents, and in many places it had to be cleared through the dense bamboo forest. Camps were in small clearings. In deteriorating weather we reached the Yonggap La on the 22nd.

As we returned from the pass to our last camp, a fierce freak storm hit the area. For the next five days there was heavy snow accumulation, prohibiting any movement. As rations ran out four porters deserted the party and made a dangerous escape down-valley. We were in contact with the army via radio, and, when a break in the weather occurred on the 27th and the cloud lifted for six hours, the Indian Air Force sent two Cheetah helicopters and evacuated us to Anini. It was a stunning display of flying in difficult conditions through the narrow valley. Three days later the four porters also returned safely.

HARISH KAPADIA, *Honorary Editor, The Himalayan Journal*

Nepal

ANNAPURNA HIMAL

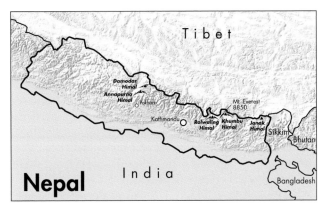

Annapurna I, east ridge, third ascent. One of the most notable accomplishments of the season was the second two-way traverse of the east ridge of Annapurna I (8,091m). When the well-known Polish climber, Piotr Pustelnik, organized his four-man team for this task, he was well aware of the difficulties they would confront on this huge ridge, which starts from Tarke Kang (a.k.a. Glacier Dome, 7,193m) in the east and runs westward over Roc Noir to the three 8,000m summits of Annapurna. However, he did not anticipate the addition of two not-so-highly skilled Tibetans on his permit and the problems one of them would present.

The first ascent of the east ridge, which resulted in an elegant traverse of Annapurna, ranks with some of the most significant events in the history of Himalayan climbing. The ridge was first attempted by Germans in 1969, and again in 1981 by a Swedish team, the latter getting as far as the East Summit of Annapurna. Both approached via the West Annapurna Glacier and the east side of the col north of Fluted Peak. In September and October 1984 a six-man expedition entirely formed of Swiss guides, established four camps from the South Annapurna Glacier, climbing to the col between Fluted Peak and Tarke Kang from the more difficult but less dangerous west side, then, in common with the Germans and Swedes, up the ridge above to Tarke Kang itself. The highest of the four camps, at 7,100m, was situated just below the summit of Tarke Kang. On October 6, Norbert Joos and Erhard Loretan constructed an igloo at 7,490m just beyond the summit of Khangsar Kang (a.k.a. Roc Noir, 7,485m), a pointed, snow-plastered rocky tower situated on the east ridge of Annapurna and first climbed in 1969 by Germans, Obster, Schubert, and Winkler, via the east ridge from the South Annapurna Glacier. The Swiss pair then descended to base camp at ca 4,200m.

Bad weather intervened but on the 22nd four of the team, Ueli Bühler, Bruno Durrer, Joos, and Loretan headed up from Camp 3 toward the igloo. Bühler and Durrer returned from Khangsar Kang, but the other two spent the night in the igloo, then on the 23rd climbed along the ridge, over the East Summit of Annapurna (8,047m) to the col between the latter and Annapurna Central (8,061m). There, at ca 8,020m, they made another igloo and spent the night inside sheltering from violent winds. On the 24th they climbed over the Central Summit to reach the Main Summit at 1:30 p.m., more or less following the crest throughout. That same day they set off for a committing on-sight descent of the north face and bivouacked at ca 6,800m. The following day they negotiated the Dutch Rib with just one ice screw and a 50m rope, and bivouacked at 5,000m. On the 26th they reached the standard base camp for the Normal Route on the north side of the mountain, where they met an expedition attempting Nilgiri. However, the other Swiss members had no news as to their whereabouts or possible success until they were all reunited on November 4 in Kathmandu.

The ridge saw its second ascent in the spring of 2002. Five climbers fixed the rock spur above the South Annapurna Glacier leading to the col between Fluted Peak and Tarke Kang. The team then established their Camp 3 at 7,100m just below the summit of Tarke Kang. From here Veikki Gustafsson, Alberto Iñurrategi, Jean Christophe Lafaille, and Ed Viesturs set off in alpine style for the summit. Gustafsson and Viesturs retreated before reaching Khangsar Kang but the other pair continued. Above 7,700m they found the ridge to be stripped bare of snow by the wind, and quite tricky. They dropped onto the north flank and traversed below the East and Central summits until they could climb up to the Main Summit via the last section of the Normal Route. However, this was only the half way point, as Iñurrategi and Lafaille had never been inspired by a descent of the dangerous north face. Instead, they reversed the route, taking a further three days to regain base camp.

Like Lafaille and Iñurrategi, Pustelnik's party had neither bottled oxygen nor Sherpa support. First they acclimatized on Cho Oyu, then on May 6 went to their base camp at 4,130m at the southern end of the Annapurna Glacier for their push to the Main Summit. After having made three more camps and two bivouacs, three members, Pustelnik, his compatriot Piotr Morawski, and Slovakian Peter Hamor, set out on May 21 from their bivouac at 7,700m for the three summits.

Tagging along with them was a Tibetan, Luo Tse, who had twelve 8,000m summits to his credit. However, all of these had been achieved with much bigger teams than his 2006 group, which comprised just two members and one Sherpa. All four crossed the East Summit of Annapurna and reached the col beyond. Onward progress looked very daunting and it took some time before the team found a practicable route down a 100m ramp on the north flank that would take them toward the Central Summit. By this time it was 4 p.m. and it was obvious that reaching the Main Summit and returning to their top bivouac would take them well into the night. At this point Pustelnik realized Luo Tse had become partly snowblind, badly dehydrated, and had no headlamp.

So Hamor went on alone, rejoined the ridge, gained the Central and Main summits and then bivouacked at 10 p.m. on his return, somewhere between these two summits. In the meantime Morawski and Pustelnik were struggling to get the Tibetan down to their last bivouac, which they eventually reached at 5 a.m. on the 22nd. The Europeans' trials were still not over: by the time they reached their last fixed camp, they had been without food for four or five days and were completely exhausted. They gave no thought to another attempt and went home.

The two Tibetans and their Sherpa stayed. They rested and then report succeeding on their second attempt in windy and cloudy weather. They reached the top on June 4 but had no visibility. However, Luo Tse is certain they reached the Main Summit because he had already seen it from the East Summit during in his first attempt with Pustelnik.

ELIZABETH HAWLEY, *AAC Honorary Member, Nepal*

Cho Oyu 2005 - blood samples at very high altitude. In the autumn of 2005, the Anglo-Irish Xtreme Everest Expedition to Cho Oyu (8,188m) undertook a number of ambitious scientific projects at high altitude. The seven-man team, which comprised Roger McMorrow (leader) with Vijay Ahuja, Nigel Hart, Mick O'Dwyer, Paul Richards, George Rodway, Piotr Szawarski and I, completed work on the effects of supplemental oxygen on well-acclimatised mountaineers during sleep, exercise, and treatment inside a portable hyperbaric chamber (a.k.a. Gamow Bag).

In addition, six members reached the summit over two consecutive days, accompanied on each occasion by Nanmygal Sherpa, who not only reached the summit twice within 24 hours but was also able to descend to Camp 1 at 6100m in just 4 hours, in order to deliver a sample of blood after the second summit bid. The sample had been obtained from inside a small, lightweight shelter erected on the summit, with Mt Everest clearly visible in the distance. This was the first attempt ever to obtain information about the concentrations of oxygen and carbon dioxide at such altitudes and provided the foundations for the Xtreme Expedition to Everest in 2007.

DR. JEREMY WINDSOR, *UK*

DAMODAR HIMAL

Pt. 6,190m and Pt. ca 5,754m, first ascents. Two members of the Kumamoto section of the Japanese Alpine Club, Koichi Kato and Makiji Kiso, made a reconnaissance of Yakawa Kang (6,482m), the peak immediately north of the Thorang La and first officially opened in 2003. The expedition lasted from October 15 through November 14, in which time they made first ascents of two nameless peaks. After descending east from the Thorang La to Manang, the team trekked to Nargaon and then north up the Labse Khola to near its head south of the Damodar Himal. Base camp was established at 4,800m at the point where the trail to the 5,595m Teri La leaves the main valley. On October 27, after having made Camp 1 at 5,400m near the head-waters of the Labse Khola, Kato with the expedition sirdar, Hari Bahadur, climbed Pt. 6,190m in the southwestern Damodar, approaching from the east. This peak may have the name of Wata.

On the 30th, again from the 4,800m base camp via a Camp 1 at 5,365m below the Teri La, Bahadur, Kato, Kiso, and a Sherpa, Rames, stood on top Pt. 5,754m (GPS measurement). This peak lies on the ridge a short distance south of the Teri La and on the northern flanks of the Putrung (a.k.a Purbung) Himal. The team turned south just before reaching the La and climbed the unnamed peak directly.

TAMOTSU NAKAMURA, *Japanese Alpine News*

Pt. 6417m correction. In *AAJ 2006*, p. 408, the dates of the first and second ascents should be September 8, 2003 and September 21, 2003 respectively and not October as stated.

PERI HIMAL

Panbari Himal, first ascent. The unclimbed Panbari Himal, a remotely situated 6,905m snow peak, was only opened to foreign expeditions in 2002. The mountain lies immediately north of the Larkya La (5,135m), a relatively spectacular pass that forms the high point on the increasingly popular Manaslu Circuit, linking the Marsyandi Khola and Buri Gandaki valleys. In the autumn, six Japanese students from five different universities arrived in Nepal to attempt the first ascent. They planned to complete the climb without any Sherpa support. In 2004, the university students' section of the Japanese Alpine Club sent a party under the leadership of Takeshi Wada to Chhiv Himal (6,650m) in the Damodar range. Five members from four differ-

Climbers at ca 6,000m moving up the Fukan Glacier toward the east face of Panbari Himal. The summit was reached via the northeast ridge (right skyline) from a col out of picture to the right. *Tamotsu Nakamura Collection*

ent universities made the first ascent of this mountain without Sherpa support (*AAJ 2005*, pp. 383-384). The Panbari Himal Expedition was the second phase of their project.

The six-member team (though one came along only as a base camp manager), under the leadership of Ms. Yoshimi Kato, approached from the west through the Marsyandi Khola and crossed the Larkya La. Descending the normal trekking route on the east side of the pass, they turned north and on September 6 established base camp at 4,865m on the right (north) side of the Fukan glacier, which rises west toward the east face of Panbari Himal. Three days later Camp 1 was placed at 5,235m.

Although the glacier looked gentle, it had complicated icefalls with unstable seracs and hidden crevasses. Camp 2 was eventually established on September 18 at 5,740m, one week behind schedule. Their final camp 3 was established on the 22nd at 6,280m below the northeast ridge, but due to whiteout conditions they had no chance to make a reconnaissance of the final ascent.

On September 27 Kato, with Gakuto Komiya, Sayaka Koyama, Kenro Nakajima, and Yousuke Urabe set off from base camp for their summit bid. These five left camp 3 at 3:30 a.m. on the 29th in fine weather and reached the start of the northeast ridge at a col between Panbari Himal and the unnamed Pt. 6,767m on the Nepal-Tibet border. A broad ridge led to the summit. It was covered with deep snow and provided a bit of a struggle but all five finally reached the summit at 9:40 a.m. Here, they were able to enjoy a fine panoramic view and were particularly impressed by the magnificent pyramid of Manaslu, the first Himalayan giant climbed by Japanese exactly 50 years ago. The team spent the next three days clearing the route of camps and fixed ropes, leaving only three snow stakes on the mountain. By October 1 they were safely back in base camp.

TSUNEMICHI IKEDA, *Japan, based on reports by* YOSHIMI KATOH *and* SAYAKA KOYAMA

MANASLU HIMAL

Manaslu, Kazakh Route. Kazakh super-high-altitude climbers, Sergei Samoilov and Denis Urubko, followed their very impressive 2005 alpine style new route on the southwest face of Broad Peak with a new route on the northeast face of 8,163m Manaslu. Together with a two-man Russian team, the pair arrived at base camp (4,700m), but were prevented from making much progress on the mountain during the first part of April due to heavy snow. They left for the Normal Route on the 20th and, climbing in alpine style, reached the summit late on the morning of the 25th.

Samoilov and Urubko initially had designs on a new route up the southwest face, but they didn't have a permit specifically for this and were concerned about the depth of new snow on the mountain. However, during their ascent they were able to study the main part of the northeast face to the left and thought it rather more windblown. The left side of this face had been climbed before in 1986, when a primarily Polish expedition led by Jerzy Kukuczka attempted the unclimbed east ridge. The Polish team spent the latter half of September and most of October of that year in bad weather and then finally gave up. On November 5, Carlos Carsolio, Artur Hajzer, and Kukuczka set off up the face immediately right of the lower ridge. Climbing in alpine style, they made four bivouacs, joined the upper section of the east ridge, made the first ascent of the East Summit (a.k.a. the East Pinnacle, 7,992m) and reached the summit plateau, where they bivouacked again at 8,000m. Next day Carsolio, who was suffering from frostbite, stayed put, leaving Hajzer and Kukuczka to force their way to the summit in extreme cold. It was the first time an 8,000m peak had been climbed in November.

Samoilov and Urubko left base camp at 2 a.m. on May 4, which later, by their own admission, was too soon after their previous ascent and did not give them quite enough rest. They left the glacier at 4,900m and started up the face a little to the right of the Polish line. Plowing through deep snow, they made their first bivouac at 5,900m and their second at 6,500m, after more deep snow and a two-hour delay finding a route through a large bergshrund. At this point they were quite close to the 1986 line.

The next day's climbing proved equally exhausting and dangerous, with the climbers setting off small avalanches as they progressed. Above their third bivouac at 7,100m, the conditions improved as they slanted right and reached the lower rocks of the Pinnacle, which they climbed (grade 5 cracks) to a bivouac at 7,450m. Now without food, on the following day they climbed up the far right flank of the East Pinnacle over difficult mixed terrain, all the time accompanied by an increasingly strong wind. Compact granite made the climbing more difficult and the crux was a rock pitch that overhung by three meters. This was thought to be 6a. That afternoon they reached the summit plateau in poor visibility and strong winds. Dumping their sacs, they climbed a 300m couloir and were on top by 6 p.m. That night they camped at 7,600m on the Normal Route and the next day, the 9th, were back at base camp, having now been on the go for the last three days without food. The "Kazakh Route" had difficulties of 70-75° ice and mixed, with 6a on rock. For this ascent the pair were awarded the newly inaugurated Piolet d'Or Asia at the ceremony taking place in Seoul later that year.

LINDSAY GRIFFIN, *Mountain INFO, CLIMB Magazine*

GANESH HIMAL

Ganesh VII, attempt and tragedy. No one knows how far four Frenchmen got on Ganesh VII (6,550m), a peak on the Tibetan border that is not on any permitted list. They had taken an inexpensive permit for the trekking peak Paldor (5,903m), but continued further up valley to climb Ganesh VII, which has no known previous attempt. When Grenoble mountaineers Stefan Cieslar, Jean-Baptiste Moreau, Raphael Perrissin, and Vincent Villedieu, failed to turn up in Kathmandu on November 5, the authorities were notified. A full rescue was organized with the help of French mountaineers, Aymeric Clouet and Christian Trommsdorff, who were in Kathmandu ready to leave for home after an unsuccessful expedition to Manaslu. In mid November the team discovered the remains of a base camp and a diary suggesting the four climbers were about to set off for an attempt on the south face to northwest ridge. Moving up the mountain, the rescuers found another tent at around 5,500m in an area covered with avalanche debris, apparently triggered by a falling serac. It appears the four French must have left their tent for a summit attempt on October 27, but conditions were far too dangerous for the rescue team to make any search for the bodies.

ELIZABETH HAWLEY, *AAC Honorary Member, Nepal*

ROWALING HIMAL

Tengkangpoche, north pillar, attempt. Paul Bride, John Furneaux, and I attempted the unclimbed north pillar of Tengkangpoche (6,487m). Base camp was at 4,350m and Paul made it as far as 5,000m, capturing an amazing series of video, digital, and film images. John and I spent 14 days on the route, climbing the hardest terrain that we have ever experienced, both physically and mentally. We started climbing on October 10 at 4,800m. Camp 1 was pitched at 5,150m after three days climbing, Camp 2 at 5,350m on day five, and Camp 3 at 5,600m on day seven. Our high point was 5,800m on day nine. On day 10 we rappelled to the base of the pillar in a seven-day storm. The route was at least ED3: we climbed pitches with difficulties up to WI6, M8, A4 and 5.11, and did not see any sign of previous passage on our chosen line. Having made it to the headwall, we only appeared to have 400m of easy splitter cracks, followed by a knife-edge ridge, to reach the summit. Records suggest we got well past

The unclimbed north pillar of Tengkangpoche, showing the line of the Furneaux-Maddaloni attempt and their camps. Their high point was 5,800m. *Matt Maddaloni*

previous high points on this pillar, and once above 5,000m the view from the wall encompassed Ama Dablam, Everest, and Makalu. I learned a lot during this trip and can't wait to return.

MATT MADDALONI, *Canada*

Kwangde Lho, north face, new route. In late autumn the French high performance team, a group of young alpinists comprising Nicolas Bernard, Laurent Bibolet, Emmanuel Chance, Nicolas Ferraud, Frédéric Gottadi, Mathieu Mauvais, Thomas Mougenot, Pierre Roy, and Sébastien Thiollier, some of them instructors or aspirant guides, plus two guides, Patrick Pessi and me, attempted several routes on the 1,200m north or Hungo face of Kwangde Lho (6,187m).

We split into three groups: Mauvais, Mougenot, and Roy would try the Breashears-Lowe Route (ED2, WI 6, 1,200m, Breashears-Lowe, December 1982); Gottadi and I would attempt a new route up a line of runnels a little further right, while the remaining members under the guidance of Pessi, would climb as two teams on a line of goulottes much further right, leading toward the summit of Kwangde Nup (6,035m).

Unfortunately, heavy spindrift proved too much for the team on the Breashears-Lowe, and Pessi's groups were no more successful. Although from afar their proposed goulottes looked feasible, in reality they comprised very thin ice over extremely compact granite.

We were more fortunate and from November 15 to 18 we managed to complete Normal Routes Have Nothing Extraordinary (ED2, WI 5+, 1,150m). The climb begins up the next main runnel right of Mandala, and after crossing through the traverse, climbs through the middle rock barrier on an ice smear right of the Breashears-Lowe crux [the upper half of this

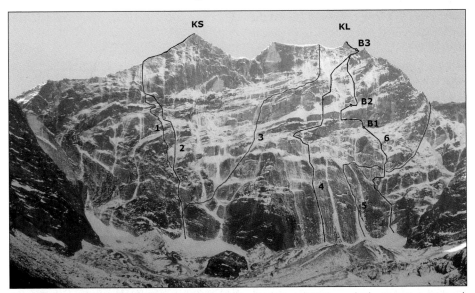

The north or Hungo face of Kwangde. (KS) Kwangde Shar (6,093m). (KL) Kwangde Lho (6,187m). (1) British variant to Extra Blue Sky (Scottish 7, Cartwright-Chinnery, 2000, not to summit). (2) Extra Blue Sky (1,200m, ED2, Beaugey-Profit-Rhem-Ruby, 1996, only Profit and Rhem to summit). (3) Japanese Route (1,200m, ED3, WI 6 M5, Ito-Nakagawa, 2002). (4) Breashears-Lowe Route (1,200m, ED2, WI 6, Breashears-Lowe, 1982). (5) Mandala (1,150m, Lorenzo-Munoz, 1985). (6) Normal Routes Have Nothing Extraordinary (1,150m, ED2, WI 5+, Benoist-Gottadi, 2006). B1, 2 and 3 mark the French bivouacs. *Stéphane Benoist*

Frédéric Gottadi on the upper section of Normal Routes Have Nothing Extraordinary (ED2, WI 5+, 1,150m) on the north face of Kwangde Lho (6,187m). The summit is directly above his head. *Stéphane Benoist*

smear had been climbed previously in 2001 by Sam Chinnery and Ali Coull as an easier variant during the second ascent of the Breashears-Lowe—Ed]. Above, we continued steeply to join the American route for its last few pitches to the summit.

The ascent was one of the most beautiful routes I have ever climbed and, overall, may be my best adventure to date. The difficulty was sustained at WI 5 and there were 12 technical pitches, the crux being WI 5+. Combating the cold proved really hard for us. There was no sun, strong winds (particularly toward the top) and temperatures down to –18°C. Three bivouacs were needed on the climb, after which we made the long descent south, down into the relatively remote Lumding Valley. After crossing a pass and making a long descent to the Dudh Kosi, we arrived in Namche Bazar three days after leaving the summit.

STÉPHANE BENOIST, *France*

Kwangde Shar, northeast ridge, alpine style winter ascent. On December 8, Corean Alpine Club Technical Committee members Yu Hak-jae and Park Seok-hee established base camp about three hours below the north face of Kwangde, with plans to make the first winter ascent of Kwangde Shar (6,093m) via the 1978 British route on the northeast ridge [the Koreans we unaware that the first ascent during the Nepalese-defined winter was made via a new route from the south on December 7, 1982, by Mick Chapman from the UK and Colin Pont from Australia. The first calendar winter ascent of the mountain, and the first winter ascent of the northeast ridge, was made on January 8, 1983, by the Japanese, Kenji Fujita, Shiniya Ikuta, Mazasru Mizukami, Yasuki Nishimoto, and Yozo Yokoyama. These five spent two weeks establishing two camps on the ridge and fixing the steeper upper section before making the final push—Ed].

Their first attempt, on December 10, was foiled by heavy snow and white-out conditions. On the 15th they set off for another attempt with the bare minimum of provisions, and after two nights on the face and three days climbing in pure alpine style, reached the summit at 11:35 a.m. on the 17th. The two men descended to the south and spent a third night at 5,140m, then on the following day crossed back over the watershed ridge and descended the north facing couloir between Kwangde Shar and Nupla, making 25 rappels and leaving only slings and pitons behind. The route was very dry and graded VI 5.9 [on the first ascent the ridge was in snowy condition and crampons were used throughout—Ed]. The following is an abbreviated account by Yu Hak-jae, beginning on the morning after the first bivouac at ca 5,300m.

Early on the 16th we melted snow from a crack in the rock, while we waited for the sun to hit us. The dirty water sufficed and we allowed the filth to sink to the bottom before trans-

The north side of the Kwangde group after heavy snowfall. On the left is Kwangde Shar (6,093m) with the 1978 northeast spur separating sunlight and shadow. This received an alpine style winter ascent last December. To the right and in shadow lies the steep Hungo Face of Kwangde Lho (6,187m), home to the recent French route. Right again and catching the morning sun is Kwangde Nup (6,035m). *The Jules Cartwright Trust*

ferring it to our three water bottles. The route seemed to become more complex the higher we climbed. By 6 p.m. we had reached 5,800m and decided to bivouac, spending three hours excavating a comfortable site for the cold night ahead, spreading the rope out in place of the mats we had decided not to bring. The wind was stronger here, and blew snow into our sleeping bags. My body was stiff, food was limited and we had only taken one gas cylinder.

Next day, each 50m pitch took more than one hour to climb and the occasional ancient fixed rope just confused my route finding. Eventually, we came to a spot on the ridge where the way ahead seemed impossible. I climbed around to the right for five meters and spotted a rusty piton five meters higher in an irregular crack. I didn't have the right gear to go up in that direction but shouted to Seok-hee to watch the tope as I crept my way up the slab. It was a bit frightening at first and I suspected that previous parties had also climbed through this section somewhat hesitantly.

Engrossed in the climbing, my stiff body began to loosen and after a thin vertical crack, I reached the narrow summit. We took a few pictures and then I wrapped a two and a half meter sling round a large rock bollard and started to rappel the south face.

YU HAK-JAE, *Corean Alpine Club (translated by Peter Jensen-Choi).*

MAHALANGUR HIMAL—KHUMBU SECTION

Palung Ri, permit confusion. A funny thing happened in connection with the first permit to be issued by the Nepalese Ministry of Tourism for Palung Ri. Two unsuspecting New Zealanders, Michael Chapman-Smith and Tim Logan, selected this mountain because they mistakenly believed it was unclimbed, and at 7,012m was just the right sort of altitude. Imagine their surprise when on the final approach to the mountain, they found a national boundary pillar and beyond it saw numerous tents comprising Cho Oyu base camp in Tibet.

Instead, they returned and climbed a 6,000er called Cho Rapsek that was definitely inside Nepal. They came back to Kathmandu to declare, as Chapman-Smith put it, that it was "morally unacceptable" for the Nepalese government to grant a permit for a mountain that wasn't theirs.

In the initial list of 103 new peaks announced by the Nepalese Government in 2002, number 49, erroneously included but subsequently never removed, was Palung Ri (7,012m), a relatively easy snow peak that lies immediately north of Cho Oyu, well into Tibet. Apparently, various people pointed out this mistake to government officials at the time, but no corrective action was ever taken. The first recorded ascent of Palung Ri took place in 1995, when the Slovenian couple, Andrej and Marija Stremfelj, reached the top via the south ridge as part of their acclimatization for an ascent of Cho Oyu. It has been climbed several times since [including autumn 2006, see the Tibet section of Climbs and Expeditions].

ELIZABETH HAWLEY, *AAC Honorary Member, Nepal*

Pasang Lhamu Chuli, south ridge attempt and tragedy. South Tyrolean mountaineers, Alois "Luis" Brugger and Hans Kammerlander returned to 7,351m Pasang Lhamu Chuli, still intent, it seems, to make the "first ascent" of this peak formerly known as Jasamba, southwest of Cho Oyu on the Nepal-Tibet frontier. Renamed in 1993 after the first Nepalese woman to climb Everest (and who died on the descent), rumors abound of the peak being climbed in the past by one or two climbers acclimatizing for fast alpine style ascents of lines on the southwest face of Cho Oyu. However the first official ascent occurred in 1986 when a Japanese expedition climbed the northwest ridge from Tibet. This ridge was gained from the Nepalese side in 1996 by both Japanese and French expeditions to make the second and third ascents. The fourth was made by Slovenians, Rok Blagus, Samo Krmelj, and Uros Samec in autumn 2004. These three climbed the southeast flank to gain the crest of the south ridge at ca 6,650m and continued to the summit (1,550m, ED, M5,): see *AAJ 2005*, pp. 391-392. Brugger, Kammerlander, and Karl Unterkircher attempted the south ridge in spring 2005. They retreated at around 6,700m (*AAJ 2006*, pp. 415-416).

In 2006 and working from a camp at 5,950m, Brugger and Kammerlander fixed ropes up the spur, as they had done before, and on May 11 pressed on up the snow fields above the steepest section to a height of just over 7,000m. Here, they decided to descend to base camp for a rest before going for the summit. Brugger went first. At 6,800m Kammerlander reached a point where he looked down and could see no sign of his partner and, impressed by the latter's apparent speed, thought he must already be well down the mountain on his way to camp. However, he then realized that the only tracks in front were coming up the mountain. Casting around, he noticed a karabiner and quick draw attached to the rope. It appears that either an equipment failure or lack of concentration on the part of Brugger had resulted in the latter became detached from the fixed rope and falling to his death. Subsequent searches, including the use of a helicopter, failed to locate the body.

Brugger (47) was a very experienced Alpine guide and snowboard instructor who climbed hard routes throughout the Dolomites and Alps in the 1980s. In 1986 he made a rapid second ascent of the West Face of Ama Dablam. On Kammerlander's return to Kathmandu, the Ministry of Tourism classified Brugger's body as abandoned rubbish on the mountain and refused to return the $2,000 environmental deposit (a similar incident took place after the death of a Czech climber on Lhotse).

LINDSAY GRIFFIN, *Mountain INFO, CLIMB Magazine* AND
ELIZABETH HAWLEY, *AAC Honorary Member, Nepal*

Nampai Gosum I, south summit. The Japan Workers Alpine Federation and the Nepal Mountaineering Association attempted to make the first ascent of Nampai Gosum. The joint expedition was organized to commemorate the 50th anniversary of the start of diplomatic relations between Japan and Nepal.

The Nampai Gosum peaks lie on a high ridge forming the Tibet-Nepal border, and confusion often surrounds their nomenclature. The most westerly peak, previously referred to as Jasamba, was renamed Pasang Lhamu Chuli (7,350m) by the Nepalese. It was first climbed in 1986 by a party from the Himalayan Association of Japan [see the previous entry in this report]. There are three other high tops that lie on the long ridge connecting Pasang Lhamu Chuli and Cho Oyu. After discussions with Ang Tsering, President of the NMA, we applied the names Nampai Gosum I, II, and III to these peaks and the Nepal Tourist Board accepted our proposal. The official Nepalese maps now show Nampai Gosum I (the most westerly of the tops and sometimes referred to as Cho Aui) as 7,321m, II as 7,296m, and III, the nearest to Cho Oyu on the latter's southwest ridge, as 7,488m. All are officially unclimbed.

Our objective was Nampai Gosum I (7,321m) and we set up base camp on October 3 at 5,250m on the Sumna Glacier. I, at 64 years of age, was overall leader, but Da Gombu Sherpa

(A) Pasang Lhamu Chuli (formerly known as Jasamba, 7,351m) with (1) the south ridge first climbed by three Slovenians in 2004. (B) Nampai Gosum I (7,321m, officially unclimbed). (D) Nampai Gosum I South (7,240m) showing (2) the line of the first ascent by a joint Nepalese-Japanese expedition. Camp 1 (5,650m), Camp 2 (6,200m), Camp 3a (6,800m) and 3b (7,050m). *Kazuyoshi Kondo*

took the role of climbing leader and his team comprised Kazuo Kozu from Japan and Sherpas, Lam Babu, Mingma Dorje, Pasang Lhamu, and Pemba Dorje. Crossing the glacier, we set up Camp 1 (5,650m) on October 6, placing it on an island of mud and rocks forming the base of the south ridge of Nampai Gosum I. From here we dropped onto the glacier, which provided a difficult route through complicated crevasse formations and unstable seracs to reach a rocky gully leading up to the lower snow crest of the south ridge.

The crest was occasionally interrupted by steeper snow steps and generally in excess of 45°. On October 14 we established Camp 2 on a flatter part of the ridge at 6,200m. Above, we climbed a huge snow face, which steepened to 60° above 6,500m. As we ran short of snow anchors the belay points used to secure our fixed rope had to be placed more than 100m apart.

We established Camp 3a at 6,800m on the 24th and one day later Camp 3b at 7,050m. Between these two the ridge became steeper and featured several rocky barriers, so we moved out left and set up camp below a 40° snow slope leading up to the south summit. To this point we fixed a total of 2,600m of rope. The following day, the 26th, all seven members progressed carefully up the final slope and reached the 7,240m South Summit. Although the main summit is less than 100m higher and, according to the map, situated only 400m distant, it looked a lot farther, so we decided to go down from this point.

KAZUYOSHI KONDO, *Japan*

The north side of the Pharilapcha group with (PE) Pharilapcha East, (PW) Pharilapcha West or Main Summit (6,017m) and (D) Dawa Peak (5,920m). (1) Bonfire of the Vanities (1,000m, M5 WI 4, Constant-Mercader, 2003). (2) Snotty's Gully (ca 1,000m of climbing, WI 5 M5+, Bracey-Bullock, 2006). (B) marks the bivouac site.
Sébastien Constant

Dawa Peak, north face, first ascent of Snotty's Gully. Jon Bracey and I landed in Lukla on October 6. Four days later we arrived at base camp, which in our case was Gokyo Resort Lodge situated at 4,800m. Day five was spent stashing gear beneath the north face of Dawa Peak (5,920m), the independent summit immediately west of Pharilapcha and named by Shuldin Sherpa (five times summiteers of Cho Oyu), the owner of the Machermo Lodge, after his daughter.

On Friday the 13th, Bracey and I bivouacked beneath a stunning gully leading directly to the pointy summit of Dawa Peak. We had spotted the line on the 10th, as we walked from Machermo village to Gokyo. It was a truly fantastic line, sporting water ice plastered to the back of a deep cleft. It promised similar climbing to the Super Couloir on the Mont Blanc du Tacul in the Mont Blanc range. The first section looked straightforward but then an imposing, overhanging rock band barred entry into the gully proper. There appeared to be a corner but as much as we tried from below, it was impossible to see into it: in fact before we started the climb we were unsure that what we hoped was a hidden, ice-filled corner, was a corner at all. The only other alternative was a direct ice-blobbed line, which looked at least WI 9 and neither of us wanted to throw ourselves at it before exploring the hidden corner option.

On the 14th we were at the base of the route by 7 a.m. An awesome chandelier led to more open ground, where we moved together for two pitches before making an 80m left to right traverse below the huge overhanging rock band. Bracey led the fifth pitch, continuing round to the corner, hoping to see hidden ice. "It should go but it looks hard," came Bracey's shout. I followed in excited anticipation: that it "should go" was good news but I wondered what the Bracey version of "hard" would entail.

The corner was vertical, mixed, and similar to the crux sections of climbs like the Beaumont on the Petites Jorasses. After 50m of M5 I constructed a belay at the top with all four of our pitons. Bracey led the next pitch at M5+, after which two more pitches of 50-60° snow and ice led to a spot where we could erect our hanging bivouac tent.

After an uncomfortable night, Bracey led pitch 10 at WI 5, running out of rope and making us move together for 10 steep meters before he could find a belay. Four more pitches, largely of unremitting, iron-hard, glass-coated ice at WI 4 and 4+, gave way to a pitch of unconsolidated snow and loose blocks leading to the ridge. The view was spectacular, the belay non-existent. Our 16th pitch led west up the ridge to a coffee-table-sized summit, which we reached at around 12:40 p.m.

The descent was four and a half hours of smooth and trouble-free rappelling, largely from Abalakovs competently constructed by Bracey, and we were back in Gokyo by 6:45 p.m. We christened our ca 1,000m route Snotty's Gully (WI 5 M5+) in memory of the late Sue Nott. Were it situated in the Alps, there would be regular queues at its base.

NICK BULLOCK, *UK*

Dawa peak, possible first ascent of west ridge; Pharilapcha, first ascent of east face via The Oracle Night. Three years after I first climbed Pharilapcha (6,017m) via a new route, Bonfire of the Vanities, on the north face (*AAJ 2004*, pp. 398-400), I was back. With Jean-Luc Bremond, Hervé Degonon, and Cécile Thomas I wanted to climb the long ridge that runs from Pharilapcha to Dawa peak (5,920m), a complete east to west traverse of the Pharilapcha group. We warmed up and acclimatized on Dawa peak, climbing the elegant west ridge. On November 10 this gave us eight pitches up snow and mixed ground to the rocky summit, which looks like a table. Although we are not sure whether this route was previously unclimbed, we named it Meditation Ridge (AD, WI 2 M2). From the top we climbed down the east ridge for 15 minutes, then at a large rock pinnacle descended a big snow gully to reach the glacier to the south (35-50°).

It's important to me that my Alpine and

The east face of Pharilapcha showing the line of the first ascent: The Oracle Night. *Sébastien Constant*

The south side of the Pharilapcha group in the Khumbu: (A) Dawa peak (5,920m), (B) Pharilapcha West (6,017m), (C) Pharilapcha East, (D) Machermo (5,766m), (E) Machermo Glacier. (1) West ridge (Meditation Ridge). (2) Descent from west ridge. (3) Original route up the northwest ridge (first official ascent by a 10-member Brazilian-Croatian-Russian-Slovenian team with Sherpa support in 2003). (4) The Bridge of Lost Desire (ca 350m, WI 3 M4, Constant-Mercader, 2003). (5) The line of descent followed by the French from the 5,650m col after their first ascent of Pharilapcha's east face. *Sébastien Constant*

Himalayan ascents are in a lightweight style with minimal equipment. Steve House has shown us new ways to be creative and I admire his thinking. In addition, a lightweight style allows you to move location, or change mountain or route, if your proposed climb is in bad shape. When we arrived in Machermo, we discovered snow conditions to be rather unstable and because our pre-trip preparations had not been the best, we decided not to attempt the long traverse as originally planned, but to go to the start and see if we could complete a route on the east face. I try not to allow ambition make me forgot that staying alive is more important than reaching the summit.

We started from Machermo on November 14 and reached the bottom of Pharilapcha's east face, which lies in a hidden cirque between the villages of Machermo and Gokyo. The following day, in an 18-hour stint from our camp below the face to the village of Machermo, we climbed The Oracle Night (750m, TD-, WI 3+ M4), a line snaking up the left side of the face to reach the 5,650m col that separates Machermo peak (5,766m) to the east from Pharilapcha to the west. This section gave climbing up to M4 with a few sections of WI 3. From the col we climbed the left side of a glacier to reach a mixed ledge at its top. We traversed this ledge right and then climbed up via amazing mixed terrain with excellent granite to the vicinity of the eastern foresummit of Pharilapcha. From here a sharp snow ridge led to the main summit, which we reached late in the afternoon. There were impressive views down the north face and incredible glowing colors on Everest and the surrounding peaks as we started our descent.

Using head torches, we down-climbed to the 5,650m col and then descended the south couloir (rock and snow to 55°), heading west at the bottom to gain the valley between Pharilapcha and Kyajo Ri at 5,200m. From there it was four hours to Machermo village, where we spent the night in a lodge, freezing despite wearing our goose down suits that we had carried with us. Two days later we collected our tents from the bottom of the east face and then spent our last two weeks exploring future possibilities.

Sébastien Constant, *France*

Tawoche, east ridge, winter ascent. For the first time in 62 years it snowed in Kathmandu. This same storm also dumped more than a meter of snow in the Khumbu, making for an interesting few days. It was February 2007 and Kristoffer Erickson, Seth Hobby, Adam Knoff, Ross Lynn, Renan Ozturk, and I were on a Mammut-sponsored winter expedition to do some new routes on 6,495m Tawoche. Prior to this we had all been part of the Khumbu Climbing School, acting as instructors for the 60 Sherpa students that signed up this year.

We set up base camp at just over 5,000m, high above the village of Pangboche. From there we had easy access to the unclimbed southwest ridge, the south ridge, and the whole east side of the mountain. After making a reconnaissance Adam, Kristoffer, Ross, and I set off for the east ridge, while Renan and Seth went for the south ridge.

The rocky east ridge snakes to the glaciated upper section of the mountain. Climbing in teams of two, we soloed, simul-climbed, and pitched the 1,000m rock ridge, which offered everything from loose scree slopes to dazzling pitches of 5.9 climbing in mountain boots.

Everest loomed above our heads the whole day, the ever-present jet steam nuking off the summit. We climbed from base camp to ca 6,000m in just 12 hours, then bivouacked in temperatures of nearly –30°C. Above the bivouac lay 500m of 70° ice and ridge climbing to the summit. The four of us topped out at 10 a.m. on February 4 in clear skies and westerly winds. We descended the same day by rappelling the southeast face between our line of ascent and the original route [possibly the so-called Japanese couloir—Ed.]. Halfway down, a snowstorm moved in and made further progress slow. Approximately eight hours after reaching the summit we arrived back at base camp from a 36-hour round trip.

During our ascent we found an empty gas canister at ca 5,500m, which had been stashed in a crack on a perfect ledge. A little above 6,000m, after the "exit pitch" that allowed us to gain the upper glacier, we discovered a large snow picket lying in the snow. This was the only evidence of gear on the ascent. We concluded the picket probably originated from a previous party descending the east

Ross Lynn working through penitents on the upper east face of Tawoche during a winter ascent. The arrow points to the camp at ca 6,000m. *Kristoffer Erickson*

The east face of Tawoche in snowy conditions showing (1) the east ridge (ca 1,300m, 5.9 AI 2, climbed in winter 2007 in dry conditions by Erickson, Knoff, Lynn, and Magro) and (2) the east-southeast face (ca 1,200m, M5 50-60°, Steck, solo, 2005). (D) is the descent used by the American quartet after their winter ascent of the east ridge. *Kristoffer Erickson*

face. It was more than likely the first piece they rapped from: it then melted out and fell down to the edge of the rocks. During the descent we found no evidence of fixed gear: most parties in the past have descended the original route on the southeast face. We graded our 1,600m route up the east ridge VI 5.9 AI 2.

[Editor's note: Although at the time of writing it cannot be confirmed, it appears that this ridge is likely the line climbed in December 1989 by the Anglo-German pair, David Etherington and Joerg Schneider. They reached the summit on the 11th, so their ascent was technically outside the calendar winter season. They made two bivouacs, at ca 5,600m and 6,140m, and on the summit day were able to make it back to the base of the mountain via a line close to the Japanese couloir. The rock ridge had previously been climbed to within 100m of the upper glacier in April 1988 by Andy Black and Mal Duff. By the time they reached their high point it had been snowing for some time. Above loomed a difficult granite wall, so they traversed left into the top section of the Japanese couloir, which Duff had climbed on a previous occasion, and descended this.]

Renan and Seth attempted the south ridge, a proud buttress of solid rock. They made it to the top of the buttress, where they bivouacked through the storm that hit us on the descent. Next morning, in unstable weather, their summit push was thwarted by a rock wall, for which they were not prepared. After a laborious descent that destroyed their ropes, they made it back to camp, where they informed us they had found a lot of fixed gear, including bolts, pins and fixed rope [this is likely the line climbed in October 1990 by Germans, who fixed ropes on the lower section, found some difficult steep rock climbing and refer to it as the southeast pillar—Ed.].

When a week of bad weather finally cleared, we had only three days left in our schedule. Adam, Kris, and I made an attempt on the southwest ridge, which had been our primary goal for this trip. We experienced mostly good rock and harder climbing than on the east ridge. At ca 5,600m we farmed out a nice bivouac ledge, with the plan being to leave sleeping gear the following morning and go lightweight for the summit. Sadly, we woke to a blizzard and were forced to rappel. This marked the end of our time and the southwest ridge will have to wait until next year. Of the 14 days we had at or above base camp only four were good weather and it's a wonder we summited at all.

After an epic descent from base camp, our journey out of the Khumbu developed into a whole new experience. It dumped over a meter of snow, burying the range. Even the locals found it a rare and beautiful sight. Once in Lukla we had to contend with a snow-covered runway, and in order to make our scheduled flight out from Kathmandu, we had to face the harsh reality of shoveling the entire runway. This was no small feat, as the runway is half a kilometer long and 30m wide. We rallied the town and spent two full days shoveling with less than adequate equipment. To our surprise, planes landed. We ended up with just three hours between our flight from the Khumbu and our flight out of Nepal: just enough time to repack, shower, and eat one final meal of dhal bhat. What a trip!

Whit Magro, *AAC*

Ama Dablam, west face. Yasuyuki Shinno and Takahiro Yoshida made a very rare ascent of the west face. It appears the pair hoped to climb a new line between the American and Smid routes but decided there was too much steep rock, so instead more or less followed the line of the American Direct (1,500m, 5.6 AI 4, Dunmire-Warner, 1990), making a small variant in the lower section. The two reached a high camp (4,600m) below the face on November 14, the same day as the avalanches [see below]. They started up the face the following day in alpine style, bivouacking at 5,950m on the 15th and 6,240m on the 16th. The next day they climbed less than 100m, bivouacking below and rather well to the left of the Dablam, before climbing to ca 6,700m on the 18th. Most of the climbing had been 50-60° but there were a couple of sections of 85°, notably reaching and bypassing the remains of the Dablam. The pair quickly reached the

The west side of Ama Dablam seen at the time of the avalanche tragedy in November. (1) Northwest ridge (2,000m, Scottish VI/7, Cartwright-Cross, 2000). (2) Japanese Route (1,400m, 5.7 55°, Ariaki-Sakashita, 1985). (3) American Direct (1,500m, 5.6 AI 4, Dunmire-Warner, 1990). (4) Smid route (1,500m, 5.6 80°, Smid, solo, 1986). (5) Yamanoi Route (1,200m, 5.7 70°, Yamanoi, solo, 1992). (6) Southwest Ridge original route (1,600m, 5.9 60°, Bishop-Gill-Romanes-Ward, 1961). (D) is the Dablam. (C3) is the site of Camp 3 on the shoulder and scene of last year's unprecedented accident. *Stephen Gandy*

6,814m summit at 9:20 a.m. on the 19th and then descended the southwest ridge all the way to Camp 1 (5,900m), which they reached at 5:40 p.m. The descent was long and tiring, with no fixed rope to follow on the ridge above Camp 3, where it had obviously been swept away by the November 14 avalanches. Yoshida had minor frostbite to the fingers.

TAMOTSU NAKAMURA, *Japanese Alpine News*

Editor's note: Glenn Dunmire and Chris Warner climbed the central rib on the west face in alpine style during December 18-21, 1990. The Japanese ascent is probably the first repeat of this route.

Ama Dablam, southwest ridge, tragedy. The southwest ridge of Ama Dablam, a beautiful peak often referred to as the Matterhorn of the Khumbu, is now one of the most popular routes in the Himalaya: commercial operators who run trips to Everest during the spring, usually reserve autumn for Ama Dablam, when there can be as many as 40 teams on the mountain. Camp 3 is situated on a shoulder, above which a steep section of ridge leads past a large serac barrier, the Dablam, which is situated out left on the west face. Camp 3 is normally considered a safe haven, but in November an unprecedented incident resulted in a fatal accident to six climbers: the British mountaineer Duncan Williams and his Sherpa Mingma Nuru, together with two Swedish climbers, Daniel Carlsson and Mikael Forsberg, plus their two Sherpas, Danuru and Tashi Dorje. Stephen Gandy, who was a member of a commercially organized expedition to the ridge, takes up the story.

On November 11 my fellow team members Duncan Williams and Mingma Nuru Sherpa left base camp for Camp 1. Clive Roberts and I had just come down from this camp after a spell of acclimatisation and needed to rest. Additionally, we had limited sleeping spaces on the mountain and it made sense to split the party, rather than carry up additional tents and stoves. Clive, Pembu Sherpa, and I set off again for Camp 1 on the following day, but later Clive descended due to difficulties with a recurring chest infection. Pembu and I continued to Camp 2 without incident.

Early on the morning of the 14th Pembu and I were woken by what sounded like an avalanche or serac fall. Approximately 15 minutes later there was a second. It seemed at the time that these came from further east and were not on Ama Dablam. Another climber at base camp put the time of the first at 4:15 a.m. A third avalanche has been reported but we didn't hear it at Camp 2.

At 7:30 a.m. we made a scheduled call to base camp and confirmed that we were ready to ascend to Camp 3. Pembu tried to raise Mingma on the radio but got no response. We assumed that either his radio batteries were dead, or that the pair were already on their way up. At 9:45 a.m. we began our ascent, with no idea that there had been any problem further up the mountain. Our radio was switched off during the ascent to conserve batteries.

At around 1:15 p.m. we were just below Camp 3, when there was another avalanche. This was not a serac fall but a snow (blocks and powder) avalanche from above the Dablam. It was directed to the right of the Dablam (looking in) and down the normal ascent route. We were sheltered by the shoulder of Camp 3. We continued and arrived at the site of the camp 10-15 minutes later. All that was left was a metal spoon to the right of the ascent route and two old ropes above some steep ground. Subsequent questioning of earlier ascensionists has shown that these were there before the avalanche.

Snow and blocks of ice weighing roughly 250-350kg covered the ca 30m by 30m area, with the 10m nearest to the Dablam heavily covered with debris and indistinguishable from the slope above: on the surface there was no evidence of Camp 3 having ever existed. We moved down the route to a safer area, where I radioed a distress message to Clive at base camp. We then descended, arriving back at Camp 2 shortly before dusk. At 4:30 p.m., a further avalanche, witnessed from base camp, again struck the site of Camp 3. Subsequent helicopter survey revealed no sign of life, though some debris was seen through binoculars, spread out ca 500m below the camp.

I believe that the initial avalanche was caused by part of the Dablam collapsing. This changed its structure, and subsequent snow avalanches from the slopes above were directed rightwards (south) onto the camp. Why the initial serac fall from the Dablam hit Camp 3 instead of following its presumably normal channel down the west face is still unclear. In initial reports several critics noted that this site has, on occasions, become too cramped, with many expeditions operating together on the mountain, forcing some teams to pitch away from the shoulder. However, I can confirm that the site was definitely not overcrowded, nor were tents situated too far to the left. In the 10 days prior to the accident there had been intermittent but certainly not heavy snowfall on the mountain, and during my ascent to Camp 3 I found the ridge to be quite firm.

I have set up a website where it is possible to make donations that will give assistance to the wives and children of the deceased Sherpas. The Himalayan Trust has agreed to act as the conduit for these funds. Please visit www.justgiving.com/amadablamwidows

STEPHEN GANDY, *UK*

Editor's note: This incident has raised the number of deaths on Ama Dablam from 11 to 17, although well over 3,000 climbers have now been on the mountain since its first ascent during the calendar winter of 1961. Before last autumn only one death had resulted from avalanche: in 1979 Ken Hyslop was killed when part of the Dablam broke while he was attempting the first ascent of the west face with fellow New Zealanders, Merv English, Geoff Gabites, and Peter Hillary. The latter was quite badly injured.

Everest. The majority of notable events on world's highest mountain took place on the Tibetan side. See that section of the *Journal* for more details.

Everest, an uncommon post-monsoon ascent and partial ski descent. Only a handful of climbers go to Everest in the autumn season because everyone knows that very few succeed in the short climbing period between the end of the monsoon rains in September and the onset of the fierce jet stream wind in October. The last ascent of Everest in the post-monsoon season was made in 2000 by a team of Slovenians led by Davo Karnicar. They needed the mountain in very snowy condition, and in early October Karnicar became the first person to descend on skis in one continuous run from the very top of Mt. Everest to base camp.

However, veteran Himalayan climber Wally Berg, owner of a business that organizes and conducts climbing expeditions, and four times Everest summiter, felt he knew how to succeed: for a seven-member team, take plenty of supplies (88 oxygen cylinders) and Sherpas (13 climbing Sherpas plus cooks and bottle-washers), go relatively early, get the camps set up, and wait for favorable weather in which to make the summit attempt. His plan worked: five members with nine Sherpas reached the summit on October 18, after having sat through continuous snowfall over several days. Three of the summiters skied major parts of their descent but broke the journey to sleep in their highest camp at the South Col. The expedition members and Sherpas consumed the contents of 84 oxygen bottles during their six-week effort, and the Sherpas fixed a total of 3,800m of rope.

ELIZABETH HAWLEY, *AAC Honorary Member, Nepal*

Lhotse south face, winter ascent (not to summit). On December 27, our six-member expedition from the Tokai Section of the Japanese Alpine Club finally climbed the south face of Lhotse (8,516m), though the successful party was not able to continue up the last section of the summit ridge due to the lateness of the hour. It was our third attempt. In 2001 we had aborted the climb at 7,600m, while it 2003 we had reached 8,250m before having to give up.

When we were defeated in 2003, I personally felt that I wouldn't be going back: for one thing, the rock fall was just too dangerous. However, in 2005 I joined a team from the Gunma Federation on Nanga Parbat and talked about Lhotse with one of the members, Noriyuki Kenmochi. He was very enthusiastic and the result was that I found myself organizing a third attempt.

On September 3, 2006, we left Japan for Xixabangma, in order to acclimatize for our Lhotse attempt. Despite heavy snow, all members reached to the main summit on October 9. After a rest in Kathmandu, we traveled to Lhotse base camp at 5,200m, where we met a Korean party led by Lee Choong-jik. They also planned to attempt a winter ascent of the south face. Fortunately, the Koreans were very friendly and good-natured, so we decided to conduct a joint operation and open the route together. In the end we would fix 5,700m of rope.

The face was in very snowy conditions but on November 18 we started climbing and on the 21st established Camp 1 at 5,900m, in exactly the same spot as 2003. Thereafter, we were harassed by strong winds: not the fierce winds you find in mid winter but still strong enough that on November 28 Atsushi Senda and Toshio Yamamoto were blown 10m across the face at an altitude of 6,800m. Fortunately, they were clipped into fixed lines. Advancing the route proved very difficult and the strong wind caused powder avalanches and rock fall, which often threatened our load-carrying Sherpas and caused several casualties.

Despite the brutal conditions, we managed to set up Camp 2 at 7,100m on December 1 and five days later establish a temporary Camp 3 at 7,300m. We'd hoped to finish the route by Christmas Day, after which, in a normal year, cold and violent gales make climbing almost impossible. However, last year the monsoon lasted longer, meaning that true winter was also late in its arrival. Even so, strong winds after December 6 prevented any climbing until the 13th.

One of the reasons for the 2003 failure was the site of Camp 3, which that year was placed 150m lower than planned. Takahiro Yamaguchi, Ngawang Tenzi Sherpa, and I took charge of pushing the route out to 8,000m, where we eventually established the 2006 Camp 3. On the 21st Noriyuki Kenmochi, Atsushi Senda, and Pema Tsering Sherpa took over and began the final push for the summit. They were joined by Ahn Chi-young of the Korean expedition. As in 2003, the final prow was avoided by the couloir on the right. In three days Senda's party reached 8,200m, then Yamaguchi, Pemba Choti Sherpa, and I took over.

On December 26 we found an old fixed rope high in the couloir. This was a major surprise, as I hadn't realized anyone had climbed in this couloir before [these originated from Polish expeditions in the 1980s—Ed.]. The last part was a vertical rock wall of 20m with no cracks. It was impossible to climb. I'd imagined that the couloir would give a direct route to the shoulder left of the main summit but actually it was a dead end. The only possible escape looked to be up the fragile rock wall on the left side of the couloir. This wall led to the summit ridge, but reaching the main summit would involve a descent and subsequent re-ascent along the crest: exhausting work at that height. That day we climbed 50m of the route up the left wall and then returned to camp.

On the 27th Yamaguchi made a bold lead up the rotten rock wall. We finished up an extremely difficult, quasi-vertical snow face and arrived on the summit ridge at 8,475m. Everest, complete with snow streams, was clearly visible ahead. The time was 3:35 p.m. I was deeply touched: my dream of climbing the south face had come true. There still remained a horizontal distance of ca 200m and a vertical gain of 41m to the summit but we had no energy left to make the necessary descent and re-ascent. At 4:17 p.m. we turned back without hesitation, finally reaching Camp 3 at 9:15 p.m. after 15 hours of demanding climbing.

Osamu Tanabe, *adapted from a translation by* Tamotsu Nakamura, *Japanese Alpine News*

Editor's note: up to Camp 3 the Japanese followed the Slovenian line of 1981, when Pavel Podogornik, Andrej Stremfelj, and Nejc Zaplotnik, in a very spirited effort and after one previous attempt, reached a height of ca 8,250m (just above the last rock step and onto the final snow arête) on the final prow. There, they were forced down by very high winds and drifting snow. In 2003 Tanabe found the start of the final ridge highly problematical and instead opted to descend 200m to the right in order to gain a prominent couloir, which leads to the summit ridge east of the highest point. This couloir did not prove easy and it took the climbers five days to fix rope from their high camp to a point 250m from the top, where they retreated. To date, the only line generally recognized to have been completed (to the summit) on Lhotse's south face is the 1990 Soviet Direttissima up the long rock rib to the right of the Japanese attempt. The main summit has only been reached by one man during the calendar winter season: a magnificent solo effort by Polish winter specialist Krzysztof Wielicki on December 31, 1988 via the Normal Route on the west face.

Lhotse south face, winter attempt. The 2006 Korean Lhotse South Face team, comprising Lee Choong-jik (leader), Kim Hyung-il, Choi Jun-yeol, Seong Nak-jong, Kang Ki-seok, and I arrived at base camp on November 14. We joined forces with the Japanese Alpine Club expedition, alternating leads and fixing rope as we opened the route. The Korean contingent was eventually forced to retreat ca 300m shy of the summit due to injuries, weather, and lack of provisions. I reached the Korean highpoint of 8,200m on Christmas Eve and the following is the story of my summit push.

Early in the morning of December 21, a group of Japanese Sherpas reached Pasang Poti, Kang Ki-seok, and me at Camp 2 (7,100m). They had to carry

Camp 2 dug precariously into the south face of Lhotse at 7,100m. One more camp was established at 8,000m before Japanese climbers made the first winter ascent to the top of the face. Unfortunately, they were unable to continue up the final ridge to the summit. *Lee Young-jun Collection*

The south face of Lhotse at the time of the Japanese-Korean winter attempt. (A) Pt. 8,426m. (B) Lhotse Main (8,516m). (C) Lhotse Middle (8,414m). (D) Lhotse Shar (8,400m). (1) The line attempted by many expeditions, leading to Pt 8,426m. In 1981 Slovenians were beaten back from a height of ca 8,250m, just short of the end of the technical difficulties. This was the line used by the Japanese-Korean winter expedition, though the final traverse and couloir are invisible. (2) Slovenians Knez and Matijevec made a last ditch attempt on the summit via this line in 1981. They reached the west ridge at 8,100m. (3) Soviet Direttissima (summit reached by Bershov and Karatayev after the pair had spent six days above 8,000m). (4) French attempt in alpine style to 7,600m (Beghin-Profit, 1989). (5) South face of Lhotse Shar Czechoslovak Route (summit first reached by Demjan, 1984). *Ahn Chi-young/Lee Young-jun Collection*

Lhotse south face in winter. A Japanese climber on the delicate traverse from Camp 3 at 8,000m toward the final couloir. *Ahn Chi-young/Lee Young-jun Collection*

gear to Camp 3 (8,000m) and get down the mountain, so we let them go ahead. The headwall above Camp 2 was particularly hard and I remembered how difficult it had been a few days earlier to hammer pitons solidly while leading through this section of continually steep mixed climbing and hard ice. To add to the difficulties, temperatures in the morning hours, when the face was in shade, would be extremely low, while afternoon sunshine would warm the face and cause showers of rock fall and spindrift. In fact, constant rock fall made this section something of a climbing hell.

At several points on this section

we jugged past Slovenian wire ladders. There were three sets of these between 7,300m and 7,500m, where the ground was very steep. Despite many areas of damage, we'd opted to use them while opening the route.

By 3 p.m. Pasang Poti and I had arrived at Camp 3 (8,000m) near the top of a steep snow face. Ki-seok's oxygen had become depleted at ca 7,860m and an hour after our arrival at camp, Pasang rappelled to help him. The Japanese found a good spot for their camp and cut a slot out of the ridge for a four-man tent. A large, mushroom-shaped lump of snow was frozen to the vertical wall and Pasang and I realized that by chopping away at it we could make enough space for a two-man tent. Unfortunately, our tent was three-man, but the ledge would have to do. That night was the first we spent tied into our harnesses.

The following morning, December 22, there was a fierce wind. Ki-seok, suffering badly from altitude, retreated to advanced base, while Noriyuki Kenmochi, Atsushi Senda, Pema Tsering Sherpa, Pasang, and I began on the route above. Unfortunately, the altitude now began to take its toll on Pasang and at 1:10 p.m. he decided to return to base camp. This left only myself from the Korean team. I'd worked very hard to get as far as this and it was great to be able to continue upward in the good company of the Japanese.

Our total for that day was five pitches. Tanabe's team had previously traversed right for 200m, fixing rope to a point where we could rappel into a couloir. From here, we alternated leads on a second traverse further to the right, which led in 300m to a second, narrower couloir rising toward the summit. The final traverse pitches were a terrifying business. On lead, the obstruction caused by my oxygen mask and thick gloves made it really difficult to maintain critical balance whilst grabbing gear off my rack and hammering pitons. At 3 p.m., Pema Tsering began having difficulty with the altitude and retreated to Camp 3. Senda and I fixed the lead rope and also started our return to camp. Next day I rested for what I hoped would be our summit bid on the 24th, while in the meantime the Japanese continued to push out the route.

The 24th proved to be the only Korean summit attempt. The weather was perfect except for the continually harsh wind, something with which we were never able to come to terms. Kenmochi, Senda, and I made up the summit team, with Senda and me setting off at 8 a.m. Kenmochi was not feeling so good and followed a little later. I deposited a bottle of oxygen between the first and second couloirs, then continued to our previous day's high point: from here, protection would primarily rely on pitons. Our line lay up the couloir between two ridges, the one on the left marking the line of the Slovenian attempt and that on the right, the Russian route. Surrounded by massive walls on both sides, we were extremely exposed to rock fall and a huge gust of wind could release loose rock at any time. We had to move quickly.

Halfway up we were hit by a small shower of rocks. Senda's goggles were shattered, Kenmochi's face was grazed and bloody, whereas I took one on the left hand. We paused and stared at each other, but knew we would have to go on. Senda led through a second ice section and gave me the signal to climb. A few meters up, a huge rock smashed into my left forearm. I screamed out in pain. Senda lowered me. I couldn't move my fingers, and when I peaked under my sleeve, I could see a huge mess of blood. Ten minutes later I was able to move my fingers again: luckily I hadn't broken any bones and felt good enough to continue.

I led the next 50m pitch and Senda led through for a second rope length. However, at 8,200m the pain in my forearm became too much to bear. I radioed base camp and told them there was nothing more I could do. The two Japanese and I agreed to rappel to Camp 3 together. That would be all for our team.

So that's the way it happened. Lhotse did not grant our wish of completing the south face to the summit in winter. I was hit and still have the scar, but am grateful to have returned alive and equally grateful to all those who helped make our efforts possible.

AHN CHI-YOUNG, *Korea (translated by Peter Jensen-choi)*

KUMBHAKARNA HIMAL

Merra, first known ascent. The name Anidesh Himal refers to the mountain range separating the Ramtang Glacier to the north and the Kumbhakarna (Jannu) Glacier to the south. The ca 10km-long massif is characterized by a striking, narrow ridge running east-west and dominated by the unclimbed mountains of Anidesh Chuli (a.k.a 6,808m) and Merra (6,334m). The Anidesh Himal is rarely visited, and the attention of most trekkers in this region is captured by the stunning north face of Jannu (7,711m), which rises above the south side of the Kumbhakarna Glacier.

In October, Thejs Ortmann and I from Denmark ventured into the remote eastern sector of the Kumbhakarna Glacier, in order to attempt Merra from the south. The mountain, which was first added to the permitted list in 2002, is a complex, four-summited peak that lies between two side glaciers: Merra southeast and Merra southwest. The limited number of groups that had attempted the peak before us had all approached from the Kumbhakarna

Camp 1 at 5,450m below Merra Peak in the Kumbhakarna Himal. The view is looking south over the Kumbhakarna Glacier directly toward the true north face of Jannu (7,711m), climbed by the Russians in 2004. To the left the northwest face catches the sun. The rounded top on the ridge left of Jannu, before it drops steeply to a col, is the unclimbed Jannu East (7,468m). *Claus Ostergaard*

The Merra massif from the northwest. The left peak is the main summit (6,334m) and received its first known ascent in 2006. The mountain has most likely not had a serious attempt from this side. *Lindsay Griffin*

Glacier, as this way is the easiest and most interesting.

Prior to the expedition, I spent a lot of time investigating whether any parties had climbed Merra at an earlier stage. To my knowledge the only groups to have made attempts from the south are: a small Japanese party, which in 1963 tried to reach the southwest summit from the Kumbhakarna glacier but turned back before the summit ridge; the French, Bouvier, Magnone, and Leroux, who in 1957 attempted the same route that I eventually climbed, but I have no idea how far they got; an unknown group of three climbers, who in 2003 took the same approach as the French and reached a subsidiary summit somewhere on the eastern flank of the mountain; one of the Russian groups that failed on the north face of Jannu and were subsequently turned back on Merra due to rotten snow on the east-northeast ridge. Information on these climbs is sparse and I've had to interpret their routes based on a few photos or fragmented notes from expedition diaries. It is likely that other teams have attempted the peak but many maps wrongly place Merra too far east (at Pt. 6,100m, a small summit). An unprepared party without the new Finnish maps would likely pick the wrong mountain, as Merra is actually a long way back from the Kumbhakarna glacier.

Our expedition attempted a route up the southeast glacier, which terminates in front of the northeast summit. Trekking from the airstrip at Taplejung, we reached base camp at Khambachen (4,040m) on October 14. Next day a small advanced base was established at 4,700m on the north side of the Kumbhakarna Glacier. Here, the glacier forms an impressive closed valley surrounded by Jannu, Yalung, and Anidesh Chuli.

Above advanced base a prominent, moraine-covered, glacial gully rises steeply to the northwest, making a wide left turn before reaching a large plateau at 5,200m. Camp 1 was established on the 16th at 5,450m on the upper plateau, in front of a rock arête splitting the southeast glacier into two distinct parts. The weather had been magnificent all week, and two nights later proved equally perfect, with no wind, moderate temperatures, and a clear star-strewn sky. We left camp at 5 a.m., and after a few hundred meters on snow-covered moraine, followed a moderate scree cone leading to an open couloir immediately east of the rock arête. Once across the heavily crevassed glacier, several short gullies led us up to the bottom of the southeast face of Merra at 5,800m. Over the last few days Ortmann had struggled with the altitude and decided to wait at this point while I continued solo. The southeast face gradually steepened to a broad 45-50° couloir at 6,000m. Here I was treated to spectacular views of Jannu, Kanchenjunga, Kangbachen and Chang Himal (Wedge Peak), as well as other fine peaks. At the top of the couloir some rock slabs, which gave slightly delicate climbing, led to the east-northeast ridge at 6,200m. The crest was narrow and exposed, and I reached the summit at 10 a.m. on the 18th, after a total of five hours from camp.

CLAUS OSTERGAARD, *Denmark*

JANAK HIMAL

Janak, first ascent. After their ascent of the 7,090m northeast summit of Pyramid Peak, north of Kangchenjunga, Slovenians Andrej Stremfelj and Rok Zalokar made the coveted first ascent of Janak (7,041m) via the southwest pillar. The 1,150m route, climbed alpine style and almost as a single push, was mostly on hard glassy ice of poor quality (often quite brittle and covered by powder), with only six pitches over mixed terrain or pure rock. Apart from these six pitches, plus a committing two-pitch traverse beneath the headwall (sustained 70° ice), the pair moved together with two or three ice screws as running belays. They were surprised by the sustained nature of the route and by the difficulties on the top part of the wall. They made one bivouac at 6,800m, using a small tent but no sleeping bags or mats. Apart from having to climb back across the traverse, descent was made via 19 rappels, mostly from Abalakov anchors. Stremfelj felt the climb was more difficult than his first ascents on Menlungtse and Gyachung Kang, and only very slightly easier than a winter ascent of the Croz Spur. A full account of this expedition appears earlier in this *Journal.*

Dome Kang, east-southeast ridge, attempt. From September 7 to October 14 a six-member Spanish expedition (Elena Goded, Emilio Lagunilla, Guillermo Mañana, Daniel Salas, Carlos Soria, and I) attempted the unclimbed Dome Kang (7,264m) in the northeast corner of Nepal. The approach to the mountain was done in classic style: three days by bus from Kathmandu to Taplejung, and then a seven-day trek from Taplejung via Ghunsa to base camp. We sited our base camp (5,330m) above Pangpema at Dyhrenfurth's 1930 Corner Camp, one of the most impressive locations in the Himalaya (a trek to Corner Camp is highly recommended). We had nine days of very poor weather to start.

Camp 1 (5,950m) to Camp II (6,100m) is a nice three-hour walk on snow. We first went to the Jongsang La (6,145m) at the base of Dome Kang's east-southeast ridge but found the initial part of the ridge, and the slopes on the Sikkim side, to be impossible. Instead, from Camp

Looking south-southeast from Camp 2 (6,100m) below the east-southeast ridge of Dome Kang toward Pathibhara Chuli (a.k.a. Pyramid Peak, 7,140m). *Salvador García-Atance*

II we climbed a 400m gully up the south flank of the ridge to the crest (mixed terrain with UIAA IV+ rock and AI 4), fixing ca 500m of rope. Snow and ice conditions were treacherous, and the level of risk was high.

Once on the crest, conditions seemed dangerous, so we used the Sikkim side of the mountain to gain as much height as possible. We reached 6,700m, where even though we had enough strength, relatively good weather and four climbing Sherpas in good shape, we decided to abandon the attempt due to avalanche danger.

As a consolation prize we were able to climb a beautiful 6,500m summit, which rises from the Jongsang glacier northeast of Camp 1 (and northwest of Pyramid Peak).

It's our intention to return in Spring 2008 to finish the project. We have the advantage of knowing how to manage the logistics and we hope that the pre-monsoon season might provide better snow and ice conditions.

SALVADOR GARCÍA-ATANCE, *Spain*

Editor's note: In 1930 six climbers from Gunter Dyrenfurth's international expedition, including the leader, climbed Jongsang (7,462m) via the northwest ridge and north face. From the summit Dyrenfurth persuaded Lewa to walk with him across the plateau to the 7,442m south summit, named Dome Kang, for its first and only ascent. However, recent maps have assigned the name Dome Kang to the lower snow dome (7,264m) east of Pt. 7,442m. This remains unclimbed and was only brought onto the permitted list in 2002. Most of the members of the Spanish expedition had already made an attempt on the east-southeast ridge in the Spring of 2004, at that occasion climbing from the Jongsang La and reaching a height of 6,650m. Prior to that the east-southeast ridge had been inspected by Slovenians in 1983 and Irish in 1998, both teams noting it would not be straightforward.

Carlos Soria between base camp and Camp 1 with the Jongsang massif in the background. The two high points in the centre are South Peak II (left) and South Peak I (7,350m). South Peak I was first climbed in 2000 by a young Slovenian pair via the central couloir on the 1,200m mixed wall facing the camera. Dome Kang (7,264m) appears in this picture as the small rounded snow dome down the ridge to the right. *Salvador García-Atance*

China

TIEN SHAN

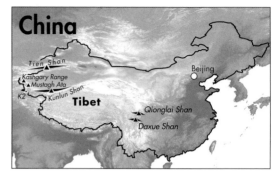

On August 20 Nikolay Dobrjaev, Anatoliy Djuliy, Aleksey Kirienko, and Vladimir Leonenko made the first ascent of the nearly 2,500m-high south ridge of Peak Voennih Topografov (Army Topographers, 6,873m) east of Pobeda. They also made the first traverse of the various Vizbora summits (5,853m-5,960m) on the south ridge of Pobeda East. A full account of these climbs and an overview of this area's potential appears earlier in the *Journal*.

KUN LUN

The route and camps on the south spur of Kokodag in the Kongur group. The main summit is 7,210m on Chinese maps, the northwest summit, the rounded snow dome to the left, is 100m lower. *Lev Ioffe*

Western Kun Lun, Kokodag, first ascent. Kokodag is the summit on the ridge extending west from Kongur and is located between Kongur Tube (7,530m on Chinese maps, 7,546m on Russian) and Aklangam (6,978m on Chinese maps, 7,004m on Russian). Chinese maps show its altitude as 7,210m; our measurements gave 50-60m less. The reason for the name is unclear, and when asked which mountain is Kokodag, locals point in different directions. The main summit is a narrow rocky crest, while the northwest summit (7,129m on Chinese maps) is a broad snow dome, 2km distant and 100m lower. The obvious line of ascent follows a rounded, south-facing, snow ridge (45-50° maximum) toward the snow dome, then traverses right on the upper snow fields to the foot of the final rock ridge. The part of the route between 5,700m and 6,200m is heavily crevassed, and there is avalanche danger on the upper traverse, especially after snowfall.

Our group of Ivan Dusharin, Lena Lebedeva, Sasha Novik, and I gathered in Kashgar on July 19. We set up base camp on July 22, after a day's trek from the Karakoram Highway. We established Camp I (5,400m) at the top of a scree slope on the 25th and Camp II (6,000m) on the 30th in a large, snow-filled crevasse, which offered good protection against wind and avalanches. We made our first summit bid on August 3 but had to turn back when a southwesterly wind decreased visibility to 10m. A period of bad weather ensued, with the wind bringing humidity and dust from the Arabian Peninsula. For our next attempt, which took place on the 9th, we moved the top camp to 6,500m but still had to turn back from the upper slopes of the dome at ca 7,000m, when visibility dropped to zero. The next day, we were able to reach the foot of the rock ridge before the weather deteriorated and then proceed to the top, disregarding the poor visibility. The last 200m involved

Climbing above a dust storm on the first ascent of Kokodag. *Lev Ioffe*

unstable rock with unreliable protection. We reached the summit late in the afternoon of the 10th. Descent was quick: by August 13 we were back in Kashgar.

LEV IOFFE, *USA*

Aksai Chin, north summit, second ascent, southeast route. As reported in *AAJ 2006*, p. 439, Aksai Chin (7,167m: sometimes referred to as Kun Lun, as it is the highest peak in this part of Kun Lun Range) was climbed in 1986 and 1997 by Japanese expeditions. On the 1986 ascent the party also traversed the summit ridge to the north summit. This lower summit, named Doufeng (6,957m), was climbed again in April-May by my client Bruno Paulet and me (guiding). We climbed a new route from the southeast directly to the top (900m, AD), taking two days for the glacier approach from base camp and reaching the summit on the third. However, we felt the easiest route to either summit was from the northwest, a flank that might provide a nice ski ascent.

CHRISTIAN TROMMSDORFF, *France*

Qong Mustagh massif, circumnavigation, reconnaissance. Our five-man team of Vasilyi Ivanov, Edmundas Jonikas, Alexander Moiseev, Tadeush Schepanyuk, and I arrived in the village of Polu on September 9. Polu is situated on the Kourab-darja River, a tributary of the Kerija on the northern slopes of the Kun Lun. With a team of donkeys and two local guides, we moved south through the Kourab Gorge, after which we crossed two high passes to the east, the Is-dawan (5,140m) and Tourpa-

The unclimbed and unnamed Pt. 6,470m, in the southwestern Qong Muztagh, as seen from the south. *Otto Chkhetiani*

Crossing the lower section of a glacier at ca 5,600m during a clockwise circumnavigation of the Qong Mustagh massif. Behind is the unclimbed and unnamed Pt. 6,710m. *Otto Chkhetiani*

The unclimbed Pt. 6,790m in the Qong Mustagh, seen from the northwest during the initial stages of a circumnavigation of the massif. This peak lies southwest of the highest mountain in the range, Qong Mustagh (6,950m). *Otto Chkhetiani*

The double-summited Qong Mustagh (East, 6,950m; West, 6,920m). The west summit was reached by Japanese in 2000 but the east remains unclimbed. *Otto Chkhetiani*

ata-dawan. We then traversed the large dry plateau of Goubaylkk, and, after six days and 100km, made a camp next to the clear waters of the Aksu, a major tributary of the Kerija. The passage through the gorge was well-described by Mark Newcomb in *AAJ 1997*, p. 129. I had also traveled through it on my 2003 and 2005 expeditions (*AAJ 2006*, pp. 438-440). Our feelings about overcoming this obstacle were no different from those of the old explorers who had passed this way: Grabzhevskyi, Przhevalskyi, and Stein.

The two guides said goodbye and left for Polu with the donkeys. Our plan was first to acclimatize in the ice-capped rocky massif to the north (5,964m or 6,198m on Shuttle Radar Topographic Mission data), then move northeast to the northern slopes of the Qong Mustagh (a.k.a. Muztag) massif. However, Moiseev suddenly developed characteristic signs of altitude sickness, and it was imperative that he descend. Moiseev's illness came as a surprise, considering his considerable high altitude experience. Jonikas accompanied him back to Polu, leaving only Ivanov, Schepanyuk, and me to continue. We had to split the essential equipment and food between the three of us, resulting in the initial weight of our rucksacks being around 55kg (28-30kg at the end of the trip). We abandoned the idea of inspecting the territory to the north and proceeded directly to Qong Mustagh.

The Kun Lun Range to the west of Qong Mustagh takes the

form of a huge arc. Maps and space shuttle images depict large glaciers. This remote range has rarely been visited, but in 2000 a Japanese expedition climbed the west (6,920m) and lower top of Qong Mustagh, a double-summited peak situated northwest of the main crest (*AAJ 2001*, pp. 406-407). According to SRTM, the east summit is 6,950m. The Japanese approached from the north and the village of Kyantokai, following the footsteps of Captain Deasy, who came this way in 1898.

A short but chilly river crossing on the southern fringes of the Qong Mustagh massif. The main peak in the background is Pt. 6,342m at the southwestern end of the massif, and the photograph was taken toward the end of a largely unsupported circumnavigation of this remote range. *Otto Chkhetiani*

Hidden farther to the east lies the unclimbed Pk. 6,946m. The map shows a valley leading southeast into the heart of the range toward 6,946m, and we decided to investigate. However, the river led to a narrow gorge, which we penetrated as far as 5,000m before being stopped. We retreated and moved around the northern and then eastern side of the range, crossing a pass of 5,800m, which we named after the Russian Geographical Society and which gave splendid views north to the 6,743m Lushtagh Ridge. We then turned south. The going was quite straightforward, but there were constant dust storms and nighttime temperatures of –22°C.

We then worked our way west around the southern slopes of the range, seeing at close quarters peaks of 6,300m-6,600m, which appeared straightforward climbing objectives, though we had no time to make any attempts. We crossed our highest pass, 5,890m, just south of the westernmost extremity of the range, and headed north, crossing a snow-covered glacier and more passes, before reaching Aksu and the Kerija River. Here we joined our outward route, which we retraced to Polu, meeting local people only when we were 5km from the finish. The three of us had spent 35 days making a clockwise circumnavigation of the Qong Mustagh massif, a roundtrip from Polu of 550km. We had only caught glimpses of the hidden 6,946m, but I plan to return in the autumn of 2007, as I now know the way to reach it.

OTTO CHKHETIANI, *Russia*

KARAKORAM

Gasherbrum II East, first ascent from China. On June 12, after two days by jeep from Kashgar to Mazar, we started our approach to base camp with 40 camels. On some of the river crossings during our trek to the Gasherbrum Glacier, the water reached the bellies of the animals, and we became anxious about our return in July, when the rivers would probably be higher and more rapid.

After five days we reached a gorgeous place for base camp at 4,300m. We then continued for a further 18 tedious kilometers across glacier and moraine, to establish advanced base at 4,800m on the East Nakpo Glacier, a safe distance from the north face of Gasherbrum II

Hard trail breaking during the first ascent of the ca 3,000m Chinese face of Gasherbrum II East (7,772m). The summit is directly above the climber's rucksack, while Gasherbrum II (8,035m) is the obvious pyramid to the right. *Hans Mitterer collection*

The summit of Gasherbrum II (8,035m) from Gasherbrum II East (7,772m). The connecting ridge has been traversed only once; in 1983 by legendary Poles, Jerzy Kukuczka and Voytek Kurtyka, who climbed the complete east ridge of Gasherbrum II over the summit of Gasherbrum II East. The normal route up Gasherbrum II slants below the rock walls from the left, to finish up the final section of the ridge. To the left and in the far distance is the Baltoro Glacier, with the Paiju and Trango groups. *Ueli Steck*

(8,035m). Our aim was the "Magic Line," the northeast pillar leading directly to the summit. However, after watching gigantic ice avalanches, emanating from large serac barriers on the right and left flanks of the pillar and sweeping the approach regularly, we looked elsewhere. We opted for an objectively safer spur on the left side of the face, leading to the crest of the east-southeast ridge. An unknown route of such length seemed hard to achieve alpine-style under prevailing conditions, so we established a second camp and fixed difficult passages.

The first section included a difficult snow mushroom that we had to bypass by rappel and a tricky traverse. Then came a huge bergschrund, crossed on partially frozen snow, and an extremely loose rock barrier: delicate mixed climbing on "vertical" scree for 65m. Above, the route to Camp 2 at 6,800m was largely an exhausting trudge up poor snow. After nine days of nonstop work in great weather, we had the camp well established, and Cedric Hählen and I, now sufficiently acclimatized, descended to base camp to prepare for a summit push. Stefan Siegrist and Ueli Steck wanted to capitalize on the good conditions and begin immediately, but they had to give up due to bad headaches.

Unsettled weather, more snowfall, one aborted attempt, and days of endless waiting chewed on our nerves. Six members decided against a further attempt, so there were only three of us: Ueli, Cedric, and I.

On July 8 we were again in Camp 1 and the following morning at 9:30 a.m. settled down for an obligatory coffee break at Camp 2. A little later all three of us broke trail to 7,100m and returned to camp. We slept from 5 p.m. to 10 p.m., thanks to a shared Dormicum pill. Half an hour later we were panting behind Cedric, as he led up our previous tracks. The pockets of our down suits were filled with everything we needed; our packs stayed behind at camp. After

Rising almost 3,000m above the Upper Nakpo Glacier is the Chinese face of the Gasherbrums. (A) Gasherbrum I (8,068m), (B) Gasherbrum II East (7,772m) and (C) Gasherbrum II (8,035m). Marked is the line climbed by Hählen, Mitterer and Steck on the left side of the northeast face of Gasherbrum II East. *Ueli Steck*

one hour the tracks ended, and the hard work began. Cedric was ill and fell behind, so Ueli and I took turns pushing through snow up to our waists. Some of the 50° passages required huge motivation.

On reaching the main ridge we found perfect snow conditions—for powder skiing. We trudged slowly along the summit ridge toward the east top of Gasherbrum II, observing far-away lights in Pakistan. At sunrise we reached the last couloir. A second ice axe would have helped to calm our nerves on the 60° ice and névé, and the ski poles we carried were just in the way. At the top of the couloir Ueli and I had to wait almost an hour for Cedric. Despite illness, he had conserved his strength and followed us, and at 7 a.m. on July 10 take the last steps with us to the 7,772m summit. As the sun's rays were already striking the avalanche-prone slopes ahead, we forewent the 300m descent and 500m ascent to Gasherbrum II. Two days later, after dismantling camps and fixed ropes, we were back at base camp, celebrating with Chinese beer our first ascent of this remote mountain face. Without support from the whole team, our ascent would not have been possible.

HANS MITTERER, *Germany*

Editor's note: This appears to be first time this high summit has been reached since its original ascent by legendary Poles Jerzy Kukuczka and Voytek Kurtyka, during their traverse of Gasherbrum II. In addition, it is only the second major route to be completed from this part of the Shaksgam Valley; the other, which took place in August 1992, was the first ascent of the Chinese (east) face of Broad Peak Central (8,006m) from the North Gasherbrum Glacier by a Spanish-Italian team.

Sichuan

Shaluli Shan

Genyen (6,204m) in the Shaluli Shan with the route up the north spur marked. *Karl Unterkircher*

Approaching the serac barrier on the north ridge of Genyen during the first ascent. *Karl Unterkircher*

Genyen, North Spur; Sachun, east face, attempt. When we left Italy, we possessed only a few satellite photos and little information on the region we had chosen for our adventure. We traveled to the area by jeep on ever-worsening roads. The last day it took almost eight hours to cover just 91km between Zhanla and Litang. Finally, with yaks and horses we walked up the Garmunei Gou Valley (called Shuta by local monks) to the heart of the Genyen group, a massif that we had been admiring for many hours. We sited base camp near Nego Gompa (a.k.a. Lengo Gompa or Rengo Monastery) at 4,060m, surrounded by granite walls leading to snow-capped summits. In the first two days we explored the secrets of the range and climbed an easy summit of 5,000m. From this viewpoint the north face of Genyen (6,204m) looked worrisome, but the surrounding valleys held a wealth of unknown peaks. Our enthusiasm was enormous.

We became an object of exploration for the monks, who had never had contact with the Western world. Our association with them became friendlier day-by-day. They told us of the origins of the valleys, in accordance with their religion, and how the mountains that rise opposite the monastery are sacred, because they cannot be reached by people, particularly Genyen with its snow-covered north and northeast faces. Were we the men who could discover the secret of Genyen?

With a good weather forecast, Simon Kehrer, Gerold Moroder, Walter Nones, and Karl Unterkircher went up to Camp 1, under the north spur, and slept there at an altitude of 5,000 m. The following day, May 16, after a climb of nine hours, we reached the flat summit of Genyen at 5:40 p.m. Snow conditions had been awful, and there had been steep sections of technically difficult climbing. Out of respect for the mountain's sacred status, we did not stand on the highest point. We then descended the south face, getting below the difficulties before making an improvised bivouac at 1 a.m. By midday on the 17th we were back at base camp.

Enthused by our success and by our meetings with the monks, listening to their beliefs and philosophies, we continued exploring the secret valleys. We discovered that though no one has climbed these mountains, the monks have names for them all. Each name has a divine meaning, representing a god's place of residence, and we won't rename these marvelous peaks.

We were attracted to the ca 5,800m peak of Sachun (the name of a Buddhist god), particularly the sheer granite east face. The monks enthusiastically helped establish Camp 1. However, monsoon-like weather hit the valley. Was it because the gods were angry with us? No, the monks assured us it was only a meteorological coincidence. However, it rained for a long time. Back at base camp we split into two parties. Walter and Karl decided to cross into one of the lateral valleys, accompanied by two monks, and return to camp by a different route. Gerold and Simon decided to have another crack at Sachun, where they had left their climbing equipment. Their aim was to complete a hard rock route up the east face with one bivouac.

Karl and Walter returned after three days of constant storm. They had unexpected meetings with nomads, yaks, and tropical forest. Karl thought he had broken a rib falling into a river, and the monks had turned back, frightened by the weather. However, Karl and Walter had explored the Zonag Valley, crossed an unnamed 5,160m pass and stumbled upon warm springs. Back at base camp the monks came to congratulate the pair. smiling and showing visible satisfaction. Unfortunately, Simon and Gerold's three-and-a-half-day attempt was unsuccessful, though they got a good distance up the wall.

Our last night was blessed by clear skies and excellent views of Genyen. The true north face, a great route that we did not climb, stands out. We will come back. There is too much we have yet to discover, and the new friends we have found, monks young and old, and orphan children the monks are looking after.

DR. LEONARDO PAGANI *and* KARL UNTERKIRCHER, *Italy*

Editor's note: This appears to be only the second climbing expedition to the massif. The first involved seven climbers from the Himalayan Association of Japan. On June 11, 1988, Tetsuro Itoh, Osamu Takita, and Kazuo Tobita reached the summit of Genyen. The three placed their base camp at 4,350m, below the south ridge of the ca 6,000m east peak of Genyen. They established camps on the ridge at 5,150m and 5,750m, before reaching the east peak and continuing up the connecting ridge to the main summit of Genyen. This information was supplied by Tamotsu Nakamura.

Genyen massif, Sachun, first ascent; Phurba, first ascent. In October Dave Anderson, Molly Loomis, Andy Tyson, and Canadian Sara Hueniken visited the Genyen massif. On the 20th Anderson and Hueniken climbed the long south ridge of Sachun in a 17-hour roundtrip from their high camp. They called the climb Dang Ba 'Dren Pa (5.10+ A0 M5 70°), a Tibetan phrase meaning to inspire, enthuse, and uplift.

The following day Loomis and Tyson climbed a ca 5,685m peak they named Phurba, due to its resemblance to the triple-bladed Tibetan dagger. Leaving base camp they scrambled unroped up loose rock and a steep snow couloir to gain the south ridge, then climbed eight pitches of mixed snow and rock (5.8) to the top. They called the route Naga (Serpent). Loomis and Tyson also climbed the southeast and east face of a peak they called Damaru (ca 5,655m), reaching a point 25 feet below the twin summits. A feature story by Molly Loomis appears earlier in the *Journal.*

DAXUE SHAN

Haizi Shan, 2003 and 2005 attempts. In October 2003 we traveled from Hong Kong to Sichuan by train. We were joined in Kanding by Neil Carruthers, Stephen Wai Wah Yip (Geordie), and Ron Yue, who arrived by plane.

After renting a horse train from the family at the trailhead, we traveled up the Yala Valley to the third lake. We then approached Haizi Shan via a gully leading to a scree fan below and left of the long ridge leading to the north summit. We then ascended an open couloir toward the left side of the north face. The following day we climbed up to and along the glacial ramp that runs parallel to and below the long northeast ridge. Geordie and Damian had started farther left and, early in their ascent, found old 6mm or 7mm fixed rope of the three-ply variety. We reached a rock buttress and from there headed up to the crest of the northeast ridge, arriving at a little rock outcrop and climbing past a broad col to the north summit. The main summit was not too far away, but the intervening ridge looked heavily corniced. Realizing that we would not make it to the top and back down before nightfall, we decided to call it good.

None of us was keen to reverse the route, so from the col we dropped straight down the face onto the glacier and descended this via a series of benches and a couple of rappels over seracs. A loose pitch, led by Geordie, across the little rock buttress gained the ascent route.

In October 2005 the two of us returned, this time with Benjamin (Benjack) Phillips and Lok Wai Keung. Ho Saam Goh from Rilong came along as base camp manager. We took the same approach to the third Yala lake but this time moved right and went to the right of the waterfall, then up a gully leading to a scree ridge. As we climbed the gully through rhododendrons behind the right side of the lake, we found the way marked by ribbons with Hongol (Korean) script. These looked to be no more than a year or two old. In the rock steps above the waterfall we also came across fixed ropes. We made a bivouac in the boulders at the base of the big rock rib that drops directly from the north summit, right of a large open snow slope. The weather then turned nasty, and we sat out a couple of nights in the boulders before bailing. We noted that this area has recently become more popular with trekkers from Chengdu.

PAUL COLLIS *and* DAMIAN RYAN, *Hong Kong*

Haizi Shan, northeast ridge, attempt. On April 28 an American expedition led by 83-year-old Fred Beckey arrived in Chengdu. The team included Dave O'Leske, Jeff Wenger, Ralf Sweeney, and I. Our objective was the first ascent of a 5,833m peak called Haizi Shan (a.k.a. Ja-Ra, Zhara, or Yala Peak). Beckey had been eyeing the mountain for over 15 years and had photos of the north and west faces from a trip he made several years ago. While our goal was to climb Haizi Shan, the team's overriding objective was to film Fred in his element, to use in a documentary of his extraordinary life story.

We drove overland to Haizi Shan and established a camp at the end of the valley, under the peak's north face. After several days acclimatizing, we moved the camp, with help from local Tibetan horsemen, to a large lake at the base of the north face. We then established our first camp at 4,580m. Nearby we discovered snow stakes of Korean origin stashed under a boulder. We shuttled gear and food to this camp over several days and then made a summit attempt via the northeast ridge. We were halted by deep snow and the heavily corniced crest. One week later, after waiting out a three-day storm that dropped a few feet of snow accompanied by strong winds, we pushed a weaving route through the icefall directly under the north summit, establishing a second camp at 5,425m. The next day we climbed to the ca 5,700m north summit, experiencing deep snow and hard ice on steeper ground.

Dave and Jeff attempted to traverse across the saddle to the main summit but were stopped by a giant crevasse spanning the ridge and effectively separating Haizi Shan into two peaks. We

Haizi Shan (5,833m) from the north. (1) The first attempt by the 2006 American expedition, which descended from its high point via (2). The combination of (2) and (3) marks the first ascent of the north summit, by a party from Hong Kong in 2003. They descended via the top section of (5) and followed (4) to regain their ascent route. A British party repeated the route in 2004, two climbers continuing toward the main summit as marked. (5) The second attempt by the American party in 2006, climbing the north summit and to the British high point on the connecting ridge to the main summit. This line is believed to have been attempted previously by a Korean expedition. (6) The north face direct, the first ascent of the mountain (Bass-Deavoll, 2006). *Malcolm Bass*

descended from the north summit to Camp 2 and continued down the next day. The weather turned bad again and never gave us an opportunity to mount another attempt. The climbing had been mostly moderate but was made difficult by fresh snow and high winds.

Haizi Shan's north summit had been previously reached, but it is unclear if another team had climbed the route we called the Beckey Direct. In the lower icefall above Camp 1 we found fixed rope, white nylon static like that used in water skiing. We presume this to have been placed for descent by a Korean team.

Climbing through the lower icefall on the north flank of Haizi Shan, during the probable third ascent of the ca 5,700m north summit. The climbers dubbed their line the Beckey Direct, but failed to cross the connecting ridge to the main top. *Todd Offenbacher*

Fred remained in base camp for most of the trip due to illness, but his mountain-awareness and route-finding proved invaluable to every aspect of the climbing. More importantly, it was a great experience to spend a month in the mountains with the legendary Beckey.

TODD OFFENBACHER, *AAC*

Late in the day, Pat Deavoll rappels the upper couloir on the north face of Haizi Shan after making the first ascent with Malcolm Bass. The two regained their tent (C) that evening. *Malcolm Bass*

Pat Deavoll below the north face of Haizi Shan (5,833m). Deavoll and Malcolm Bass made the coveted first ascent via the big snow gully to the right, which leads directly to the summit ridge right of the highest point. *Malcolm Bass*

Haizi Shan, first ascent. When Pat Deavoll from New Zealand suggested a trip to Sichuan or Tibet, I jumped at the opportunity, especially as Pat had experience of the country from her successful 2005 expedition to Xiashe with the late Karen McNeill. We only had time for a short trip, so Haizi Shan's accessibility from Chengdu commended the mountain to us.

By our reckoning this 5,833m mountain has three commonly used names. Haizi is its Mandarin Chinese name, but local Tibetans call it either Yala or Zhara. It stands in proud isolation on the edge of the Tagong grasslands, and has a reputation as a bad-weather magnet. It had seen about 10 previous attempts, mostly by the long northeast ridge. Photographs of the north side suggested a direct line might be possible up the 1,150m north face to the main summit. Such a line would not only be aesthetically pleasing but hopefully quicker, giving us more chance of snatching an ascent during a typically short weather window.

Getting to the mountain was relatively straightforward, except for an anxious delay while Pat's bags were extricated from the chaos of the new Bangkok airport. A day on good roads took us to Kanding, where we picked up our permit from the Ganzi Tibetan Autonomous Region Mountaineering Association. The next day's driving was superb, taking us over high grasslands to an inspiring view of the south side of Haizi. The road circled to the west and then around to birch and larch woods north of the mountain. At this point we turned on to a small rough track that took us bumpily past a zinc mine to a grassy camp site. Haizi's north face hung ethereally above.

Over the next eight days we found a way up from the Tai Zhan Valley to the basin beneath the north face, and then spent a few days at 4,500m acclimatizing and face-watching. The route into the basin followed a 400m snow gully through steep lower cliffs and was rather fraught, as it drained the whole basin and north face above. We narrowly escaped obliteration when a serac fell on the north face, 10 minutes after we'd descended the gully.

On October 11 there was snowfall down to the level of base camp. This forced us to delay our first attempt for two days, while we let the face clear. On the 13th we went back up the gully, into the basin, and camped 200m below the face. The most prominent feature on the north face is an arête dropping from just west of the main summit. Gully systems fall to the foot of the face from either side of this nose. We decided we'd climb a rib between these two gullies, then drop into the right-hand gully and follow it to the west ridge near the summit. On the 14th we climbed 800m onto and then up the rib as planned. Snow conditions varied from firm to knee-deep. The climbing was straightforward; we took turns breaking trail and didn't rope up. There was a shallow couloir, on the rib, that we mostly stayed in, finding snow conditions better. At 5,200m we moved back onto the rib proper and hacked out a tent platform. This was a fine, safe bivouac site, with a good view over the serac-threatened face to the east. The early part of the evening was a bit worrying, as thunderstorms played over the surrounding lower hills, and the odd shower of hail blew in on gusty winds. Eventually the weather passed around and below us and the night grew quiet.

Next morning, with just over 600m to gain, we left the tent pitched and set off into the darkness with light sacks. We made a rising traverse into the right hand couloir, which we reached at dawn. Snow conditions were good, and again we were able to climb unroped, until we encountered loose snow over granite slabs at 5,500m. At this point we roped, as it got a bit scratchy, and belayed two pitches. The best of these was a groove in the gully wall, skirting some particularly blank slabs in the gully bed at about Scottish IV. We stopped belaying and trailed the ropes, leaving the gully and moving left. The cornice at the top of the face took a while to break through, and I asked Pat for a body belay when I became convinced that, having surmounted it, I'd fall down the south face. But this didn't happen, and we were soon able to relax, albeit briefly, on the broad west ridge. As the excitement of having climbed the face faded, tiredness began to tell on our pace. We stayed roped, as the ridge was corniced to the north. Eventually a promising top ahead began to look like a summit. Pat led out, vanishing into the cloud as she surmounted a last step. So far from maritime Scotland and New Zealand, and still not a ropelength of visibility.

And that was it, the summit: a sharp little point above a big northerly cornice. Obligingly the clouds parted, and we were enraptured by expansive views west to grasslands, south to the hot springs valley, north to our base camp, visible only as a clearing in the woods, and east to a vividly colored glacial lake. The final section of the oft-attempted northeast ridge looked particularly corniced and resembled a roller coaster.

And then down, rappelling the top of the face in pink evening light and downclimbing into the encroaching gloom, till the GPS guided us onto the traverse back to our tent. We descended to base camp next day, the 16th.

We encountered no problems with bureaucracy throughout the trip. The Ganzi Tibetan Autonomous Region Mountaineering Association and our agent Lenny (Chen Zheng Lin) worked well together. There is considerable potential for new routes on Haizi Shan, both on rock ridges and ribs to the west and south, and on steep mixed routes in the couloirs and chimneys between. However, the latter would need to be done early or late in the year.

MALCOLM BASS, *Alpine Club*

Haizi Shan, second ascent. Piecing together the evidence, it appears that the late Christine Boskoff and Charlie Fowler made the second ascent of Haizi Shan on October 22. They appear to have walked into the peak, presumably from the north, and climbed it straight off. However, they were later buried by an avalanche below Genyen, and sadly we will never know the details.

QONGLAI SHAN

SIGUNIANG NATIONAL PARK

The north face of Banji North (5,400m) above the Bipeng Valley. The face was attempted during the winter of 2006 via a line toward the right edge. A marks the high point. *Bob Keaty*

Bipeng Valley, Banji North, north face, attempt. Banji (Banji Feng; Half Ridge Peak, 5,430m) was the first main peak to be climbed in the Bipeng Valley. It was first ascended in May 2004 from the west via the drainage that flows down to the valley below (north of) Shanghaizi (see *AAJ 2005*, pp. 418-419). I climbed Banji the following October via the same route. Beyond the approach, the route ascends the north flank of the mountain and is mostly glacier travel of the order Alpine F/PD. It has become a *voie normale* and sees three or four repeats every year. Jon Otto's company (Otto made the first ascent) guides it at least twice a year (May and October); that's a lot of traffic by Chinese standards.

Driving up to the Bipeng Reception Center, you cannot help but be impressed by Banji North's huge north wall, dominating the southern skyline up and left from the main valley. The face is 600-800m high, and the summit of Banji North is marked as 5,400m on the Chinese topographic map. Banji North is connected by a knife-edge ridge to the main summit, and when I first I photographed these peaks, I began to dream about a traverse along the jagged skyline between the two summits.

On January 21 Cosmin Andron, a Rumanian living in Guangzhou, and I, an American living in Shanghai, arrived at the accommodation in Shanghaizi (3,600m; GPS N 31° 14.776', E 102° 52.778') after driving that day from Chengdu. Cosmin had food poisoning, so the following day we did a couple of new icefalls in the valley. On the 25th we went down to Lixain for a night's sleep in a warm room and the next day, with two porters, walked up to camp in the basin below the wall. A direct line up the center of this wall proved too difficult to access due to deep powder snow, so we chose a line toward the right side. Cosmin led off on granite that was mossy, particularly in the cracks, requiring a lot of cleaning for gear placements. We climbed three pitches before settling down for a cramped bivouac.

The next morning, as the sky lightened, we could clearly see the distant Outaiji, a magnificent lone peak near Heishui. Also visible were spectacular peaks with high icefalls splitting blank rock walls. These lay to the east, probably in the Tazi Valley. There is no shortage of stunning peaks in this area. Most of them have never been explored or named, and none has been climbed. The only difference between these peaks and their counterparts in Europe and the Americas is a climbing history. Once climbers start putting up routes in these mountains, they should be recognized as classic, beautiful climbs. And these mountains are becoming more accessible. A plane ride to Chengdu, followed by a five-hour drive into the canyons, and you are near the base of giants waiting for new lines. The rock quality is great, the avalanche danger relatively low, and the various forms of accommodation are getting more comfortable.

On day two the line was obvious: straight up a dihedral with great cracks. The temperature was only –6°C, though it felt colder because of a chilly wind. The first pitch took three hours, and it was dark by the time we were on the third. The bivouac was as uncomfortable as the previous. The next day we climbed a pitch, before we realized we had bitten off more than we could chew. The route would require more aid gear, food, and fuel, and at least three more days. By evening we had reached the foot of the face and our high camp in the basin.

BOB KEATY, *Shanghai*

Bipeng Valley, Longgesali. On September 3-4 Saburo Mizobuchi, Keiichi Nagatomo, Naoki Ohuchi, and Tomohiro Sugai climbed a new route (400m, 13 pitches, IV A0) on Longgesali (a.k.a. Panyanjuhui, 5,420m). They also made unsuccessful attempts on the pointed rock summit of Pt. 5,513m and Jiang Jun Feng (5,260m).

TAMOTSU NAKAMURA, *Editor, Japanese Alpine News*

Shuangqiao Valley, Daogou West, first ascent. In late September Vaughn Thomas (Australia) and I made the first ascent of the granite peak of Daogou West (5,422m), via the south face. The weather was unstable during most of our stay, with the best weather windows occurring at the end of September and beginning of October.

During one of these good spells we made two attempts on the face, on the second of which we reached the summit. The south face is 600m high, and we climbed it in nine pitches, plus some

The south face of Daogou West (5,422m), with the line of the Australian-New Zealand first ascent (700m, 5.10 A0). This side of the mountain is approached from the Shuangqiao Valley. *Kester Brown*

scrambling, to a foresummit. We then followed the ridge rightward for three more pitches to the base of the main summit, which we climbed in two pitches. The route has 700m of vertical gain and is mostly free rock climbing, with snow ledges and ramps. We made one small pendulum and a 10m rappel to avoid a gendarme in the upper section. The grade was 5.10 A0 and the rock of the highest quality for the entire route.

We climbed and descended the route in a day from a bivouac at the foot. We descended mostly by rappel, with a deviation to avoid reversing the ridge. We left a single nut or knotted sling at each anchor. There remain many unclimbed granite ridges and faces in and around the Shuangqiao and Changping valleys, and even a few impressive summits yet to bear a flag.

KESTER BROWN, *Aotearoa/New Zealand*

Editor's note: Daogou West lies in a side valley that drains west into the upper Shuangqiao Gou. It was possibly first visited by climbers in 2000, when Italians Gianluca Belin and Diego Stefani climbed Shuangqiao Peak (a.k.a. Wong Shan). It was visited in 2003 by Andrej and Tanja Grmovsek (see AAJ 2004, pp. 420-422), who climbed the south face of Tan Shan, and in 2005 by Boris Cujic and Ivica Matkovic (see AAJ 2006, pp. 451-453), who climbed three peaks. That same year Americans Chad Kellogg, Joe Puryear, and Stoney Richards climbed Daogou (5,466m) by the south face. They reached the head of the valley from the east, walking up the Chiwen Gorge and crossing a pass (see AAJ 2006, pp. 446-448).

The east face of Celestial Peak (5,413m) above the Changping Valley, showing the line of the new Russian winter route. The left skyline was climbed in 1985 by Keith Brown, solo, while the American first ascent in 1983 was made from the far side via the southwest face. *Anna Piunova collection*

Changping Valley, Celestial Peak, east face. From February 7-19 the Russian team of Kolesov, Shelkovnikov, and Sherstnev climbed a major new line up the east face of Celestial Peak (5,413m). The accompanying photograph shows the line but no further details have been forthcoming.

ANNA PIUNOVA, *www.mountain.ru, Russia*

Changping Valley, Thorn, first ascent; Falcon, first ascent; Camel Peak, southwest face, attempt. In October Josh Butson and I ventured to the Quonglai mountains, inspired by conversations with Charlie Fowler, Keith Brown, and information lifted from recent volumes of the *Japanese Alpine News*. The two of us were hungry for a remote adventure and first ascents on virgin granite. I purchased a plane ticket to Chengdu, armed with a tip from Salt Lake climber Tommy Chandler that our first discovery would be a man named Tong Wei in a bar called the Iced Rock. By the time we found him, we had flown for two days, been held up on the road to Rilong, and pushed a Yugo over a 4,000m pass in a blizzard. On our first overcast morning in the heart of Sichuan, we woke worried and uncertain we were in the right place. We could see no mountains.

We ambled about town, rendezvoused with Tong Wei, and met a government man named Gao Wei. A heated negotiation, tense with cigarette smoke and bulleted by broken but deliberate English, forged an agreement over a stream of Heinikens and $85US. We hadn't expected contact with the Sichuan Mountaineering Association but its representative, Gao Wei, was fair. We could climb in any style, but not on any mountain. We were granted a permit to explore unclimbed 5,000m peaks in the Changping Goa. It was scrawled on cheap waxy paper.

Ben Clark seconding a pitch of M6 during an unsuccessful attempt on the southwest face of Camel Peak West (5,484m) in the Changping Valley. *Josh Butson*

We hiked from the mouth of the valley with just rucksacks, post-holing through miles of mud deep enough to inhale our plastic boots and exhale belches like a fifth grader. We established a base camp in the hanging valley north of Celestial Peak. The valley, which rises west out of the Changping, was steep and offered little room but ample water. Our first alpine foray was adventurous climbing on two unclimbed 5,000m peaks: a twin-peak formation we called The Thorn and a second peak that looked like a Falcon. We established a run-out 5.9+ on The Thorn and climbed a long steep couloir to a previously unclimbed summit on The Falcon. The couloir was the

The Falcon (ca 5,250m), which lies in a cirque on the north side of the hanging valley north of Celestial Peak. Marked is the line of the first ascent, No Cupcake Couloir (ca 1,500m). *Ben Clark*

only weakness in the granite cirque north of Celestial Peak; we found it to be interesting but not altogether difficult: 50°, with third- and fourth-class mixed moves to surmount a small saddle, after which we scooted up to the tiny, exposed summit. We felt The Falcon to be no more than 150m lower than Celestial (5,413m), and as tree line is ca 3,700m, our route, which we named No Cupcake Couloir, must have been ca 1,500m long.

Our final reconnaissance was an endurance march as far up valley as we could see. For four days we approached the unclimbed southwest face of the highest of the previously climbed Camel Peaks [Camel Peak West, 5,484m, first climbed in 1994 by Charlie Fowler]. This face looked demanding, with powder-covered, polished, exfoliating granite slabs, which rose over 600m to a long, steep shoulder.

We burned every bit of the next day's sunlight establishing an absorbing but incomplete route we named Up the Gullet. The climbing was run-out and mixed, with difficulties of AI 5+ 5.7 M8. The pitch of M8 was an unprotected runout up a 35m corner of s'nice. When I returned to the belay after having pounded in the only piece of pro, a stubby LA, and then tenuously rapped down the scrappy corner, Josh commented on what a mentally challenging lead it must have been. I handed the next lead to Josh, and we continued onward, finding more steep, fun climbing through the heart of the throaty route. However, at 6 p.m., when we were over 400m up the face, we became enveloped in winter's icy blast. We were only one overhanging pitch from the long snowfield that led to the summit but decided to bail. Both the rock and the climbing had been great, and we were content, but we were well aware that the weather of the Changping does not forgive.

Darkness stripped away the light as ominously as the featureless granite devoured our 11-pin rack in the maelstrom. Seven rappels led to the wind-scoured ramp below our gully. I dropped to my knees once while blindly traversing the rarely recognizable lower moraine, ready for a night out. Hours passed before the relentless gale ceased, and a momentary break in the cloud revealed the tent. The guy lines were reflecting eerily back at us like a ghost ship. We hugged like brothers and sat outside the tiny structure, finishing our water and flushing our senses.

The walk out took three more days; our trip total was 27. Wild is the Changping Goa. How lucky we were to have traveled there. How irrevocable our will to return.

                                                                    BEN CLARK

Changping Valley, Dorsal Peak, first ascent; Jiang Jun Feng, southwest ridge. On April 3 two friends and I found ourselves on top a previously unclimbed peak for the first time in our lives. This was not the culmination of a lengthy expedition to one of the most remote places in the world, nor the completion of one of the sport's most challenging new routes. Rather, we were in the first half of a three-week trip, climbing at a grade achievable by many enthusiastic mountaineers.

One of the beauties of the Siguniang National Park, an area that has become a popular Chinese tourist destination and hit the climbing headlines in 2002 with Mick Fowler and Paul Ramsden's award-winning ascent on Siguniang itself, is its accessibility and lack of bureaucracy. Ian Gibb, Felix Hoddinott, and I left London on a Saturday and were in base camp by Wednesday, largely thanks to our Mr. Fix-It, a man known as Lion, whom we had contacted on the Internet. Lion is a young Chinese climber who has acted as an interpreter/guide for several Western expeditions. He proved to be an invaluable asset, whether arranging park fees, introducing us to boiled rabbit heads, scaring off yaks, or getting the local party official drunk. In Chengdu we were able to buy our food at a large Western-style supermarket and purchase a few items of Black Diamond equipment, after one of us found he had forgotten his harness.

In Rilong we stayed at Mr. Ma's hostel. Although Ma proved to be a skillful negotiator when it came to renting horses to carry our equipment, he was a man of his word and treated us as a family guest. His mother even offered to disinfect Felix's cut finger by having her grandson urinate on it: a rare level of hospitality. With Mr. Ma and his horses, we established base camp at 3,800m, two-thirds of the way up the Changping. On the third day after our arrival, we set off for the northwest ridge of what we named Dorsal Peak, after its distinctive curved arête. Dorsal Peak lies on the east rim of the Changping, south of Peak 5,666m, climbed by Charlie Fowler in 1997, on the ridge running south towards the Siguniang peaks. After a bivouac at 4,200m,

The line taken by the British expedition on the south flank of Peak 5,260m at the head of the Changping Valley. The high point on this unclimbed mountain in Siguniang National Park was ca. 5,000m. *Jeremy Thornley collection*

Looking southwest toward Daogou (5,465m, left) and Daogou West (5,422m) from the north side of the upper Changping Valley. Both peaks have been climbed from the far side; the former by an American team in 2005, and the latter by an Australian-New Zealand pair in 2006. *Jeremy Thornley collection*

Kitting up before an unsuccessful attempt on the unclimbed Peak 5,260m at the head of the Changping Valley. Behind are Putala Shan (5,428m, left) and, closer to the camera, the unclimbed Peak 5,592m (a.k.a Barbarian Peak). *Ian Gibb*

we were slowed by regularly falling into chest-deep hidden, snow-covered fissures between boulders. The ridge posed a more technical challenge, with delicate traverses across excellent rock covered in powder snow. The summit was a pleasingly small, pointed, 5,050m peak and our route around PD+ in standard. There were no signs of a previous ascent, and we felt confident that our 6mm tat left on top was the first sign of human presence on the mountain.

On the sixth day of relatively stable weather we ascended the path towards Bipeng Pass (4,644m) at the head of the valley. We made a comfortable bivouac in the snow just under the pass, before starting up our second objective: the southwest ridge of the peak immediately east of the pass, known locally as Ding Ding (5,202m). We circumnavigated the initial gendarmes by traversing the south flank of the ridge, then passed through a notch in a subsidiary ridge running north-south. From there we followed a couloir through a rock band to reach an awkward step, which led onto the main ridge and amazing views. Without an accurate map or knowledge of the summit height, we found the ridge to present a frustrating series of false summits. However, the climbing was enjoyable and became steadily more technical. A delicate step down to an exposed traverse led to steep, exposed snow-smothered rock and finally the fairytale summit. We were disappointed to discover a small but unmistakable cairn, and we subsequently discovered that the peak is also known as Jiang Jun Feng and had been climbed from the Bipeng Valley the previous year by Tommy Chandler and Pat Goodman (see *AAJ 2006*, pp. 445-446). The grade of our ascent, which took place on April 6, was AD.

The second half of the trip was dominated by afternoon snowstorms. Toward the end we made an attempt on the south flank and west ridge of Peak 5,260m, at the head of the Changping, the second peak west of Bipeng Pass. The route seemed feasible and worthwhile (about AD), but we had only reached 5,000m when heavy snowfall forced retreat.

Despite mixed weather, the team had enjoyed their first taste of new ascents in the greater ranges and is grateful to the Mount Everest Foundation and The British Mountaineering Council (U.K. Sport) for supporting the expedition.

JEREMY THORNLEY, *U.K.*

The southwest face of Siguniang IV (the Fourth Sister of Siguniang Shan, a ca 4,950m summit on the long southwest ridge of 6,250m Siguniang) rises out of the jungle above the east side of the Changping Valley. Marked is Suffering First Class (ca 450m, V A3 5.10). *Cosmin Andron*

Cosmin Andron following the initial cracks of Suffering First Class (V A3 5.10), the first route climbed on the southwest face of the ca 4,950m Fourth Sister of Siguniang, Qonglai Shan. *Wai Wah Yip/ Cosmin Andron collection*

Siguniang IV, southwest face. Our initial team of four, which intended a leisurely trip to Siguniang National Park, saw itself reduced to two: Steve Wai Wah Yip (Geordie) and I. We decided to play on granite faces in the Changping Gou, walls that I remembered from a trip the year before. However, our visit turned out jinxed, and it appeared that disasters ready to happen were lurking around every corner. First we missed our flight. Then our luggage was rejected. We were sent to board the plane with ice axes, were turned back again, and missed the next two flights fighting with the challenging-to-deal-with staff of Sichuan Airlines. Then our local fixer didn't show up as agreed, and we ended up overcharged and dumped halfway to base camp by charming porters and their lovely horses. We had to randomly choose a wall, pay more money to have our gear ferried there, and then the weather crapped out. I then got sick. It seemed as though we'd got the perfect recipe for disaster, but we managed to improve on it.

We got onto our wall, a splendid blank face with two parallel cracks running for 200m. Too bad they were off-width, and for most of their length we only had two pieces of gear that would fit. Geordie leapfrogged a Camalot 5, cute and cozy, and a wobbly, screeching 4.5. Above this section we had a roof, then a system of overhangs and chimneys, all seasoned by a several-days downpour, a sprinkle of high winds, and a fist-full of mist.

Ours was the first ascent of the southwest face of Siguniang IV (the Fourth Sister of

Siguniang Shan, a ca 4,950m summit on the long southwest ridge of 6,250m Siguniang). The wall topped out on the ridge, where at 2:45 a.m. on June 8 we intersected a previously climbed route. However, we were unable to follow it to the summit due to time constraints. We climbed the 400-450m wall bolt-free (and in places brain-free) and left behind only a few pegs, nuts, and slings for rappel anchors.

We named our route Suffering First Class and graded it V A3 5.10. However, getting to and back from the route got A6 in my book. I'm entirely to blame, because when our teacher was instructing my classmates to the meaning of "monsoon," I was playing truant and bouldering on the school's wall. As she said, "You can learn things the easy way or the hard way." I made my choice.

As we descended the wall after a 24-hour day, a belay in an expando crack blew, nearly sending me to the valley floor air express. Somehow we got off the wall with all limbs attached, to find out that we were again hijacked by our porters, who refused, halfway through the descent, to take us to the nearest village. This would have meant we were doomed, once again, to miss our flights. For me this included the one back to my home country, Romania. Finally, after a shouting championship, we concluded our 36-hour day in the van taking us to Chengdu's airport. To top it all we received a $300 fine for not having a climbing permit (which our fixer was supposed to have arranged) and later realized that the porters had lost some of our precious gear. The last mix-up that befell us was that by mistake we ended up flying…first class. Somehow this made for a happy ending.

So, I'm writing this report sitting on my Zion haul bag, which I'll be sending this afternoon to Chengdu. And guess where are we headed next Saturday? Yep! But I've heard that in winter it doesn't rain.

COSMIN ANDRON, Guangzhou, China

Siguniang, south face to southwest ridge, not to summit; Siguniang North, first ascent, southwest face. I'm at 5,500m. The ice is hard. My crampons rebound, blunted after three weeks. For the last eight years in Haute Savoie the Committee of the French Alpine Club has selected people 16-26 years old for a "young alpinists" group. For two years the young men and women are trained in various aspects of mountaineering by a professional guide, and at the end of this period they organize an expedition. In 2006 the project was a new route on Siguniang (6,250m) in Sichuan, an area still ignored by many Europeans but having exceptional potential.

Our flight landed in Chengdu on October 9. Chengdu is a model of the modern Chinese city, soaked in Western culture. With McDonald's, KFC, Pizza Hut, posters for Oréal, Cartier, Vuitton, Sony, it doesn't correspond to my image of a communist country; the Cultural Revolution seems far away. The city appears to be under construction, with 40-floor apartment blocks. There are many cars: Is Audi the symbol of the new Communism? Is China is becoming modernized too quickly? Economists calculate that if the 1.2 billion Chinese had the same amount of stuff as Westerners, there would be no more oil on the planet in 20 years.

The road to Rilong has been greatly upgraded since the Siguniang National Park became a World Heritage Site. In Rilong, Audis are replaced by horses and yaks. The walk to our base camp at 3,500m in the Changping Valley takes four hours. Our site is next to a wooden hut, where two Tibetans live. They have no running water or electricity, just a wood stove. They have a few pigs and yaks, and sell kebabs to Chinese tourists.

(A) Siguniang North (5,700m) and (B) Siguniang (6,250m) from the west-northwest. (1) Southwest face (V 4+ M4, Batoux-Blair-Bodin-Jacquemond-Rolinet-Valla, 2006). (2) North ridge, used in descent by Fowler and Ramsden after their ascent of the north couloir. (3) North couloir - The Inside Line (WI 6, Fowler-Ramsden, 2002). (4) Northwest buttress attempted in 2005 by an American team. (5) Northwest face, with the proposed line attempted by Americans in 1981 and British in 2004. The solid line ends at the approximate high point of 5,400m. (6) The unclimbed southwest ridge. *Philippe Batoux*

Maile, our translator, has always lived in Beijing and Chengdu, and it is his first time outside a large city. He is so happy to discover the Milky Way and a billion other stars. The pollution in Chinese cities only allows people to see the most brilliant planets. Chengdu and Rilong: two cities in the same China but separated by 100 years.

The mountains of Siguniang are splendid. The peaks are of the most beautiful granite, smooth and compact, a Yosemite Valley with virgin tops between 5,000 and 6,000m. Jérôme Berton, Guillaume Blair, Guillaume Bodin, Clémont Jacquemond, Aurélie Lévèque, David Rolinet, Théo Valla, and I hoped to climb the prominent central couloir on the south face of Siguniang. However, last autumn this gully, more than 1,000m high, was quite dry and the top section completely rocky. Instead, we chose a steep ice line leading out left, up the right side of the rock pillar taken by the eight-member Japanese team, which in 1992 sieged the south buttress and upper southwest ridge to make the second ascent of the mountain. [The French line may be similar to that tried by a Russian team, which attempted a route west of the central couloir but was forced down by stonefall and avalanches—Ed.]

We established a high camp at 5,000m and fixed 500m of rope on the initial difficulties. On October 24 we tried to make a one-day lightweight push to the summit. Leaving camp at 1 a.m., we jumared the ropes and continued on the upper snow slopes, crossing the Japanese Route to reach the crest of the southwest ridge. Here we were slowed by poor conditions. At 5,950m a horizontal rocky ridge, covered in soft snow and impossible to protect, barred the way. An accident at this point would have been serious. Some of the team were already quite tired. It was now 3 p.m. If we continued to the summit, we would certainly have had to bivouac

The south face of Siguniang (6,250m) above the Changping Valley. (1) The long unclimbed southwest ridge. (2) South buttress and upper southwest ridge (Japanese, July 1992, eight climbers led by Chiharu Yoshimura, 600m of fixed rope). (3) The 2006 French attempt, which joined the upper section of (2) and reached a high point H, using 500m of fixed rope. Russians have also attempted a line in this vicinity. (4) South face and southeast ridge (Charlie Fowler, solo, September 1994 in alpine style). (5) Original route via the southeast ridge (Japanese, July 1981, Suita and Sumiya were the first to summit, 2,000m of fixed rope). *Philippe Batoux*

above 6,000m without equipment. I made the decision to go down. The difficulties of our incomplete line, which joined the existing Japanese route on the ridge, were V (WI) 4 M5+.

Four days later we made an attempt on the original 1981 Japanese Route on the southeast ridge, but more bad snow and cold forced us down from 5,600m.

We returned to base camp for a new objective, Siguniang North (5,700m). At 2 a.m. on November 1 all except Berton and Lévèque left the camp at 4,500m and started up the southwest face. This is the open snow and ice slope left of (and opposite) the northwest face Siguniang and was partially followed in descent by Mick Fowler and Paul Ramsden after their successful ascent of the stunning north-facing couloir, The Inside Line.

The face was granite flagstone, covered by a 5cm layer of snow and ice. The ice was good. The climbing wasn't difficult, but we couldn't protect ourselves. Higher, a mixed section, followed by a short vertical ice wall formed by a bergschrund, led to the summit slopes. A ridge led to the highest point. Our joy at being the first to reach this summit was immense. The difficulties of our route were V WI4+ M4.

On our way back to Rilong, we detoured to look at the Shuangqiao, the parallel valley west of the Changping. This valley is famous for its icefalls: more than 50 higher than 400m. Most end up at 5,000m. These lines were not in condition, but there was another surprise. Less than a day's walk from the road we saw several granite walls at least 1,000m high, major objectives to justify many trips to this land of pandas. This is the new Eldorado, and I believe part of alpinism's future development will take place on these walls.

PHILIPPE BATOUX, *France*

Tibet

CENTRAL TIBET

Shahkangsham, correction. In *AAJ 2006*, pp. 454-455, we reported the first ascent of Pt. 6,603m to the south of the main summit of Shahkangsham. Actually, Pt. 6,603m was previously climbed on October 7, 2002, by a three-member British party, which approached from the east, traversed both east and west summits, and then continued north along the ridge to bag the main 6,822m summit of Shahkangsham. This is believed to be the first time all these summits have been climbed.

NYANCHEN TANGLHA WEST

Sha Mo Karpo Ri (White Cap mountain, 6,261m) at the head of the valley southwest of the Nyanchen Tanglha massif. The main glacier rises to a high pass, which leads toward the Nam Tso, the second largest saltwater lake in Tibet. The route of ascent took the tributary glacier to the left and climbed onto the left ridge leading north to the summit. *Christian Haas*

Sha Mo Karpo Ri (Mt. White Cap), first ascent. In September and October I returned to the Nyanchen Tanglha Range, situated about 80km north of Lhasa. It was my third visit to this region, so we celebrated the return heartily with the local inhabitants. Our expedition comprised just two people: Hansjoerg Pfaundler and I. As in previous years, we went into the valley immediately southwest of the huge Nyanchen Tanglha massif, a line of three summits above 7,000m.

Before our visit we acclimatized by spending a week in the delightful Siguniang Mountains of Sichuan and then a second week around Lhasa. We then moved to our base camp, which we reached on October 2. In 2006 the weather proved to be extremely changeable. There was hardly a day without rapid transformations from sunshine to snowfall. On the 4th we went up a 6,000m peak named Bella Vista, where we had some good views of the surroundings. From this vantage point we could see our proposed summit for the following day, a high snowy peak on the horizon. This stood left of the pass leading to the second largest saltwater lake of Tibet, Nam Tso, which lies just north of the Nyanchen Tanglha. Because of its shape, we named the summit Mt. White Cap, or Sha Mo Karpo Ri in Tibetan.

We left base camp at 8:40 a.m. on October 5. The weather was cold, the sky was blue, and there was no sign of clouds. We passed a moraine lake in a steep slope of boulders at the end of the valley, crossed the big silt plain behind the lake, and reached the contorted glacier tongue. The main glacier led up to a pass on the watershed to the north, but we soon left it, following a tributary to the west. Clouds were now beginning to build on the northwest summit (7,162m) of Nyanchen Tanglha, and snow on the glacier reached knee deep.

After several hours trail-breaking between huge crevasses in moderately angled terrain, we arrived at the bottom of the final ridge, which rose north to the summit. In good visibility we slowly climbed the 40-45° ridge in deep snow, arriving on the summit at 3:50 p.m. GPS measurements gave the height as 6,261m and the location as N 30° 22,641', E 90° 30,015'. For a few minutes we could see our route across the glacier, but then we were shrouded in mist, and it started to snow. We started descending, but soon the tracks disappeared, so our GPS did the route-finding until we reached the main glacier, where visibility was sufficient for us to find our way back to base camp. We reached the tents at 7 p.m. in falling snow and windy conditions. Next day the weather was perfect, with no sign of there having been a storm, apart from a 10cm covering of fresh snow.

After several foiled attempts on 7,117m Nyanchen Tanglha Central (GPS N 30° 22,218', E 90° 35,181') we finally reached the summit at 5:30 p.m. on October 12 after a one-day marathon. We left base camp at 6 a.m. and returned at 9:30 p.m., having followed the normal route on the southwest ridge, which has a vertical gain of ca 1,850m. We had good conditions but in the upper part found the trail breaking hard going in deep snow. During our descent we once again had to rely on the GPS for short sections, because of the wind and mist.

CHRISTIAN HAAS, *Austria*

Editor's note: The three main summits of Nyanchen Tanglha are generally referred to as I (northwest or main summit, 7,162m), II (central, 7177m), and III (southeast, 7,046m). Summit I was first climbed in 1986 by a Japanese expedition via the west ridge. II was climbed in 1989 by an Austrian expedition via the southwest ridge, again in 1992 by Chinese, a multi-national expedition in 2001, and Austrians in 2002. The Haas- Pfaundler ascent was probably the fifth. III was first climbed by Japanese in 1995 and again by Austrians in 2002.

First ascents from valleys east of Nam Tso. I spent 23 days from November 9 to December 1 climbing in an area of the Western Nyanchen Tanglha not far from Samdain Kangsang (6,590m), the main peak in this area. I reached this region from Lhasa in less than a full day's drive by Land Cruiser. I carefully documented each peak by GPS and photographs, and researched the history of each area by using my interpreter to conduct interviews in each village with local Tibetans. I experienced tem-

Sean Burch celebrating on a summit above base camp 5 in the Lakyem area. He climbed most of the peaks visible in the background during a 63-peak spree in 23 days. *Sean Burch*

peratures below −18°C, high winds, avalanches, rockfall, crevasses and, surprisingly, wild dogs and bears. During summer these summits would be bare, but during my time there they were snow-covered and rather nice. The daily dispatches for the expedition can be read at my website, www.SeanBurch.com. I reached 63 summits in 23 days, though some other summits I attained have not been included in the list below due to lack of proper altitude, etc. The list of summits reached is as follows:

From base camp #1, within the Samdain Kangsang area:
1. N30° 46.580', E 091° 30.323' (17,565 feet)
2. N30° 46.152', E 091° 31.248' (17,147 feet)

From base camp #2, near Nam Tso Cho River:
3. N30° 32.786', E 091° 04.801' (16,343 feet)
4. N30° 33.943', E 091° 04.113' (17,909 feet)
5. N30° 33.544', E 091° 04.796' (16,784 feet)
6. N30° 32.806', E 091° 02.882' (18,132 feet)

From base camp #3, within the Lungring area:
7. N30° 28.491', E 091° 17.105' (16,093 feet)
8. N30° 28.587', E 091° 15.851' (16,509 feet)
9. N30° 27.310', E 091° 16.188' (18,097 feet)
10. N30° 26.561', E 091° 16.435' (16,605 feet)
11. N30° 25.863', E 091° 16.641' (17,427 feet)
12. N30° 27.287', E 091° 18.085' (16,334 feet)
13. N30° 27.511', E 091° 17.889' (16,628 feet)
14. N30° 27.795', E 091° 16.897' (17,332 feet)

From base camp #4, in the Nagdrak area:
15. N30° 25.626', E 091° 04.064' (16,767 feet)
16. N30° 25.151', E 091° 04.620' (17,737 feet)
17. N30° 24.850', E 091° 04.719' (17,683 feet)
18. N30° 25.067', E 091° 03.976' (16,648 feet)
19. N30° 24.574', E 091° 04.207' (17,917 feet)
20. N30° 24.185', E 091° 04.357' (18,177 feet)
21. N30° 24.105', E 091° 03.682' (18,222 feet)
22. N30° 24.051', E 091° 04.254' (18,054 feet)
23. N30° 24.412', E 091° 04.723' (18,249 feet)
24. N30° 24.781', E 091° 05.338' (18,142 feet)
25. N30° 24.926', E 091° 06.227' (18,139 feet)
26. N30° 25.110', E 091° 06.716' (17,904 feet)
27. N30° 24.733', E 091° 05.682' (18,164 feet)
28. N30° 25.570', E 091° 05.541' (16,915 feet)

From base camp #5, in the Lakyem area:
29. N30° 20.405', E 091° 02.823' (16,120 feet)
30. N30° 18.936', E 091° 01.513' (18,411 feet)
31. N30° 19.186', E 091° 01.261' (18,253 feet)
32. N30° 19.232', E 091° 02.007' (17,509 feet)
33. N30° 18.812', E 091° 01.932' (18,294 feet)
34. N30° 18,771', E 091° 02.541' (18,607 feet)
35. N30° 20.077', E 090° 59.967' (17,586 feet)
36. N30° 19.736', E 091° 00.175' (18,022 feet)
37. N30° 20.190', E 090° 59.678' (17,194 feet)
38. N30° 20.961', E 091° 00.334' (17,008 feet)
39. N30° 20.821', E 091° 01.899' (16,065 feet)

From base camp #6, within Nam Tso Park:
40. N30° 35.056', E 091° 06.350' (16,494 feet)
41. N30° 35.784', E 091° 05.382' (18,255 feet)
42. N30° 35.998', E 091° 04.991' (18,481 feet)
43. N30° 35.463', E 091° 05.079' (17,784 feet)
44. N30° 35.138', E 091° 05.185' (18,552 feet)

From base camp #7, in the Bhaknag area:
45. N30° 10.747', E 090° 41.557' (17,074 feet)
46. N30° 10.551', E 090° 41.458' (17,280 feet)
47. N30° 09.860', E 090° 40.773' (18,708 feet)
48. N30° 09.484', E 090° 40.552' (18,819 feet)
49. N30° 08.960', E 090° 40.768' (18,912 feet)
50. N30° 09.164', E 090° 41.178' (18,745 feet)
51. N30° 09.116', E 090° 44.595' (18,059 feet)
52. N30° 08.420', E 090° 44.927' (18,957 feet)
53. N30° 08.685', E 090° 45.244' (18,884 feet)
54. N30° 08.807', E 090° 45.437' (18,909 feet)
55. N30° 09.205', E 090° 45.302' (18,944 feet)
56. N30° 09.306', E 090° 45.335' (18,845 feet)
57. N30° 09.645', E 090° 45.293' (18,809 feet)
58. N30° 11.574', E 090° 42.457' (16,701 feet)
59. N30° 10.022', E 090° 42.082' (17,611 feet)
60. N30° 09.821', E 090° 42.737' (17,500 feet)
61. N30° 09.036', E 090° 42.187' (18,548 feet)
62. N30° 08.980', E 090° 42.541' (18,829 feet)
63. N30° 09.350', E 090° 42.534' (18,459 feet)

SEAN BURCH, *AAC*

NYANCHEN TANGLHA EAST

Access and potential climbing in the range between Lhari and Lake Basong. In November 2006 I trekked from Niwu to Punkar over the Laqin La, passing the highest and steepest peaks of the central range. The following information on access and climbing potential may be useful.

The unclimbed Jiongmudazhi (6,590m), Nyanchen Tanglha East, seen from the north. *Bruce Normand*

Access:

Niwu is currently accessible only "from above," i.e. from the Tibetan plateau, via a 110km drive from Lhari (Jiali). The last 50km of this road are closed by landslides in summer and are reopened during the latter half of October. However, they are in poor condition until repaired, usually in early November. Only Land Cruisers should be considered for this road before November, and one should allow two full days from Lhasa (one and a half by mid-November). It is promised that a much better road will be completed "from below," i.e. from Tongmi, in 2008, which would radically alter access to the area. The road from Lhasa directly to Lhari appears passable all the time, despite at least one high pass, and is far quicker than the northern route via Nagchu.

Nenang (6,870m), the highest unclimbed mountain in the Nyanchen Tanglha East, seen from above the Niwu Valley to the north. In 2006 British mountaineer Jim Lowther, with Americans Mark Richey and Mark Wilford, made an alpine style attempt on the east ridge but were stopped ca 300m below the summit by an enormous crevasse bisecting the crest. They retreated to their high camp at ca 6,200m in hopes of finding an alternative route, but after two days' bad weather and with all their food eaten, were forced to retreat. *Bruce Normand*

The road from Bahel (on the Lhasa-Bayi highway) is paved to Lake Basong; from the turn-off there are 53km on a relatively good dirt road to Punkar, with few of the problems of the Niwu road. The valley floor is flat, so there are no canyon walls causing landslides, but mud can be a problem in September and early October; thereafter, Lhasa-Punkar should be one long day's drive.

Once past the roadhead, the valleys are narrow and densely forested, which, combined with the hanging nature of the main valley, means many peaks have never even been seen. Every side valley I attempted to reconnoiter did have a reasonable grazing trail, but this may not be the case for some of the narrower, north-facing side valleys.

Logistics:

The people around Niwu are strange and not easy to work with. Generally, other Tibetans regard East Tibetans as rude, crude, and unhelpful. In Niwu these features are compounded by a special medicinal grass that grows well in the area, so the people are relatively rich. They are inundated every summer by traders (Tibetans, usually from Amdo and Kham), who are prepared to pay top dollar for their services. The current price is 100Y per day per horse and 100Y per horseman per three horses. A horse carries 50-60kg. There is no negotiation for anyone or at any time of year: apparently they would prefer not to work than to earn 80% of this amount during a period when they and their horses are otherwise idle. I suspect that there is a strong cartel system, and anyone violating it is penalized by other horsemen. However, if you pay the going rate, you will move 180kg (three horses) 16-20km up valley for around $50; this speed and price are difficult to match in Nepal. Horse prices may fall if the main road, and perhaps a drivable road from Niwu to Upper Niwu, is completed. On the plus side, the people neither steal nor beg, although like all Tibetans they crowd around a camp to see what the strange foreigners are doing and therefore have plenty of opportunity for both. As more foreigners enter the area, it would be good if these two attributes could be maintained, particularly as potential trekkers may be manifestly no richer than the traders.

Climbing:

The region contains a wealth of steep, spectacular, and unclimbed peaks. The monsoon comes in May and lasts until late October, so climbing activities involve, by necessity, wintry conditions. To date only Kajaqiao and Birutaso have been climbed, while Nenang and Chukporisum have been attempted. Other extremely inviting targets include Lumboganzegabo, Jiongmudazhi, and Chuchepo. The majority of the high peaks are guarded on their approaches by extensive icefalls, particularly on their northern aspects, and prospective climbers should budget their time accordingly. Climbing officially in the East Nyanchen Tanglha requires contacting the CTMA and paying a virgin-peak fee of $8,000 for everything except Kajaqiao and Birutaso (both climbed with permits in 2005), plus approximately $3,000 per climber for a guide/liaison officer and vehicles.

Unauthorized climbing is not an option for anyone approaching from Lake Basong, and probably not from Punkar. It did not appear that it would be a problem farther from the paved

Unclimbed peaks toward the head of the upper Niwu Valley, Nyanchen Tanglha East. *Bruce Normand*

road, where locals know little and climbers are generally in remote side valleys. However, this situation will not last. As has happened once already around Lake Basong, the first group of unauthorized climbers to be caught will cause a major clampdown, destroy the plans of all the expeditions aiming to go there the following season, and end up paying at minimum all of the costs they forgot to pay the first time. They may also be banned from China for some period and damage the livelihoods of the agency employees that provided their basic logistics.

Information:

The best information and sketch maps are available in the recent publications of Tamotsu Nakamura (see, for example, the article in *AAJ 2003* and the annual editions of the *Japanese Alpine News*). The summit heights in these sketches are based on Chinese maps; Russian military maps also exist. The maps are reasonable for general topography but poor for peak heights.

BRUCE NORMAND, *Switzerland*

KANGRI GARPO RANGE

Lhagu Glacier, ski expedition and probable first ascent of Pt. 5,928m. In the past our Silver Turtle Group, composed of elderly mountaineers, has climbed several 8,000m peaks. More recently we have been concentrating on unexplored regions, notably the Lhagu Glacier in the Kangri Garpo Range of southeast Tibet. The Lhagu has the largest surface area of any glacier in Tibet and appears to be retreating quite fast. We first visited the glacier in 2000 but were not able to progress very far up it. We returned in 2001 and 2002 but were still not able to make much progress due to poor conditions and soft snow. As we had only snowshoes and crampons, walking proved difficult.

In 2006 we planned to ascend the glacier on skis and finish our exploratory work. The expedition comprised Takeo Honjo (64, leader), Kaneshige Ikeda (67), Haruhisa Kato (62), Isamu Moriyama (67), and Hiroshi Sagano (61). We drove from Lhasa to Rawu via Bomi, finding the Sichuan-Tibet

The unattempted Pt. 5,480m on the Lhagu Glacier, Kangri Garpo Range. *Kaneshige Ikeda/Tamotsu Nakamura Collection*

The north face of unclimbed Pt. 6,006m on the Lhagu Glacier, Kangri Garpo Range. *Kaneshige Ikeda/Tamotsu Nakamura collection*

The north face of unclimbed Pt. 6,321m on the Lhagu Glacier, Kangri Garpo Range. *Kaneshige Ikeda/Tamotsu Nakamura collection*

highway vastly improved, with most of it paved. On October 21 we set up a temporary base camp near Dapa Bridge on the way from Rawu to Lhagu village. Three days with horses took us to a base camp at 4,730m on the moraine of the Lhagu Glacier, where the yak trails ended.

On the 27th we established Camp 1 at 5,200m in a crevassed zone of the glacier, and Camp 2 at 5,260m. All the time we followed the north bank; in 2000 we had tried to go up the south. Above Camp 2 we decided to split into two groups: one would try to reach the headwaters of the glacier, while the other would try some nearer peaks.

On the 31st we were blessed with fine weather (in the autumn of 2006 the weather in this region was much better than normal) and left camp at 8:30 a.m. Unfortunately, although the temperature had fallen to –10°C the previous night, the snow remained unexpectedly soft, and ski tracks were still 10cm deep. Ikeda and Sagano skied up toward the glacier head and, after identifying surrounding peaks from a point just before the watershed with the Midoi Glacier. Meanwhile Kato and Moriyama headed up toward the 6,260m peak of Hamokongga on the northern rim, a little farther west of Camp 2 and skied up a 5,928m peak called Snow Dome.

By November 2 all members had returned to base camp, having enjoyed continuously fine weather since arriving on the glacier. The following day, as we waited for horses, Honjo suddenly became ill. His breathing became difficult, and after 15 minutes he lost consciousness. After a further 15 minutes his pulse stopped, and he passed away. There had been no time to perform even emergency measures.

Several photographs accompanying this report show some of the unclimbed peaks on the southern rim toward the head of the glacier.

KANESHIGE IKEDA, *Japan*

Editor's note: The first team to reach the upper Lhagu Glacier and the only team to climb a peak prior to the Japanese was a group of New Zealand climbers in 2001. They also hoped to try one of the major peaks at the head of the glacier (the highest is Pt. 6,606m) but had to be content with Pt. 5,750m. The Japanese explorer Tamotsu Nakamura, editor of the Japanese Alpine News, was also in this area at the same time. He noted that Rawu Lake and the entrance to the Lhagu Glacier were becoming tourist spots, and an entrance fee of 20Rmb is collected from foreigners at Lhagu village. Nakamura and his party also visited the neighboring Midoi and Mimei glaciers, noting that the local government is developing the Midoi Glacier for tourism (there was a group of Chinese tourists on the glacier) and that the north faces of Gemosongu (6,450m) and Hamogongga (6,260m) were most impressive. The Mimei Glacier was surveyed by the Chinese Academy of Science in the 1980s, but only porters rather than animals are available for load carrying. Three 6,000m peaks were seen in the distance, but they were not particularly attractive. This was part of a greater journey that included treks toward the glaciers north of the Yigong Tso and, farther east, toward the mountains north of Bomi via the village of Yur, all in the Eastern Nyanchen Tanglha.

Himalaya

Xixabangma, new variant to normal north side route. On October 3 Inaki Ochoa de Olza reached the main summit of Xixabangma (8,012m) having made what is believed to be a new variant on the north face. The Spanish climber followed the normal route to Camp 3 (7,440m), the point where it climbs onto the final ridge leading up to the central summit (7,999m, Chinese map). From there he moved down and east, descending 150m before continuing his leftward traverse. He crossed a bergschrund and climbed to a rocky buttress, which he passed on the left flank via a step of UIAA III. He then continued up the northeast face (60°) to hit the southeast ridge at 7,950m, more or less at the same point where the 1982 British route emerges from the southwest face. From here it is a short distance back right to the summit.

Ochoa de Olza left Camp 1 (6,400m) at 1 a.m. and reached the main summit at 2 p.m. He has christened his 800m variant Lorpen-Diario de Navarra. Some years ago a Russian team left the standard route and climbed out onto the face below the summit, but this was rather higher and a completely different line. This new line avoids some of the problems that often occur with avalanche-prone snow high on the mountain, either in following the Chinese traverse or the sharp connecting ridge from the central to main summits.

Ochoa de Olza's solo ascent was the first to the main summit of the season, despite almost 100 climbers working on the mountain from the north. It is his 11th 8,000m peak and his fourth attempt to climb to the highest point of Xixabangma. He reached the central summit in 1995.

Lindsay Griffin, *Mountain INFO, CLIMB Magazine*

Palung Ri, south face. During my days spent acclimatizing for an ascent of Cho Oyu, I noticed a good line on the neighboring peak of Palung Ri (7,100m). I was working in this area as a guide, but bad conditions above 7,000m had confined us to base camp. The south face of Palung Ri is composed of steep snow and ice, interspersed with rock bands. It is not too difficult and offers good climbing in couloirs and mixed terrain. Higher up, the face becomes more open and leads to the summit ridge, where I found dangerous wind-blown snow and scary cornices.

I left base camp on the morning of September 19 and walked along the moraine to the bottom of the south face. I began climbing on rock and mixed terrain, with difficulties up to 4 and M4, and then continued up nice gullies with short steps of steep ice (80-90°). Difficulties were not sustained, just 10m of steep ground here and there in the long narrow couloir. Above this section the climb finished on snow and ice (50-60°) and became easier

The south face of Palung Ri showing Jan. After his ascent, the Spanish climber descended the west ridge (left skyline). *Jordi Tozas*

as I reached the summit ridge. I decided to descend the west ridge, as this led me closer to base camp, and the glacier at its base is not as crevassed as the one below the Palung La. I took only crampons, ice axes, energy food, and drink. I climbed alone and without a rope, completing the climb to the summit in a round trip of eight hours from base camp. I named the 900m route Jan. Although I had climbed solo in this style before, I had never done so in the Himalaya; it was a great experience.

JORDI TOZAS, *Spain*

Cho Oyu, shooting of Tibetan refugees. When shots rang out near Cho Oyu's crowded advance base camp on September 30, climbers ventured out to see what was going on. A professional photographer from Romania, Sergiu Matei, took his camera and was in time to film a queue of Tibetans snaking up the trail to the Nangpa La, the high pass into Nepal used every year by hundreds of Tibetans fleeing their homeland to join the Dalai Lama in India. His pictures show a line of unarmed Tibetans trudging uphill. Then a shot is heard, and a figure falls to the ground. Behind them can be seen Chinese border police, who had fired at their retreating backs. The figure was a 17-year-old nun, Kelsang Namtso, who had put up no resistance and died where she lay in the snow.

The first official Chinese account said the Tibetans had attacked the armed police, who were then forced to defend themselves. Later, her death was officially attributed to altitude sickness. A Czech expedition leader, Josef Simunek, who witnessed the shooting, told a pro-Tibetan organization based in Washington, "We felt as though it was 20 years ago during communist times in our country, when Czech soldiers killed Czech citizens in their escape over the Iron Curtain."

ELIZABETH HAWLEY, *AAC Honorary Member, Nepal*

Cho Oyu, southwest face to west ridge, partial new route. On October 2 the accomplished Slovenian mountaineer Pavle Kozjek soloed a partial new route to the summit of 8,188m Cho Oyu. Starting from an advanced base at 6,200m on the Gyabrag Lho Glacier, Kozjek soloed a new line on the southwest face, left of the existing Japanese and Swiss-Polish routes. Most of the 1,100m face gave snow and ice climbing at 50-60° but at ca 7,200m, near the exit, his way was barred by a steep ice fall, which the Slovenian avoided by climbing rock to the right (UIAA V-). At ca 7,300m he joined the 1986 Polish Route, up which he continued for the remaining 900m to the top, completing his ascent in a single push of 14.5 hours. After reaching the summit at 6 p.m., he descended to Camp 2 at 7,000m on the normal route. Next day he continued down

The summit of Cho Oyu (8,188m) on February 1977, as photographed from Emil Wick's Pilatus Porter. (1) West ridge complete (international team led by Krzysztof Wielicki, 1993; original west ridge by Poles, 1986). (2) Southwest face, Slovenian Route (Kozjek, solo, 2006). (3) Southwest face, Japanese Route (Yamanoi, solo, 1994). (4) Southwest face, Swiss-Polish Route (Kurtyka-Loretan-Troillet, 1990). *Jacques Belge*

to base camp, reaching it after a total of 30 hours. Kozjek's ascent marks the first time that a new route on an 8,000m peak has been soloed in a single push and in a day. His account of this climb, for which he won the People's Choice at this year's Piolet d'Or, appears earlier in the *Journal*

Hungchi, north face. A five-member party led by Toshiya Nakajima made the first ascent of Hungchi (7,038m) from the north in the autumn. The summit was reached by Naoyuki Momose and the leader on November 1. Hungchi, a border peak a little west of Everest, was first climbed in 2003 by a Japanese expedition from the Nepalese side. The same year another Japanese expedition attempted the mountain from the north, making a long approach from Everest base camp up the Central and Western Rongbuk glaciers. The team climbed the north face to a 6,600m col on the northwest ridge and then continued up the crest, partly on the Nepalese flank, before retreating 200m below the summit (see *AAJ 2004*, p. 426). It is not clear whether the 2006 ascensionists followed this route.

TAMOTSU NAKAMURA, *Editor, Japanese Alpine News*

Everest statistics and records in the spring season. The number of teams on Everest during the spring was 94. These ranged in size from one member with no Sherpa helpers to 29 members and 22 Sherpas. Perhaps surprisingly, the number of expeditions was five fewer than the 2005 total of 99, but it was actually larger on the Tibetan side during the spring of 2006, up from 57 to 64. On the Nepalese side there was a big drop, down from 42 to 30.

In terms of number of summiters, there was an even greater difference between the Tibetan and Nepalese sides. A total of 276 people went to the top from Tibet, not counting the possibility that David Sharp summited and died during his descent; his movements above 8,500m are not known. From Nepal only 192 people succeeded.

One explanation for the fall in numbers summiting from the Nepalese side was the worrisome situation created by the 10-year-old armed rebellion of the Communist Party of Nepal (Maoist) and its increasing use of force throughout the country. In addition, this spring's political unrest spilled onto the streets of Kathmandu and other towns nationwide, organized by conventional parties angered by the King's "autocratic" actions. It took the form of protest marches, public rallies, and general strikes, including bans on motorized travel. The international news media gave increasing attention to all this, and some expeditions canceled their plans to visit Nepal.

As usual, Everest records were set. They included the oldest summiteer and the first double amputee. On May 17 Takao Arayama, a 70-year-old Japanese, became the oldest climber—by three days—to reach the top, having climbed the Tibetan side of the mountain.

The first successful double amputee, 46-year-old New Zealander Mark Inglis, had summited two days earlier, also from the Tibetan side. There have been two single-amputee summiters, each of whom had lost a substantial part of one leg: American Tom Whittaker in 1998 and a Sherpa six years later. Both climbed from the Nepalese side. The first double amputee to try was an American, Ed Hommer, in the autumn of 2001, but when he reached 7,500m, he found the scar tissue on his left stump had cracked open in the dry air and was bleeding slightly. He abandoned the climb.

Twenty-five years ago Inglis had been marooned in a storm for two weeks on New Zealand's highest peak, Mt. Cook, and his badly frostbitten legs had to be amputated at mid-calf. His cleverly engineered artificial legs have the flexibility to enable him to handle technical climbing, but when he was going down the fixed rope early in his attempt on Everest this spring, an anchor pulled, he did a couple of somersaults and found himself sitting in the snow with one leg lying beside him. He got out some duct tape, did a field fix, and descended carefully to advanced base camp. A new leg was brought to him from base camp, and he went back up.

Inglis said he felt "huge satisfaction" at having summited Everest. "If you are a climber, as I have been all my life, the skills are already there. My problem is not going up but coming down. You have to be very careful; there is more wear and tear on the stumps." And indeed he got frostbitten. In his descent to advanced base camp on the day after his success, he was lowered by one his guides on his bottom and two days later reached base camp astride a yak. Back in New Zealand he underwent an operation on his stumps.

ELIZABETH HAWLEY, *AAC Honorary Member, Nepal*

Everest, cross-border traverses. Everest traverses seem to have become the latest fashion, with an unprecedented four successfully completed in the spring season. Three had received permission from both the Chinese and Nepalese authorities; one had not, but managed to get away with it—at a price, literally.

The Italian Simone Moro had no permit to make a traverse. According to him, he had intended to reach the summit from Nepal via the South Col, then descend the Tibetan north face via the Hornbein Couloir, move across to the west ridge and down the Nepalese flank into the Western Cwm, where he had left a camp. But, he claimed, he became lost in the moonless dark and had to follow the fixed ropes down the normal Tibetan route, pulling them out of the snow as he went. An Italian friend, who lives in Lhasa and speaks Chinese and Tibetan, met him in base camp and explained to the authorities, both there and at the nearest police post, how he had innocently gotten lost. The police sold him a pass that allowed him to cross the border into Nepal.

Others who were on the mountain at the same time point out that Moro had taken his passport with him, which is most unusual when climbing from Nepal. They also say there was a tent and an oxygen bottle labeled "MORO" placed by two Italians, Marco Astori and Roberto Piantoni, at 8,100-8,200m on the normal Tibetan route. His friend was already waiting for him at base camp when he arrived, but Moro had no satellite phone, so their meeting must have been pre-arranged. He had to pay $3,000 for his permit to cross the border.

Those who did have permits came from three other expeditions. The Swiss, Mario Julen, with Sherpa Da Nima, crossed from south to north. Korean Park Young-Seok and Serap Jangbu Sherpa, and at a different time Dawa Sherpa alone, traversed from north to south. Dawa rightly claimed a traverse speed record with his elapsed time of 20 hours and 15 minutes, verified by the leaders of teams he left on the north side and joined on the south side. He used two bottles of oxygen, starting at 8,300m during his ascent and finishing at 8,500m on the descent.

ELIZABETH HAWLEY, *AAC Honorary Member, Nepal*

Everest, deaths during the spring. "I imagine you guys are surprised to see me here" were Australian Lincoln Hall's words upon being discovered miraculously alive on the north side of Everest on May 26, after having been reported dead the day before. He was speaking to Dan Mazur and his party, who were on their way to the summit. "Can you please tell me how I got here? ... You guys on this boat too?" Mazur said that Hall was behaving like a three-old-year child.

Mazur's account of the rescue appears below but it took several days and reportedly at least 15 Sherpas and 50 cylinders of oxygen to get Hall to base camp. A yak took him the last distance because of his weakness and seriously frostbitten fingers and big toe. Mazur's summit party, knowing it was then too late to go for the top, turned around and went down to advance base camp.

Lincoln Hall at ca 8,550m on Everest's north ridge on the morning of May 26, after being discovered by Dan Mazur's party and revived with oxygen, warm tea, and food. *Dan Mazur*

The Hall saga is reminiscent of an incident during the disastrous spring of 1996, when the resurrected American, Beck Weathers, suddenly appeared alone at his camp on the South Col, saying, "It's great to be alive." Weathers was alive, but after having been out in the open for 20 hours at very high altitude and presumed dead when last seen. He was nearly blind and very badly frostbitten on his nose and the fingers of both hands.

Although Lincoln Hall did not die, eleven people did, making spring 2006 the second deadliest season on the great mountain (a dozen died in spring 1996). On the south side three Nepalese Sherpas, Lhakpa Tshering, Dawa Temba, and Phinzo, perished when a massive chunk of the notorious Khumbu Icefall collapsed on top of them. The remaining eight deaths occurred on the Tibetan side. A Russian, Igor Plyushkin, and a Nepalese, Tuk Bahadur Thapa Magar, succumbed to acute altitude sickness. German Thomas Weber died of a stroke. Two were killed in falls: a Swedish skier, Tomas Olsson, when one ski reportedly cracked while descending the Great Couloir, and an Indian soldier, Sri Kishan. And three died, as Hall nearly did, from exhaustion, exposure, and frostbite: a Briton, David Sharp, a Brazilian, Vitor Negrete, and Jacques Letrange from France.

There was much outraged commentary, including entries on mountaineering websites, about how as many as 30 people may have passed the dying David Sharp at 8,500m as they went for the top or descended from their summit bids. Their actions were depicted as heartless and reflected a supposed deterioration in climbing ethics due to the advent of large numbers of "amateurs" in recent years. But armchair critics can fail to take into account possible reasons:

* Many simply did not see him. It was a dark night, and headlamps focus on restricted areas. The day was cold, so passersby would have had hoods around their faces. Almost all were wearing oxygen masks, which limit viewing areas. Sharp was in a shallow cave, where he was difficult to spot.

* Some may have seen him but thought he was a long-dead Indian, the body of whom he was actually lying on top of.

* Others may have seen—even recognized—him and thought he was dead already.

Some climbers did stop and try to give him help. Turks tried, but they were occupied rescuing their own member and could give only limited assistance. Sherpas from other teams also tried, but they were themselves exhausted, and their oxygen supplies were running low. Sharp did not have a Sherpa helping him; he reportedly refused to have one. He wanted to climb alone, and so he did. It is extremely difficult to piece together his movements. He climbed alone and died alone.

Although reports of this kind of alleged callous behavior by climbers, all determined to fulfill their personal ambitions to get to the summit regardless of others' predicaments, made good newspaper stories, there were several instances in which "amateurs" sacrificed their own summit successes to help strangers in distress. The reaction of Dan Mazur's party when they came upon Lincoln Hall was not unique.

ELIZABETH HAWLEY, *AAC Honorary Member, Nepal*

Everest, the rescue of Lincoln Hall. At 7:30 a.m. on May 26 a team of four climbers comprising Andrew Brash from Canada, Myles Osborne from the UK, Jangbu Sherpa from Nepal, and I, an American living in Bristol, UK, were at 8,550m, about two hours from the summit of Everest via the North Ridge, when we rounded a corner at the "Mushroom Rock" and stumbled upon the Australian Lincoln Hall. He was sitting on the trail with his jacket around his waist, was wearing neither hat nor gloves, and was mumbling deliriously. He held his frostbitten fingers aloft like so many frozen, waxy, candlesticks. Our group found he was suffering from symptoms of cerebral edema, frostbite, hypothermia, and dehydration. He seemed generally incoherent in responses to offers of help and believed that he was on a boat ride. Apparently Hall had collapsed the previous day on his way down from the summit, and his commercially organized team, assuming he was dead, removed his oxygen, rucksack, and ice axe, taking it down the mountain.

We replaced the hat, jacket, and gloves that Hall had discarded, anchored him to the mountain, and gave him our own oxygen, food, and water. We then radioed his team and convinced the members that he was alive and must be saved. They took some persuading, which used valuable time, depleting our oxygen. Our team was small, compact, and lightweight with just one Sherpa. In contrast we discovered that Hall's team had around 30 members and 20 Sherpas. It took several hours for the team to agree to send up some of its Sherpas to help with the evacuation. For four hours we stayed with Hall, not wanting to leave, as we were unsure whether we might have to carry him down. By the time the Sherpa team arrived and took over life support, it was too late for us to continue toward the summit. With another member of our expedition, Phil Crampton from the UK, coordinating our movements from his location at the 7,900m high camp, and Kipa Sherpa acting as liaison to Hall's team at advanced base, we carried out the rescue. During the time we were trying to help Hall, several climbers passed by on their way to the summit. They declined to help in the rescue, saying they did not speak English. During the afternoon, as we worked our way down the mountain, we became engulfed by strong winds and a snowstorm.

DAN MAZUR, *AAC*

Everest, rescue of Lincoln Hall, Alex Abramov response. The leader of Lincoln Hall's expedition was the Russian, Alex Abramov, who in a reply to Dan Mazur's report above noted that Lincoln Hall began to have problems at around 10 a.m. on May 25 after having reached the summit. From that time until 7 p.m. four Sherpas who had accompanied Hall tried to help him down the mountain, descending from the "Rock Triangle" at 8,800m to the "Mushroom Rock" at 8,550m. Bringing him down the Second Step alone took four hours. During the day, as the news reached Abramov, he sent two more Sherpas, carrying oxygen, from advanced base to the top camp at 8,300m. Eleven more Sherpas were sent to the North Col (7,000m) to further assist in the rescue of the stricken climber, should it become necessary. With each hour Hall's condition became worse; he didn't move and finally stopped speaking. His breathing was reported to be very bad. It came as little surprise to Abramov when his Sherpas radioed down at 7:30 p.m. to say that Hall had died. That evening the two Sherpas reached the top camp and organized rescue of their four compatriots higher on the mountain, who were now extremely tired (and two were already snow blind).

At 7 a.m. next day, when Abramov was radioed by Mazur to say that Hall was still alive, the Russian asked the six Sherpas, who were still at the top camp, if they could climb up and help with the rescue. Only two were fit enough to go. He then asked the 11 Sherpas at the North Col to climb to the Second Step, using expedition oxygen so they could move as fast as possible.

At 9 p.m. Hall arrived at the North Col, where he was met by expedition doctor Andrey Selivanov, who attended to the casualty through the night. The following day the Sherpas brought Hall down to advanced base, where he spent two more nights under doctor's supervision, before being carried by yak to base camp. Abramov admits there was a wrong diagnosis by his Sherpas but feels that at the time Hall must have been close to death. Fortunately, the night was unusually warm, the Australian got some rest and a bit of sleep, and by the following morning had improved slightly. It was lucky that Mazur found him in time.

From notes provided by ALEX ABRAMOV, *RUSSIA*

Everest, post-monsoon attempt on the north face. There was one post-monsoon expedition to the Tibetan side of Everest: three strong and highly experienced Spaniards, Alberto Inurrategi, Ferran Latorre, and Juan Vallejo, who had a total of at least twenty-three 8,000m summit successes to their credit. They took no Sherpas, no oxygen bottles and no rope to fix on their chosen route up the steep, never-ending north face via the Japanese and Hornbein Couloirs. They were just three men equipped with their mountaineering expertise and motivation.

First they acclimatized on the normal route from Tibet, climbing to the North Col at 7,000m. They then went to a 5,900m camp at the bottom of the north face. They started their summit push on September 30 in alpine style and after three bivouacs had reached the Hornbein Couloir. Here, on October 3 at 8,200m, Latorre stopped, not feeling strong. However, his teammates carried on to 8,500m, where the Hornbein opens out. At this point Vallejo felt his strength ebbing, and Inurrategi turned back with him, not wanting to continue alone—and "maybe I was beginning to get tired too," he said. They seemed satisfied with what they had accomplished. "We made a good push," Inurrategi commented.

ELIZABETH HAWLEY, *AAC Honorary Member, Nepal*

Everest, new fees and restrictions on climbers. International publicity about the Nangpa La shooting led some journalists to see it as a factor in the Chinese authorities' decision to place restrictions on teams going to Everest in spring 2007. But the Chinese Mountaineering Association's formal announcement, distributed in November to trekking agencies in Kathmandu, made it clear that the cause was actually related to the 2008 Olympic Games in Beijing and China's plan to take the Olympic torch to the summit of Everest, before running it in relays to the Beijing stadium.

A covering letter from the secretary of CMA's Exchange Department, Li Guowei, to one Kathmandu agent said, "We have some temporary measures to limit the climbers in 2007 and 2008." However, at least part of what is now billed as temporary is expected to become permanent, according to a CTMA official in an interview during December 2006. He estimated that the number of teams in 2007 could be half the number in spring '06. Asked whether any teams besides the official 50-member expedition would be permitted in 2008, he replied, "I don't know."

The official explained that during the coming years the rules will gradually be tightened. Improving the quality of expeditions on the mountain would be implemented in 2007 by including a requirement that climbers have mountaineering skills; some do not possess these when they arrive at base camp. Expeditions would also need to be equipped with walkie-talkies and other safety-enhancing equipment. Although he did not expand on this topic, it might mean that agents will no longer be able simply to obtain a climbing permit and then sign up a collection of independent climbers who have never met and who don't even speak a common language.

The requirement that all Everest climbers must have been to 8,000m previously will disqualify a lot of would-be Everesters, especially those who would normally join a "collection." A significant percentage of the hundreds of people who go each year to nearby Cho Oyu, which is the least difficult of all the 8,000ers, do so as a run-up to an Everest attempt. But many of them turn back before reaching the magic altitude of 8,000m and thus will not be considered by the CMA and CTMA to be fit to attempt the Tibetan side of the mountain.

The rules from 2007 onward may be a boon to the government of Nepal, which charges a steep fee for climbs on its side of the mountain. They will certainly be effective in reducing crowding at campsites and at the ladder placed beside the Second Step, and in eliminating the quasi-competent men and women wanting to be able to boast back home that they have climbed to the highest point on earth.

The cost increases in Tibet were spelled out soon after the initial notice. They add $1,000 to the current $3,900 per foreign climber, $500 more to the $1,700 payable per climbing Sherpa and $300 more to the $1,100 per kitchen staff worker. Despite these increases, the rates will still be substantially below Nepal's permit fees, although numerous unexpected charges keep being added to the total cost in Tibet.

ELIZABETH HAWLEY, *AAC Honorary Member, Nepal*

Chomo Lonzo North, southwest face to summit ridge.
Although we left Kathmandu on April 15, it was not
until the 24th that I arrived at my 4,750m base camp
below Chomo Lonzo. There had been so much snow
on the approach that in places I had to break a waist-
deep trail for the yaks to follow. The depth of snow also
promised much hard work establishing my proposed
advanced base at 5,900m below my goal, the unclimbed
west face of Chomo Lonzo (7,790m). Most mornings
were sunny, but at midday the clouds rolled in, and by 3
p.m. it was snowing. I eventually managed to get all my
equipment to the higher camp on May 2 and the following day made an attempt on the west face. On my second attempt I reached 6,600m and realized that this year
I was not going to climb the face. Steep glassy ice led to
smooth slabs of yellow granite. I estimated it would take
me around six or seven days to reach the summit, and
there were few places for even a sitting bivouac.

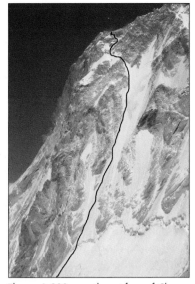

The ca 1,200m southwest face of Chomo
Lonzo North (7,199m) showing the line of
Little Prince, which terminated on the summit
ridge at 7,100m. *Valeri Babanov*

Back at advanced base I came up with an alternative idea: a new route to Chomo Lonzo North (7,199m).
The southwest face rose from the glacier on which my
camp was situated, and right of the summit fall line was
a prominent steep ice couloir topped by a rock barrier. The face was ca 1,200m high, and there
seemed to be several options through the upper cliffs to gain the summit ridge. Two routes had
been climbed to this summit in 2005 by a French expedition. My proposed line looked logical
and safe, and being mostly ice could be climbed fairly fast. I planned to spend no more than two
or three days on the route and therefore did not take much food.

I crossed the bergschrund at 7 a.m. on the 16th with two 60m ropes, a hammock tent,
light sleeping bag, gas stove, and jacket. As the top part of the route would require climbing
rock, I also had Friends, stoppers, and pitons. It all came in handy, especially on the descent. I
was able to climb unroped until ca 6,400m, after which the ice became harder and steeper and
I needed to haul my 15-16kg sack.

Above, my protection in the couloir was rather symbolic: two screws per belay and for most
of the time nothing in the intervening 60m. As normal, it began snowing at 2 p.m. By 9 p.m., I
had reached the rock band at ca 6,800m and then during the remaining minutes of daylight, I
managed to gain another 30m of height in a rock and ice couloir. I never did manage to find a
comfortable spot for a bivouac. Half-sitting, half-lying, I survived that night without sleep.

I estimated that it should take me seven to eight hours to reach the summit, so I took only
bare necessities. However, by 8 p.m. not only was I not at the summit, I had not even reached the
summit ridge. There were times when the steep ice was as hard as granite. In darkening twilight
I climbed the final rope length to the ridge. It was 9 p.m. and a voice in my head said, "That's it,
enough, stop! You are already at the limit. Go down." I did not resist. I descended to my bivouac
site then on down the couloir, reaching the glacier at 5 the following morning, crazy with thirst.

My route, Little Prince (1,100m, TD+ M4), joined the existing French route on the ridge
connecting Chomo Lonzo North and Central at ca 7,100m, and most likely the top section

of Unforgiven, the mixed route on the west face climbed by Stéphane Benoist and Patrice Glairon-Rappaz (*AAJ 2006*, pp. 35-45). It took a round trip of 47 hours from advanced base. This may not be a long time in real terms, but by the intensity of the experience it could hold several years of a lifetime.

VALERI BABANOV, *Canada*

Chomolhari, north face, and Chomolhari, northwest pillar. A Slovenian expedition comprising Rok Blagus, Tine Cuder, Matej Kladnik, Samo Krmelj, Boris Lorencic, and Marko Prezelj, accompanied by a doctor, Damijan Mesko, established base camp at 5,000m below Chomolhari, a 7,326m peak on the remote Bhutan-Tibet border. For acclimatization the team first climbed three peaks of 5,700m-5,800m on side ridges above base camp and then turned to the north face of Chomolhari II (Tserimkang or possibly Jangmo Gopsha, 6,972m on the Chinese map), which they climbed up the left side via a line between seracs, with short 60° sections. This brought them to the east summit, which is around 50m lower than the west summit. In mid-October, Blagus, Cuder, Kladnik, and Krmelj reached the summit of Chomolhari by a new route toward the left side of the north face, a steep snow-and-ice couloir that they climbed in four days roundtrip from base camp. The couloir led to the upper section of the east ridge, which they followed to the summit on the 14th (1,900m, TD+ 80°). At the same time Lorencic and Prezelj climbed the magnificent and much-eyed northwest pillar in a six-day round trip from base camp, reaching the summit on the 15th. Prezelj led every pitch (1,950m, ED2 M6+ 80°). All routes were climbed in alpine style. Prezelj's account of this expedition appears earlier in the *Journal*.

The view east along the Tibet-Bhutan border from Chomolhari (7,326m). The route marked was first climbed by a Slovenian team in 2006 as acclimatization for more difficult ascents on Chomolhari. It leads to the previously unclimbed Chomolhari II East (ca 6,920m). The higher west summit is 6,972m. The lower (triangular sunlit) summit just left of Chomolhari II East is Pt. 6,706m, also unclimbed. A little further back and to the right is the unclimbed Kungphu (6,532m). A line of smaller summits continues along the border toward Masa Kang (ca 7,200m), climbed by Japanese in 1985. *Marko Prezelj*

Mongolia

ALTAI MOUNTAINS

Huiten, a.k.a Khuiten Uul, first winter ascent of north ridge. On the winter solstice, December 22, Graham Taylor and I summited Huiten (4,374m), the highest mountain in Outer Mongolia. Taylor had made two previous winter attempts, in 1999 and 2000. Both were unsuccessful due to severe cold and weather conditions. Both of us have now been resident in Mongolia for over six years, Taylor as a director of an adventure tour outfitter and I as an exploration geologist.

Huiten or Khuiten Uul, meaning "Cold Mountain" in Mongolian, is located in the extensive Altai Range in the northwest corner of Mongolia. The Altai Range spans over 1,500km, emerging from the pebbly plains of southwest Mongolia's Gobi desert and running along the Mongolian border northwestward into Siberian Russia. Huiten is the highest point in the Tavan Bogd (Five Holy Peaks) sector of the Altai, a dense cluster of alpine peaks that contain a compact but complex system of glaciers. Huiten is located only 3km south of the ice-dome summit of Naraimdal Uul (Friendship Peak, 4,184m), the geopolitical triple point where Mongolia, Russia, and China converge.

The first ascent was completed in 1967 by Russians, and later most of the surrounding significant peaks were climbed. Because of the remoteness of the Altai frontier and the extremely cold climate, it was only in 1998 that Huiten was climbed in winter. This ascent took place via the southeast ridge (*AAJ 2003*).

We chose to climb the mountain by the north ridge, which connects with Naraimdal Uul via a north-south trending ridge and col. Following a 15km snowshoe approach (the snowline was 2,400m), we established a base camp along the margin of the Potaniin Glacier's northern-flanking lateral moraine. Our ascent route continued westward up the central longitudinal axis of the Potaniin Glacier. Crevasses on the middle slopes of the glacier were mostly covered with hard, wind-packed snow that presented no significant hazard. The moderate (30-40°) slopes on the upper glacier contained more complex terrain, including open and partly buried crevasses and sections of hard ice that required more diligent route-finding. From the upper glacier we traversed southwest and gained the north col, which connects directly to the summit ridge. On the narrow corniced col we swapped our snowshoes for crampons, in preparation for ascending the north ridge to the summit. The ascent up the 45° hard, snow-packed north ridge took one and a half hours. From the false summit located on the southwest part of the summit ridge, we traversed another 15 minutes to the true summit. Visibility from the north col to the summit was limited by blowing snow driven by a winter storm. Summit conditions included temperatures of -20°C and were accompanied by gusts exceeding 100 km/hr. A rapid descent was necessitated by the conditions. Including the 15km approach from the Tavan Bogd National Park entrance, we completed the climb in a 30-hour alpine-style push, beginning on December 21. The ascent from base camp to the summit took 11 hours and the descent back to base camp a further five hours. The overall grade was PD+.

Taylor's third winter attempt resulted in the first winter ascent via the north ridge, the second winter ascent, and the first ascent on the shortest day of the year, when there is only eight hours of daylight.

GREGORY LEONARD, *Ulaanbaatar, Mongolia*

New Zealand

AUTUMN 2006-AUTUMN 2007

Mayan Smith-Gobat during the first free ascent of Shadowlands (27), Sinbad Gully Headwall, Fiordland. *Craig Jefferies*

Derek Thatcher on the fourth pitch (24) of an as-yet-unnamed 11-pitch route on the upper Kaipo Wall, Darran Mountains, Fiordland. *Craig Jefferies*

The Darran Mountains, summary. The alpine and rock climbing region of the Darran Mountains (Fiordland) continues to be the area of New Zealand that is generating the most climbing news and new routes of note. In late 2006 the New Zealand Alpine Club published Craig Jefferies' new guidebook to the Darrans. The guidebook's 312 pages capture more than a decade's worth of new route activity since the last edition, as well as revealing the enormous scope for new climbs that this region still provides.

A Hillary Expedition grant from the Government organisation SPARC enabled a group of (mostly young) and highly motivated individuals to make some major first ascents this summer. The "Rock Solid Progression" team of Kester Brown, Craig Jefferies, Paul Rogers, Mayan Smith-Gobat, and Derek Thatcher pooled their talents to make the first free ascent of Shadowlands (27) on the remote Sinbad Gully headwall, near Mitre Peak. This sustained 300m route has multiple pitches of hard climbing, including three of 27 and two of 26.

Following this, they helicoptered onto the Ngapunatoru ice plateau and rappelled into the isolated 1,300m Kaipo Wall, adding the first new route since the 1974 first ascent. The team rappelled to a shelf at the base of the upper wall, placing bolt belays, and then Smith-Gobat and Thatcher climbed back out via 11 pitches of varied and often difficult, committing climbing up to grade 25. The first ascent of the Kaipo Wall was made by Graham Dingle, Mike Gill, and Murray Jones, who reached the base from the Hollyford River by raft, kayak, and foot. The three then climbed the entire 1,300m face from the valley floor via a prominent corner/ramp in the upper section. The crux pitch was 17.

Early in the summer Smith-Gobat and Thatcher teamed with the 2006 CMC/Macpac Mountaineer of the Year, Jonathon Clearwater, for a quick and inspired first ascent on the northwest face of an iconic Darrans mountain, Sabre Peak (2,162m). Tora Tora Tora (24) takes a direct line up the face right of the Original Line and was established on sight, ground up and with no fixed protection. It is the first new route on the face in over 20 years.

Closer to the climbing base at the Homer Hut, a four-pitch project on the Mate's Little Brother was completed to give the hardest alpine free climb in the Darrans: Armageddon (21,

28, 28, 25). This powerful route climbs directly through the Second Coming roofs and was redpointed by Stefan Hadfield and Derek Thatcher.

The Barrier Face (Gertrude Valley) saw a new five-pitch line established 200m right of Joker by Sam Bossard and Al Ritchie. Scrabble (18, 18, 20, 18, 22) was bolted and climbed over several days. Late March saw two new routes added to the northeast face of Barrier Knob by Kristen Foley and Mark Watson. Utu (25, 22, 24) is the hardest line on Barrier Knob and features intricate slab and face climbing, while Forgotten Silver (16, 18, 20) climbs a sweep of nicely featured rock. Both routes were bolted and climbed over four days.

New route activity continues at Babylon with the pace driven by Bruce Dowrick and Jon Sedon. Attention has recently turned to the reportedly Arapiles-like Little Babylon, a very promising cave above Babylon. A number of new routes were completed.

MARK WATSON, *New Zealand Alpine Club*

The upper half of the isolated 1,300m Kaipo Wall in the Darran Mountains. The as-yet-unnamed 11-pitch route climbed in 2006 is marked. The only other route on the wall climbs its full height, finishing up the prominent rightward sloping ramp. *Derek Thatcher/NZAC*

Queenstown region, summary. Winter saw the development of Cigar Creek in the Eyre Mountains as an ice climbing venue. A few new routes were established. Johnny Davison and Rupert Gardiner made first ascents of Kapa O Panga (WI 5) and the Cold Light of Day (WI 4+), the latter reportedly fell down soon after being climbed! Davison and Andy Mills climbed Balloons and Knives (WI 4), with Mills taking a huge whipper off the top of the route, narrowly missing the ground. Dave Bolger climbed a potentially classic 60m moderate, Divine Symmetry (WI 3), and a second route he named Hybrid (WI 3+). In South Wye Valley Adrian Camm and Mal Haskins put up Bush Lawyer (WI 4), while in great early season conditions Bolger and Rupert Gardiner climbed a new route on the southwest face of Double Cone in the Remarkables. The route follows mixed terrain and is called Warthog.

MARK WATSON, *New Zealand Alpine Club*

Barron Saddle – Mt. Brewster Region, summary. With plums still to be picked, this extensive and remote mountain tract between the Aoraki Mt. Cook and Mt. Aspiring areas has seen continued activity from a motivated few. Guidebook author Ross Cullen teamed up with Nick Shearer to make the first ascent of the East Ridge of Mt. Hiwiroa (2,281m), a seven-hour scramble. Paul Hersey with various partners has made number of notable first ascents. During winter he climbed The Grr Room (WI 4, four pitches) with Mat Woods on Peak 2,200m. Also during the winter Kester Brown and Jono Clarke climbed a very obvious thin ice flow at the head of North Temple Valley: Temple of Doom (M6 WI 4). New ice routes were also climbed in Bush Stream, off the Aoraki Mt. Cook Highway.

Hersey's name pops up again, this time with Graham Zimmermann. The pair made a first ascent on the south face of Taiaha Peak. The classic-looking line was named I've Found Cod (500m, 4+ WI3). In February 2007, Hersey, this time with Danny Baille, headed into the Ahuriri and climbed a 700m new route on the south face of Mt. Huxley. Hey I Ordered a Cheeseburger (4- 16) followed rock most of the way, with a mixed section at the top. The same pair also made the first ascent of the east face of Peak 2,237m in the west branch of South Temple Valley. This gave a 400-500m rock route with a crux of 14 (3+ overall). On Glen Lyon at the entrance to the Hopkins Valley, Hersey with Mat Woods climbed Vote For Hillary, a six-pitch 15. Glen Lyon now has a number of multi-pitch rock routes on its flanks.

MARK WATSON, *New Zealand Alpine Club*

Aoraki Mt. Cook and Westland, summary. The Aoraki Mt. Cook region has been particularly quiet in terms of new route activity or ascents of harder routes, suggesting that there are less people heading into the mountains for hard climbing, or that they are direct-ing their focus elsewhere. Perhaps it's to the Westland névés, as this region is seeing increased activity and busier huts. The pop-ularity is probably due in part to the relative ease of access to routes once climbers are based at a hut, and the scope for technical and mixed climbs.

The west face of Lendenfield (3,194m) in the Aoraki Mt. Cook region. Marked is the line of the 2006 route, The Mutant (6+, Robinson-Uren-White). *Adventure Consultants/Mark Watson Collection*

Winter at Aoraki Mt. Cook saw an ascent of the east face of Mt. Sefton (3,151m) via the Direct Route by Jon Loeffer, Andrew Rennie, and Graham Zimmer-mann. During August a new mixed route was climbed on the southwest face of Conway Peak (2,899m): Life in the Fridge was completed by Johnny Davison and Allan Uren, and was graded 4.

Also on Conway peak but later in the season, Uren com-pleted his project, The Vision, at a grade of 6+ A1 mixed. The route had thwarted previous attempts due to marginal climbing and a scarcity of protection. Uren finally succumbed and placed two bolts on lead at the crux. In the process he may have pointed the way for future ascents in the region with bolt protection.

In contrast to this style Uren then climbed a long and sinuous mixed route named The Mutant (6+) on the west face of Mt. Lendenfeld (3,194m). The ascent took place in December with Tim Robinson and Julian White. Uren said, "the lower five pitches contain some of the most sustained and difficult climbing I've done up there, and some of the most aesthetic."

Canterbury climber Guy McKinnon has once again been showing his drive for daring solo ascents. In September he made the first ascent of the 1,400m north face of Hochstetter Dome (2,827m). This was one of New Zealand's largest remaining unclimbed faces. In January 2007 he completed an oft-looked-at line, an 800m buttress on Mt. Whataroa (1,988m), which is visible from the West Coast Highway. It's great to see the adventurous spirit of first ascents in New Zealand's mountains being retained with stylish ascents like McKinnon's.

Back over the Divide, Steven Barratt and Daniel Joll climbed a new route on Nun's Veil in the Liebig Range (east Tasman Valley): Curb Your Enthusiasm (4+) takes a line up the southeast buttress.

MARK WATSON, *New Zealand Alpine Club*

Canterbury region, summary. A couple of new alpine routes were climbed in the Canterbury mountains. Guy McKinnon, alone again, climbed a new 350m route on the east face of Mt. Evans (2,620m), while Don French and James Wright climbed a new route up the southeast face of Mt. Franklin (2,145m) in the Arthur's Pass National Park. The eight-pitch route is graded 5-.

MARK WATSON, *New Zealand Alpine Club*

Central North Island, summary. Richard Thomson's new guidebook to the Tongariro National Park may have kicked off some fresh enthusiasm, or maybe it was the good early season conditions. Either way some great-looking ice and mixed routes were climbed last winter. In the Mangaturuturu Cirque, Kester Brown and Jono Clarke climbed Free Radicals (WI 5), The Glass Spider (M 4), Pope's Pillar (WI 5), and Strung Out (WI 5). On Puggy's Buttress on the southwest face of Matiaho, Clarke climbed Scratch and Win (M5).

MARK WATSON, *New Zealand Alpine Club*

AMERICAN ALPINE CLUB GRANTS

Fall 2005 and Spring 2006

The American Alpine Club provides resources for climbers and explorers to attempt new challenges, conduct scientific research, and conserve mountain environments. The AAC gives out more than $35,000 annually, although the size and number of awards vary from year to year. In 2006, the Zack Martin Breaking Barriers Grant was awarded for the first time; this grant goes to an expedition that combines a serious climbing objective with a humanitarian mission. For more information on all the grant programs, please visit www.americanalpineclub.org.

Grant recipients' original objectives are reported below; in some cases, they may have decided to attempt other objectives. Expeditions labeled with an asterisk (*) are reported in this *Journal*.

LYMAN SPITZER CUTTING EDGE AWARDS (2006)

Mike Libecki, Salt Lake City, Utah*
Attempts on new routes in remote valleys in Uzbekistan and Kyrgyzstan
$2,500

Will Mayo, Northfield, Vermont*
Attempt on new line on the south face of Mt. Foraker in Alaska
$1,500

Mike Schaefer, Snohomish, Washington*
Attempt on the direct east face of Uli Biaho in Pakistan
$5,000

Josh Wharton, Rifle, Colorado*
Attempt on the north ridge of Shingu Charpa in Pakistan
$3,000

MOUNTAIN FELLOWSHIP AWARDS (FALL 2005)

Michael Buchanan, Salt Lake City, Utah
Attempts on new routes on Peak 11,300' and the northwest face of the Rooster Comb, Alaska
$800 (John R. Hudson Fund)

Adam Fruh and Aaron Thrasher, Bozeman, Montana
Attempt on the south face of Kichatna Spire, Alaska
$900 each

MOUNTAIN FELLOWSHIP AWARDS (SPRING 2006)

Alison Criscitiello (Winchester, MA) and Jessica Drees (Seattle, WA)
Climb the three highest peaks in Ecuador
$500 each (REI Challenge Fund)

Elena Mihaly and Jeremy Roop, Colorado Springs, Colorado
Attempt on a new route in the Cirque of the Unclimbables, Northwest Territories, Canada
$800 each (REI Challenge Fund)

Mark Thomas, Berkeley, California
Attempt on a new route on Peak 11,300' and ice lines on the northwest shoulder of the Rooster Comb in Alaska
$700 (Boyd Everett Jr. Fund)

Tim Tormey, Fort Collins, Colorado
Attempt to link the North and South Howser Towers in Canada's Bugaboos in a push
$800 (REI Challenge Fund)

Dave Turner, Sacramento, California*
Major objectives in the Cordillera Blanca of Peru and Paine region of Patagonia
$600 (Rick Mosher Fund)

2006 RESEARCH GRANTS
*The Arthur K. Gilkey Memorial Research Fund,
the William Putnam Research Fund, and the
Bedayn Research Fund*

Tana Beus, Bellingham, Washington
*Decline of mountain goats in their historic
range in the North Cascades*
$400

Keith Bosak, Boone, North Carolina
*Mountain tourism, information technologies,
and women's empowerment in the Nanda Devi
Biosphere Reserve, Garhwal Himalaya, India*
$500

Monica Bruckner, Bozeman, Montana
*Biochemical changes in alpine catchments in
response to glacial retreat*
$1,000

Teresa Chuang, Berkeley, California
*Species shift as a result of climate change in
the Sierra Nevada*
$1,000

Adam French, Missoula, Montana
*Analyzing local livelihood needs and crafting
strategies for community-managed protected
areas in the Cordillera Huayhuash of Peru*
$500

Will Mayo wondering just what his Lyman Spitzer Award
has gotten him into on Mt. Foraker. *Maxime Turgeon*

Jason Gulley, Richmond, Kentucky
*Subglacial and englacial conduits of the
Matanuska Glacier, Alaska*
$500

Micah Jessup, Blacksburg, Virginia
*Updated high-resolution map of the
Everest region*
$1,000

Sarah Laxton, Cincinnati, Ohio
*Reconstruction of late Holocene glacier activity
in the Lahul and Garhwal Himalaya, India*
$1,000

Koren Nydick, Silverton, Colorado
*Alpine plants in the San Juan Mountains of
southern Colorado and their response to
climate change*
$600

Kurt Refsnider, Madison, Wisconsin
*Glacial and paleoclimate history of the Sangre de
Cristo Range, Colorado*
$600

Clint Rogers, Piedmont, California
*Subsistence trade in the borderlands of
Nepal-Tibet*
$1,000

ZACK MARTIN BREAKING BARRIERS GRANT (2006)

Adam French, Missoula, Montana
*Attempt on the east ridge of Huantsan in
Peru's Cordillera Blanca and construction of
a composting toilet in the Ishinca Valley in
Huascarán National Park*
$2,500

BOOK REVIEWS

EDITED BY DAVID STEVENSON

The Boys of Everest: Chris Bonington and the Tragedy of Climbing's Greatest Generation. CLINT WILLIS. NEW YORK: CARROLL AND GRAF, 2006. BLACK AND WHITE PHOTOS. 535 PAGES. HARDCOVER. $27.95.

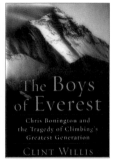

I confess my initial reaction to hearing the title of Clint Willis' latest offering was something along the lines of, oh god, do we really need another book about Chris Bonington and company? After all, in the four decades since the publication of Bonington's *I Chose to Climb*, he has been nothing if not prolific as a chronicler of his own climbing career, amassing a pile of titles that includes such classics of expeditionary narrative as *Annapurna South Face* and *Everest: The Hard Way*. And many of the "Bonington Boys," the cohort of British climbers who accompanied him to the Eiger, Annapurna, Everest, Changabang, and elsewhere in the 1960s, 70s and 80s, have offered their own accounts of the accomplishments of what Willis terms "climbing's greatest generation," ranging from Dougal Haston's terse *In High Places* to Pete Boardman's lyric *The Shining Mountain*. And, if all that doesn't suffice, we also have Jim Curran's fine 1999 biography, *High Achiever: The Life and Climbs of Chris Bonington*.

But it turns out there is room for at least one more book about Bonington and his mates. Willis, whose many publishing credits include editing a series in which several of Bonington's expedition books are reprinted, is a knowledgeable student of recent mountaineering. He proves himself equally adept at discussing innovations in climbing technique and the manufacture of climbing celebrities—both considerations equally relevant to a discussion of Chris Bonington's significance to mountaineering history.

If you don't happen to have the collected works of Chris Bonington close at hand, and want an abbreviated compendium of his greatest climbs, *The Boys of Everest* is an excellent substitute. Willis' writing has a breathless you-are-there quality that puts the reader next to the climber on the mountain's face as he tackles one challenging pitch after another, with occasional forays on the part of the author into the climber's mind and emotions. "Chris felt surprisingly strong this morning," Willis writes of the second day of Bonington's first ascent of Mount Blanc's Central Pillar of Frêney in 1961, in the company of Don Whillans, Ian Clough, and Jan Dlugosz. "[I]n any case, he planned on aiding the crack. He did so by taking pebbles from the back of the crack, and wedging them into place, then threading slings around the pebbles. That done, he clipped his etriers—the loops of webbing that could serve as awkward steps—to the slings and then stood in the steps to gain height." Note the effortless insertion into the text of that critical bit of technical arcana, the definition of etriers, without breaking narrative stride.

Willis offers an equally astute assessment of Bonington's emergence as the public face of British mountaineering in the 1960s, a process which received a powerful boost from a BBC television special devoted to his climb of The Old Man of Hoy in Scotland's Orkney Islands:

"The broadcast, aired live in the summer of 1967, was a huge hit—perhaps the most widely watched climbing film since the one that documented the 1953 first ascent of Everest. Chris—with his youth, his upscale accent and his earnest desire to appeal to his audience—made an especially pleasing impression on the millions of viewers who tuned in." Bonington was not the only one of his contemporaries with telegenic charisma. As Willis notes, Dougal Haston was often compared to one or another sixties pop-star. Unlike Dougal and so many of his contemporaries, however, Bonington was not given to pub-brawls. As a result, there was a knighthood in his future, while it's inconceivable there ever would have been a Sir Dougal.

The Boys of Everest is both entertaining and enlightening. I am bothered by only two aspects of the book. One is Willis' decision to present us with the final moments of the many Bonington Boys who died while climbing. "He made a mistake and he is ready to forgive it, but there is no apparent need," Willis writes, for example, of the moment after Mick Burke broke through a cornice on his descent from Everest's summit in 1975, and plunged thousands of feet downwards toward the Kangshung Glacier. "He's grateful for that, but he is distracted. He is swimming in a blue, blue light—it reminds him of something—and the snow keeps falling; the flakes touch the ocean and vanish." Well, perhaps. Or perhaps all he experienced was stark terror. We'll never know, and it would have been better, more tasteful certainly, not to go there.

The other problem lies with the notion offered in Willis' sub-title, but never really explained or justified in the book, that his subject is "climbing's greatest generation." How could any meaningful definition of "greatest" exclude the generations of Himalayan climbers who made their reputations from the 1930s through the 1950s—Eric Shipton, Bill Tilman, Raymond Lambert, Herbert Tichy, Ricardo Cassin, Walter Bonatti, Hermann Buhl, Lionel Terray, Charlie Houston? When the Bonington Boys climbed Annapurna by its South Face in 1970 they changed the calculus for the possible in Himalayan climbing. But was theirs a "greater" achievement than the original ascent of the mountain in 1950, the first time an 8,000-meter peak had ever been climbed? As Bonington himself noted in *Annapurna South Face*, with the generosity to predecessors that characterizes his books, "when Maurice Herzog and his team arrived at the foot of Annapurna in 1950, their biggest problem was finding a route onto the mountain. We didn't even need a map to find ours." As far as determining degrees of greatness goes, Sir Isaac Newton said it best back in 1676: "If I have seen further it is by standing on ye shoulders of Giants."

MAURICE ISSERMAN

The Wall: A Thriller. JEFF LONG. NEW YORK: SIMON AND SCHUSTER, 2006. 294 PAGES. $24.00.

Midway through their lives' journeys, two former Camp 4 dirtbags, Hugh and Lewis, find themselves in a dark wood at the base of El Cap; the forests and walls of their youth now transformed into a macabre dreamscape, complete with a prophesizing wildman, witches and mysterious screams—a tangle of savage birds, lost souls, nightmares and menacing visions. This Dantesque vision rises out of the modern-day setting with a seamlessness that proves, once more, Jeff Long's ability to forge a sense of authentic myth—and in the process to tell a gripping story.

Readers of his cult novel, *Angels of Light,* will recognize certain familiar elements: a motley cast of climbers and rangers; a mystery that draws its protagonists high up the cliffs and deeper into an atmosphere of impending doom. Yet this new novel takes the same preoccupation with lost innocence and karmic retribution onto a far more ambitious scale—at times reminiscent of *Moby Dick,* the Old Testament, Greek tragedies, the paintings of Hieronymous Bosch, and the tradition of medieval allegory, in ways both strangely beautiful (as in the glittering deluge of insects descending on El Cap after a forest fire) and not so subtle (just in case the reader misses these allusions, Long is careful to offer reminders, such as "The Ten Commandments drama of plague and apocalypse grew tiresome, and finally ugly").

The rest of the prose's delicacy, however, makes up for any occasional heavy-handedness. The climbing scenes are so deeply woven into psychological story that the borders between the characters' internal and external worlds fade; when Hugh desperately searches for holds as he tries to make a second ascent of a new El Cap route, the suspense becomes not only whether or not he will fall, but also what he will learn about the first ascensionist by uncovering her line. Appropriate to a book about crossing boundaries, Long's imagery becomes most poignant in moments of transition and metamorphosis: the air cooling from gold to blue the instant a climber realizes she's falling to her death; the face of a woman's corpse turning from rose to gray when a man touches her shoulder; the strands of a rope unfurling as they break: "Fifty feet overhead, right where it bends from sight, the rope bursts into flower. It happens in a small, white explosion of nylon fibers. It looks like a magician's trick, like a bouquet springing from a wand."

For the novel's characters, each in his or her own way tragic, such beauty might be the only consolation, an all-too-brief, and dangerously seductive, burst of light before darkness falls. The aging Hugh and Lewis, in an effort to recapture their youth, start back up their most legendary first ascent and become involved, instead, in a perilous rescue attempt. As they climb higher, the threads of the plot tighten around them, until they begin to wonder whether they've been drawn into some plan of ghostly vengeance.

By the time the reader gets to the end, he or she realizes that behind each word and act lays the author's impeccable design, an exquisite and deliberately contrived plot. This ornate artifice provides both some of the delight and the potential frustration of reading the book. "We didn't ask to be part of this," one character protests about the sequence of events. Perhaps the book's greatest unanswered question is why so many people's fates would be arranged around one man's punishment. Maybe all climbers are somehow implicated because our pursuit takes us into forbidden realms, bringing our unconscious close to the surface, encouraging our hubris, feeding off our much-cited personal demons. Or maybe it's simply that in the book's self-proclaimed genre as a "thriller," no one is innocent, no one is safe. The ultimate message of ghost stories might be why we're so drawn to them: being haunted is better than facing a complete void. As he struggles up the wall, Hugh thinks, "If he could finish this thing and get to the top, then the smoke would part and the floor would be revealed and he would surely be able to read his own fate."

Haven't each of us hoped for such adrenaline-induced epiphanies, at one time or another, and most often in vain, as we've started up some climb, full of our own existential questions? With *The Wall,* Long has firmly established himself as the voice of our subculture's collective unconscious, invoking images that continue to haunt, long after the shivers of reading have subsided.

KATIE IVES

Note: The Wall won the Grand Prize at the Banff Mountain Book Festival 2006.

Strange and Dangerous Dreams: The Fine Line Between Adventure and Madness. GEOFF POWTER. SEATTLE: THE MOUNTAINEERS BOOKS, 2006. 8 PAGES OF BLACK & WHITE PHOTOGRAPHS. 245 PAGES. $22.95 HARDCOVER.

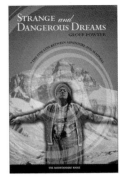

A bit of ancient wisdom has it that no matter how far the freedom-seeker travels, he always carries his own chains with him. This venerable insight is amply confirmed by Geoff Powter's extraordinary book, which consists of eleven elegantly written case histories of grim adventuring, ranging from Meriwether Lewis to Guy and Johnny Waterman. Although the term "case history" accurately describes these pieces, it comes nowhere close to conveying the mesmerizing narrative force of Powter's prose. As the author explains in his introduction, "everyone in this book has been called 'mad.'" The lives of these haunted souls are not to be read as profiles in courage but as proverbs of pixilation. Powter—a psychologist with a clinical practice in Canmore, BC, and editor of the *Canadian Alpine Journal*—is uniquely positioned to make this distinctive contribution to mountaineering literature.

Certainly every adventurer who has ever paused to reflect has confronted the question of what constitutes acceptable risk versus what is just plain crazy. Unfortunately for the men and women whose lives are examined in this book, none had the inclination or opportunity to engage in any therapeutic soul-searching; instead they threw themselves into—and *against*—the world. The inevitable result was tragedy. "In each of these stories," Powter tells us, "darkness of some kind—ambition, ego, a thirst for redemption, the need to please others—carried these characters in a perilous direction." When it comes to stories in the annals of adventure that involve tragic death, very few are untainted by some kind of controversy. As both psychologist and mountaineer, Powter feels a special responsibility to offer explanation to those outside the adventuring community who look askance upon risky activities: "I was convinced that there were right and wrong adventures, but I often found it a challenge to explain the difference to non-adventurers who often saw any voluntary risk as a sign of stupidity or lunacy." Thus he selected stories of individuals in whom "the line between adventure and madness is less distinct," figures such as Robert Falcon Scott, Jean Batten, and Earl Denman. The dismal destination of these tortured souls was the same, only the routes they chose varied.

For alpinists, the exemplar case in the book is perhaps that of Maurice Wilson, a shell-shocked survivor of the bloody trenches of Flanders in World War I. Wilson was a man who took post-traumatic stress to new heights—by concocting a scheme to become the first to ascend Everest. The plan entailed landing a plane on—or more precisely, crashing it into—the higher slopes of the peak. Then he would just hop out and scoot to the top. To the chagrin and horror of contemporary climbers, Wilson was quoted in the newspapers as saying: "All you need to climb a mountain is a tent, a sleeping bag, warm clothing, food and faith." That this man had no mountaineering experience nor indeed any particular interest in mountains prior to coming up with his cockamamie idea only adds absurdity to the apparent insanity. But as Powter so aptly phrases it, "Wilson's story is a perfect illustration of how so many aspects of any risky adventure start to look abnormal when judged through the narrow perspective of 'normal' safety-conscious lives." To nobody's surprise, Wilson's plans were grounded by the colonial authorities in India, but this did not stop him from sneaking off and walking the long distance to the base of the peak and then making a pair of solo attempts, the latter ending in his death. That second attempt has been a source of much speculation over the years as to whether Wilson was in fact bent on suicide. "The crux of Wilson's tale," Powter explains, "lies in whether his return to the mountain was truly a dedicated last shot, or more honestly a sad resignation to fate—as though he simply ended the journey by going up rather than down." In the end, such profoundly disturbing questions must remain unanswered, and Powter's great strength as a writer is to defer from any psychological vandalism, leaving undisturbed the inner recesses of a human heart racked with suffering.

There is no denying the pain and melancholy that seem to throb from the pages of this book. Yet, as Powter summarizes it in his epilogue, "the best way to understand how the mind and body work is to observe illness or dysfunction; the stories of what went *wrong* here might offer clues to what goes right in the best cases." For readers who prefer stories of triumphant ascents, *Strange and Dangerous Dreams* will be a real downer. But for those who agree with Socrates that the unexamined life is not worth living, this book should offer genuine hope and immense reading pleasure.

JOHN P. O'GRADY

Note: Strange and Dangerous Dreams received the Special Jury Mention Award at the Banff Mountain Book Festival 2006.

The Climbing Essays. JIM PERRIN. GLASGOW: THE IN PINN, 2006. 8 PAGES OF BLACK AND WHITE PHOTOS; 6 OF COLOR. 320 PAGES. HARDCOVER. £18. $44.95.

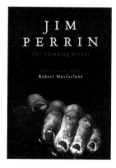

In *The Climbing Essays* Jim Perrin has collected nearly 40 years of essays, 60 of them in all. I cannot think of a book in our literature that can match it for depth, elegance of language, clarity of vision, or its sheer, yet somehow modest, brilliance. Robert Macfarlane contributes a fine introduction to the volume, reminding me that his *Mountains of the Mind* (2003) surely deserves another read. Perrin introduces the essays with a dozen "Autobiographical Sketches" covering about 20 pages—the effect of which is of reading a book-length memoir—it's intimate and gorgeous, a deeply textured fabric against which the climbing will be counterpoised.

In keeping with Tim O'Brien's dictum that great writing should be greeted with a kind of "holy silence" perhaps I should stop now before I make any noise that might distract anyone from the book itself. Another strategy might be to just extract a dozen passages from these essays and let these speak for themselves. Or just one, for example, this from "Adventuring on the Lllewn" (1991):

"We dawdled around, drank more coffee, and towards midday sauntered out of the house. This may have been a mistake. We were setting off on a miserable December day to drive for the best part of an hour to do a 700-ft route with a complex and frightening approach, difficult route-finding, seven or eight pitches, poor belays. All this, as you know intuitively at the time, adds up to the trap closing behind you. But you carry on because to commit yourself to it brings into play a primal reliance on your own resources that's close to the essence of why we climb."

This is plain writing but it has the great virtue of honesty, not to mention a stated purpose: to strike towards "the essence of why we climb." I think all Perrin's essays do this, sometimes overtly and sometimes slyly, wherein "climb" and "live" and "love" are either metonymic, or indistinguishable, or all one thing. In fact, this passage may not "typify" Perrin's prose style, which often employs elevated diction, literary references, and British place names— all of which I find very appealing. I am reading, after all, to learn something of what I don't know, not merely to have my own observations   confirmed.

Having never climbed in Great Britain, I only recognize a handful of routes by name; *Cenotaph Corner* and *A Dream of White Horses* come most readily to mind (yes, they appear in these pages). Thus, Perrin mentions dozens of climbs, climbing areas, and persons that are unknown to me—it's like some marvelous fictional world and works as a purely literary achievement.

Macfarlane astutely notes that "(Beinn A'Chaoruinn and) The Vision of Glory" is a great essay in which Perrin best articulates the transcendental moments he experiences in the mountains. Perrin tells us: "I do not know how you can adequately describe these moments and their effect on our lives." About their effect on our lives he says: "Our essential life, the joy-life, is a sequence of these moments." And later: "The moments seem to come more easily in the mountains." He is equally "adequate" in describing the moments themselves. Along the way he cites Wordsworth and Shipton, and it's a reasonably clear literary lineage that may be extrapolated. In other essays we are unsurprised to learn of his admiration for Murray and Tillman, and for his prose style, the great essayist, William Hazlitt.

Perrin's own favorite among his work is "Vision and Virians" about climbing on the sea cliffs of west Britain with his son Will, then 15 years old. This is the essay he chose for inclusion in Pat Ament's excellent and undervalued *Climber's Choice* (2002). At the time, both 1995 when he wrote it and when he selected it, he could not have known that Will would live only a few more years. Nonetheless, Perrin observes near the end of the essay: "For me, it is both a pleasure and painful responsibility to see him habituating to this environment of deadly beauty in which so many of my friends have died." Its companion piece, "Will" (2004) is Perrin's funeral address for his son, an expression of love and broken-heartedness that is miraculously free of self-pity and sentimentality. I felt honored its author would share it with me.

In "For Arnold Pines," an essay first written in 1979 and revised for broadcast in 1993, Perrin invokes Montaigne: "ever since I can remember nothing has occupied my imagination more than death...." Yet, his is not a morbid fascination. "You can scarcely disagree," he says, "that the risk of death is indissociable from the thrill of climbing." It's not so much that climbers would disagree, rather, many would pretend it were otherwise. What Perrin understands is that "In great danger, there is great joy." Two sides of a single coin spinning on a tabletop.

After the "Autobiographical Sketches" the book is separated into three sections: "Climbs," "The Climbers," and "On Climbing." Each section is imbued with elements of the other two. Add to this that the pieces are not ordered chronologically, but rather "plotted." The effect is recursive—I felt like I was always being returned back into the book, which felt to me like an inexhaustible universe.

Although *The Climbing Essays* was awarded the Jon White Award for Mountain Literature at the Banff Mountain Book Festival in 2006 it has, as of this moment, yet to find a North American publisher. This seems a shameful commentary on the state of publishing here, where the market rules and editors pander to the reading public's lowest common denominator. The

climbing world is small and somewhat insular, given to value what may ultimately lack significance. We need Perrin's vision—expansively human and literate—to awaken us to what climbing,
love, and life might be.

DAVID STEVENSON

K2: The Price of Conquest. LINO LACEDELLI & GIOVANNI CENACCHI.
SEATTLE: THE MOUNTAINEERS BOOKS, 2006. 124 PAGES. 30
BLACK & WHITE PHOTOS. $16.95.

Was there ever a large climbing expedition that did not spew out
rancor, *ressentiment* and the whine of wounded pride in its wake?
Perhaps, but damn few. For a display of the very worst in human
nature that mountaineering can bring out, surely none tops the Italian
first ascent of K2 in 1954, whose summiteers were Achille Compagnoni and Lino Lacedelli. The chief whiner in this sordid opera has
been the much-calumnied Walter Bonatti. From his efforts to clear
his name, and correct a false official narrative, the climbing community
has learnt something of this climb's internal politics. And now there is
more, much more—courtesy of the US publication of *K2: The Price of Conquest* (first published
in Italy in 2004 to mark the 50th anniversary) in which Lacedelli now purports to tell all.

   One cannot get very far into this book before questioning Lacedelli's credentials as a
truth teller. In the half century since his climb, he has not merely stuck his head in the sand.
He mutely supported many untruths promulgated by the late Compagnoni and Ardito Desio,
the martinet leader, even in joint press appearances. But the trouble is that mani pulliti (dirty
hands) cannot be washed clean with the assertion that "I went along to get along." Even on the
mountain, out of range of the universally hated Desio, where Lacedelli was the stronger and
more talented, on the pre-summit day he uncomplainingly deferred to Compagnoni's decision
to locate their tent where they were at needless risk.

   Of his long history of lacunae and evasions, he says "Sometimes I confirmed things even
when I knew they hadn't happened exactly like that" in the first minute of the interview with
Cenecchi that is the heart of the book. Why? That is the enigma. Here is a sport that is supposed
to build character, and what we have is a gentle giant who tolerated scores of others' falsehoods
by making himself invisible when truth cried out to be heard—not a morally edifying sight.

   In the end he is of some help to Bonatti's version of the metanarrative. He confirms
Bonatti's picture of the events on the pre-summit day, but insists, contra Bonatti, that the summiters ran out of oxygen before topping out. (Sorting out this and other domains of conflict,
agreement, and speculative reenactment is beyond the scope of this review.)

   "Ripeness is all," declaims one of Shakespeare's heroes. Alas, Lacedelli's chronic lack of it
cannot, as he doubtless now imagines, be compensated for at this late date. Nor by the character
assassination of Desio and Compagnoni. As Bad Guys they are worse than I'd imagined, real
villains. But Lacedelli is a bad guy of a different, yet no more savory kind, the empty suit.

JOHN THACKRAY

To the Ends of the Earth: Adventures of an Expedition Photographer. Gordon Wiltsie. New York: W.W. Norton, 2006. Hardback. 224 pages. $35.00.

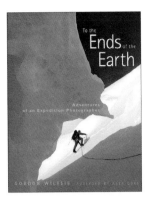

Gordon Wiltsie's *To the Ends of the Earth* is a merry carnival of destinations, a shiny ride that spins readers through the globe's far-flung mountains. Wiltsie's book will please you as a glittering photographic tour, though it may disappoint as a sustained narrative. Gordon Wiltsie's career from Bishop climber to *National Geographic* regular makes him a perfect writer for a book like this, and WW Norton Publishing has come through with first-rate reproductions. This book offers insight into both sides of the camera—the places in front of the lens, and the man behind it.

To the Ends of the Earth opens with a biographical chapter called "Getting Started" which details Wiltsie's early Bishop climbing days, and his formative acquaintance with mountain legends Galen Rowell and Doug Robinson. Not surprisingly, Wiltsie's photo career started with shots of climbing trips, and progressed to what he defines as "Expedition Photography." That means a "complicated exploratory endeavor that may be very expensive, involves years of planning, and involves risks far beyond what most people would consider acceptable." And those endeavors and that risk fill the rest of the book's nine chapters.

First and foremost, this is a book of cool photos. Wiltsie's chapters take us to the Arctic, to Baffin, to Nepal, to the Antarctic, to Mongolia and Peru and Chile and Nepal. It's a wild ride. And beyond the photos, Wiltsie's ambition is to "step out of the shadows" and be recognized as "a full-fledged team member" on these hard expeditions. Every climber and wannabe Shipton will love the photos; whether Wiltsie deserves varsity status as an explorer and climber each reader can decide. One thing I know, it's very hard to climb peaks and also get good photos. So full credit to anyone who can do either. If it's only a rare talent like Galen Rowell who can do both at the highest level, then all the more reason to appreciate the clear colors and careful framing in Wiltsie's photography.

If the volume has a shortcoming it lies in the narrative, which is presented, in staccato bursts of information. I suppose the point really is the photographs, but I do like the writing best where it sustains a point of view and develops instead of describes characters and situations. Unfortunately, much of the book reads like *National Geographic* captions stitched together—informational but superficial.

On the plus side, Wiltsie emphasizes that photography is much more than a mirror to the physical world. Photography is a series of choices that shapes, frames, and even manipulates that world. Therein lies the art, and therein lies a particular power for the modern photographer. You see, on this threatened planet people need a reason to care about places and creatures beyond their own lawns. Wiltsie's lens and doughty explorations make him one bridge between ourselves and these other places and other beings. I'm reminded of John Muir and the Preservationist ideal of getting people into the wild so they can see for themselves, and then become caring wilderness defenders, too. In Wiltsie's case this guiding hand is extended through his photography. That environmental desideratum is made real with the presence of great spirits like Alex Lowe who appears throughout the volume to remind us that climbing's joy is connected to the places and the people that host it.

To the Ends of the Earth is a collection of powerful photographs from beautiful places. If you're looking for a treasury of crisp images, and some understanding of the hand that holds the camera, well this is the book for you.

JEFF MCCARTHY

No Shortcuts to the Top: Climbing the World's Highest 14 Peaks. ED VIESTURS AND DAVID ROBERTS. NEW YORK: BROADWAY BOOKS, 2006. 368 PAGES. $23.95.

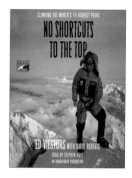

The old adage about bold climbers and old climbers is hackneyed jargon to most of us, but in Ed Viesturs fascinating account of his quest to climb the fourteen 8,000ers (without bottled oxygen), few sayings have rarely been as apropos. Himalayan climbing legends typically seem to get away with seemingly impossible feats on a diet of sheer balls and superhuman willpower—at least from the public's vantage. *No Shortcuts to the Top* undermines that notion by describing how one extremely careful mountaineer managed to climb all fourteen peaks, but did so within his own, very healthy, margins of safety.

The story begins with a truly hairy account of Viesturs' 1992 ascent of K2, and describes a heroic effort by Viesturs and Fischer to rescue the late Chantal Maudit and Thor Keiser from high on the mountain. His subsequent climb to the top with Fischer and Charley Mace introduces the reader to Viesturs' notion of "acceptable risk"—a theme that is repeated, quite appropriately, throughout the rest of the book.

From there, the story jumps back and gets real, so to speak, and describes Viesturs' upbringing in the Midwest and his subsequent collegiate life, as well as the on-again off-again life of a guy trying to fit a professional career into the climbing life (eventually climbing wins). As a Rainier guide, "acceptable risk" became a theme in Viesturs' life, as did his adage "getting down is mandatory."

Through the 1990s, as Viesturs juggles work and climbing more and more 8,000ers, the tale becomes, honestly, more and more frightening as super-safe Ed watches the many accidents, illnesses, mistakes, and deaths that are, literally, waiting around every corner.

At one point he even lists a handful of his early '90s climbing partners and friends, commenting, sadly, that they'd all since died.

The final section of the book includes a white-knuckle series of attempts on Annapurna, from the north, from the east, from the north again. While Viesturs' own obsession with the mountain is quite a story, he weaves it together with the haunting Annapurna-obsession story of the late Jean-Christophe LaFaille, one of his partners on the east ridge.

One of the best parts of *No Shortcuts* deals with a story about an article on Viesturs written for *Men's Journal*, and the author of that piece, who was, apparently, something of a statistician. Viesturs describes the writer's theory of risk on high mountains ("…[he] had counted up all the members of all the expeditions that had gone to 8,000-meter peaks and divided them by the number of deaths on those expeditions…"), and then goes on to explain that so safety conscious was Viesturs' own approach to mountaineering—one nurtured by years as a Rainier guide—that the numbers simply didn't apply.

Take a chapter from Ed if you ever need to explain the risk/safety equation of mountaineering to a critic. But don't forget the underpinning lesson: this sport is dangerous and only an individual can assess his or her own vulnerability in life-threatening situations.

Pete Athans once told me "you can't believe your own press releases." That's clear here, and Viesturs clearly is a man who knows what the headlines are, how many are true, and what the real story is. This is a humble, honest book by one of the world's greatest mountaineers—the best thing is he just happens to be a real person, too.

CAMERON M. BURNS

World Climbing: Images from the Edge. Simon Carter. BLACKHEATH, NEW SOUTH WALES, AUSTRALIA: ONSIGHT PHOTOGRAPHY AND PUBLISHING. 2005. 192 PAGES; 230 COLOR PHOTOS. $40.00.

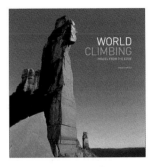

What makes a climbing photo a stunner is not necessarily the climber. Rather, the texture and color of the rock can make for images that transcend the conventional shot. Simon Carter has done a superb job portraying such textures in this lavish coffee-table book of climbing photographs. For example, take a look at the bizarre formations of seaside Thailand. Or the marvelous conglomerates of Riglos, in Spain. Or the sheen emanating from the slate quarries of Wales. Or the gray and gold limestone of the Verdon. Such images make one want to rush to such places on the next flight, to climb or simply to gaze upon such fascinating geology.

Had this book been published thirty years ago we would have been astonished at the lush colors, the pristine reproductions, and, of course, the dramatic climbing. Nowadays, sad to say, the glossies that arrive every month or two are full of almost identical images. I think most of us who look at this book will say: I've seen these before. This, of course, is not Carter's fault. It's simply to say that there's not much new in climbing photography. It appears to have hit a dead end (perhaps it's the same with surfing, skiing, and skydiving?).

We see overhangs surmounted by the obligatory topless men with Popeye muscles. We see 17 photos of the photographer's lithe girlfriend (but why not?). We see some world-renowned climbers: Lynn Hill, Chris Sharma, Leo Houlding, and Alex Huber. We see obviously staged shots, many dozens of them, though Carter claims, "I do not ask climbers...to adopt a particular pose." We see the familiar shots taken from rappel, looking down, and slightly off to the side. Perhaps I am jaded. A youth just beginning to climb will be mesmerized by these images; this would be a dream gift for such a person.

Carter has certainly traveled the world in his quest for photos. Australia is represented by the Grampians, Mount Arapiles, the Blue Mountains, and Tasmania (where the photos of Lynn Hill and Nancy Feagin on the fearsome Totem Pole are among the best of the book). Canada is under-represented, as is New Zealand. Croatia, Spain, France, Thailand, and the UK, among other countries, are featured. The United States is allotted 35 pages (about the same number given to Australia), highlighting Yosemite, the desert spires and cracks, Red Rocks, and the Bishop boulders. It's a bit odd that only three states are represented. You would think Carter might have visited the Tetons, Eldorado, the Gunks, the fabulous gorges of the Southeast, or many other places in this varied country of ours. But to feast our eyes on so many worldwide locales is well worth this lapse.

STEVE ROPER

Note: World Climbing received the Mountain Image Award at the Banff Mountain Book Festival 2006.

Three Cups of Tea: One Man's Mission to Fight Terrorism and Build Nations–One School at a Time, GREG MORTENSON AND DAVID OLIVER RELIN. NEW YORK: PENGUIN, 2006. BLACK AND WHITE PHOTOS. 338 PAGES. $25.95.

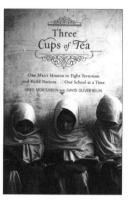

Three Cups of Tea tells the compelling story of Mortenson's struggle to help the world. Mortenson had been a fairly active and committed climber until he embarked, almost by chance, on what at first cynical glance would have seemed like a Quixotic undertaking. Retreating from a profoundly discouraging attempt on K2 in 1993, Mortenson barely makes it out the Baltoro Glacier alive. Essentially alone and lost, he is overwhelmed by the kindness and concern shown him by Balti porters and villagers. He resolves to personally build a school for a remote and abysmally poor and powerless village in Pakistan.

One has no difficulty understanding why Mortenson was profoundly moved by the village's children going through the motions of attending school without teachers, crouched outdoors in the dirt of the high and harsh Karakoram. But then most good people similarly moved would return to the "real" world. They might go as far as contacting a Pakistani official of some sort to alert him to the plight of the Balti people, and then at home they might look to see if there wasn't already some existing governmental organization dedicated to funding schools for poor people. If we are talking about really good people, they'd devote themselves to digging into the problem until the bureaucratic impossibilities utterly defeated them and they'd go on with their lives.

Mortenson's approach turns out to be radically different and refreshingly backward. Returning to Berkeley and the Bay Area, he transitions rather easily from being a climbing bum to living in extreme frugality so as to save up the $12,000 that he has determined will build a school in remote Pakistan. Mortenson writes letters to famous people he doesn't know, asking for money… which might not strike you as being an especially unique practice in this day and age, but when he also sells his precious climbing gear and his mountaineering books to help make his target, you begin to understand his devotion to his goal. He doesn't bother talking to anyone in either the US government or the Pakistani government and it is clear that in his mind it has nothing whatsoever to do with such irrelevant entities. He is totally focused on a simple way to improve the lives of others and so he doesn't bother to seek permission to do so.

It won't spoil your enjoyment of the book to learn that Greg Mortenson succeeds in building not just one school, but dozens. He becomes the director of the Central Asia Institute, finds funding and more funding and devotes himself absolutely to building schools and helping the rural poor in Pakistan and eventually Afghanistan. Most amazingly, he learns the languages and customs and is accepted and beloved by people that most Americans are terrified by. When, inevitably, he runs afoul of those that disagree with his desire to educate Muslim girls in his schools, the dreaded "Fatwas" are issued and instead of running for cover, Mortenson and his growing cadre of Pakistani allies successfully challenge the edicts in the upper levels of the conservative religious institutions that most would assume could never favor an American infidel.

When the attacks of September 11, 2001 take place, the world focuses intently on the very places and peoples that Mortenson has devoted himself to. The book reminds us of how clear it was back in the days when we were dismantling the Taliban in Afghanistan that such a vacuum could not be left once again to be exploited by Al Quaida and the fanatics. Of course, as a nation, we were going to rebuild Afghanistan and prove to those people just how genuinely good Americans could be. But in following Mortenson's struggles to do just that, on a shoestring budget and with little or no official assistance... it becomes clear that the moment was missed. Outside of Kabul, "aid" turned into security expenditures and other wars. Mortenson went on alone anyway, "fighting terrorism" by caring for people. If this idea is sometimes overstated in the book and comes across as too simplistic, then compare it to the prevailing simplistic idea that terrorism will be ended when enough terrorists are killed.

Climbing turns out to be a backdrop to the great stories this book tells, but climbers shouldn't be overly concerned with the minor mountaineering specific flaws that proofing missed. It is hard to imagine that any climbers would not want to take great pride in what one of their own has accomplished. The book's title, "Three Cups of Tea," refers to a traditional approach to bringing strangers into the close-knit mountain communities that many of us have passed through on our way to summits. Most of us don't drink that first cup. Too much salt and yak butter and third world in it ... but we like and respect the people just the same, don't we? Greg Mortenson drinks the tea ... and he eats the weird food, and he sleeps in the dirty beds, and crowds in with unwashed poor people and he wears the clothes and messes up his life in order to make a real difference.

It isn't like the rest of us are going to give up our mountains to do all that, but I'd be surprised if, after reading *Three Cups of Tea*, that you won't want to reach out and help the guy by simply scratching out a check. Even if you don't want to save the world, the book just makes for great reading. It is well plotted, honest, avoids preaching and is set in the rugged mountains that we all dream of visiting.

Dave Hahn

Note: This is the second review Hahn was written for the AAJ and sent electronically from Everest Base Camp.

An Eye at the Top of the World: The Terrifying Legacy of the Cold War's Most Daring CIA Operation. Pete Takeda. New York: Thunder's Mouth Press, 2006. Hardcover. 304 pages. $26.95.

Of all the idiotic things the CIA has dreamed up in its half-century of existence, dragging a nuclear-powered listening device to the top of a remote Himalayan peak in order to spy on the Chinese may top the list. Not surprisingly, this Cold War operation involving Indian and US spooks and elite climbers repeatedly failed with potentially devastating effects for future generations. While the CIA will neither confirm nor deny what transpired high in the Nanda Devi region some four decades ago, a missing load of plutonium, hidden in the belly of a glacier, is likely crawling ever closer to the Ganges River where it will no doubt wreak unimaginable havoc.

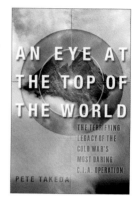

Takeda stumbled upon what he calls "the most bizarre and unheralded espionage escapade of the Cold War" around a Yosemite campfire. As Takeda describes in the opening chapters, pursuing this rumor grew into an obsession. Leaving his job behind, Takeda dove headfirst into a three-year process of research and writing on this elusive Cold War subject. *An Eye at the Top of the World* is the final product of this long journey. While Takeda's writing is superb, making the book extremely gripping and entertaining, the work unfortunately suffers from an organizational drawback.

Contrary to what the title suggests, the book is not focused exclusively on the CIA operation, but in fact dedicates more space to Takeda's journey in pursuing the story. In the first half of the book, Takeda manages to weave the narrative between these two parallel subjects. The reader learns about the intricacies of plutonium and the global conditions that lead the US and Indian governments to believe that this outrageous operation was in their interest. Intertwined with this are the confessions of a professional climbing bum with the ability to "squander so much money on such an obscure passion." At times the connections and transitions between these two subjects are fluid and logical; other times they are forced.

The opening chapters set the scene for the second half of the book, which one would expect to contain a culmination of both the CIA story and Takeda's personal story. It fails to reach this dual crescendo, however. The CIA story is increasingly eclipsed in the second half of the book by the gripping account of Takeda and friends' climbing and near-death experience. While superbly written, especially the harrowing description of being repeatedly buried by avalanches high on Nanda Kot—a section that leaves the reader gasping for air—the connections to the purported main subject of the book are almost completely absent from the last 100 pages, including from the epilogue. This is a weakness of the book, leaving the reader with the feeling of having read two books.

Nevertheless the book is well worth a read. Takeda has done his homework and clearly commands the facts. His second chapter, "A Cold War," is a first-rate sketch of the complicated and ever-changing Cold War international landscape. Equally compelling is his chapter on plutonium. In both of these chapters, which are on par with exposés by the most distinguished foreign correspondents, Takeda proves himself a master of his craft. Furthermore, Takeda's honesty pervades the work. His is not afraid to be critical, especially of himself. This becomes most evident in the chapters covering his expedition to Nanda Kot and Nanda Devi East, which radiate with lucid self-reflection.

It should be noted that the intended audience is the average layperson, and mountaineers may find several parts of the book unnecessarily descriptive or drawn-out. Everything from belaying to living in base camp is explained in painstaking detail. This must be forgiven, of course, since it is a necessary component of a book aimed at a wider crowd. In writing to this audience, it is clear that Takeda is concerned with setting himself apart from your average weekend mountaineer. He employs the terms, "elite," "hard core," "tribe," and so on, to describe his climbing circle. Although it is surely warranted for Takeda to avoid being compared to the novice mountaineers encountered in certain "epic" books, some readers may find that he crosses the fine line between useful clarification and condescending elitism.

Regardless of these shortcomings, the book is extremely insightful and entertaining. It is a genuine page-turner. Takeda's writing strikes a refreshing balance between erudite and clear, factual and entertaining, humorous and solemn. The fact that the connection between the CIA operation and Takeda's own experience is sometimes lacking—again, in many cases it is not—does not diminish the appeal of the individual tales. Certain readers, caught up in the adventure and beautiful language of the book, may not even be bothered by the fact that the focus is sometimes blurred. Others, such as this reviewer, may get hung up on it. Either way, in no other work will one discover such memorable mountain wisdom as why buying a single wall tent is like buying a bikini.

MARTIN GUTMANN

Thin Ice: Unlocking the Secrets of Climate in the World's Highest Mountains. MARK BOWEN. NEW YORK: HOLT PAPERBACK. 2006. 320 PAGES. $17.50.

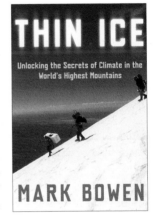

Glaciers worldwide are dying. Our warming climate is killing them off drip by drip. While many climbers have developed an intuitive sense of this loss through repeat trips to familiar mountain ranges, Ohio State University paleoclimatologist Lonnie Thompson has made a career of studying them. *Thin Ice* is principally the profile of his many groundbreaking scientific research expeditions to glaciers around the world, though it also serves as well as a well-researched overview of global warming theory and a passionate clarion call for saving the world's glaciers from almost certain destruction.

Thin Ice covers much ground, yet is a lively, approachable read. Author Mark Bowen, a climber (and sometime AAC member) with a doctorate in physics from MIT, writes with clarity and excitement, resulting in a book that details Thompson's contributions to hard science while also providing the thrilling adventure of his expeditions. The coverage of climate change science is thorough, yet approachable to the lay reader, giving one a clear sense of how, when, and why scientists began to understand that something had fundamentally shifted in our climate system. He discusses how past climactic swings have affected civilizations and postulates about what the future might be like for us.

One can't help but become fascinated with Thompson, his expeditions, and his revolutionary scientific theories. His under-funded, ragtag expeditions head off to areas thought to be of little consequence to the global climate system and attempt to drill ice in improbable locations with inadequate equipment. Yet they emerge with findings that shock the scientific world and spur new theories about how our climate system works. Because he chose to focus on the regions others thought unimportant, Thompson's unique perspective allows him to gain insight into unresolved questions, ultimately developing a revolutionary theory that has the equatorial areas as the drivers of global climate, not the poles as the scientific establishment had long assumed.

Thompson emerges as a bit of an enigma. While he has spent more time at extreme altitude than most leading high-altitude mountaineers, Thompson doesn't consider himself a climber. He climbs the world's high peaks solely because that is where he can extract the longest, most complete glacial cores possible from temperate regions of the globe. Thompson clearly is moved by the changes occurring in the alpine environment, but his is the more detached perspective of a scientist. Yet Thompson is the person whose 2001 announcement that the snows of Kilimanjaro likely will be gone by 2015 shook the alpine world in a way no other has been able to do.

Climbers will appreciate *Thin Ice* for the detail Bowen includes about expedition logistics, what it is like to live for weeks in such high, remote terrain and the sublime beauty of these high places. Anyone who has struggled through the obstacles posed by climbing in the developing world will smile at many of Thompson's scrapes with recalcitrant bureaucrats, striking porters, and broken equipment. While science is the focus of the scruffy band of eccentrics Thompson has assembled, they feel strikingly similar to many climbing teams.

Bowen does not shy away from the politics of global warming. While he fairly covers the many theories and perspectives about climate change, one clearly understands that he believes this to be one of the most serious threats to our planet. Bowen also charts the role of politics in climate change science, for example documenting the many career moves of James Hansen, the scientist whose pronouncements about global warming draw the ire of Republican presidents from Reagan through the two Bushes, causing his funding to dry up at the Department of Energy and the Environmental Protection Agency. (On the day I began reading *Thin Ice*, Hansen was again in the news as the story broke over Bush political operatives without scientific backgrounds censoring reports by Hansen and other NASA scientists.)

Though Al Gore's *Inconvenient Truth* has gained most of the public attention about global warming, *Thin Ice* is a must read for climbers curious about the changes going on in the mountains, as well as for those wanting to gain a better understanding about the science behind these changes.

LLOYD ATHEARN

IN BRIEF: NOTES FROM THE BANFF MOUNTAIN BOOK FESTIVAL, 2006

The 2006 Banff Mountain Book Festival competition—the 14th annual—received 113 books from nine countries. Those were narrowed down to 29 finalists by a committee, and then to eight winners by jury members Audrey Salkeld, David Stevenson, and David Leach. Each fall, the festival brings the spirit of outdoor adventure and the tradition of mountain literature to Banff, featuring guest speakers, readings, seminars, an international book competition, a book fair, and book signings and launches. To see the 2006 competition results or to enter a book in an upcoming year, go to www.banffmountainfestivals.ca

A brief selection of some noteworthy Banff entries not reviewed in this *AAJ*:

Summit: 150 Years of the Alpine Club, by George Band (HarperCollins £25), is a large format history with excellent photography, told in short self-contained episodes. One jury member found its contribution greater in the book's second half wherein the histories are not already so familiar as the early years.

Himalaya: Personal Stories of Grandeur, Challenge & Hope, edited by Richard C. Blum, Erica Stone, and Broughton Coburn (National Geographic Society $35), is an elegantly presented book of photography and newly-commissioned pieces by well-known Himalayan figures, including many Sherpa writers. A joint project of the American Himalayan Foundation and the National Geographic Society, its purpose is a call for compassion and humanitarian aid.

Ice Soldiers, by Paul Watkins (Henry Holt $25), is a work of fiction set in the Italian Alps in the years following World War II. Jury members found it "engaging, if not always quite believable in its climbing scenes."

Illustrated Atlas of the Himalaya, by David Zurick and Julsun Pacheco (University of Kentucky Press $50). Attractively illustrated with maps, this is a combination coffee table book and work of general science and geography.

Burbage, Millstone and Beyond, edited by David Simmonite; Niall Grimes, series editor (British Mountaineering Council £19). An expert and exhaustive guidebook to England's Peak District with a detailed mix of history, first-ascent lore, lists of bouldering problems, maps, and photography. Jury member Audrey Salkeld says the book "seems to have learned all the lessons of what constitutes a good and easily accessible guide."

SHANNON O'DONAGHUE, *Director, Banff Mountain Book Festival 2006*

IN MEMORIAM

EDITED BY CAMERON M. BURNS

DOUG COOMBS 1957-2006

Doug Coombs died last spring in a skiing accident in the French Alps while trying to aid a friend who had fallen over a cliff. He was 48 years old. Many writers and magazine editors will recall that Doug took skiing to a new level, pushed the boundaries of the sport, that sort of talk. Maybe. But those boundaries had previously been drawn by guys like Patrick Vallencent and Pierre Tardivel for steep, you-fall-you-die skiing; by Scott Schmidt for big air and fluidity; by Bill Briggs for technical ski mountaineering; by Hans Kammerlander and others in Himalayan ski mountaineering.

Doug Coombs *Wade McKoy, focusproductions.com*

What Doug did bring to skiing in the late 1980s was a liquid-smooth, deceivingly powerful, utterly natural turn the likes of which had not been seen before. His incomprehensibly fast reaction speed and sixth sense kept him always on—but never over—the sharp edge of disaster. It was this combination of qualities that made him unique in the realm of big mountains and big faces. He was truly the king of steeps.

Cameramen loved Coombs. His speed, power, and keen sense for the perfect line made him the ideal skier to film. He could look at a slope and know immediately how water would flow down it, and he would take the same line, deftly stepping out of the way of his slough, or juicing it and simply outrunning the cascading plume.

We're talking about skiing 50-60 miles per hour in extreme terrain. For those of us who often tried following his tracks, where he was making perfect turns, we were hesitant, making twice as many turns and picking our way slowly down.

But what really set him apart was his personality. Always laughing, always enthusiastic, always upbeat and positive, he was utterly approachable whether you were a total novice or a fellow pro. He loved skiing and he loved pushing himself, but he also loved seeing others push themselves, acquire new skills, and improve. Doug had a way of communicating clear, direct, uncomplicated instructions to clients that would at once calm their fears and get them to ski terrain beyond what they thought themselves capable of. His was a joyful, romping pursuit of perfection.

He never followed. Not anyone. Not Scott Schmidt. Not Dominique Perret. He led, you followed; you tried to keep up, you rarely did. But you learned. The angulation, the pole plant, the counter rotation, the power, the deft touch in variable snow. And in the bar, his remarkable memory rehashed the day: this turn here, that turn there, that terrain feature. He physically skied every run, then mentally skied them all again, often out loud. And again, you sat and listened and learned. And laughed. A lot.

I met Doug as he was pushing into the realm of, shall we say, non-lift-assisted ski mountaineering. Along with being king of the steeps, he was also the king of the poach, finagling more free lift, tram, and heli rides than any ten ski bums put together. Ultimately, though, he loved the mountains and realized that many stunning lines could only be accessed the old fashioned way—by climbing or hiking.

I watched Doug's mountain climbing skills progress from the beginner walls at the local rock climbing gym (I first taught him how to use the belay device there) to waltzing up 5.11 rock climbs and passing his AMGA rock-guide exam (with very strict requirements on rock-climbing ability). And his mountaineering skills and judgment made a similarly steep and rapid progression.

Raw energy ... endless energy. No body fat, just steel cables in ceaseless motion. Until a deep low-pressure and a big storm, at which point he could sleep for hours. In Antarctica, during a storm, he slept for *twenty* hours straight.

And I never saw him lose a chess match. Probably not something people knew him for—he was a brilliant chess player. And he ran his field operations at Valdez Heli-Ski Guides like a chess game, carefully placing all his pawns—us mere mortal guides—so that we never beat him to the best line of the day. If we ever did, he was just as enthusiastic about our accomplishment as he would have been if it were he on that perfect, fluted face.

"I think I'm getting rusty," Doug told me once during an Exum Ski Mountaineering Camp. "I haven't skied much for a while." It was June 10.

"Really?" I replied, wondering if the transition back from Europe, the moving, the visiting family, etc., had kept him his off his skis for a few weeks or even a month. "How long has it been?"

"Five days." He replied with a straight face.

Then he laughed.

We all laughed.

MARK NEWCOMB, *AAC*

CHARLES DUNCAN FOWLER 1954-2006

I first met Charlie Fowler in about 1977 in Eldorado Springs Canyon, Colorado. Already Charlie had made his vision-altering free solos of the Diamond on Long's Peak and the DNB on Middle Cathedral Rock in Yosemite. The shy, fresh-faced young fellow with a bowl-shaped mop of blondish hair making plans to climb with me seemed an unlikely perpetrator of such bold deeds. Next day on the rock, however, Charlie demonstrated his ability to rise to any challenge, a characteristic that became a life-long trademark. That day we headed up to Hawk Eagle Ridge. Just before reaching our intended climb we eyed an attractive roof and corner not listed in the guidebook and decided that this would be our first climb together. I recall being surprised when Charlie seemed a lit-

Charlie Fowler at Camp Bridwell, Patagonia. *Cameron M. Burns*

tle shaky on what proved to be only 5.9 or easy 5.10 terrain. Could he be one of those mediocre climbers who manage to get up impressive climbs above their skill-level by accepting huge risks? By the end of the day that question was definitively answered.

After pioneering our little first ascent we stuck to climbs in the guidebook. We had done half a dozen routes before we finished up with the big roof/corner of Dead On Arrival, which at the time was a respected, not super-well-protected 5.11c. I remember Charlie leading that climb with no struggle at all. Following his lead, I knew he was the real deal. The more difficult and serious the climbing became, the more focus and skill Charlie displayed.

With Charlie, what you saw was what you got, at least in the climbing arena. Whatever he *desired* to climb, he almost always climbed. What those of us who knew, admired, and followed his ascendant life-path and got to marvel at—again and again and again as he strode over the peaks of the globe, a compact unassuming figure donning seven-league ice boots or magic rock slippers—was to witness an inspired artist pushing the limits of his brush and canvas, expanding the limits of his own expression and ours at the same time (through witnessing his).

Soon after our first day in Eldorado, Charlie left for Patagonia with Mike Munger. They were headed for the 5,000-foot Super Couloir on Fitz Roy. With the successful third or fourth ascent of that amazing vein of ice, Charlie laid a deep foundation on which he would build a huge pyramid of such experience. A couple of months later, in reply to a query of what he thought of the Super Couloir, his answer was vintage Charlie: "Pretty wild! Really good." Four words from Charlie for one of the era's most fabled and respected climbs.

I began to imagine a new rating system. The Charlie Word Count System went from one to sixteen. The system begins where most climbers will never go. An example in the first category would be Charlie's report of his un-roped second ascent of David Breashears's unprotected 5.11 Eldorado face climb, Perilous Journey. "Scary," said Charlie, and not one word more.

In the early days this reticence was could be a challenge. When you finally could get Charlie to open up, it was remarkably rewarding. Charlie was educated, well-read, widely curious, and keenly observant of human nature, animal nature, and nature nature. To my regret, I drifted away from travels with Charlie. I did stay tuned into Charlie's channel, though, listening to a constant stream of hits. In the summer of 1979, after we had spent a month or two doing new rock climbs in Colorado and the Wind Rivers, and a new ice route on the Grand Teton's north face, Charlie, still a relative alpine initiate, headed off for his first season in the Alps. In late August I received an aer-o-gram from Charlie reporting the climbs he'd done. In two short paragraphs he related about a dozen routes, some of them the most notorious of the era, half of them solo. He had accomplished more in weeks than most alpine hardmen manage in a decade. The Fowler Word Count Rating System again at work.

Charlie never denigrated others' approach to climbing. When sport climbing made its debut in America in the mid-1980s, Charlie quickly caught on to the new game, and incorporated the extra free-climbing skills and strengths developed by clipping bolts on extremely hard routes into his repertoire. He obviously preferred climbing to debating the merits of various styles. In the Andes and China he developed his own unique style. Often he would guide a client or two up a few good climbs, then take off on more extreme adventures of his own, putting up amazing routes wherever he went.

Charlie did it all in a low-cost, low-hype, low-impact, simple, straightforward, and exemplary manner. He never went in for big sponsorship, big media, or posturing of any sort. His social confidence increased and his shyness decreased over the years until he became an articulate speaker, writer, and climbing film personality, but he was never full of himself. In fact, his amazing solos of beautiful but little-known peaks in China, often first ascents, are little known not because he tried to hide them, but because they were buried in plain view in a sentence or two in the *AAJ* or in person in his usual laconic drawl, and which gave no indication of the scale or difficulty of the accomplishments. "Yeah," he told me, "I soloed the south face of Siguniang. That was a pretty damn hard route—really good." Yes, indeed, a world-class first ascent on one of the most alluring of the world's mountain beauties summed up in 16 words. Rarely in the history of mankind have 16 words led so many off the track.

But there was much more to Charlie. To his family he was their proud and adventurous son and brother. His sister spoke at his memorial in Telluride with heart-breaking love, affection, and respect. To his friends and neighbors in Norwood, Colorado, where he made his home, he was that friendly guy who helped design and build the climbing gym and teach the kids how to climb at the local school. Several women hold him deep in their hearts, their personal Orion helping guide their passage through life, a reference point on sometimes dark nights. To people around the world he had met during his travels he was a goodwill ambassador of both his country and his sport, showing respect and kindness to everyone. Charlie was the type of man who made me feel good about being a climber and gave me hope that I live in an America filled with mostly good and generous people. At the Telluride celebration, which was packed with old friends of mine and many new faces, all of whom were friends of Charlie, of course, a short video was played that had been quickly but skillfully edited from recovered footage shot by Charlie and Christine Boskoff on their last fateful journey in China together, where they disappeared, most likely under an avalanche.

I was struck by the clean way the pair went about the business of inserting themselves almost seamlessly into the culture. They rode on buses engaging in verbal and pantomimed conversations with the locals, who took them in as friends. When they finally reached their drop off point, which was as far as the bus went, they simply walked off toward their mountain, each carrying one pack in front and another monster on their back. Then there is a scene that must have been shot by Christine. Charlie's head and trunk are sticking out of the entrance of a tiny red tent in the midst of raging winds and storm. Over the noise of the flapping tent fabric, in Charlie's distinct nasal monotone, he says something like, "Oh, yeah, as soon as this wind stops we're in a great position to go for the summit." There's not a bit of concern in his voice over the wind. Charlie himself was unflappable. In Christine he seemed to have found a match. For those of us left behind to mourn their passing, there is some solace that they had each other at the end.

JEFF LOWE

JOHANN WOLFGANG "HANS" GMOSER 1932-2006

It is beyond the capability of this aging wordsmith to come up with a simple summary of the eventful and productive life of a brilliant but complex man, who was also a good friend to so many and accomplished so much in the mountains of North America. Hans was born in Braunau am Inn, Austria (the same place where Adolf Hitler had been born a long generation earlier), and moved to Canada in 1951. After a few rocky years, Hans started guiding, following somewhat in the footsteps of his fellow countryman, Conrad Kain, another long generation earlier. In concert with fellow Austrian expatriate, Leo Grillmair, he developed the idea of using helicopters to gain access to the better skiing above timber-

Hans Gmoser *Brad White*

line. This was the beginning of a whole industry that now features a great number of competitive off-shoots and mountain chalets, while providing gainful employment to hundreds of guides in the mountains of Western Canada.

It was Brookie Dodge, son of the White Mountains' legendary Joe Dodge, who first brought moneyed American skiers to the Bugaboos, thus giving credence to this novel approach to better skiing. As time went on, Hans found he also needed further employment for his guides and arranged for summer activities, culminating in the 1970s with the formal establishment of heli-hiking, a program that now uses most of the seven Canadian Mountain Holidays backcountry lodges as bases for bringing hundreds of new people to see and enjoy the beauty of alpine regions every summer. To some purists, who may think the world's mountains are personal property, this process was anathema, but to the many thousands who were thus enabled to appreciate the beauty—and the need for the protection—of the world's mountains, Hans's most famous lifework has thus been an enormous service to the cause of mountain protection and conservation.

Besides his work as founder of Canadian Mountain Holidays, Hans led numerous great ascents, from the Yamnuska of the Frontal Rockies to the Wickersham Wall of Denali. He was also one of the very few non-native-borns to be elected to the Order of Canada and honored during his lifetime with honorary membership in the Alpine Club of Canada, the honorary presidency of the Association of Canadian Mountain Guides, and honorary membership in the UIAGM; and—in death—with a full-page obituary in Canada's national newspaper.

I first met Hans when he visited Fairy Meadow in 1957 with some friends, who have also now crossed the final divide. It was a difficult introduction for two "Type A" persons, but we both survived it. He then visited us in his promotional travels, and was interviewed on television several times by my wife, Kitty. In due course, I was tabbed as an "arm's-length" investor to meet a requirement of Canadian revenue rules. This turned out to be the best use of $5,000 I ever made. At about that time, he asked me if I could conjure up a few first ascents that he could offer to summertime clients. So, I did that for 10 years—mostly in the Frontal Ranges of the Canadian Rockies. With various accompanying personages—often malamutes—I would visit the Gmoser home in Harvie Heights, either coming or going to the hills, and was always welcomed, generally with some fine Scotch, which Hans kept around for my pleasure. I sort of grew up with his two boys, Conrad and Robson (the fruit of his marriage in 1966 to Margaret MacGougan), who all visited with me at Battle Abbey (our "home for geriatric alpinists," which they helped build) on many occasions, in summer and winter.

Hans's most notable trait was his invariable custom of standing back from the limelight and giving credit to others, some of whom deserved it. Besides all that, Hans Gmoser was the finest gentleman this writer has ever met.

WILLIAM LOWELL PUTNAM, *AAC*

SAMUEL HARLOW GOODHUE 1922-2006

Sam was recruited by Joe Dodge in 1947 to do "useful" things around the Old Rockpile. Over the span of the next 60 years, that list of useful things came to be an enormous litany of accomplishment. In the days when the Mt. Washington Observatory and the Appalachian Mountain Club were somewhat inseparable—under Joe's all-inclusive and heavenly mandated management style—it was hard to determine where the one organization left off and the other began. As a good worker, Sam was always in demand, mostly for matters requiring his engineering skills, but always in demand, nevertheless.

Sam did not withhold his opinions, on practically any topic, and never let his arguments become mired with unwelcome fact, or less strong because of any dearth thereof; and, like Joe, generally damned Democrats as being responsible for most of the ills of the State of "Cow Hampshire," the nation, and the world. Sam's opinion on the Mt. Washington Observatory, however, evolved over time to the effect that it had gradually become more of a valued institution to the North Country than the Appalachian Mountain Club, which had unintentionally given birth to the "Obs."

But Sam had given very generously to the AMC, of his time and talents, before it became a staff-driven organization. In time he came to head the Club's two committees most concerned with North Country activities—Trails and Huts. In those same years, he was contributing most usefully to the Committee on Mountain Leadership. Sam's barn, shed, and house on Thorn Hill became unofficial storage areas for the materiel (and personnel) pertinent to those committees, and Sam's foresight led to the construction of the AMC's newest off-road facility—the Mizpah Springs Hut. But, being a mainstay of the Mt. Washington Volunteer Ski Patrol, he never let go of his interest in the Old Rockpile, which always had free accommodations at the "Obs" on the summit.

He even managed to get good mileage out of a lot of Army surplus wire that Joe (who never told us which war that wire was surplus from) had obtained for ski patrol communications. There's probably a good bit of that wire still draped through the scrub and stumps of the Gulf of Slides.

But, the old goat was not immured in New Hampshire's hills, then or now. After very creditable service in the 84th Infantry Division (Battle of the Bulge—Bronze Star and Purple Heart) he misspent one of his post-War years in Aspen, as that area was in development just after World War II, before graduation from the University of New Hampshire with a degree in engineering. In later years he misspent even more time in the mountains of Western Canada, where he was a party to a lot of backcountry alpine skiing and quests for summertime first ascents.

Sam was enormously proud of his long Yankee heritage, which began in 1638 with the arrival in Ipswich of his tenth-generation forebear, William Goodhue (1612-1669), who had emigrated from Ipswich, in East Suffolk, England. Sam's family tree included many a Salem ship-owner and captain as well as Charles Leonard Goodhue, America's great waterworks engineer. Making things work was obviously a trait which carried down in Yankee families, for Sam worked for 30 years for the Foxboro Company, traveling the world—from the deserts of Iran to arctic Canada—as a trouble-shooter in process control installations.

For all of his "loner" attitude and appearance, Sam was beloved by the few younger folk who knew him well. But, he died—as he lived—a self-sustaining loner, who paid his own way through the world. Samuel H. Goodhue was rightfully proud of the fact that he consistently put more into American society than he took out, and invested wisely in the future, thereby leaving far more of an estate than did his parents. Sam left half to the Mt. Washington Observatory and half to the Lowell Observatory.

WILLIAM L. PUTNAM, *AAC*

RICHARD K IRVIN 1930-2006

Richard Irvin died on March 10, 2006 at his home in Boise, Idaho after a long battle with cancer. It was the end of an eventful life. Dick's participation in a climb frequently guaranteed success and always guaranteed a good time for his companions. I remember a late afternoon in 1951 standing on a ledge under the Second Tower of the East Ridge of the Grand Teton with Dick, John Mowat, and Leigh Ortenburger, who had taken a day off from guiding. We asked Leigh, our Teton guru, where the route went. "The route goes up there," he said, pointing to a difficult-looking chimney. "Dick, you lead." Irvin scampered up the chimney and soon we were at the top. Later we found out that the proven route traversed the Tower.

Dick Irvin *Kris Carter*

Leigh had seized the opportunity to use Dick's talents to make a first ascent.

Born in 1930 in Berkeley, California, Dick's lifelong dedication to mountains and mountaineering began when he was five and his parents took him on a camping trip in the Sierra Nevada. Later he continued his camping with the Boy Scouts where he became an Eagle Scout. He climbed and hiked on his own throughout the Sierra, making an ascent of Mt. Ritter when he was 15. He started rock climbing with Sierra Club Rock Climbing Section in 1948 and climbed extensively in Pinnacles National Monument and Yosemite.

In 1951, Dick spent the summer vagabonding and climbing in the Tetons and the Canadian Rockies, making several first ascents and new routes. The trip triggered a lifetime of mountaineering around the world. From hikes in the Pennines in England to Rakaposhi and Hidden Peak in the Karakoram, Dick did anything anywhere. He climbed Mt. St. Elias in Alaska and Ararat in Turkey. He did scores of climbs throughout North America and the Alps. He did new routes on Mt. Aspiring and Mt. Cook in New Zealand, and early ascents in the Cordillera Blanca of Peru, including the second ascent of Chopicalqui in 1954. Accounts of his climbs would fill an entire *AAJ*. Pull out a map of the world and randomly stick a pin in a mountain range. Dick had probably climbed there. He was the mountaineering equivalent of Kilroy. No matter where you went, he had been there first.

Although he was a member of the successful Gasherbrum I (Hidden Peak) expedition in 1958, he did not get the opportunity to climb high on the mountain because of the early success of the party. But Dick's most remarkable expedition was the four-man attempt on Rakaposhi, 25,550 feet, in 1956. Dick, Bob Swift, Mike Banks, and Hamish McInnes tackled that giant with a budget of $5,000. It was an epic. Among other things, everyone fell more than 100 feet at one time or another. Somehow they reached 23,500 feet, a new high point, before having to turn back. Later, when Dick was asked how close they had come to the summit, he immediately replied, "We were $5,000 short."

Dick was also absorbed in the history and literature of mountaineering. With limited resources, he assembled an excellent mountaineering library. He was always thinking about books. When we reached Urdukas on the way out from Hidden Peak, he said to me with a sly grin, "One more expedition like this and we can put our names in our books and increase their value."

Later in life Dick led trips for Mountain Travel and then took up birding, which he pursued with his usual dedication until his life list included 6,002 species. It is hard to believe that Dick had another life, but he did. He graduated in 1953 with a degree in anthropology from San Francisco State University. For many years he taught math at Saratoga High School. Of all the many achievements in his life, he was most proud of the number of students he had inspired to go into science and mathematics. He was also proud of the four children he had by his first wife, Heidi Irvin. In 1998 he married Kris Carter, who warmed the remaining years of his life.

One's memory of him is good climbs and good times. Often when I think of a climb, I realize, "I did it with Dick Irvin." He was the kind of friend that when he went, a piece of you went with him. Now he has moved on. "The route goes up there. Dick, you lead!"

NICK CLINCH, *AAC*

SUE NOTT 1970-2006

Sue Nott *Courtesy Mountain Hardwear*

In 2003, in Chamonix, France, conditions were good, and alpinists in heaven. I heard whispers in the lift lines of an American woman, an accomplished alpinist. The whispers carried awe, respect, and stories of the Croz Spur on the north face of the Grand Jorasses, the 1938 route on the north face of the Eiger, the north face of the Droites, Scotch On The Rocks—all names of routes I could only dream of ticking. I wanted to meet this woman. I want to *be* this woman. I think a lot of the people passing whispers wanted the same.

A native of Vail, Colorado, Sue was at home in the mountains, when alpine climbing, on expeditions, or big technical objectives. Wintering in Chamonix, for the ease of access to big, hard, alpine lines, Sue could only be found in town, or on the stair stepper, if weather was bad and avalanche hazards high. She was most commonly found in the winter rooms of the refuges or on snowy, icy, north faces.

Over the past few years I shared a rope, ski tours, bivies, many dinner parties, too many bottles of wine, and a thousand dreams with Sue. I watched her float down ski slopes in mountaineering boots, because they were more comfortable than ski boots. I watched her float up hard mixed climbs slow and steady, always in control. I saw her pass smiling and giggling, always in pink, up and down the West Buttress of Denali as she tackled Mt. Hunter, Mt. Foraker, and Denali in one month—climbing the Cassin on the first all-women's team. I received emails of a new route on Kalanka in the Gharwal Himalaya. Each note, each interaction, each adventure an inspiration.

In the spring of 2006, I shared a winter in the Alps with Sue and a spring in Alaska. Each morning in Chamonix, my phone would beep with a text: "Off running, call me when you wake up. We'll go skinning." Evenings we'd convene in her small apartment for a gourmet meal served on paper plates to a heaving crew of hungry mouths. She nudged us out touring on days so filled with snow we'd break trail downhill as well as up. We'd lust over topos of Mt. Hunter's Moonflower Buttress on bad weather days in coffee shops. Sue's motivation and drive were endless.

In April 2006, we landed on the Kahiltna basecamp, with over a 1,000 pounds of supplies. As John Varco and I, hypo-glycemic and lost in a sea of poles, attempted to construct the dome tent, Mamma Sue, affectionately referred to as "Grubby," produced a handful of cheesy, bacon quesadillas, her hands glistening with butter. In a few hours we had constructed our compound, which would be Sue's home for the next month and a half. Each day she unveiled a new treat: candy necklaces, a small paddle-ball set, pink cups and straws to drink cocktails, facials, toe-nail polish, even a razor to shave her legs. On snow days Sue sat reading fashion magazines and business journals. We chatted about our families, and what we would do when we were old. Sue calmed me in the mountains, I calmed her in town.

We packed to make an attempt on Deprivation. I stared skeptically at the handful of energy gels and bars, the few hundred calories per day, the light sleeping bags. Sue smiled. She knew she could suffer; I wasn't so sure I could. She looked at me as we lifted our packs to leave the boys behind at camp and said, "Zoe, I picked out your pitches. I don't care how slow you go, but I want you to share some leads." I smiled. Sue was far stronger than I, tougher, and more experienced, and yet for some reason she had confidence in me. She saw a potential I can only dream of living up to. That's how she saw everyone.

We suffered slowly up hard dry-tooling, a route of ice and dry rock, Sue picking slowly, clearing away sugary snow and finding minute gear placements. We found a bivy spot, chopped away at the snow, and created a platform big enough for one set of shoulders not two, two feet, not four. I looked quizzically at Sue. She smiled and giggled, "It's ok, we'll just hang the tent, and I'll sleep on the outside cradled by the tent." I stuffed myself in the drooping tent while Sue patiently handed each item in to me. She finished melting water and crawled into her half-sized bed, snuggled into her sleeping bag, and smiled. After a few days of slow movement and heavy packs, we decided to descend. At the base Sue looked up and said "That route's stupid." Giggling, "We'll get it next year."

Sue's passion and comfort in the mountain environment was bred deep and young, her childhood was spent in the mountains on skis. A successful downhill ski racer, Sue learned the attributes of a committed training regime and high goals and expectations early in life. Eventually storing her skis, Sue ventured into rock and ice climbing for the first time in 1989. Showing her natural athleticism, she led the Fang in Vail (WI 6+) a year later. After a few years of university and collegiate running, Sue traded in her books for a full time climbing life and buggered off to Yosemite.

Shortly after, in typical Sue style, she decided the best way to properly learn to ice climb would be to winter in Valdez, climbing things like the Glass Onion (WI 5-). The long, cold, gray winter was likely good training for her alpine climbing career to come. Sue's adventures and expeditions took her across the globe, from India to China, Peru, Europe, North America, and beyond. She set standards, opened new routes, and pushed limits that few people, let alone women, have pushed. All the while with a smile and a small puffy pink jacket. I will forever remember Sue as an alpine goddess, one of the ladies in pink, climbing hard, with a handful of sweets, an enormous smile, and an inspiration to us all.

ZOE HART

Editor's note: Sue Nott and Karen McNeill disappeared together on the south face of Mt. Foraker in May 2006. The McNeill-Nott Memorial Route, recounted on page 42 of this Journal, remembers them.

John Cameron Oberlin 1914-2006

John Cameron Oberlin, President of the American Alpine Club from 1956 to 1958, represented the AAC at the centenary of the Alpine Club in London. He strongly supported the international aspects of mountaineering. He was best known for the second ascent of Mt. Alberta in the Canadian Rockies, with Fred Ayres, in 1948. It had first been climbed by six Japanese climbers and three Swiss guides.

John Cameron Oberlin

John grew up in Cleveland, Ohio. As a boy he climbed trees, walls, and limestone ledges. After some early climbs in the White Mountains with fellow Clevelander David Green, a chance encounter with Fred Ayres led to the Tetons and Canada's Rocky Mountains, where he climbed in the Selkirks and the Bugaboos. With the formation of the U.S. mountain troops in World War II, John was among the first to arrive at Fort Lewis to join the 87th Mountain Infantry Regiment. Happily, as a private, he was assigned to instructing rock and ice climbing on Mt. Rainier. When he left for OCS, he had expected to return to the 87th Infantry but was instead assigned to chemical warfare because of his chemistry degree from Harvard and his experience as a patent lawyer dealing with chemical companies.

After the war he returned to climbing in the Canadian Rockies, making first ascents of Mt. Erasmus and Oppy Mountain, the highest unclimbed peak in the Canadian Rockies, as well as a determined attempt on the Wishbone Arête of Mt. Robson. His climb with Fred Ayres of Mt. Alberta in 1948 led to one of the most pleasant episodes of his climbing career: contact and friendly exchanges with the four remaining members of the 1925 Mt. Alberta first ascent team, of which Yuko Maki was the Japanese leader. There was an exchange of gifts, including a "silver" ice axe sent to the Japanese as it had been rumored that one had been left on the summit in 1925.

In the early 1950s, he was among the earliest Americans to climb in the Peruvian Andes. He joined the French-American expedition to Salcantay, which included the French climbers Bernard Pierre and Claude Kogan. In the 1950s he continued climbing in the Wind Rivers and the Alps with his brother-in-law Bob Bates, and he climbed the Matterhorn by the Zmutt Ridge with Bob Dodson.

After marriage to Corinne Albinson, he settled in the hills south of Palo Alto, enjoying another consuming interest: horticulture, and growing all of the exotic plants he could establish in that climate. He leaves his wife, daughter, and two grandchildren.

Robert Bates *and* Gail Oberlin Bates, *AAC*

Todd Richard Skinner 1957-2006

Todd is gone, fallen from life. My greatest friend, my chosen brother, a part of my heart and world for 30 years. We have lost a contagious source of energy, which fueled the lives and dreams of countless people.

Todd was born in Sun Valley Idaho on October 28, 1958 and lived life to the fullest right up to the moment he died in a climbing accident in Yosemite on October 21, 2006—just a week before his 48th birthday. The accident occurred while working on a new free climb (of the direct aid route "Jesus Built My Hot Rod") on the Leaning Tower. As Todd and his partner (Jim Hewitt) were rappelling, Todd's terribly worn belay loop broke and he was gone. Jim told me that he had pointed out that Todd's harness was very worn and that Todd told him he had one on order and that his harness "would do" until the new one arrived. When Jim told me that Todd's belay loop had broken, I thought he might be mistaken, as I had never heard of a belay loop failing. However, Jim was correct about the belay loop. This makes Todd's loss even more tragic because this accident could have been prevented.

From his earliest days, Todd joined his family at the Skinner Brothers Wilderness School, based in Pinedale, Wyoming. On the short crags near Burnt Lake, Todd, his older brother Orion and younger sister Holly were taken top-roping. Todd's Dad, Bob Skinner, along with uncles Monte, Court, and Oly taught the kids how to thrive in an alpine environment. Bob and Court inspired

Todd Skinner on Trango Tower. *Bobby Model*

Todd to read the exploits of Shackleton, Herzog, Shipton and Tilman, and especially Mawson, and his incredible story of survival in the Antarctic.

Todd climbed Wyoming's highest point, Gannett Peak, when he was 11 years old. Seven years later, with his Dad and Uncle Court, he made the first winter ascent of the 13,804-foot mountain. This bitterly cold winter expedition to Gannett Peak would serve as perhaps the most seminal learning experience of his life.

In the closing days of 1978, I met Todd at the University of Wyoming in Laramie and we began our higher education to a lesser extent within the halls of academe, and to a larger extent by making dozens of first ascents at nearby Vedauwoo, in the Black Hills, Needles, and in the thin corners of Devils Tower. We quickly discovered that we shared an unquenchable desire to explore yet-to-be-free-climbed routes. We began searching for potential in travel books, geology texts, and rumors shared by other climbers.

In the early 1980s, after graduation with a degree in finance, Todd began his life of climbing and exploration. Naturally talented and driven, Todd had the ability to free climb the most difficult routes—and he became one of the climbers who were nudging the difficulty ratings ever higher. For years, he traveled the country to test himself on the hardest climbs and often contributed new routes of even greater difficulty at the areas he visited. Soon the magazines took note. In postcards and letters from that era, he wrote not so much about the climbing, but about new friends he had met. The colorful characters he was climbing with were a source of inspiration. These formed the basis of a variety of slide presentations, which were performed at climbing shops, college adventure clubs, and youth group meetings—and supplemented his meager annual income. Eventually, his skills as a raconteur evolved into a career. Todd, in association with Extreme Connection, became a sought-after motivational speaker.

Members of the AAC may remember the 1988 annual banquet in Atlanta. There, the club honored Todd and me with the Underhill Award for Lifetime Achievement. Up to that point Todd and I (but especially Todd) had climbed many, many, new routes across the country. However, the award was certainly given due to our free climb of the Salathé Wall a few months earlier. During that ascent, Todd and I employed many of the techniques we had been using for years, the most controversial at the time being "hang-dogging." Neither of us would hesitate to hang at a given point of difficulty on a pitch of climbing in order to "hang dog the moves"—meaning, we would take numerous short falls to rehearse crux sections. When we had choreographed the difficulties, we would lead the pitch without falling. Friends who were serious detractors, believing we were cheating, would watch from El Cap meadow and entertain us by shouting "Haaaaang-dogs!" Both sides of the argument were sincerely convinced that their approach was the best; however, with the passage of nearly 20 years, hang-dogging seems de rigueur. Todd and I both felt that our willingness (read: stubbornness) to spend nearly 40 days and nights learning to live and free climb on El Cap was our greatest attribute.

Prior to success on the Salathé, Todd was principally known as the author of some of the most difficult short free climbs in North America. The Gunfighter at Hueco Tanks, City Park at Index, and Throwin' The Houlihan at Wild Iris are but a few of the hundreds of 5.13 and harder climbs Todd established. For us, the Salathé was proof of concept, demonstrating that our dreams of free climbing other big walls were reasonable. Together and with numerous talented friends, we shared in the free ascents of Mt. Hooker in the Wind River Range; The Great Canadian Knife in The Cirque of the Unclimbables; The Direct Northwest Face of Half Dome; Harmattan Rodeo on The Hand of Fatima in Mali; War & Poetry on Ulamertorsuaq in Greenland; and True At First Light, on Poi, in the Northern Frontier District in Kenya.

Many consider Todd's finest hour to be a free ascent of the 20,500-foot Trango Tower with Steve and Jeff Bechtel, Bobby Model, Mike Lilygren, and Bill Hatcher. This climb summoned everything Todd ever learned about climbing and keeping team members motivated and working in order to grow together in strength, resolve, and perseverance. When the climbers succeeded in free-climbing Trango Tower, they had lived on the wall for 60 days through the deadliest season in Karakoram history and established the world's first Grade VII free climb.

But simply to write about the climbs would be to ignore the most personal stories—the glorious days of tipi life at Devils Tower and in the Needles, where I watched Todd and Amy climb together and fall in love. I wish everyone could have seen his enraptured face when Hannah was born. After the twins, Jake and Sarah, came along, the three kids would flop over Todd like blankets, insisting he tell (for the millionth time) about when "Finger-biter the Piranha" bit me in the Amazon, or "The Legend of Stumpy Model," or of "Gypsy Dave," or "Tennessee Jim," and the many other friends who had become characters in the stories he told his kids as they drifted off to sleep.

Some might say that Todd experienced and achieved more in his short life than almost everyone. Todd lived, loved, climbed, and thought more passionately than anyone I've ever known. Still, I believe his greatest achievements were still ahead.

How would Todd finish this remembrance? I think he would leave us with inspiration. He might say: "The next time you stand below a route that you have only dreamed of climbing, begin it with all of your heart and soul.

"The next time you find yourself with your toes against a blank spot on the map, take another step.

"The next time you are too tired to go on, think of a team high on Trango Tower after 59 freezing days of climbing—and persevere.

"The next time you don't know where to turn, think about where you want to be in 20 years, and start moving, not worrying if your goal is straight ahead, and never, never give up."

Todd is survived by wife Amy Whistler Skinner, son Jake, daughters Hannah and Sarah, brother Orion, and sister Holly. Sadly, a month before Todd's death, his mother, Doris Skinner, passed. Todd's father, Bob Skinner, passed a month after his son. A memorial fund has been established for Todd's family. To donate please send contributions to: Todd Skinner Memorial Fund c/o Atlantic City Federal Credit Union, 704 W. Main Street, Lander, Wyoming, 82520.

PAUL PIANA

HENRY BRADFORD WASHBURN, JR. 1910-2007

On January 10, 2007 we lost a visionary, a world-class mountaineer and explorer, a scientist and teacher, and perhaps the
most prolific mountain photographer of all time when Brad
Washburn passed away at the age of 96.

I first met Brad only 15 years ago, but as a climber I had
known of him and his many accomplishments a long time.
Brad and Barbara came to visit, as Brad wanted a look at one
of my photographs of Everest that he thought might be useful. Never ones to procrastinate, they arrived just 45 minutes
after our first conversation, already in their eighties but still
with the energy to put most people half their age to shame.
They were busy with Brad's latest innovative project to re-
measure the exact height of Mt. Everest using state-of-the-
art technology and some top climbers who were to plant a

Brad Washburn   © Bradford
Washburn, Courtesy Panopticon
Gallery, Boston, MA

GPS receiver on the highest rock projection near the summit. They did it the next year, and I
remember when the new official height of Everest—29,035 feet—was read aloud at the National
Geographic Society in Washington DC.

We spent a lovely afternoon with them that first evening. I'll never forget Brad explain-
ing to me with contagious enthusiasm how maps were made—for the first time I really understood! What made Brad a great teacher was his own insatiable interest in so many things.

Most everyone is familiar with Brad's many ascents of Mt McKinley, including the
first ascent of the West Buttress, and, of course, the landmark 1947 ascent with Barbara, who
became the first woman to climb McKinley. And there were the first ascents of mounts Crillon
and Bertha, and that marvelous picture of Brad and Barbara on top.

But not everyone knows that Brad was climbing in the Alps as a teenager and was one
of the most accomplished American alpinists of his day with ascents of the Matterhorn, Mt.
Blanc, the Charmoz, and the airy needle of the Grepon. His greatest and most technical climb
(according to Brad) occurred in the French Alps when he was just 19. Along with local guides
Albert Coutier and Georges Charlet, Brad made the first ascent of the 4,000-foot sheer north
face of the Aguille Vert in a single day. A good feat even by today's standards, and Brad did it
in 1929. He published stories for boys of his early adventures in his popular series "Among the
Alps with Bradford," which helped pay his way through Harvard.

Perhaps the most famous and harrowing of Brad's climbs took place in the remote Saint
Elias Range of the Yukon, where he and Bob Bates made the first ascent of Mt. Lucania in 1937.
It is one of the great epic stories of survival, exploration, and comradeship in all of mountaineering lore. Upon realizing they were stranded at the foot of Lucania after their bush pilot,
Bob Reeves, barely escaped the unseasonable slushy conditions on the glacier, the intrepid pair
resolved to focus on the climb and worry about finding their way back to civilization—some
120 miles of desolate glaciers, rivers, and wilderness—later.

After 20 days they reached Lucania's elusive summit and, if that weren't enough, they
carried on to bag the second ascent of nearby Mt. Steele! The real epic however was yet to
unfold, as Bob and Brad spent the next several weeks crossing uncharted territory, negotiating
swollen rivers, and eating squirrels and rabbits that Bob shot with his revolver as they made
their way back to a tiny trading post.

The stories from these adventures were endless and what often amazed me was Brad's ability to recall specific details from so many years ago, even in his final years when his short-term memory had suffered so much.

If all Brad and Barbara had done was climb mountains they would be famous enough, but they of course did so much more. When we speak of mountain photography I believe there are few if any equals to Brad Washburn. The precision and artistry of his work puts him in a tiny group of visionaries like Vittorio Sella and Ansel Adams. And frankly, in many ways, Brad was better. You can always tell a Washburn. The detail is so exceptional you feel you are right there, peering through the open door of a small aircraft into the cold Alaskan wilderness. And yet in each photo there is something unique and personal, the curious eye of a relentless explorer. No matter how much you magnify a Washburn you will always find more.

From a mountaineer's perspective, it is hard to fathom the enormous impact his photos have had on exploratory climbing and first ascents as practically every serious expedition to Alaska has been planned and plotted over an 8×10-inch black and white of the intended ridge or vertical wall taken by Brad during one of his countless flights over Alaska. We climbers owe him a great debt.

This quote from one of Brad's early mentors sums it up: "Brad Washburn is one of the very few people who have combined spectacular experience in the wilderness with equally spectacular achievements in the world of civilization. One never knows what to expect next from this roving genius of mind and mountains, but whatever it is, we know it will be excellent and effective." (That comment was from Ansel Adams in 1983.)

As a professional cartographer, Brad produced the most accurate and useful maps in existence of Mt McKinley, the Grand Canyon, the Western Yukon, and Mt. Everest, as well as the Everest and Presidential Range scale models. I dare say that the full impact and importance of Brad and Barbara's work will not be known or fully appreciated for many years, the scope is simply so vast.

In 1939, not long after graduating from Harvard, Brad accepted a position as Director of the Museum of Natural History in Boston. This would lead to Brad's instrumental role in founding and developing Boston's Museum of Science and his extraordinary gift to public education. Under Brad's imaginative leadership and effective administration, the Museum of Science has become one of the finest teaching museums in the world. "Museums should be a place where learning is fun and exciting," Brad often remarked, and his museum would set a new standard for interactive exhibits. It was also the first major museum to incorporate all the sciences under one roof. Brad's work with the museum was a lifelong commitment. Forty-one years as its director and well into his eighties, Brad could be found in his office enthusiastically involved in a new exhibit or program.

The museum is also where he met Barbara, who came to interview for a secretarial position at the original natural history museum. She declined at first, and, as she said, "I had no interest in working in that dusty old place filled with a bunch of decaying stuffed animals." But Brad knew a good thing when he saw it, and like everything else he pursued in life, Brad didn't give up easily. After endless pestering from Brad, Barbara eventually accepted the position and they married shortly thereafter. So began a remarkable lifelong partnership, a busy and adventurous life; they were inseparable as they were always working together on some new project. And yet they still found time to raise three wonderful children.

Inevitable as Brad's passing was, it is hard to accept that he is actually gone. Brad's death marks the end of an era, the final chapter in a visionary life spent so productively that there is no doubt his legacy will survive a very long time, inspiring future climbers, scientists and artists around the world. More than anything else, I'll miss Brad's contagious love for living life to it's fullest. One of Brad's favorite quotes was from Rudyard Kipling's 1898 poem "The Explorer": "Something hidden. Go and find it. Go and look behind the ranges. Lost and waiting for you—Go!"

Brad is survived by his wife Barbara and his three children, Dorothy, Betsy, and Edward.

MARK RICHEY, *AAC*

Brief obituaries of other AAC members may be found in the quarterly American Alpine News.

NECROLOGY

Charles Borgh
Doug Coombs
Edward R. Cummings
Hans Gmoser
Willi Ashton Hirst
Richard K. Irvin
Edward B. Keller, M.D.
Robert G. Kelley
Susan Nott
John C. Oberlin
Daniel Scott
Todd R. Skinner

Club Activities

Edited by Frederick O. Johnson

Alaska Section. The slide shows in Anchorage have been a great way to bring our members and others together on a regular basis to network and find out what concerns the public has on climbing related issues. Eight of these popular shows were presented in 2006. In January Sam Johnson described a new route he had completed on Trango 2 in Pakistan. In February Alaska Range veteran Mark Westman talked on "Once Were Warriors," a new route on Mount Grosvenor, and Alaska Range pilot Paul Roderick showed aerial photos from his amazing collection. In March the Section hosted the preview of Joe Puryear's guidebook to the Alaska Range, and Joe highlighted his new route, the Black Crystal Arete, on Kichatna Spire. April featured Ralph Baldwin's climb of Mt. Stanley in the Ruwenzori Mountains in Uganda and other Rwandan adventures. After the summer break, the slide shows resumed in September with Matt Szundy from the local guiding company, The Ascending Path, discussing Ama Dablam and his time working in Antarctica. In October local legend and AAC secretary, Charlie Sassara, described his recent trip to Patagonia. In November USGS geologist Peter Haeussler reviewed his climbs in the Ruth Gorge and discussed the fracture faults of the Alaska Range and why Denali got to be the Mountain it is today. At the final slide show in December, Dave Hart spoke about his ascents of the 20 highest summits in Canada and Alaska.

The Alaska Section was active in 2006 with public service projects. With funding from the AAC and the Matanuska-Susitna Borough's Community Development Department we were able to build the Webfoot Latrine, located at the best alpine rock climbing area with road access in south-central Alaska. Also, funds raised from a benefit showing of Steve House's climb of the Rupal Face of Nanga Parbat enabled the Section to purchase the Snowbird Hut. Formerly owned privately, this hut in the Talkeetna Mountains offers fantastic spring skiing along with great multi-pitch rock climbs in a great alpine setting about a three-hour walk from the road. It will be open to the public on a first-come, no-reservation basis, pack it in, take it out, including human waste. The Alaska Section would like to thank the BP Energy Center and its staff for opening its doors for our use, with thanks also to the speakers who presented their fine programs.

Harry Hunt, *Chair*

Oregon Section. Bob McGown, Section chair, was on four continents this year, so Richard Bence took over some of his duties. Bence also maintains the Oregon Section and Madrone Wall Web sites, www.ors.alpine.org and www.savemadrone.org. The Oregon Section sponsors the Madrone Wall Web site. In a public study session, Clackamas County unanimously accepted the Parks Advisory Board recommendation not to sell the site for a private quarry or housing development and to move forward to establish a public park. Letters of support were written by over 500 citizens and by organizations including the Oregon Section. AAC member Keith Daellenbach is the founder and long time director of the Friends of Madrone Wall Preservation Committee.

In late fall 2005 the Section sent $2,500 to Pakistan and collected tents and clothing that were shipped by the AAC. In January at the Hollywood Theater, Jeff Alzner organized the Cascade Mountain Film Festival, which raised an additional $6,000 for Pakistani relief efforts. Other contributions came from the Banff Film Festival participants who donated use of their films: Sandra Wroten and Gary Beck. There were also significant donations from Jill Kellogg, Jeff Alzner, Richard Bence, Richard Humphrey, Bob McGown, and others. Mazama president Wendy Carlton acted as MC in making the Pakistan Earthquake Village evening a success. We had over a dozen volunteers from the AAC and the Mazamas, and an estimated 350 people attended. The chair of Mercy Corps, headquartered in Portland, introduced the program.

Bob Speik organized a fundraiser featuring Royal Robbins' program, "40 Years of Adventure," on March 22 at the Tower Theater in Bend. The proceeds were donated to the Deschutes Basin Land Trust. Jeff Alzner, who climbed Mt. Stuart and several peaks in the Canadian Rockies in 2005, presented us with a large number of excellent photographs soon to appear on the Section's website, along with his descriptions of the climbs. Jeff continues to work on a memorial video honoring Mike Bearzi, who was one of the first people to develop the M grading system for mixed ice and rock.

Wayne Wallace gave two fine talks about his adventures in the Picket Range for the Oregon Section at the Old Market Pub. Wayne, who has completed difficult traverses in the Pickets with his Seattle climbing partners, recently earned the Fred Beckey Award. The Fred Beckey Award is given by the Oregon Section to members who have done outstanding routes in the Cascades. Mike Layton gave a benefit slide show with Wayne Wallace for Madrone Wall. Layton completed the first ascent of Mox Peak's southeast face and the Washington Pass traverse (See Climbs and Expeditions in this *Journal*).

On behalf of the Section, Bob Speik placed a geo-cache in the vicinity of one of the AAC-donated rescue caches at Smith Rock.

In September, Neale Creamer, Jim Onstott, Bob Moshier, and Mark Roddy together with the Friends of Silcox Hut and Timberline Lodge joined to perform the difficult annual maintenance tasks at the Silcox Hut. The Friends also provide hut hosting at Silcox in May to give climbers access to this 1933 WPA structure at 7,000' on Mt. Hood. It serves as an excellent base camp for south side rescues.

In November, Kellie Rice, Access Fund coordinator, put on a Rocky Butte cleanup assisted by AAC members. The cleanup drew 40 volunteers and was a great success in keeping the Butte in good condition.

Bob McGown and Matt Brewster climbed a new route called the Pioneer Anomaly on Newton Pinnacle on the north face ridge of Mt. Hood with three 5.9 pitches. They also ascended an overhanging face climb named Gravity's Rainbow, developing a new 5.10 route on Newton Pinnacle's south face.

Keith Daellenbach was the leader of an expedition to make the first ascent of Mt. Blachnitzky in southeastern Alaska. Dr Maynard Miller's glaciological research program is conducted in this glacial region of the Coast Range.

Our members Bob Lockerby, Tom Bennett, Clint Veilbig, Keith Campbell, Gary Beck, Bob McGown, and many others continued to volunteer for the construction of the new Mazama headquarters building, which is an old classic church and Masons' Hall in Portland. The Mazamas, with 50 active volunteers, construction manager Jay Levins, and climber-contractor Jim Brewer have completed their headquarters building for the grand opening in January 2007.

BOB MCGOWN, *Chair*

SIERRA NEVADA SECTION. The Sierra Nevada Section had an active 2006 promoting the AAC's goals of Knowledge, Conservation, and Community. The Section hosted nine events at which it welcomed AAC members, their guests, visiting climbers, and the public to share mountain fellowship, learn and preserve the rich history of climbing, and contribute to the conservation of the mountains and crags we love.

In February we hosted our first annual Ice Climb-munity based from the off-the-grid Lost Trail Lodge in Coldstream Canyon near Truckee. Sierra Nevada Section Climb-munity events are intended to get both AAC members and nonmembers out climbing together and promote AAC membership. Despite challenging weather, we enjoyed a variety of climbs from moderate smears to steep pillars and a little mixed climbing. Great meals, a warm fire and some live music each evening at the lodge kept spirits high.

Yosemite Valley in late April saw the Section hosting the Yosemite premiere of the award winning documentary film *Monumental*, a biography of climber and conservation icon David Brower. Along with the movie, we hosted a free beer and wine reception where we welcomed Park Superintendent Mike Tollefson and many climbers from Camp 4. A number of Section members attended to help with the event and to share the joy of springtime climbing in the Valley. *Monumental* was produced by Kelley Duane, daughter of our member Dick Duane, with financial support from the Sierra Nevada Section. Screenings of the film are now part of the climbers' interpretive program in Yosemite. This wonderful addition is the latest in the ongoing efforts of Section member Linda McMillan in leading the AAC's work to preserve and promote the historical importance of Camp 4 and climbing in Yosemite Valley.

Section members and friends gathered on Donner Summit in June to enjoy superb granite cragging. We camped within walking distance of the climbs on undeveloped property owned by our member Bela Vadasz of Alpine Skills International and enjoyed a barbeque and campfire. This event featured the debut of the Sierra Nevada Section's newly acquired portable Wag Bag human waste system, which allows us to cost effectively reduce the impact of our larger groups when camped informally on undeveloped land or gathered in other locations without facilities. The Section is promoting human waste management practices consistent with the AAC's Clean Mountain Can initiative on Denali and its Wag Bag kiosk in Indian Creek south of Moab, Utah.

In July the Section took its Climb-munity series of gatherings to Tioga Pass and Tuolumne Meadows. With some last minute good fortune, we were able to secure a group campsite in the Meadows. This allowed outreach to the climbing community by sharing our site with quite a few climbers whom we invited in after they were shut out of the full camp-ground. Great weather on Saturday saw members hitting the crags and heading for nearby peaks. That evening we shared the campfire with our new friends. Our guests were impressed to learn about the AAC's ongoing initiatives, from those right in front of them in Yosemite National Park to our Pakistan earthquake relief efforts. On Sunday morning, the AAC-sup-ported weekly coffee with climbing ranger Jesse McGahey included a discussion of the Park

Service's management plans for Tuolumne Meadows and the Tuolumne Wild and Scenic River. Sunday's climbing had most of the group enjoying a number of fine routes on Dozier Dome recently established by Section member George Ridgely and friends.

AAC President Jim Donini and his crew of fellow Club members from Colorado joined us for the Donner Summit Climb-munity II in late August. The weather was splitter, and everyone enjoyed great cragging and another fun barbeque and campfire on Bela Vadasz's beautiful Donner Pass property. Bela has begun exploring the possibility of establishing an AAC-affiliated hut on the property, providing access to the nearby cragging and excellent winter ski-mountaineering terrain.

The Section kicked off its series of fall events with the ever-popular Pinecrest Climb-In hosted by Royal and Liz Robbins and Tom Frost in late September. Members and friends gathered to enjoy cragging at Gianelli Edges with crisp fall weather and a wonderful party at the Robbins cabin. Attendees included climbers from the Yosemite Golden Age like Pat Ament and Mike Sherrick, along with his wife Natalie, as well as local Sonora Pass area guidebook author Brad Young. Our thanks to Royal, Liz, and Tom for their usual warm hospitality.

Sierra Nevada Section members were part of history by attending the Camp 4 Historic Registration celebration on September 30th and October 1st in Yosemite Valley. A ceremony placing the plaque marking Camp 4's inclusion in the National Register of Historic Places was held at Columbia Boulder. The Section helped host the celebration including food and refreshments, and clips from a wonderful home movie of an early ascent of the Salathé Wall by Allen Steck and Steve Roper. Luminaries in attendance included National Park Service officials and AAC past President Nick Clinch, who spoke eloquently of the AAC's leadership and perseverance in saving Camp 4. We also began the sale of Camp 4 commemorative t-shirts and insulated mugs (they work equally well for hot coffee and cold beer) to raise money for the Section's ongoing conservation efforts and promote awareness of the AAC. Contact the Section Chair to order yours today! Our members also participated in the tremendous effort of the Yosemite Facelift cleanup organized by the Yosemite Climbers Association.

In early November, the Section hosted a fun and successful event with our "Fall High Ball" in Bishop. Quite a few folks made the trip to the Eastside of the Sierra to join our local members for some good bouldering and climbing. And over 100 people attended our party and slide show at Mill Creek Station Saturday evening. This included a good number of road-tripping climbers we met at the campground, boulders, and crags.

Thanks to Roger and Mary Lou Derryberry, the owners of Mill Creek Station, for the cool venue and to Lisa Rands for an enthusiastic and exciting slide presentation featuring not only her world-class bouldering, but also hard grit routes in the U.K. and climbing in Patagonia. We also had a successful gear raffle thanks to our supporters at Wilson's Eastside Sports, Climb-It, Mammoth Mountaineering Supply, Big Sur Bar, and Great Basin Bakery. Thanks also to our own Andy Selters and everyone on the Eastside who helped us promote the event. With the net proceeds of the event, the Sierra Nevada Section was pleased to support two climbing community conservation initiatives on the Eastside. First, we supplied our friend Scott Justham of the BLM with enough coffee to run the 2006-07 season series of Sunday morning free climbers' coffee at the Pleasant Valley Pit campground. Second, we were proud to contribute the remaining net proceeds of $400 to the Eastern Sierra Climbers Coalition in support of a human waste management solution for the popular Buttermilk bouldering area.

On December 3 the Sierra Nevada Section wrapped up the year with our Annual Holiday Dinner at Spenger's Fish Grotto in Berkeley. Members and guests enjoyed drinks, a dinner buffet, video and photos from this year's Section events, a gear raffle, and a Big Wall Triple Header: Our own Peter Mayfield and Steve Schneider were joined by fellow AAC member Mike Libecki to present *Big Walls After the Golden Age—From Yosemite to the Greater Ranges.* The general public was invited to join us just for the slideshow, and about 20 folks did so. Peter shared his 1980s first ascents of the A5 El Cap routes, Aurora and Zenyatta Mondatta, and the Big Chill on Half Dome, the latter two with Jim Bridwell. Former Section Chair Steve Schneider told us of his free ascent of El Cap via the route Golden Gate and of his ascent of "Welcome to the Slabs of Koricancha" (V 5.13b, 650m, 13 pitches) on La Esfinge in the Cordillera Blanca with a then 14-year old Scott Corey. And our guest Mike Libecki showed a film of his solo trip to the remote East coast of Greenland (85 hours of three-mph boat travel through a choked icepack!), where he made the first ascent of a 5,000-foot wall. What a fantastic show! The Section also presented certificates of appreciation to our members Linda McMillan and Dick Duane for their tremendous efforts on behalf of the AAC and all of the climbing community in preserving Yosemite's Camp 4.

DAVE RIGGS, *Chair*

NORTHERN ROCKIES SECTION. In March, Access Fund Policy Director Jason Keith asked the Section to rally a letter writing campaign in support of re-opening the Twin Sisters at Idaho's City of Rocks for climbing. Thanks are due to all who responded. The revised City of Rocks Climbing Management Plan is in draft, and there should be a further comment period sometime in 2007. For those who may not know, the Access Fund logo is based on the outline of the Twin Sisters.

On September 30 members pitched in with the Salt Lake City Climbers' Alliance and the Access Fund for Adopt-a-Crag day at the Salt Lake Slips in Big Cottonwood Canyon near Salt Lake City. The Slips climbing area needed a better access trail and more stable staging areas. A large turnout of hard workers pitched in to insure a successful day. Particular thanks were extended by the Natural Resource Manager of the Wasatch Cache National Forest.

The annual Moondance at City of Rocks National Reserve, hosted by the Section, was held on the first full-moon weekend in October, which landed on the weekend of October 7. Despite cold weather and rain at the start, 32 people showed up to be rewarded by a surprise appearance of the full moon itself. Doug Colwell donated a fully functional barbeque for the gala party, at which folks ate and reveled around the campfire until the wee hours of the night. AAC members journeyed from Boise, Missoula, Sun Valley/Ketchum, Salt City City, and elsewhere in the area to share the mountaineering camaraderie.

Our former Chair, Doug Colwell, was awarded the Access Fund's Sharp End Award in recognition of his longtime activism for the climbing community and countless hours spent promoting climbers' interests at Twin Sisters at City of Rocks, Castle Rock State Park, and, in Arizona, at the Oak Flat/Queen Creek climbing area.

Local Organizations/Web sites of interest of interest to climbers in our territory: http://www.boiseclimbers.org, http://www.saltlakeclimbers.org; http://montanaclimbers.org, http://seracclub.org, http://www.wasatchmountainclub.org.

BRIAN CABE, *Chair*

CENTRAL ROCKIES SECTION. On January 21 the Section hosted the debut showing of *Skiing Mount Everest and the High Himalayas* in the Foss Auditorium of the American Mountaineering Center in Golden. The movie was produced by Aspen resident and AAC member Mike Marolt. In May 2000 Mike and his twin brother Steve, along with lifelong friends, skied from the central summit of Shishapangma in Tibet, becoming the first Western Hemisphere skiers to ski from above 8,000m. In May 2003 under formidable conditions—ferocious wind, cold temperatures, no Sherpa porters, no supplemental oxygen—the same group took a giant leap toward the ultimate high altitude ski run, the north face of Mt. Everest. The team climbed the north ridge of Everest and proceeded to ski it, the first Americans to do so. The film provides the only known ski footage from these altitudes and shows what can happen when a group of friends set their sights high and work together to reach their goals.

In February the CRS, for the sixth consecutive year, sponsored and helped fund the Waterfall Ice Roundup in Cody, Wyoming. This year it partnered with AAC headquarters with Executive Director Phil Powers attending. Known as the "friendliest little ice festival in the Rockies," the Roundup invites climbers to sample over 99 ice routes, demo equipment, and enjoy the catered food and the evening slide programs.

The Colorado 14ers Initiative (CFI) has been doing trail rehabilitation work for nearly a decade on the popular giant mountains throughout Colorado. This year's volunteers, including our members Fred Barth, Bill Oliver, Charlotte Fox, and Gerard Vanderbeek, continued work begun last year on Pyramid Peak (14,018') in the popular Maroon Bells-Snowmass Wilderness. Vegetation trampling and subsequent erosion have resulted in several gullied areas up to four feet deep and 15 feet wide. A new, sustainable route combining new construction and restoration will provide climbers with access to the amphitheater, from which they can explore Pyramid's crumbling rock face and complex network of couloirs and ridges.

October 15th marked the sixth consecutive year that the AAC has hosted the Lumpy Trails Day at Lumpy Ridge in Rocky Mountain National Park. This fine climbing destination in Estes Park, which offers high quality granite on one- to six-pitch long routes, has been selected as part of the Access Fund's Adopt-a-Crag program. The volunteers, 49 in number, included Front Range climbers, Club members, locals, and Park Service employees, who collaborated to continue improving climber access trails. The access trail to the Pear received significant work with the addition of over 70 wood and rock steps and seven drains.

Finally, Greg Sievers, as one of the original members of the Hut Committee and its past Chairman, was excited that Bison Willy's became the third AAC Hut in 1998. He now continues to work toward adding facilities to the "rustic" end of the options list. That bunkhouse is located in the heart of the Southfork Valley southwest of Cody, Wyoming. Opening in 1999, it became an instant hit with climbers coming to enjoy the world-class ice climbing. Its convenient location saves the arduous hour's drive from Cody to the valley. Last year the bunkhouse was closed pending a lease with the new owners of the Double Diamond X Ranch, but is expected to re-open in 2008. Hutmaster, local climber and Section member, Kenny Gasch, and his late wife Carrie opened two other facilities—the Base Camp and Spike Camp—last year in downtown Cody to provide year-round service to travelers visiting the area. For more on Bison Willy's Bunkhouse, check the Web site at www.bisonwillys.com.

GREG SIEVERS, *Chair*

NORTH CENTRAL SECTION. The North Central Section was without a chairman in 2006 as the former chair of eight years, Scott Christensen, resigned to finish his Ph D. in comparative physiology. Because of this, communication within the Section was a problem, as the position is still unfilled. However, there were activities and climbing taking place! Major projects for 2006 were patterned after those of 2005: further work to develop a sorely needed Section Web site, clean-up days at two areas, and further communication with the Minnesota Department of Natural Resources (DNR) regarding closed areas at the most popular climbing destination in the Minneapolis/St. Paul area. The clean-up days were held. The Web site is still incomplete. In addition, a small social was again held at an indoor climbing gym and restaurant in Stillwater, Minnesota, in October, and an AAC table was manned at Midwest Mountaineering's gigantic Winter Fest in Minneapolis in November.

As background, Inter-State State Park lies along the St Croix River bordering Minnesota and Wisconsin. Because of the river valley, the geological formations are spectacular. The routed climbs vary from 5.3 to 5.12 and are about 50 feet long. In July of 2001 there was a large rock fall that necessitated closing 40 percent of the Minnesota side. The North Central Section continues to work with the DNR to point out the closed areas as well as plan for the possible re-opening of part of the area. In addition we had a garbage pick-up day at the park in June. There were five members on hand, and the day included some climbing and a barbeque, along with a meeting with the State Park staff. There were two other clean-up days in other parts of the summer at this crag. One of them, organized by the Access Fund, was attended by four of our members. The Section was represented again this year at a clean-up day on July 6 at Blue Mounds State Park in Luverne, Minnesota, along the Minnesota-South Dakota border. This is an area that has had a big increase in the number of climber visits over the past 10 years with growing maintenance needs

SCOTT CHRISTENSEN, *Past Chair*

NEW YORK SECTION. New York Section members, like everyone else, love rituals, and one of our most enduring, second in longevity to our black tie dinner in the fall, is our Adirondack Winter Outing, now in its 16th year. Historically the weather in the third week of January is the coldest of the year, making the event an unusually invigorating exercise. Not in 2006, however, as January turned out to be the warmest on record in the Northeast. Thankfully, a cold snap just a few days before the event made the ice climbable, although not all routes were in condition. Anyhow, if the climbing wasn't world class, the happy hour, dinner and slide show afterward definitely were top notch, making the trip worthwhile for the 36 members and guests. A special treat was Fritz Selby's show on his expedition to Mongolia the summer before. In addition, a number of Club members and guests arrived early on Friday to take in Olaf Soot's exhibit of Adirondack photos at the Lake Placid Center for the Arts. These may be found in his new coffee table book, *Adirondacks Alive,* co-authored by Don Mellor, the well-known Adirondack climber and writer.

In February the Section launched a new collaboration with the Rubin Museum of Art in Manhattan. Housing an extraordinary collection of Himalayan art and artifacts, the Museum, in the Chelsea District of Manhattan, also has a first-class theater seating over 150 people. It was at this location in February that the Section co-sponsored a special tribute to Heinrich Harrer, who had passed away the month before. Hosted by David Breashears, with the participation of the U.S. representative of the Dalai Lama, the sold-out event featured a presentation of Harrer's historic photographs of Lhasa in the late 1940s. In March we organized another lecture at the Rubin on Extreme Medicine, given by Dr. Ken Kamler. Ken, a high altitude climber himself, was high up on Everest when the 1996 disaster occurred and administered first aid to the injured climbers, who included Beck Weathers. Finally, in June the Section helped organize The Great Everest Sleepover of 2006, a simulated, overnight climb of Everest inside the Museum for 40 kids ages 11-14. Assisting Chief Guide Luis Benitez were five "guides" from the New York Section who instructed their young charges on basic mountain safety and techniques. Saturday night was spent in tents at "Camp Six" (the sixth floor) of the Museum. Nobody got much sleep, especially when the yeti arrived at midnight! This imaginative event got national publicity with a special report in *The New Yorker.*

Our Twenty-Seventh Annual Black Tie Dinner on November 11 featuring Dr. Charles Houston, M.D., was one of the most eagerly anticipated and the earliest sellout in Dinner history. The topic was the 1953 American Expedition to K2, best known for Pete Schoening's miraculous ice-axe belay, which saved six lives including Houston's. The selfless heroism of the team members in attempting to evacuate a fatally stricken Art Gilkey stood in sharp contrast to those recent Everest climbers who were reported to have bypassed a dying climber as they pursued their summit ambitions. Houston showed a film with historic footage aptly entitled *The Brotherhood of the Rope.* Other program highlights, included a nine-minute film, *A Peak Experience,* on The Great Everest Sleepover discussed above, and the introduction of 12 new members.

Special thanks go to Richard Ryan and Howard Sebold for creating this fun, imaginative and well-edited film which no doubt will do well at various mountain film festivals. The Dinner raised a record contribution for the Library. At the end of the evening, special plaques were awarded to Todd Fairbairn, Richard Ryan, and Holly Edelston recognizing the long hours they dedicated to soliciting, assembling and shipping much needed cold weather gear and supplies to Pakistan in connection with the Club's Earthquake Relief Initiative. At the Dinner the New York Section Flag was introduced. This flag will accompany future expeditions or other significant ascents by New York Section members. The first such flag was awarded to Dr. Samuel Silverstein to accompany the 40th anniversary attempt on Mt. Vinson in Antarctica, scheduled for January 2007. Sam was a member of the AAC team that made the first ascent of all the significant peaks in the Ellsworth Range back in 1966. That original first ascent team included Nick Clinch and the late Pete Schoening, among others.

Section members were also busy in the summer months of 2006 climbing in far-flung places: Dan Lochner, with his old Everest partner Dan Meggitt, attempted 7,000-meter Khan Tegri in Kazakhstan, only to be thwarted by difficult logistics. As a consolation prize they climbed nearby Chapuyeva, a challenging 6,200-meter satellite peak. In September Fritz Selby led a group of section members to the rarely visited Minya Konka area in China's Sichuan Province. Others in the group included Mark Kassner, Roland Puton, Joe diSaverio, and Carlo and Manuela Filiaci.

The New York Section is blessed with a number of active, inspired and hardworking volunteers without whom these ambitious undertakings would not be possible. Among those not already mentioned above who should be singled out are Mike Barker, who also chairs our membership committee, Martin Torresquintero, Michael Lederer, and Vic Benes, our webmaster.

Stay up to date on Section events at http://nysalpineclub.org.

Philip Erard, Chair

NEW ENGLAND SECTION. As noted elsewhere in this *Journal*, Section member Mark Richey, with Steve Swenson and Doug Chabot, achieved the summit of Latok II (7,108m) in Pakistan in August, for the first time in alpine style. On a somewhat lesser scale, Nancy Savickas climbed ice in Cogne, Italy, with British friends and also climbed in Zion National Park and the Verdon Gorge in France. In February many of us made it to the AAC Annual Meeting, held at the Grand Summit Hotel at Attitash in New Hampshire's White Mountains. Longtime Section Chair Bill Atkinson was awarded the Angelo Heilprin Citation for service to the Club.

On March 18 we staged what many have agreed was the best New England Section dinner ever. It was our tenth and featured the legacy of Kenneth Henderson, whose climbing films of the 1930s have been a continuing inspiration for our efforts. Seventy members and guests attended, among them Ken's son-in-law, Harold Frost, and his two grandchildren, William and Josephine Frost. AAC President Jim Donini came all the way from Ouray, Colorado, to provide some inspirational remarks. We screened one of the best of the Henderson reels: a 10-minute film of a 1930s ascent of Old Cannon on the 1,200-foot Cannon cliff in New Hampshire, for which notes and background music had been arranged by Bill Clack. Germane to the theme, Ed Webster followed the film with a marvelous hour-long pictorial tribute to Ken and the early pioneers of New England mountaineering, with many images seeing the projection light for the first time. Among those in the van were Ken himself, Bob and Miriam O'Brien Underhill, Lincoln O'Brien, Bill House, and Fritz Wiessner. Bill reported that an archival repository for Ken's footage has been found in Maine, the same facility that houses Charlie Houston's film records.

Club pins were presented to three new members: Zak Hampton, Jake Stabile, and Justus Zimmerman. At the reception AAC artist and Canadian Rockies legend Glen Boles of Alberta exhibited six of his beautiful and detailed ink-and-pencil drawings of selected Canadian peaks.

Basecamp at Nancy Savickas's alpine refuge in Albany, New Hampshire, has become a tradition. At our annual gathering in June, 23 members showed up. Some were returning from serious climbs that day, while others came up from wherever they call home. Notably, we had the honor of meeting Anne Parmenter, who had reached the summit of Everest a few weeks earlier.

On August 5, at the end of a nasty heat wave, Bob Clark, Chad Hussey, and Bill Atkinson hosted a day of climbing and camaraderie at the Traprock crags in central Connecticut. On Ragged Mountain the climbers enjoyed excellent weather for ascents of area classics that included Wiessner Slab, Broadway, YMC, and Unconquerable Crack.

Post-climb we arrived at Chad's remote outback station. Slides under the stars featured Bill Atkinson's climbs in the Shawangunks from the 1950s, followed by his ascent years ago of the East Ridge of the Grand Teton. Chuck Boyd treated the audience to an overview of backcountry rock climbs in the Adirondacks; rock climbing in Montserrat and Siurana, Spain; and an excellent DVD of the 2004 Connecticut Everest Expedition. Chuck summitted Everest on May 20, 2004. Finally, Bob Clark gave a multimedia presentation featuring images of New England rock climbing in Connecticut, the 'Gunks, and the White Mountains by Bob Clark and Chad Hussey.

The year's final event was the by-now annual fall gathering at Nancy's alpine refuge. Eighteen people gathered to enjoy her Halloween hospitality and elegant hors d'oeuvres after a day of climbing the nearby cliffs in New Hampshire.

BILL ATKINSON, *CHAIR, and* NANCY SAVICKAS, *Vice Chair*

INDEX

COMPILED BY RALPH FERRARA AND EVE TALLMAN

Mountains are listed by their official names. Ranges and geographic locations are also indexed. Unnamed peaks (eg. Peak 2,340) are listed under P. Abbreviations are used for some states and countries and for the following: Article: art.; Cordillera: C.; Mountains: Mts.; National Park: Nat'l Park; Obituary: obit. Most personnel are listed for major articles. Expedition leaders and persons supplying information in Climbs and Expeditions are also cited here. Indexed photographs are listed in bold type. Reviewed books are listed alphabetically under Book Reviews.

SUBMISSIONS GUIDELINES

The *American Alpine Journal* records the significant climbing accomplishments of the world in an annual volume. We encourage climbers to submit brief (250-500 words) factual accounts of their climbs and expeditions. Accounts should be submitted by e-mail whenever possible. Alternatively, submit accounts by regular post on CD, zip, or floppy disk. Please provide complete contact information, including e-mail address, postal address, fax, and phone. The deadline is December 31, through earlier submissions will be looked on very kindly! For photo guidelines and other information, please see the complete Submissions Guidelines document at the American Alpine Journal section of www.AmericanAlpineClub.org.

Please address all correspondences to:

The American Alpine Journal, 710 Tenth Street, Suite 140, Golden, CO 80401 USA; tel.: (303) 384 0110; fax: (303) 384 0111; aaj@americanalpineclub.org; www.AmericanAlpineClub.org